Y0-EOE-749

THE LETTERS OF CATHERINE OF SIENA

Volume II

Medieval and Renaissance Texts and Studies

Volume 203

THE LETTERS OF CATHERINE OF SIENA

Volume II

Translated with
introduction and notes
by

Suzanne Noffke, O.P.

Arizona Center for Medieval and Renaissance Studies
Tempe, Arizona
2001

Istituto Italiano di Cultura

A generous grant from the General Division of Cultural Co-operation of the Ministry of Foreign Affairs for Italy has helped meet the publication costs of this book.

© Copyright 2001
Arizona Board of Regents for Arizona State University

Library of Congress Cataloging-in-Publication Data
Catherine, of Siena, Saint, 1347–1380.
[Correspondence]
The letters of Catherine of Siena / Catherine of Siena ; translated with introduction and notes by Suzanne Noffke.—2nd ed.
p. cm. — (Medieval and Renaissance texts and studies ; v. 202, 203)
Includes bibliographical references and index.
ISBN 0-86698-244-2, v. 1; ISBN 0-86698-245-0, v. 2.
1. Catherine, of Siena, Saint, 1347–1380—Correspondence. 2. Christian women saints—Italy—Siena—Correspondence. I. Noffke, Suzanne. II. Title. III. Medieval & Renaissance Texts & Studies (Series) ; v. 202, 203.
BX4700.C4 A4 1999
282'.092--dc21
[B] 99–054886

∞
This book is made to last.
It is set in Garamond Antiqua typeface,
smythe-sewn and printed on acid-free paper
to library specifications.

Printed in the United States of America

TABLE OF CONTENTS

VI

SIENA AND BELCARO: (LATE DECEMBER 1376 THROUGH EARLY SUMMER 1377)

APPENDIX

BIBLIOGRAPHY

A NOTE OF GRATITUDE

The project out of which have developed the volumes of this English edition of *The Letters of Catherine of Siena* first began in 1979 under the auspices of the PARABLE Conference for Dominican Life and Mission. It was to have been a simple collaborative venture in which drafts of the letters prepared by three translators were to be brought together by a general editor (Suzanne Noffke, O.P.) and published.

Mary Carola Parks, O.P. († 7 July 1998), Adrian, Michigan, prepared Letters T1 through T153.

Mary Janet La Giglia, O.P. († 21 April 1998), Springfield, Illinois, prepared Letters T154 through T260.

Juliana D'Amato, O.P., Columbus, Ohio, prepared Letters T261 through T381.

As will be explained in the Introduction, the work has since undergone years of significant further development. Among other things, continuing research necessitated a full reworking of the draft translations initially provided. It would, however, be remiss not to especially acknowledge the work of those who spent so much time and effort on the earlier project and who waited so long to see its fruition. Two of the team, Janet La Giglia and Mary Carola Parks, lived to see only the first fruits, in the form of the original first volume of 1988. May this new beginning honor their memory! And may it bring some measure of satisfaction to the third, Juliana D'Amato, most of whose labors will be reflected only in later volumes.

ABBREVIATIONS

Biblical books are cited as in *The New American Bible.* Manuscripts of the *Letters* are designated by the abbreviations given in Appendix One, Volume I.

Dial.	*The Dialogue of Catherine of Siena*, trans. Suzanne Noffke (New York: Paulist Press, 1980)
DT	Eugenio Dupré Theseider
G	Girolamo Gigli
It.	Italian
Let.	Letter
Life	*The Life of Catherine of Siena* (Raimondo da Capua's *Legenda major*), trans. Conleth Kearns (Wilmington: Michael Glazier, 1980)
PG	*Patrologiae Cursus Completus, Series Graeca*, ed. J. P. Migne (Tournhout: Brepols, 1969).
PL	*Patrologiae Cursus Completus, Series Latina*, ed. J. P. Migne (Paris: Garnier Frères, 1958–)
T	*Lettere di S. Caterina da Siena*, ed. Niccolò Tommasèo (Florence: Barbera, 1860)
Vulg.	Vulgate

TEXTUAL NOTES

The following conventions are used in the textual notes:

MS:	The manuscript code followed by a colon indicates the manuscript or manuscripts in which the variant is found.
From MS	Indicates that the translation is in this instance based on the specified manuscript rather than on the manuscript used for the rest of the letter.
/	Signifies "in place of."
[ ]	Signify that the text enclosed is omitted.
It.	Signifies the form in the original.

THE LETTERS OF CATHERINE OF SIENA

Volume II

the WORLD of CATHERINE of SIENA

1347 – 1380

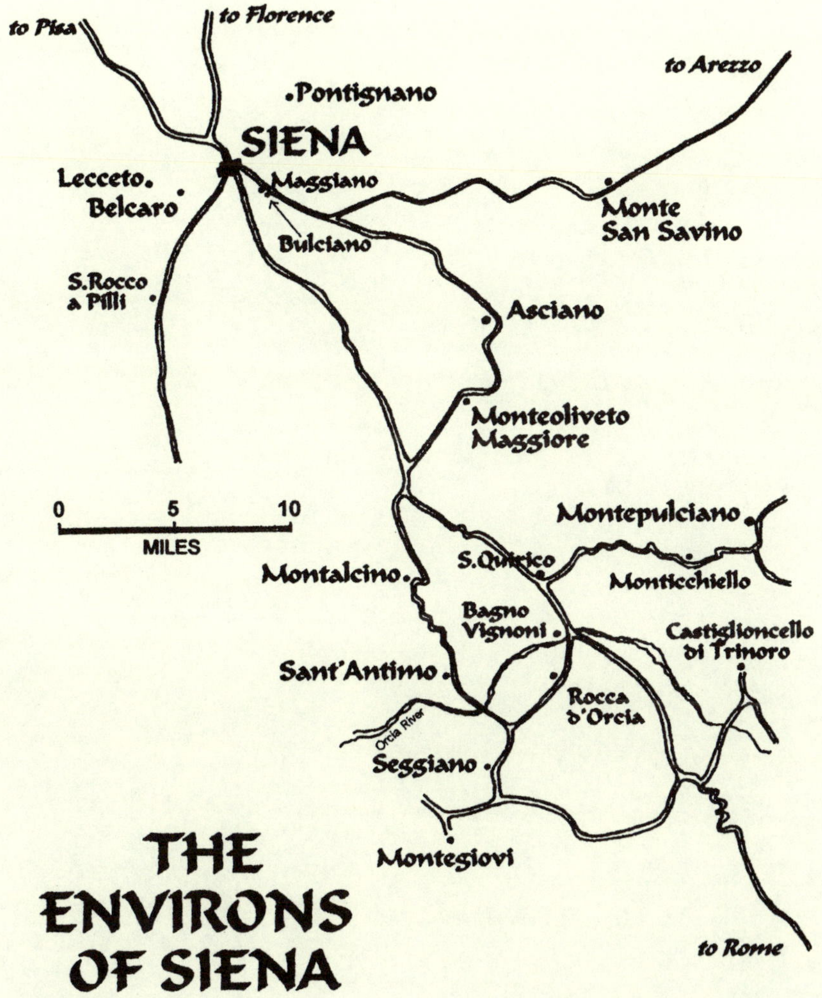
to Pisa
to Florence
Pontignano
to Arezzo
SIENA
Lecceto
Belcaro
Maggiano
Bulciano
Monte San Savino
S.Rocco a Pilli
Asciano
Monteoliveto Maggiore
0 5 10
MILES
Montepulciano
S.Quirico
Montalcino
Monticchiello
Bagno Vignoni
Castiglioncello di Trinoro
Sant'Antimo
Rocca d'Orcia
Orcia River
Seggiano
Montegiovi
THE ENVIRONS OF SIENA
to Rome

Catherine of Siena addresses Pope Gregory XI. A woodcut from a German translation of Raimondo da Capua's *Legenda Major* entitled *Hystori und wunderbarlich legend Katharine von Senis, der hailigen junckfrawen* … (Augspurg: Gedruckt durch Hannsen Otmar, Jn verlegung des herten Johann Rynman, 1515).

Part IV:
Preludes to Catherine's Avignon Mission (February through April 1376)

According to Raimondo da Capua,[1] the Florentines under the burden of interdict and the threat of military attack were seeking the mediation of persons known to enjoy the pope's favor. Having heard that Catherine, on account of her reputation for holiness, was one such person, they took the initial step of arranging that her confessor Raimondo should make a first approach to the pontiff in Catherine's name.[2] It was probably in late February of 1376 that he and a few companions set out for Avignon, stopping perhaps first in Florence and then surely in Pisa (documented by Catherine's correspondence with them there).

Catherine herself remained in Siena for a few more months, occupied not only with the growing divisions within the Church, but also with the more intimate concerns of those dear to her. She corresponded with citizens of Lucca who had recently become her friends and disciples. She pursued her plans for the establishment of a monastery for women. She took up various causes commended to her by acquaintances.

---

[1] Appendix One provides brief biographical notes on the various persons mentioned in the course of this volume.

[2] *Life*, III, vi, 420, pp. 380–381.

LETTER T226/G89[1]
To Frate Raimondo da Capua
About 17 February 1376

A number of events and letters must be related in order to date this letter.[2]

On 11 February 1377 Pope Gregory XI issued a personal ultimatum to all who had held office in Florence since the previous June; they were to appear before him in Avignon before the end of March. In the communication he enumerated their offenses in such terms that the Florentines called it "too atrocious to be addressed even to schismatics and infidels."[3] This would have been a logical time for the Florentines to look for a mediator. So this may well have been the time Raimondo refers to when he says that they asked him first to go to Avignon "in Catherine's name" to sue for peace, calling for Catherine herself only later.[4] Catherine later sent a letter commending Raimondo to Gregory XI (T206/DT63, in this volume), in which she mentioned "what has happened in Bologna," a reference almost certainly to the revolt of Bologna against the papacy on the night of 20 March 1376. Catherine probably was not thinking as she wrote the letter that Raimondo was as yet actually in Avignon. Still, that letter of recommendation must have been written before 31 March, when Gregory XI actually imposed an interdict on Florence. And by very shortly after 1 April, when she wrote Let. T219/DT65 to Raimondo, Catherine was

---

[1] MSS: Mo-*c*, P4; translation based on Mo-*c*, with variants from P4 based on an unpublished transcription by A. Volpato.

[2] Fawtier (II, pp. 197–198), following Burlamacchi, dates this letter in 1378, taking the elevation of "the archbishop" to refer to the conclave of 8 April 1378, in which Urban VI was elected. The results of this 1378 conclave were known in Florence by the next Wednesday, 14 April, Wednesday of Holy Week, when the gospel from Luke was read that could have furnished the Passover theme for the letter.

Gardner (*Saint Catherine of Siena*, p. 168) puts the letter in 1376, but after Raimondo's arrival in Avignon. This poses a problem regarding the women disciples mentioned at the end of the letter, since no women went with Raimondo, Giovanni Tantucci, and Felice da Massa when they set out for Avignon.

Dupré Theseider in his unpublished notes speculates about 1376, but in the end dates the letter to spring of 1378 for several reasons: (1) He thinks it unlikely that Neri would have been sent to Avignon; (2) T226 could hardly be before T219 because of its Easter references; (3) There is no mention of the pope's return to Rome in T226, whereas it is mentioned several times in T219; (4) Catherine would not have expected any special peace to come from the appointment of Iacopo da Itri. However, placing the letter in 1378 needs to assume an unrecorded trip by Raimondo to Pisa from Rome (where he had been since about mid-September 1377 as prior of Santa Maria sopra Minerva), and also that Catherine somehow and somewhere had a chance to see him along the way.

[3] Gardner, *Saint Catherine of Siena*, p. 157 (no source cited).

[4] *Life*, III, vi, 420, pp. 380–381.

assuming that he and his companions would be in Avignon by the time the letter reached there.[5]

It is within this framework that the present letter, T226, seems to fit. I would *hypothesize* the following sequence of events:

- Sometime after 11 February 1376 (the date of Gregory's ultimatum), at the request of the Florentines and at Catherine's behest, Raimondo leaves for Avignon by way of Pisa, almost certainly stopping first in Florence (since he is on mission in the interests of that city). A certain Papo has apparently gone with Raimondo. Along the way Raimondo learns that Iacopo da Itri has, as of 18 January, been appointed Patriarch of Constantinople. He writes this news to Catherine, who is still in Siena.

- Shortly after Raimondo's departure (possibly about 17 February), she receives his letter and writes this one (T226) to him. (Mention of Tommaso dalla Fonte is a very probable indication that Catherine is still in Siena.) By now she is thinking that she should send Neri di Landoccio Pagliaresi to join Raimondo.[6] (She can spare him because Stefano Maconi has recently joined her circle and can serve her as secretary, as well as the "Francesco" who will apparently be the scribe for T228.[7]) In case the pope should want to send her any verbal message, Neri will be freer than Raimondo to come back with it. She does in fact send Neri (perhaps with Let. T226), but leaves to Raimondo the decision whether or not to send him (or take him along) to Avignon.

- Neri leaves Siena possibly about 18 to 20 February, and joins Raimondo and Papo in Pisa shortly thereafter. Catherine writes Let. T228 to Neri and Papo there, perhaps still in late February, including greetings to Raimondo. Sometime after this Raimondo and Neri (and possibly Papo—though the latter is never mentioned again), with Giovanni Tantucci, Felice da Massa, and others, leave for Avignon, perhaps at the end of February or in early March.

- After 20 March (the revolt of Bologna), Catherine writes Let. T206/DT63 to Gregory XI concerning the latter event and commends Rai-

---

[5] The rubric of B says the letter was written "to Master Raimondo, before Pope Gregory came to Rome, and to Master Giovanni and to Frate Felice and certain others of her sons in Christ whom she had sent to Avignon."

[6] Gardner proposes this hypothesis (*Saint Catherine of Siena*, p. 168). There is no direct evidence of it. We know that Neri was eventually in Avignon with Catherine, but are not told with which party he went there. It does not seem unreasonable to hypothesize that he was one of the "certain others" mentioned in the rubric of B for the present letter.

[7] Probably Francesco Malavolti. Let. T228 follows the present letter in this volume.

mondo to him. It is quite plausible that this commendation (possibly along with Let. T280) reaches Raimondo while he is still in Pisa, or possibly it is waiting for him at his arrival in Avignon (so that he can deliver it personally to the pope).[8]

- Very soon after this, but before she receives word of the interdict pronounced on Florence on 31 March, Catherine writes Let. T196/DT64 to Gregory, urging him to return to Rome and to use peaceful means to win back the rebellious republics.

- On 1 April, Catherine has the vision of which she writes to Raimondo and his companions in Let. T219/DT65.[9]

This placement of the present letter is powerfully supported by the linguistic evidence.[10] Paschal references[11] and the mention of the nearness of spring would also fit well in mid-February.

---

[8] Gardner (*Saint Catherine of Siena*, p. 162) guesses that the party left for Avignon about the fourth week of March.

[9] The journey of Raimondo and the others from Pisa to Avignon could well have taken a few weeks, given the spring weather and the possible modes of transportation. They may have traveled either by sea or land route to Genoa and then, since the Dominicans did not use horses, by foot and/or mule to Avignon. (Later in the year both Gregory XI, who came from Avignon by sea, and Catherine's party, who came by land, would pass through Pisa.) This would still give them time to have arrived in Avignon before a letter written in late March would reach them over the same route.

[10] Of the five letters which share nineteen or more of this one's ninety-nine analyzed patterns, three are from February through April 1376. (Another is from mid-1375 and the fifth from 1377.) By far the most dense concentration of significant clusters within individual patterns is in this same period, with the placement around 17 February 1376 most closely supported by clusters of CARNPUZ, CONDOTT, CONSUMAM, CONVERSD, DESIDDE, MAESTRVE, MANGGUST, MARPACIF, MEMBPUTR, MUOIO, RIMEDIO, SCUOLA, SERVEFIG, TEMPAPRS, VASDILEZ. (Cf. Vol. I, Appendix IV for interpretation of these patterns.)

[11] Lent began on 26 February in 1376.

§

In the name of Jesus Christ crucified and of gentle Mary.

Dearest, very loved father and son in Christ Jesus, given me by that gentle mother Mary,[12]

I Caterina, servant and slave of the servants of Jesus Christ, am writing to you and to Papo[13] in his precious blood. I long to see you true sons and trumpeters of the incarnate Word, God's Son, not only with your voices but in your actions.[14] Learn from the Master of truth, who preached virtue only after he had practiced it.[15] In this way you will produce fruit and will be channels through whom God will offer his grace within the hearts of those who hear you.

Realize, my sons, that it is impossible for us either to learn about or to have the good life, or to be hungry for God's honor and the salvation of souls, unless we go to the school of the Word, the Lamb slain and abandoned on the cross, because it is there that the true teaching is found.[16] This is what he said: "I am way and truth and life." And no one can go to the Father except through him.[17] Let your mind's eye be opened to see, and unplug your ears and listen to the teaching he gives you. Look at yourselves, for in him you will find yourselves, and in yourselves, him.[18] What I mean is that you will find yourselves in him in that he is creating you in his own image and likeness—gratuitously, and not because he owes it to you—and within yourselves you will discover God's boundless goodness in having taken on our likeness by the union the divine nature has

---

[12] She uses the same title for Raimondo in Let. T373/DT70 (15 February 1380).

[13] Also spelled Papi (over an erasure of *Papo* in the manuscript Mo). He is mentioned also in Let. T228 to Neri di Landoccio Pagliaresi (in this volume). His identity, however, is unknown.

[14] In the Middle Ages, great proclamations were signaled by trumpeters. So Catherine naturally links the proclamation of God's word with this image. Later in this letter (and elsewhere) she calls St. Paul a trumpeter. And in Let. T87 to Giovanna Pazza (in this volume), she says that the greatest revelation of God's word, Christ's blood, "was heralded with the trumpet of mercy, with the fire of the Holy Spirit as trumpeter, so that whoever wants some of this blood can come for it."

[15] Acts 1, 1, a passage frequently cited in medieval devotional literature. Cf. *Dial.* 29, p. 69: "He taught you more by example than with words, always doing first what he talked about."

[16] Cf. Let. T242/DT23 (in this volume): "He is that Master who has taken his chair to teach us the doctrine of truth. . . . And he is the way we must walk to get to this school—I mean, by following his example."

[17] Jn. 14, 6.

[18] A summary of Catherine's core teaching on the integration of knowledge of self and knowledge of God.

effected with our human nature.[19] Let our hearts explode wide open, then, as we contemplate a flame and fire of love so great that God has engrafted himself into us and us into himself![20] Oh unimaginable love! It would be enough if we had even appreciated it![21] To this wonderful school, then, my sons! For this energy[22] and love will lead you on and will be your life!

Open your ears, I tell you, to hear his teaching—and it is this: voluntary poverty; patience in the face of injury; returning good to those who do us evil; being little, humble, oppressed and forsaken in the world; [putting up] with ridicule, torment, wrongs, insults, detraction, gossip, difficulties, and harassment from the world, from devils seen and unseen, and from our own stinking flesh which (rebel that it is) is always wanting to defy its Creator and fight against the spirit.[23] It means suffering with patience and resisting [the devils] with the weapons of hatred and of love. Oh sweet and pleasant teaching! This is the treasure he chose for himself and left to his disciples, left it as the greatest wealth he could have left. If divine Goodness had seen that pleasure and delight and amusement and selfishness and vanity and frivolity of heart were good, he would have chosen them for himself. But Wisdom the incarnate Word saw and knew that all this other was the best part, and so he loved it immediately and lovingly clothed himself in it. And this is what his servants and his children do, when they follow in their Father's footsteps.[24]

I don't want you, then, to be overcome by ignorance or to pull back from this sweet, delightful way and pleasant school. No, as true sons wrap this garment round you, and make it so much part of yourself that it will never be lifted from you except when life is, when we will leave behind the garment of suffering, and will stand there clothed in the garment of

---

[19] P4 has "with our human wool." If this is indeed the original, it is a unique and not uncharacteristic image for Catherine! Here she is speaking of Jesus as the Lamb of God. In Let. T64/DT24 to the wool-worker Sano di Maco (1378), she says that the bond of our debt to God "was written on nothing less than lambskin, the skin of the spotless Lamb. He inscribed us on himself and then tore up the lambskin!" In any case, as for the intimacy of the union of which she speaks, cf. *Dial.* 13, p. 50: "We are your image, and now by making yourself one with us you have become our image, veiling your eternal divinity in the wretched cloud and dung heap of Adam. And why? For love! You, God, became human and we have been made divine!"

[20] In Prayer 17, pp. 147–154, the image of engrafting is much expanded.

[21] The meaning of this sentence has been questioned (*Se l'uomo l'avesse avuto in pregione si bastarebbe*). Gigli in his edition of the letter (*Opere*, I) speculated that *pregione* ("appreciation") should be split into *pregio, ne*, so that the sentence would read: "Even if we had appreciated it, that would not be enough!"

[22] It. *affetto*.

[23] Cf. Rom. 7, 21–23.

[24] This is one of a few instances in which Catherine refers to Christ as father.

delight.[25] And at the table of the Lamb we shall eat the fruit that comes as a result of our labors.

This is what the dear trumpeter Paul did. He clothed himself in Christ crucified, and was stripped of the joy of [seeing] the divine Essence.[26] He clothed himself in the human Christ—that is, in the sufferings and humiliations of Christ crucified, and wanted no other joy. He even said, "I refuse to glory except in the cross of Christ crucified."[27] And that pleased him so much that—as the same apostle once said to a servant of his, "My dear daughter, I so clasped it to myself with the bond of affection and love that it was never lifted, never loosened a bit, except when life was taken from me."[28] Dear Paul seemed truly to have studied this teaching. He knew it so thoroughly that he became a person who ate and savored souls. He became like a sponge absorbing water, so that as he traveled along the way of humiliation he absorbed the boundless charity and goodness with which God supremely loves his creatures. He saw that [Christ's] will is for the eternal Father's honor and our salvation and holiness,[29] and that he gave himself up to death in order to realize this holiness in us. Paul grasped and understood this, and once he had understood it he at once devoted himself to giving honor to God and his best efforts to his neighbors. Courageously he proclaimed the truth. He was zealous, not holding back for lack of concern. And he became a vessel of love[30] filled with fire, to carry and preach God's Word.

Now this is my soul's desire. With tremendous blazing desire I have longed to celebrate this Pasch with you, that is, to see my desire fulfilled and accomplished.[31] How blessed will my soul be now when I see you, more than all the others, established, confirmed, and secured in your goal, Christ crucified, feeding and nourishing yourself on spiritual food![a] For those who see themselves not selfishly but for God, and who see God for

---

[25] The garment of suffering is ultimately the same as the wedding garment one must have to enter the eternal banquet (referred to in the next sentence). Cf. Let. T221 to Suor Bartolomea della Seta (in this volume): "Now what greater pleasure can a bride have than to be like her bridegroom, to be dressed in a garment like his? So because Christ crucified in his life chose nothing but the cross and suffering, and clothed himself in this garment, his bride considers herself blessed to see herself dressed in the same garment."

[26] Cf. Prayer 4, pp. 42–45; Rom. 13, 14.

[27] Gal. 6, 14.

[28] She is certainly referring, in her usual third-person formula, to a mystical experience of her own. Paul is speaking of the garment of Christ's suffering.

[29] 1 Thes. 4, 3.

[30] As often elsewhere she misquotes Acts 9, 15, having apparently misheard the Vulgate as *vas delectionis* rather than *vas electionis*.

[31] Cf. Lk. 22, 15. If this letter is correctly placed in mid-February of 1376 (that is, very near the beginning of Lent), the Pasch referred to would be the same referred to in the gospel, Christ's death—though *pasqua* in the Italian can refer to any feast.

God (as he is supreme eternal Goodness and is deserving of our love), when they contemplate God in blazing, consumed love discover the image of the human person in God. And they discover themselves, God's image, in God. I mean the love they see God having for us, that same love they extend to everyone else. For when they look at their reflection in the fountain, the sea of the divine Being, they feel at once compelled to love their neighbors as they love themselves, because they see that God loves them supremely. Desire then disposes them to love themselves in God, and God in themselves, just as we, when we look into a fountain and see our image, take pleasure in it and love ourselves.[32] But if we are wise, we are moved to love the fountain before we love ourselves. For if we hadn't seen ourselves we wouldn't have loved ourselves or taken pleasure in ourselves. Nor would we have corrected what was faulty about the face we saw in the fountain![33]

So think, my dearest sons. There is no other way we can see either our dignity or the faults that mar our soul's beauty, except by going to look into the quiet sea of the divine Being. There, in that Being, we see our reflection. Why? Because we came forth from there when God's wisdom created us in God's image and likeness. There we discover the union of the Word engrafted into our humanity; we discover and see and experience the blazing furnace of his charity,[34] the means by which God gave us to ourselves and later united the Word with us and us with the Word when he took on our human nature. That charity was the strong bond that held him nailed fast to the cross.[35] And all this we will see when we see ourselves in God's goodness. In no other way could we ever experience him in everlasting life or see him face to face, except by first experiencing him in this life through affection and love and desire in the way I've described.

We can't show God this affection by the service we might be able to do

---

[32] She certainly has in mind a fountain such as Fonte Branda near her home in Siena, where the waters of the source collect in a quiet and shaded pool. The surface of the fountain is therefore like a mirror.

[33] Cf. *Dial.* 167, pp. 365–366: "Truly this light [faith] is a sea, for it nourishes the soul in you, peaceful sea, eternal Trinity. Its water is not sluggish; so the soul is not afraid because she knows the truth. It distills, revealing hidden things, so that here, where the most abundant light of faith abounds, the soul has a guarantee [or, in another manuscript, 'a clarification'] of what she believes. This water is a mirror in which you, eternal Trinity, grant me knowledge; for when I look into this mirror, holding it in the hand of love, it shows me myself, as your creation, in you, and you in me through the union you have brought about of the Godhead with our humanity."

[34] So for Catherine, the water and the fire are ultimately one—in Christ's blood.

[35] Catherine was probably familiar with this concept from Cavalca (*Specchio di croce*, p. 41): "No bond of iron could have held Christ nailed or bound—only charity, the bond of perfection." She uses it often, as do other medieval writers such as Ludolphus de Saxonia and Feo Belcari.

for him, because he has no need of the good we do; but we can and must show it in the persons of our brothers and sisters by seeking the glory and praise of God's name in them. No more indifference, then! No more sleeping in unawareness! No, with bold and blazing heart stretch your sweet loving desires to go and give honor to God and your best efforts to your neighbors, never losing sight of your goal, Christ crucified.[36]

Understand that he is the wall on which you must lean in order to look at yourselves in the fountain.[37] Run, run to get there! And lock yourselves within the wounds of Christ crucified. Be glad, be exultantly glad! For the time is near when spring will offer us the fragrant flowers.[38] And don't be surprised if you've seen the opposite happening. In fact, let that make you more certain than ever.

Oimé! Oimé! My poor unfortunate soul! For I don't want ever to rest until I see a sword slash my throat for God's honor, so that my blood would be shed in the mystic body of holy Church! Oimé! Oimé! I am dying and cannot die! I'll say no more. Forgive my foolishness, father.[39] And let your own heart melt and burst in so much of love's heat!

I'm not writing to you about what God has done and is still doing, because there is no language or pen up to the task. You sent me word telling me to be glad and rejoice. You also sent me such news as to give me special joy.[40] Well, the day after I was separated from you[41] gentle First Truth, my eternal Spouse, decided to treat me as a father does his daughter, or a bridegroom his bride, not being able to bear her grieving at all but finding new ways to give her joy. Imagine, father! The supreme eternal Word and exalted Godhead gave me such joy that even the parts of my body felt as if they were melting, disintegrating like wax in the fire.[b]

---

[36] Literally, "never losing hold. . . ." Cf. Prayer 4, pp. 42–43, where she is addressing St. Paul: "[Y]ou truly knew where you had come from and where you were going—and not only where you were going but even the road you were traveling, for you had come to know your origin and your goal and the road by which you would travel to your goal. . . . You joined your power of understanding with the Son, the Word, understanding perfectly the whole order ordained by wisdom itself, the Word, the order that is to lead created things to their goal—and their goal is the same as their origin."

[37] Again, in order to sense the full force of the image, one must recall the public fountains of Siena, especially Fonte Branda already referred to. On its low wall one can easily lean or sit, and see one's face reflected on the dark still surface of the water. Catherine must have done that often, especially as a child.

[38] She is hoping for an end to the rebellion of the Italian republics, for which purpose Raimondo is on his way to Avignon. The season is an appropriate image, since winter is in its last weeks when this is written.

[39] Here Catherine seems to shift her attention and her words to Raimondo alone.

[40] Possibly the news of the appointment of Jacopo da Itri as Patriarch of Constantinople.

[41] That is, after Raimondo's departure for Pisa on his way to Avignon.

My soul was at that time making three dwellings.[42] One was with the devils, both in knowledge of myself and in all the battles and threats and torments they were piling up on me, never for a moment ceasing their knocking at the door of my conscience. At that point I rose up with a sort of hatred and went with it to hell. I wanted to make my confession to you; but divine Goodness gave me more than I was asking for, since when I asked for you he gave me himself, and gave me absolution and remission of both my sins and yours. He repeated the lessons he had spoken at another time and overshadowed me with a great fire of love, with so great a certainty and spiritual purity that words cannot describe it. And to complete the consolation within me, he gave me the dwelling of Christ on earth.[43] [We were] walking as one walks along a road—or so it seemed. There seemed to be a road from supreme Exaltedness, the eternal Trinity, where one received indescribable light and knowledge of God's goodness. As [he] spoke of future things, and as [I] was walking and conversing with the truly joyful as well as with Christ's little family on earth, I saw coming new news of great exultation and peace. And I heard the voice of gentle First Truth saying, "My daughter, I do not spurn true and holy desires; in fact, I fulfill them.[44] So take heart, and be a good and courageous instrument to announce the truth, for I will always be with you." I seemed to sense the elevation of our archbishop. Later, when I learned from your letter what had happened, I was overcome with joy upon joy.[45]

---

[42] Dupré Theseider, in his unpublished notes, interprets these "three dwellings" as three successive stages of spiritual growth. The first, "with the devils," is repentance and self-knowledge. (Cf. Is. 38, 10: "In the noontime of my life I depart for the gates of hell"; *Dial.* 66, p. 125, where the devil curses Catherine for hounding him "even in hell" with her humility. Also Bernard de Clairvaux, to the monks of Montedei, cited by Giovanni dalle Celle, ed. Cividali, p. 429: "From one's cell one often ascends to heaven, but scarcely ever does one descend into hell from one's cell—except as the psalm [54, 16, Vulg.] says, 'Let them descend while alive into hell; not when they are dead.' ") The second dwelling, "with the family of Christ on earth," and the third, "with the truly joyful" in heaven, merge into one another, as Catherine herself explains. But in the third Catherine senses future events, the same events (speculates Dupré Theseider) as those she rejoices to find spoken of later in Raimondo's letter. To me, however, it seems rather that Catherine is speaking of simultaneous experiences within one present moment, that she finds herself at the same time in the presence of evil and of good, in the present and in the future. (The word "prophecy" is written by a later hand into the margin of the manuscript; whoever wrote this gloss must have interpreted the "dwellings" as images of the present and future states of the Church.)

[43] The Italian, as the English here, is ambiguous. "Christ on earth" may be the pope, to whom Catherine so often gives this name and with whom Catherine is, of course, very immediately concerned; the sense could also be "Christ's dwelling on earth," that is, the whole Church.

[44] Cf. *Dial.* 4, p. 31: "I do not spurn their tears and sweat and humble prayers; no, I accept them."

[45] In January 1376, Catherine had written to Iacopo da Itri, then in Avignon (Let. T183/DT56, vol. I). He had apparently written to Catherine about the pope's intentions

Oh my dear son! I am revealing to you my stubborn hard heart, so that you may, for me, ask vengeance and punishment on it for not exploding wide open from so much of love's heat. Oimé! How these three dwellings in some wonderful fashion didn't get in each others' way, but each seasoned the others! Just as salt and oil season and perfect the cooking, so did my association with the devil in humility and hatred, and my hunger and association with holy church in love and desire, make me experience and actually be in everlasting life with the truly joyful.[46] I don't want to say any more. Imagine how I am bursting, yet cannot burst!

I'll tell you news of my father, Frate Tommaso, who by God's grace has conquered the devil with virtue. He has become a completely different person from what he used to be: his heart is at rest in great affection and love. Please write to him sometime, and open your heart to him. Celebrate, because my lost children have been found and have returned to the fold! They have come out of the darkness! No one will be telling me any more to do anything I don't want to do.[47]

I Caterina, your unworthy daughter, ask your blessing. I commend to you all my sons and daughters; take good care of them lest the infernal wolf take any of them from me.[48]

I think Neri will be coming there, for it seems to me it would be good to send him to the court.[49] Inform him as to what needs to be done for

---

regarding his return to Rome and a crusade, and she was heartened; she had told him not to be discouraged and to encourage Gregory. She had said also that Raimondo could come any time it might be useful. This closeness could justify Catherine's calling Iacopo da Itri "our archbishop." She could very likely see hope for peace in his appointment as Patriarch of Constantinople (of which she had not yet known when she had written to him) because of her impression that the Moslems were fast closing in toward Europe, taking Christian lands as they went. (Cf. Let. T145/DT40 to Queen Mother Elizabeth of Hungary, vol. I.)

[46] This seems to support an interpretation of the experience as one of being simultaneously immersed in evil and in good.

[47] The meaning of this paragraph is unclear. Frate Tommaso is almost certainly Tommaso dalla Fonte, Catherine's earliest confessor. The implication seems to be that he and others were in some sort of disagreement with Catherine on what she ought to be doing. Did it perhaps have something to do with her willingness to mediate with the pope on behalf of the Florentines? with attitudes toward the antipapal revolt? She may well be consciously and teasingly exaggerating their situation as being "lost" and "out of the fold."

[48] This implied presence of women disciples at the place where Raimondo is seems again to narrow the possibilities to Pisa. There were women there who had become Catherine's disciples during her stay in 1375. On the other hand (looking at other proposed placements of this letter), there were no women disciples that we know of in the Avignon party itself until Catherine herself went, nor any we know of in Rome before Catherine's arrival there. There is, however, the less likely possibility that she is referring to a kind of concern from a distance.

[49] Neri di Landoccio Pagliaresi. If my placement of this letter is correct, Neri will in fact leave to join Raimondo shortly after this letter. Though Dupré Theseider dismisses the plausibility of Neri's being considered for an Avignon mission because he was unknown to

the peace of these rotten members who are rebelling against holy Church, since there seems to be no sweeter solution than this for both spiritual and material reconciliation. Act zealously in regard to this and whatever else is necessary, concerned always for God's honor and nothing else. Still, even though I tell you this, do whatever God would have you do, and whatever seems best to you, either sending him or not.

Keep living in God's holy and tender love.

Jesus! Gentle Jesus! Jesus! Jesus!

Textual Notes

a. P4: *the food of souls / spiritual food.*

b. P4: [*Imagine .... fire.*]

the pope, it would not, I think, be unlike Catherine to presume that Gregory might have some message for her in her mediation efforts in Florence, and Neri could easily be entrusted with such a message. Also, she wants Raimondo to give Neri instructions as to "what needs to be done [by Catherine, presumably] for these rotten members." The implication in either case seems to be that Neri will return to Catherine in Tuscany. It seems very likely, then, that she has not at this time decided yet on her own eventual journey to Avignon.

LETTER T228/G278[1]
To Neri di Landoccio Pagliaresi
About 25 to 28 February 1376

The rubrics of three manuscripts (P3, P5, T) tell us that this letter was written while Neri was in Pisa, having been sent by Catherine to the holy father. Fawtier places it in June 1378, speculating that Neri has been sent to see the newly elected Urban VI in Rome, and that he was going there by sea (and would therefore have traveled through Pisa). He argues for several reasons that the letter could not have been written in 1376: (1) Catherine would not have entrusted to Neri the task of carrying "Christ's name and mysteries" to the pope in Avignon when Raimondo was already on his way there; (2) No greetings are sent to Giovanni Tantucci and Felice da Massa, who accompanied Raimondo to Avignon.[2] Dupré Theseider accepts Fawtier's reasoning, though he admits that this makes it difficult to explain the letter's mentions of the indulgence and the pope's desire, as well as the greetings to Raimondo, who was not in Pisa but in Rome in June 1378.[3]

The linguistic evidence, on the other hand, points strongly toward early 1376.[4]

The arguments raised against the hypothesis that Catherine sent Neri to join Raimondo in the last weeks of February 1376[5] are not difficult to eliminate. (1) Since we do not know at which point Giovanni Tantucci and Felice da Massa joined Raimondo, the fact that no explicit greetings are sent to them is not really problematic; (2) As for the exhortation that Neri should carry "Christ's name and mysteries" before the pope, she might have so exhorted any of her disciples who would see the pontiff.[6]

---

[1] MSS: Mo, B, P2, T, P5, F2, P3, S3, P4; translation based on Mo-*a*, corrected by *b*, with reference to T, P3, P5.

[2] II, pp. 277–279.

[3] Such a scenario would require either Raimondo's making a trip to Pisa from Rome, or Neri's conveying the greetings when he would actually arrive in Rome.

[4] Three of the four letters which share six or more of this one's twenty-five analyzed patterns are from February through April 1376 (with the fourth in 1380). Granted, one of these is Let. T226, which Fawtier and Dupré Theseider place with this one in 1378 (though the linguistic evidence supports its placement in 1376). The argument for 1376 is further supported by the concentration of the patterns PORTNOME, UNITRAS, and VASDILEZ in this same short period. On the other hand, this letter has very little in common linguistically with 1378 letters.

[5] Cf. the introduction to Let. T226, the previous letter in this volume.

[6] Note, for example, her later message to Pope Urban VI (Let. T306, October 1378), in which she includes all of her followers: "We are all ready to obey your holiness—I and those God has given me to love with a special love—and to suffer even to the point of death, helping you with the arms of holy prayer and sowing and proclaiming the truth wherever it may please God's gentle will—proclaiming it even to your holiness."

I would, then, place this letter after Raimondo's departure for Avignon in 1376, allowing time for his communication to Catherine concerning Iacopo da Itri[7] and for Neri's own joining of Raimondo, perhaps still in late February.

§

In the name of Jesus Christ crucified and of gentle Mary.

Dearest and very loved son in Christ Jesus,[a]

I Caterina, servant and slave of the servants of Jesus Christ, am writing to you in his precious blood. I long to see you united with and[b] transformed in the fire of blazing charity, so that you may be a vessel of love[8] to carry the name of God's Word and his great mysteries before our dear Christ on earth, and to be effective in igniting his desire.[9] So I want you, my son, to open your mind's eye and focus it on Christ crucified, for he is the fountain where we can drink to the full,[c] drawing from him sweet loving desires. These are the desires I want you to pour out on the body of holy[d] Church for God's honor and every person's salvation.[10] If you do, your words and actions will become like an arrow drawn red-hot out of the fire, that wherever it is shot[e] sets on fire everything it strikes, since it can't help sharing what it has. So, son, think of your soul as entering the fiery furnace of divine charity, and love's power will make you shoot out and share what you have drawn from the fire.[11]

---

[7] Again, cf. introduction to Let. T226.

[8] As she often does in her letters of this period, Catherine repeats Acts 9, 15 as she misheard or misread it: *vas delectionis* (It. *vasello di dilectione*) instead of *vas electionis* (It. *vasello d'electione*). T corrects it to correspond with the biblical text.

[9] Catherine was concerned with igniting everyone's desire, not only the pope's. So there is no need to identify a specific desire the pope may have manifested about the time this letter was written (see Dupré Theseider's concern mentioned earlier).

[10] Cf. Let. T208/DT6 to Bartolomeo Dominici (in this volume), where desire for others' salvation is "poured out" over them as wine from a drunkard's enflamed stomach: "Do as a heavy drinker does who loses himself and can no longer see himself. If he really likes the wine he drinks even more, till his stomach becomes so warmed by the wine that he can no longer hold it, and out it comes! Truly, son, here is the table on which we find this wine: I mean the pierced side of God's Son. This is the blood that warms, that drives out all chill, clears the voice of the one who drinks it, and gladdens heart and soul. For this blood is shed with the fire of divine charity. It so warms us that out *we* come from our very selves—and from that point on, we cannot see ourselves selfishly, but only for God, and we see God for God, and we see our neighbors for God. And when we have drunk enough, out it comes over the heads of our sisters and brothers."

[11] Cf. Let. T198/DT4 to Bartolomeo Dominici (in this volume), where the same image is used. (I have speculated that both that letter and Let. T208/DT6, just cited, were written

And what have you drawn from God[f] in this way? Hatred and contempt for yourself, and love for virtue, and hunger for the salvation of souls and the honor of the eternal Father; for that is all that is found in this gentle Word. You see, it was for hunger that he died.[12] So intense was that hunger that the force of love produced a sweat not of water but of drops of blood. How could a heart be so hard and stubborn as not to burst with emotion from the warmth and heat of this fire?[13] Contemplating it, we can only be like flax stubble thrown into the fire;[14] it can't help burning, since it is the nature of fire to burn[g] and to transform into itself whatever comes near it. So we, when we contemplate our Creator's love, are drawn at once to love him and turn our affection completely to him. In him all the dampness of selfishness is dried up, and we take on the likeness of the Holy Spirit's fire.[15] And the sign that we have received it

---

during Lent of 1376.) The sword as an image of God's word occurs several times in Scripture, for example, Is. 49, 2: "[God] made of me a sharp-edged sword"; Heb. 4, 12: "Indeed, God's word is living and effective, sharper than any two-edged sword, penetrating and dividing soul and spirit"; Rv. 19, 15: "Out of his [the rider of the white horse, symbolizing Christ] mouth came a sharp sword." Elsewhere God's word is fire, for example, Pr. 30, 5: "Every word of God is afire." (all Vulg.) Cavalca brings the two concepts together in *Trenta stoltizie*, p. 33B: "[The preachers'] word is like a sharp sword, and their words blaze like a torch."

[12] The concept of Christ's dying of hunger is developed in Let. T11 to Cardinal Pierre d'Estaing (in this volume): "You know very well that divine Goodness has set you within the mystic body of holy Church and nourished you at the breast of this dear bride only to have you eat the food of God's honor and the salvation of souls at the table of the most holy cross. It is his will that this food be eaten only on the cross, that is, by bearing physical difficulties with constant restless desire. This is what God's Son did. As he endured torments in his body he endured also the pain of desire, and the cross of desire was greater than the physical cross. And this was his desire: hunger for our redemption in fulfillment of his eternal Father's commission—and he suffered until he saw this accomplished. . . . This was the crucified desire he bore from beginning to end. And when he had given his life the cross of desire ended, but not desire itself."

[13] Cf. *Dial.* 4, pp. 31–32: "They have, with the hand of free choice, encrusted their heart in a diamond rock that can never be shattered except by blood. Still, I tell you, in spite of their hardness, let them while they still have time and freedom to choose seek the blood of my Son and with that same hand let them pour it over the hardness of their heart. It will shatter the diamond and they will know the fruit of that blood which was paid out for them." (In medieval lore, the only force capable of shattering a diamond was the fresh warm blood of a goat. Cf. Heb. 9, 13–14.)

[14] This imagery occurs nowhere else in Catherine's extant writings.

[15] The imagery of wood transformed in fire is developed in Let. T137/DT45 to Matteo di Fazio dei Cenni (vol. I): "I long to see you so totally ablaze with loving fire that you become one with gentle First Truth. Truly the soul's being united with and transformed into him is like fire consuming the dampness in logs. Once the logs are heated through and through, the fire burns and changes them into itself, giving them its own color and warmth and power. It is just so with us when we look at our Creator and his boundless charity. We begin to experience the heat of self-knowledge—which consumes all the dampness of our selfish love for ourselves. As the heat increases, we throw ourselves with blazing desire into God's measureless goodness, which we discover within our very selves. We are then sharing

is that we at once become lovers of what God loves and haters of what God hates.

This is why my soul longs to see you[h] so truly united with and transformed in the fire of God's charity. Strive for that with all your might, my dearest son, so that you may fulfill God's will as well as your poor sad mother's. Keep living in God's holy and tender love.[i]

Tell Nanni and Papo[16] to shout so loudly that I will pay attention to their voices. Tell Gherardo my son to respond to the voice of his mother, who is calling him, and to hurry, because I'm waiting for him.[17] Give Vanni a hug for me, and also Missere Francesco, Monna Nella, and Caterina—all of them.[18] Bless them by setting the most holy cross in your midst. And the same to *babbo* for me.[19]

Jesus! Gentle Jesus!

Francesco says he is not obligated, and bad, lazy Francesco[20] also says you should commend him to Frate Raimondo a thousand times in Christ Jesus and tell him to pray to God for him.

Jesus! Jesus!

You know that when I received from the holy father the indulgence for sin and punishment,[21] he imposed on me the obligation of saying every

---

in his warmth and in his power, in that we begin at once to feed on and savor souls. And we in turn change every other person into ourselves in love and desire, by giving *them* the color and taste for virtue that we have drawn from the wood of the most holy cross." Also Let. T151 (in this volume) and Prayer 15.

16 Nanni is unidentified. Papo is all but certainly the same as is mentioned in Let. T226, but other than his being named in these two letters we know nothing of him.

17 Neither Fawtier nor Dupré Theseider questions why Catherine should be waiting for Gherardo Buonconti. One can only guess, but perhaps she is wanting his assistance as scribe. If he was the scribe for Let. T183/DT56 (written in January 1376), he would have to have been in Siena also when that letter was written. He will also accompany Catherine to Florence and Avignon in May (presumably from Siena). It seems just a bit strange that he would spend so much of his time away from home, since he is married. Recall that he and his wife Caterina were Catherine's hosts during her 1375 stay in Pisa. (Let. T161, in this volume, will be addressed to Caterina.)

18 These are all members of the Buonconti family. Niccolò and Nella are the parents; Vanni, Francesco, and Gherardo are three of their sons. Caterina is Gherardo's wife.

19 The informality of the greeting would lead me to suspect that *babbo* here is Raimondo. She clearly calls him by that nickname ("Daddy") in Let. T295 (1378) and T192 (1379).

20 These seem to be two different Francescos. The second may be the scribe who is writing this letter (because Catherine's scribes often label themselves pejoratively), probably Francesco Malavolti, a lay disciple who says that he did occasionally serve Catherine in that role. Malavolti was something of a playboy, and sometimes wandered back into his old ways. The other Francesco is unidentified.

21 A "plenary indulgence" is the Catholic Church's remission of all sin and of all punishment due that sin. Such indulgences could be given for a specific time or in view of the moment of death if at that moment certain conditions would be fulfilled. The former sort

Friday thirty-three *Pater nosters* and thirty-three *Ave Marias*, plus seventy-two more *Ave Marias*. But I would be happy now if you would (if it seems good to you) ask him to impose on me a fast of bread and water every Friday. Don't forget this—if it seems good to you to ask that.[22]

Jesus! Jesus![j]

Textual Notes

a. B, P2, P5, F2: *Christ gentle Jesus / Christ Jesus.*

b. T, P3, B, P2, P5, F2: [*united with and*].

c. Literally, "get drunk."

d. P3: *most holy / holy.*

e. P5, F2: *It follows then then / that wherever it is shot* (an apparent scribal error).

f. T, P3, B, P2, P5, F2: *God's Son / God.*

g. P5, F2 add: *and to consume.*

h. Mo, T, B, P2, P3: *to see effected in you / to see in you* (Volpato speculates that the addition is out of scrupulosity for orthodoxy).

i. B, P2, T: *Keep living, etc. Jesus, etc.*; P3: *Keep living, etc. Jesus love.*; P5, F2: ... *madre tua in Christ gentle Jesus. Amen.*

j. S3: *Gentle Jesus! Jesus love! / Jesus! Jesus!*

---

of indulgence could be received many times during life, whereas one would presumably need the latter sort only once. We know that Catherine had received an indulgence from Gregory XI in spring of 1374 (cf. Let T127/DT20, vol. I). We are not told either in Let. T127/DT20 or in the present letter which sort of plenary indulgence is involved, though we do know from the *Leggenda minore* (III, iv, Grottanelli, p. 164) that at some point Catherine received from Gregory XI an indulgence for the moment of death, an indulgence which was renewed by Urban VI.

[22] This would seem to exclude any claim that, at least at the time this letter was written, Catherine was fasting so extremely as to be consuming nothing but the Eucharist. To have considered fasting on bread and water a penance, she must have been customarily eating more than that. Stefano Maconi, in fact, testifies (*Processo Castellano*, ed. Laurent, p. 267) that her being able to tolerate "not even a drop of water" occurred while she was in Rome, and Barduccio Canigiani, in a letter to Suor Caterina Petriboni, (published in Gigli, *Opere*, IV, pp. 484–489.) places this change in January 1380, four months before her death. Stefano says that "her usual way of living over a long time—which I witnessed for many years—was this. She had a genuine horror of meat and wine, as well as of things prepared with eggs. Her companions continually furnished her with raw greens (what we call 'salad') when they could find them, and sometimes with cooked greens seasoned with oil. Of eels, she would eat only the head and the tail. Cheese she would eat only when it was already spoiled—and other such things as well. And this she ate sometimes with bread, sometimes without bread. She would swallow the juice of the greens and spit out the rest. Most often she drank only water." As for her request concerning the *Paters* and *Aves*, Catherine, who cautions others about simply "getting in their quotas of Our Fathers" (Let. T213), seems herself to have been disinclined to repetitive vocal prayers such as the series imposed on her for this indulgence.

LETTER T196/G4/DT64[1]
To Pope Gregory XI, in Avignon
February 1376

Tensions between the republics of the Italian peninsula deepened as the pope's representatives there exercised their authority through increasingly oppressive measures. During the first three months of 1376 one Tuscan city after another took up arms against the Church, expelled the papal garrisons, and entered into league with Florence and her allies.[2] The urgent tone of the present letter probably reflects this situation. I would guess, however, that it was written before the pope's failed overture of peace to Florence in the first half of March.[3]

§

In the name of Jesus Christ crucified and of gentle Mary.

My most reverend and holy father in Christ gentle Jesus,

I Caterina, your poor unworthy daughter, servant and slave of the servants of Jesus Christ, am writing to you in his precious blood. I long to see you a good shepherd, my dear *babbo*, for I see the infernal[a] wolf carrying off your little sheep, and there is no one to rescue[b] them. So I am turning to you, our father and shepherd, begging you in the name of Christ crucified to learn from him who with such blazing love gave himself up to the shameful death of the most holy cross to save this little lost sheep, the human race, from the devils' hands. Because of its rebellion against God, here are the devils, holding this sheep as their own possession.[4] Then along comes God's infinite goodness and sees the sheep's sorry state, its ruin and damnation. He knows he cannot use wrath or war to entice it away from them. Supreme eternal wisdom doesn't want to do it that way, even though the sheep has wronged him (for humankind, by its rebellion

---

[1] MSS: Mo, M, S5, S6, Ro, S2, P4, S4; translation based on Mo-*a*, corrected by *b*. Other variants based on Dupré Theseider.

[2] See Brucker, *Florentine Politics and Society*, p. 308; Gardner, *Saint Catherine of Siena*, pp. 157–160.

[3] The linguistic evidence supports the historical basis for the placement of this letter only broadly, adding little to the historical arguments for its date. Seckendorff (*Politische Tätigkeit*, pp. 88–89), Fawtier (II, pp. 143–144), and Dupré Theseider (n. 1) place the letter between mid-February and the end of March 1376.

[4] In Let. T97 (in this volume) to Monna Pavola da Siena, Catherine will refer to the human race as Christ's spouse, who "because she was an adulteress" had been in the devil's possession.

in disobedience, was deserving of infinite punishment). No, he finds a delightful way—the most sweet and loving way possible; for he sees that the human heart is drawn by love as by nothing else, since it is made of love.[5]

This seems to be why human beings love so much, because they are made of nothing but love, body and soul. In love God created them in his own image and likeness, and in love father and mother conceive and bring forth their children, giving them a share in their own substance.[6] So God, seeing that humankind is so quick to love, throws out to us right away the hook of love,[7] giving us the Word, his only-begotten Son. He takes on our humanity to make a great peace. But justice wants vengeance for the wrong done to God. So along comes divine mercy and ineffable charity and, to satisfy justice as well as mercy, condemns his Son to death once he has clothed him in our humanity, in the clay of Adam who had sinned.[8] So by his death the Father's anger is appeased and justice is satisfied by the sentence passed on the person of his Son. And mercy is satisfied because he has snatched humankind from the devils' hands!

This Word played life against death and death against life in tournament on the wood of the most holy cross, so that by his death he destroyed our death, and to give us life he spent his own bodily life.[9] With

---

[5] Cf. *Dial.* 26, p. 65: "The human heart is always drawn by love." And 110, pp. 207–208: "And your candle is love, because it was for love that I created you, so without love you cannot have life."

[6] Cf. Let. GardI/DT52 (vol. I): "The very first garment we ever had was love, for it was only by love that we were created in God's image and likeness. So we cannot exist without love since we are made of nothing less than love. Whatever we have, physically or spiritually, we have because of love—for it is by love alone, with the help of God's grace, that a mother and father give their child existence (I mean bodily existence)."

[7] In *Dial.* 139, p. 286, God uses Mary as a bait to catch his creatures. There are a number of other instances in which the image of the hook has different referents, for example, the Word catching the devil on the hook of humanity (Let. T136/DT37), or God catching the devil on the hook of divinity with the bait of humanity (*Dial.* 135, p. 278; Prayer 13, p. 109); the devil catching the soul with the hook of spiritual pleasure (*Dial.* 71, p. 133).

[8] Catherine here summarizes the Augustinian and medieval theology of redemption: original sin, because it was an offense against the infinite God, required atonement by the humanity that had sinned but at the same time by an infinite being, a requirement met by Jesus as both human and divine.

[9] Cf. *Dial.* 30, p. 71: "Your mercy made your Son play life against death on the wood of the cross. In him life confounded the death that is our sin, even while that same death of sin robbed the spotless Lamb of his bodily life. But who was conquered? Death! And how? By your mercy!" Also 2 Tim. 1, 10: "He has robbed death of its power and has brought life and immortality into clear light through the gospel." Heb. 2, 14–15: "that by his death he might rob the devil, the prince of death, of his power, and free those who through fear of death had been slaves their whole life long." Catherine may also be thinking of the Easter Sequence: "Death and life in battle—wondrous conflict!—the Captain of life, though killed, reigns alive," or the hymn *Vexilla Regis*: "He endured death, and by death brought forth

love, then, he has so drawn us and with his kindness so conquered our malice that every heart should be won over. For a person can show no greater love (he said so himself) than to give his or her life for a friend.[10] And if he praises the love that gives one's life for a friend, what shall we say of the consummate blazing love that gave his life for his enemy?[11] For through sin we had become God's enemies. *Oh gentle loving Word, with love you recovered your little sheep, and with love gave them life. You brought them back to the fold by restoring to them the grace they had lost.*

Oh my dear most holy *babbo*! I see no other way, no other help for getting back your little sheep who have left the fold of holy Church as rebels disobedient and unsubmissive to you their father. So I am begging you in the name of Christ crucified, and I want you to do me this favor: use your kindness to conquer their malice. We are yours, father, and I know for certain that all of them realize they have done wrong. And even though there is no excuse for wrongdoing, still, because of all the suffering and injustice and unfairness they were enduring from bad pastors and administrators, it didn't seem to them they had any alternative. They smelled the stinking lives of these bad administrators (who you know are devils incarnate) and they became so terribly fearful that, like Pilate, who killed Christ so as not to lose his authority, they attacked you rather than lose their position.[12] So I am asking your mercy for them, father.

Don't look at your children's pride and foolishness. No, with the bait of love and of your own kindness give peace to us poor children who have sinned, adding whatever sweet discipline and kind rebuke may please your holiness. I tell you, dear Christ on earth, in the name of Christ in heaven, if you do this without creating a storm or tempest, they will all come and lay their heads in your lap in sorrow for what they've done. Then you will be happy and so will we, because by love you will have put your little lost sheep back in the fold of holy Church. And then, my dear *babbo*, you can carry out your desire and God's will—I mean the holy crusade. I invite you in his name to do it soon, without putting it off. These same people have been ready and will be ready to give their lives eagerly for Christ.[13]

---

life." Also Jacopo Passavanti, *Lo specchio di vera penitentia*, Dist. II, chap. VII: "As St. Gregory says (PL LXXIX, 28), by his passion and death he conquered our death."

[10] Jn. 15, 13.

[11] Cf. Rom. 5, 6–10.

[12] Cf. Cavalca, *Specchio dei peccati*, p. 90: "Pilate had [Christ] crucified, even though he knew he was blameless, for fear of losing the emperor's friendship, as the Jews were threatening, if he would let him go."

[13] Dupré Theseider (n. 9 to this letter) sees this as possibly an allusion to a promise the Tuscan communes have made to Catherine, that they would contribute to an eventual crusade. If such a promise was in fact made (and was not simply a pious wish on Catherine's part), it was probably nothing but an attempt to appease the pope.

Oimé! *God sweet love!* Do raise the standard of the most holy cross soon, *babbo*, and you will see the wolves become lambs. Peace! Peace! Peace!—so that war may not delay this sweet time! But if you want vengeance and strict justice, take it out on this poor wretch; give me any pain and torment you please, even death. I believe the stench of my sins has been the cause of much evil, discord, and great misfortune. So take as much vengeance on me your miserable daughter as you like.

Oimé! Father, I am dying of grief and cannot die![14] Come, come; don't resist any longer the will of God who is calling you! The starving little sheep are waiting for you to come and take possession of the place of your predecessor and model, the apostle Peter. You, as Christ's vicar, ought to be residing in your proper place.[15] Come! Come! Come! Don't put it off any longer! Take heart, and don't be afraid of anything that might happen, for God will be with you. I humbly ask your blessing for myself and for all my children. And I beg you to pardon my presumption. I'll say no more.

Keep living in God's holy and tender love.

Gentle Jesus! Jesus love!

Textual Notes

a. M: [*infernal*].

b. M: *redeem / rescue.*

[14] Catherine uses this expression quite often. Giovanni Colombini speaks in a similar way in his letters. (Let. 18: "You can imagine the pain and torture this poor thing lives in—he lives dying." Let. 103: "I am dying of love for Jesus Christ and for holy charity, and I don't know what to do with myself." Let. 77 "I cannot think of Christ my joy without bursting and dying.")

[15] Many fourteenth-century writers, according to Dupré Theseider (n. 12 to this letter) believed that the pope could in principle live anywhere. (Cavalca writes in *Specchio di croce*, p. 135: "There is a common proverb that says, 'Where the pope is, there is Rome.' ") But Rome, in the view of these same writers, is the *proper* place, since Peter lived in Rome. Cf. also Dupré Theseider, *I papi di Avignone* (Firenze: Felice Le Monnier, 1939), pp. XXI, 72.

LETTER T171/G217/DT60[1]

To Niccolò Soderini, one of the *priori delle Arti* of Florence
Late February 1376

Niccolò di Ruggero (Geri) Soderini, who had become Catherine's friend and disciple probably during her 1374 stay in his city, was one of the *priori delle Arti* in Florence during January and February of 1376. The rubric of B and of P2 indicates that this letter to him was written while he held that office, and while the antipapal league was still in formation.

Throughout this letter Catherine plays on the word *legare* ("to bind") and its associated forms, *lega* ("league") and *legame* ("bond"). Though Pisa and Lucca will not seal their allegiance to the antipapal league until 12 March 1376, the determination of Florence has already been clear for several months as Catherine is writing. That city formally joined the league on 24 July 1375.[2]

[1] MSS: Mo-*c*, B, P2, R1, T, P5, F2, P3, S3; translation based on Mo-*c*, with variants based on Dupré Theseider.

[2] The early 1376 placement required by the rubric is strongly supported by the linguistic data. Six other letters, all from mid-1375 to early 1376, share eighteen or more of this letter's sixty-one analyzed patterns. There are, further, a good number of significant clusters within individual patterns concentrated in this time period, with several of these ending or beginning in the first three months of 1376: AMPRIM, ANGELTER, ARBPIANT, COLTODAM, EREDITA, ESALT, JERUSAL, MARIAMAD, MEMBPUTR, OCCHIO, OFFIZIO, PACEUNIO, PORTBASS, RIBELCRE, SUPERBPR, SUSTPADR, VERMINE, VOGLIO.

§

In the name of Jesus Christ crucified and of gentle Mary, mother of God's Son.

Dearest and very loved brother and son in Christ Jesus,

I Caterina, servant and slave of the servants of Jesus Christ, am writing to you in his precious blood. I long to see you a member so tightly bound in the bond of true charity that you will share in this true love. For since you have been placed in leadership and appointed to the *Signoria*,[3] you could be the means of helping bind all of your townspeople, so that they might not be in such physical and spiritual danger.

You know that a member cut off from its head cannot live, for it is not joined with the source of its life. It is the same, I tell you, with people cut off from God's love and charity—I mean those who do not follow their Creator but harass him with insults and deadly sins that are clear from signs and behavior we see every day. And you know what I'm talking about. Now who are we—poor, miserable, proud, and wicked as we are—that we should act against our head? Oimé! Oimé! The blind sight of our pride and arrogance shows us the flower of prestige and power, but we don't see the worm that has gotten under this flowering plant and is gnawing away at it.[4] And it will soon die if it doesn't set itself right. It must, then, set itself right[a] by the light of true sweet humility's reasonableness—for those who love this virtue are always exalted, while the proud, as Christ said, are always humbled.[5] Such people cannot have life, since they are members cut off from the gentle bond of charity.[6]

Now what worse can befall us than to be deprived of God? Oh, we could have plenty of connections, once the league is sealed, and be in league with many persons and cities.[7] But if God's bonding and help are not there, they would be useless to us. You know that those who guard

---

[3] Soderini, as one of the *priori delle Arti*, is a member of the *Signoria*, or ruling body of the city.

[4] As frequent as the image of the flower is in Catherine's works, she is probably in this case playing directly on the name of Florence—*Fiorenza*, often interpreted as "the city of flowers." She has earlier used the same imagery in writing to the pope (Let. T185/DT54, vol. I): *"Oh sweet true knowledge! You thrust out your hand, holy desire, bearing the knife of hatred, to cut out and kill the worm of selfish self-centeredness that so gnaws at and cripples the root of our tree that it can produce no fruit of life. The tree withers and its fruits dry up, and its freshness does not last."*

[5] Lk. 14, 11.

[6] Cf. Jn. 15, 6: "Anyone who does not live in me is like a withered, rejected branch, picked up to be thrown into the fire and burned."

[7] An allusion to the antipapal league being advocated by Florence. Catherine is playing on the words *legare* ("to bind") and *lega* ("league").

the city are wearing themselves out for nothing if God is not keeping guard.[8] So what shall we do, unfortunate, blind, and obstinate in our sins, since God is the one who guards and preserves the city and the whole universe, and I have rebelled against him, the one who is? And if I should say, "I am not acting against God!" I'm telling you that you do act against God when you act against his vicar, who takes his place.[9] Realize that you are so weakened by your rebellion that there is scarcely any strength left, for we are deprived of our strength. Oimé! Dearest brother and son, open your eyes and look at the danger, the destruction of soul and body! I beg you not to wait for disaster and divine judgment. For the worm could grow so big that the flower would shrivel up and die. Its fragrance has already faded because we have rebelled against Christ. You know that the fragrance of grace cannot last in those who act against their Creator, but the remedy is there if we are willing to take it. And I beg you as strongly as I know how in Christ gentle Jesus to take it, you and your fellow citizens. As for you yourself, do what you can.

Humble yourselves; make peace in your hearts and minds.[b] We cannot pass through the low door with our head held high unless we want to crack it.[10] And the door we have to pass through is Christ crucified, who humbled himself down to the level of us witless fools. If you do humble yourselves, you will peaceably and meekly ask for peace with our head, Christ on earth. Be willing to show that you are children, members bound, not cut off, and you will find mercy and kindness and will be exalted soul and body. You know that necessity must force us to do this even if love does not.[11]

A young lad cannot get along without his father's help, for he has no power or energy whatever of his own. (Whatever he has, he has from

---

[8] Ps. 127, 1.

[9] This is the same argument as in Let. T28/DT17 to Bernabò Visconti (vol. I).

[10] Cf. Cavalca, *Specchio di croce*, p. 212: "We have to bow our head low in fear when we enter through the low door, so as not to strike it or, in fear that something might be banged against our head." Cavalca cites Augustine, referring perhaps to a passage in *In Ioannis evangelium tractatus XLV* (PL XXXV, 1721): "Christ our God is a low door. All who enter through this door must humble themselves in order to enter with head intact." Also Simone Fidati da Cascia, *Expositiones super totum corpus evangeliorum*, p. 41: "The door to paradise is very narrow and low. The rich, dressed in love of riches, cannot go through it; nor the proud with head held high, bloated with the wind of vainglory. They might crack and break their heads."

[11] Cf. *Dial.* 159, p. 341 (where the reference is to members of religious orders, who make a vow of obedience): "[The disobedient] walk proudly, carrying the head of self-will high. And if they are sometimes forced to obey they do not bow down in humility but pass through [the door] proudly. So their head is bent by a force that breaks their self-will, because they obey with contempt."

God.[12]) It behooves him, therefore, to stay in his father's good graces. If there is hatred and bitterness between them, the help will stop coming—and when the help fails, so will he. So you must go—and quickly—to ask for your Father's (I mean God's) help. But we have to ask his vicar too. Since God has given him the key to heaven, we[c] have to yield the leadership to this doorkeeper.[13] For whatever he does is done; what he does not do is not done. Christ said to Saint Peter, "Whatever you bind on earth will be bound in heaven, and whatever you loose on earth will be loosed in heaven."[14] Since this vicar is so strong and has so much power and authority that he opens and shuts the doors to eternal life, shall we rotten members, children rebelling against our father, be so stupid as to act against him? It is very clear that without[d] him we are powerless. If you are against holy Church, how can you have a share in Christ's blood, since the Church is none other than that same Christ? It is Christ who gives and administers the sacraments to us—the sacraments that give us life through the life they derive from the blood of Christ.[15] For before we were given that blood, neither virtue nor anything else could give us eternal life.[16]

How, then, can we be so brazen as to scorn this blood? And if you should say to me, "I'm not scorning [Christ's] blood!" I say that is not so. Whoever scorns this dear vicar is scorning the blood, because whoever acts against the one is acting against the other, since they are inseparable. How can you tell me that you can attack a body without attacking the blood within the body? Don't you know that this is a mystic body holding within itself the blood of Christ? Understand that it is the same here as with the son and father: no matter how much the father may offend his son, the son never has a case against his father. No, the son neither can nor should offend his father without courting death and condemnation. He is forever indebted to his father for the existence his father has given him. The son never asked his father to give him a share of his own flesh, and

---

[12] She alternates between the metaphor of a human father and son, and her underlying meaning, that the father is God.

[13] She clearly derives the image of the pope as doorkeeper from the words of Christ to Peter cited next. Cf. *Dial.* 154, p. 328; also Giordano da Rivalto, *Prediche inedite*, ed. Narducci, p. 140: "He is the doorkeeper; when you confess [your sins], you are asking him to open the door for you."

[14] Mt. 16, 19. Cf. *Dial.* 115, p. 215, where the concept is further developed. Also Let. T28/DT17 (vol. I).

[15] Cf. *Dial.* 115, p. 215: "And from this blood all the sacraments derive their life-giving power."

[16] In *The Dialogue*, Catherine speaks of heaven's gate closed by sin and of the broken roadway; the blood of Christ is the key that unlocks heaven, and the mystical bridge built in his Passion rejoins earth to heaven. Cf. also Aquinas, *Summa Theologica*, III, q. 49, a. 5: "Before Christ's Passion no one could enter the kingdom of heaven."

yet he did, moved by the love he had for his son even before he existed. How much less, then, should we foolish heedless ungrateful children be able to bear offending our true Father! For he loved us without being loved.[17] Out of love he created us, and then created us anew to grace in his blood. He gave his life with such blazing love that we at the very thought of it should rather endure hunger and thirst and every exigency, even to the point of death, before we would rebel against his vicar. For through his vicar we receive the fruit of Christ's blood—and all this not because it is due us, but by grace.

So no more, my brothers! Sleep no more in so little light and knowledge. Let us dig out the worm of pride and selfish self-love. Let us kill it with the knife of hatred and love—with love for God and reverence for holy Church, with hatred and contempt for the sin committed against God and the Church. Then you will have made an engrafting into the tree of life. You will be delivered from death and your life restored. Your weakness will be taken away (for we have already said that you have been deprived of God, who is our strength, because of your[e] attacks against his bride).

By using this hatred and contempt to replace this division with unity, you will be so strengthened in spiritual gifts (in which we have to share if we want the life of grace) and in temporal ones, that no one will be able to harm you. It is better for you to live in peace and unity, not only with your head but with everyone—for we are not Jews or Saracens, but Christians ransomed and bathed[f] in Christ's blood.[18] How foolish we are to be all wrapped up in our craving for greatness and, for fear of losing status, taking on and doing the devils' work by going about enticing others to do the same evil you are doing! Yes, this is how the devils acted. They were angels, but those who fell joined in league to rebel against God. They wanted to be high, but they became low.

Please, I don't want you behaving like them, joining in league to act against Christ's bride. If you do, just when you think you are bound together and exalted, you will be more divided and lower than ever. No more of this, dearest brothers! Bond together in the league[g] of blazing charity; ask to return to peace and unity with your head, so that you may

---

[17] Cf. *Dial.* 119, p. 226: "I loved you before you came into being."

[18] See, in contrast, Let. T346 to Pope Urban VI (1378): "What I mean is, [we must] find sadness and bitterness only in our sins and in the dishonor done to God in the universal body of the Christian religion and in the mystic body of holy Church, as well as in the harm being done the souls of the unbelievers, who like us were ransomed by Christ's blood— the blood to which you, most holy father, hold the keys—and whom we see in the hands of the devils."

not be members cut off.[19] You have a father so kind that if you repent he will not only pardon you but will invite you to peace in spite of the abuse he has had from you.

It may perhaps seem to you that you are the ones who have been abused, but if this is the case it is because you have so little light in you. This is very dangerous; in fact, it's the reason people don't repent or correct themselves. They don't see their fault, and because they don't see it they don't heap hatred and contempt on it. So we have to see our faults in order to acknowledge them, so that acknowledging them we can correct them. As for the vice we see in others, we mustn't love the vice, but we should love and reverence the person and the authority God has placed in his ministers. And as for their sins, leave the judgment and chastisement to God, for he is the supreme Judge who rightly passes judgment and justly gives everyone what is due, rightly and as each deserves. It would be altogether unfitting for us to judge, for we have fallen under the same sentence as they. I beg you not to let yourselves be guided any more by such naiveté. Rather with heart courageous and virtuous bind yourselves to your head so that, as the moment of death arrives when we cannot excuse ourselves, we may share in and receive the fruit of Christ's blood.

I beg you, Niccolò, by the ineffable love with which God created you and so kindly redeemed you, to try as hard as you can (for God has put you in your position not without great mystery[20]) to bring about peace and unity between yourselves and holy Church, so that you and all of Tuscany may not be endangered. It doesn't seem to me that war is so lovely a thing that we should go running after it when we can prevent it. But is there anything lovelier than peace? Certainly not.[h] This is the sweet testament and lesson[i] Christ left to his disciples. He told them, "You will be known as my disciples not by working miracles, nor by knowing the future, nor by showing great holiness in externals, but only by having charity and peace and love among you."[21]

I want you, then, to take on the work of the angels (who are mediators) by making an effort to reconcile us with God. Do what you can. Don't be swayed either by pleasure or displeasure, but be concerned only for God's honor and your salvation. Even if it should cost you your life, never hold back from speaking the truth because of any fear the devil or

---

[19] The Florentines will not be subjected to the ultimate "cutting off," interdict, until 31 March 1376.

[20] "Mystery" is a favorite concept to Catherine. It implies all of God's relating with humanity, the sacramentality of all of life in Christ. Cf. Let. T13 to Marco Bindi (1378): "In whatever God gives or permits he is exercising his providence. Everything is done with mystery and out of love, not out of hatred."

[21] She is elaborating on Jn. 13, 35.

anyone else may try to instill in you. Take for your shield and defense the fear of God, knowing that his eyes are upon us[22] and that he always looks kindly on our will and intention when it is directed to him.

If you do this my desire for you will be fulfilled, since I told you I want you to be a member bound and united in the bond of charity—and not only for yourself but as a mediator for binding all the others. Get them to see, as much as you can, the danger and the evil state they are in. For I guarantee that if you don't make an effort to ask for peace and accept it graciously, you will fall into the greatest disaster you've ever fallen into.

I fear lest the same thing could be said [to you] as Christ said when he was going to his shameful death on the cross for us miserable wretches who are ungrateful for such a great favor. He turned and said, "Daughters of Jerusalem, weep not for me but for yourselves and your children."[23] And on Palm Sunday, when he was coming down from the mount, he said, "Jerusalem! Jerusalem! You are joyful because today is your day, but the time will come when you will weep."[24] Now, for love of God, don't wait till such a time but put on true joy, the joy of peace and unity. In this way you will be true children and you will share in and possess the inheritance of the eternal Father.

I'll say no more. For such is the pain and sorrow I bear for your spiritual and physical destruction that to prevent it I would give my life in great desire a thousand times if I could.

So let that be my excuse for rambling on, for I would surely bring my desire to realization quickly if I could.[j] I pray divine providence to give you, son, and all the others light, knowledge, fear, and holy love of God, and to free you from all darkness, selfish love, and slavish fear, from which all evil comes.

Keep living[k] in God's holy and tender love.

I am sending you the bearer of this letter, this year's preacher, a member of the Order of Friars Minor.[25] He is a true and good servant of God, and will help, advise, and direct you in the way of truth and in all you have to do, you yourself and the whole city in general. I beg you to accept

---

[22] Cf. Ps. 33, 18: "The eyes of the Lord are upon those who fear him, upon those who hope in his kindness."

[23] Lk. 23, 28.

[24] Cf. Lk. 19, 41–44. (Vulg.)

[25] In 1376 Lent began on 26 February. Catherine is confiding this letter to a religious who is leaving Siena for Florence, evidently to preach a Lenten series there. We do not know for certain who this is, but it may well be Fra Lazzarino da Pisa, who in fact will preach in Florence in Lent of 1376 to the great satisfaction of the *Signoria*. (Dupré Theseider, n. 22 to this letter) Lazzarino is by this time a disciple of Catherine's, having been converted by her from a rather sumptuous lifestyle.

and hold on to his advice. Let there be nothing so secret or hidden in your mind that you do not openly share it with him. I hope that by divine grace, because of his love and affection for your and everyone else's salvation, he will receive light from God to advise you rightly. Treat him as if he were another me.

Bless and encourage Monna Costanza[26] and the whole family.

Textual Notes

a. P2: [*It must, then, set itself right*].
b. B, P2: [*and minds*].
c. From B, P2; others have *you*.
d. P2: *against / without*.
e. Literally: *our*. (The pronouns here shift between first and second person pl.; this instance, however, may be significant in that Catherine often refers to the sins of others as her own as well.)
f. B, P2: *baptized / bathed*.
g. B, P2: *hands / league* (*nelle mani / nel legame*).
h. P2: [*But ... not*].
i. B, P2: *election / lesson*.
j. Mo: [*So ... could*] (supplied from B, P2).
k. B, P2 close here with *&c*.

---

[26] Costanza is Niccolò's wife (cf. Pompeo Litta, "Famiglia Soderini," table II, in *Famiglie celebri italiane*).

LETTER T164/G348/DT58[1]
To Monna Melina, wife of Bartolomeo Barbani of Lucca[a]
Mid-February to March 1376

Catherine was in Lucca at some point in January 1376 (almost surely a second visit), possibly at the suggestion of Pope Gregory XI, to attempt to persuade that city, teetering on the brink of joining the antipapal league, to maintain its loyalty to the pope. During at least one of her visits to Lucca she was the guest of the noble family of Bartolomeo Barbani (or Balbani), and after her departure Bartolomeo's wife Melina and other women who had grown close to Catherine during that visit and her probable stay the previous September apparently let Catherine know how painfully they were missing her.

The linguistic evidence reinforces the probability that this letter of response to their pain was written still in the early months of 1376.[2] If Catherine left Lucca only after 14 January (cf. Let. T168/DT53, vol. I), this letter could scarcely have been written before mid-February, since it seems to imply that she has heard from Melina. And because she says she intends the letter also for "Caterina, Monna Chiara, Monna Bartolomea, Monna Lagina, and Monna Colomba," it cannot be contemporary with Let. T162 or T165/DT59 (to some of those women), both of which seem to have been written during Lent of 1376 (26 February to 6 April). I would therefore place this letter most probably between mid-February and March of 1376, but before T162 and T165/DT59.

§

In the name of Jesus Christ crucified and of gentle Mary,
mother of God's Son.

My daughter in Christ Jesus,

I Caterina, servant and slave of the servants of Jesus Christ, am writing to encourage you in his precious blood. I long to see you so transformed and fused into the fire of divine charity that nobody and nothing will ever

---

[1] MSS: Mo-*c*, B, P2, R1, T, P5, F2, F1, P3, S3; translation based on Mo-*c*, corrected by *b*. Other variants based on Dupré Theseider.

[2] The only two letters with which this one shares twelve or more patterns are from February or March 1376. Besides, there are several significant clusters within individual patterns which end by March or early April of that year: AMASNZAM, MAGDALEN, MANGGUST, SANGMUR. And a number of patterns do not occur before early 1376: ACQUGRAZ, SANGMUR, TENEREZZ, VIRTVITA.

separate you from it.[3] You know, my dear beloved daughter, that to join two things together there must be nothing between them or there cannot be a perfect fusion.[4] Now realize that this is how God wants our soul to be, without any selfish love of ourselves or of others in between, just as God loves us without anything in between. Freely and generously he loved us, gratuitously and not because he had to: he loved us without being loved.[5] For us it is impossible to love the way God does. We are always obligated in duty to love since we are constantly being given a share in God's goodness and blessings. So we have to love with this second sort of love. But let this love be so clean and free that we love no one, nothing, spiritually or temporally, apart from God.

And if you say to me, "How can I have this sort of love?" I tell you, daughter, that we cannot have it or draw it from any source but the fountain of First Truth.[6] At this fountain you will discover your soul's dignity and beauty. You will see the Word, the slain Lamb who gave himself as your ransom and as your food. And he was moved only by the fire of his charity and not by any service he could have received from us, from whom he had received nothing but offense. I am saying, then, that when we gaze into this fountain thirsty and hungry for virtue, we begin at once to drink. We do not see or love[b] ourselves or anything else selfishly, because[c] we see everything in the fountain of God's goodness. In him we love what we love, and we love nothing without him.

Now how could the soul who has seen such immeasurable goodness on God's part do anything but love? This, it seems, is what gentle First Truth

---

[3] Cf. Rom. 8, 35–39: "Who will separate us from the love of Christ? Trial, or distress, or persecution, or hunger, or nakedness, or danger, or the sword? .... I am certain that neither death nor life, neither angels nor principalities, neither the present nor the future, nor powers, neither height nor depth nor any other creature, will be able to separate us from the love of God that comes to us in Christ Jesus, our Lord."

[4] Cf. Cavalca, *Trattato della mondizia del cuore* (a version of a writing attributed to St. Bonaventure, *De modo confitendi et de puritate conscientiae*, vol. VII of his *Works*, ed. Roma, 1596), p. 106: "Let there be nothing between your heart and God. And since it is impossible not to love anything that is less than God and yourself, at least don't love anything apart from God. So love every creature you love simply and completely in God and for God; then nothing in between will encumber your affection, but will be helpful and accommodating." Also Giovanni Colombini, Let. I: "... give yourself to God without anything in between." Later on Catherine uses the same word, *mezzo* ("in-between" as interfering, or as medium, or as intermediary) in its positive sense. The whole letter, in fact, plays on the multiple senses of the word *mezzo*.

[5] Catherine repeats this axiom often.

[6] The fountain in Catherine's writings variously images divine life and goodness poured out in the blood of Christ and the fire of the Spirit. This is the only instance, however, in which she uses the expression, "the fountain of First Truth." The nearest parallel is in *Dial.* 53, p. 106, where she comments on the passage from Jn. 7 which she will shortly cite here, and refers to Christ as "Truth."

invited us to when he cried out with heartfelt earnestness in the temple: "Let anyone who is thirsty come to me and drink, for I am the fountain of living water!"[7] You see, daughter, it is the thirsty who are invited. He does not say, "anyone who is not thirsty," but "anyone who is thirsty." So God insists that we bring with us the vessel of our free will, with a thirst and willingness to love. Let us go, then, to the fountain[d] of God's sweet goodness. There we shall discover the knowledge of ourselves and of God.[8] And when we dip our vessel in, we shall draw out the water of divine grace, powerful enough to give us everlasting life.[9]

But remember: we wouldn't be able to make any progress if we were burdened with a heavy load. This is why I don't want you to clothe yourself with love for me or anyone else, but to be clothed only in love for God.[10] I'm telling you this because I know from your letter the pain you suffered at my departure.[11] I want you to learn from gentle First Truth. Neither attachment to his mother nor to any of his disciples kept him from running like one in love to the shameful death of the cross, leaving Mary and his disciples behind. Yet he loved them immensely.[12] And later on[e] they left one another for the greater honor of God and other people's salvation, because their concern was not for themselves.[f] They gave up their own consolations for God's praise and glory, as people who eat and savor souls. You must believe that when they were so distressed they

---

[7] Jn. 7, 37.

[8] Cf. Let. T226 to Raimondo da Capua (in this volume), where Catherine develops in detail the image of the fountain in relation to knowledge of God and self: "[W]hen they contemplate God in blazing consumed love, [they] discover the image of the human person in God. And they discover themselves, God's image, in God. . . . Desire then disposes them to love themselves in God, and God in themselves, just as we, when we look into a fountain and see our image, take pleasure in it and love ourselves. But if we are wise, we are moved to love the fountain before we love ourselves. For if we hadn't seen ourselves we wouldn't have loved ourselves or taken pleasure in ourselves. Nor would we have corrected what was faulty about the face we saw in the fountain! . . .

"There is no other way we can see either our dignity or the faults that mar our soul's beauty, except by going to look into the quiet sea of the divine Being. There, in that Being, we see our reflection. Why? Because we came forth from there when God's wisdom created us in God's image and likeness. There we discover the union of the Word engrafted into our humanity; we discover and see and experience the blazing furnace of his charity, the means by which God gave us to ourselves and later united the Word with us and us with the Word when he took on our human nature."

[9] Cf. Jn. 4, 14: "Those who drink the water I give them will never be thirsty. The water I give shall become a fountain within them, leaping up into eternal life." (Vulg.)

[10] This imagery of love or charity as a garment is developed in vivid detail in Let. T182 to Suor Bartolomea della Seta (in this volume).

[11] Catherine must have left Lucca after 14 January, since she was aware of the elders' decision of that date, to side in principle with the antipapal league.

[12] The departure of the disciples from Mary (referred to also in Let. T30/DT1, vol. I, and elsewhere) is a theme often found in medieval legend.

would gladly have stayed with Mary, whom they loved so much. Yet they all left. For they did not love themselves or their neighbors or God selfishly. No, they loved God because he was supremely good and worthy of love, and themselves and[g] their neighbors and everything else they loved in God.

Now this is how I want you and the others to love. Look at me[h] only in terms of giving honor to God and your best efforts[13] to your neighbors. For though we may feel a certain sadness when someone we love leaves us, still we accept it graciously if our love is true, rooted only in God's honor and concerned more for the salvation of souls than for ourselves. Now then, don't let me see any more sadness, because this would be an interference that would hinder your being conformed and united with Christ.[i] It is because I think God asks us to give ourselves freely, as he did, that I said I want you and my other dear daughters to be transformed in and united with God by love, getting rid of any medium, anything that gets in between—except divine charity, which is a sweet and glorious medium that doesn't separate but unites.

Really, it seems just like the master mason. He gathers many stones and fits them together, and the result is called both "stones" and "a wall." He does this by using mortar as his medium.[14] Without the medium the stones would fall apart more scattered and broken than ever. So now imagine how our soul has to gather all people and be united with them in love and desire for their salvation, so that they may be sharers in the blood of the Lamb. So here this wall stands—many people, yet they are one. This, it seems, is what Saint Paul was inviting us to when he said that many run the race, but only one wins,[15] and the winner is the one who has used this medium, divine charity.

But you could say to me what the disciples said to Christ when he said, "A little while and you shall not see me, and again a little while and you shall see me."[16] They said,[j] "What is he going to do, that he says, 'A little while and you shall not see me, and again a little while and you shall see me'?" So you could say, "First you tell us that God doesn't want anything between us and him, and now you tell us to put something in between!" My answer is that you must use the medium that doesn't put anything between us and God,[k] the fire of divine charity, which becomes one with [God] as wood put into the fire. Would you say the wood remains wood?

---

[13] It. *fadiga.*

[14] The mortar—a medium that does not divide but unites—is confected with the blood of Christ, as explained in Let. T181/DT55 (vol. I), where the image of the mason (there, as the "master architect") is developed in greater detail.

[15] 1 Cor. 9, 24.

[16] Jn. 16, 16–18.

No, it becomes one with the fire.[17] But if you were to use as medium your selfish love for yourself, you would be using a medium that would separate you from God, even though it is nothing[18] (because sins have their root in nothing but selfish love and pleasure and enjoyment apart from God). For just as all virtue proceeds from charity, which gives it life, so all vice proceeds from selfish love, which deals death and eats away every virtue in the soul. This is why I said that God doesn't want anything between himself and us, and that any love not set in the true medium [of divine charity] does not last.

Run, my beloved daughters! Let's sleep no longer! I've felt sorry about your pain, and this is why I am giving you this remedy of loving God without anything between you and him. But if you still want poor wretched me as intermediary, I want to show you where to find me without being separated from this true love. Go with the dear loving Magdalen to the most sweet venerable cross. There you will find the Lamb and me, and there you can graze and feed and fulfill your desires. This is the way I want you to seek me and every created thing. Let this cross be your standard and comfort.[19] And don't imagine, because I am physically far away from you, that my affection and my concern for your salvation are far away. No, I am even closer than when I am there physically.

Don't you know that the holy disciples had a greater awareness and knowledge of the Master after he had left them than before?[20] They had

---

[17] Cf. Let. T137/DT45 to Matteo di Fazio dei Cenni (vol. I), where the wood transformed in the fire in turn becomes transforming: "Truly the soul's being united with and transformed into him is like fire consuming the dampness in logs. Once the logs are heated through and through, the fire burns and changes them into itself, giving them its own color and warmth and power. It is just so with us when we look at our Creator and his boundless charity. We begin to experience the heat of self-knowledge—which consumes all the dampness of our selfish love for ourselves. As the heat increases, we throw ourselves with blazing desire into God's measureless goodness, which we discover within our very selves. We are then sharing in his warmth and in his power, in that we begin at once to feed on and savor souls. And we in turn change every other person into ourselves in love and desire, by giving them the color and taste for virtue that we have drawn from the wood of the most holy cross."

[18] Sin is nothingness because it is contrary to God, who is pure Being.

[19] Cf. Let. T61/DT2 to Monna Agnesa Malavolti and the *Mantellate* of Siena (vol. I) on Mary Magdalen. The feast of the Triumph of the Cross is a solemn one in Lucca, honoring a crucifix (called the *Volto santo*, or "Holy Face") supposedly carved by Jesus' disciple Nicodemus and transported miraculously from the Holy Land during a crusade. Dupré Theseider (n. 17 to this letter) rejects, however, Tommasèo's contention, taken from Burlamacchi, that Catherine has in mind here that image. Yet Catherine certainly knew of that crucifix and had probably even made her first journey to Lucca the previous September to celebrate the feast at which it was venerated. In any case, the cross of Christ is a central mystery for Catherine.

[20] She picks up again what she had said earlier about the disciples, this time adding a new dimension: the disciples' love was imperfect because they were too attached to Christ's

been so taken up with his humanity that they hadn't looked beyond it. But after his departure they began to know and understand his goodness. This is why First Truth said, "I have to go; otherwise the Paraclete will not come to you."[21] So I say I had to leave you so you would begin to seek God in truth and not through any intermediary. I tell you, you will be better off than before, if you enter into yourselves to ponder the words[l] and teaching you have been given. In this way you will receive the fullness of grace by the very grace of God.

I'll write no more, because I have no more time for writing.

I'm sending this letter primarily to you, Melina, and then to Caterina, Monna Chiara, Monna Bartolomea, Monna Lagina, and Monna Colomba. Warm greetings from all of us!

Keep living in God's holy and tender love.

Textual Notes

a. In the rubrics of the various manuscripts the spelling *Barbani* predominates. Only B, P2 have *Balbani.*
b. B, P2: [*or love*].
c. B, P2: *and / because*; *b*: *but / because.*
d. Mo: *Let's go then to the love / Let's . . . fountain.*
e. From *b*; others have *But.*
f. P2: *In the same way the holy disciples, after they had received the Holy Spirit, parted ways, one going here, another there, for God's honor and other people's salvation. They did this because they chose not to be concerned about themselves. / But for . . . themselves.*
g. P2: [*themselves and*].
h. P2: *each other / me.*
i. B, P2: *Christ crucified / Christ.*
j. *b*: *So they were saying among themselves / They said.*
k. Literally, *which is not a medium.*
l. B, P2: *word / words.*

---

physical presence as long as he was among them before his death. Cf. Bernard de Clairvaux, *In Cantico sermo XX*, 5 (PL CLXXXIII, p. 869): "They loved him dearly but less wisely; they loved him in the flesh but not reasonably; they loved him with their whole heart but not with their whole soul."

[21] Jn. 16, 7.

Letter T170/G208/DT67[1]
To Pietro del Monte Santa Maria
Late February to March 1376

This is the third of Catherine's extant letters to Pietro del Monte Santa Maria.[2] In the present letter she is appealing to the senator for assistance in apprehending a young man who has been tormenting the nuns of the monastery of San Michele Angelo da Vico in Siena, apparently threatening rape. Her intimate acquaintance with the problem would suggest that she is almost certainly writing from Siena. Because of the linguistic evidence, I would place the letter after her return from Lucca (late January 1376) and before the end of March, but certainly before her departure for Florence and Avignon in early May.[3] The emphasis on discipline might further narrow the probability to Lent, and therefore between 26 February and 6 April.

§

In the name of Jesus Christ crucified and of gentle Mary.

Dearest father in Christ Jesus,

I Caterina, servant and slave of the servants of Jesus Christ, greet you in the precious blood of God's Son. I long to see you as Christ's true servant and knight, always fighting courageously against vice and sin, not apathetically but with genuine holy zeal. Then when we reach the sweet moment of death we will return victorious to our true city, Jerusalem, vision of peace,[4] where we will not find our flesh rebelling against our spirit.

But note, father, if we would have everlasting life we must let go of our flesh, before death comes and our flesh lets go of us. I mean we must let go of our carnal appetites, desires, and feelings. Oimé! Don't wait for an invitation to let go of them, for there is no time. And there is nothing that

---

[1] MSS: Mo-*b*, S3; translation based on Mo-*b*. No relevant variants.

[2] The earlier ones are Let. T148/DT36 and T135/DT42, both in vol. I.

[3] The only two letters with which this one shares six or more of its fifteen analyzed patterns are from January to April 1376. Further, there are significant clusters of the patterns ALLUMIN, DIGNITA, and VISIOPAC which end by April 1376, and clusters of GIUSTMIS and RICCPOV which do not begin until early 1376.

[4] The name Jerusalem means "city of peace." The expression "vision of peace" in reference to Jerusalem is not unique to her; it was used by, among others, Simone Fidati da Cascia (*Expositiones super totum corpus evangeliorum*, p. 459) in regard to eternal life. Catherine may have picked up the use of the expression in relation to Jerusalem while in Pisa, where there were so many graphic reminders of the crusades. She first used the expression during that year in Pisa, in Let. T143/DT39 (vol. I).

makes a person so bestial as this wicked vice. How stupid for a person to give up so much dignity for such a paltry thing, and turn into a brute animal!

So let's fight and root out this vice and every other with the fragrance of holy continence and integrity, and with the shield of the most holy cross, let's fend off the blows. Then you will be a true judge and lord in the position to which God has appointed you. And you will give fairly to rich and poor alike what is due them in holy justice—justice always seasoned with mercy. I'll say no more here.

I call to your attention something that has happened at the monastery of Santo Michele angelo a Vico.[5] It concerns a young man whose name you will be told in the letter the abbess of that monastery is sending you.[6] For a good long time he has been tormenting them, even to the point of entering the monastery whenever he pleases by breaking in through a window. He threatens those who refuse to cooperate, saying he is going to set fire to the monastery and burn them up inside, according to what they have told me. So I am asking you, please, to do what seems best to you to help them, so that an end is made of this abomination. I would not, however, want the young man to lose his life, though any other punishment would relieve me.[7]

I'll say no more on this subject. May the Holy Spirit enlighten you on this and on everything else.

Praised be Jesus!

---

[5] The Benedictine monastery of S. Michele Angelo a Vico was about a mile from Siena. It was suppressed in 1480 by Cardinal Francesco Piccolomini, archbishop of Siena (later Pope Pius III) when nuns no longer resided there. The revenues of the monastery were given as a benefice to two canons by the name of Piccolomini. Tommasèo in his note to this letter says, "It surely would have been possible to find a more charitable use than to contribute to the fortunes of two canons what had served for a whole convent of nuns! And not to load the Piccolomini hands with such a fortune would have been the height of charity!"

[6] The episode Catherine alludes to is, according to Dupré Theseider (n. 2 to this letter), not documented anywhere else. The expression, "according to what they have told me," makes it all but certain that she is writing from Siena. In fact, the letter may have been written to accompany the account written by the abbess and to commend the latter to the senator's attention.

[7] In Catherine's day it was much to ask that a convicted criminal's life be spared. This was so much more the case since these nuns were Benedictines, who were usually from illustrious families, and some of whose relatives would probably have cried out for blood (Tommasèo, *Lettere*, vol. III, p. 64, n. 5).

Letter T165/G351/DT59[1]
To Monna Bartolomea di Salvatico of Lucca
Between 26 February (Ash Wednesday) and 6 April (Palm Sunday) 1376

Monna Bartolomea[2] was one of the group of pious women Catherine had befriended while in Lucca, but the saint singles her out in this letter because of her recent conversion "because new plants need more help."

In this letter she greets Colomba, Giovanna d'Azzolino, Melina (probably Barbani), Caterina, and Lagina, and says she is not writing to them separately. Let. T162, on the other hand, is addressed to Franceschina, Caterina, and two other unnamed women of Lucca. "Caterina" is mentioned in both letters, but otherwise there is no duplication of greeting between T162 and T165, so they could well have been written and sent at the same time, especially since the themes in T165 also could be related to the Lenten season. For this reason as well as the linguistic evidence, I would place this letter within the first four months of 1376. Catherine is possibly writing it during Lent, that is, between late February and March.[3] It is, on the other hand, probably not too near Let. T164/DT58 to Melina Barbani, since the latter is greeted here and Catherine says she is *not* writing to her separately; nor too near T166 to Colomba, who is also greeted in the present letter, and Bartolomea in Let. T164/DT58.[4]

---

[1] MSS: Mo-*c*, S3; translation based on Mo-*c*, corrected by *b*. No relevant variants.

[2] See Let. T164/DT58, in this volume.

[3] The fact that the letter is addressed to Lucca would almost certainly place it after Catherine's first visit to that city (probably mid-September 1375). The eight other letters which share thirteen or more of this letter's fifty-eight analyzed patterns are broadly scattered from mid-1375 through mid-1379 (though all but one of those dated later than early 1376 are very long letters). A placement in early 1376 is, however, strongly supported by a heavy concentration of significant clusters within individual patterns during that period, with several of these not occurring before that time: CALDCAR, EBBRAMOR, FATTVIA, GLORCROC, GLORTRIB, MADRLATT, MAGDALEN, MANGFRUT, MARIAMAD, MEZZOPER, PASCNOTR, PORTBASS, STACARIT, TRIBCONS, VERSANG, VIAPENE.

[4] Dupré Theseider assigns the present letter with some hesitation to early 1376, but prior in any case to Catherine's departure for Florence and Avignon (April 1376).

§

In the name of Jesus Christ crucified and of gentle Mary,
mother of God's Son.

Dearest and very loved daughter in Christ Jesus,

I Caterina, servant and slave of the servants of Jesus Christ, am writing to you in his precious blood. I long to see you always feeding and nursing at the breast of the gentle mother, charity, for I am convinced no one can have life without the milk this glorious mother gives us. She is so sweet and mild to souls who taste her that in her everything bitter becomes sweet, and every heavy burden light. This doesn't surprise me, because when we live in this charity and love, we are living in God. This is what Saint John says: "God is charity, and when we live in charity we are living in God, and God in us."[5]

So if we have God we cannot have any bitterness, since God is supreme delight, supreme sweetness and joy. This is why God's servants are always happy. If they are ill or hungry, thirsty, poor, afflicted, troubled, or persecuted by others, they are happy. It doesn't bother God's servants if their reputation is torn to shreds. They are happy, jubilant about everything because they have God, who is all the rest they need, and they have tasted the milk of divine charity. And just as a baby draws milk through its mother's breast, so souls in love with God draw him to themselves through Christ crucified.[6] They always follow in his footsteps, choosing to follow him along the road of disgrace, suffering, and abuse. They want to find their delight only in Christ crucified, and they refuse to boast of anything but the cross. Such people say with Saint Paul, "I glory in difficulties for love of my Lord Jesus Christ, through whom the world is crucified to me, and I to the world."[7] So they embrace the wood of the most holy cross and with the face of holy desire upturned, gaze on the consum-

---

[5] 1 Jn. 4, 16.

[6] The imagery is developed especially in *Dial.* 96, p. 179: "Such a soul receives the fruit of spiritual calm, a union of the emotions with my gentle divine nature in which she tastes milk, just as an infant when quieted rests on its mother's breast, takes her nipple, and drinks her milk through her flesh. This is how the soul who has reached this final stage [of love] rests on the breast of my divine charity and takes into the mouth of her holy desire the flesh of Christ crucified." She goes on to explain that this means becoming one with Christ in his redemptive suffering. Since charity is the fire of the Holy Spirit, it is this fire one drinks in the blood of the crucified Christ. See also *Dial.* 70, p. 132, and 72, p. 134, where the imagery is not as completely developed.

[7] Cf. Gal. 6, 14: "May I never boast of anything but the cross of our Lord Jesus Christ! Through it, the world has been crucified to me and I to the world."

mate blazing love that has torn open his body, which in love is pouring out blood from every part.[8]

I'm not surprised, then, that these souls are patient in difficulties, since in love and with a free will they have rejected worldly consolations, and have become close friends with toil and persecution. For they have seen that this was the garment of God's Son, the garment he chose as the most precious and glorious he could find. This is the pearl our gentle Savior tells us of. The person who discovers it sells everything he or she has to buy it.[9]

What is this thing that is ours, given us by God, that neither the devil nor anyone else can take from us? It is our will. To whom shall we sell this treasure, our will? To Christ crucified. I mean that voluntarily and with wholesome[10] patience we will renounce our perverse will, which, when it is set on God, is a treasure. And with this treasure we will buy the pearl of suffering, and from it we will in patience draw the fruit we eat at the table of everlasting life.

Now it is to this food, this table, this milk that I am inviting you, my dearest daughter, and I beg you to accept it eagerly. Rise from the sleep of indifference, for I don't want you to be caught sleeping when you are summoned by First Truth. Oh sweet gentle summons that relieves us of our body's heaviness, that perverse interloper[11] that has always rebelled against its Creator by ill-ordered indulgence and pleasure, making of these a god for us![12] We used to be so blind that we didn't see our nothingness.[13] Proud as we were, we thought we could get through the narrow door loaded with the baggage of our pathetic perverse love of the world, which is the death of our soul.

So I want us to get rid of the baggage of all worldly vanity and selfish love for ourselves. Do you know why he says that the door through which we must pass is narrow? Because we have to narrow down our love and

---

[8] Cf. Let. T136/DT37 to Bishop Angelo Ricasoli (vol. I), where the Holy Spirit is the hand that taps the cask of Christ's body to spill the wine of his blood.

[9] Mt. 13, 45–46.

[10] It. *buona* ("good").

[11] Again the Italian is *mezzo*; the body, meant to be a medium of service and worship, is made a means of sin, an "interloper" between ourselves and God.

[12] Phil. 3, 19: "Their god is their belly." Cf. Cavalca, *Descrizione de' dieci comandamenti*, I: "As St. Augustine says, 'Whatever a person loves more than anything else is that person's god. This is why St. Paul says of certain people that they make a god of their belly, and others of money. He says this because they love these things excessively, more than God. So to put too much faith or hope or love in creatures is to make them God.' "

[13] Cf. Prayer 19, p. 179: "Ah, eternal Father! Grant that we may not be foolish, blind, or cold, or see so darkly that we do not see ourselves, but give us the gift of knowing your will."

desires for all worldly pleasure and consolation, and transform ourselves in our sweet mother charity, as I've said. I say we have to bow our head because the door is low, and if we carry our head high we will crack it.[14] We have to be willing to bow down in true holy humility, seeing that God has stooped down to us. I want you to regard yourself, as you should, as the lowest of all. And mind you don't turn back for anything whatever—neither for the devil's deceits nor for anything your husband or anyone else might say. Persevere courageously in your holy resolution. For you know that Christ says, "Do not turn back to look at what you've plowed."[15] It is perseverance that is crowned.[16]

Turn in affectionate love, with the dear loving Magdalen, and embrace the sweet venerable cross. There you will find all the sweet solid virtues, since it is there we find the God-Man. Reflect that the fire of divine charity has so crushed that venerable and tender body that it pours out blood from every part. He is so patient and loving that not a cry of complaint is heard from this Lamb, humble and despised, sated with disgrace.[17] Let your heart and soul burst with the heat of love [as you drink] at this breast of charity through the flesh of Christ crucified.[18] There is no other way you can taste or have virtue, because he *is* the way and truth, and whoever holds to this way and truth cannot be deceived.

Realize that the whole world is against you. Don't turn back, but with heart courageous and true prepare yourself ahead of time, with shield in hand, to receive the blows. You know that a shield is three-sided;[19] so you need to have three virtues. You need hatred and contempt for the sins

---

[14] In *Dial.* 159, p. 341, this is developed in the context of obedience. Cf. Cavalca, *Specchio di croce*, p. 212: "If we want to enter through a low door we have to bow our head low in fear of bumping it, or in fear of something being banged against our head. In the same way, we have to bow down and humble ourselves if we want to enter through the door and the narrow way that is Christ, who said, I am the door and I am the way. This is what Saint Augustine said: 'You who want to enter through this door, bow low so that you don't crack your head.' " Also Simone Fidati da Cascia, *Expositiones in totum corpus evangeliorum*, p. 41: "The door to paradise is very narrow and low. The rich, dressed in love of riches, cannot go through it; nor the proud with head held high, bloated with the wind of vainglory. They might crack and break their heads."

[15] Cf. Lk. 9, 62, but with a slight shift in meaning. Christ says that a person must not look back after putting hand to plow. Cf. *Dial.* 12, p. 46, n. 32; also Let. T126 to Alessa dei Saracini and Cecca di Clemente Gori (in this volume): "Christ said no one should turn back to look at what has already been plowed, that is, to look back at earlier pleasures or at work already done."

[16] Mt. 10, 22: "Whoever perseveres to the end will be saved." (Vulg.)

[17] Cf. Is. 53, 7.

[18] *as you drink* supplied by Dupré Theseider.

[19] Catherine has in mind the shields of medieval infantrymen, which usually were in the form of an isosceles triangle, with the sides slightly rounded. This is the only occurrence of this image in Catherine's writings.

you have committed against your Creator, particularly in the past when you were a devil because you were following in the devil's footsteps. Next I am saying that you need to have love, considering the goodness of God, who has loved you so much, and not because he had to but gratuitously. Moved by his ineffable love, he did not take your soul from your body while you were rebelling against him. No, the gentle Jesus snatched you from the devil's hands and brought you grace. And I tell you, as soon as you have this perfect love and hatred, the third virtue will be born to you.[20] I mean patience, so that not only will you not be saddened by any hurtful words or actions, nor moved to impatience by any suffering you may have to bear, but you will endure these things joyfully, holding them in reverence and considering yourself unworthy of such grace. There will be no blow, from the devil or anyone else, that can harm you if you have this shield of hatred, love, and true patience. For these are the three sturdy pillars that free the soul from weakness and keep it strong.

The dear Magdalen took up this shield in such a way that she thought no more of herself but with true heart clothed herself in Christ crucified. She no longer turned to prestige or grandeur or her own vanities. She took no more pleasure or delight in the world. She didn't think or worry about anything but how she could follow Christ. No sooner had she set her affection on him and come to know herself than she embraced him and took the path of lowliness. For God's sake she despised herself, for she saw that there is no other way to follow or to please him. She realized that she was the lowliest of all people. She was no more self-conscious than a drunken woman, whether alone or with others.[21] Otherwise she would never have been among those soldiers of Pilate, nor would she have gone and stayed alone at the tomb. Love kept her from thinking, "What will it look like? Will people speak ill of me because I am rich and beautiful?"[22] Her thoughts weren't here, but only on how she might find and follow her Master. She, then, is the companion I am giving you. I want you to follow her because she knew the way so well that she has been made our teacher.

Run, my daughter and my daughters! Don't fall asleep on me any more, for time is racing on and won't wait even a moment for you. I don't want to say any more.

---

[20] Cf. *Dial.* 7, p. 36: "Virtue, once conceived, must come to birth."

[21] Cf. Let. T25 to Tommaso dalla Fonte (early 1378): "One who is drunk loses all self-consciousness and feels nothing but the wine; all feeling is immersed in the wine. So it is when we are drunk on the blood of Christ crucified. We lose all selfish self-consciousness."

[22] The *Legenda aurea* depicts Mary Magdalen as "born of parents who were of noble station, and of royal lineage," and "as beautiful as she was rich." Also, Catherine follows medieval tradition in identifying as one Mary of Bethany, Mary Magdalen, and the sinful woman who anointed Jesus.

Encourage Madonna Colomba, as I am sending this to her as well as to you, and to Monna Giovanna d'Azzolino as well. Bless Monna Melina and Caterina and Monna Lagina and all my other daughters in Christ Jesus for me.[23] They shouldn't be surprised or feel badly because I haven't written to them separately. I consider you all as one body, and I've done it this way because new plants need more help.[24]

Courage in Christ Jesus from all of us. Keep living in God's holy and tender love.

Textual Notes

a. Text has *t'abbraccia*, which has no relevance to the context.

[23] All women of Lucca, at least some of whom are named together in other letters, for example, Let. T164/DT58 (in this volume). We know nothing more about any of them, except perhaps Lagina, who may have been one of the Trente family (Dupré Theseider, n. 17 to this letter), and of Melina, who is probably the same to whom Let. T164/DT58 (in this volume) is addressed.

[24] This is apparently a reference to the recent conversion of Monna Bartolomea. Usually Catherine uses the imagery of "new plants" to refer to persons new in religious life or ecclesiastical office.

Letter T162/G350[1]
To Monna Franceschina, Monna Caterina, and two other spiritual companions in Lucca
Between Ash Wednesday (26 February) and Palm Sunday (6 April) 1376

In this letter we meet again some of the women Catherine befriended in Lucca. Because of the linguistic evidence as well as the letter's Lenten themes, I am inclined to place it between late February and March 1376.[2] It could very possibly have been written and sent at the same time as T165/DT59.[3]

§

In the name of Christ[a] crucified and of gentle Mary.

My very loved and dearest daughters and sisters in Christ Jesus,

I Caterina, servant and slave of the servants of God, am writing to encourage you all in the precious blood of God's Son. I long to see you true daughters, true brides consecrated to the eternal bridegroom, who gave his life for us with such burning charity. Do the same, and follow the standard of the most holy cross courageously and with blazing desire; follow in his footsteps along the way of suffering and of crucified loving desires. For the son or daughter should always be glad to follow his or her father, and the bride her bridegroom, so that if our father and bridegroom is in pain we conform ourselves with him in pain, and if he is joyful we conform ourselves with him in joy.[4] Thus the apostle Paul, that man in love, said of himself: "I rejoice with those who rejoice, and I weep with those who

---

[1] MSS: Mo, S3; translation based on Mo-*a*, corrected by *b*. Variants from S3 based on an unpublished transcription by A. Volpato.

[2] Fawtier (II, pp. 304–305) speculates that the letter was written shortly after Catherine's departure from Lucca. Dupré Theseider (unpublished notes) declines to date it. Of the six other letters which share eleven or more of this letter's thirty-seven analyzed patterns, five are dated between January and March 1376. Further, eight patterns do not occur before that time (CRESCVIR, CROCDESI, GAUDLET, SAZFAST, TERMMORT, TRIBCONS, VIAPENE, VIAVERIT), and seven significant clusters within individual patterns end by March or April 1376 (CRESCVIR, GAUDLET, SAZFAST, SPENDTEM, STACARIT, TERMMORT, TRIBCONS). One pattern, GAUDLET, occurs only from January to March 1376.

[3] See the introduction to that letter.

[4] A variation on her much more common theme of loving what God loves and hating what God hates.

weep."[5] This is how we act if we are living in perfect charity, and by so doing we realize in ourselves what the apostle[b] Paul said: that those who share in the suffering, the cross of Christ, will also share in the consolation, will be in glory with Christ.[6] Justly will God give them his inheritance, since for love they have left behind the inheritance and concerns of the world, have given up worldly pleasure and consolation and followed the cross of Christ crucified. They[c] have embraced pain and disgrace and dishonor for love of him.[d]

This, my dearest daughters, is the fire in which your souls must burn[e] with enflamed and loving desires. In nothing else must you take pleasure, for every other way is dark and obscure for us and leads to eternal death. So don't be careless. Be conscientious on this lovely straight way, Christ Jesus. He said, "I am way and truth and life. Whoever walks by me walks in the light and not in darkness, and comes to the true life that will not be taken away for ever."[7] Don't let selfish love or inattentiveness take control of you, because this is what keeps us from running, so that we stall along the way and keep turning back to look at what we've already plowed.[8] But the true daughter and bride, who is conscientious, never turns back; she runs continually forward with the oil of humility and the fire of blazing charity.[9] This is her endeavor,[f] and this is how she presents herself constantly to serve her most gentle Savior.

I urge you then, for love of Christ crucified—because our good gentle Jesus is so noble and generous—let us dally no longer. Let's keep in mind how short our time is. Let's redeem with holy sorrow and grief the time we have spent carelessly or lost, and in this way we shall regain the past.

---

[5] Cf. Rom. 12, 15. As Paul states it, it is a command to his readers in regard to their love for others, whereas Catherine here uses it to bolster her description of love for Christ—not inconsistent with her identification of the two loves.

[6] Cf. 2 Cor. 1, 5: "As we have shared much in the suffering of Christ, so through Christ do we share abundantly in his consolation. . . . Our hope for you is firm because we know that just as you share in the sufferings, so you will share in the consolation."

[7] Cf. Jn. 14, 6; 8, 12; 6, 50. Catherine here intertwines elements from all three passages.

[8] Cf. Lk. 9, 62: "No one who puts a hand to the plow and looks back is fit for the kingdom of God." Repeatedly, Catherine interpolates looking back at what one has plowed (*arato* rather than *aratro*), and often, as here, adds a reference to looking ahead or moving forward. A farmer guiding a medieval hand plow pulled by an animal or even another human being could never make a straight furrow without watching straight ahead. Only in three instances, all late, does she use the word *aratro*, "plow."

[9] In Let. T30/DT1 to the Abbess and Suora Niccolosa of the Monastery of Santa Marta in Siena (vol. I) Catherine related the oil and the fire to Saints Lucy (whose name means "light") and Agnes: "Anyone on a journey needs a light in order not to stray from the road. I have found a light, that sweet Roman virgin who gifts us with light [that is, St. Lucy]. . . . [A]nd of Agnesa, who is a lamb, we will ask meekness and humility. So Lucy gives us light, . . . and Agnesa, the oil of humility."

I'll say no more. I pray First Truth to make you grow from strength to strength[10] until you reach that end where there is life without death, satiety without boredom, hunger without pain,[g] joy without sadness; where there is every good with no evil at all. God's peace be always in your souls.[11] Keep living in God's holy love.

Gentle Jesus! Jesus! Jesus!

Textual Notes

a. S3: *Gesù Cristo / Cristo.*
b. *b*,S3 add *apostolo* (*b* over erasure).
c. *b*,S3: *consolation, and following . . . crucified, they / consolation. . . . They* (*b* over erasure).
d. *of him* by *b* over erasure; original may have been *of God.*
e. S3: *enter* (*andare*) / *burn* (*ardere*).
f. *b* adds *always.*
g. *hunger without pain* added by *b.*

---

[10] Ps. 84, 7: "They shall advance from strength to strength." (Vulg.)

[11] Catherine would have encountered this saying of Pseudo-Augustine (*Meditatio XXVII*, PL XL, 921) in Cavalca who repeats it in several places, for example, in *Specchio di croce*, p. 184: "Sated, we shall be hungry, and hungering we shall be sated, but our satiety will be far from boredom, and our hunger far from pain."

LETTER T163/G347[1]
To Monna Franceschina in Lucca
January to April 1376

As with Catherine's other female disciples in Lucca, we know nothing of Franceschina except her name and her association with other women of Lucca with whom she is named in Catherine's letters.

There are few clues to date this letter. One may presume it post-dates Catherine's first visit to Lucca (probably in September 1375). Also, it must also be seen in relation to Let. T162, also addressed to Franceschina along with Monna Caterina and two other spiritual companions in Lucca. I have placed Let. T162 in February or March 1376 because of its apparently Lenten themes. In fact, there are so many similarities in theme between this letter and Let. T162 that it seems impossible to guess which might have been written first. I am therefore placing them together, guessing that both must have been written within the first four months of 1376. The linguistic evidence supports such a placement.[2]

---

[1] MSS: Mo, B, P2, T, R1, P5, F2, F1, P3, S3; translation based on Mo-*a*, corrected by *b*, with variants from B based on an unpublished transcription by Dupré Theseider.

[2] There are three other letters which share eleven or more of this letter's forty-five analyzed patterns, and all three are dated between February and April 1376. A good number of significant clusters within individual patterns also are concentrated in this period: AMAODDIO, CRESCVIR, GAUDLET, LARGCUOR, LETTNEGL, MAGDALEN, MANGGUST, MENSCIBO, SAETTA, SERVEFIG, STANC, VIAPENE. Dupré Theseider (unpublished notes) simply considers all of the Lucca letters undatable, since "it is not stated that Catherine wrote only once to Lucca, or which letters were from that one time." Fawtier (II, pp. 304–305) speculates that all of the Lucca letters may date to shortly after Catherine's stay there, that is, early 1376.

§

In the name of Jesus Christ crucified and of gentle Mary.

Very loved and dearest sister[a] in Christ gentle Jesus,

I Caterina, servant and slave of the servants of Jesus Christ, am writing to encourage you in his precious blood. I long to see you a true servant and daughter of the good gentle Jesus, bathed and clothed in the blood of God's Son, so that every garment of selfish love may be stripped from you, along with any ignorance and indifference.

So I want you to follow the Magdalen, that lovely woman in love, who never let go of the tree of the most holy cross. No, with perseverance she was bathed in the blood of God's Son; she got drunk on it; she so filled her memory and heart and understanding with it that she became incapable of loving anything but Christ Jesus.[3] This is what I want you to do right up to the end of your life, growing from strength to strength.[4] Persevere day after day. Never give up. Be a true pilgrim, never letting tiredness make you turn back. Don't take to apathetically sitting down. No, I want you to take up the staff of the most holy cross, upon which all the virtues are planted and rooted,[5] and contemplate the Lamb, slain for us with such blazing fire[b] that it must burn and consume whatever coldness or hardheartedness or self-love there might be in our soul.

Oh how can a bride not follow in the footsteps of her bridegroom? How can she not suffer with love and walk along the way of pain in whatever way God may grant her to? So get up with true humility and a willingness to suffer,[6] and follow the meek Lamb with a heart free and generous and filled with charity. Abandon yourself for him, learning from this Jesus who in order to give you the life of grace gave up his bodily life. And as a sign of his generosity he opened up his whole self by creating a

---

[3] In Let. T165/DT59 to Monna Bartolomea di Salvatica, also of Lucca (a letter written in this same general period), she develops the Magdalen theme in much greater detail.

[4] Ps. 84, 7. In Latin and in Catherine's Tuscan, the word *virtus/virtù* is both "strength" and "virtue." Catherine clearly has both senses in mind here.

[5] The image of the cross as staff is used only in two letters from early 1376, this one and Let. T60 (vol. I), and again in Let. T266 (1378). Cf. also Let. T138/DT41 to Giovanna d'Angiò (vol. I): "Take hold of the tree of the most holy cross and let it be planted in the garden of your soul, because this is a tree laden with fruits, the true solid virtues. For you see very well that beyond God's union with his creature he has joined himself to the most holy cross. And he wills, he insists, that we too join ourselves to this sweet tree in love and desire. Then our garden cannot help producing sweet and tender fruit."

[6] It. *pazienza*. Though it can often be translated literally as "patience," it often clearly connotes an explicit willingness to suffer.

bath within his open side after he had died, to show us his love.[7] Do you want to live in security? Then hide yourself within this side and see that you are never found outside this opened heart[c]—though once you enter, you will discover such joy and sweetness that you will never want to leave. For it is an open storehouse filled with spices,[8] overflowing with mercy. And that mercy gives grace and leads to everlasting life, where there is life without death, satiety without boredom, hunger without pain, perfect and complete joy with no bitterness at all.[9] There our appetite and taste are satisfied. *Oh indescribable,*[d] *immeasurable charity! What drove you to give us this true good? Only the boundless love with which you made us, your creatures, not because you had any obligation—for it is we who are obligated to you, not you to us.*

But remember, dearest sister in Christ gentle Jesus, we cannot attain such a great good as seeing God without first making an effort in this life to experience him through burning, blazing love, a love that attracts and embraces all the virtues. Anyone who has been wounded by the arrow of divine charity will not be lacking in virtue, and that charity is gotten at the table of the most holy cross, where the spotless Lamb is table, food, and waiter.[10]

Now how can we keep from loving our gentle Savior, when we see how much we have been loved by him? It is the character and way of love always to return love for love, and lover is transformed into beloved. So it is with the soul, Christ's bride, who sees herself loved by him: let her show that she wants to make a return to him by returning his love. I mean, let her because of her love be willing to endure pain and dishonor for him, and she will thus be transformed and become one with him through love and desire. She will love what God loves and hate what God

---

[7] Cf. *Dial.* 75, p. 138, where this mystery of the "secret of Christ's heart" is developed.

[8] She may be recalling references to spices in the Song of Songs, for example, 5, 13; 6, 2; 8, 14. While she often refers to Christ's heart as a *bottiga* (shop or storehouse or hostelry), this is the only time she explicitly adds spices to the image.

[9] The thought is originally from Pseudo-Augustine (*Meditatio XXVII*, PL XL, 921. Catherine, however, probably encountered the passage in one of Cavalca's works, for example, *Descrizione de' dieci comandamenti*, p. 306: "We shall desire though we are sated, and we shall be sated even in our desiring. Yet satiety will not be a source of boredom, nor desire be accompanied by pain, as happens in this world."

[10] Cf. Let. T97 to Pavola da Siena and her disciples (in this volume): "Those who live in charity live in God, and God in them. But the bride of Christ, who has been pierced by this arrow of charity, never stops working—like a fresh wound that makes our heart beat constantly harder. For every day all over again new arrows are shot—I mean arrows of blazing charity—since not a moment passes but God's goodness is not heaping burning coals upon our head." (Cf. Rom. 12, 20: "But if your enemy is hungry, feed him; if he is thirsty, give him something to drink; by doing this you will heap burning coals upon his head.") For Catherine these "burning coals" are always burning with the fire of charity.

hates, for she will see that the gentle Jesus found his greatest joy in enduring the burdensome cross for love of the Father's honor and our salvation, as one who ate and relished souls. And we must relish them in the same way, and conform ourselves with him.

So let's run! Let's sleep no longer in the bed of apathy! Let's run to get to this true good! I'll say no more. Keep living in God's holy and tender love.

Gentle Jesus! Jesus love!

Textual Notes

a. *b*, B: *sister and daughter / sister.*

b. B: *fire of love / fire.*

c. B: *within, and see that this opened heart is never found outside / within . . . heart*—but B's version makes no sense in Catherine's context.

d. B: *delight / indescribable.*

LETTER Dupré Theseider I[1]

To Monna Tora of Lucca and to Monna Giovanna, Tora's daughter and wife of Giovanni Trenta of Lucca. Between Ash Wednesday (26 February) and Palm Sunday (6 April) 1376

Catherine has already written to Giovanna's husband, Giovanni Trenta, counseling detachment from wealth and honor after the example of the newborn Christ (Let. T152). One has the impression from that letter that the marriage of the younger couple has not been entirely happy, or at least that Giovanni is not one with his wife in the quest for virtue, specifically the virtue of voluntary poverty.

In the present letter Catherine seems to be urging Giovanna's mother Tora to the same voluntary poverty. However, for the daughter, Giovanna, she now has in mind a more extreme detachment: sexual abstinence within her marriage. (It is not clear whether this step is Giovanna's own idea or whether Catherine has in fact counseled it. She tells Tora that Giovanna "wants freely and with desire to enter the state of perfection, that is, to keep herself in the fragrance of purity and continence.") If Giovanni has found it difficult to join his wife in renouncing wealth and prestige, how much more support the latter would need to persuade him to sexual abstinence! Giovanni may not, however, have welcomed that support quite as warmly as his wife.

So when might this letter have been written? The linguistic evidence points strongly to February through April 1376.[2] Lent, moreover, would have been a very appropriate time to suggest such a drastic form of detachment. It is not unlikely, therefore, that this letter was written during Lent of 1376 and possibly sent with the same courier who carried Let. T162 and T165 to Lucca.

---

[1] MSS: Mo; translation based on Dupré Theseider's edited text of Mo-*a* (corrected by *b*) in "Un codice inedito dell'Epistolario di S. Caterina," *Bullettino dell'Istituto storico italiano e Archivio Muratoriano* 48 (1931), pp. 18–56.

[2] Six other letters, all between 1372 and early 1376, share eleven or more of this letter's fifty-one analyzed patterns. Of these letters, three are from February to April 1376. Further, a large number of significant clusters within individual patterns beginning and/or ending between February and April 1376 support even more strongly a placement in that period (ANGELTER, CARCONFU, CONSUM, CRESCVIR, CUORAFFE, GAUDLET, GITTODOR, ISPIRAZ, MONDCONT, OCCHIO, OFFIZIO, PACEUNIO, PARTECBN, POMPVANI, PREZRICO, SANTPROP, SCRVCNBN, TERMMORT, VEDFACC, VERGINIT, VISIOPAC).

§

In the name of Jesus Christ crucified and of gentle Mary.

Very loved and dearest mother and daughter in Christ Jesus,

I Caterina, servant and slave of the servants of Jesus Christ, encourage[a] and bless you in the precious blood of God's Son.[b] I long to see your heart and affection raised above earth to complete freedom, since I am aware that your affection is misdirected to worldly vanity and ostentation. This is why my soul longs to see you totally stripped of these things, for the world has nothing in common with Christ. The world seeks honor and glory, enjoyment and carnal pleasure and gratification.[c] Christ chose the exact opposite. He spurned honor and embraced outrage, disgrace, and pain, insult, derision, and abuse.[d] He had a consummate love for continence and virginity as a way of life. *Oh dearest love! How pleasing to you and how fragrant is the state of holy continence, especially in those you have chosen for marriage and who for love of virtue abstain and so move from the common state to the perfect because they feel they are so called by the Holy Spirit!* And when does the Holy Spirit call you? When he sends you good holy inspirations; when he lets you recognize our human weakness and the wretched instability and fickleness of the world.

Oh, let our hearts not become lukewarm, but let them rise up to respond to the Holy Spirit who is calling, and follow the way of perfection! And see to it, my daughter,[3] if you hear the Holy Spirit calling you—both within yourself and within your husband—that you pay no attention to what other people say or to what the devil may suggest. No, act courageously, not like a child, and with the lamp of fortitude follow the light of the Holy Spirit.[4] Answer as the glorious martyr Reparata[e] did when the tyrant said to her, "Why are you giving up your physical beauty and youth?" Her response was wise and filled with blazing desire: "It is enough for me, wicked tyrant, to have seen the world's pleasure."[5] So, my daughter, do the same; rise above the world's vanity and pleasure. Oh how blessed your soul will be that you know how to and want to rise with Christ crucified above conformity with the world!

And you, dearest mother,[6] I beg you, if you see that your daughter is

---

[3] Catherine is now addressing Giovanna specifically.

[4] While Catherine couples light and fortitude elsewhere, this is the only instance in which she actually uses a lamp as an image of fortitude.

[5] The story of Reparata is reported in *Acta Sanctorum*, vol. IV, for 8 October. It is now considered "spurious," but was popular in medieval Tuscany because Saint Reparata was patron of Florence.

[6] She now turns her attention to Giovanna's mother, Monna Tora.

so growing from strength to strength[7] as to freely and eagerly[8] want to enter the state of perfection, that is, to keep herself in the fragrance of purity and continence, see to it that you don't stand in her way.[9] That would be very displeasing to God. You would be doing the work of the devils, since it is their work to lure people away from their holy resolution and lead them to the world's wretched vanity. No, I don't want that to happen. I want you to have the work of the angels, who are always there to help souls and to rescue them from wretchedness and lead them into the way of salvation.

Always keep your eyes on God.[10] Let everything you do be directed toward God. Let each of you try to grow from strength to strength, never turning back to look at the world but keeping your heart constantly fixed on the thought of how short our time is. Ponder the price at which you have been so tenderly ransomed[11] and the reward given to those who clothe themselves in virtue. In this way you[12] will be a support for her, to sustain her and help her grow more and more in holy desire. Then at end of your life you will [both] come, bound in love and in charity, to that perfect union and vision of peace where there is joy and happiness completely free of sadness or bitterness. There there is no selfish love but only a familial charity in which each one shares in the good of the other.[13] So let us be exultantly happy, experiencing through charity in this life what we shall see face to face in the next.

Love, love each other! Keep living in God's holy love.

Gentle Jesus! Jesus! Jesus!

---

[7] Cf. Ps. 84, 8. The sense is inherently ambivalent, since *di virtù in virtù* connotes both "from strength to strength" and "from virtue to virtue."

[8] Literally, "with desire."

[9] Recall that Tora's daughter Giovanna is married. So what Catherine is counseling is sexual abstinence within marriage, which was at the time considered more perfect than a sexual relationship and was often referred to as "spiritual marriage." It was in fact usually undertaken on the initiative of the bride or wife, sometimes with her husband's cooperation, but sometimes through ruses and subterfuges.

[10] The rest of the letter is directed to both women.

[11] Cf. 1 Cor. 6, 20: "You have been purchased, and at a great price. So glorify God in your body."

[12] Tora, the mother.

[13] Cf. *Dial.* 40, p. 83, where God says of the blessed in heaven: "And though they are all joined in the bond of charity, they know a special kind of sharing with those whom they loved most closely and with a special love in the world, a love through which they grew in grace and virtue. . . . So now in everlasting life they have not lost that love; no, they still love and share with each other even more closely and fully, adding their love to the good of all. For I would not have you think this special good they have is only for themselves. No, it is shared by all their just companions, my beloved children, and by all the angels."

Textual Notes

a. *b*: *am writing to encourage* / *encourage*.
b. *b*: *his precious blood* / *the precious ... Son*.
c. *b*: [*and gratification*].
d. The six last nouns written by *b* over erasures.
e. *Reparata* supplied by *b*.

LETTER T161/G340[1]
To Monna Nella, widow of Niccolò Buonconti of Pisa, and to Monna Caterina, wife of Gherardo di Niccolò Buonconti
March or April 1376

Since Gherardo was Catherine's host during her stay in Pisa, this letter to his mother and to his wife was surely not written before the saint's return from Pisa to Siena near Christmas of 1375. The linguistic evidence would in fact place the letter quite certainly within the first four months of 1376.[2] I am inclined to place it most probably in March or April 1376 because of its Lenten themes and because one pattern (ODORVIRT) does not otherwise occur before April of that year.[3]

One might be tempted to speculate from the references to lost time and the inconstancy of the world that Nella Buonconti has recently lost her husband. However, both later letters to Nella address Nella's need for patience and detachment, so it may simply be a matter of character.[4]

---

[1] MSS: Mo, S3; translation based on Mo-*a*, corrected by *b*, with variants based on an unpublished transcription by A. Volpato.

[2] Of the seven letters which share eleven or more of this letter's forty-eight analyzed patterns, five are from the first four months of 1376. A number of strong clusters within individual patterns begin only in early 1376 (CARCONFU, LEVUNION, ODORVIRT, PENAFAME, SAZFAST, SENZPENA, STACARIT, VINCCAR), and several end by April of the same year (JERUSAL, LAUDATO, LEVUNION, SAZFAST, VINCCAR, VISIOPAC).

[3] Both Fawtier (II, p. 309) and Dupré Theseider (unpublished notes) consider this letter undatable.

[4] The other letters to Nella are Let. T167, written in late 1377 or 1378 while three of Nella's sons were with Catherine in Avignon, and Let. T151a (in this volume), written in autumn of 1377.

§

In the name of Jesus Christ crucified and of gentle Mary.

Dearest mother Monna Nella and dearest daughter[a] Caterina in Christ Jesus,

I Caterina, servant and slave of the servants of Jesus Christ, encourage and bless you in the precious blood of God's Son.[b] I long to see you bound and united by the chain of charity that held God's Son nailed fast to the cross. Oh sweetest measureless charity! How strong is this bond that held the God-Man on the wood of the cross, wounded and lacerated! There he bore the weight of our sins; there they were hammered out as [on] an anvil under the hammer.[5] This is how the soul is shaped—in the sufferings of Christ, with the fire of his charity as agent. *Oh how sweetly and perfectly have you, God, united yourself with humanity!*

So I want you[c] to make a real effort[6] to become so one [with each other] that neither the devils nor anyone else will be able to separate you.[7] This is a union bequeathed to us by God (as a commandment, in fact), for he had nothing more dear to give.[8] Is there anything more dear than to possess God and to live[d] in this perfect union of God's charity? For God is charity, and those who live in charity are living in God, and God in them.[9] This is what First Truth says: "If you keep my word, I will live in you and you in me, and I will reveal myself to you."[10] *Oh most tender love! What are we, that you should reveal yourself to us human beings?*[11] *What is the revelation that you make to the soul? Nothing less than an indescribable love, love that is a mother who conceives the fragrance of virtue. And just as a mother nurses her children at her breast, so this mother charity*

[5] The text has "as an anvil," but in other places, the anvil is always the body of Christ. The image is one which began to appear in Catherine's writings in late 1375.

[6] It. *che vi leviate con perfetta sollecitudine.*

[7] It. *Fate una unione che non sia né dimonia né creatura che vi possa separare.* In every other instance in Catherine's writings the expression *fare una unione* refers to the union between the soul and God or between God and human nature in the incarnation. But here the biblical reference Catherine uses to buttress her admonition makes it clear that the reference is to a union of love between the two women.

[8] Jn. 13, 34: "I give you a new commandment: love one another! Such as my love has been for you, so must your love be for each other."

[9] Cf. 1 Jn. 4, 16. (Most recent translations have *love* here; the Vulgate has *caritas*, and this is what Catherine uses.)

[10] She is bringing together elements of two texts: Jn. 14, 23, "Those who love me will keep my word, and my Father will love them, and we will come to them and make our dwelling place with them," and Jn. 14, 21–22, "But those who love me will be loved by my Father, and I will love them and will reveal myself to them."

[11] Cf. Ps. 8, 5: "What is humankind, that you should take notice of us?" (Vulg.)

nurses her children the virtues,[e] *and she carries the fruit into everlasting life.*

So rise up, up with unstinted energy, dearest mother and daughter! Pursue[f] virtue. Lean on this glorious breast of charity. And if you should ask me, "How can I find this glorious mother?" I'll tell you where: on the tree of the venerable and most holy cross, onto which was engrafted the incarnate Word, God's Son. There you will find the open stream[12] of the blood of God's Son,[g] shed with such a fire of love. And when you turn your mind's eye towards the divine charity that constantly rests on us,[h] your heart won't be able to keep itself from loving, seeing that you are loved so much.

And little by little[i] a hatred and contempt for yourself will follow, along with contempt for the world. Because of this you will make light of pleasure and honor and will embrace insult and disgrace; it will be really easy for you to suffer when you contemplate how your Creator was mocked.

Oh how ignorant and vile is the heart that would prefer a road different from the one taken by its Master—even though anyone who wants everlasting life *must* follow in that Master's footsteps! He said as much: "I am way and truth and life. Whoever walks in me is not walking in the dark but reaches the light."[13] And in[j] another place he says, "No one can come to the Father except through me."[14]

Now we have seen what great love has been poured into our soul.[15] And we are necessarily compelled to raise our affection and desire above the world. For the world is inconstant and fickle, full of darkness and bitterness; it has nothing in common with Christ crucified, because Christ is alive and the world is dead.

So let us rise up courageously, dearest mother and daughter! Leave behind the vanity and ostentation of the world, so that right now[k] you may, in sorrow for the time you've lost, choose to make up for it in the present, which you have. And realize that you will be asked to give an account of time at that final moment of death. Oh how confounded they will be who have spent their time carelessly and sinfully! I don't want us waiting to be embarrassed like this. No, let us live so virtuously that when our life is finished we shall find ourselves afire with virtue, with our gentle mother

---

[12] It. *vena.*

[13] Jn. 14, 6; 8, 12: "I am the light of the world; whoever follows me does not walk in the dark but has the light of life." Again, as she often does, Catherine brings together elements of two biblical passages into a single statement, an indication of her assimilation of the scriptures.

[14] Jn. 14, 6 again, except that the biblical text (in the *Vulgate*) does not have "can."

[15] Cf. Rom. 5, 5: "For the charity of God has been poured out in our hearts by the Spirit of God, who has been given to us." (Vulg.)

charity in the true city of Jerusalem. There we shall rest in that vision of peace where there is life without death, light without darkness, satiety without boredom, and hunger without pain.[16]

Oh how tender and kind is our God, who gives us the infinite for leaving behind the finite! No more carelessness or ingratitude, then, but let's follow in the footsteps of Christ crucified!

Love, love each other, dearest mother and sister! Keep living in holy love.[l] Praised be Jesus Christ![m]

Textual Notes

a. *b* adds *dearest daughter in margin.*

b. *b*, S3: *his blood* (in Mo, over erasure of *a*).

c. *b* has *Voglio du~q* over an erasure of the same length. Original illegible.

d. *b* has *e stare* (*and to live*) over an erasure of something slightly longer.

e. *the virtues* added by *b.*

f. *b*, S3: *daughter, to pursue / daughter. Pursue.*

g. *b*: [*There . . . Son*], clearly a scribal error.

h. S3: *you / us.* In Mo the pronoun is followed by an erasure of three words, the first of which is *non*, perhaps because of a mistaken repetition of *non si potra.*

i. S3: *Thus, loving / And . . . little* (*Onde amando / admano admano*, with *Unde* inserted by *b*).

j. *And in* written by *b* over a slightly shorter erasure.

k. *b* has written *In qsto* over a shorter word (*nel?*). Was the original (prior to Mo) perhaps Catherine's more usual *in questo punto del tempo che. . . .* (*in this bit of time still left to us?*)

l. S3: *Keep living in God's holy and tender love / Keep . . . love.*

m. S3 adds *Gentle Jesus! Jesus love!*

[16] Catherine probably encountered this thought of Pseudo-Augustine (*Meditatio XXVII*, PL XL, 921) in the works of Cavalca, for example, *Specchio di croce*, p. 184: "Sated, we shall be hungry, and hungering we shall be sated, but our satiety will be far from boredom, and our hunger far from pain." The thought appears frequently in her letters from this period.

LETTER T280/G98[1]
To Frate Raimondo da Capua
Late March 1376

The linguistic evidence places this letter among the others Catherine wrote to Raimondo and his companions while they were on their way to Avignon, some time between late February (by which time at least Neri di Landoccio Pagliaresi and Papo were with Raimondo[2]) and late March (when the group was probably on the road, so that Catherine would have needed to know where to direct a letter to them).[3] I would guess that this letter was written a bit later than Let. T226 and T228 because of its rather urgent exhortations not to fear and the mention of flowers ready to bloom. It may have been sent at the same time as Let. T206/DT63, in which Catherine commends Raimondo to the pope, which would place it in late March.[4]

§

In the name of Jesus Christ crucified and of gentle Mary.

Dearest father in Christ Jesus,[a]

I Caterina, servant and slave of the servants of Jesus Christ, am writing to you in his precious blood. I long to see you a vessel of love,[5] carrying the truth with fire and proclaiming it with daring, sowing the seed of God's word in everyone, but right now especially in our dear Christ on earth.[6] Up, dearest father and children![7] Go, for me, as proclaimers[8] who are

---

[1] MSS: Mo-*c*, P4. Translation based on Mo-*c*, with variants from an unpublished transcription by A. Volpato.

[2] Neri will accompany Raimondo to Avignon, as will the Augustinians Felice da Massa and Giovanni Tantucci. On Papo (or Papi), see the introduction and note 13 for Let. T226.

[3] Only two letters share eight or more of this one's sixteen analyzed patterns, and both are from that period. Further, beyond its elements of non-standardized protocol, SEMPAROL and VASDILEZ are clustered all but exclusively up to April 1376.

[4] Fawtier (II, p. 202) declines to date this letter. Dupré Theseider in his unpublished notes vacillates among the various possibilities, but seems to conclude finally that the letter is from 1378, some time before Let. T226, which he places in June 1378. Volpato concludes that because of its non-standardized protocol it must be from before 1377.

[5] As she often does in her letters from this period, she misquotes Acts 9, 15, having apparently misheard *vas delectionis* (It. *vasello di dilectione*) rather than *vas electionis* (It. *vasello d'electione*, "chosen vessel").

[6] Pope Gregory XI.

[7] That is, Raimondo and the others who have been sent ahead to Avignon.

[8] The It. *banditori* connotes the trumpeters whose fanfare announced important news.

poor yet taking with you the wealth of faith along with hope and the strong bond of charity. Remember the sweet words of First Truth: "You will send these children of yours as lambs among wolves. Let them go confidently, for I will be with them. And if human help should fail them, my divine help will always be with them."[9]

Oh my father and sons, who wants any other joy or comfort? Who will yield to fear? Those who aren't trusting, yes, but not those who are about to die of hunger for God's honor and the salvation of souls,[b] and to be consumed in the fire of divine charity, bathed and immersed and consumed in the blood of the slain Lamb.

Oimé! Oimé, my unfortunate soul, for I am dying yet cannot die! My heart is breaking, my bones are straining as long as the longed-for season hasn't come.[10] Even though spring[c] is ready to begin producing flowers, that isn't enough for me; we live not on flowers but on fruits. My *babbo* and my sons, help this poor thing, I say, for I am dying of hunger! Beg gentle First Truth to give us some fruits without waiting any longer.

I'll say no more. Keep living in God's holy and tender love.

Gentle Jesus! Jesus! Jesus![d]

Textual Notes

a. P4: *Christ gentle Jesus / Christ Jesus.*

b. Mo has singular; P4 has plural.

c. P4: *First Truth* (*prima verità*) / *spring* (*primavera*).

d. P4: *Jesus love! / Jesus! Jesus!*

---

[9] Cf. Mt. 10, 16; 28, 2; Lk. 10, 3; Heb. 13, 5–6. Catherine may here be paraphrasing the message she recalls from her own near-death experience in the summer of 1370: "For the salvation of souls you will even have to leave your own city. But I will be with you always. I will lead you forth, and will lead you back again, and you will carry with you the honor of my name." (*Life*, II, vi, 216, p. 205)

[10] That is, the time of reform and the calling of a crusade.

LETTER T206/G5/DT63[1]
To Pope Gregory XI, in Avignon
Late March 1376

This letter clearly serves as Catherine's commendation of Raimondo and his companions to Gregory XI. Because of the mention of the revolt of Bologna, which took place on the night of 20 March 1376, it must have been written very shortly after Catherine heard of that event. This would place it in late March, when Raimondo and the others are certainly already en route for Avignon. Catherine, however, may be sending the letter to Avignon, assuming that Raimondo's party will arrive there shortly.[2]

The date is broadly supported by the linguistic evidence.[3]

§

In the name of Jesus Christ crucified and of gentle Mary.

Dearest, most holy and gracious father in Christ Jesus,[a]

Your poor unworthy daughter Caterina, servant and slave of the servants of Jesus Christ, is writing to you in his precious blood. With desire have I desired[4] to see you so filled with divine grace that you may be the instrument and means, by divine grace,[b] of bringing peace to the whole world. So I beg you, my dear father,[c] to use your authority and power diligently and with hungry longing for peace, God's honor, and the salvation of souls.

You may say to me, father, "The world is in such a sorry state! How can I bring it peace?" I tell you in the name of Christ crucified that you must use your authority to do three essential things. You are in charge of the garden[d] of holy Church. So [first of all] uproot from that garden the stinking weeds full of impurity and avarice, and bloated with pride (I mean the evil pastors and administrators who poison and corrupt the garden). Oimé! *Use* your authority, you who are in charge of us! Uproot these weeds and throw them out where they will have nothing to administer!

---

[1] MSS: B, P2, H, P1, P5, F2, P3, P4, V; translation based on B as edited by Dupré Theseider, with reference to H, V. Other variants based on Dupré Theseider.

[2] See the introduction to Let. T226 (in this volume) to Raimondo da Capua for the possible chronology of the mission to Avignon.

[3] All seven of the letters which share twelve or more of this one's forty-seven analyzed patterns range from late 1375 to very early 1377, and a number of significant clusters within individual patterns (PACEUNIO, PASTRETT, PERDSCUS, PIENGRAZ, STATPRIM, VITUPDIO) are concentrated in the same period.

[4] Lk. 22, 15. (Vulg.)

Tell them to tend to administering themselves by a good holy life. Plant fragrant flowers in this garden for us, pastors and administrators who will be true servants of Jesus Christ crucified,[e] who will seek only God's honor and the salvation of souls, who will be fathers to the poor.[5]

Oimé! What a shame this is! They ought to be mirrors of freely chosen poverty, humble lambs, giving out the Church's possessions to the poor.[6] Yet here they are, living in worldly luxury and ambition and pretentious vanity a thousand times worse than if they belonged to the world! In fact, many layfolk put them to shame by their good holy lives.[7] But it seems supreme eternal Goodness is making us do under coercion what we haven't done for love. It seems he is permitting his bride to be stripped of prestige and luxury, as if to show that he wants holy Church to return to being poor, humble, and meek as she was in those holy[f] early days, when she was concerned only with God's honor and the salvation of souls, taken up not with material things but with the spiritual.[8] For ever since the Church has paid more attention to the material than to the spiritual, things have gone from bad to worse.[9]

This is why you have seen God in his just judgment permitting the Church to suffer so many persecutions and trials. But take heart, father, and don't be afraid, no matter what has happened or may yet happen. God is doing it to make the Church perfect once again, so that lambs may feed in this garden instead of the wolves who are devouring the honor that belongs to God by stealing it for themselves. Take heart in Christ gentle Jesus, for I trust that his help, the fullness of divine grace, will come soon to your support and aid. If you do as I've told you, you will emerge from war into the greatest peace, from persecution to complete unity—not by

---

[5] She has asked the same of Archbishop Angelo Ricasoli in Let. T88/DT28 (vol. I), calling him as well "father to the poor."

[6] Cf. *Dial.* 119, pp. 225–226, for praise of the exemplary life of the good prelates who "embraced voluntary poverty" and "generously gave out the Church's possessions to the poor."

[7] Lk. 16, 8: "The children of this world are wiser in dealing with their own kind than are the children of light." (Vulg.) Cf. also Bernard de Clairvaux, *Sermo XXXVI*, 3, *De diversis* (PL CLXXXIII, 639): "Would that we could be at least equal to [worldly people]! For it would be a great shame—a very great shame—if they should want evil more ardently than we desire good, if they should race toward death more speedily than we to life." Catherine may have encountered the citation in Cavalca's *Disciplina degli spirituali* (p. 5A) or in his *Pungilingua* (VII, p. 58, and XVII, p. 166).

[8] Catherine speaks much of "voluntary poverty" after the example of Christ, but she speaks only here and in *Dial.* 151 (pp. 319–320) of the poverty of the apostles and the early Church. She will again in Let. T209, also to Gregory XI (in this volume), refer to the Church's "original lovely state."

[9] Cf. *Dial.* 127, p. 250: "If they were filled with virtue and careful for spiritual things as they ought to be, they would have plenty of the temporal as well. So many rebellions has my bride suffered that she should not have had!"

human power but by holy virtue—and you will defeat the devils we can see (evil people) as well as those we cannot see—though they never take their eyes off us.

But just think, my dear father,[g] how difficult it will be to do what I've been talking about unless you do the other two essential things:[h] I mean your return [to Rome] and the raising of the standard of the most holy cross.[10] Don't let your holy desire falter on account of any dissent or rebellion you might see or hear about on the part of the cities. Rather, let your holy desire be even more enkindled to act soon. Don't put off your coming because of it. Don't believe the devil. He knows he is the loser, and so he is trying to put obstacles in your way to make you give up what is yours. He wants to make you lose love and charity, and prevent your coming. I tell you, father in Christ Jesus, to come soon, like a gentle lamb. Respond to the Holy Spirit, who is calling you! I tell you, come! Come! Come! Don't wait for time, because time isn't waiting for you. Then you will be acting like the slain Lamb, whose place you hold. With unarmed hand he slew[i] our enemies.[11] He came as a gentle Lamb, using the power of love as his only weapon, looking only to care for spiritual things and to the restoration of grace to humankind, who had lost it through sin.

Oimé! My dear father![j] I am begging you, I am *telling* you: come! Conquer our[k] enemies with the same gentle hand. In the name of Christ crucified I am telling you! Don't choose to listen to the devil's advisors. They would like to block your holy and good resolution. Be a courageous man for me, not a coward. Respond to God, who is calling you to come and take possession of the place of the glorious shepherd,[l] Saint Peter, whose vicar you still are.[12] And there raise the standard of the holy cross. For as we were freed through the cross (as said our dear Paul[13]), so by raising this standard (which I see as relief for Christians[14]) we shall be freed—we from war[15] and divisions and many sins, and the unbelievers from their unbelief. And by doing these [two] things you will come to see the reform[m] of holy Church in the persons of good pastors. You will bring back

---

[10] The "three essential things" that will bring peace to the world are the reform of the Church, the return of the papacy to Rome, and the crusade; Catherine sees them as intimately related.

[11] Cf. Cavalca, *Specchio di croce*, XXXII, p. 133: "As Saint Augustine says, with unarmed hand and nailed to the cross, he conquered the devils."

[12] Her assumption is that the pope should always reside in Rome because Peter resided there.

[13] Cf. Gal. 5, 1: "for which freedom Christ freed us." (Vulg.) Catherine calls Paul, here and frequently elsewhere, by the affectionate nickname *Pavoloccio*.

[14] It. *refrigerio de' cristiani*. Nowhere else does she use this expression.

[15] One of Catherine's views of the projected crusade is that it will divert Christian armies from fighting against the papacy by uniting them in a common external cause.

to her faded face the color of blazing charity—for so much blood has been sucked from her by wicked gluttons that she is all pale.[16]

But take heart and come, father! Don't make God's servants, tormented with desire, wait any longer. I, poor wretch, *cannot* wait any more. Though I am alive, I feel as if I am dying of anguish, seeing God so insulted. Don't back off from making peace because of what has happened in Bologna.[17] Just come, for I tell you, the ferocious wolves will lay their heads in your lap meek as lambs, and will ask you for mercy.

Father, I'll say no more. I beg you to hear and listen to what Frate Raimondo my father and my other sons who are in his company have to say to you.[18] They come in the name of Christ crucified and in mine, for they are true servants of God[n] and sons of holy Church.

Pardon my foolishness, father, and let the love and sorrow that make me speak be my excuse in the presence of your kindness. Give me your blessing.

Keep living in God's holy and tender love.

Jesus, gentle Jesus![o]

Textual Notes

a. From V; others have *gentle Jesus / Jesus*
b. *so filled ... by divine grace* from B, P2; missing in B.
c. H: *babbo / father.*
d. H: [*You ... garden*].
e. H: [*crucified*].
f. P2: [*holy*].
g. H: *babbo / father.*
h. Lit: *think ... with what difficulty you would be able to do this if you did not accomplish the other two things that go to make up the three.*
i. P2: *conquered and slew / slew.*
j. H: *babbo / father.*
k. P2: *your / our.*
l. P2: *father / shepherd.*
m. Reading from P2; others: *'nformatione / riformatione.*
n. H: *Christ / God.*
o. From V; others have *Gentle Jesus! Jesus love!*

---

[16] Behind this imagery is Catherine's identification of the blood of Christ with the fire of the Spirit which is charity.

[17] Bologna joined the antipapal revolt on 21 March 1376.

[18] These "other sons" are Giovanni (Terzo) Tantucci, Felice da Massa, and Neri di Landoccio Pagliaresi.

Letter T101/G27/DT23[1]
To Cardinal Iacopo Orsini
Latter half of March 1376

One of a line of twenty-two Orsini cardinals in the twelfth to sixteenth centuries, Iacopo (or Iacomo) Orsini was titular cardinal of San Giorgio in Velabro and official protector of Siena at the papal court (salaried as such by the commune). He was an ambitious man whose sights were set on wearing the papal tiara. In July of 1376, the Florentine government would use both Cardinals Orsini and Corsini in a sense against Catherine by asking them to use their influence with Gregory XI on behalf of the very ambassadors who were refusing to deal with Catherine. The two cardinals would maintain their neutrality concerning Gregory's leaving Avignon for Rome. Orsini, in fact, seems to have taken an outward stance of neutrality in anything that might affect his own political interests (though he would openly oppose the election of Urban VI in 1378).[2] All of Catherine's extant letters to him (this one, Let. T223 in this volume, and T310, written in 1378) express dissatisfaction with his personal life.

Since Let. T223 and this one share a number of themes, their dating must be addressed in relation to each other. These themes—crusade expectations, rebellion, the need for reform and the appointment of good pastors as a remedy for rebellion (rather than resorting to war), and, in this letter, the pope's return to Rome—are all themes which appear in Catherine's letters after her return from Pisa and Lucca in early 1376. The linguistic evidence strongly supports placing both between late January and early April of that year.

The strong passion themes of this letter suggest that it may have been written during Lent (26 February to 12 April).[3] The fact that Let. T223 has more in common with other letters closer to April, plus the reference in that letter to the cardinal's falling "again," incline me to place the present letter earlier, but still in Lent, perhaps, around the latter half of March.[4]

---

[1] MSS: Mo, S2, P4, S4; translation based on Mo-*a*, corrected by *b*. No relevant variants.

[2] Cf. Gardner, *Saint Catherine of Siena*, pp. 181, 184, 186, 256.

[3] Dupré Theseider places this letter in late 1374, a placement which is not supported by the linguistic data. Both Fawtier (II, p. 167) and Dupré Theseider (unpublished notes) place Let. T223 in the summer of 1377, after Gregory's return from Rome, a placement which again is not linguistically supported. Gardner (*Saint Catherine of Siena*, p. 159) places Let. T223 in early 1376.

[4] Five letters share nineteen or more of this one's eighty-seven analyzed patterns, and all are dated between summer of 1375 and March 1376. The fact that this letter represents the earliest occurrence of a number of patterns which otherwise begin to occur only in February 1376 (CARCONFU, COGNAMA, GITTODOR, GODPENA, LAVDIFET,

§

In the name of Jesus Christ crucified and of gentle Mary, mother of God's Son.

Dearest and very loved father in Christ Jesus,

I Caterina, servant and slave of the servants of Jesus Christ, am writing to you in his precious blood. I long to see you bound by the same blazing divine charity that moved God to draw us from within himself, from his infinite wisdom, so that we might share in and enjoy his supreme eternal good.[5] This is the bond that bound and united God to human nature and engrafted him into us after we had lost grace through our sin. Life was engrafted into death so that we who were dead acquired life through that union. For God was so engrafted into humanity that one who was both God and human ran like one in love to the shameful death of the cross. This incarnate Word wanted to be engrafted onto that tree. And it was not the cross or the nails that held him there. These were not strong enough to hold the God-Man. No, it was love that held him there.[6]

He is that Master who has taken his chair to teach us the doctrine of truth.[7] The soul who follows his teaching can never fall into darkness. And he is the way we must walk to get to this school—I mean, by following his example. He said, "I am way and truth and life."[8] He truly is, father. For those who through being wronged, through anguish and abuse, through disgrace, suffering, and torment follow this Word in true holy poverty, those who bear with injury, and suffer humbly and meekly and with genuine good patience, learning from this Master who is himself the

---

PARTECBN, PENADES) support the hypothesis of its being a Lenten letter from that year. Several significant clusters within individual patterns end by March or April 1376 (AMAODDIO, AMASNZAM, APPOGG, CUORDUR, FATTVIA, PARTECBN, PIENGRAZ, TERMMORT, UNITRAS, VERSSANG, VISTAVED).

[5] Cf. *Dial.* 13, p. 49: "Why did you so dignify us? With unimaginable love you looked upon your creatures within your very self, and you fell in love with us. So it was love that made you create us and give us being just so that we might taste your supreme eternal good."

[6] Cf. Cavalca, *Specchio di croce*, p. 41: "No bond of iron could have held Christ nailed or bound—only charity, the bond of perfection." This is a concept Catherine refers to often, for example, *Dial.* 14, p. 52; 77, p. 143. Though it is found in other authors as well, she most probably was acquainted with it from her reading or hearing of Cavalca. The imagery of engrafting is particularly developed in Prayer 24, pp. 207–208.

[7] Cf. Augustine, *Sermo CCXXXIV* (PL XXXVIII, 1116): "That cross was a school, where the teacher taught the thief. The wood on which he hung became a chair for teaching." Cavalca, *Specchio di croce, Prologo*, p. 2: "Christ . . . on the cross is like a teacher occupying his chair, for he teaches . . . every perfect doctrine."

[8] Jn. 14, 6.

way (for he constructed it and kept to it, was himself faithful to it)—such people give everyone good for evil. Such is his teaching.

It is easy to see his patient forbearance then and now in the face of our sins, how he seems to pretend not to see. (Yet when that final moment of death comes he will prove that he has seen, because every sin will be punished and every good deed rewarded.) What great patience, that he disregards the wrongs done him! On the cross he hears the clamor of the Jews, who first shouted, "Crucify him!" and now challenge him to come down from the cross. And he cries, "Father, forgive them!" He does not move when they shout that he should come down, but stays there till the end.[9]

Then he joyously shouts, "It is finished!"[10] Yes, those seem to be sorrowful words, but they were words of joy to that soul aflame and consumed in the fire of divine charity, the soul of the incarnate Word, God's Son. It is as if the gentle Jesus wanted to say, "I have completely fulfilled what was written of me. Fulfilled too is my painful desire to redeem the human race. I am happy, exultant, that I have finished this suffering.[a] I have fulfilled the commission given me by my Father, a commission I so longed to accomplish."[11] *Oh gentle Master, well have you taught us your way and your teaching! Truly indeed did you say that you are way and truth and life. For those who follow your way and teaching cannot have death within themselves. No, they receive everlasting life within themselves, and they cannot be robbed of it by devils or by other people or by any wrong they may suffer, unless they themselves so choose.*

Shame, shame on our human pride, our self-complacency, our self-centeredness, when we see how good God has been to us, how many gifts and graces he has given us—and not because he has to but because he wants to![12] Obtuse as we are, we seem not to see or feel this love so hot that, if we were made of stone, it would long ago have burst us open![13] Oimé! Oimé! Unhappy me! I can see no other reason except that the eye of our understanding is not focused on the tree of the cross. For there is revealed such warm love, such gently persuasive teaching filled with life-giving

---

[9] These references to the Passion are based primarily on Lk. 23.

[10] Jn. 19, 30.

[11] These remarks resonate with Catherine's conviction, expressed to Raimondo da Capua (and with which he disagreed), that when Jesus asked in Gethsemani that "this cup be taken away," he was asking it not out of fear but out of eagerness to accomplish his mission. (*Life*, II, vi, 208–209, pp. 198–199)

[12] Cf. Rom. 4, 4–5: "A worker's wages are not considered a free gift but something owed. But when we do nothing, yet believe in him who justifies the sinful, our faith is considered as justice because of God's free gift." (Vulg.)

[13] Cf. Let. T34, to the prior of Monteoliveto (1378): "It would surely have to be a heart hard as diamond that would not be dissolved by such measureless love!"

fruits, such generosity that he has torn open his very body, has shed his life's blood, and with that blood has baptized and bathed us. We can and should make use of that baptism every day with continual remembrance and great love.[14] For just as baptism with water cleanses us of original sin and gives us grace, so in the blood we will wash away our sins and our unwillingness to suffer. There all wounds will be healed: not only will we cease to brood on them or seek revenge, but we will receive the fullness of grace to lead us along the right path.

If we see this, I tell you, we will not be able to bear *not* drowning and killing this disordered sensual will of ours that is always rebelling against ourselves as well as against our Creator.[15] In love with God's honor and the salvation of his creatures, we will forget ourselves. We will *act* like people in love, whose heart and will are centered not in themselves but in the object of their love. Love is so powerful that it makes one heart and one will of lover and beloved.[16] Whatever the one loves, so does the other; if it were otherwise, it would not be perfect love. I have often noticed that when we love something—either because it would be useful to us or because it would give us some gratification or pleasure—we don't care what sort of abuse or injury or pain we might have to endure to get it. The effort means nothing to us. We are concerned only with satisfying our desire for the thing we love.

Oh dearest father, let us not disgrace ourselves before the children of darkness![17] What a shame that would be for the children of light—I mean God's servants chosen and taken from the world,[18] and especially those

---

[14] Cf. Cavalca, *Specchio di croce*, p. 191: "To wash us, Christ made a bath for us of his most holy blood. A figure of this, says St. Paul [Heb. 9, 11–12] is that in the Old Testament everything is purified with the blood of slain animals—a prefiguring of Christ crucified. And it was to symbolize this that from Christ's side came blood and water: blood for our redemption, water for our sanctification. It is by the power of this blood and water that baptism has power to purify us from sin." This argument is developed in detail in *Dial.* 75, pp. 138–139, where baptism of blood and continual baptism are explained.

[15] Cf. Rom. 7, 22–23: "My inner self agrees with the law of God, but I see in my body's members another law at war with the law of my mind."

[16] Cf. *Dial.* 60, pp. 115–116: "Love transforms one into what one loves." Giordano da Rivalto, *Prediche*, ed. D. Moreni, II, p. 122: "Love is a passion in the soul that transforms lover into beloved." Also Cavalca, *Trattato della mondizia del cuore*, p. 22: "As Saint Paul says, anyone who approaches God in love is one spirit with him. And as Saint Denis says [*De divino nomine*, c. IV, n. 12—PG III, 709], love is a unitive virtue that transforms the lover into the one loved. And St. Augustine says [*De Trinitate* VIII, 10—PL XLII, 960], 'I know, my soul, that you are transformed into the likeness of whatever you perfectly unite yourself with.' " Also Aquinas, *Summa Theologica*, I–II, q. 26, a. 2.

[17] Lk. 16, 8: "The children of this world are wiser in dealing with their own kind than are the children of light." (Vulg.)

[18] Jn. 15, 19.

who have been set as flowers and pillars in the garden of holy Church! You ought to be a fragrant flower, not a stinking weed.[19] You should be clothed in purity's white, fragrant with patience and blazing with love. You should be magnanimous and generous, not stingy. Learn from First Truth, who in his generosity gave up his life. This is the fragrance you ought to shed on Christ's dear bride, who rests in this garden.[20] Oh how this gentle bride delights in these lovely and genuine virtues! When we have them we are her trueborn children, so she feeds and nourishes us at her breast, giving us the milk of divine grace, which is fully able to impart to us the life of seeing God eternally.[21] This is what Christ said to Paul: "My grace is enough for you, Paul."[22]

I say you are a pillar set up to keep this bride's home safe. So you must be strong, not weak; for weak things topple with the slightest wind—whether that wind is difficulty, or some wrong that may be done to us, or too much of the world's abundance and prosperity, pleasure and grandeur.[23] I want you to be strong then, since God has made you a pillar in his Church. Is there a way to shore up our weakness? Yes indeed: the way is love. Yet not every sort of love will do. Love of status or wealth would not do; nor would love of our own pride, or of our anger and hatred against those who wrong us; nor attachment to any created thing apart from God. Not only do these sorts of love fail to shore us up. They sap whatever strength we have. So wretchedly miserable is such love that it

---

[19] In Let. T24/DT10 (in this volume) she will use this imagery to admonish the priest Biringhieri degli Arzocchi: "Please, please be the fragrant flower you ought to be, breathing out a sweet perfume in God's gracious presence! You know well that flowers that stand too long in water give off a stench instead of fragrance. It really seems to me, father, that you and other ministers ought to be like flowers. But the water this flower has been put into is the wickedness and filth of sin and worldly wretchedness." And in Let. T206/DT63 and T270 (both in this volume) she urges Gregory XI to root up such stinking weeds from the Church.

[20] Catherine often speaks of the Church as a garden or as the bride of Christ, but this is the only instance in which she refers to the Church as a bride resting in the garden. Actually, here the Church is both bride and garden. Cf. Sg. 4, 12: "You are an enclosed garden, my sister, my bride."

[21] In Let. T239/DT81 to Gregory XI (in this volume), she refers to the Moslems as "these bastard children who have not yet been legitimized through holy baptism." Christians, in contrast, are "your legitimate children, who feed at the breasts of Christ's bride." There she goes on to say, "But I am hoping, by God's goodness, that if your legitimate children go to them [the Moslems] with your authority, with the divine power of the sword of the holy word, and with human power and force, these [unbelievers] will return to their mother, holy Church, and you will legitimize them."

[22] Catherine uses the affectionate nickname *Pavoloccio*. The biblical passage is 2 Cor. 12, 9.

[23] From the parable of the house built on sand in Mt. 7, 26–27. Cf. also *Dial.* 49, p. 101.

leads us to the most perverse slavery there is, making us servants and slaves of what is not,[24] and depriving us of our greatness and dignity. It is reasonable that we should suffer for this, because we ourselves have deprived ourselves of God.

There is only one thing to do then, and that is to invest our affection, our desire, our love in something stronger than ourselves—I mean in God, the source of all strength.[25] He is our God who loved us without being loved. And once we have discovered and experienced such a gentle love, strong beyond all other strength, we cannot cling to or desire any other love but him. Apart from him there is nothing at all we seek or want. Such people are strong then, because they are bound to and supported by what is firm and stable, what no eventuality will ever change. They follow always in the footsteps and ways of the one they love, because they have been made one heart and one will with him. They see that Christ more than anyone else found his delight in suffering and lowliness. Even though he was God's Son, he shared our company like a lowly, docile, despised Lamb.[26] This is why his servants delight in that sort of life. They hate and despise and avoid whatever is opposed to it. They have been made one with him, so they love what God loves and hate what God hates. This gives them such strength that nothing can harm them. They act like true knights who never consider any rising storm so great that they are daunted by it. They have no fear because it is not in themselves that they trust. No, all their faith and trust is in God, whom they love, because they see that he is strong, and that he is willing and able to help them. So with Saint Paul they say very humbly, "I can do all things in Christ crucified, who is in me and who strengthens me."[27]

So sleep no longer, father! Since by yourself you are a weak pillar, engraft yourself onto the tree of the cross.[28] Bind yourself by love, by measureless, infinite charity, to the slain Lamb who pours out his blood from every part of his body. Let these hearts of ours be broken open! No more hardness, no more carelessness—for time does not sleep but runs its course

---

[24] That is, sin, which Catherine consistently defines as "that which is not," "a nothing," in contrast to God, "the one who is."

[25] Cf. Ps. 43, 2: "For you, oh God, are my strength."

[26] Cf. Is. 53, 3, where the Lord's servant is called "despised and the least of men." (Vulg.)

[27] Phil. 4, 13.

[28] She also speaks in Let. T171/DT60 to Niccolò Soderini (in this volume) of losing one's weakness when one is engrafted into the tree of life. But the present instance is the only time she combines the image of the pillar with that of engrafting.

relentlessly! Let us make our dwelling place with him[29] in love and holy desire, and we need never be afraid again.

Here is the sweet holy remedy [for fear]: that we creatures recognize that of ourselves we are nothing, that we are moreover constantly doing that nothingness which is sin, and that everything else we have is from God. Once we have come to know ourselves we come to know also God's goodness to us. And knowing that, we love God and hate ourselves—not the self that is [God's] creation, but the self we see rebelling against our Creator.[30] If we walk in this true and holy knowledge, we will not stray from the path but will go forward courageously, because we are united with and transformed into the one who is way and truth and life. And he has made us so strong that neither the devil nor anyone else can take away our strength, so completely one with God are we.

This is what I want for you: to see you bound fast in that firm yet gentle bond. I will see that you are so bound—and this is one of the chief signs we have to show that we are disciples bound to Christ—if we are returning good for evil. (Otherwise you will be like the damned, and that is very displeasing to God in anyone, but especially in people like you who are set up in holy Church as mirrors where the laity look for a reflection of what they should be.) Certainly we must consider the offense we offer the infinite God by our sins greater than any offense a finite person could offer us. Nevertheless we want God to pardon us and make peace with us; we would like him to pretend not to see our offenses. Well, we ought to do the same for *our* enemies.[31] I beg you—I charge you—in the name of Christ crucified, to do just that for God's honor and your own salvation.

I'll say no more. Pardon my foolishness: my tongue babbles on too much because my heart is so full.[32]

I beg you, by his ineffable love, to be a champion for me in holy Church, seeking always God's honor and exaltation, not your own, as one who eats and savors souls. Try to do all you can, begging the holy father to come soon and to put it off no longer. Encourage him to raise the standard of the holy cross very soon and go against the unbelievers, so that the war Christians are waging against each other may be waged against

---

[29] Cf. Jn. 14, 23.

[30] Here Catherine is very explicit that by "self-hatred" she means only the hatred of what is sinful in oneself.

[31] Cf. Mt. 6, 12: "And forgive us the wrong we have done as we forgive those who wrong us."

[32] Mt. 12, 34 and Lk. 6, 45: "The mouth speaks what fills the mind."

them.[33] Don't be afraid of anything you may see arising, because divine help is with us.

Keep living in God's holy and tender love.

Textual Notes

a. There follows in Mo an erasure of one or two short words.

[33] A reference to the war between France and England—the two countries that have always made the greatest contribution to the crusades. Now they have all but lost interest in such ventures, so peace between these two is considered essential before a crusade can be mounted. Catherine is, in fact, a firm and vocal supporter of the projected crusade for reasons she sees as legitimate: the reclaiming of the Christian holy places, the conversion of the Moslems, the uniting of Christians in a common cause in support of rather than against the papacy, and her own probable martyrdom when she joins in the venture.

LETTER T77/G128[1]
To Brother William Flete (Guglielmo d'Inghilterra), at Lecceto[2]
Late March or very early April 1376

The only earlier extant letter to William is T66/DT35 (vol. I), written probably in late summer of 1375. In that letter, Antonio da Nizza is mentioned only to send him warm greetings and encouragement. In the present letter, however, there are indications of some tension between the two men.

The content of this letter in itself gives no clue as to the year it might have been written. But there are linguistic clues by which it can confidently be placed in late March or very early April 1376. Only a single letter shares twelve of this one's thirty-two analyzed patterns, T101/DT23 to Cardinal Iacopo Orsini, which seems to be from about the second half of March 1376. Because that letter is to a cardinal and not to a religious as the present letter is (thereby making the argument of common themes even more striking), one is tempted to speculate that the two letters might have been written about the same time. If one looks to significant clusters within individual patterns, the case becomes stronger still.[3]

The image of the incarnation as the seed of the Word sown in Mary as in a field might possibly reflect proximity to the feast of the Annunciation, 25 March. On the other hand, the twelfth chapter of the Gospel according to John, with the reference to Christ's being "lifted up," was read on the Saturday of the fifth week of Lent, 5 April that year. In any case, the themes of the letter seem strongly Lenten. I would therefore hypothesize that this letter was written about the same time as T101/DT23, most probably in late March or very early April, all but certainly before Easter.

---

[1] MSS: T, P3, P5, F2, R1, V; translation based on R1.

[2] The rubric has: "To Brother William of England, Bachelor, or the Order of Hermits of St. Augustine at Selva di Lago." (Selva di Lago is a name more particular to the precise location of the monastery.)

[3] Two earlier letters, but none later, share ten patterns. The patterns AMANSIEM, ARBFRUTT, and CAMPOMAR are clustered mainly in this general period. Also, the theme of knowledge related to love (GOGNAMA, COGNVERI) occurs for the first time in this letter and in T101. There are only two isolated instances of TITUL after April 1376, and UNITRAS never occurs again after that date. The letter contains a number of expressions unusual or even unique in Catherine's letters: *maestro della grazia*, "Master of grace" (in contrast with the more usual *maestro della verità*, "Master of truth"), unique here; *l'amore e l'ignorantia che noi abiamo a noi medesimi* ("our selfish love and our lack of self-knowledge"), not expressed in just this way anywhere else, though the idea is common; *à uperto lo 'ntendimento* ("opening one's understanding"), usually expressed as *aprendo l'occhio dell'intendimento* ("opening the eye of one's understanding"); *infinito essere* ("infinite being"), unique here. I am at a loss to explain these, unless perhaps they reflect the influence—and liberty—of a scribe not usually employed by Catherine. Both Fawtier and Dupré Theseider consider the letter undatable.

§

In the name of Jesus Christ and of gentle Mary.

Most reverend and very loved father in Christ Jesus,[a]

I Caterina, servant and slave of the servants of Jesus Christ, commend myself to you and encourage you in his precious blood.[b] I long to see us united with his boundless charity and transformed there, so that we who are sterile, unproductive, fruitless trees may be engrafted into the tree of life and so bear a sweet and flavorful fruit—not of ourselves but because of the Master of grace[4] who is within us. Just as the body is alive because of the soul, the soul is alive because of God. And because of the incarnate Word, we have been delivered from death and given life.[c] As a human being the incarnate Word could not restore the life of grace to us. But in virtue of his being God,[5] his divine Essence[6] could and wanted to do so for love.[7,d]

Oh fire! Oh abyss of charity! So that we would not be separated from you, you chose to engraft yourself into me, and this was when you sowed your Word in Mary as in a field.[8] *It is really true, then, that my soul is alive because of you, and the price of the overflowing blood shed for me had its value from the love of the divine Essence.* I am not surprised, dearest father, that God's Wisdom, the incarnate Word,[e] says: "If I am lifted up high, I will draw everything to myself."[9] Oh hardened hearts! Oh foolish children of Adam! It is indeed a wretched and miserable heart that refuses to be drawn

---

[4] Nowhere else does Catherine use this title, "Master of grace." The image of engrafting into Christ the tree of life is one she began to develop in some of her earliest letters and uses heavily through early 1376. She continues to use and elaborate on it occasionally through the rest of her life.

[5] Literally, "as God."

[6] Other than *The Dialogue* and Prayer 23 (25 January 1377), there are no other instances of Catherine's using "divine Essence" as a title for God.

[7] Later in her correspondence and *The Dialogue*, Catherine will develop this thought into the theme that God "knows how to, can, and wants to" do all that is for our good, paralleling the trilogy of Father as power ("can"), the Son as wisdom ("knows how"), and the Spirit as mercy ("wants").

[8] The image has occurred just three times earlier (in Let. T144/DT34, T342, and T138/DT41, all in vol. I) and never occurs again in Catherine's extant writings in these exact terms (though in Prayer 18, p. 156, in 1379, she will speak of Mary as "fertile soil"). For the fullest development of the image, cf. Let. T144/DT34 to Monna Pavola (vol. I): "Human pride must really blush to see God so humbled in gentle Mary's womb. She was the field wherein was sown the seed of the incarnate Word, God's Son. Truly, dearest sister, in that lovely blessed field the Word was engrafted into Mary's flesh as a seed is sown in the earth. In the sun's warmth it sprouts and blossoms and bears fruit, while the seed's husk remains in the ground. This is exactly what the fire and warmth of God's divine charity for the human race did after he had sown the seed of his Word in the field that was Mary."

[9] Jn. 12, 32.

to so tender a father! He says: "If I am lifted up." Why? Only to make us run![10]

I don't see anything to hinder us,[11] dearest father, except our selfish love and our lack of self-knowledge, and our scant light and knowledge of God. Those who do not know cannot love, and those who know also love.[12] I don't want us[f] living any longer in such ignorance, since it keeps us from being engrafted into life. No, I want our mind's eye to be lifted up above ourselves to see and know this supreme eternal Truth,[g] who cannot want anything other than that we be made holy.[13] Every circumstance of time and place, whether in life or in death, whether in persecution on the part of devils or of other people, [God] gives for this purpose only, that we may be made holy.[14]

I tell you, as soon as we open our understanding we become lovers of God's honor and of other people. We become lovers of suffering and find our pleasure only on the cross with him. This is no great wonder, for we had already seen that God's goodness cannot want anything but good and that everything comes from God. Already we had been freed from the selfish love that brought us darkness and kept us from seeing the light. Oh father, let's wait no longer; let's engraft ourselves into the productive tree so that the Master may not be lifted up without us![15] Let's take[h] the bond and chain of his blazing charity which held him nailed fast to the wood of the most holy cross! Let's run, run[i] with eagerness, for the infinite Good calls for infinite desire![16] This is how the soul is. Because it has infinite

---

[10] Cf. Sg. 1, 3 (Vulg.): "Draw me! We will run after you!"

[11] Literally, "any weight."

[12] This is the standard scholastic axiom of knowledge (intellect) preceding love (will).

[13] 1 Thes. 4, 3.

[14] Literally, "may have our sanctification."

[15] Cf. Let. T139 to Tommaso dalla Fonte (vol. I): "How I long to see you massacred on the tree of the sweet beloved cross—but not without me! I see no other refreshment for us, dearest father, but to agonize up there in blazing love."

[16] T and V have *percotiamo* here, which seems to make no sense. In every other instance in Catherine's writings this verb either carries some sense of striking or striking out at, with an object expressed, or of striking on (such as knocking on a door, striking a reef). Nowhere, on the other hand, does Catherine use the verb *percorrere* ("to run on"), so that one might guess this to be a miscopying of that verb. She does, however, often call on her addressees to "run," using the verb *correre*. In fact, there are several passages in which the exhortation is used in reference to desire (Let. T66/DT35, T69/DT24, T137/DT45, all in vol. I; T163 in this volume; T271, written in 1378); to the bond of charity (Let. T137/DT45 and T225 in vol. I, T172 in this volume); and to engrafting onto the wood of the cross (Let. T144/DT34, vol. I). A number of these passages contain the expression *Or corriamo* ("now let's run"), which could easily have been miscopied at some point as *Percotiamo*. I would therefore conjecture that this is how the original read, and have so translated it here. Also, all but one of the parallel passages cited are dated in 1375 through 1376, which would further support the placement of this letter in the same general period.

being, it desires infinitely and will never be satisfied until it is joined with the infinite.[17] So let our heart be lifted up with its every movement to love the one who loves without being loved. *Oh boundless love! To hammer out our souls*[18] *you made an anvil of your own body.* So Christ's body satisfies for the punishment, his soul has contempt for sin, and his divine nature [satisfies] with its power. See with what fidelity we have been redeemed![19] And why? Because he was lifted up on high. Let us submit our stubborn will then to the yoke of God's will, which wants nothing but our good. And because we are unworthy of such good, let us accept every difficulty with reverence.

In the name of Christ crucified I am telling you that you are to say Mass in the convent not only the few times a week that the prior asks it, but every day if you see that to be his wish.[20] Even though you may be giving up your comfort, you are not for all that losing the state of grace but rather gaining it by giving up your own will. So that we may show ourselves to be eaters of souls,[j] savorers of our neighbors,[21] I want us to be concerned not just about our own comfort but about listening to and seeing and having compassion on our neighbors' problems,[k] particularly those neighbors with whom we are joined in one and the same charity.[22] To do otherwise would be a very serious failing. I want you, therefore, to lend your ears and listen to Frate Antonio's difficulty, and I ask and want Frate Antonio to listen to you.[23] I'm begging you in Christ's name and my own to do this, and in this way you will preserve true charity within you. Otherwise you would be giving the devil room to sow disharmony.

I'll say no more, except to beg you urgently in the name of Christ[l] to

---

[17] In Let. T264 to Jacoma, widow of Trincio de' Trincio (in this volume) she also calls the soul "infinite." And in *Dial.* 92, p. 170, and Let. T213 to Daniela of Orvieto (1378) she speaks of God's wish to be served with what is infinite, and that the only infinite thing the soul has is desire.

[18] Usually Catherine speaks of hammering out our wickedness (*iniquitadi*) on the anvil of Christ's body. There is, however, one other instance in which the object is our souls, Let. T161 to Nella and Caterina Buonconti (in this volume). That letter seems to be from March or April 1376, yet another reason to conjecture that the present letter may be from near the same time.

[19] Cf. 2 Tim. 2, 13: "If we are unfaithful he will still remain faithful, for he cannot deny himself."

[20] The hermits at Lecceto spent most of their time in their own hermitages on the monastery grounds, and gathered in the central building (the "convent") only for certain functions.

[21] It.: *mangiatori e gustatori dell'anime*, that is, people who in Catherine's imagery "eat souls" and enjoy it.

[22] That is, in William's case, with his brothers in community.

[23] Antonia da Nizza, another hermit of Lecceto and William's good friend. But this comment may indicate that the two are having some difficulty in their relationship.

be united and bound into this tree, Christ crucified, and transformed in him.

Jesus, gentle Jesus![m]

Textual Notes

a. Dupré Theseider in his unpublished transcription has: *gentle Jesus / Jesus.* He does not indicate the manuscript on which the transcription is based.
b. V: [*commend myself to you and encourage you*]; DT: *writing to commend myself to you in the precious blood of God's Son.*
c. From V; R1: [*And because ... life*].
d. V: [*but as God, his divine; for love*], clearly a copyist's error.
e. V: *speaks in charity* (*parla in carità*) / *the incarnate Word* (*parola incarnata*).
f. V: *you / us.*
g. V: *Life / Truth.*
h. V: *cut* (*tagliamo*) / *take* (*tolliamo*), clearly an error in this context.
i. V: *run / run, run.*
j. V: [*eaters of souls*].
k. V: *neighbors / neighbors' problems.*
l. *in the name of Christ* supplied from V.
m. Dupré Theseider: ... *bound into this tree, Christ gentle Jesus crucified, and transformed in him.*

LETTER T204/G109/DT5[1]
To Frate Bartolomeo Dominici, in Asciano
Lent (26 February to 12 April) 1376

The Dominicans Bartolomeo Dominici and Simone da Cortona were in Asciano probably in 1372 to preach a Lenten mission. (See Let. T99/DT7 in Volume I and the four letters which follow it.) The linguistic evidence in Catherine's letters addressed to persons in that town compels me to conclude that the same two friars conducted a second Asciano Lenten mission at least a few years later. This could not have been in 1375, since Bartolomeo was in Florence that Lent. The best possibility seems to be 1376.[2] The linguistic evidence for this is reinforced by a number of clues within this letter. There is no evidence in the sources to indicate that Bartolomeo was with Catherine continually between her return from Pisa and their departure for Florence and Avignon. There are greetings to Simone, but with no hint that he is depressed. Above all, there is no reference to the presence of Neri di Landoccio Pagliaresi as there was in the letters I have placed in 1372.[3] Catherine is still chiding Bartolomeo for his small-heartedness.

The scribe is clearly Cecca (Francesca di Clemente Gori), with greetings also from "fat Alessa" (Alessa dei Saracini) and Lisa (Catherine's sister-in-law).[4]

---

[1] MSS: Mo, P4, Pa; translation based on Mo-*a*, corrected by *b*. No other relevant variants.

[2] Of the thirty-six patterns analyzed, a number of individual patterns show significant concentrations beginning in mid-1375 to early 1376 and ending by mid-1376 (APPDISORD, ANNEGAFF, CARCONFU, FINECRE, LIBROVIT, MORTDIST, OGGETOCC, VASDILEZ). This plus the fact that only three significantly clustered non-protocol patterns (INNAMOR, OCCHINT, PERDMED) begin earlier than this strongly reinforces the probability of a second Asciano mission. Further, all three of the letters which share eleven or more patterns with this one have been dated in early 1376. Fawtier (II, p. 207) and Dupré Theseider place all of the Asciano letters together, associating them with a single mission sometime before 1374, with Fawtier specifying "most probably 1372–1373."

[3] If this Asciano mission is rightly placed, Neri is on his way to Avignon by the time these letters are being written.

[4] See also the notes for Let. T198/DT4 in this volume. The fact that Cecca serves as scribe for the Asciano letters which I have placed in 1376 is my only cause for hesitation in this placement, since by this time Catherine seems to be more generally employing her male disciples in this capacity.

§

In the name of Jesus Christ crucified and of gentle Mary.

My dearest and very loved brother in Christ Jesus,

I Caterina, servant and slave of God's servants, am writing to encourage you in the precious blood of God's Son. I long to see you so engulfed and set on fire in Christ Jesus that you will be completely lost to yourself. But I don't see how you can unless your mind's eye rises above yourself in true desire to gaze into the eye of the divine charity with which God looked on his creatures before he created us. And so he still looks on us.

For he looked on us within himself and fell so boundlessly in love with us that for love he created us to share and enjoy the good he possessed in himself.[5] But because of Adam's sin his desire was not realized. So God, moved by the fire of divine charity, sent the gentle incarnate Word, his Son, to ransom us and rescue us from slavery. And his Son ran to surrender himself to the shame of the cross. He eagerly associated with sinners, with publicans,[6] with outcasts, with all sorts of people. For there is no putting laws or limits to charity: it is not self-centered or self-seeking.[7] Since the first man had fallen from the height of grace through selfish love of himself, God had to act in the opposite way—so he sent this spotless Lamb with an indescribably great-hearted charity, seeking not himself but only the Father's honor and our salvation.

Oh gentle loving Knight, you made nothing of your death, your life, or your shame. No, on the cross you did battle with the death that is our sin, and though death destroyed your bodily life, your death destroyed our death.[8] Love

---

[5] Cf. *Dial.* 13, p. 49: "Why did you so dignify us? With unimaginable love you looked upon your creatures within your very self, and you fell in love with us. So it was love that made you create us and give us being just so that we might taste your supreme eternal good." She continues with a commentary on sin and redemption. Also *Dial.* 119, p. 226: "I loved you before you came into being." The same ideas are developed by Aquinas, *Summa Theologica*, I, q. 44, a. 4, and II–II, q. 104, a. 3.

[6] Dupré Theseider points out (n. 4) that, according to popular interpretations of Catherine's time, "publicans were so called after the emperor Publius, who first established their function." (Simone Fidati da Cascia, *Expositiones super totum corpus evangeliorum*, p. 74). Cf. also Franco Sacchetti, *Sermo III*: "It seems that every public sinner was called a publican."

[7] 1 Cor. 13, 5.

[8] Cf. *Dial.* 30, p. 71: "Your mercy made your Son play life against death on the wood of the cross. In him life confounded the death that is our sin, even while that same death of sin robbed the spotless Lamb of his bodily life. But who was conquered? Death! And how? By your mercy!" Also 2 Tim. 1, 10: "He has robbed death of its power and has brought life and immortality into clear light through the gospel." Heb. 2, 14–15: "that by his death he might rob the devil, the prince of death, of his power, and free those who through fear of death had been slaves their whole life long." Also Augustine, *Enarratio in Ps. CXLIX*, 6 (PL XXXVII, 1952): "When he did battle for us he seemed to be conquered, but in fact he was

is the reason, you see; for his eye was fixed on nothing but his Father's honor and on realizing his desire for us, that we might experience God—which is why he had created us.

Oh my very dear and cherished son, I want you to imitate this Word who is our rule, and[a] the saints who followed him. Then you will become one with him and will have a share in his great-heartedness to replace [your own] small-heartedness. I tell you again, unless you rise up, open your eyes, and take as your model the boundless goodness and love God has shown to his creatures, you will never attain such perfect greatness of soul but will be so small-hearted that you will have no room either for yourself *or* for your neighbors.

This is why I want you, as I said, to be engulfed and set on fire in him, constantly gazing into the gentle eye of his charity, for then you will love perfectly what he loves, and hate what he hates. Lift up, lift up your puny heart, your small disordered conscience! Don't give any leverage to the wicked devil, who wants to prevent so much good and doesn't want to be thrown out of his city. No, I want you, with courageous heart and perfect zeal, to realize that the Holy Spirit's law is quite different from ours. Imitate that dear Paul, who was so in love, and be a vessel of affection[9] that bears and proclaims the name of Jesus. It seems to me that Paul gazed into this eye and lost himself in it. And he was granted such a great soul that he was willing and even desired to be separated from God, an outcast, for the sake of his brothers and sisters.[10] Paul was in love with whatever God was in love with. He saw that charity is never scandalized, is never confounded.

Moses, too, looked to the honor of God; this is why he wished to be struck out of the book of life rather than have the people die.[11] So I urge you in Christ—I want you—to be determined in rooting out vice and planting virtue. Follow First Truth, as I have said, and the saints who have

---

the conqueror. He was crucified, and from the cross to which he was nailed he killed the devil." Catherine may also be thinking of the Easter Sequence: "Death and life in battle—wondrous conflict!—the Captain of life, though killed, reigns alive," or the hymn *Vexilla Regis*: "He endured death, and by death brought forth life." Also Jacopo Passavanti, *Lo specchio di vera penitentia*, Dist. II, chap. VII: "As St. Gregory says (PL LXXIX, 28), by his passion and death he conquered our death."

[9] Cf. Acts 9, 15; Catherine's allusion probably reflects her hearing rather than reading. The Latin *vas electionis* (It. *vasello d'elezione*) is heard as *vas delectionis* (It. *vasello di dilezione*). She does the same in many other instances.

[10] Rom. 9, 3.

[11] Ex. 32, 32: "If only you would forgive their sin! If not, then strike me out of the book you have written."

walked in his footsteps. Set no rule or limit to your desire, which he wants to be without limit.[12] Accept the fact that you are in the midst of an unfaithful people, outcasts full of wickedness. Love demands that you associate with them, but I would have you know that when you do, charity rather than they themselves will be your companion—the love, I mean, that you have for their salvation.[13] For if you were associating with them for selfish reasons or for the personal gratification it brings you, whether temporal or spiritual, and not for this hunger [for their salvation], then you should well fear and flee their company. So get rid of all petty resentment, and trust more in others than in yourself. And if the devil should still try to trouble your conscience, tell him to deal with *me*—about this and about everything else—for a mother is accountable for her child! So that is how zealous I want you to be! For nothing, no situation, is so hard that charity cannot break through it, even as it makes you stronger.

Bless my son Frate Simone for me,[14] and tell him to run on with holy desire—I mean the holy cross—as his staff.[15] Let me know how you are and how God's honor is faring.

Fat Alessa[16] says that you are praying for her and asks you please to

---

[12] Aquinas, *Summa Theologica*, II–II, q. 27, a. 6, concludes that God is to be loved without measure, that "the more we love God, the better our love is." He cites Bernard de Clairvaux, *De diligendo Deo*, I (PL CLXXXII, 974): "God himself is the reason for loving God; the measure of loving him is to love him without measure." Catherine does not, however, seem to have made a conscious connection between this "measureless love" and the "infinite desire" of which she speaks here and elsewhere, except perhaps in *Dial.* 3, p. 28: "True contrition satisfies for sin and its penalty not by virtue of any finite suffering you may bear, but by virtue of your infinite desire. For God, who is infinite, would have infinite love and infinite sorrow."

[13] Bartolomeo has evidently complained to Catherine about the wickedness of the people to whom he is preaching and has expressed some fear that he will be corrupted by it. This is not the only occasion Catherine has had to chide the friar for his lack of magnanimity. As for the wickedness of the people of Asciano, Catherine will in Let. T24/DT10 (in this volume) admonish their pastor: "Correct vice and strengthen the virtuous in doing good. The failure to correct causes decay just as surely as does a gangrenous organ in the human body. Keep a watchful eye on yourself and on those in your care. Don't think it harsh to root out these thorns; the fruit will be far sweeter than the effort is bitter."

[14] Dupré Theseider points out (n. 17 to this letter) that a marginal gloss of the same period as the manuscript reads, "Frater Simon Antonii, one of the witnesses examined in the Process of Venice." Frate Simone da Cortona, who was a witness for that Process, the *Processo Castellano*, is certainly the one referred to here, but his father's name was Neri (Rainiero), not Antonio.

[15] Cf. Franco Sacchetti, *Sermo XLVIII*, where Christ is compared to a pilgrim "who carried a staff (that is, the wood of the cross) on which he leaned when he was crucified, and with which he defended himself against the dogs."

[16] It. *Alessa grassotta*, Alessa dei Saracini. The scribe, her friend Cecca, uses one of those derogatory but affectionate epithets so characteristically used among Catherine's disciples.

keep praying for her. Pray for me too, Cecca the time-waster.[17] And pray for Lisa.[18]

Keep living in God's holy peace and love.

Textual Notes

a. *b* adds *that of,* thus changing the sense.

---

[17] Cecca di Clemente Gori, clearly the writer of this letter.

[18] This is almost certainly Catherine's sister-in-law Lisa, wife of Bartolomeo. The 1352 list of Sienese *Mantellate* (Laurent, *Fontes*, I, *Documenti*, p. 24) lists together *domina Lisa Bartoli, domina Cecca Clementis, domina Alessa.*

LETTER T198/G110/DT4[1]
To Frate Bartolomeo Dominici, in Asciano
Early April (before 13 April, Easter) 1376

The linguistic evidence in this letter reinforces my hypothesis that there may have been a preaching mission to Asciano later than the one I have posited for 1372.[2] This particular letter contains other clues as well: (1) There are greetings to Simone, but no indication that he is particularly depressed; (2) There is no reference to Neri's presence; (3) Catherine writes to Bartolomeo that Raimondo (who, so far as we know, was not associated with Catherine before May 1374) has *sent* word from Nicola da Osimo concerning a crusade.[3] Now Raimondo was sent on his way to Avignon probably in late February of 1376, and just after 1 April, Catherine addresses a letter to Raimondo *in* Avignon. She has already written to Nicola da Osimo in Avignon about January 1376. Presumably, since he was Gregory XI's notary and secretary, Nicola was fairly constantly in Avignon. So it would seem that Raimondo too must be in Avignon when he sends word "from Nicola da Osimo";[4] (4) Further, a certain "Nanni" is with Catherine. This could well be Nanni di Ser Vanni. She must have negotiated with him for Belcaro before she herself went to Avignon, since while there she obtained Gregory's permission for her foundation specifically at Belcaro.[5]

What of Catherine's begging for Sant'Agnesa toward the end of the letter? Besides the present letter, such begging is referred to in Let. T105/DT8 to Bartolomeo in 1372, and again in Let. T88/DT28 to Angelo Ricasoli and Let. T129/DT29 to Bartolomeo, both in spring of 1375.[6] So this would not necessarily link the present letter to the earlier Asciano mission.

The scribe is *perdatrice del tempo* ("the time-waster" or perhaps "procrastinator"), probably Cecca; Alessa also sends greetings. These women could still have served Catherine in this role even after Neri di Landoccio Pagliaresi had joined Catherine's circle. In fact, if the letter is correctly

---

[1] MSS: Mo, P4; translation based on Mo-*a*, corrected by *b*. No relevant variants.

[2] Of eighteen patterns analyzed, there is fairly strong sharing up to mid-1376, with four patterns (one, COLTPARO) ending at that point. More telling, however, is the fact that while a good number of patterns begin early, there are three which do not begin at all until early 1376 (BOCCDESI, COLTPARO, MAMELLE).

[3] Nicola's name is sometimes given as *Niccolò*, but I have rendered it consistently as *Nicola* in order to avoid confusion.

[4] I can see no reason for Dupré Theseider's supposition that the reference is from before 1374, and thus his conclusion that Raimondo must have known Catherine before 1374.

[5] Details of the foundation of the monastery at Belcaro are given in the introduction to the next section, and in notes to Let. T112 in this volume.

[6] All of these letters are to be found in Volume I.

placed in April 1376, Raimondo has already left for Avignon, and Neri has been sent to join him (though Stefano Maconi was available by this time as well, since he would accompany Catherine to Florence in May).

For all of the above reasons, but especially on the basis of the reference to Raimondo's letter, I would date this letter to early April of 1376, before Easter (13 April).

§

In the name of Jesus Christ and of gentle Mary.

My very loved and dearest son in Christ Jesus,

I Caterina, servant and slave of God's servants, am writing to encourage you in the precious blood of God's Son. I long to see you so strong and filled to overflowing with that Holy Spirit who came upon the holy disciples, that God's gentle word will be able to grow and bear fruit in you and in your neighbors as well. After the fire of the Holy Spirit had descended on them they mounted the pulpit of the blazing cross,[7] where they felt and tasted the hunger of God's Son, his love for humankind. Then their words came forth as does a red-hot knife from a furnace,[8] and with its heat they pierced their listeners to the heart and cast out the devils. Since they had lost themselves, they saw not themselves but only God's glory and honor and our salvation.[9]

So, my dearest son, I beg you—it is my will in Christ Jesus—make your home in the pulpit of the cross. There be engulfed,[10] lose yourself completely, with insatiable desire. Draw the red-hot knife and strike the devils, seen and unseen, who want continually to disturb your conscience by nipping people's fruit in the bud. Don't give in to this wicked devil—especially now, when it is time for harvesting and sowing. Tell the devil to deal with me instead of with you! Forward then, courageously!

---

[7] The pulpit or chair of the cross is a frequent image in Catherine, for example, in her letter (T101/DT23 in this volume) to Cardinal Iacopo Orsini.

[8] She may or may not be consciously combining the biblical image of the two-edged sword (Is. 49, 2; Heb. 4, 12) with the image in Proverbs of God's word as fire (Prv. 30, 5, Vulg.). She may be echoing Cavalca, who brings the two concepts together in *Trenta stoltizie* (p. 33B): "Their word is like a sharp sword, and their words blaze like a torch." Or the image may be her own.

[9] Cf. Gal. 2, 20: "The life I live now is not my own; Christ is living in me. I still live my human life, but it is a life of faith in the Son of God."

[10] The Italian *anegarsi* as derived from the Latin *abnegare semetipsum* has the sense of "denying oneself," as in Mt. 16, 24. When derived from the colloquial Latin *adnecare*, however, it has the sense of immersing oneself or drowning; this is the sense in which Catherine most often uses it.

Let's sleep no more, for the time is near. I am so glad that so much fruit is apparently being produced there.[11] I'm also happy for some good news about the crusade, which Frate Raimondo had from Messer Nicola da Osimo and sent on to me.[12] Rejoice and be glad, for our desires will soon be fulfilled! I have no time for writing. Nanni is very well and happy.[13]

Bless my son Frate Simone, and tell him to get the mouth of his desire ready for milk, for his mamma will send him some.[14]

Keep in mind the young girl who was commended to you in that will, as well as my Sant'Agnesa,[15] in case you have a little extra or anything else to give.

Keep living in God's holy love.

Alessa and the time-waster[16] send you many many greetings.

---

[11] The sentence is not entirely clear, but the reference is certainly to the work in Asciano.

[12] Nicola da Osimo is one of the secretaries of Pope Gregory XI. He has informed Raimondo (already at the Curia in Avignon, if my placement of this letter is correct) of the pope's intentions regarding the projected crusade, and Raimondo has sent the word on to Catherine. Catherine often uses the expression "the time is near" in connection with the crusade, but it could also refer in this case to Catherine's other desires.

[13] The name Nanni (Giovanni) occurs a number of times in the letters, and the reference may or may not always be to the same person. If this letter is correctly placed in 1376, the Nanni referred to in this instance could well be Nanni di Ser Vanni Savini, as mentioned in the introduction. Burlamacchi (Gigli, *Opere*, II, p. 615) is of the opinion that it is Frate Giovanni Piccolomini. Innocenzo Taurisano (*Fioretti*, 2nd ed., p. 143, n. 3) thinks it is the Bavarian Frate Giovanni Simons, who had been a mercenary and had joined the Dominicans in Siena under Catherine's inspiration. He is cited in the Necrology of San Domenico for his humility, peaceableness, mildness, and lovableness, and as a confessor especially sought after by women (cf. Seckendorff, *Kirchenpolitische Tätigkeit*, pp. 83–84 and 160, and *Fioretti*, pp. 175–177).

[14] The reference is to Frate Simone di Neri da Cortona, once again Bartolomeo's companion in Asciano. He is remembered not only in this letter, but in letters from the earlier Asciano mission as well. It seems from the references that he is again (as he seems often to have been) going through some sort of spiritual crisis, and Catherine is watching over and guiding him even from a distance. Her words are reminiscent of Heb. 5, 12: "You need milk, not solid food." Since Catherine makes frequent use of this image of milk (for example, Let. T200/DT9, vol. I) in reference to the blood of Christ and to the fire of the Spirit as "solid food" for those who are mature in faith, one may guess that there is a kind of teasing in her remark here.

[15] That is, the monastery of Sant'Agnesa in Montepulciano. The young girl is not identified, nor is there any clue as to whose will is referred to.

[16] Almost certainly Cecca di Clemente Gori, who is writing the letter for Catherine. Alessa is Alessa dei Saracini.

LETTER T208/G111/DT6[1]
To Frate Bartolomeo Dominici, in Asciano
About 6 to 11 April (Holy Week) 1376

Again, because of the linguistic evidence, I would place this letter within the context of a 1376 Lenten mission to Asciano.[2]

Burlamacchi sees the "Monna Giovanna" who sends greetings at the end of the letter as Stefano Maconi's mother, whom Catherine did not know before 1376. There are, however, other Giovannas referred to by this title. Giovanna di Capo is "Monna Giovanna" in the rubric of Let. T108 (late 1377); a "Monna Giovanna" (whom Dupré Theseider thinks is also Giovanna di Capo) sends blessings in Let. T127 (vol. I, clearly written near 26 March 1374).

"Crazy Giovanna" (*Giovanna pazza*) is apparently the scribe for this letter. I would guess from all occurrences that Catherine's disciple Giovanna dei Pazzi had that nickname within the family (she is *Giovanna Pazza* even in the rubric of Let. T87 in this volume). Since both "crazy Giovanna" and "Monna Giovanna" are mentioned, I would posit the presence of both Giovanna dei Pazzi and Giovanna di Capo.[3]

There are admonitions to the parish priest Biringhieri (cf. Let. T24/DT10 in this volume). There are greetings to Simone da Cortona (who may or may not be depressed at this point, judging from the tone of the remark). "Crazy Giovanna," Monna Giovanna, Lisa (presumably Catherine's sister-in-law), Alessa dei Saracini, and Cecca di Clemente Gori send greetings. Significantly, there is no reference to Neri di Landoccio Pagliaresi, who was with Bartolomeo on the 1372 mission.

My chief hesitation about placing this letter in conjunction with a 1376 Lenten mission to Asciano is in Catherine's "If I can, I will come," since she also was trying to come to Asciano during the earlier mission. How likely is it that Catherine would have promised to try to come to Asciano on two different occasions? It seems to be specifically Biringhieri's problem that prompts her desire to come this time. Or possibly the Dominicans want her to come because she was *not* able to come the previous time. In

---

[1] MSS: Mo, P4; translation based on Mo-*a*, corrected by *b*. No relevant variants.

[2] There is only a single letter, T189 from Holy Week of 1376 (in this volume), which shares fifteen or more of the thirty-four patterns analyzed for this letter. Several clusters within individual patterns also point to early 1376 (CUORMESC, FUNE, RICHIAM, UTILPROS beginning in early 1376, and DESIDDE, GIOVPAZ, LAUDATO, and a significant cluster of SANGACQU ending there).

[3] The latter was for certain *not* with Catherine at the time of Let. T132 (vol. I, December 1375) and Let. T118 (in this volume, October 1377), but *was* with her at the time of Let. T127 (vol. I, about 26 March 1374), Let. T41 (vol. I, before May 1374), Let. T144 (vol. I, July 1375), and Let. T152 (vol. I, January 1376).

any case, this does not seem sufficient grounds to back off positing two missions to Asciano, one in 1372 and one in 1376, given the other evidence. Judging from the references to Passover (*Pasqua*), I would guess that the letter was written around Holy Week (6 to 11 April in 1376).

§

In the name of Jesus Christ crucified.

My very loved and dearest son in Christ Jesus,

I Caterina, servant and slave of God's servants, bless and encourage you in the precious blood of Jesus Christ. "How I have longed to celebrate this Passover with you before I die!"[4] This is the Passover I want us to celebrate: I want to see us at the table of the spotless Lamb, who is food, table, and waiter.[5] The fruits on this table are the true solid virtues. No other table bears fruit, but this one's fruit is perfect, because this table is life-giving. This table has been furrowed, with channels everywhere flowing with blood. But among them all there is one channel flowing with blood and water mixed with fire, and to the eye that rests on this channel is revealed the secret of his heart.[6]

This blood is a wine on which our soul gets drunk. The more we drink, the more we would like to drink, and we are never fully satisfied, because his flesh and his blood are joined with the infinite God. Oh dearest son in Christ Jesus, let us eagerly run to this table!

Fulfill my desire for you, so that I may celebrate the Passover. Do as a heavy drinker does who loses himself and can no longer see himself. If he really likes the wine he drinks even more, till his stomach becomes so warmed by the wine that he can no longer hold it, and out it comes! Truly, son, here is the table on which we find this wine: I mean the pierced side of God's Son. This is the blood that warms, that drives out all chill, clears the voice of the one who drinks it, and gladdens heart and soul.[7]

---

[4] Cf. Lk. 22, 15. (Vulg.)

[5] This imagery (usually explicitly Trinitarian) is developed in *Dial.* 78, pp. 145–146, and elsewhere. Cf. Augustine, *Sermones*, CCCXXIX (PL XXXVIII, 1455): "The table is large where the table's very Lord holds his banquet. No one comes to eat at his or her own invitation; the Lord Christ does this: he is the one who invites, he is the food and drink."

[6] Cf. Bernard de Clairvaux, *In Cantico sermo LXI* (PL CLXXXIII, 1072): "The secret of his heart is revealed through the wounding of his body." Also *Dial.* 75, p. 138: "My longing for humankind was infinite, but the actual deed of bearing pain and torment was finite and could never show all the love I had. This is why I wanted you to see my inmost heart, so that you would see that I loved you more than finite suffering could show."

[7] Cf. Ps. 104, 15: "and wine to gladden people's hearts."

For this blood is shed with the fire of divine charity. It so warms us that out *we* come from our very selves—and from that point on, we cannot see ourselves selfishly, but only for God, and we see God for God, and we see our neighbors for God.[8] And when we have drunk enough, out it comes over the heads of our sisters and brothers.[9] We have taken our example from the one who is continually pouring out his blood at this table—and not for his own good but for ours. We who eat at this table and become like the food we eat[10] begin to do as he does—not for our own good but for God's honor and for our neighbors' salvation. This is why *you* were sent. Be encouraged by the thought that this fire will give you your voice and relieve your hoarseness.[11]

If I can, I will come, and very gladly. Plead with Christ and ask him to let me come. Tell Messer Biringhieri[12] to find his courage in Christ Jesus, and to think about the brevity of time and the price that was paid for him. I will come to see him if I can.

Tell Frate Simone I will take the cord of charity and keep him tied to my heart as a mother keeps her child.[13]

I feel good about this priest, who seems to be well-disposed. Take him

---

[8] In this definition of charity Catherine is close to Augustine, *De doctrina christiana* III, 16 (PL XXXIV, 72): "I call charity the movement of the soul toward the enjoyment of God for his own sake, and of herself and her neighbor for God's sake." (Also *Sermones*, CCCXXXVI, 2, PL XXXVIII, 1472.) This is picked up and developed at length in Bernard de Clairvaux, *De diligendo Deo*, VIII–X, XV (PL CLXXXII), where four degrees are distinguished: loving oneself for oneself, God for one's own sake, God for God's sake, and self for God's sake. (Also Peter Lombard, *Sententiae*, III, 27, 2) The image of the drinker is found also in Augustine, *Enarratio in Ps. XXXV* (PL XXXVI, 351).

[9] Cf. Ps. 45, 2: "My heart overflows with a goodly theme." Also Augustine, *Enarratio in Ps. CXLIV*, 7 (PL XXXVII, 1874–1875): "When you are learning you are eating; when you are teaching you are overflowing. When you are listening you are eating; when you are preaching you are overflowing. . . . If you want to overflow with grace, drink grace." The concept appears in other letters of Catherine as well. Giovanni dalle Celle (ed. Cividali, p. 436) says of Catherine: "She can appropriately say with the spouse in the Song of Songs (1, 3): 'The king brought me into his wine cellar,' that is, into the wounds of Jesus Christ where, drunk on the blood of the Savior, she poured forth the gift that you see in her letters."

[10] Cf. Augustine, *Confessiones*, VII, 10 (PL XXXII, 742): "I am a greater food. . . . You do not change me into yourself as you do with bodily food, but you are changed into me." This passage occurred in the Dominican Breviary in the First Nocturn for 28 August, the feast of Saint Augustine.

[11] Catherine is perhaps simply expanding on her own metaphor. However, given Catherine's frequent admonitions to Bartolomeo about his "small-heartedness," I would guess that the excuse was real. Cf. her remarks at the end of Let. T204/DT5 in this volume.

[12] Biringhieri degli Arzocchi, the parish priest of Asciano. Let. T24/DT10 (in this volume) is addressed to him, but besides this, nothing is known of him.

[13] The text has *to his heart*, which makes no sense. Cf. Hos. 11, 4: "I drew them with human cords, with bands of love; I fostered them like one who raises an infant to his cheeks."

to the brothers at Monteoliveto, and get him to settle his affairs as soon as possible.[14] And do be zealous.

Monna Giovanna[15] encourages and blesses you. Remember crazy Giovanna,[16] possessed by the fire of the slain Lamb. Lisa, Monna Alessa, and Cecca wish to be remembered to you a hundred thousand times.

Praised be Jesus! Jesus! Jesus!

---

[14] The Benedictine Monastery of Monteoliveto Maggiore was just a few miles south of Asciano. It is not clear who "this priest" is. None of the editions either questions or explains the reference.

[15] Burlamacchi presumes that this is Stefano Maconi's mother. This is possible, but a number of the *Mantellate* in the 1352 list have the name *domina Iohanna*. So the identity of this Giovanna is not certain. I would guess it is Giovanna di Capo, a frequent companion of Catherine.

[16] Giovanna dei Pazzi is often called *Giovanna pazza*, or "crazy Giovanna," in Catherine's circle of friends. The derogatory epithet is a probable indication that she is the scribe who is writing this letter for Catherine.

LETTER T219/G87/DT65[1]

To Frate Raimondo da Capua and others of his company, in Avignon
Early April 1376

On the night of 1 April 1376, Catherine has an experience in prayer that remarkably expresses her motivation for all of her great public concerns: the return of the pope to Rome, the reform and unity of the Church, the crusade. In this letter, written very shortly thereafter, she attempts to describe the experience to Raimondo and others of her disciples who have gone ahead of her to Avignon.[2]

§

In the name of Jesus Christ crucified and of gentle Mary.

My very loved sons in Christ Jesus,

I your poor mother have desired with anguished desire to see you nailed, heart and affection, to the cross—bound and united in the same bond that bound and engrafted God into humanity and humanity into God. This is how my soul longs[a] to see your hearts and affections engrafted into the incarnate Word, gentle Jesus—so engrafted that neither the devil nor anyone else can ever separate you.

But I'm sure that if you are bound and set ablaze in the gentle Jesus, all the devils of hell with all their cunning will never be able to tear you away from so sweet a union. So, since this bonding is so strong and so necessary for you, I don't want you ever to stop throwing wood on the fire of holy desire—I mean the wood of self-knowledge. This is the wood that feeds the fire of divine charity,[3] the charity that is gained by knowing[b] God's

---

[1] MSS: Mo-*b*, B, P2, H, S1, P1, P5, F2, P3, S2, P4; translation based on Mo-*b*, with reference to H. Other variants based on Dupré Theseider.

[2] The linguistic evidence reinforces the historically attested date. Most of the letter's thirty-three analyzed patterns range from early to late with random frequency, but there are a few with significant clusters beginning in early 1376 (DAFIGLIO, FUNE, MUOIO, ODORVIRT). Only two other letters share eleven or more of Let. T219's patterns, one from May 1376 and the other (the very long Let. T272) from 1377, both in this volume.

[3] Cf. Cavalca, *Specchio di croce*, p. 215: "It is a proverb that love never grows weary. Whoever is really strong accomplishes more, and the more we accomplish, the more our desire grows, the same as fire: the more wood we put on it, the more it blazes and grows." Also especially *Trattato dello Spirito Santo*, p. 15: "God commanded in the Old Law [Lev. 6, 5]: 'I want fire to be always burning on my altar. Let the priest add wood to it every day so as to feed it.' St. Gregory expounds on this wood, saying [*Libri moralium*, XXV, 7: PL LXXVI] that the altar is our heart, where we must feed this fire of love, adding wood to it every day by pondering God's constant and boundless blessings." Also *Dial.* 162, p. 352:

boundless charity.

Then we become one with our neighbors as well, and the more fuel we put on the fire (I mean the wood of self-knowledge), the more intense grows the heat of our love for Christ and for our neighbors. Stay hid, then, within self-knowledge, and don't be caught outside yourselves, lest Malatasca[4] catch you with all sorts of illusory imaginings against[c] one another—for he would do this to rob you of the unity of divine charity. This is why I want you, and I command you, to be submissive to one another. Learn from gentle First Truth to bear each other's shortcomings. He chose to make himself[d] the least, and humbly bore all of our sins and shortcomings, and this is what I want you to do, my sons.[e]

Love, love, love one another! Be glad, be jubilant! Summertime is coming! For on the night of April first[5] God disclosed his secrets more than usual. He showed his marvels in such a way that my soul seemed to be outside my body and was so overwhelmed with joy that I can't really describe it in words.[6] He told and explained bit by bit the mystery of the persecution holy Church is now enduring, and of the renewal and exaltation to come. He said that what is happening now is being permitted to restore her to her original condition. First Truth cited a few words from the holy gospel: "It is inevitable that scandal should come into the world,[f] but woe to the one by whom the scandal comes!"[7] It was as if he were saying, "I am permitting this time of persecution in order to uproot the thorns from my bride, for she is all hedged in with thorns. But people have no permission from me for their evil plottings. Do you know what I am doing? I am doing as I did when I was in the world, when I made the whip of cords and drove out those who were selling and buying in the Temple,[g] since I didn't want my Father's[h] house to be made a robbers' den.[8] In the same way, I tell you, I've made a whip now of certain people, and with that whip I am driving out the filthy, greedy, avaricious dealers

---

"Let them take the wood of self-knowledge along with contempt for their self-complacency and self-conceit, and put these into the fire of my divine charity."

[4] Cf. *Life*, II, ii, 128, p. 123: "That was her name for the devil. He is a sack of wickedness (*malus saccus*) for souls; and in Catherine's country a little sack or pouch is called a *tasca* by the common people." Jorgensen (*Saint Catherine of Siena*, p. 425, n. 8) points out that the expression is not original, but can be found earlier in Giovanni Colombini (*Lettere*, pp. 105, 219), and is reminiscent of Dante's *Malacoda* ("Evil Tail," *Inferno*, XXI, 76) and *Malebranche* ("Evil Claws," ibid., 37).

[5] 1 April 1376.

[6] Cf. 2 Cor. 12, 2–4.

[7] Mt. 18, 7.

[8] Mt. 21,13; Mk. 11,17; Lk. 19, 46. Catherine refers to this gospel incident also in *Dial.* 127, p. 248, where she applies it to the avarice of the clergy who sell their services, making "the grace of the Holy Spirit a piece of merchandise."

bloated with pride, who are selling and buying the graces and gifts of the Holy Spirit." So with the whip of human persecution he was driving them out—I mean he was using suffering and persecution to free them from their shameful disordered way of living.

The fire of holy desire was growing within me as I gazed. And I saw the people, Christians and unbelievers, entering the side of Christ crucified. In desire and impelled by love I walked through their midst and entered with them into Christ gentle Jesus. And with me were my father Saint Dominic, the beloved John,[9] and all my children. Then he placed the cross on my shoulder and put the olive branch in my hand, as if he wanted me (and so he told me) to carry it to the Christians and unbelievers alike. And he said to me: "Tell them, 'I am bringing you news of great joy!' "[10]

Then my soul was fuller than ever. It was immersed in the divine Being, along with the truly joyful, in union and love's affection. So great was my soul's delight that I was no longer conscious of the pain I had felt at seeing God offended. In fact, I said, "Oh happy blessed fault!"[11] Then the gentle Jesus smiled and said, "Is sin blessed now? Sin, which is nothingness? Do you know what Gregory meant when he said, 'happy blessed fault'? What aspect of sin do you see as blessed and happy, and what was Saint Gregory talking about?"

I answered as he made me answer, "I see well, my dear Lord, and I know well that sin is not worthy of blessedness, and so it is neither blessed nor happy.[i] But the fruit that comes from sin is. This, it seems to me, is what Gregory meant, that because of Adam's sin God gave us the Word, his only-begotten Son. And the Word gave his blood; by giving his life he restored grace[j] to us with such[k] blazing love. So sin is blessed not because

---

[9] *Iohanni singulare.* Cf. *Life,* I, xii, 115, p. 107, where Saints John the evangelist, Paul, and Dominic are present at Catherine's mystical espousals. Giordano da Rivalto, *Prediche inedite,* ed. Narducci, p. 430, speaks of the evangelist in the same way: "What was so singular and special about St. John the evangelist, that he should be singled out among all the others? He himself tells us what his singularity was. And what was it? It was Christ's love, and this is why he says, 'This was the disciple who was loved by Christ.' This gift, this singularity he had among all the other disciples, was that he was singularly loved by Christ."

[10] Lk. 2, 10.

[11] From the hymn for the Easter Vigil, the *Exultet:* "Oh truly necessary sin of Adam, that was blotted out by Christ's death! Oh happy fault, that merited to have such and so great a Redeemer!" (PL LXXII, 269) F. Cabrol and H. Leclercq have written amply about the authorship of the *Exultet* (*Dictionnaire d'archéologie chrétienne et de liturgie,* "Paques," XIII, 2, p. 1568f.), but in Catherine's day the hymn was attributed to Gregory the Great. Cf. Giovanni Dominici, *Il libro d'amore,* p. 244: "In this way St. Gregory sang joyfully about the sin of Adam when he said, 'O happy fault. . . .' "

it is sin, but for the fruit and the gift we receive[l] because of that sin. Yes, that's the way it is!"

So from the sin wicked Christians[m] commit by persecuting Christ's bride come exaltation, light, and the fragrance of virtue in this bride. And this was so sweet that there seemed to be no comparison between the offense and the immeasurable goodness and generosity God was showing this bride. Then I was marvelously happy. I was so confident about the future that it seemed I was already possessing and enjoying it. Then I said, like Simeon, "Now you can dismiss your servant, Lord. . . ."[12,n] And there were such mysteries as words can never describe, nor heart imagine, nor eye see.[13] Now what words could ever describe the wonderful things of God? None from this poor wretch! So I'd rather keep silent and give myself completely to seeking God's honor, the salvation of souls, and the renewal and exaltation[o] of holy Church. And by the grace and power of the Holy Spirit I intend to persevere until I die.

With this desire I called and will continue to call our Christ on earth, and you, father, and all my dear children with great love and compassion.

I asked for and obtained what you had asked.[14] Be happy; be jubilantly happy! *Oh sweet*[p] *God, love, fulfill quickly your servants' desires!* I don't want to say any more; I've said nothing anyway. In my anguish I am dying of desire. Be compassionate to me! Beg divine Goodness and Christ on earth to hurry.[15]

Keep living in God's holy and tender love. Drown yourselves in the blood of Christ crucified. Don't let anything make you waver; no, be more encouraged than ever. Be happy, be happy in your sweet labors. Love, love, love one another!

Gentle Jesus! Good Jesus! Jesus love! Jesus, Jesus!

Textual Notes

a. Mo: *My soul considers / This . . . longs* (*considera / cosi desidera*).
b. B, Mo: *by knowledge in / by knowing* (the latter reading from P2).
c. From Mo, H; B: *with / against.*
d. Mo: *be / make himself.*
e. Mo: *dearest sons / sons.*
f. Mo inserts *but then he added.*

---

[12] Lk. 2, 29.

[13] Cf. 1 Cor. 2, 9.

[14] Perhaps Raimondo has asked Catherine to pray for something in particular.

[15] She may be referring to her desire for the calling of the projected crusade, or she may be alluding to her conviction that the pope should return to Rome.

g. *in the Temple* from Mo; missing in B, P2.
h. Mo: *God's / my Father's.*
i. Mo: *happy in itself / happy.*
j. Mo, H: *life / grace.*
k. Mo: *a great / such.*
l. Mo: [*we receive*].
m. P2: *people / Christians.*
n. Mo, H add: *according to your word in peace.*
o. *and exaltation* from Mo; missing in B, P2.
p. H: [*Oh sweet*].

LETTER T177/G29/DT61[1]
To Cardinal Pietro Corsini of Florence, in Avignon
Most probably near Palm Sunday (6 April) 1376

Pietro di Tommaso Corsini, former bishop of Florence (1363–1370) and titular cardinal of Porto and San Rufino, has been asked by the Florentines to support their cause in their conflict with the papacy. Catherine writes in this letter to him that "Christians have risen and are continuing to rise up in rebellion." Yet it is clear from her remarks that Gregory XI is still in Avignon. One might connect the letter with the date Florence joined the antipapal league (24 July 1375), but given the mention of Christians "continuing to rise up in rebellion," it seems more logical to associate it with the rebellion (on 12 March 1376) of Pisa and Lucca, cities Catherine has tried so hard to hold to the papal cause. And the call for Cardinal Corsini to roar like a lion to "help bring back to life the children lying dead" could well be related to his own city of Florence being placed under interdict by Gregory XI on 31 March, since the ecclesiastical penalty of interdict deprived the offender (in this case, the entire city) of access to the sacraments and public worship.

The linguistic evidence supports this choice far more strongly than the earlier date.[2] Also, a Lenten date would be consistent with the theme of Christ as the slain Lamb as well as with the Palm Sunday themes of kingship and humility. I would therefore guess that the letter was almost surely written between February and early April 1376, but most probably near Palm Sunday (6 April), thus putting it shortly after the above-mentioned events of 12 and 31 March.[3]

---

[1] MSS: Mo-*c*, B, P2, H, P1, P3, S2, P4, S4; translation based on Mo-*c*, with reference to H. Other variants based on Dupré Theseider.

[2] First, two of the three letters which share twenty-three or more of its eighty-two analyzed patterns are from February to March 1376 (the third from June to July 1375). An even stronger argument lies in the concentration of individual patterns which do not begin until early 1376: ARREND, GIACMORT, GIOCBRAC, MADCHIES, MORTDIST, PLACIRA, TORNIELL, VERIANUN.

[3] Both Fawtier (II, p. 168) and Dupré Theseider place the letter in February or March 1376.

§

In the name of Jesus Christ crucified and of gentle Mary,
mother of God's Son.

Very loved reverend father and brother in Christ Jesus,

I Caterina, unworthy servant and slave of the servants of Jesus Christ, am writing to you in his precious blood. I long to see you a meek humble lamb. I want you to learn from the spotless Lamb, who was so humble and meek that no cry of complaint was heard from him. No, he let himself be led like a defenseless lamb to the slaughter[4] of the most holy and hard cross.[5]

Oh boundless fire of love! You have given us your flesh as food and your blood as drink![6] You are the Lamb roasted in the fire[a] of blazing charity![7] Father, I see no other way we can have virtue except by keeping this Lamb before our mind's eye, for in him we find true deep humility, great meekness, and patience. And although he is God's Son, he neither comes nor lives as a king,[8] because he is not proud or self-centered. He comes, in fact,[b] as a lowly servant. He is not self-seeking but concerned only about giving honor and glory to the Father, and restoring to us the life we had lost through sin. And he does this for love alone, to fulfill the Father's will for us. For God had created us in his image and likeness simply that we might experience and enjoy him in everlasting life. But because we had rebelled against God, the road to life was so broken up that God's purpose in creating us was not being realized—I mean our possession of everlasting life, the only end we were created for.[9]

---

[4] Is. 53, 7.

[5] It. *dura croce*, an expression found only here.

[6] Cf. Cavalca, *Trattato dello Spirito Santo*, p. 41: "A certain saint says, 'This giver is indeed generous who has given us his flesh as food, his blood as drink, his soul as ransom, his wounds as healing, his arms as refuge, his cross as shield, his open heart as a sign of love, water as bath, his sweat as medicine, the nails as support, his crown of thorns as ornament, his teaching as instruction, and his life as example.' " Elsewhere (*Specchio di croce*, prologue) he attributes the passage to Bernard de Clairvaux, but Dupré Theseider (n. 3) looked for it there without success.

[7] Cf. Ex. 12. Also Cavalca, *Specchio di croce*, p. 154: "He had his flesh roasted over the fire of great torment on the wood of the cross, so as to offer it to us as food." Also Bianco da Siena, *Lauda XVII*, 93: "We shall see the humble soul of Jesus, the kind King, with his noble flesh that he roasted on the wood." In Let. T52 (in this volume) Catherine explicitly images the cross as the spit on which the Lamb of God was roasted.

[8] The allusion may well be to Palm Sunday.

[9] Cf. *Dial.* 21, p. 58: "I told you that I have made a bridge of the Word, my only-begotten Son, and such is the truth. I want you to realize, my children, that by Adam's sinful disobedience the road was so broken up that no one could reach everlasting life. . . . I created them in my image and likeness so that they might have eternal life, sharing in my being and enjoying my supreme eternal tenderness and goodness. But because of their sin they never

Moved, then, by the same boundless charity with which he had created us, God gave us the Word, his only-begotten Son, in order to realize his will for us. So God's Son was concerned not for himself but only for fulfilling this gracious purpose.[c] He was made mediator between God and humankind, and he turned the great war into a great peace.[10] With his humility he conquered the world's pride. This is why he said, "Rejoice, for I have overcome the world."[11] What he meant is our pride. For none of us is so puffed up, so proud, so impatient that we would not become humble and meek on seeing and contemplating such great profound love as to see God stoop down to our humanity.

This is why God's true holy servants, wanting to reciprocate, always humble themselves and give God all the praise and glory. They recognize that all they have is from God alone, and they are conscious of their own nothingness. Whatever they love, they love in God, regardless of their own position or greatness. For the greater we are, the more we should humble ourselves and recognize our own nothingness. If we know ourselves, we humble ourselves, not holding our head high or becoming bloated with pride. Rather we bow our head in acknowledgment of the goodness God has showered on us. This is how we acquire the virtues of humility and love: the former is governess and wet nurse of the latter, and without them we cannot have life.[12]

Who, oh who would be so stupid, so bestial, as not to return love for love, and completely get rid of perverse selfish love, the source and root of our every evil? I can't imagine anyone so hardened as not to respond to love by loving—except those who have put out the light with their selfish love. What visible sign do lovers give? Let's ask them.

Look at Jerome, for he was in the same position as you are.[13] He disciplined his flesh by fasting, watching, and prayer. He killed his pride by wearing shabby clothes, and he was very careful to avoid seeking worldly status and honor. Yet God exalts those who humble themselves.[14] Though such persons have status, it does not make them lose their virtue.

---

reached this goal and never fulfilled my truth, for sin closed heaven and the door of my mercy."

[10] Cf. Prayer 1, p. 17: "And you, Jesus Christ, our reconciler, our refashioner, our redeemer—you, Word and love, were made our mediator. You turned our great war with God into a great peace." Also Eph. 2, 14: "It is he who is our peace."

[11] Jn. 16, 33.

[12] Cf. *Dial.* 154, p. 328: "This humility is also charity's governess and wet nurse, and she nurtures the virtue of obedience with the very same milk."

[13] She is referring to the popular belief, expressed in many art works of her time, that Saint Jerome was a cardinal. The earliest indication of this is found in Pseudo-Augustine, *Ad fratres de eremo sermo XXIV* (PL XL, 1274): "We read that our holy father Jerome was a cardinal of the church of St. Lawrence, martyr."

[14] Lk. 14, 11.

No, they refine it, like gold in the fire,[15] by adding to it the virtue of charity. They begin to eat and savor souls, and have no fear of losing their bodily life, because they have put on the form and garment of the gentle Lamb, Jesus.[16] They do not love themselves or their neighbors or God selfishly, but in God they love everything. Neither life nor death nor persecution nor any pain they might suffer worries them; they are concerned only for the honor of supreme eternal Truth.

These, then, are the signs of God's true servants. Be one of these, father: it is my prayer and my wish. Bring me the sign of true humility by being not overly ambitious in your position, but lowly. Don't be impatient over any pain or abuse you might suffer, but endure within the body of holy Church by the firm power of patience, even to the point of death. When you speak and proclaim the truth, whether in giving counsel or in any other role, do it fearlessly, looking only to God's honor, the salvation of souls, and the advancement of holy Church, as her true son, nurtured by so tender a mother. In this way you will demonstrate gentle divine charity, and patience as well. Be generous in your charity—spiritually, as I've already said, but materially too. Reflect that the hands of the poor are helping you to offer and receive[d] divine grace.[17] I want you to begin a new life, a new way of living. Slumber no more in the sleep of foolish indifference. Be a real champion for me, please.

I told you that I want you to be a lamb, a follower of the true Lamb. Now I'm telling you that I want you to be a lion, roaring loudly in holy Church, your virtue and your voice so strong that you help bring back to life the children lying dead within her.[18] Perhaps you are asking: "Where can I get such a strong roaring voice?" From the Lamb, who in his humanity remains meek and does not cry out, but whose divinity lends

---

[15] Cf. Sir. 2, 5: "For gold and silver are tested in fire, and worthy people in the crucible of humiliation." (Vulg.) The saying was often cited by medieval spiritual writers.

[16] Cf. Phil. 2, 6–7: "Though he was in the form of God, he did not deem equality with God something to be grasped at. Rather, he emptied himself and took the form of a slave."

[17] Cf. Giovanni dalle Celle, Let. XXV, ed. Sorio, p. 165: "I call you poor, and St. Gregory [*Homiliae quadraginta in Evangelia II, homilia XL*, 10—PL LXXVI, 1310] calls you patrons. He says, 'They shouldn't be called poor, but patrons through whose hands our alms are borne into the presence of God, and through whose prayers we receive mercy.' "

[18] This is a common theme in medieval bestiaries. Cf. *Bestiario toscano*, p. 33: "It is the nature of lions to kill their young. They remain dead for three days, after which the father comes and roars loudly over them, so that the lion cubs come to life." Further (p. 81) on the lion is described allegorically as Christ raised to life on the third day and saving the whole human race. We find this image in Bernard de Clairvaux as well (*In die sanctae Paschae sermo*, 5—PL CLXXXIII, 277): "The cub has been raised by the father lion's voice." Also in Giordano da Rivalto, *Prediche*, ed. D. Moreni, I, p. 15. Catherine sometimes uses this lion imagery without actually naming the lion, for example, in Let. T286/DT57 (25 January 1378).

power to the Son's cry with the voice of its immeasurable charity. And so, by the strength and power of divine Being and of the love that joined God with humanity, the Lamb becomes a Lion. From the chair of the cross[19] he roared so loudly over the dead child, the human race, that he freed us from death and gave us life. It is from him, then, that we will receive strength, for the love we will drink from the gentle Jesus will give us a share in the Father's power. (You can easily see that this is so, for neither the devil nor anyone else can force us to a single deadly sin, since Christ has made us free and given us power over ourselves.) And in this love we share in the light and strength of the Holy Spirit, who is an intermediary[e] binding our soul with our Creator, and enlightening our understanding and knowledge so that we can share in the wisdom of God's Son.[f]

Oh dearest father, our heart should burst right out of our body at the realization of the status and dignity to which infinite Goodness has appointed us—first by creating us in his own image, and then by joining his divine nature with our humanity to ransom us and create us anew![g] More than this he could not give: to give himself to those who by sin had become his enemies.

Oh ineffable[h] *consummate love! You really are in love with what you have made! You, God, cannot suffer,*[20] *yet you wanted to make peace with us, and the sin we had committed had to be punished. But we are not capable of satisfying in any way for the great injustice done to you, eternal Father. So in your love for us you found a way. You clothed the Word in our flesh, and he at one and the same time offered you honor and appeased your anger by bearing the punishment in his own flesh, taken from Adam's clay that had sinned. How then can we do anything but surrender ourselves? We see how he wrestled on the cross and let himself be conquered even as he won. For death*[i] *conquered death even as death conquered life, and life conquered and killed and destroyed death. They jousted, and death was completely defeated, and life rose to life in us.*[21]

---

[19] Cf. Augustine, *Sermo CCXXXIV* (PL XXXVIII, 1116): "That cross was a school, where the teacher taught the thief. The wood on which he hung became a chair for teaching." Cavalca, *Specchio di croce, Prologo*, p. 2: "Christ . . . on the cross is like a teacher occupying his chair, for he teaches . . . every perfect doctrine."

[20] Cf. Bernard de Clairvaux, *De diversis sermo XXXIV* (PL CLXXXIII, 631): "[God] who could not suffer in his divinity assumed a body in which he could suffer." *Dial.* 14, pp. 51–53, has much in common with this letter.

[21] Cf. *Dial.* 30, p. 71: "Your mercy made your Son play life against death on the wood of the cross. In him life confounded the death that is our sin, even while that same death of sin robbed the spotless Lamb of his bodily life. But who was conquered? Death! And how? By your mercy!" 2 Tim. 1, 10: "He has robbed death of its power and has brought life and immortality into clear light through the gospel." Heb. 2, 14–15: "that by his death he might rob the devil, the prince of death, of his power, and free those who through fear of death had been slaves their whole life long." Also Augustine, *Enarratio in Ps. CXLIX*, 6 (PL

So let your heart hold back no longer. Let the city of your soul surrender. If it does not surrender to anything else, it will have to surrender to fire—for Christ has set fire everywhere, and there is nowhere you can turn, physically or spiritually, without encountering the fire of love.[22]

I want you, please, to encourage Christ on earth a little. Ask him about his return. And urge him to raise the standard of the most holy cross soon against the unbelievers. Don't wonder, you or the others, why Christians have risen and are continuing to rise up in rebellion, like rotten members against their dear head. This will be the way to placate them and make them return as his children. Ask him for this, and have others ask him to do it soon.

Forgive my foolishness in presuming to babble on so; love is my excuse, as is my desire for your salvation and for the renewal and advancement of holy Church, so pale that the color of charity seems to have all but faded away. For everyone is robbing her; they take her color and paint it on themselves—I mean, in their selfish love for themselves they attend only to their own welfare and advancement.[23,j] This is the sign of the proud, who for their own swollen-headed greatness don't care that the Church is being destroyed and that the devil is devouring souls. The sign of these people, who are rapacious wolves, is very different from that of God's servants, who are lambs and follow the sign of the Lamb. So my soul longs to see you a lamb.

I'll say no more, because if I went on as long as I'd like, I'd never stop. Remember me warmly in Christ Jesus to Christ on earth, and encourage him; let him not be afraid, no matter what happens.

Keep living in God's holy and tender love.[k]

XXXVII, 1952): "When he did battle for us he seemed to be conquered, but in fact he was the conqueror. He was crucified, and from the cross to which he was nailed he killed the devil." Catherine may also be thinking of the Easter Sequence: "Death and life in battle—wondrous conflict!—the Captain of life, though killed, reigns alive," or the hymn *Vexilla Regis:* "He endured death, and by death brought forth life." Also Jacopo Passavanti, *Lo specchio di vera penitentia*, Dist. II, chap. VII: "As St. Gregory says (PL LXXIX, 28), by his passion and death he conquered our death."

[22] Cf. Lk. 12, 49: "I have come to light a fire on the earth. How I wish the blaze were ignited!"

[23] It is charity, the fire of the Spirit, the blood of Christ, that gives color to the face of the bride of Christ, the Church. Cf. *Dial.* 132, p. 271 "[They] suck the blood of my bride, holy Church. By their sins they have left her pallid. The loving charity they ought to have had for this bride they have lavished on themselves." The image is somewhat different in *Dial.* 14, p. 50: "But look how my bride has disfigured her face! She is leprous with impurity and selfishness." Cf. also Prayer 3, p. 38: "You [Christ] are pallid because your creatures are constantly throwing your graces away, plundering your one bride."

Textual Notes

a. B, P2: [*in the fire*].
b. Mo: *And this is why he comes / He . . . fact.*
c. P2: *truth / purpose.*
d. B: *enter into / receive.*
e. P2: *a light and intermediary / an intermediary.*
f. B, P2: *the Son / God's Son.*
g. Mo: [*and create us anew*].
h. P2: *immeasurable / ineffable.*
i. B, P2: *love / death* (*l'amore / la morte*).
j. Mo-*b*: *I mean by selfish love of themselves, when they should be attending only to her welfare and advancement / I mean . . . advancement.*
k. B, P2 invert the order of the last two sentences and add *Gentle Jesus! Jesus love!*

LETTER T97/G370[1]
To Monna Pavola da Siena and her disciples
Early April 1376

In early July 1375, Catherine wrote to a Monna Pavola (Let. T144/DT34, vol. I) in Fiesole to invite her and her "daughters" to prepare to join the projected crusade. And the rubric of Mo states that the present letter was written "while she [presumably Pavola] was at Fiesole." Later, while Catherine is in Rome, she will mention a Monna Pavola in several letters to Bartalo Usimbardi and Francesco di Pipino and their wives. There seems to be no reason at all not to suppose that the present letter is written to the same Pavola.[2] In fact, Mo positions this letter just after T144/DT34, stating in the rubric that it is written "to the same Monna Pavola."

There is no clue in the content of the letter to date it, but the linguistic evidence would support its placement in March to April 1376.[3] Because of the strong Paschal references, it could well have been written near the end of Lent, therefore in early April 1376.

---

[1] MSS: Mo, S3; translation based on Mo-*a*, corrected by *b*.

[2] See introduction to Let. T144/DT34. If Monna Pavola is indeed a monastic prioress, it might seem strange that Catherine refers here to her "disciples." But perhaps her popularity was such that she did in fact have disciples beyond her monastic community of Santo Giorgio.

[3] There are only two other letters which share thirteen or more of this one's fifty-two analyzed patterns, and both are from March and April 1376. Further, a good number of significant clusters within individual patterns either begin or end in those months: ARATO, CARBONI, DAFIGLIO, GIOCBRACC, LAVDIFET, PARTECBN, PARTUR, PIEDCOST, DESIDDE, FABBRIC.

§

In the name of Jesus Christ crucified. Amen.

Very loved and dearest daughter and sister in Christ Jesus,

I Caterina, servant and slave of the servants of Jesus Christ, am writing to you, encourage you, bless you in the blood of that same gentle Son of God.[a] With desire have I desired[4] to see you all united in his blazing charity, the charity that makes the soul become one thing with God.

Oh charity, filled with joy and gladness and utter serenity[b]*—so much so that everything stormy becomes peaceful and calm! Oh dearest mother, gentle charity! It was you who gave birth to all the virtues as your children.*

Understand, my very loved sister, that no virtue is alive without charity. So said that dear Paul, so in love, that vessel of love:[5] "If I had an angelic tongue, and if I gave everything to the poor, and did not have charity, it would profit me nothing."[6] And that's the way it really is, for those who are not living in charity cannot do anything that would please God. Instead they give birth to virtues that are stillborn. Why are they stillborn? Because God is not there to give them life, that is, charity.[7] Those who live in charity live in God, and God in them.[8] But the bride of Christ, who has been pierced by this arrow of charity, never stops working—like a fresh wound that makes our heart beat constantly harder. For every day all over again new arrows are shot—I mean arrows of blazing charity—since not a moment passes but God's goodness is not heaping burning coals upon our head.[9]

And if we turn to look at the being[10] God's goodness has given us, we

---

[4] Cf. Lk. 22, 15.

[5] Cf. Acts 9, 15. As almost always, Catherine cites this description of Paul apparently from her mishearing the Latin *vas electionis* ("chosen vessel") as *vas delectionis.*

[6] 1 Cor. 13, 1–3, slightly contracted.

[7] Cf. *Dial.* 11, p. 45: "If a woman has conceived a child but never brings it to birth for people to see, her husband will consider himself childless. Just so, I am the spouse of the soul, and unless she gives birth to the virtue she has conceived [by showing it] in her charity to her neighbors . . . , then I insist that she has never in truth even conceived virtue within her." And 46, p. 94: "Just as a woman bears a living child and presents it living to her husband, so [these people] would have presented me, the soul's spouse, with living virtues. But these wretched people do just the opposite. They reach the age of discernment when they ought to . . . give birth to virtues with the life of grace. Instead they give birth to dead virtues. They are dead because all their actions, being done in deadly sin and bereft of the light of faith, are dead."

[8] 1 Jn. 4, 16.

[9] Cf. Rom. 12, 20: "But if your enemy is hungry, feed him; if he is thirsty, give him something to drink; by doing this you will heap burning coals upon his head." For Catherine these "burning coals" are always burning with the fire of charity.

[10] In the scholastic sense of essence as opposed to simple existence.

see that he created us only out of pure charity, so that we might enjoy the good he had in himself, and to give us eternal life. This is why Saint Paul says that God wants nothing else but that we be made holy.[11] And whatever God gives, he gives for this purpose: that we may be made holy in him. *Oh supreme eternal Truth! You have shown us this so clearly!* Once we had lost grace we were unable to share in this good. So God, seeing that because of sin this will of his could not be fulfilled, and driven by his mad love for us, sent his only-begotten Son to hammer out our sins upon his own body.[12] As soon as this Word was engrafted into our flesh in Mary's womb, God sentenced him to the shameful death of the cross by having set him on the field of this life to do battle for his spouse and to rescue her from the hands of the devil, who because she was an adulteress had possession of her.[13] This knight came, as Saint Bernard says, and mounted[c] his horse, the wood of the most holy cross. He took on the crown of thorns, tightly fit, as his helmet; the nails into his hands and feet; and the lance into his side to reveal to us the secret of his heart.[14]

Oimé! Love! Love! Don't you think this gentle Savior of ours is well armed? Let us take heart, for he has won[d] the battle for us. He said as much to his disciples: "Be happy, because I have overcome the prince of the world."[15] And Saint Augustine says that he has overcome the devils with hands nailed fast.[16]

So I don't want any devil, seen or unseen, visiting fear on you, my dearest daughters. But if the devil should trouble you with all sorts of struggles and illusions or with fear of not being able to persevere in the works you've begun, take heart and say, "I will be able to do everything

---

[11] 1 Thes. 4, 3.

[12] The image is that of the anvil, as in Let. T76 to Giovanni di Bindo (in this volume): "We surely know that if sin were not very displeasing to God and extremely destructive of our salvation, he would not have given up the Word, his only-begotten Son. He would not have been willing to make his Son an anvil in order to take out on his body the punishment for our sins and so work out justice for the sin we had committed."

[13] Cf. Hos. 2, 4–7, for the image of God's people as a harlot. There is a parallel reference in Let. T107/DT11 (vol. I) to humankind as an adulteress in the hands of the devil.

[14] Cf. Cavalca, *Specchio di Croce*, p. 21: "And so Saint Bernard says, 'This steward is so generous. He has given us his flesh as food and his blood as drink; his life as ransom, his wounds as remedy, his outstretched arms as refuge, the cross as shield, his open heart as a sign of love, the water [from his side] as bath, his sweat as medicine, the nails and the crown of thorns as adornment, his words as teaching, his whole life and death as an example. He gave his clothing to those who crucified him, his mother to his disciple, paradise to the thief.' "

[15] Cf. Jn. 16, 33.

[16] Cf. Cavalca, *Specchio di croce*, p. 133: "And as Saint Augustine says, 'With hands unarmed and nailed to the cross he conquered the devils.' "

through Christ crucified,[17] for he has overcome the devils for me." *Oh sweetest love, Jesus! You jousted with death on the cross and death conquered life while life conquered death.* By this I mean that by his bodily death he destroyed our death, and because of our death he destroyed his bodily life.[18] *Oh boundless love, charity! All of this reveals to us your love and will and purpose in creating us: that you did it only to give us eternal life.*

Oh tender love! What heart[e] will shield itself, then, from being set ablaze by such a fire of love? For God has given us his only-begotten Son, and the Son has given us his life with such great desire that he seems to have been unable to express it when he said, "With desire have I desired to celebrate the Pasch with you before I die."[19] *Oh sweetest love! Were you referring to the Pasch of eating with them? No,*[f] *you were speaking of sacrificing your own body to the Father for us. Oh love! With what charity and joy you spoke that word about making a sacrifice of yourself—because you saw that you were nearing the end! You were acting like someone who has had a tremendous desire to do a grand deed and is joyful and happy when it is all but finished.*

This is the sort of joy with which this man in love ran to the shameful death of the cross. So I am begging you, sister (and you, daughters) let's find our joy in this—in bearing his disgrace, I mean. Put your mouth to the open side of God's Son, put it there; for his side is a mouth that emits the fire of charity and pours out blood to wash away your[g] sins.[20] I tell you, those who rest there and who with their mind's eye contemplate the heart consumed and opened up for love receive such conformity with him when they see themselves so loved, that they cannot help loving. And then they become well-ordered, because whatever they love they love for God, and they love nothing apart from him. Thus they become another him by desire because they have no will but God's.

Don't be apathetic, then, but run constantly, always[h] breaking your own wills. Keep living, my daughters, in God's holy love. See to it that

---

[17] Cf. Phil. 4, 13.

[18] Cf. 2 Tim. 1, 10: "He has robbed death of its power and has brought life and immortality into clear light through the gospel." Heb. 2, 14–15: "that by his death he might rob the devil, the prince of death, of his power, and free those who through fear of death had been slaves their whole life long." Catherine may also be thinking of the Easter Sequence: "Death and life in battle—wondrous conflict!—the Captain of life, though killed, reigns alive," or the hymn *Vexilla Regis*: "He endured death, and by death brought forth life."

[19] Cf. Lk. 22, 15.

[20] The nuns are invited to drink from the heart of Christ. This is the "kiss of peace" referred to, for example, in *Dial.* 76, p. 141: "She found her spiritual peace and quiet in the mouth. You know that peace is given with the mouth." Only in the present letter, however, does Catherine join this "kiss of peace" to the forgiveness of sin.

you fulfill my desire, so that I may see you united and transformed as one thing in him.

Caterina,
servant and slave
of the servants of Jesus Christ

Encourage Monna Bartolomea[21] and all the others, and tell them[i] not to turn back to look at what they have plowed[22] but always to persevere in their holy resolution, for without perseverance you wouldn't be able to receive the crown. Praised be Jesus Christ![j]

Textual Notes

a. *b* has simply *his blood*, but *suo* is written at the head of a long erasure which Dupré Theseider conjectures to be *desso dolce figluolo di Dio.*
b. S3: *security / serenity.*
c. S3: *So this knight, as Saint Bernard says, mounted / This . . . mounted.*
d. S3: *will have* (*avera*) */ has won* (*a venta*).
e. S3: *fire / heart.*
f. S3: [*Were. . . . No*].
g. S3: *our / your.*
h. S3: [*always*].
i. *and tell them* added by *b.*
j. S3 adds *Gentle Jesus! Jesus love!*

---

[21] Meattini (*Epistolario*, p. 1082) identifies her as Bartolomea di Andrea Mei da Siena, possibly because this is the only Bartolomea mentioned in the letters who is known to be Sienese.

[22] Cf. Lk. 9, 62, which Catherine always quotes this way.

Letter T159/G120[1]
To Frate Ranieri of the Dominican Church of Santa Caterina in Pisa
Near Holy Week (6 to 11 April) 1376

We know little of the addressee except from this letter, which indicates that he has recently entered the Dominican Order at the priory associated with the church of Santa Caterina (St. Catherine of Alexandria) in Pisa.[2] Catherine may have become acquainted with him while she was in Pisa. Using this evidence alone the letter could be placed any time after either of Catherine's visits to Pisa (most of 1375 and fall of 1376).

Umberto Meattini, in fact, states that Ranieri had been rector of the church of Santa Cristina in Pisa before joining the Dominicans, though he gives no source for this information.[3] If the information is correct, Catherine, who during her 1375 stay in Pisa had lived just behind Santa Cristina and had prayed in the church often, would certainly have gotten to know its rector well. She had perhaps confronted him about his uninhibited lifestyle because in the present letter she expresses obvious delight at the news that he has become a Dominican and sees the step as a kind of reparation for his earlier liberties. Meattini says further that Ranieri entered the order on the feast of St. Thomas Aquinas (then celebrated on 7 March) at the age of thirty-six, and that he died in Pisa on the same feast at the age of fifty-six.[4]

The linguistic evidence convincingly supports placement of Catherine's single extant letter to Ranieri in the early months of 1376.[5] The letter's content, however, so centered on the Passion of Christ, would correspond very well with the placement required if Ranieri did indeed enter the order on 7 March. The very explicit emphasis on the Passion would place the letter near Holy Week (the first week of April), thus allowing a full month for the news to have reached Catherine in Siena.

---

[1] MSS: R1, P5, F2, P3; translation based on R1, with relevant variants based on Dupré Theseider's unpublished transcription of P3.

[2] Burlamacchi in his notes to the letter states that Aldo Manuzio's edition (as does R1) places the addressee at Santa Cristina rather than Santa Caterina (but still identifies Santa Cristina—mistakenly—as Dominican). If Ranieri was indeed the former rector at Santa Cristina, as Meattini states (*Epistolario*, p. 1254) this could explain the confusion.

[3] *Epistolario*, in his notes prefacing Catherine's letters to friars, p. 1254.

[4] *Epistolario*, p. 1254. Again, he does not cite a source.

[5] Of the five other letters which share nineteen or more of this letter's eighty-two analyzed patterns, four are from June 1375 to early 1376 (with the fifth in 1377). But clusters within individual patterns point strongly toward a placement in the first four months of 1376. Beyond traces of non-standardized protocol, a large number of patterns (twenty, in fact) do not occur before 1376. The strongest and most direct support, however, is in those clusters which are concentrated in the first four months of 1376: CONFICCR, CORRAZ, GLORCROC, IMPUGNSP, LAVDIFETT, VERSANG.

§

In the name of Jesus Christ crucified and of gentle Mary.

Reverend father—out of reverence for that sweetest of sacraments—[a] in Christ Jesus,

I Caterina, servant and slave of the servants of God, am writing to you in the precious blood of God's Son.[b] I long to see you a real knight, fighting against every vice and temptation for Christ crucified with a true holy perseverance. For it is perseverance that is crowned. You know that victory is achieved by fighting and by perseverance. In this life we are set as on a battlefield and we must fight courageously, not dodging the blows or retreating, but keeping our eyes on our captain, Christ crucified, who always persevered. He didn't give up when the Jews said, "Come down from the cross!"[6] Nor did the devil or our ingratitude make him give up fulfilling the Father's command and our salvation. No, he persevered right up to the end, when he returned to the eternal Father with the victory he had achieved, the victory of having rescued humankind from darkness and given us the light of grace once again by conquering the devil and the world with all its pleasures. And it killed him: this Lamb took death for himself in order to give us life; by his dying he destroyed our death.[7]

This captain's blood and his perseverance ought to inspire[c] us for every battle—for enduring pain, slander, reproach and abuse for love of him. It should inspire us to voluntary poverty, humility of heart,[8] and total and perfect obedience. In this way, when the cloud of our body is destroyed, we will return victorious to the city of eternal life. We will have conquered the devil, the world, and the flesh, our three wicked enemies—and especially the flesh, which is always pricking at us and fighting against the spirit.[9] We must subdue it and discipline it with fasting and vigils and

[6] Mt. 27, 40.

[7] Cf. Heb. 2, 14–15: "that by his death he might rob the devil, the prince of death, of his power, and free those who through fear of death had been slaves their whole life long." Catherine may also be thinking of the Easter Sequence: "Death and life in battle—wondrous conflict!—the Captain of life, though killed, reigns alive," or the hymn *Vexilla Regis*: "He endured death, and by death brought forth life."

[8] The Italian is *humiliazione di cuore*, reminiscent of Ps. 51, "A heart humbled and contrite you will not despise" (in the Vulgate: *cor contritum et humiliatum*).

[9] Except for the last clause, the personal pronouns in this sentence in the original are third person singular. Tommasèo interprets them as referring still to Christ, but this does not really fit the context, which has switched to a consideration of ourselves. Nor does the punctuation of P3 support Tommasèo's introduction of a new paragraph (or even new sentence) with *and especially*. It. *la carne che sempre ci stimola e inpugna contra lo spirito.* Cf. 2 Cor. 12, 7, "a thorn (Vulg. *stimulus*) in the flesh"; Gal. 5, 17: "The flesh lusts against the spirit."

prayer. And the evil thoughts that come we must constantly chase out with holy images—pondering and imagining how great is the fire of blazing charity; how much it has done for us freely and not because it was our due.

For the Father gave us the Word, his only-begotten Son. And the Son gave his life—for it was out of love that he tore open his body so that blood poured out from every part. He washed away the stains of our sin with blood. When we contemplate such love we are consumed by love, and it seems to us we cannot do as much; nor could we. Even if we were to give our body up to every sort of pain and torment, we could not pay for the great love and all the blessings we receive from our Creator. He is our dear God, who loved us without being loved.

Yes, this is the way you will chase out the devil's evil thoughts.

But you might say to me, father, "Since you want me to be a courageous knight, and since I am on the battlefield being attacked by many enemies, I need armor. Tell me what sort of armor to use." I answer that I don't want you to be unarmed. I want you to be armed as was dear Paul, that man in love,[d] who was as human as you are. I mean armed with the cuirass of true and deep humility and the breastplate of blazing charity. For just as the cuirass is joined to the breastplate and the breastplate to the cuirass, so is humility the nurse of charity, and charity the nourisher of humility.[10] This is the armor I am giving you, since it can withstand all the poisoned arrows the devil, the world, and the flesh can shoot, without being penetrated by a single one.[11] For when we are in love with Christ crucified no arrow of deadly sin will penetrate us—I mean through the

---

[10] Only in this letter and in T58 to Suor Cristofora of Montepulciano (1379) does Catherine clearly speak of this mutual nurturing relationship between humility and charity. Elsewhere it is always humility which nurses and nurtures charity.

[11] There is a close parallel to this in Let. T148/DT36 to Pietro del Monte Santa Maria (August 1375, vol. I): "We have three specific enemies: the world, the flesh, and the devil. But let's not be afraid, because divine providence has outfitted us so well that we have no reason for fear. Our armor is good, and our helper the best. For our helper is God, and he is such that no one can withstand him. As long as we continue to look to this strong loving helper, we cannot be weakened by the thought of our own frailty. It seems this is what that dear lover Paul saw when he said, 'I can do all things in Christ crucified, who is in me and strengthens me.' For when Paul felt the annoyance and pricking of the flesh, he found strength not in himself, because he knew he was weak, but in Christ Jesus. It was because of Christ Jesus and that fine strong armor God had given him, his strong freedom, that he could say, 'I can do all things.' For neither the devil nor anyone else can force me to commit a single deadly sin against my will. We can never be overcome unless we give up this armor and turn it over to the devil by our willing consent. The temptations and wiles of the devils, the flesh, and the world may come shooting poisoned arrows—the flesh with ugly thoughts and sensations, the devil with his assorted temptations and deceit and trickery, the world with its pretentiousness and pride. But unless lady freedom consents to these disordered suggestions, she never sins, because sin is in the will alone." Most often in Catherine's writings the arrow is the burning arrow of charity.

consent of our will. We are so strong that neither the devil nor anyone else can force us to do more than we want.

You must also have a knife in your hand to defend yourself against your enemies, and it must be a double-edged knife. One edge is hatred and contempt for yourself, for the time you've often spent with scant concern for virtue and in great wretchedness and sin and frequent offenses against our Savior. We must hate this sin, and we must hate ourselves in so far as we have sinned. For once we have conceived such a hatred we want to make up for our past life and endure every sort of suffering for love of Christ and in payment for our sins.[12] [We want to] make up for pride with humility, for avarice and greed with charity and generosity, for the liberties of selfishness with obedience. This is the holy reparation we must make when we carry this knife of hatred and of love.

But I am exultantly happy over the glorious news I've heard about you, since you've apparently made reparation for your liberties by taking on the yoke of holy obedience.[13] You cannot have done better than to have renounced your own will and the world with its pleasures and enjoyment. I urge you for love of Christ crucified to stay on this battlefield with courage and with a holy perseverance. Never retreat in order to evade any blow of trouble or temptation. No, unwavering and armed as I've described, use those arms to withstand and deflect whatever blows may come, and the double-edged knife of hatred and of love to defend yourself against your enemies.

I want the tree of the cross to be planted in your heart and soul.[14]

---

[12] This love of virtue, of all that God loves, is the other edge of the knife. This two-edged knife is drawn from the knowledge of self and of God which we discover in the blood of Christ (Let. T99/DT7, vol. I; T128, in this volume; T329, written in early 1379; *Dial.* 23). It is to be held in the hand of free choice (Let. T154, written in late 1378 or early 1379; *Dial.* 23), defending what is of God, striking down and cutting off what is not of God.

[13] Word must have reached Catherine that Ranieri has joined the Dominicans in Pisa.

[14] This image, with further development, is found in two other letters from this general period: Let. T138/DT41 to Giovanna d'Angiò (vol. I): "Take hold of the tree of the most holy cross and let it be planted in the garden of your soul, because this is a tree laden with fruits, the true solid virtues. For you see very well that beyond God's union with his creature he has joined himself to the most holy cross. And he wills, he insists, that we too join ourselves to this sweet tree in love and desire. Then our garden cannot help producing sweet and tender fruit." And Let. T52 to Jeronimo da Siena (in this volume): "Look at the Lamb slain on the wood of the most holy cross! There is no other way we can eat at this sweet venerable table. See to it that the tree of the most holy cross is always firmly planted in the cell of your soul, for from this tree you will gather the fruit of true obedience, of patience, and of deep humility. All complacency and selfish love will die in you, and you will acquire a hunger for eating and relishing souls when you see that in hunger for our salvation and his Father's honor [Christ] humbled himself and gave himself up to the shameful death of the cross as one madly, drunkenly in love with us."

Conform yourself with Christ crucified. Hide yourself in the wounds of Christ crucified. Bathe in the blood of Christ crucified. Get drunk on Christ crucified and clothe yourself in him. As Paul says, glory in the cross of Christ crucified.[15] Eat your fill of disgrace and shame and dishonor by suffering for love of Christ crucified. Fasten your heart and affection to the cross with Christ, for the cross has been made a ship for you and a port that will lead you to the [ultimate] port, salvation.[16] And the nails have been made keys for you to open the kingdom of heaven.[17]

So up, dearest father and brother! No more sleeping in the bed of indifference! No, fight as a courageous and fearless knight against every adversary. For God will give you the fullness of grace, so that when your life is finished you will after your labors come to rest and see the supreme eternal beauty and vision that is God, where your soul is quieted and stilled.

---

[15] Cf. Gal. 6, 14: "May I never glory except in the cross of our Lord Jesus Christ." (Vulg.)

[16] The ship is for Catherine an image sometimes of the Church, sometimes of religious life, and sometimes, as here, of the cross. In each case, however, it is fundamentally an image of security against the forces inimical to salvation. Much later, in Let. T275 to Raimondo da Capua (1378), she will elaborate on the ship as image of the cross: "We must climb up into the little ship of the most holy cross and navigate fearlessly in this stormy sea. Those who are in this little ship have no reason for slavish fear, because the ship is provisioned with every food the soul can imagine. And if head winds blow that would beat against us and delay us so that we cannot fulfill our desires, we are not concerned. We stay there in living faith, because we have plenty to eat and the little ship is so strong that no wind, no matter how terrible, can dash it against the rocks and wreck it. True, [God] may often allow the little ship to be swamped by the sea's waves. But he does this not to drown us, but to make us better and more perfectly able to discern peaceful weather from stormy, so that we will not be over-confident in peaceful weather but will turn in holy fear, with continual humble prayer, and with holy and burning desire to seek his honor and the salvation of souls in this little ship, the cross. This is why he permits the devil, the flesh, and the world, with all their harassment, to swamp us with their stormy waves. But those on board shouldn't simply stand at the edge but should leap into the hold at the heart of the ship, into the abyss of the blazing and anguished love of Christ crucified, and the waves won't hurt them at all. In fact, once they have experienced and tasted divine providence in the waves, they will energy more strengthened and courageous, willing to endure pain and weariness and reproach in the world without sinning."

[17] The image of nails being made into keys occurs in only three other letters (T112, T184, and T207/DT68, all in this volume), the last of which was written near Easter of 1376, the other two in early 1377. In many other places, however, Christ's blood, his obedience, is the key which opens heaven. The image and the underlying idea are brought together in a text Catherine certainly knew, Cavalca's *Descrizione de' dieci comandamenti* (p. 284): "St. Bernard also says, 'Christ's nail has become my key, so that I can open him up and see within his compassionate heart. And through the opening in his side the tenderness of his heart is revealed to me.' " The passage from Bernard de Clairvaux is in *In Cantico sermo LXI*, 4 (PL CLXXXIII, 1072): "The piercing nail becomes for me an unlocking key. . . . He reveals the secret of his heart through the opening of his body." The secret of Christ's heart is God's infinite love, revealed in the shedding of Christ's blood (*Dial.* 75, p. 138), bringing humankind to salvation. So Catherine has in fact carried Bernard's image to an integration far beyond Bernard's text.

Every suffering and evil ended, you will receive every good, satiety without boredom and hunger without pain.[18] Finish your life on the cross.[19] Keep living in God's holy and tender love.[e]

Gentle Jesus! Jesus love!

Textual Notes

a. From P3; R1: [*out of . . . sacraments*].

b. A. Volpato ("*Analisi diplomatistica,*" p. 7) points out that this letter is preserved only in the Maconian codices, where a clumsy correction makes the opening read: *serva e schiava de' servi di Dio, scrivo nel pretioso sangue suo. . . .* He hypothesizes that the text originally read . . . *pretioso sangue del figliuolo di Dio.*

c. From P3; R1: *fill us with love* (*ci . . . innamorare*) / *inspire us* (*ci . . . innanimare*).

d. P3 adds *that man in love.*

e. Manuscripts have simply *Keep living, etc.*

[18] Catherine probably encountered this thought of Pseudo-Augustine (*Meditatio XXVII*, PL XL, 921) in the works of Cavalca, for example, *Specchio di croce*, p. 184: "Sated, we shall be hungry, and hungering we shall be sated, but our satiety will be far from boredom, and our hunger far from pain." It occurs also in *Descrizione de' dieci comandamenti*, p. 306: "We shall desire though we are sated, and we shall be sated even in our desiring. Yet satiety will not be a source of boredom, nor desire be accompanied by pain, as happens in this world."

[19] This is an admonition Catherine does not repeat anywhere else.

LETTER T16/G38[1]
To a great prelate
February to April 1376,
but most likely near Holy Week (6 to 12 April)

Catherine writes this letter to an unidentified prelate (presumably a bishop or cardinal) at a time when the need for the reform of the clergy is very much on her mind. She sees her addressee as someone who must speak out in these matters. And because she wants him to use his influence to see that the crusade is called soon, it is fairly likely that he is near the pope. Beyond these clues, we have only the linguistic evidence to place this letter chronologically.[2]

Among the letter's themes, the image of wolves carrying off the flock occurs with the call for a crusade only in letters between April and September 1376, with most of these being from March to April. The heavy emphasis on the passion, especially since a good deal of it is expressed in the present tense, could be a reflection of the proximity of Holy Week. This is reinforced by the expectation of flowers appearing soon. Therefore, I would posit that this letter is most probably from spring of 1376, with a good possibility that it was written near Holy Week (6 to 12 April).

Such a date would place the addressee in Avignon. Catherine has already written to two cardinals there, Iacopo Orsini (Let. T101/DT23 and T223, both in this volume) and Pietro Corsini (Let. T177/DT61, in this volume), as well as to the pope's secretary, Nicola da Osima (Let. T181/DT55, vol. I). But since Let. T223 and T177/DT61 were probably written near April 1376 as well, it is quite likely that this letter is to some other cardinal in Avignon, possibly Pierre d'Estaing, with whom Catherine will be in contact later in 1376 and who we know was at the papal court well before Catherine's arrival there in June.

---

1 MSS: B, P2,T, R1, P5, F2, F1, P3, P4, Pa; translation based on R1, with reference to P4.

2 The only two other letters which share fifteen or more of this one's fifty-seven analyzed patterns are from February and April 1376. Further, there are a number of significant clusters within individual patterns which begin and/or end in the months immediately preceding Catherine's departure for Avignon (ACQUGRAZ, CONDOTT, CROCDES, CUORSCOP, FAMESAL, GLORTRIB, MUOIO, NASCPIAG, PADMANIF, PENADES, PENAFIN, SCEM, SEMPAROL, SIMONIA). Dupré Theseider (unpublished notes) considers the letter undatable. Fawtier (II, pp. 166–167) places it simply in 1377.

§

In the name of Jesus Christ crucified and of gentle Mary.

Dearest reverend father in Christ Jesus,

I Caterina, servant and slave of the servants of Jesus Christ crucified, am writing to you in his precious blood. I long to see you hungering to have people as your food for God's honor. Learn from gentle First Truth, who dies in his hunger and thirst for our salvation. It seems this spotless Lamb cannot be satisfied: on the cross, saturated with humiliation, he cries out that he is thirsty.[3] Though he was physically thirsty, his thirst of holy longing for the salvation of souls was greater.[4]

Oh wonderful boundless charity! It seems it wasn't enough that you gave so much in surrendering yourself to such torments! You wanted even more. And love was the reason for it all.[5] *I'm not surprised, because your love was infinite and the suffering was finite. So the cross of desire was greater than the physical cross.*[6]

I recall the good gentle Jesus explaining this once to a servant of his. When she saw in him both the cross of desire and the physical cross, she asked, "My dear Lord, which was worse for you, the physical pain or the pain of desire?"

He responded kindly and sweetly, "My daughter, have no doubt; I would have you be sure of this. It is impossible to make comparisons between the finite and the infinite. Reflect, therefore, that my physical pain was finite; yet holy desire has no bounds. This is why I carried the cross of holy desire.[7] And don't you remember, my daughter, how once when

---

[3] Jn. 19, 28.

[4] Cf. Cavalca, *Specchio di croce*, XXXIII, pp. 136–137: "One must certainly believe that, though he was physically thirsty, he had even more thirst and desire for our salvation, and this is why he said, 'I am thirsty.' He meant, 'I long for human salvation.' He wanted to make us understand that he loved us more than he could show. For though by dying he demonstrated the most perfect love possible, even this deed was finite, and he could not demonstrate the infinite with something finite. And this is why he said, 'I am thirsty.' It is as if he were saying, 'I have more ardor, fervor, and longing in my heart than can be shown in deeds."

[5] Tommasèo's text inserts an additional clause and changes the punctuation, with a result that not only makes little sense grammatically but is not consistent with the logic of the rest of the letter: . . . *non pare che tu dia tanto, dandoti a tanti tormenti,* ***che non rimanga maggiore il desiderio che egli aveva della salute dell'anime*** *di più voler dare tutto. N'è cagione l'amore.*

[6] This contrast between the physical cross and the cross of desire occurs also in *Dial.* 78, p. 146, and in Let. T11 to Cardinal Pierre d'Estaing (in this volume).

[7] Cf. *Dial.* 75, p. 139: "The eternal Divinity took to itself the suffering I [Christ] bore with such burning love. For this reason what I did can be called infinite. Not that either the actual bodily suffering or the pain of my longing to accomplish your redemption was infi-

I showed you my birth, you saw me as a little infant born with a cross on my shoulder? So I want you to know that even as I, the incarnate Word, was sown [as a seed] in Mary's womb, the cross of desire began for me.[8] This was the cross of obedience to my Father, of realizing his will for humankind—that is, that humankind should be restored to grace and receive that for which you had been created. This cross was more painful for me than any other suffering I ever bore physically. This is why my spirit exulted with such great joy when I saw myself being led to the end point, especially at Holy Thursday's supper. This is why I said, 'With desire have I longed to celebrate this Passover,'[9] that is, to sacrifice my body to the Father. I was tremendously happy and consoled to see the time approaching when I would be relieved of this cross of desire. So the closer I saw myself coming to the physical scourging and torment, the less intense my suffering became.[a] For the physical pain dispelled the pain of desire, since I was seeing the realization of what I longed for."

She answered, "Oh my gentle Lord, you say that on the cross this pain of the cross of desire left you. How so? Did you then lose your desire for me?"

"My dear daughter! No!" he said. "When I died on the cross, the pain of holy desire ended at the same moment as my life. But my desire and hunger for your salvation did not end. In fact, if the unspeakable love I had and still have for the human race had ended and ceased, you would not exist! For just as love drew you from my Father's breast, creating you with wisdom, so this same love preserves you; you are made of nothing less than love. If God were to withdraw back into himself the love and power and wisdom with which he created you, you would not exist. I, God's only-begotten Son, the Word, have been made a channel that brings you the water of grace. I reveal to you my Father's love, since whatever love he has, I have also, and whatever I have, he has. I am one with the Father, and the Father is one with me,[10] and he has used me to reveal

nite, for all of that ended on the cross when my soul left my body. But the fruit was infinite that comes from my suffering and from my desire for your salvation, and therefore you receive it without limit."

[8] Cf. Prayer 18, pp. 162–163: "I see that this Word, once written in you, [Mary,] was never without the cross of holy desire. Even as he was conceived within you, desire to die for the salvation of humankind was engrafted and bound into him. This is why he had been made flesh. So it was a great cross for him to carry for such a long time that desire, when he would have liked to see it realized at once."

[9] Lk. 22, 15.

[10] Jn. 10, 30.

himself. This is why I said, 'Whatever I have from my Father, I have revealed to you.'[11] Love is the reason for everything."[12]

So you see clearly, reverend father, that the good gentle Jesus, love, dies of thirst and hunger for our salvation. I beg you for love of Christ crucified to keep your eyes on the hunger of this Lamb. This is what my soul desires: to see you dying of true and holy desire, that is, of the vigorous love you will have for God's honor, the salvation of souls, and the exaltation of holy Church. I want to see this hunger grow so intense in you that you die of it. Just as God's Son died of hunger (as we've said), so may you be left dead to every selfish love for yourself. And may your will and appetite be left dead to every sensual passion, to earthly prestige and pleasure, to human respect and worldly ostentation.

I have no doubt that if you turn your understanding's eye to look at yourself and realize that you are not, you will discover with what blazing love your being has been given you. I tell you, your heart and affection will not be able to keep from exploding for love.[13] Selfishness will not be able to live there. You will seek yourself not for your own sake, for your own advantage, but for God's honor. You will seek your neighbors not for your own sake, for your own advantage, but will love them and long for their salvation for the praise and glory of God's name. For you will see that God loves people above all else, and this is why God's servants love other people so much—because they see that the Creator loves them above all else. I love what the person I love loves; that's the nature of love. God's servants, I say, love God not for their own sake but because God is supreme eternal Goodness and deserves to be loved.

Truly, father, God's servants have put an end to life, because they no longer think of themselves. They want nothing but suffering, anguish, torment, and abuse from the world. They have only contempt for all the world's torments,[b] since the cross they bear when they see God offended

---

[11] Jn. 15, 15.

[12] Cf. *Dial.* 82, pp. 151–152, where this is expressed in almost the same words: "The Word, my Son, in his painful death on the cross ended the pain of that tormenting desire he had borne from the beginning when I sent him into the world right to the moment of his death for your salvation. Not that he ended his desire for your salvation—no, only the pain. For if my loving charity, which I had revealed to you in his person, had at that point been ended and finished for you, you would not even exist, because you are created through love. And if I had taken back my love and ceased to love your being, you would not exist. But my love did create you and my love preserves you. And because I am one with my Truth, the incarnate Word, and he is one with me, he put an end to desire's pain, but not its love." Such a close parallel with *The Dialogue* (matter which does not appear in Let. T272, *The Dialogue*'s prototype, in this volume) would suggest, as do other such parallels, that Catherine consulted past letters in her editing of that work. The *Dialogue* passage, in its entire context, also seems to reflect an earlier mystical experience.

[13] It. *l'affetto vostro non potrà tenersi che non si spasimi per amore.*

and vilified and other people damned is so much greater. This pain is so great that they forget any feeling for their own life. Not only do they not run away from suffering; they delight in it and go looking for it. They are in agreement with that dear Paul, so in love, who gloried in tribulations for love of Christ crucified.[14] So I am asking you and I want you to follow this dear trumpeter.

Oimé! Oimé! My unfortunate soul! Open your eyes and look at the evil of death that has come into the world, and especially into the body of holy Church! Oimé! Let your heart and soul break to see God so offended! Look, father, how the infernal wolf is carrying people off, carrying off the little sheep who are feeding in the garden of holy Church—and no one is making a move to snatch them from his mouth! The shepherds are sleeping in selfish love for themselves, in concupiscence and indecency. They are so drunk with pride that they are asleep and senseless, even while they see the devil, the infernal wolf, snatching the life of grace from them and even from those in their charge. They aren't concerned. And the reason for all this is the evil of selfish love.[15]

Oh how dangerous this love is, whether in those in authority or in those subject to them! Those in authority who love selfishly do not correct the sins of their subjects, because those who love themselves for their own sake fall into slavish fear and so do not reprove. For if they loved themselves for God's sake, they would not fear with this slavish fear. They would with courageous heart reprove sin and not be silent or pretend not to see. I don't want you to have this sort of love, dearest father! I beg you to act in such a way that First Truth's hard word of reproach will not be said of you: "Cursed are you who were silent!"

Oimé! No more silence! Shout out with a hundred thousand tongues! I am seeing the world going to ruin because people are not speaking out! I am seeing Christ's bride made pallid, her color drained, because her blood is being sucked from behind her back. I mean that by their pride they are stealing Christ's blood (given gratuitously and not because it is owed us), taking the honor that ought to be God's and giving it to themselves.[16] They are robbing by their simony, selling the graces and gifts

---

[14] Rom. 5, 3 (Vulg.).

[15] Cf. *Dial.* 129, p. 257: "And the little sheep who have no shepherd who cares about them or knows how to guide them easily go astray and are often snatched and devoured by wolves. . . . [I]f the shepherd has no rod and no dog of conscience his sheep will perish. And he will not even be concerned, because the dog of his own conscience is so weakened for want of feeding that it cannot bark."

[16] Cf. *Dial.* 132, p. 271 "[They] suck the blood of my bride, holy Church. By their sins they have left her pallid. The loving charity they ought to have had for this bride they have lavished on themselves." She writes in the same imagery to Cardinal Pietro Corsini in Avignon in T177/DT61 (in this volume), which I have placed around Palm Sunday, 1376.

given us gratuitously at the price of the blood of God's Son.[17] Oimé! I am dying and cannot die!

No more sleeping in apathy! Do whatever can be done in this present time. I believe another time will come when you can do even more, but for now I am inviting you to strip your heart of all selfish love and clothe it in hunger and in virtue true and solid, for God's honor and the salvation of souls. Take courage in Christ Jesus, gentle love; for soon we shall see the flowers appear. Try to have the standard of the cross raised soon.[18] And let not your heart and affection fail because of any trouble you may see coming. No, be even more encouraged then, reflecting that Christ crucified will be the one who realizes and fulfils the passionate desires of God's servants.

I'll say no more. Keep living in God's holy and tender love.[c] Immerse yourself in the blood of Christ crucified. Put yourself on the cross with Christ crucified. Hide in the wounds of Christ crucified. Make the blood of Christ crucified your bath.

Forgive my presumption, father.

Gentle Jesus! Jesus love!

Textual Notes

a. From P4; R1: [*the less intense my suffering became*], an apparent scribal error.

b. From the Tommasèo text; R1, P4 [*They have only contempt for all the world's torments.*]

c. R1, P4 have for this sentence simply: *Permanete, etc.*

---

[17] She has written much the same in Let. T88/DT28 to Bishop Angelo Ricasoli in early January 1376 (vol. I). The idea will reappear in *Dial.* 121, p. 232: "Not only do they not give what they are in duty bound to give to the poor, but they rob them through simony and their hankering after money, selling the grace of the Holy Spirit."

[18] That is, try to influence the pope to call the crusade he has proposed.

LETTER T52/G132[1]

To Frate Jeronimo da Siena of the Hermits of Saint Augustine February to April 1376, with a good probability of Holy Week (6 to 12 April)

Jeronimo, a native of Siena, was one of the Augustinians of Lecceto.[2] Tommaso Caffarini calls him not a hermit but a preacher. He tells us also that after Catherine had written her brief prayer to the Holy Spirit during her stay at Rocca d'Orcia in 1377, that document was given (by Catherine or someone else) to Jeronimo "as a special memento."[3]

This single extant letter to Jeronimo addresses the issue of friendship. It seems from Catherine's remarks that she is concerned about the quality of the Augustinian's relationship with some particular person, perhaps someone to whom he is ministering, since what Catherine says of friendship flows from admonitions about motivations for service.

Basically, only the linguistic evidence is helpful in placing this letter, and this points to a probable date somewhere between February and April 1376.[4] In fact, I would place this letter with a great deal of confidence between February and April 1376, with the strong paschal imagery inclining me to guess that it may well be from Holy Week (6 to 12 April).

---

[1] MSS: Mo, P4, Pa; translation based on Mo-*a*, corrected by *b*. Other relevant variants based on an unpublished transcription by A. Volpato.

[2] See the introduction to Let. T66/DT35 to William Flete (vol. I).

[3] *Libellus de Supplemento*, I, i, p. 17. Caffarini goes on to say that Jeronimo eventually gave the parchment to another preacher while on a preaching mission to Venice. This preacher gave it to Caffarini, who in turn gave it to the *Mantellate* of Venice. It has not been discovered. The prayer is Prayer 6 in the collection of Catherine's prayers, p. 54.

[4] There are a good number of very striking vertical clusters within individual patterns between February and April 1376: ACQUAVIV, AGNELARR, ARBPIANT, BANPAROL, CARCONFU, LETTO, MENSCIBO, OPERATOR, PIENGRAZ, PORTNOME, SEMPAROL, VASDILEZ. No other period shows anywhere near the same density of sharing. Further, of the six letters which share thirteen or more of this one's fifty-seven analyzed patterns, four are from this same period, with one only a few months earlier and one very long one in 1377.

§

In the name of Jesus Christ crucified and of gentle Mary.[a]

Very loved and dearest father and son in Christ Jesus,

I Caterina, servant and slave of the servants of Jesus Christ,[b] am writing to you in his precious blood,[c] recalling our Savior's words to his disciples, "With desire have I desired to celebrate the Pasch with you before I die."[5] I say the same to you, Frate Jeronimo, my dearest father and son. And if you ask me, "What Pasch are you desiring to celebrate with us?"[d] I answer, "There is no other Pasch but that of the spotless Lamb, the same Pasch he made of himself for his dear disciples."

Oh tender Lamb, roasted over the fire of divine charity on the spit of the most holy cross! Oh sweetest of foods, filled with joy and happiness and consolation! You lack nothing, because for those who serve you in truth you are made table and food and waiter. We see well that the Father is a table for us, and a bed where the soul can rest. And we see the Word, his only-begotten Son, who has given himself to us as food with such burning love. And who has brought him to us? The waiter, the Holy Spirit—and because of his boundless love he is not satisfied[e] to have anyone else wait on us but wants to serve as waiter himself.

Now it is at this table that my soul desires to celebrate this Pasch together with you before I die, because once life is past we cannot do it. And understand, my son, that we must go to this table stripped and clothed. By "stripped" I mean stripped of all selfish love and desire to please the world, stripped of apathy and sadness and spiritual discouragement (because inordinate sadness dries up the soul). But we must dress up in his blazing charity,[6] and this we cannot have without opening the eye of self-knowledge so as to see that we are not (and that we are therefore doers of what is not because we are not[7]), and to know within ourselves God's infinite goodness.[f]

When we contemplate our Creator and the infinite goodness we find in

---

[5] Cf. Lk. 22, 15 (Vulg.).

[6] This garment of charity, the fire of love, is the scarlet garment of Christ's blood. Cf. Let. T384, addressed simply to "her children"(late 1377): "This blood makes the soul drunk. It clothes us in the fire of divine charity, because there is no blood without fire, no fire without blood. Oh how sweet and wonderful it is to be drunk on and clothed in such a gentle loving fire, to lose ourselves completely in it! It consumes the dampness of selfish love and the delight we take in our own comfort [and] in all human pleasure. We now delight not in pleasing others but only in pleasing our Creator. Why? Because of our self-contempt. For the sole source of our desire to please is the pleasure we take in ourselves. And the fire of charity which we find in [Christ's] blood consumes all of this." It is also the garment of the parable of the wedding feast (Mt. 22, 1–14).

[7] "What is not" is sin, which is opposed to all that shares in the being of God.

him, we cannot help loving. And love at once clothes us in true solid virtue. We would sooner die than do anything against the one we love, but seek constantly and eagerly to do what would please him. What he loves we spontaneously love, and we hate what he hates, for by love we have been made another himself.[8] This is the love that strips us of all apathy and ignorance and sadness. For our memory rises up to celebrate with our Father by holding in remembrance God's favors. Our understanding celebrates with the Son by knowing and loving God's will with wisdom and knowledge. At once we lift up our love and desire[9] and become lovers of supreme eternal Truth—so much so that we neither can nor want to love or desire anything but Christ crucified.[10] Nothing gives us pleasure except bearing his pain and disgrace, and this so pleases and satisfies us that we are suspicious of anything else. Pain and scorn and persecution from the world or the devil—we consider it glory to suffer these for Christ.[11]

Light, light the fire of holy desire! Look at the Lamb slain on the wood of the most holy cross! There is no other way we can eat at this sweet venerable table. See to it that the tree of the most holy cross is always firmly planted in the cell of your soul, for from this tree you will gather the fruit of true obedience, of patience, and of deep humility. All complacency and selfish love will die in you, and you will acquire a hunger for eating and savoring souls when you see that in hunger for our salvation and his Father's honor [Christ] humbled himself and gave himself up to the shameful death of the cross as one madly, drunkenly in love with us.[12]

This is the Pasch I desire to celebrate with you. And since we said we

---

[8] Cf. *Dial.* 1, p. 26: "Open your mind's eye and look within me, and you will see the dignity and beauty of my reasoning creature. But beyond the beauty I have given the soul by creating her in my image and likeness, look at those who are clothed in the wedding garment of charity, adorned with many true virtues. They are united with me through love. So I say, if you should ask me who they are, I would answer . . . that they are another me; for they have lost and drowned their own will and have clothed themselves and united themselves and conformed themselves with mine."

[9] That is, the will, the third power of the soul in Catherine's framework.

[10] Cf. 1 Cor. 2, 2: "I determined that while I was with you I would speak of nothing but Jesus Christ and him crucified."

[11] Cf. Gal. 6, 14 (Vulg.): "May I glory in nothing but in the cross of our Lord Jesus Christ."

[12] In Let. T145/DT40 to Elizabeth of Hungary (vol. I) the tree of the cross is planted in the garden of the Church: "I invite you and your son to this sweet food, and we have found the place where you can share in it. The time has already come, and the fruit is ripe. The place is the garden of most holy Church. That is where all faithful Christians feed, since there is planted the tree of the cross with its burden, the fruit of the Lamb slain for us with such blazing love that it should set every heart afire. Oh mildest of fruits, full of gladness and joy and consolation!" In every case, she calls her correspondents to "eat souls at the table of the cross," that is, to feed on the salvation of others in imitation of Christ, whose insatiable hunger for that salvation led him to the cross.

ought to be people who eat and savor souls, this is what my soul longs to see in you, because you are a proclaimer of God's word.[13] I want you to be a vessel of love,[14] filled with the fire of blazing charity, to carry the sweet name of Jesus[g] and sow the seed of this incarnate Word in the field of the soul.[15] But when you gather in the harvest[16] (that is, when your work with people is productive), I want and encourage you to store it within the eternal Father's honor by giving him the glory and honor and letting go of all self-complacent gloating. Otherwise we would be thieves, because we would be stealing what belongs to God and taking it for ourselves. But I believe that, by God's grace, this doesn't apply to you, since it seems certain to me that your primary motivation and starting point[17] rests purely in God's honor and the salvation of souls. Still, you *are* often subject to a bit of self-serving in [your relationships with] others.[18]

But because I want you to be perfect and to bear the fruit of perfection, I don't want you loving anyone, either in general or individually, except in God alone. Listen carefully, though, to how I say this, for I know that you love spiritually and in God—but sometimes, either inadvertently or through human inclination (and you *are* human),[h] while you love spiritually, you take pleasure and satisfaction in the love to such an extent that sensuality sometimes does play a role,[i] though always under the pretext of spirituality.

---

[13] This is consistent with Caffarini's reference to Jeronimo as a preacher.

[14] Here, as often elsewhere, Catherine renders the title given to Paul in Acts 9, 15 as she may well have misheard it (*vasello di dilezione* or *vas delectionis*, "vessel of love / predilection" rather than *vasello d'elezione* or *vas electionis*, "chosen vessel"): "This man is a chosen vessel for me, to carry my name." (Vulg.)

[15] This is the only direct reference to the soul as the field in which the Word is sown. Usually the image is applied to Mary, as in Let. T144/DT34 to Monna Pavola (vol. I): "*Oh ineffably tender love, how sweet this union of yourself with humanity! You have indeed shown ineffable love by all your graces and gifts to your creatures, but most of all by the gift of your Son's incarnation, the gift of seeing supreme exaltedness bend down as low as to our humanity.* Human pride must really blush to see God so humbled in gentle Mary's womb. She was the field wherein was sown the seed of the incarnate Word, God's Son. Truly, dearest sister, in that lovely blessed field the Word was engrafted into Mary's flesh as a seed is sown in the earth. In the sun's warmth it sprouts and blossoms and bears fruit, while the seed's husk remains in the ground. This is exactly what the fire and warmth of God's divine charity for the human race did after he had sown the seed of his Word in the field that was Mary." Catherine does, however, in several places, speak of sowing the word (*parola* vs. *Verbo*) of God, or the truth, in people.

[16] Literally, "seed."

[17] It. *principio*.

[18] The placement of this sentence as a bridge between what she has to say about ministry and her remarks about friendship seems to justify this interpretation. The original is more literally: "Still, you are often subject to some self-satisfaction in others."

You may say, "What will alert me to the presence of this imperfection?" I'll tell you.[j] When you see that the person you love is somehow falling short of your expectations, when he or she isn't talking to you as usual or seems to you to be loving someone else more than you, if then you become resentful and slightly chagrined, slacking off in the love that was there before, take it for certain that this love is still imperfect.[19] And how can we perfect it? I give[k] you no other way, dearest son, but that which was given to a servant of his[l] by First Truth.[20] He said, "My dearest daughter, I don't want you to act like a person who draws a vessel filled with water from the fountain and, after taking it out, drinks it, draining the vessel empty without even noticing that it's empty. No, when you fill the vessel of your soul by joining yourself in love and affection as one with someone you love for love of me, don't carry it even one step away from me,[m] the fountain of living water.[21] Instead hold that person whom you love for love of me just as you would a vessel in the water. In this way neither you nor the person you love will become empty, but both of you will always be filled with divine grace, with the fire of blazing charity. Then you will never experience resentment or chagrin. For as long as one who loves sees that the beloved is living in sweet solid virtue, he or she feels no troubling pain[22] even on seeing the beloved becoming somewhat distant or acting differently,[23] because the love has not been selfish but for God. This does not mean you may not feel a bit of holy sensitivity when you see yourself distanced from the object of your love."

---

[19] Cf. *Dial.* 144, pp. 302–303, where this theme is further developed: "She will love others with the same measure of perfection with which she loves me. And how does this [special love] let her know this? . . . Whenever the soul loves someone with a special love, she feels pain when the pleasure or comfort or companionship she has become accustomed to, and which gave her great consolation, is lessened. Or she suffers if she sees that person keeping more company with someone else than with her. This pain makes her enter into knowledge of herself. And if she is willing to walk wisely in the light as she ought, she will come to love that special person more perfectly, for with self-knowledge and the contempt she has conceived for her selfish feelings, she will cast off imperfection and come to perfection. Once she is more perfect, a greater and more perfect love for others in general will follow, as well as for the special person my goodness has given her."

[20] The reference (feminine singular) is, as often in cases such as this, to herself. The message is echoed more briefly in *Dial.* 64, pp. 120–121.

[21] Cf. Jer. 2, 13 (Vulg.): "They have left me, the fountain of living water, and have made cisterns for themselves—leaky cisterns which hold no water."

[22] For the sense of "troubling pain," cf. *Dial.* 4, p. 30: "Still, this is not a pain that troubles or shrivels up the soul. On the contrary, it makes her grow fat. For she suffers because she loves me, not would she suffer if she did not love me." Catherine frequently contrasts these two sorts of pain, the one unhealthy, the other healthy.

[23] The Italian object of "seeing" here is *molti modi*, literally, "many ways," which I have translated as "acting differently" on the basis of the preceding text and that of *Dial.* 144 cited earlier.

This, then, is the rule and measure I want you to hold to so that you may be perfect rather than imperfect.

I'll say no more. Keep living in God's holy and tender love.

Textual Notes

a. The invocation is missing in Pa, and in Mo it precedes the inscription naming the addressee.

b. Pa: *God / Jesus Christ.*

c. Mo-*a* had first written *his precious blood*, changing it to *the precious of God's Son.* Mo-*b* corrects it again to its original form; P4, Pa also have *his.*

d. P4, Pa: *What Pasch do I desire to celebrate with you?*

e. *he is satisfied* (*è contento*) written by *b* over erasure.

f. *b*: *And so we are doers of what is not because we do not know God's infinite goodness within ourselves / and therefore . . . goodness.*

g. P4, Pa: *Christ / Jesus.*

h. P4, Pa, as well as a correction by *b* shift this to the third person indefinite: *or because human nature—which you share—inclines people to love spiritually. . . .*

i. Mo-*a* had again inserted *of pleasure and satisfaction*, an error corrected by *b.*

j. Mo-*a*, Pa: [*I'll tell you.*]

k. P4, Pa: *tell / give.*

l. From Pa; Mo, P4 have simply *una* ("a").

m. P4: *don't draw it outside of me / don't carry it even one step away from me.*

Letter T36/G83[1]

To Frate Simone di Giovanni, Frate Francesco di Pascuale, Frate Iacomo di Sano di Maco, and others, all from Siena and novices of the Order of Monteoliveto at the Convent of San Michele in Bosco in Bologna[2]

Holy Week, 6 to 12 April 1376

For years there had been a convent of Augustinian Canons Regular in the pleasant hills of San Michele in Bosco ("St. Michael in the Woods") near Bologna. The plague of 1348 and the wars of the period had, however, reduced the number of monks to three, and their prior at that point had requested of Pope Urban V that their convent be permanently joined to the Benedictine Order of Monteoliveto, which had its center at Monteoliveto Maggiore near Siena.[3] The union was effected on 29 June 1364, and Monteolivetan monks had come to San Michele under a new prior of their own, Fra Michele da Prato.[4]

We know that two young men recommended to the order by Catherine in 1378, the Florentines Filippo di Vannuccio and Nicolò di Piero, became novices at San Michele.[5] Of the novices to whom the present letter is addressed, however, we know only that they are natives of Siena and that one of them, Iacomo, is the son of Catherine's disciple Sano di Maco of Siena.[6] So these young men also may be at San Michele on Catherine's recommendation.

The linguistic evidence strongly suggests that this letter to the novices was written close to April 1376.[7] This is supported by the strong paschal

---

[1] MSS: B, P2, T, R1, P5, F2, P3, V, P4, Pa; translation based on R1, with V as guide to glosses and standardizations added by other manuscripts.

[2] Rubric from V. Other manuscripts have: "To certain novices of the order of Santa Maria di Monteoliveto." There was an Olivetan monastery of Santa Maria Nova in Rome, but Meattini (*Epistolario*, p. 1474) speculates that here it simply refers to the order in general, perhaps because of its intense devotion to the Virgin Mary as an infant. The rubric from V is almost certainly older, though it is possible that the same letter was sent both to Bologna and to Monteoliveto Maggiore near Siena.

[3] Cf. Let. T32 (vol. I).

[4] *Tabularium S. Mariae Novae*, III, 29 June 1364, cited in *Spicilegium Montolivetense*, II (Florence,1903), p. 150, n. 1. These notes on San Michele are based on P. Lugano, "L'Istituzione di Montoliveto nella seconda metà del Trecento," p. 52. While Lugano comments on other letters of Catherine to Olivetans, he does not mention this one.

[5] Lugano, "L'Istituzione di Montoliveto nella seconda metà del Trecento," p. 69, citing *Familiarum Tabulae*, I, fol. 2v (ad annum 1379). He does not give any further information concerning this source, but the nature of the citation leads me to suspect it is the same as the *Tabularium S. Mariae Novae* mentioned in the previous note.

[6] It is not implausible that Catherine may in fact have written this letter at Sano's request.

[7] Though the eight letters sharing fourteen or more of this letter's sixty-five analyzed

theme, which would suggest Holy Week (6 to 12 April). Therefore, this is where I am most inclined to place the letter.

§

In the name of Jesus Christ crucified and of gentle Mary.

Dearest sons in Christ Jesus,[a]

I Caterina, servant and slave of the servants of Jesus Christ, am writing to you in his precious blood. I long to see you as children obedient even to the point of death, learning from the spotless Lamb,[8] who was obedient to the Father even to the point of a shameful death on a cross. Realize that he is the rule and the way that you and everyone else must follow. I want you to keep your spiritual sights set on him. See how obedient he is, this Word! He does not find the great burden imposed on him by the Father repugnant.[9] In fact, he runs to it with tremendous desire. He expressed this at the Holy Thursday supper when he said, "How I have longed to celebrate the Pasch with you before I die!"[10] That is, he intended to celebrate the Pasch by fulfilling the Father's will and command,[11] and so he was exultantly happy to see that the time had almost come. In the end he saw that he must sacrifice his body to the Father for us, and he said, "How I have desired [it]!"

The Pasch he was talking about was the gift of himself as food, and the sacrifice of his body in obedience to the Father. For he had often celebrated the other Pasch, eating it with his disciples, but never this Pasch. *Oh boundless sweet blazing charity! You do not think about your own pain or your shameful death; if you did, you would never go so joyfully, nor would you ever call it a Pasch!*

Think of this gentle Lamb as a real eagle, my sons. He does not look down at the earth, his humanity, but fixes his eyes on the circle of the sun,

---

patterns include one in 1377 and three from late 1378 to 1379, those four are all very long letters. The other four range from late 1375 through May 1376. The strongest concentration of significant clusters within individual patterns occurs from February through April 1376, with a number of these clusters suggesting that the letter is more likely from later in that period rather than earlier (AMAINSIE, CONDOTT, CONSUM, DESIDDE, NAVICREL, OBEDLUNG, OBEDSANG, SANGSANT, TIEPID).

[8] Quite possibly the fact that Iacomo's father was a wool-worker inspires Catherine's frequent references to Christ as Lamb in this letter.

[9] Usually she speaks of the "obedience" or "command" laid on Jesus by the Father.

[10] Lk. 22, 15.

[11] It. *la volontà del Padre e l'obedienzia sua* could also be interpreted as the Father's will and Jesus' responsibility to obey.

his eternal Father.[12] For within his very self he sees that the Father's will is this: that we be made holy in him.[13] Because of our first father Adam's sin we have no access to this holiness. So we have to have an intermediary, a means of making the fulfillment of God's will possible for us.[14] The Word sees that he is the one God has appointed, that God has given him the human race as his bride. The Father has commanded him to make his blood our intermediary so that God's will might be fulfilled in us, so that in Jesus' blood we might be made holy.[15]

This, then, is the sweet Pasch this spotless Lamb is inaugurating. With tremendous eagerness and desire he fulfills the Father's will for us even as he acknowledges and fulfills his own responsibility.[16] *Oh sweet boundless love! You have joined and conformed*[b] *creature with Creator, as one does when matching stone with stone, joining them with active lime mixed with water so that when the wind comes they will not be knocked down.*[17] *You, Word incarnate, have given this stone, your creature, a foundation. You have imbedded it in its Creator. You have joined us with a mortar made from the living lime of the divine Being mixed with your blood by means of the union you have formed with human nature. You have provided for all the foul winds that beat against our soul, inflicted on us by the devil, by other people, and by our own flesh—fierce battles and temptations, and all sorts of sufferings and torments.*[c] *I see, gentle First Truth, that because of the blood you have put between us, this wall is so strong that no foul wind can knock it down. Your creature has good reason, then, to love only you, sweetest Love, and not to be afraid of any fantasy*[18] *that may come along.*

So I beg you, my dear sons in Christ gentle Jesus: never be afraid. Trust in the blood of Christ crucified. Don't let emotions or fantasies make you

---

[12] Cf. Prayer 11, pp. 89–90; Prayer 19, p. 170, for expansions on the double image of the sun/circle. According to medieval belief, the eagle is the only animal that can focus its eyes on the sun. The eagle thus becomes a symbol of the holy person who can look into the divine light without being blinded. Cf. *Bestiario toscano*, p. 57: "[The mother eagle] tests her young by seeing whether they can look steadily into the eye of the sun as she can. She turns toward the sun and beats her wings to make sure that they are like her and that she can trust that they really are offspring of hers."

[13] 1 Thes. 4, 3.

[14] The next sentences play on the It. *mezzo* ("means" or "intermediary"). Let. T164/DT58 to Melina Barbani (in this volume), has a much expanded treatment of the same theme.

[15] Heb. 9, 13–14.

[16] There is here the same ambivalence as above: *obedienzia* could be either God's command or Jesus' responsibility to obey.

[17] Cf. the parable of those who build on sand and on rock, Mt. 7, 26–27.

[18] It. *illusione*, which Catherine normally uses to refer to diabolical deceit, and below she makes this diabolical connection explicit.

fall apart.[19] Never ever be afraid of anything—neither apprehension about not being able to persevere, nor the prospect that bearing up under obedience and the rule may be painful, nor anything that might happen. Keep your will good and holy, for your will is master of this wall, and with the pick-axe of free choice can maintain or demolish it as it[d] chooses.[20]

So I want you never to be afraid. May you be free of any slavish fear. Respond to the devils' fantasies and to your own heart's lukewarmness by saying with that dear Paul, who was so in love: "Bear up today, my soul! I can do anything because of Christ crucified, for he who strengthens me is in me through desire and love."[21] Love! Love! Love! Get drunk on the blood of this gentle Lamb, who has made the fortress of your soul strong, who has delivered it from slavery to the devil's perverse tyranny and given it back to you a free woman.[22] For there is no one who can take away your mastery unless you so choose, and this is something [God] has given to everyone.[23]

But I call your attention to the fact that divine providence has put you in a ship, so that you will not sink in the stormy sea of this darksome life. That ship is genuine and holy religious life.[24] It is maneuvered under the yoke of sincere and holy obedience.[25] Just think how great a favor God

---

[19] It. *dissolvete.* The image of the wall continues: if the mortar is strong, it will not dissolve or crumble in a storm.

[20] Cf. Let. GardI/DT52 to Bartolomeo della Pace Smeducci (vol. I): "For just as lime mixed with water is put between stone and stone to mold them securely together, so God has put between himself and his creature the blood of his only-begotten Son, mixed into the living lime, the fire of his blazing charity—because there is no blood without fire, nor fire without blood. The blood was shed with the fire of God's love for the human race. This wall makes the soul so strong that no foul wind can topple it unless we ourselves choose to demolish it by putting the pick-axe of deadly sin to it." But here the pick-axe is also a construction tool.

[21] Cf. Phil. 4, 13.

[22] Literally, "free, and a woman," the soul being feminine for Catherine both grammatically and conceptually. The image here is mixed: the soul is both fortress and a free woman.

[23] Catherine uses the pronoun *he*, which must here mean God, since it is God who in creation gives us free will. But contextually the antecedent is the Lamb, who has given back our full freedom through his blood. This, however, raises the theological questions of 1) the relationship of redemption to human freedom and 2) the universality of the effects of Christ's redemptive gift as Catherine understood it.

[24] The section of *The Dialogue* entitled "Obedience" (pp. 335–360) elaborates on this image of religious life as a ship. She is explicitly contrasting the state of these novices ("But. . . .") with that of "everyone" else.

[25] The original (*La quale navicella è menata col giogo della santa e vera obedienzia*) is a bit problematic, since *giogo* can refer to one of the banks of oars in a galley. This interpretation, however, does not seem possible in light of Let. T287 (in this volume), where Catherine describes the *giogo* with which a religious sails as *dolce e soave*, echoing the gospel reference to the yoke of Christ (Mt. 11, 29–30). It is therefore probable that, in the context of the ship image, she is thinking of the chains which bind the rowers of the Mediterranean

has done you because he knows how weak your arms are! For those who are in the world navigate this sea on their own power, but those in religious life navigate on the power of others.[26] When we are truly obedient we are not accountable for ourselves; rather the order is accountable for us—if we have been obedient to our superiors.[27,e] I will know that you are following the slain Lamb if you are obedient.[28] I have already told you that I want you to learn from the good gentle Jesus, who was obedient even to the point of death, who fulfilled the Father's will and command. That is what God wants you to do: to fulfill his will by keeping your rule and using it as a mirror.[29] Choose death rather than ever going against the command of your superior. However, if it should ever happen (may God in his compassion prevent it!) that your superior should command something that is not of God, then not even I would want you to obey,[f] nor should you, for we must never obey a creature in preference to the Creator. But in every other case be willing to obey always.[30]

Do not look to your own comfort, whether spiritual or material. I say this because sometimes the devil makes us see things under the guise of virtue or greater devotion. We would like to have circumstances suit our fancy, and so we say, "In such and such a time or place my soul experiences more consolation and peace."[g] But sometimes obedience will not have it so. What I am saying is that you should prefer obedience to your own consolation, and that is what I want you to do. Be aware that this is

---

galleys, who in her day are usually slaves or prisoners. (This interpretation would be borne out by the following reference to weak arms.) She does not, however, anywhere speak of members of religious orders as slaves or prisoners, but only as servants. Except for naming herself "servant and slave," she reserves the term *slavery* for servitude to sin.

[26] Literally, "on the arms of others," carrying through the rowing image.

[27] "Keep the rule and the rule will keep you," was a common saying among members of religious orders. The usual interpretation was that if the superior commanded something lawful but foolish, the responsibility for the foolishness rested not with the obedient subject but with the superior.

[28] Rev. 14, 4.

[29] Cf. Let. T173 to a brother who has left the order (in this volume): "If they are laypersons, they are good laypersons; if they are religious, they are perfect religious and navigate in the ship of true obedience, never leaving it. The mirror in which they look to see themselves is the rule and its customs and observances, and they are constantly trying to realize these in themselves." In many other letters to religious, she reminds them that they in turn are to be "mirrors of virtue" in whose lives layfolk can see how they ought to live.

[30] Cf. Aquinas, *Summa Theologica*, II–II, q. 104, a. 5, reply to obj. 3: "Religious profess obedience in regard to a way of life governed by a rule, and in this regard they are subject to their superiors. Because of this they are bound to obey only in those matters which pertain to the regular way of life, and this obedience suffices for salvation. If they are willing to obey even in other matters, this pertains to the super-abundance of perfection—provided always that such things are not contrary to God or to the rule they profess, for obedience in this case would be unlawful."

a subtle snare encountered by all of God's servants, and under the pretext of serving God they do the opposite.

Understand that it is only our will that serves or fails to serve. If you as a religious have the will, the devil will not try to entice you with gross external things, for you have already given these up by leaving the world. Instead he will tempt you interiorly with spiritual things. You say, "It seems to me I have more peace and love for God when I am in such and such a place than I do here." And to get your way, you resist obeying. Or if you simply must obey, you do it grudgingly. So in seeking peace you cut yourself off from peace. It is better, then, to put aside your own will and not to think of yourself at all, but to be concerned only about fulfilling God's will and that of the holy rule, and obeying your superior.

I am certain that you will be young eaglets and that you will learn from the real Eagle.[31]

Here is how worldly people act who cut themselves off from their Creator's will. When God permits them some trial or persecution they say, "It's not the suffering that makes me not want these things so much as that they seem to separate me from God." But they are deluded, for that is misguided sensual passion. The devil's deceptiveness makes suffering repugnant to them, and they are more afraid of suffering than they are of sin. The devil uses this trick in every generation.[32] So we have to deny this will of ours: obedient layfolk by observing God's commandments, and religious by observing both the commandments and the counsels as they have vowed in holy religion.

So up, my sons! Be obedient, in true solid virtue, even to the point of death. Understand that you will be as obedient as you are humble, because humility is born from the spring of obedience,[h] and obedience from humility, and both well up from the stream of blazing charity. And you will tap this stream of charity at the open side of Christ crucified.[33] That is where I want you to go to get it, and this is the place I am giving you for

---

[31] Cf. Deut. 32, 11: "As an eagle incites its nestlings forth by hovering over its brood, so he spread his wings to receive them and bore them up on his pinions." Cf. also Let. T134 (vol. I), T259 (in this volume).

[32] Cf. Cavalca, *Specchio di croce*, VI, p. 24: "Of this [sensual] love St. Bernard says, 'Many people, O good Jesus, want to come to you because they know you are the source of delight. They want to follow you in pleasure and consolation, but not in trials. They are certainly deceived, however. For, as the apostle Paul says, those who do not share in trials will not share in consolations. So whoever wants to see Christ in heaven as blessed must follow his example of humility.' "

[33] In Let. T145/DT40 to Elizabeth of Hungary (vol. I) it is the water of humility that enkindles the fire of charity in us: "From that knowledge [of God's goodness] there arises a spring of deep humility—refreshing water that extinguishes the fire of pride but enkindles the flame of blazing divine charity given us in our recognition of God's goodness to us."

your home.[i] You know that a religious outside of the cell is as dead as a fish out of water.[34] This is why I refer to Christ's side as the cell where you will find knowledge of yourself and of his goodness.

So now get up with tremendous blazing desire. Go to this sweet home; enter in and stay there, and there will be no devil or anyone else who can take grace from you or keep you from reaching your destination of seeing and tasting God.[35]

I'll say no more. Be obedient even to the point of death, following the Lamb, who is your rule and your way. Bathe in the blood of Christ crucified and hide yourselves in the wounds of Christ crucified. Keep living in God's holy and tender love. Love, love each other! Jesus! Gentle Jesus![j]

Textual Notes

a. From V; R1, T, B, P2, P3, P4 have *Christ gentle Jesus.*

b. V: [*and conformed*].

c. V: [*fierce battles and temptations, and all sorts of sufferings and torments].*

d. The text actually has *as the master, good will, chooses.* The adjective does not make sense in view of the option to "demolish"; nor does Tommasèo's interpretation, "as the Master of good will chooses," for the same reason.

e. V: [*if we have been obedient to our superiors*].

f. P4: *consent or agree / obey.*

g. V: [*and peace*].

h. T: *true obedience / the spring of obedience.*

i. From V, where the text reads *E questo vi do per luogo e abitazione*; others have *a questo modo per luogo e abitazione*, which makes no sense.

j. Ending from V. R1, T: *Keep living. ... Love, love each other! Gentle Jesus! Jesus love! Mary!* P3, P4 as R1, T, except for *Mary!* B: *Keep living, etc.* P2, same as B, but adds *Gentle Jesus! Jesus, etc.*

---

[34] The *Legenda aurea,* life of Anthony of the Desert, says that a monk outside his cell is like a fish out of water.

[35] Ps. 34, 9: "Taste and see how good the Lord is!"

LETTER T189/G52/DT84[1]
To the monks of the Monastery of San Girolamo at Cervaia
and
To Giovanni di Bindo, Nicolò di Ghida,
and other monks of Monteoliveto Maggiore
Early April 1376

Catherine sends this same letter, without modification, to two different monasteries: to the Benedictines of San Girolamo (St. Jerome) at Cervaia, about twenty-five miles from Genoa, and to several monks at Monteoliveto Maggiore near Siena. Because Catherine may have become acquainted with the monks at Cervaia, perhaps even paying them a visit while she was staying in Genoa on her way home from Avignon (as did the pope on 1 November, when his ship was held up by a storm in the Bay of Portofino), Dupré Theseider places the letter, at least the version sent to Cervaia, near that time. The linguistic evidence, however, strongly suggests a date much earlier in 1376, and the letter has scarcely anything in common with letters written in autumn of that year.[2]

Raimondo da Capua and his companions could very possibly have stopped at Cervaia to rest on their way to Avignon around late March, and Raimondo could have informed Catherine of affairs there in the same communication referred to in Let. T198/DT4, thus motivating this letter to Cervaia. In fact, this seems more plausible to me than supposing that she wrote it shortly after having seen the monks on her way back from Avignon.

The letter was very probably sent to Monteoliveto about the same time, that is, early April 1376.

---

[1] MSS: The first letter is in Mo, P5, F2, S2, P4, Pa; the second is in B, P2, H, P1, P5, F2, P3, S2, P4. Translation based on Mo-*a*, corrected by *b*, with reference to H. Other relevant variants based on Dupré Theseider.

[2] Of the six letters which share fifteen or more of this one's seventy-five analyzed patterns, four are from March to May 1376, two from mid-1375, and two from 1377. Further, the strongest concentration of significant clusters within individual patterns is centered between March and May 1376, with especially telling clusters of ACQUAVIV, CAPOGESU, CARCONFU, GODPENA, INDOMNJC, OBEDSANG, SANGACQU, SANGVAL, TEMPTENE.

§

In the name of Jesus Christ crucified and of gentle Mary.

Dearest and very loved brothers in Christ Jesus,

I Caterina, servant and slave of the servants of Jesus Christ, am writing to encourage you in the precious blood of God's Son.[a] That blood was shed with such burning fire that it must surely draw everyone's heart and affection to itself.[3,b] No wonder the memory of the blood lives on in the hearts of God's servants, for it is mixed with fire![4]

I remember in this regard what First Truth once said to one of his servants.[5] She asked, "Once you were dead, why did you want your side to be opened and to pour out such a torrent of blood?" And he said, "There are many reasons, but I will tell you two important ones. First of all, I wanted this because by having my side opened I showed you the secret of my heart. For my heart held more love for humankind than any external physical act could show. The other reason was the baptism that was given to the human race because of the merits of my blood."

You know that he poured out blood and water. The water was for Christian baptism, which gives us the life and form of grace, and which divine eternal Goodness provided through the merits of the blood of the Lamb as a remedy for our poverty and ignorance.

And for those who might not be able to have baptism by water, he instituted the baptism of blood and of fire. Their blood[c] would be their baptism, as it was for the holy innocents.[6] It would have value for them because of the blood of God's Son; I mean the martyrs' blood had and still has worth because of his blood. But we poor wretched Christians who

---

[3] Cf. Jn. 12, 32: "I, if I am lifted up, will draw all to myself."

[4] Cf. Let. Gardner I to Bartolomeo Smeducci (vol. I): "For just as lime mixed with water is put between stone and stone to mold them securely together, so God has put between himself and his creature the blood of his only-begotten Son, mixed into the living lime, the fire of his blazing charity—because there is no blood without fire, nor fire without blood."

[5] Catherine is alluding to an experience she herself had in prayer at an earlier date. The same experience is recounted more at length in *Dial.* 75, pp. 138–139. The concept of the opening of Christ's side is from Bernard de Clairvaux. On the baptism of water and of blood, cf. Cavalca, *Specchio di croce*, p. 191: "To wash us, Christ made a bath for us of his most holy blood. A figure of this, says St. Paul [Heb. 9, 11–12] is that in the Old Testament everything is purified with the blood of slain animals—a prefiguring of Christ crucified. And it was to symbolize this that from Christ's side came blood and water: blood for our redemption, water for our sanctification. It is by the power of this blood and water that baptism has power to purify us from sin."

[6] She is referring to the infants slain by order of Herod on hearing of the birth of Christ (Mt. 2, 16–18). These "holy innocents" were considered martyrs in the liturgical tradition of the Church in the West as early as the fifth century.

have already received grace—why doesn't our cold heart, full of selfish love and ignorance, rise up at the sight of such an ineffable fire of love and its wisdom? We know that our sin causes us to lose the grace and purity we receive in holy baptism. So our heart ought to melt with gratitude at the thought of such a great gift,[d] such a marvelous thing that it can be received only once!

Yet let's take heart, my brothers! Our sin, or any diabolical illusion or temptation, however repulsive, filthy, and ugly it may be, need not make us falter; for our doctor[7] has given us a medicine for any sickness we may have. I mean the baptism of blood and of fire in which the soul cleanses and washes away every sin, consumes and burns away every diabolical temptation and illusion—for the fire is steeped in blood,[8] so it truly does burn. This fire is the love that is the Holy Spirit, for love was the hand that pierced God's Son and made him shed his blood. [The fire and the blood] became one, and so perfect was their uniting that we cannot have fire without blood, nor blood without fire.

And because[e] we live in the corruptible prison of our body, which is a perverse law that is always inclining and inviting us to sin, the dear good God provided this ongoing remedy to strengthen our reason and freedom. I am referring to the ongoing medicine that is the Holy Spirit, the fire God never takes away from us. No, God is constantly setting in motion his gifts and graces, so that every day we can and should make use of this sweet holy baptism, given us as a gift and not because we had earned it.

When we look into ourselves and see there such a marvelous strength as is this fire, the Holy Spirit, we become so drunk with love for our Creator that we completely lose ourselves. We live as if we were dead, feeling within ourselves no creaturely love or pleasure, since our memory is already filled with love for our Creator. Our understanding does not reach out to see or grasp at any created thing apart from God, but sees and understands only our own nothingness and God's goodness to us. And we see that this infinite goodness wants nothing but what is good for us. Now our love for God has become perfect, since we no longer hold or understand anything but God. And now there is no holding back the swift course of desire. We run untrammeled and unbound, for we have cut off and thrown aside every weight that might have impeded our running. And we are so yoked with Christ that we love ourselves for God, and God for God, and our neighbors for God.

---

[7] Cf. Bianco da Siena, *Laude*, XIII, 5: "In his infinite compassion for us sinners the great doctor came; to heal the cut of our wounded hearts he made a bath of his blood."

[8] Cf. *Dial.* 75, p. 138: "Nor is there any baptism of fire without blood, for the blood has been fused with the fire of divine charity, because it was shed for love."

It is to this perfection, dearest brothers,[f] that you have been invited. You have been drawn by the Holy Spirit from a worldly life,[g] bound with the cord of holy true obedience,[9] and led to eat honeycombs in the garden of holy Church.[10] So I am begging you, since it is so delightful, never let any trouble or temptation the devil might give you make you look back; never let your soul give in to sadness or discouragement, for the devil would like nothing better. He likes to give us lots of annoyances and different sorts of struggles, and suggest false judgments against what we are commanded in obedience. He doesn't do this thinking we will fall at the first stroke, but only to lead us to unreasonable sadness and spiritual discouragement. For once he has brought us to sadness and discouragement, we become frustrated with ourselves and abandon our spiritual practices, thinking God must not be pleased or satisfied with what we have been doing, since we are experiencing so much darkness and coldheartedness. We seem to have lost the warmth of charity, and so we think it better to let go of these practices than to keep them up. Then the devil is happy, because he sees we are ready to be led into despair—and this is the one way he can get us.[h]

For if all the sins there are were collected in my one body, and I still had true hope and lively faith in infinite mercy, nobody would be able to keep me from receiving and sharing in the fruit of the blood of God's Son, which the gentle Jesus shed to fulfill his Father's command and to save us. And because his only will was to do his Father's will, all the pain, torment, scorn, and death were turned for him into the greatest sweetness—so much so that coming to his sufferings seemed to him like coming to a Pasch. This, it seems, is what he was showing at the supper when he said to his disciples, "How I have longed to celebrate this Pasch!"[11] This *was* the Pasch, for he saw that the time had finally come that he had so longed for, the time to sacrifice his body to the Father for us on the wood of the most holy cross.

Now this is how I want you to act. Why? Because this is how people act who are in love with God. They don't evade the troubles they encounter, whether from the devil or because of obedience. No, the more

---

[9] Cf. *Dial.* 155–156, pp. 329–334, for a fuller development of the images Catherine associates with obedience. Obedience is a key tied "with the cord of lowliness and contempt for yourself and the world" to the "belt of desire to please me your Creator."

[10] Cf. Prv. 24, 13–14: "My son, eat honey, for it is good, and the honeycomb is very sweet to your taste. So is the teaching of wisdom to your soul: when you find her, you will have hope for the future, a hope that will never die." Ps. 18, 10–11: "The judgments of the Lord are . . . sweeter than honey and the honeycomb." Sg. 5, 1: "I have come into my garden, my sister, my bride; . . . I have eaten my honeycomb with my honey." (All Vulg.)

[11] Lk. 22, 15. The sense of *Pasch* here could be either "Passover" or simply a feast.

they find to suffer, the happier they are. And the more strictly they are held to obedience by their superiors, the more they rejoice. For they know that the more their love and will are bound here below, the more generous they are, and the more closely they are bound to Christ.

You may say to me, "What can I do when I experience such darkness and blindness of spirit that there doesn't seem to be a thread of light by which I can hang on to hope?" I'll tell you, my brothers and sons. You know that sin can live only in a perverse and evil will.[12] When you know you have a good will, and know you would rather die than actually offend your Creator, then you must let go of your discouragement and walk by the light of the grace hidden within your soul, the grace God has given you in safeguarding your good will. This is the table at which you must eat by being faithful to all your good works. Answer the devil's discouragement by saying, "If divine grace were not in me, I would have no good will but would be following your tricks and my own evil thoughts. But I trust in our Lord, Jesus Christ, who will keep me safe right up to the end of my life."

My brothers, I want you to open the eye of your reason and you will see that[i] knowledge of ourselves makes us humble. We come to such knowledge [precisely] through all the darkness and all the devils' annoyances. And we grow in zeal and in love for God because we see that without God there is no defending ourselves. And we discover God in ourselves by discovering our good and holy will.

So we have seen how we find God in time of darkness, how in bitter things we find sweetness—only through the impassioned, consummate love we conceive and continually discover in this baptism of the blood and of the fire that is the Holy Spirit. This Spirit is our beginning, our rule, our intermediary, and our end. And in this end we are no longer pilgrim travelers in this life, but are securely settled in the eternal vision of God, where we receive the fruit of our every effort. So let's run on, my dear sons! Let's never avoid or run away from difficulty, but follow our leader, Christ Jesus.

I'll say no more. Fly on the wings of deep humility and blazing charity! Keep living in God's holy and tender love.[j]

---

[12] Cf. Let. T148/DT36 to Pietro del Monte Santa Maria (vol. I): "The temptations and wiles of the devils, the flesh, and the world may come shooting poisoned arrows—the flesh with ugly thoughts and sensations, the devil with his assorted temptations and deceit and trickery, the world with its pretentiousness and pride. But unless lady freedom consents to these disordered suggestions, she never sins, because sin is in the will alone."

Textual Notes

a. B, P2: *his precious blood / the blood . . . Son* (the entire phrase erased in Mo).

b. *to itself* from Mo-*b*.

c. Mo-*b*: *blood, shed for God, / blood.*

d. Mo: [*So . . . gift*]; *b* adds the sentence: *he has ordained the baptism of blood and of fire, which we can receive continually* (but this notion appears anyway in the next sentence).

e. The text here either lacks a verb, or has an unnecessary *perchè* or *mentre che*. Still the intended sense is clear, and I have translated it without *mentre che* ("while").

f. B, P2, H: *brothers and sons in Christ gentle Jesus / brothers.*

g. *b* adds *to the state of holy religion.*

h. *b* adds *so we must never do this.*

i. *b*: *to know yourselves, for / and . . . that.*

j. B, P2, H add *Gentle Jesus! Jesus love!*

LETTER T207/G198/DT68[1]
To the *Signori* of Florence
Early April 1376, perhaps Holy Week

The rubric of this letter says that it is addressed not to the *Signoria* (the governing body) but to the *Signori* ("lords") of Florence. Catherine may therefore be writing not to the entire governing body of Florence, but to specific individuals. Given the severity of her condemnation, I would guess that it is not her Guelf supporters she is addressing but rather those members of the ruling populist party who have led Florence's collusion in the antipapal league.[2] Many references make it clear that the letter is being written after Florence has been placed under interdict on 31 March 1376, and the fact that Catherine says she would rather say in person what she is writing seems to indicate that she is not yet in Florence. More precisely, the paschal references suggest that she is writing near Easter (13 April 1376), perhaps still during Holy Week.[3]

§

In the name of Jesus Christ crucified and of gentle Mary,
mother of God's Son.

Dearest, very loved brothers in Christ Jesus,

I Caterina, servant and slave of the servants of Jesus Christ, am writing to you in his precious blood. I am thinking of our Savior's words to his disciples, "With desire have I desired to celebrate the Pasch with you before I die."[4] Now our Savior had been celebrating the Pasch with them for a long time, so what Pasch was he referring to?[5] He was speaking of the

---

[1] MSS: Mo, S3; translation based on Mo-*a*, corrected by *b*. No other relevant variants.

[2] Fawtier (II, p. 242) believes Catherine is addressing only some of the Guelf leaders.

[3] Such a placement is supported by the linguistic evidence. Of seven letters sharing seventeen or more of this one's sixty-six analyzed patterns, five are from January to early April 1376. (One of the others is from mid-1375, the other from June 1376.) There are, besides, a number of significant clusters within individual patterns which either begin or end in these same months: ALEUMCAR, CALDCAR, CAPOGESU, CHIOVCHI, DAREVITA, DESIDDE, DILPROSS, EREDITA, MEMBCAPO, MEMBPUTR, ODIOAMPR, PACEUNIO, PASQUA. Fawtier (II, p. 243) places the letter precisely on 13 April 1376 (Easter). Dupré Theseider places it simply in the early months of 1376, preceding Catherine's departure for Avignon.

[4] Lk. 22, 15.

[5] In the language of Catherine's day every solemn feast was called a "pasch" (*pasqua*), but it is not unlikely that the reference here is actually to Passover, especially since Catherine's elaboration has overtones of Christ's Passion.

very last Pasch which he was celebrating by communicating to them his very self. He shows clearly how in love he is with our salvation. He does not say, "I desire," but "with desire have I desired," as if to say, "For a long time I have desired to accomplish your redemption, to give myself to you as food, and to give myself up to death to restore life to you."

This is the Pasch he was desiring, and so he is happy, rejoices, and celebrates within himself because he is seeing his desire fulfilled that he has so longed for. And as a sign that this makes him happy, he calls it a Pasch. Then he leaves them peace and unity and the command to love one another. He leaves this to them as a testament and as a sign by which people can recognize Christ's children and true disciples.[6] This true Father is leaving this to *us* as a testament. And we his children must not renounce our Father's testament, for whoever renounces the testament is not entitled to the inheritance.[7]

This is why I desire with tremendous desire to see you true children, not rebellious against your father, not renouncing the testament of peace but realizing that peace by being bound and united in the bond, the love, of blazing charity. If you live in this love he will give himself to you as food, and you will receive the fruit of the blood of God's Son, through which we receive eternal life as our inheritance. For before his blood was shed eternal life was closed to us. None of us could journey to our goal, God—though this is why we were created.[8] But death entered the picture because humankind would not live under the yoke of obedience but disobediently rebelled against God's commandment.[9] Then God, moved by

---

[6] Jn. 13, 34–35.

[7] Cf. Let. T133/DT32 to Giovanna d'Angiò (vol. I): "True sons and daughters, I tell you, would rather die than offend their father—not for fear of him or of his punishment, but only out of respect and love. These are the children who should receive the inheritance, because they have not betrayed their father's legacy but have cherished and followed his example." The reference is also reminiscent of Heb. 9, 15–18. This is one of several instances in which Catherine refers to Christ as "Father."

[8] In the section of *The Dialogue* entitled "The Bridge" (pp. 64–160) Catherine develops this concept at great length under the imagery of the crucified Christ as the bridge which reconstitutes the road between humanity and God. (She first used the image in Let. T272 to Raimondo da Capua, the letter on which *The Dialogue* was based. These are, in fact, the only places the image occurs.)

[9] A Pauline concept (cf. Rom. 9 and elsewhere). Also Augustine, *Propositio ex Epistole ad Romanos, Expositio XLVI* (PL XXXV, 2072): "[Paul] says that the law of sin, because of Adam's transgression, is mortality, by which we become mortal." Also *Contra Faustum* XIV, 3 (PL XLII, 296): "Human death comes as the punishment for sin, so that death itself is called sin, not because we sin by dying, but because sin is the reason we must die." Bernard de Clairvaux, *Ad milites Templi*, XI (PL CLXXXII, 933): "Sin is certainly the forerunner of death, for if humankind had avoided it they would surely not experience death in eternity." And *In feriis IV hebdomadis sanctae sermo*, 6 (PL CLXXXIII, 265): "Adam, . . . in whom we all sinned and on account of whom we all die."

the fire of his divine charity, gave us the Word, his only-begotten Son. And he, in obedience to his Father, gave us his blood with such warm love that any proud foolish heart should be ashamed not to acknowledge[a] such an enormous favor. His blood became a bath to wash away our weaknesses,[b] and the nails became keys[c] that unlocked the door to heaven.[10] So, my sons and brothers, I don't want you to be ungrateful or unappreciative for all the boundless love God is showing you—for you are well aware that ingratitude dries up the fountain of piety.[11]

This[d] is the Pasch my soul longs to celebrate with you: your becoming peaceable children, not rebellious against your head but submissive and obedient even to the point of death. You know well that Christ left us his vicar, and he left him as a help for our souls. There is nowhere we can have salvation except in the mystic body of holy Church, whose head is Christ and whose members we are.[12] Whoever disobeys Christ on earth, who takes the place of Christ in heaven, will have no share in the fruit of the blood of God's Son. For God has decreed that through his hands this blood will be communicated and given to us, as well as all the sacraments of holy Church, which receive life from this blood.[13] We cannot journey by any other road, nor can we enter through any other door, for First Truth said, "I am way and truth and life."[14] Whoever keeps to this road

---

[10] Cf. Cavalca, *Descrizione de' dieci comandamenti*, p. 284: "St. Bernard also says, 'Christ's nail has become my key, so that I can open him up and see within his compassionate heart. And through the opening in his side the tenderness of his heart is revealed to me.' " The passage from Bernard de Clairvaux is in *In Cantico sermo LXI*, 4 (PL CLXXXIII, 1072): "The piercing nail becomes for me an unlocking key. . . . He reveals the secret of his heart through the opening of his body." The "opening of his side" is addressed at length in Let. T189/DT84 to the monks of the Monastery of San Girolamo at Cervaia (in this volume). Regarding the blood of Christ as our bath, cf. Cavalca, *Specchio di croce*, p. 191: "To wash us, Christ made a bath for us of his most holy blood. A figure of this, says St. Paul [Heb. 9, 11–12] is that in the Old Testament everything is purified with the blood of slain animals—a prefiguring of Christ crucified. And it was to symbolize this that from Christ's side came blood and water: blood for our redemption, water for our sanctification. It is by the power of this blood and water that baptism has power to purify us from sin." This argument is developed in detail in *Dial.* 75, pp. 138–139.

[11] Cf. Bernard de Clairvaux, *De caritate*, XIX (PL CLXXXIV, 615): "Ingratitude is a blast, . . . a blight, . . . a wind shattering the gentle distillations of piety, and drying up the dew of grace and the fountain of mercy." (Cited also by Giovanni Colombini, Let. V, and by Jacopo Passavanti, *Lo specchio di vera penitentia*, p. 195). The sense of "piety" is filial devotion and loyalty.

[12] Cf. Eph. 5, 30: "For we are members of his body"; 1 Cor. 12, 12: "The body is one and has many members . . . and so it is with Christ." Pope Boniface VIII, in the decree *Unam sanctam* in 1302, had declared that "it is altogether necessary for salvation that every human creature be subject to the Roman pontiff."

[13] Cf. Let. T28/DT17 to Bernabò Visconti (vol. I), with which the present letter has much in common.

[14] Jn. 14, 6.

is walking by way of truth, not falsehood. This is a way of hatred for the sin[e] of selfish love of self, which is the cause of all evil. This way gives us love for the virtues, which give life to our souls and through which we are blessed with love and unity with our neighbors, so that we would rather die than sin against them. It becomes clear that if we sin against other creatures we sin against their Creator. So this is the way of truth. And it seems to me it is also the door[15] through which we must enter once we have completed our journey, for he said, "No one can come to the Father except through me."[16]

So you see, my dearest sons, that whoever like a gangrenous limb rebels against holy Church and against our father, Christ on earth, has fallen under the sentence of death, because whatever we do to him we are doing to Christ in heaven, whether it is reverence or dishonor. It is clear that by your disobedience and persecution (believe me, my brothers, I am saying this with heartfelt sorrow and tears), you have fallen into death and into hatred and contempt for God. And nothing worse could happen to you than to be deprived of his grace. Human power would be of little use without divine power. Alas, those who guard the city are wearing themselves out for nothing unless God is guarding the city![17] If God has declared war on you because of the wrong you have done your father, his vicar, you are weak indeed, having lost his help. It's true that many do not believe they are offending God by this. It seems to them they are offering sacrifice to him. If they persecute the Church and its pastors they defend themselves by saying, "They are bad, and they are doing all kinds of evil."[18] But I'm telling you that God wills, and has[f] so commanded, that even if the pastors and Christ on earth were devils incarnate (rather than good kind fathers), we must be submissive and obedient to them—not for what they are in themselves but out of obedience to God, because they take the place of Christ, who wants us to obey them.[g] You know that a son never has a just case against his father, no matter how bad and unjust the latter may be, for the gift the son has received[h] from his father, his very being, is so great that nothing can ever repay so great a debt.[19] Now reflect that in the same way the being, the gift of grace, that we draw from the mystic body of holy Church is so great that no reverence or works we might offer could be[i] sufficient to pay back this debt.

[15] Cf. Jn. 10, 7: "I am the sheepgate."

[16] Jn. 14, 6.

[17] Ps. 127, 1.

[18] Again, cf. Let. T28/DT17 to Bernabò Visconti, where Catherine reasons in much the same way.

[19] Many of these same concerns are addressed to Niccolò Soderini of Florence in Let. T171/DT60 (in this volume).

Oimé! Oimé! My sons, I tell you weeping: I beg you, I urge you, in the name of Christ crucified, to be reconciled and make peace with him. Continue the war no longer. Don't wait for God's wrath to descend on you—for I tell you, he considers this wrong as done to him, and so it is. Make your decision to take shelter under the wings of love and fear of God, humbling yourselves and being willing to seek peace and unity with your father. Open, open the eye of your understanding, and don't walk so blindly! For we are not Jews or Saracens, but Christians baptized and ransomed in the blood of Christ. So we must not go against our head, no matter what injustice may have been done us. Nor must one Christian go against another. No, we should be going together against the unbelievers who are doing us an injustice because they are holding what is not theirs but ours.[20]

Now, for love of God, no more sleeping in such unenlightened foolish obstinacy! Get up and run to your father's arms! If you do, he will receive you kindly, and you will have spiritual as well as material peace and tranquility, you and all of Tuscany. All this warring here will be turned against the unbelievers, by the raising of the standard of the most holy cross. But if you do not make any effort toward a wholesome peace, you and all of Tuscany will have a worse time than our ancestors ever had.[21] Don't think that God is sleeping while his bride is being wronged. No, he is watching! It may not seem so to us, because we see things going well—but under the prosperity is hidden the discipline of God's powerful hand. Since God is ready to offer us his mercy, my brothers, don't be unyielding any more. Humble yourselves now, while you have time. For those who humble themselves will always be exalted (so said Christ[22]), and those who exalt themselves will be humbled by God's discipline and whippings and beatings.

Walk in peace and unity. This is the Pasch I long to celebrate with you. And the only court in which we can celebrate this Pasch is the body of holy Church, because there we have the blood of God's Son as a bath to wash away the filth of our sins. There is the food that nourishes and satisfies our soul. And there is found the wedding garment we must have if we want to get into the wedding feast of eternal life, to which we are invited by the Lamb who was abandoned and slain on the cross for us.[23] This is

---

[20] As in Let. T140/DT30 to John Hawkwood (vol. I), Catherine expresses the common conviction of the medieval Church that the Holy Land belongs by right to Christians.

[21] Cf. Let. T171/DT60 to Niccolò Soderini: "If you don't make an effort to ask for peace and accept it graciously, you will fall into the greatest disaster you've ever fallen into."

[22] Lk. 14, 11.

[23] Cf. Mt. 22, 2–13.

the garment of peace that calms our heart and covers the shame of our nakedness (I mean all our wretchedness and sin and divisiveness, which are the things that strip us of the garment of grace). Once God's gentle goodness gives us back this garment, don't be slow to put it on and go bravely and earnestly to your head,[24] so that death won't find you naked. For we must die, but we don't know when. Don't wait for time, for time isn't waiting for you. It would be great folly to wait and rely on what I don't have and am not sure of having.

I'll say no more. Pardon my presumption, and blame it on my love for your well-being, physical as well as spiritual, and on my sorrow over the spiritual and temporal harm you are suffering. Keep in mind that I would rather say these things to you in person than by letter. If I can be of any use in advancing the honor of God and your reconciliation with holy Church, I am ready if necessary to give my life.

Keep living in God's holy and tender love.

Gentle Jesus! Jesus!

Textual Notes

a. Original *ricognoscetite*? (Ending *-endo* written over an erasure.)

b. *Weaknesses* written over an erasure; a second word, also erased, followed.

c. It: *li chiovi ci sono fatte chiave.*

d. *b*: *And this is why this / this.*

e. *b*: *hatred for sin, and not / hatred for the sin.*

f. *wills and has* written over an erasure.

g. Singular and plural are significantly inconsistent in the text. Literally, ... *even if the pastors and Christ on earth were devils incarnate (rather than a good and kind father), we must be submissive and obedient to him, not for what they are in themselves but out of obedience to God, because he is the vicar of Christ, who wants us to act this way.*

h. *has received* written over an erasure.

i. A word is erased after *be*.

[24] Christ, the head of the "mystical body" of the Church, and the pope as his representative.

Letter T21/G306[1]
To an unnamed person
February to April 1376, possibly Holy Week (6 to 11 April)

The language of this letter, so typical of references to homosexuality (or "sodomy") from biblical times until even very recently, leads to the conclusion that the person Catherine is addressing has been involved in homosexual behavior. Catherine's attitudes toward homosexuality are typical of her age, as is evident from her comments to this "unnamed person." Still, she does not hesitate to write lovingly and frankly to one whose behavior she admits finding it hard even to talk about.

The name of the addressee was apparently removed by a very early copyist, for it survives in no extant manuscript. The rubric in T (and other manuscripts) reads: "This is a letter which Catherine dictated and sent to a person whose name I don't know how I can write because of some words used in this letter. The reader (or one who hears it read) should not be surprised if some things seem not to hang together, for wherever *etc.* is written, we have omitted some words unfitting for anyone to know. Nor should anyone know the name of the one to whom the letter went." (There is, in fact, only one such omission obvious, and the deleted content seems to have referred to something Catherine regarded as even worse than homosexual behavior.) The rubrical comment seems to imply that the scribe who wrote it knew the name of the addressee.

Because all of the manuscripts in which this letter occurs (with the exception of V) are from the manuscript family of Stefano Maconi, who was Sienese, it is tempting to speculate that Maconi was the original scribe and that the addressee, known to him, was also from Siena. This would place the letter most probably in a period during which Catherine was in Siena. Given this possibility in combination with the linguistic evidence (inconclusive as that is), I would place the letter tentatively between February and April of 1376, with a greater likelihood that it is later in that period. It is quite possible, judging from its tone, that it was written during Holy Week.[2]

---

[1] MSS: B, P2, T, R1, P5, F2, P3, V; translation based on T, with V for initial and closing protocol; textual notes from B, P2 based on an unpublished transcription by Dupré Theseider.

[2] The linguistic evidence for the dating of this otherwise undated letter is not conclusive. Three of the four letters which share fourteen or more of this one's sixty-six analyzed patterns are dated from mid-1375 to early 1376. (Of these four, the heaviest sharing is, not surprisingly, in Let. T276, written to a prostitute [vol. I]. The other three have no such common base.) As far as clusterings within individual patterns are concerned, however, the picture is not quite so clear. While there are a number of clusters beginning and ending between late 1375 and early 1376 (CAPOGESU, CARNPUZ, CRENPREG, CUORANIM,

§

Dearest brother in Christ Jesus.[a]

I Caterina, servant and slave[b] of Jesus Christ, am writing to you in his precious blood. I long to see you an honorable debtor, paying what you owe your Creator.[3] You know we are all in God's debt: all that we have, we have only because of grace and boundless[c] love. We never asked to be created.[4] Moved by the fire of love, God created us in his own image and likeness.[d] He created us in such dignity that no tongue can express nor eye see nor heart imagine how great our dignity is.[5]

This is the debt we have incurred with God, and God wants this debt repaid: love for love. It is a matter of justice and fairness that those who see they are loved should love. God, in fact, showed us the greatest love possible by giving his life for us. For when God saw that we had lost our dignity because of our sin and had become the devil's bond-servants, supreme eternal Goodness, in love as he was with his creature, came along wanting to restore us and release us from our bondage. He sends the Word, his only-begotten Son, and condemns him to death in order to give us back the life of grace.[6] He sends him to stand security for us,[7] to free

---

CUORSCOP, DIGNUNIO, DORMMORT, LUPDIVOR, SAZFAST, TERRAAPE), there are also some patterns in which this letter, if placed early, represents an isolated pre-1377 occurrence: ANIMAL, SEDIACON, TENRAGIO.

[3] Cf. Let. T311 to the Defenders of Siena (1379): "Like thieves and wicked debtors, we take from others very unjustly. I mean, the honor and love we ought to be giving to God and to our neighbor we bestow on ourselves. Proud, we give ourselves honor by seeking worldly status, pleasure, and greatness. We offend God. We regard as our own and take credit for what we know and possess. And, ignorant as we are, we insult God. To God we give hatred, and to ourselves love—not rational love but sensual. To God we give the stench and to ourselves the fragrance, by pursuing human pleasure and satisfaction." Also *Dial.* 25, p. 63: "What could move you [God] to such mercy? Neither duty nor any need you have of us (we are sinful and wicked debtors!)—but only love! If I see clearly at all, supreme eternal Truth, it is I who am the thief, and you have been executed in my place."

[4] The notion is Augustinian, and Catherine repeats it often.

[5] Adapted from 1 Cor. 2, 9.

[6] She suddenly shifts to present tense. Cf. Prayer 18, pp. 159–160, where this "atonement" theology of redemption is developed: "I see, then, that whatever your wisdom saw, in that great eternal council of yours, as best for our salvation, is what your mercy willed, and what your power has today accomplished. So in that council your power, your wisdom, and your mercy agreed on our salvation, O eternal Trinity. In that council your great mercy chose to be merciful to your creature, and you, eternal Trinity, chose to fulfill your truth in us by giving us eternal life. . . . But your justice disagreed with this, protesting in the great council that justice, which lasts for ever, is just as much your hallmark as is mercy. . . . So what did you do? . . . You arranged to give us the Word, your only-begotten Son. He would take on the clay of our flesh which had offended you so that when he suffered in that humanity your justice would be satisfied—not by humanity's power, but by the power of the divinity united with that humanity. And so your truth was fulfilled, and both justice and mercy were satisfied."

us from the prison of sin and from the devil's hands.

Oh gentle loving Word, Son of God, boundless charity most tender! You stood security for us; you paid our debt; you tore up the parchment that bonded humankind to the devil (for because of sin we were in bondage to him). Yes, by tearing up the parchment that was your body you set us free.[8] *Oimé, my Lord, who would not be swallowed up in such a great fire of love? Those who day after day renew their bond with the devil, paying no attention to you, Jesus Christ, God and human, scourged, saturated with scorn!*[9] Oimé! Oimé These people make a stable of their bodies, harboring totally mindless beasts within!

Oimé, dearest brother! Sleep no longer in the death of mortal sin. I tell you, the axe is already laid to the root of the tree.[10] Pick up the shovel of holy fear of God and let the hand of love guide it. Come! Shovel out the filth from your soul and body![11] Don't be cruel to yourself—your own executioner, in fact—by cutting yourself off from your head, the gentle Christ, good Jesus. No more filth! No more impurity! Run back to your Creator. Open your soul's eye[12] and see how great is the fire of his charity, that he has put up with you and hasn't commanded the earth to open and swallow you, or the wild beasts to devour you.[13] On the contrary, the earth has shared its fruits with you, the sun its warmth and light, and the sky its movement,[14] so that you might live, giving you a bit of time

---

[7] That is, to "bail us out."

[8] Cf. Let. T69/DT24 to Sano di Maco di Mazzacorno (vol. I), where the image is developed in finer detail: "For the devil was holding on to us as his own property, as slaves and prisoners, and Jesus rescued us. He assumed responsibility [that is, stood security] for us, paid our debt, and then tore up the bond. . . . That bond was written on nothing less than lambskin, the skin of the spotless Lamb. He inscribed us on himself and then tore up the lambskin! So let our souls find strength in knowing that the parchment our bond was written on has been torn up, and our opponent and adversary can never again demand to have us back!" Also Col. 2, 14.

[9] Cf. Lam. 3, 30.

[10] Mt. 3, 10.

[11] This is the only use of the shovel image in Catherine's extant writings.

[12] Cf. Let. T51 to Felice da Massa (in this volume): "Our soul's eye is understanding, and it has the light of faith to the extent that the veil of selfish love hasn't covered it up."

[13] Cf. Nm. 16, 28–30: "Moses said, 'This is how you shall know that it was the Lord who sent me to do all I have done, and that it was not I who planned it: if these men die an ordinary death, merely suffering the fate common to all humankind, then it was not the Lord who sent me. But if the Lord does something entirely new, and the ground opens its mouth and swallows them alive down into the nether world, then you will know that these men have defied the Lord.' " Also Jer. 15, 3: "Four kinds of scourge I have decreed against them, says the Lord: the sword to slay them; dogs to drag them about; the birds of the sky and the beasts of the earth to devour and destroy them."

[14] Cf. Aquinas, *Summa Theologica*, I, q. 115, a. 3: "The more immovable certain things are, the more are they the cause of those things which are most moveable. Now the heavenly bodies are of all bodies the most immovable, for they are not moved save locally.

that you might be able to change your ways. And this he has done for love alone.

Oh foolish debtor thief! Don't wait any longer; make a sacrifice to Christ crucified of your mind, your soul, and your body.[15] I don't mean you are to put yourself to death in the sense of separation from bodily life (any more than you may be willing to); I mean death in your sensual appetites. Let your will be dead and reason alive, following the example of Christ crucified.[16] Then you will be paying what you owe.

Give to God what is God's and to the earth what belongs to the earth.[17] To God one must give one's heart and soul and affection—with energy, not apathetically.[18] Everything you do ought to have its foundation in God. And what ought one to give to the earth, to this sensual part of oneself? Just what it deserves. What does a killer deserve? A killer deserves to be dead. Just so, we have to kill this will by scourging our flesh, afflicting it, imposing on it the yoke of God's holy commandments.

Don't you see that this flesh is mortal? Its freshness soon passes away, like a flower plucked from its roots. Don't be like this any more, for love of Christ crucified! I assure you that God will not endure such abomination and such wickedness; if you do not change your ways he will pass the severest of judgments on you. I tell you, it is not only God, supreme purity,[e] who cannot endure it; not even the devils can! For all other sins are comprehensible[19]—but not this sin against nature.[20] Or are you a beast or a mindless[f] animal? I see well enough that you have the form of a human being, but this human being has in fact been turned into a stable, and inside are the beasts of deadly sins.

Oimé, for love of God, no more of this! Pay, pay attention to your salvation; respond to Christ, who is calling you! You were made to be a temple of God;[21] you ought to be receiving Christ[g] by grace, living virtuously, and sharing in the blood of the Lamb, in which our sins are washed away.

Oimé! Oimé! My unfortunate soul! I don't know how to get my hands

---

Therefore the movements of bodies here below ... must be referred to the movement of the heavenly bodies, as to their cause."

[15] Cf. Rom. 12, 1: "I beg you ... to offer your bodies as a living sacrifice holy and acceptable to God, your spiritual worship."

[16] Cf. 1 Pet. 2, 21.

[17] Cf. Mk. 12, 17: "Give to Caesar what is Caesar's, but give to God what is God's."

[18] Deut. 6, 5; Mt. 22, 37; Mk. 12, 30; Lk. 10, 27.

[19] It. *stanno a vedere*.

[20] Cf. *Dial.* 124, p. 237, where (also without naming homosexuality) she goes on more at length about "that accursed unnatural sin."

[21] Cf. 1 Cor. 3, 16.

on my sins and yours![22] How cruel and ruthless your soul and your bestial sensual passion, that beyond the sin against nature you. . . .[23] Oimé! Let our hearts burst! Let the earth split open! Let the rocks roll down upon us and the wolves devour us![24] Let them not endure such wickedness, such filth and sin against God and against your own soul! My brother, all our language and sensibility fail us! Oimé! I want no more of this! Put an end and a stop to this wretchedness; don't be so willing to be at ease with your longstanding involvement in it.[25] I've told you and I tell you again that God will not endure it if you do not change your ways.

I assure you, if you decide to reform your life in the bit of time that is still left for you, God is so gracious and merciful that he will have mercy on you and receive you graciously into his arms. He will allow you to share in the fruit of the blood of the Lamb, poured out with such blazing love that no one is too great a sinner to find mercy. For God's mercy is greater than our sins, so long as we are willing to change and to vomit out the filth of sin in holy confession with a determination to choose death rather than return to our vomit.[26] In this way you will regain your dignity, lost by sin, and we shall pay the debt we owe to God.[27] Realize that if you don't pay it, you will land in the darkest prison you can imagine. Realize that when this debt of confession and contempt for sin is not paid, there is no need for anyone else to bother to pick it up.[28] You will go all by yourself, in the company of the devils your lords whom you have served, into the depths of hell.

My dear brother in Christ gentle Jesus, I don't want this prison and damnation to be your lot. No, I want you, I beg you, and I wish to help you in the name of Christ crucified to escape from the devil's hands. Pay the debt of holy confession, with hatred for the offense against God and with determination not to fall back into such wretchedness. Remember Christ crucified; neutralize the poison in your flesh with remembrance of

---

[22] As she does so often, Catherine identifies her own sinfulness with that of the person to whom she is writing.

[23] This is one of those omissions referred to by the copyist in the rubric (see introduction).

[24] Cf. Lk. 23, 30 (and Hos. 10, 8): "Then they will begin saying to the mountains, 'Fall on us,' and to the hills, 'Cover us.' " However, as above, Catherine's sense is one of punishment, not relief. She makes these references in a number of places, but this is the only instance in which she makes the beasts wolves.

[25] Literally: Don't be willing to get accustomed to your long perseverance in such wretchedness.

[26] Cf. 2 Pet. 2, 22.

[27] The switch in pronominal reference is hers.

[28] Her reference is probably both to Christ, who took up our debt, and to herself, since above and again just below she implies her willingness to take his sinfulness upon herself.

the scourged flesh of Christ crucified, God and human. For through the union of the divine nature with human nature, our flesh attained such dignity that it is exalted above all the choirs of angels.

Surely Adam's stupid children should be ashamed to give themselves up[h] to such wretchedness and to lose their dignity![29] Set Christ crucified before you; hide yourself in the wounds of Christ crucified; drown yourself in the blood of Christ crucified.[i] And don't dally; don't wait for time, because time won't wait for you.

And if your weakness wants to give you trouble, pronounce judgment on yourself like a good judge. Mount the judgment seat of your conscience and don't let pass any feelings that haven't been corrected by you with a holy sweet remembrance of God.[30] Invite yourself to put up resistance, and don't consent to sin or actually carry it out. No, say to yourself:[j] "My soul, put up today with this little bit of suffering. Resist, and don't give in. Tomorrow perhaps your life will come to an end, and even if you're still alive you'll do what God will have you do; do the same today."

I tell you, if you act in this way your soul and your body, which are now turned into a stable, will become a temple where God will find his delight, dwelling within you by grace. Then when your life comes to an end you will receive the eternal[k] vision of God, where there is life without death and satiety without boredom.[31] Don't choose the loss of so great a good over a pitiful pleasure.

I'll say no more. Keep living in God's love.[l] Forgive my foolishness. Perhaps I've burdened you with too many[m] words and have said what we[32] perhaps[n] don't want to hear. Hold me excused, because my affection and love for the salvation of[o] your soul have made me say it. For if I didn't love you I wouldn't have bothered myself about it, nor would it

---

[29] There are only three instances where she refers to the "stupid" children of Adam, and all three seem to be early in her letter-writing years (Let. T28/DT17, vol. I; T77/DT17 in this volume; and the present letter).

[30] Cf. *Dial.* 63, p. 120: "She would find the root of her spiritual selfishness and have reason to know it for what it is and to rise above herself and mount the judgment seat of her conscience. She . . . would not let pass any feeling that had not been corrected by reproof." Also *Dial.* 73, p. 135: "And if difficulties make her selfish sensuality want to rise up against reason, her conscience must use hatred to pronounce judgment and not let any impulse pass uncorrected."

[31] Catherine probably encountered this thought of Pseudo-Augustine (*Meditatio XXVII*, PL XL, 921) in the works of Cavalca, for example, *Specchio di croce*, p. 184: "Sated, we shall be hungry, and hungering we shall be sated, but our satiety will be far from boredom, and our hunger far from pain." It occurs also in Cavalca's *Descrizione de' dieci comandamenti*, p. 306: "We shall desire though we are sated, and we shall be sated even in our desiring. Yet satiety will not be a source of boredom, nor desire be accompanied by pain, as happens in this world."

[32] Again, the switch of pronominal reference is hers.

have troubled me to see you in the devil's hands—but because I love you I cannot bear it. I want you to share in the blood of God's Son.

Gentle Jesus! Jesus love! Gentle Mary![p]

Textual Notes

a. From V; B, P2: *gentle Jesus / Jesus.*
b. From V; B, P2: *slave of the servants / slave.*
c. From P2; B, V: [boundless].
d. *in . . . likeness* from P2, V; lacking in B.
e. V: *supreme eternal / supreme.*
f. From P2; B, V: [*mindless*].
g. P, V: *God / Christ.*
h. V: *the foolish children should be ashamed to condemn themselves* (*si debono vergognare gli stolti figliuoli di dannificarsi*) / *the foolish . . . themselves up* (*. . . figliuoli d'Adam di darsi*).
i. V: [*hide . . . drown . . . crucified*].
j. V has *di dio porta* (which does not make sense here) for *dite all'anima vostra.*
k. V: [*eternal*].
l. From V; others have only *Permanete ec.*.
m. From P2; B, V: [*too many*].
n. V: [*perhaps*].
o. V: [*the salvation of*].
p. *Gentle Mary!* from T, R1.

LETTER T172/G80[1]
To Frate Niccolò of the Brothers of Monteoliveto in the monastery of Florence
Near Holy Saturday (12 April) 1376

Placido Lugano tells us[2] that in 1379, and possibly earlier as well, there were two monks named Niccolò in the Olivetan monastery of Florence: "frater Nicholaus Gerini" and "frater Nicholaus de burgo s. Nicholai," both Florentines, and that either of these may have been the addressee of this letter.

The linguistic evidence would situate this letter somewhere between late 1375 and the first few months of 1376.[3] Lugano assumes, surely because of the reference to Christ's freeing the souls in limbo (popularly called the "harrowing of hell"), that the letter was written at Eastertime. He is probably right. The prominence of that mystery in this letter would seem to reflect that some liturgical or sermon reference would have brought it to Catherine's mind, especially since limbo is a concept she refers to only three other times. I am inclined to place this letter very near Holy Saturday (12 April in 1376), when references to the harrowing of hell were most likely to be made.[4]

---

[1] MSS: Mo, B, P2, T, R1, P5, F2, P3, S2, P4, Pa; translation based on Mo-*a*, corrected by *b*, with reference to B as edited by Dupré Theseider (unpublished notes).

[2] "L'Istituzione di Montoliveto nella seconda metà del Trecento," p. 77.

[3] This letter shares heavily in content with only four other letters, all from October 1375 to the first four months of 1376. Also, one of the tree images used in this letter (ARBSTER) occurs only once after early 1376, and another (ARBFRUT) only three times. Other significant clusters within individual patterns are: AGNELCON, BRIGATA, CALDCAR, CAPOGESU, CONSUMAM, CUORAFFE, DISTEND, SACRIFIC (the last two of which occur *only* from mid-1375 through early 1376), SANINFER, TIEPID.

[4] Fawtier (II, pp. 193–194), while declining to date the letter, remarks: "If, as we believe, the text of these letters was conserved for us through the mediation of Francesco di Ser Vanni Malavolti [a disciple of Catherine who after her death became a monk at Monteoliveto Maggiore], one cannot be more happy that the whole collection of St. Catherine's letters was not entrusted to him, for he seems to have been especially severe in his treatment of the correspondence, unless the saint sent these Olivetan religious nothing but mystical considerations without—with few exceptions—any relationship to current events."

§

In the name of Christ crucified and of gentle Mary.

Most reverend and dearest father in Christ Jesus,

I Caterina, servant and slave of the servants of God, am writing, and commend myself to you, in the precious blood of God's[a] Son. I long to see us with heart and affection and desire raised to this dear Christ Jesus at the head of the troop he brought out of limbo. For a long time they had waited in intense darkness for their redemption.[5] Let us raise our hearts to him; let us contemplate the consummate, affectionate love God has demonstrated in all his dealings with humankind. Then let us consider the sweet desire our holy and venerable ancestors had simply waiting for the coming of God's Son. And let our inattentiveness and coldness and indifference be confounded and obliterated within us—for we[b] have experienced and seen and felt the fire of divine charity! Oh, what an astonishing thing this is! They burned[c] at the very thought, and[d] we see God engrafted into our flesh, made one with us, and we don't react at all![e]

Oh true and sweet engrafting! Humankind was sterile, with no access to the water of grace, and he[f] made us productive.[6] We have only to spread our wings of holy desire[7] and attach ourselves to the tree of the most holy cross, where we will find this sweet and holy engrafting of the incarnate Word, God's Son. There we will find the virtues, fruits ripened on the body of the Lamb slain and consumed for us.[8] So let our hearts

[5] Thomas Aquinas (*Summa Theologica, Supplementum*, q. 69, aa. 4–6) recognizes a "limbo of the fathers," a temporary abode of those who died in holiness before the redemption, and a "limbo of children," a permanent state of those who die without baptism but also without personal mortal sin. Consistent with the tradition before him, Thomas associates both states with hell in the sense that they lack the beatific vision of God. Though Catherine does refer twice to the death of baptized infants (whom she assumes are saved purely through the merits of Christ), she never mentions the fate of unbaptized infants. As for the "limbo of the fathers," she refers to it three other times besides this (Let. T47, written in 1379); *Dial.* 15; 32), and in the same terms as Thomas: it is the abode of the saints who are redeemed when Christ after his death "plunders" it to give them their "full reward" for having "in truth served him." These are, for her, only the holy people of the former Jewish dispensation. When she speaks of the pagan philosophers, she consigns them to "eternal death" in spite of the continence and poverty they embraced for the sake of knowledge. She says they "could not be saved" because they did not have faith (Prayer 24, p. 209).

[6] Cf. Prayer 17, pp. 147–152, for an extended meditation on this theme.

[7] This is the only instance in which Catherine uses wings as an image of desire. Elsewhere she uses the hand of holy desire (Let. T185/DT54, vol. I; *Dial.* 155, p. 331, and 163, p. 353); but her most common image is "the arms of holy desire."

[8] This is the most detailed treatment of the fruits of virtue maturing on the body of Christ crucified. However, there is one further embellishment in Let. T354 to Pentella of Naples (1379): "He had such love for virtue that he ripened all of them in his blood. As the tree of life, he brought forth these fruits of virtue for us. For after the redemption we

and desires rise up, and with true and perfect eagerness let us receive these lovely fruits. And let our apathy be confounded because we do not wait with the same desire as our ancient ancestors.[g]

What sweet fruits are these that we should be gathering? We have[h] a real need for the fruit of true patience. In him this fruit was so mature that he was never influenced by unwillingness to suffer or by our ingratitude or inattention; no, he suffered and bore our sins on the wood of the most holy cross like one in love. And there you will find the fruit that gives life to the dead, light to those who had been blind, and health to the sick—the fruit of most holy charity. Charity was the bond that held God on the cross, for neither[i] the nails nor the cross would have been enough to hold him fastened to the cross; it was the bond of charity alone that held him. These fruits, then, are well ripened.

Let our[j] hearts hold back no longer, but let them rise up eagerly to contemplate this unspeakable love that God has had for us. If we do,[k] I tell you, there will be no devil or anyone else who can hinder our true and holy desire. For the devils run away from the heart and desire set ablaze in the fire of divine charity just as the fly retreats and doesn't land on a boiling pot—because he sees there his death, ready-made, in the scorching heat of the fire. But when the pot is lukewarm, [both fly and devil][9] hurry in, feeling right at home, and feed there. No lukewarmness, for love of God! No, let us run toward the heat of divine charity, following in the footsteps of Christ crucified. Let us enter into the wounds of Christ[l] so that we may be inspired to bear everything for him and to make a sacrifice of our bodies.[10]

I'll say no more. Provision the boat of your soul,[m] for the time is short. Keep living in God's holy love.[n]

Textual Notes

a. *b*, B: *his / God's.*

b. *b*: *we, I say / we.*

c. S2: *they rejoiced / they burned.*

d. *b*, S2: *and now / and.*

e. *and we . . . all* added in margin of Mo.

---

received in the blood, the fruits of the virtues all became of value to us for eternal life."

[9] A plural pronoun here may refer just to "the devils" above, or it may signal Catherine's inclusion now of both devils and fly.

[10] Note the paradox here: the devils find death in the heat of charity, and so do we, but in our case the death is life-giving. The reference to "sacrificing our bodies" occurs only three times, very close together chronologically, and it seems to be a reference to the proclaimed crusade.

f. *b*, S2: *you* / *he*.

g. *a*: *we do not await those desires of our ancient ancestors; let our indifference be confounded*; *b*'s correction brings sense out of the otherwise very obscure passage, making it consistent with the rest of the text.

h. *b*, S2 add *I say*.

i. *a*: [*God ... neither*], but this is clearly a copyist's error.

j. *a* has simply *hearts*; *b* adds *our*; S2 has *your hearts*.

k. *b*, S2 supply *If we do* and *there will be*.

l. *b*, S2: *his wounds* / *the wounds of Christ*.

m. S2: *your boat* / *the boat of your soul*.

n. B: *Keep living in God's holy and tender love. Gentle Jesus! Jesus love!* / *Keep ... love*.

LETTER T24/G44/DT10[1]

To Biringhieri degli Arzocchi, parish priest of Asciano

Shortly after Easter (13 April) 1376

Biringhieri degli Arzocchi was parish priest at Asciano. We know nothing of him apart from this letter to him (the tone of which indicates that Catherine is not too pleased with his behavior at the time of the writing), and the mention of him in Let. T200/DT9 (vol. I) and T208/DT6 (in this volume).

Since there are no greetings except to "the whole family" (presumably Biringhieri's congregation), it is quite likely that the letter is being written after one of the missions to Asciano, based on reports Catherine has received from the missionaries on their return (therefore, shortly after Easter). However, in the letters which definitely seem to belong to a 1372 mission, there is no indication that Biringhieri is in any particular trouble, whereas this *is* the case in Let. T208/DT6, which I have placed in late Lent of 1376. And the present letter is certainly an admonition! The linguistic evidence is broadly supportive of a 1376 placement.[2] I would, therefore, place this letter shortly after the 1376 Lenten mission of Bartolomeo Dominici and Simone da Cortona to Asciano, and so shortly after 13 April, the date of Easter that year.[3]

---

[1] MSS: Mo-*a* corrected by *b*, S2, P4, S4; translation based on Mo-*a*.

[2] Only two letters share eleven or more of this one's thirty-three analyzed patterns, and they are from mid-1375 and April 1376. Also, significant clusters of BENEDIZ, CUORDUM, and GITTODOR, as well as the patterns associated with the image of the pig rolling in the mud (LOTOINVO, PORCO), either begin or end in early 1376.

[3] Both Fawtier (II, p. 180) and Dupré Theseider place it probably about the same time as the other six letters to Asciano, which they group in a single period.

§

In the name of Christ and of gentle Mary.

My very dear and reverend father in Christ Jesus,

I Caterina, servant and slave of God's servants, am writing to commend myself to you in the precious blood of God's Son. I long to see you his true minister, following always in his footsteps. Please, please be the fragrant flower you ought to be, breathing out a sweet perfume in God's gracious presence!

You know well that flowers that stand too long in water give off a stench instead of fragrance. It really seems to me, father, that you and other ministers ought to be like flowers. But the water this flower has been put into is the wickedness and filth of sin and worldly wretchedness.[a] Oh how miserably wretched, since this man was put as a flower in holy Church, to be answerable for those in his care![4] As you know, God demands integrity and purity of such men.[5] But—oimé! Venerable father, God is finding just the opposite: not only are they themselves corrupt and putrid, but they corrupt all who come near them! Get up then! No more sleeping![6] We've slept so long we are dead to the state of grace. We have no more time; the call to judgment has been sounded and we are condemned to death.[7] Oh dearest father, give a little thought to your perilous state! In what great danger you are, drowning in this bitter sea of deadly sin! Don't we really believe that we must eventually come to the moment of death? Let's not doubt it: no one can escape it because of riches or rank! And then that poor wretched soul—who mirrors the carnal pleasures in which he wallows like a pig in mud[8]—changes from a person into an ani-

---

[4] Cf. Cavalca, *Disciplina degli spirituali*, p. 66: "Let us perseveringly turn to Christ if we have been separated from him. He is called a fragrant flower, and leads us ever along a joyful flowered path." Catherine, however, applies the image to priests and laity alike: *Dial.* 113, p. 212: "I have appointed them to be my ministers to you and have sent them like fragrant flowers into the mystic body of holy Church"; and 119, p. 223: "They grew up as fragrant flowers in the mystic body of holy Church because my ministers fearlessly gave them the correction they needed"; and 122, p. 234: "That garden was well cultivated . . . and it was adorned with an abundance of fragrant flowers, because good shepherds . . . kept their subjects from living evil lives."

[5] Cf. *Dial.* 113, p. 213: "Just as these ministers want the chalice . . . to be clean, so I demand that they themselves be clean in heart and soul and mind. And I want them to keep their bodies . . . in perfect purity."

[6] Rom. 13, 11: "It is now the hour for us to rise from sleep." (Vulg.)

[7] Cf. Franco Sacchetti, *Canzione LXVII*: "What are people happy about here; what are people boasting of; what are people dancing and singing about? For everyone is before the bugler and the sentence is being pronounced that leads us all quickly to death!"

[8] 2 Pet. 2, 22: "A sow bathes by wallowing in the mire." Cf. Augustine, *Enarratio in Ps. CXLI* (PL XXXVII, 1834): "The pig stands for the filth of forgetful stupidity." Also

mal in that putrid avarice of his![b] Many times in his greed and avarice he sells spiritual gifts and graces.[9] He becomes swollen with pride, and spends his whole life seeking honor. And what should be given to serve the poor he spends on banquets and a host of servants and well-fed horses.[10] These are the deeds that are presented at the moment of death for judgment and justice.[11,c] He thought he was acting against God, but in reality he was acting against himself. He has become his own judge, and has condemned himself, since he has made himself deserving of eternal death. Let's not be naive: it is the height of stupidity to make oneself deserving of death when one could have life.

It is up to us, then, to use the freedom we have been given to choose life or death. So I beg you as lovingly and tenderly as I can to be the sort of flower that breathes out a fragrance before God and for those in your care. Be a true shepherd, ready to give your life for your sheep.[12,d] Correct vice and strengthen the virtuous in doing good. The failure to correct causes decay just as surely as does a gangrenous organ in the human body. Keep a watchful eye on yourself and on those in your care. Don't think it harsh to root out these thorns; the fruit will be far sweeter than the effort is bitter.[13]

Oh father, consider God's ineffable love for your salvation; open your eyes and you will see his boundless blessings and gifts. Is there a greater love than to give one's life for one's friends?[14] How much more deserving of praise is the One who gave his life for his enemies![15]

Cavalca, *Trattato dello Spirito Santo*, p. 78: "Human dignity resides in this gift of understanding, in which we are made in the image and likeness of God. So whoever loses this gift becomes like a beast. This is why the psalmist says [Ps. 49, 21], 'Human beings, for all their honor, are without understanding, so they are like brute beasts.' "

[9] Catherine rails against simony in a number of places in *The Dialogue*, for example, chapters 113, 119, 121, and especially 127.

[10] There are similar descriptions in *Dial.* 113, 121, 127. Catherine often uses these "well-fed horses" as a tangible symbol of greed. Cf. also Giordano da Rivalto, *Prediche inedite*, ed. Narducci, p. 319: "You would see these bishops with fat stallions. Their many ladies are well-dressed, and they care nothing for the poor." Cavalca, *Specchio di croce*, p. 99, puts this rebuke into the mouth of Christ: "What I won with my nailed hands you spend and squander with evil crowds. What I won hanging naked on the cross you spend on a bed and fancy clothes. What I won in disgrace and torment you eat up in disordered priorities." And a bit further on: "Like gentlemen they want big horses for hawking, and to be at grand parties."

[11] Catherine describes the sinner's death in detail in *Dial.* 132, pp. 266–271.

[12] Jn. 10, 11.

[13] This would seem to support Bartolomeo Dominici's complaints about the wickedness of the people in Asciano (cf. Let. T204/DT5 to him, in this volume).

[14] Jn. 15, 13.

[15] Rom. 5, 7–8: "It is rare that anyone should lay down his life for a just person, though it is barely possible that for a good person someone may have the courage to die. It is

So let our hearts be on the defensive no longer, but let hardness be driven out and let these hearts not be stone forever.[16] Let that binding chain be broken with which the devil so often keeps us bound. The power of holy desire, scorn for vice and love for virtue, will break all these bonds. Fall in love with true virtue: its effect is the opposite of that of vice, because sin brings bitterness while virtue brings sweetness and even in this life a foretaste of the next. When the sweet hour of death comes, the virtue we have lived answers for us and shields us from God's judgment. It gives security and drives out confusion. It leads us into everlasting life, where we possess life without death, health without sickness, riches without poverty, honor without shame, dominion without slavery. There all are sovereigns, and the smaller we have been in this life, the greater we will be in the next. But the greater we would have liked to be in this life, the smaller we will be in the next.[17]

So be small in deep and genuine humility. Look at God, who lowered himself to your humanity. Don't make yourself unworthy of what God has made you worthy of—I mean the precious blood of his Son, by which you were ransomed with such blazing love.[18] We are ransomed servants;[19] we can no longer sell ourselves. But when we are in deadly sin we do blindly sell ourselves to the devil. I beg you, for love of Christ crucified: let's get out of such slavery! I'll say no more, but let me tell you this much: my own sins are numberless. So I promise you that I will take both mine and yours and make of them a bundle of myrrh which I will keep in my breast with constant bitter weeping.[20] This sort of bitterness,

---

precisely in this that God proves his love for us: that while we were still sinners Christ died for us."

[16] Cf. Ez. 11, 19: "I will remove the stony heart from their bodies, and replace it with a natural heart." The same image occurs in Ez. 36, 26.

[17] Mt. 23, 11–12.

[18] Cf. *Dial.* 71, p. 133: "I look not to her unworthiness but to my worth, and so make her worthy to receive me."

[19] 1 Pet. 1, 18-19: "You were ransomed not with corruptible gold or silver ... but with the precious blood of Christ, the spotless Lamb"; 1 Cor. 7, 23: "You have been bought with a price; do not make yourselves slaves to human beings." (Vulg.)

[20] Cf. Sg. 1, 13: "My beloved is a bundle of myrrh to rest in my bosom." (Vulg.) Pseudo-Bernardus, *Vitis mystica*, ch. IV (PL CLXXXIV, 647) interprets the bundle of myrrh as the coalescence of the human passions. Albert the Great, *Sermones de tempore*, XIII, I, i, 20, calls the Passion of Christ "the bundle of myrrh which every Christian should keep in the chamber of his or her heart." Catherine, however, here associates the bitter-tasting myrrh with sin. Cf. Let. T321 to the Company of the Virgin at La Scala Hospital (autumn of 1378): "[Grace] gives us the milk of divine sweetness, along with the bitter myrrh of the cross and of sorrow over God's having been offended." Also Let. T313 to Onorato Gaetano (also autumn of 1378), where the myrrh is simply "the bitterness of the cross, that is, of the sufferings borne by God's Son."

based on true charity, will bring us to the real sweetness and consolation of everlasting life.

Forgive my presumption and arrogance. Give the whole family my greetings and bless them in Christ Jesus. I pray that he will grant you his sweet eternal benediction, and that it may be so strong as to break and shatter all the bonds that would take you away from him.

Keep living in God's holy love.

Textual Notes

a. *b*: *But this flower, when it is put into the water ... gives forth not fragrance but stench.*

b. *b*: *Oh how poor and wretched that soul will be! Then that soul who like a mirror ... mud, so that this rational creature becomes a brute animal wallowing still in his putrid avarice.*

c. *b* adds *before that unfortunate soul.*

d. *b* adds *if necessary.*

LETTER T223/G28[1]
To Cardinal Iacopo Orsini
April 1376, perhaps shortly after Easter, 13 April

This letter is clearly related to Let. T101/DT23, also written to Cardinal Orsini. The fact that in the present letter Catherine refers to the cardinal's falling "again" into the same sorts of faults to which she referred in Let. T101/DT23 leads me to suppose that the present letter is a bit later than that one, which I have placed in Lent of 1376, probably in the latter half of March or very early April.[2] Since this letter dwells more on the theme of Christ as mediator than on his passion as such, it could very possibly be from shortly after Easter, 13 April. The linguistic evidence would support such a placement.[3]

---

[1] MSS: B, P2, P1, H, P3, P5, F2, V, P4; translation based on B, with reference to V, H.

[2] See the notes to Let. T101/DT23 for further details both of this history and of the linguistic evidence for the two letters.

[3] All four of the letters which share eighteen or more of this letter's sixty-nine analyzed patterns range from very late 1375 to early April 1376, and it shares by far most heavily with Let. T177, which I have placed in Holy Week of that year. Placing this letter in the second half of April would be supported by a number of significant clusters within individual patterns: ARREND, ONORFADP, PLACIRA, PROPPIAC, SENSRAG.

§

In the name of Jesus Christ crucified and of gentle Mary.

Dearest and very loved father in Christ Jesus,

I Caterina, servant and slave[a] of the servants of Jesus Christ, am writing to you in his precious blood. I long to see you set up as a strong and steady pillar of support[4] within the garden of holy Church because of all the contrary winds that are blowing. If such a pillar were not of stone and well-grounded it would fall.[5] Its foundation has to be dug deep. If it were shallow, the pillar would be weak. Oh father in Christ Jesus! You are a pillar set in humility, a humility that is learned in true self-knowledge.[6]

It is through lack of self-knowledge that people fall into pride, for if they knew their own nothingness they would not be proud. No, whatever being we have, we have received from God alone. We never asked God to create us. He was moved by the fire of his divine charity, by his love for his creatures. Seeing us within himself, he fell in love with our beauty, with the work of his own hands.[7] Bit by bit, as we look within ourselves, we come to[b] discover God's goodness, and we grow in such a fire of love that we can no longer love or desire anything but God alone, in whom we have found such boundless goodness. We see that within us is the stone that held up the standard of the most holy cross—for except for the force of God's love[c] for us, the stone[d] could never have held [the cross] nor could the nails[e] have held [Christ] fast.[8] I remember this being said once to one of his servants. She in her boundless desire said, "Oh my Lord,

---

[4] Literally, "to nurture" (*a notricare*). Catherine often uses the pillar as an image for members of the hierarchy.

[5] Cf. Mt. 7, 24–27, the parable of the house built on a rock.

[6] Cf. Let. T113 to Bandeçça Salimbeni (in this volume), where it is the soul, imaged as a tree, which must be set in the soil of humility: "[I]f this worker, free choice, plants the tree [of the soul] where it ought to be planted, that is, in the soil of true humility (for it should not put it on the mountain of pride, but in the valley of humility), then it will produce fragrant blossoms of virtue, especially that topmost blossom of glory and praise for God's name. . . . I want to tell in what field this sort of soil is, so that you'll not make a mistake. The soil is true humility, as I've said, and the place you'll find it is the enclosed garden of self-knowledge."

[7] Cf. Let. T28/DT17 to Bernabò Visconti (vol. I): "Ponder the fact that you were loved before ever you loved. For God looked within himself and fell in love with the beauty of his creature and so created us. He was moved by the fire of his ineffable charity to one purpose only: that we should have eternal life and enjoy the infinite good God was enjoying in himself."

[8] Cf. *Dial.* 14, p. 52; 77, p. 143; Prayer 24, p. 207. Catherine may have encountered the concept in Cavalca's *Specchio di croce*, p. 41: "No bond of iron could have held Christ nailed or bound—only charity, the bond of perfection." Other writers of the time use it as well, for example, Ludolphus de Saxonia and Feo Belcari.

what grace it would have been for me if I had been some of the stone or soil in which your cross was set, for I would have received some of your blood that flowed down from the cross!" Gentle First Truth answered, "My dearest daughter, you *were* the stone that held me, you and everyone else—I mean my love for you—for nothing else could have held me."[f]

Shame then on those wretchedly proud hearts, given up completely to the miserable crass things of this dark life, to worldly grandeur, prestige, and pleasure! Such people make their foundation so very shallow with self-centeredness, because they are unwilling to endure weariness or to keep to the way of disgrace and lowliness and voluntary poverty that the good gentle Jesus walked. I tell you, dearest brother,[9] such [pillars] will not last. Any slightest wind will topple them because their foundation, their motivating love, is set in what is empty, flimsy, as passing[g] as the wind.

It is clear that nothing has any stability of itself, except God. As for life, it fails. We go from life to death, from health to illness, from honor to shame, from wealth to poverty. Everything is passing.[h] Oh how foolish to devote one's whole energy to such things! People invest their energy there because they love themselves with a sensual love; they love whatever agrees with that puny sensual aspect of themselves rather than loving themselves reasonably, with a love grounded in virtue. For if they did love themselves reasonably, they would love whatever else they love reasonably and virtuously, and not for the sensual pleasure of selfish love, for worldly pleasure and delight, set on pleasing themselves and other people rather than God. And if they did fail they would lose nothing, nor would they suffer any pain, because that is not where their love is.

For pain afflicts only those who love apart from God; but no pain afflicts those whose priorities are God's, who love themselves and everything else[i] within the reasonableness of true knowledge grounded in their Creator. They see clearly that God does nothing—neither gives nor takes anything, spiritually or materially—except to make us holy.[10] And then, with this light and with the knowledge they have acquired of themselves and of God's goodness and boundless charity, they humble themselves, digging out a foundation of self-hatred and self-contempt.[11] There is born within them a willingness to bear any pain, injury, scorn, or abuse they might suffer; they are happy to suffer pain when they reflect that they have been rebels against their Creator.[12]

---

[9] This is the only instance in which Catherine addresses a member of the hierarchy as "brother."

[10] Cf. 1 Thes. 4, 3.

[11] Cf. *Dial.* 63, pp. 118–120, for Catherine's concept of self-contempt. She does not say that one should hate the self created by God, but only the sin that does violence to that self.

[12] That is, pain as punishment for sin.

Once they have dug their foundation, they become strong and stable stone set on the rock, Christ Jesus, and made firm there by following in his footsteps.[13] They cannot love or want or find pleasure in anything except what God loves, and they hate what God hates. And then they receive so much pleasure, strength, and consolation that nothing at all, no devil or anyone else, can weaken them or cause them any bitterness—because where God is, is all good. Let our heart never again be drawn away from such love! No more carelessness or foolishness! For me, follow the slain Lamb, opened up on the wood of the most holy cross. Otherwise, dearest father, you who are a pillar set up to help and sustain the bride of this Lamb in whatever way you can. . . .[14] You are there not because of your own goodness but[j] because of his, so that you might give him the honor, and give your best efforts to your neighbors. Be, oh be one who eats and savors souls—for that was his food.

You are very aware that after we lost grace because of our first father's[k] sin, the eternal Father's will was not being realized in us. He had created us for no other destiny but to experience and enjoy his beauty, everlasting life without death, and this will of his was not being realized. Moved by the same fire of love with which he created us, he wants to show that it is for no other destiny he has created[l] us, and he finds a way to realize this will of his. In love he gives us the Word, his only-begotten Son, and in his person punishes our weakness and sin.[15,m] *Oh sweet fire of love! You strike one blow. You punish sin in your own person by suffering your passion and death, saturating yourself with disgrace and shame and dishonor in order to give us back the honor we lost because of our sin. And with the same blow you placate your Father's wrath. By taking the sentence on yourself for me, you make up for the offense done to your eternal Father. So have you made peace out of the great war.*[16] That dear Paul, so in love, really spoke the truth: that Christ is our peace and our mediator.[17] For he was the instrument of peace between God and humanity.[18] This, then, is the sweet and tender way God used to give us the destiny for which he created us. He revealed it in what he did and in its effect—not only in that he did it, but that he continues to do it, showing us tremendous signs of love.

---

[13] Cf. 1 Pet. 2, 4: "Come to [Christ], a living stone."

[14] There seems to be a lacuna in the manuscripts here, since the sentence as it stands has no predicate. Aldo and Gigli in their respective editions propose their own additions to complete the sense, but neither has any real basis in the text itself as it has come to us.

[15] This concept is developed in *Dial.* 21, p. 58; Let. T204/DT5, T177/DT61 (both in this volume); Prayer 13, p. 112.

[16] The concept occurs elsewhere, for example, *Dial.* 13, p. 50; Prayer 1, p. 17.

[17] Col. 1, 20–22.

[18] Cf. 1 Tim. 2, 5.

All of this you will discover if you will look within yourself, because all of it has been done for you. Let the city of your soul surrender—surrender to fire if to nothing else![19] Oimé! Oimé! Sleep no longer, you and the other champions of holy Church! Stop attending merely to these passing things, but be concerned about the salvation of souls. For you see that the devil never stops devouring the little sheep that were bought back at so dear a price,[n] and all because of the poor care of their shepherds, who have become devourers of souls![20]

Pay attention to us, for love of God! With our[o] dear Christ on earth do what you can about seeing to the appointment of good pastors and administrators. *Oh God, Love!* Don't make us[p] and God's other servants keep dying of heartbreak! No, be concerned enough to do what you can to show that you are hungry for God's honor and the salvation of souls—and not only for the Christian people but for the unbelievers as well.[21] Beg Christ on earth to raise the standard of the most holy cross against them soon. And don't be afraid of any war or scandal that may come, but take action courageously. That will be the way to achieve peace. I beg you, for love of Christ crucified: take hold of the war you are waging with these rotten members who are rebelling against their head,[q] and beg the holy father to be decisive about seeking reconciliation and peace with them.[22] For if you can have peace by using the means demanded for the good of holy Church, that is better than using war. Yes, they have done us wrong, but in spite of that, we have to discern what is the greater good. I am begging you in this regard as strongly as I can, so that later we may be able to go bravely to give our lives for Christ.

I'll say no more. Be a strong pillar, strengthened and stabilized on the strong rock, Christ. Keep living in God's holy and tender love. Forgive my audacity in presuming to write to you. Let my love for the sweet bride of Christ Jesus and for our salvation[r] be my excuse.[s]

Jesus! Gentle Jesus![t]

---

[19] That is, to the fire of love.

[20] Cf. Let. T2 to Andrea dei Vitroni (1378): "The people I've been speaking of become cruel to themselves once they have become the devils' companions. They are living with the devils before it is time! And they show the same cruelty to others because they are bereft of charity's love for their neighbors. They are not guardians but devourers of souls, for they personally put souls into the clutches of the infernal wolf."

[21] It is clear from this that Catherine sees the projected crusade as a means of converting the unbelievers. She has no idea of the violent outrages the crusades actually involve.

[22] The reference is to the Italian republics which have rebelled against the papacy.

Textual Notes

a. V: *sichiama / schiava*, clearly a scribal error.

b. P2: [*come to*].

c. From other manuscripts; B: *heart* (*cuore*) / *love* (*amore*).

d. P4: *compassion* (*pieta*) / *stone* (*pietra*).

e. P5: *stone / nails*.

f. P1, H, P3, P5, P4 add *the God-Man*.

g. P2: [*flimsy*]; P1, H, P3, P5, P4, V add *and transitory*.

h. P4, H, P3, P5, P4, V add *and runs away*.

i. P5: *those whose priorities are Christ's and who love everything in themselves / those . . . everything else*.

j. P2, P4, H, P3, P5: *but only / but*.

k. P2: *the first man's*; P1: *our first parent's / our first father's*.

l. P2, H, P3, P5, P4: *made / created*.

m. V: *he laid our weakness and sin on him / in . . . sin*.

n. P5: *by such sweet blood / at . . . price*.

o. P3: *your / our*.

p. B, P2, P3, P5, V: *yourselves / us*, but this is almost surely an error.

q. P5: *their head and ours / their head*.

r. P2: [*Jesus and for our salvation*]; P1, H, P3, P5, V: *Jesus Christ / Christ Jesus*.

s. P5 adds: *I'll say no more. Keep living in the holy and tender love of the good gentle Jesus. Amen*.

t. From V.

Letter T211/G88/DT70[1]
To Frate Raimondo da Capua, in Avignon
Late April 1376

Both the rubric and her reference to impatience for the pope to act make it clear that Catherine is writing this letter when she is certain that Raimondo will be in Avignon to receive it. (She was already aware of his arrival there when she wrote T219/DT65 to him in early April.) It is also clear that Catherine herself is not yet in Avignon. The level of Catherine's own agitation could indicate that she is very near her departure for the papal court. Like a number of other letters from the first four months of 1376, this one contains the admonition not to fear what may yet happen. It also seems to imply that something bad has already happened—though here it seems to be a matter of Raimondo's personal life. I would therefore guess that Catherine is writing this letter in late April, while she is still in Siena.[2]

---

[1] MSS: B, P2, H, P1, S1, P5, F2, P3, P4; translation based on B as edited by Dupré Theseider, with reference to H. Relevant variants (other than H) based on Dupré Theseider.

[2] Linguistically this letter shares most with others dated between February and April 1376, including four of the five which share fifteen or more of its fifty-one analyzed patterns. Moreover, a number of significant clusters within individual patterns begin or end or are concentrated in those months: AGNELCON, CARCONFU, EBBRAMOR, GODPENA, ODORVIRT, POTERE, RIBELSP. Fawtier (II, p. 195) places the letter in April or May, but "more probably in May." Dupré Theseider places it between early May and Catherine's arrival in Avignon.

§

In the name of Jesus Christ crucified and of gentle Mary.

My revered father in Christ Jesus,

I Caterina, servant and slave of the servants of Jesus Christ, am writing to you in his precious blood. I long to see you and the rest of my children clothed in the wedding garment that covers all our sin and[a] nakedness.[3] This is a suit of armor that does not let the blows of our enemy the devil mortally wound us,[4,b] and it gets stronger rather than weaker with each blow of temptation or harassment from the devil or other people or our own flesh (which would like to rebel against the spirit[5]). Not only are these blows not injurious, I say, but they will be precious stones and pearls set onto this garment of blazing charity.

Now what sort of soul would refuse to endure any difficulty or temptation, from whatever source or in whatever way God would send it? Such a soul would have no proven virtue, for virtue is proved by its opposite.[6] How is purity proved, and how is it learned? Through its opposite, that is, the temptation to impurity. For an impure person wouldn't need to be molested by impure thoughts. But if it seems that our will no longer consents to what is perverse, and is purified of every stain by a true holy desire to please our Creator, then the devil, the world, and the flesh *will* harass us. So opposites always drive each other out. See [for another example] how humility is learned because of pride. When we see ourselves pestered by the vice of pride we humble ourselves, recognizing that we *are* sinful and proud. Were it not for this temptation, we would not come to know ourselves so well. Once we have humbled ourselves and seen what we are, we conceive such a contempt [for ourselves] that we are happy and glad for any pain or injustice we might suffer. Such people are like courageous knights. They do not avoid the blows, but even consider themselves unworthy of what seems to them—and is—a very great grace: to bear pain, temptation, and harassment for Christ crucified. All of this comes from their contempt for themselves and the love they have conceived for virtue.

---

[3] Cf. 1 Pt. 4, 8: "for love covers a multitude of sins."

[4] Cf. *Dial.* 77, p. 143: "This is a suit of armor that keeps blows from piercing them through if only they do not take off the armor and let go of the knife and give it into the hands of their enemies."

[5] Cf. Rom. 7, 21–23.

[6] This concept is more fully developed in *Dial.* 8, pp. 38–39, and 98, pp. 184–186. It is found also, a bit differently developed, in Cavalca, *Medicina del cuore*, p. 206: "The stronger opposition and the more provocation it has, the greater the virtue." Also *Trenta stoltizie*, p. 13: "Briefly, we must resist every vice with its opposite, not nourish it with what is like it; for, as one holy father says, no one resists the heat very well by putting on winter clothes."

You see, then, that we must not complain or run away in time of darkness, because out of the darkness is born the light.[7] *Oh God, tender love, what sweet teaching you give us—that virtue is learned through what is contrary to it!*[c] Because of impatience, patience is acquired, for people who are conscious of [their own] impatience become patient because of what they suffer. They are impatient with [their] impatience,[d] more sad that they are sad at all than for anything else. And so out of opposites we come to learn perfection without even noticing it. We discover that we have become perfect in the midst of storms and temptations. And there is no other way one can ever arrive at the port of perfection. So reflect on this: we cannot receive or even desire virtue unless we have desires and harassment and temptation to suffer with true holy patience for love of Christ crucified. We must, then, be happy and glad in time of struggle, temptation, and darkness, since they are the source of so much virtue and joy.

Oimé, son given me by that sweet mother Mary![8] I don't want you to yield to weariness or confusion, no matter what may trouble your spirit. No, I want you to keep the good, holy, and true faithful will that I know God in his mercy[e] has given you. I know you would rather die than offend him mortally. So I want you to gain knowledge of yourself, without confusion, from the darkness. And from your good will I want you to gain knowledge of God's infinite goodness and boundless charity. In such knowledge may your soul live and grow fat. Realize that in his love God preserves your good will and doesn't let it run with consent and pleasure after the devil's suggestions. So it is in love that he has permitted you and me and his other servants all these temptations and illusions from the devil, from other people, and from our own flesh, simply to rouse us from our indifference and bring us to a real sense of responsibility, true humility, and blazing charity. This humility comes from self-knowledge, and this charity from knowledge of God's goodness. And there the soul becomes drunk and consumed with love.

Be glad, father; celebrate! Without any slavish fear, take courage. Don't be afraid, no matter what has happened, no matter what you see coming. Take courage, for perfection is very accessible. Answer the devil by telling him it is not *my* doing that virtue has been at work in you, because it was not in me. It was the doing of grace, of God's infinite compassion and

---

[7] In Let. T270 (in this volume) she will write analogously to Gregory XI: "Don't be afraid when you see all these trials and troubles; take heart in Christ gentle Jesus. For the rose is being born among the thorns, and from among all these persecutions will come the reform of holy Church, light to relieve Christians of darkness, life for the unbelievers, and the raising of the holy cross."

[8] She refers to Raimondo in the same terms in Let. T226 (in this volume) and T373 (15 February 1380).

mercy.[9] So in Christ crucified you can do anything.[10] Do everything you do with lively faith. And don't be surprised at anything that might come along apparently in opposition to what you are doing.

Take courage, take courage, because gentle First Truth has promised to fulfill your own and my desire for you. In burning desire give yourself unsparingly with the Lamb who was consumed in his unsparing gift of himself. Find your rest on the cross with Christ crucified; find your joy in Christ crucified; find your joy in suffering. Satiate yourself with humiliation for Christ crucified. Engraft your heart and your affection onto the tree of the most holy cross with Christ crucified, and in his wounds make your home.[11]

Forgive me, the cause and instrument of all your pain and imperfection (for were I an instrument of virtue, you and the others would be experiencing its fragrance). I don't say these things to cause you pain—for your pain would be mine. I only want you and my other children to have pity on my wretchedness. I firmly believe and trust that the Holy Spirit will graciously put an end to all that is not within God's will.

Think of it! Here I am, poor wretch, living in my body, yet in desire constantly outside my body! *Oimé! Good gentle Jesus! I am dying and cannot die!* I am bursting and cannot burst[12] because of my desire for the renewal of holy Church, for God's honor, and for everyone's salvation—and my desire to see you and the others clothed in purity, and set afire, consumed in his blazing charity. Tell Christ on earth not to make me wait

---

[9] While the reference to perfection makes it likely that Catherine is referring to something in Raimondo's own spiritual life, the references to his activity might point also to external events in Avignon.

[10] Cf. Phil. 4, 13.

[11] This is the only instance in which Catherine explicitly joins the image of engrafting with that of dwelling within Christ's wounds. But cf. Let. T27 to Abbot Martino of Passignano (vol. I), where the image of clothing is so joined: "This Word made an engrafting on the wood of the holy cross and bathed us in his precious blood, making the true solid virtues sprout as flowers and fruits. The bonding of love accomplished all this. This warm, shining, engaging love ripened the fruits of virtue, drawing all the bitterness out of them—all because of the engrafting of the divine Word into human nature and of the Word to the wood of the most holy cross. . . . But I tell you, even with all this exquisitely sweet bonding, we do not and cannot share in grace unless we clothe ourselves, through the movement of love, in the crucified love of God's Son, by following in the footsteps of Christ crucified. For we sterile and completely fruitless trees have to be joined with Christ gentle Jesus, the fruitful tree, as I've said."

[12] Catherine uses this expression often. There are similar expressions in Giovanni Colombini, for example, Let. XVIII: "You can imagine the pain and torture this poor thing lives in—he lives dying"; Let. CIII: "I am dying of love for Jesus Christ and for holy charity, and I don't know what to do with myself"; Let. LXXVII "I cannot think of Christ my joy without bursting and dying."

any longer.[13] When I see it happen I shall sing with that dear old Simeon, "Now, Lord, you can let your servant go in peace, according to your word."[14]

I'll say no more, for if I followed my inclination, I'd begin all over again!

Let me see and sense that you are all so bound, so nailed to the cross with Christ gentle Jesus, that neither the devil nor anyone else will ever be able to free you from so sweet and pleasant a bond. Love, love, love one another! Keep living in God's holy and tender love.

Gentle Jesus! Jesus love!

Textual Notes

a. H: [*sin and*].

b. P2: *take us prisoner or mortally wound / mortally wound.*

c. *that* . . . *it* taken from P3, lacking in B, P2; H: . . . *teaching do you give us? That virtue.* . . .

d. H, P2: [*become* . . . *impatience*].

e. P2: *holy mercy / mercy.*

[13] In Let. T219/DT65, earlier in the same month of April, she has written to Raimondo: "Beg divine Goodness and Christ on earth to hurry," urging the pope's speedy return to Rome.

[14] Lk. 2, 29 (Vulg.). Catherine cites it in Latin, probably because of her familiarity with the canticle from its daily occurrence in Vespers of the liturgical office.

LETTER T187/G60[1]
To Don Giovanni dei Sabbatini of Bologna and Don Taddeo dei Malavolti of Siena, Carthusian monks of Belriguardo
Late April 1376

The Carthusian monastery of Belriguardo, founded by Niccolò Cinughi not long before Catherine's birth, was about three miles northwest of Siena. Catherine had written to Don Giovanni there while she was in Pisa in the summer of 1375 (Let. T141/DT38, vol. I), and in that letter seems to have been encouraging the monk to prepare to join the projected crusade. The present letter refers to some command of a superior which Giovanni and Taddeo are apparently resisting. Perhaps Catherine's remarks about embracing the cross in their cells is an indication that the two have been told they cannot go on crusade but must remain in their monastery.

Linguistic evidence supports the placement of this letter sometime after Catherine's return to Siena from Pisa and Lucca.[2] Also, the letter admonishes Giovanni and Taddeo not to be afraid of what may happen, an admonition which occurs in a number of other letters from the first four months of 1376. This, as well as the subject matter of the letter and the place to which it is addressed, lead me to place it not long before Catherine's departure for Florence and Avignon in May. Very possibly, since it has so much in common linguistically and thematically with T211/DT70 to Raimondo da Capua, it was written about the same time as that letter—that is, about late April 1376.[3]

---

[1] MSS: B, P2, S7, H, P1, P2, P5, F2, P3, V; translation based on S7 (from an unpublished transcription by A. Volpato), with reference to H, V for protocol only.

[2] The two letters which share fourteen or more of its forty-two analyzed patterns are from May 1376 and (a very long one) from 1377. Several patterns do not occur at all before February 1376 (CONTRAR, CUORLIBE, GODPENA, SALUPERF, SENZPENA). Further, significant clusters of CONTRAR and VESTCRUC respectively begin in April 1376 and end in September of the same year.

[3] Fawtier (II, p. 188) and Dupré Theseider (unpublished notes) decline to date this letter.

§

Dearest sons in Christ Jesus,[a]

I Caterina, servant and slave of the servants of Jesus Christ, am writing to you in his precious blood, longing to see you courageous knights completely free of slavish fear. This is what our[b] gentle Savior wants: that we fear him, and not worldly people. Thus he said, "Do not be afraid of those who can kill the body, but of me, who can send soul and body to hell."[4] I want you therefore to be immersed[c] in the blood of God's Son, set ablaze in the fire of divine charity, because there you will lose all slavish fear and keep only reverential fear.

Now what can the world or the devil and his servants[d] do to those who live in this immeasurable love, who have the blood as their focus?[5] Nothing! In fact, they are instrumental in giving us virtue, in proving virtue in us, since virtue is proved through its opposite.[6] So we ought to be happy and glad, and in our suffering always look for Christ crucified, and humble and abase ourselves for him, finding constant joy in suffering and in the cross. If you want suffering you will have joy, and if you want joy you will have suffering.[7]

So it is better to immerse ourselves in the blood and to kill our perverse wills with a heart generous toward our Creator and with no pity for ourselves. Then your joy and happiness will be complete.[8] You will wait without crippling weariness.[9] No command we have been given ought to cause us pain but rather delight, for there is no command of human origin that could deprive us of God. On the contrary, these commands are occa-

---

[4] Cf. Lk. 12, 4–5: "Do not be afraid of those who kill the body and after that can do no more. I will show you whom you should fear: fear him who after he has killed has the power to send to Gehenna." (Vulg.)

[5] It. *obietto.*

[6] Cf. *Dial.* 8, pp. 38–39, for the development of this notion so central in Catherine's thought.

[7] The idea here is often reiterated by Catherine, but nowhere else so concisely. Cf., for example, *Dial.* 68, p. 129: If a soul "runs only after pleasure in her own way rather than mine, she will experience pain and unbearable confusion when the object of her delight, as her mind sees it, seems to be taken away."

[8] The change from first person to second is Catherine's.

[9] Catherine often contrasts "crippling" (*affliggitiva*) pain, that is, pain which does one no good because it is not received with willingness to be acted upon by God and to be joined with the sufferings of Christ, with "fattening" (*ingrassativa*) pain. The latter "fattens" because it is "eaten at the table of the cross." Cf. Let. T359 to Leonardo Frescobaldi (1378): "Oh dearest will [of God]! . . . You relieve us of all spiritually crippling pain and fatten us in the fragrance of virtue. You clothe us in the wedding garment that is the fire of divine charity, and you make us eat the food that is God's honor and the salvation of souls at the table of the cross."

sions for giving us the virtue of patience. They make us more conscientious about hastening to our cell to embrace the tree of the cross,[e] to seek there the unseen vision that cannot be taken away from us.[10] For affection and charity are never lost unless we so choose. What sweet joy it would be to be persecuted for the sake of Christ crucified! This is where I want you to find your joy, no matter how God may give you the cross—not choosing to have it your way but as he would have it who gives it to you, considering yourself unworthy of so great a grace as to be persecuted for the sake of Christ crucified.[11]

Realize, my dear sons in Christ Jesus, that this is the way of the saints who followed the path of Christ. There is no other path that would lead us to life.[f] And this is why I want you to make every effort to follow this lovely straight path conscientiously and with a holy contempt for yourselves. Bring to the holy place of prayer whatever wholesome zeal and perseverance the Holy Spirit offers you. Do not shun or avoid prayer even if it should cost you your life. Never relax out of self-indulgence or pity for your body, for the devil wants nothing more than to rob us of prayer, whether out of self-pity or softness or spiritual weariness. So we must not let any of these things make us relax in our practice of prayer. Rather let us dispel the devil's suggestions and our own self-indulgence with the thought of God's goodness and the recognition of our own sinfulness. Hide yourselves in the wounds of Christ crucified. Love one another for the sake of Christ crucified.[g] Don't be afraid of what may happen. You will be able to do all things through Christ crucified, who will be within you and who will strengthen you.[12]

Be obedient even to the point of death in whatever you may be commanded to do, no matter how burdensome. Don't forego the fruit in order to avoid the effort—even though the devil may make you feel like evading this thing or that under pretext of virtue, saying: "What I had[13] was my soul's consolation, and helped me to grow in virtue." Don't believe him. But have confidence and believe that whatever God was giving you before through that consolation he will give you simply by himself, in his good-

---

[10] This "unseen vision" (*visio invisibile*) occurs in only one other letter, T200/DT9 to Bartolomeo Dominici (vol. I): "I will be at your side, never leaving you, with that invisible presence which the Holy Spirit makes possible." In the present case, the reference is probably to the experience of mystical prayer.

[11] Since in Let. T141/DT38 she seems to have been encouraging Niccolò to prepare to join the crusade (that is, "take the cross"), the command in question here could be that he remain in his monastery. If that is the case, Catherine is now encouraging him and Taddeo to "take the cross" that is offered in that command of their superiors.

[12] Cf. Phil. 4, 13: "I can do all things in the one who strengthens me."

[13] It. *Questa*, which I take to refer to whatever is being threatened by the command they are tempted to evade.

ness. You know very well that not a leaf falls from a tree without his providence. In the same way, whatever he may permit the devil or anyone else to do to us is done with his providence, either because it is necessary for our salvation or to help us grow in perfection. So I want you to hold it in reverence.

Also, strip your heart and affections of material things apart from what you really need. Clothe yourselves in Christ crucified and immerse yourselves in his blood. There you will find perfect joy and peace.

I'll say no more. Keep living in the holy faith of the dear God. Love, love, love one another!

Jesus, gentle Jesus![h]

Textual Notes

a. B, P2, H include standard opening invocation: *In the name of Jesus Christ crucified and of gentle Mary*. V, however, does not have it, and in regard to opening and closing protocols, Volpato has shown V to be more probably closer to the original form. H: *in Christ gentle Jesus / in . . . Jesus.*

b. H, P2: *your / our.*

c. P1: *lambs / immersed.*

d. H: *scorn / servants.*

e. Tommasèo: [*of the cross*].

f. V: *eternal life / life.*

g. V: *Love . . . crucified*, but this is clearly a copyist's error.

h. Closing from V; others have: *Keep living, etc. Love, love one another. Gentle Jesus! Jesus love!*

Letter T4/G64[1]
To an Imprisoned Carthusian Monk
Late April to early May 1376

Thirteen letters survive from Catherine's correspondence with members of Carthusian monasteries.[2]

During her lifetime there were three such monasteries near Siena: Maggiano, Pontignano (where Stefano Maconi would, after Catherine's death, enter the order and eventually become prior), and Belriguardo. Let. T287 (in this volume) is addressed to Pietro di Viva of the Maggiano monastery, and T39 (vol. I) to Giacomo Tondi of Pontignano. We know from Raimondo da Capua that the prior of Belriguardo, Dom Cristoforo, confided in Catherine on at least one occasion.[3] This was in Siena, during the period when Raimondo "had just begun to know something of Catherine . . . ," therefore somewhere between Raimondo's coming to Siena in late June of 1374 and the journey to Pisa in February of 1375. At least three of her letters (T141/DT38, vol. I; T169, written in early 1378; and T187 in this volume) were addressed to monks at Belriguardo.

It was probably during her stay in Pisa in 1375 that Catherine came to know Dom Bartolomeo Serafini, the prior of the newly-founded Carthusian monastery on the island of Gorgona off the Tyrrhenian coast southwest of that city. Sometime during the warm season of 1375 she visited there at his request and over time she directed at least three letters to Gorgona (T150, T154, and T323, all written in late 1378 or 1379).

Let. T189/DT84 and T246/DT85 (both in this volume) are addressed to the monastery at Cervaia near Genoa, Let. T315 and T331 (1378 to 1379) to Dom Pietro da Milano, Let. T201 (1378) to a Carthusian at Rome, and Let. T335 (in this volume) to Dom Cristoforo while he was at the Carthusian monastery of San Martino in Naples. And she directed one letter (T55, in this volume) to the general of the order, Dom Guillaume Raynaud, at the Grande Chartreuse in France.[4]

Only the present letter among those to Carthusians remains unidentified by either name or place. Given Catherine's relationship with the

---

[1] MSS. Mo, S2, P4, Pa; translation based on Mo-*a*, corrected by *b*. Other relevant variants based on an unpublished transcription by A. Volpato.

[2] For an extended commentary on Catherine's relationship with the Carthusians see A. Baglioni, "S. Caterina da Siena e l'Ordine della Certosa," *Quaderni cateriniani: Inquadramenti storici* 9, Rome, 1975, pp. 65–107.

[3] *Life*, II, xii, pp. 293–297. The prior had come seeking to confer with Catherine on "an urgent question of conscience."

[4] There is also a non-extant letter to Guillaume, referred to by Stefano Maconi in a letter reproduced in the Laurent edition of the *Processo Castellano*, pp. 256–257, n. 1.

priors of Belriguardo and Gorgona, it is not unlikely that the imprisoned monk she addresses here may be at one of those two monasteries, especially since the linguistic evidence of the text places it during a period when Catherine is in close contact with both places.[5] If the monk in question is at Gorgona, the letter may be contemporary with T221 (in this volume), addressed to Suor Bartholomea in Pisa.

Since the Carthusians lived a quasi-eremitical life, coming together even among themselves only for certain community exercises, it is hardly to be supposed that this monk is in a civil prison. The Carthusian rule, as most other monastic rules of the time, punished certain serious offenses by isolation in a "prison" cell within the confines of the monastery, and this is almost certainly the context of the present letter.

§

In the name of Christ[a] and of gentle Mary.

My[b] dearest and very loved brother in Christ Jesus,

I Caterina, servant and slave of the servants of God, am writing to encourage you in the precious blood of God's[c] Son. I long to see you united with and transformed in the consummate love of God's Son, heart and soul. For without this true love we cannot have the life of grace, nor can we bear our burdens with good and perfect patience. And I don't see, dearest brother, how we can have this true charity unless we ponder God's immeasurable love for us—especially when we see him bleeding to death on the wood of the most holy cross, where[d] love alone kept him nailed fast.[6] I tell you,[e] there is no bitterness that does not become sweet, nor any burden, however great, that does not become light at the thought of the blood of God's Son.[7,f]

I've heard about all your troubles and difficulties—what we *consider* to be troubles, that is. If, however, we open the eyes of our self-knowledge

---

[5] Four letters share ten or more of the thirty-eight patterns analyzed for this letter. All of them are dated from July 1375 to early 1377, with two in April 1376. Also, several significant clusters within individual patterns (INDOMNJC, PAREOFFE, PUNIGRAZ, VESTPENA) would support placing the letter near the two from April 1376 with which it shares so heavily (T189/DT84, T221).

[6] Catherine would have been familiar with this concept, which she uses often, from authors such as Ludolphus de Saxonia and Feo Belcari. (Belcari, *Parte della vita di alcuni Gesuati*, p. 131: "Not all the wood that ever was cut in this world, nor all the nails ever made, could have held Christ on the cross. No, only love for our salvation held him.")

[7] Mt. 11, 30. Cf. Cavalca, *Specchio di croce*, VIII, p. 31: "If we held Christ's passion in memory, nothing would be so hard that it would not seem light, nor so bitter that it would not seem to us to be sweet."

and knowledge of God's goodness, these troubles appear as great consolations. When I say self-knowledge I mean the realization that we *are not*, that we have always been the perpetrators of every sort of sin and wickedness. When we reflect how we have offended our Creator, supreme eternal Goodness, we so grow in contempt for ourselves that we want to punish and take vengeance on ourselves, happy to suffer any penalty or pain to satisfy for the offense we have committed against our Creator. And we consider it a very great grace if God punishes us in this life rather than waiting to punish us in the next, where punishments are unending.[8]

Oh dearest brother in Christ Jesus, if we would only consider what a great advantage it is to endure sufferings in this life, while we are pilgrims always running on toward our end in death![g] Many good things come from being in trouble. One is that we become like Christ crucified in his suffering and reproach—and what greater treasure can we have than to be clothed in his reproach and suffering? Another is this, that God gives us difficulties because he wants to repay us for our sufferings and our efforts, and we [can] use these to punish ourselves, to cancel out our sins and failings, to grow in grace, and to carry the treasure into everlasting life.

Don't be afraid, my dearest brother, though you may have seen or may still see the devil sending you spiritual discouragement and darkness by filling you with all sorts of evil thoughts and preoccupations in order to disturb the peace and patience of your heart and soul. It will even seem that your body wants to rebel against your spirit.[9] Sometimes[h] the spirit of blasphemy[10] will try to seduce your heart through other sorts of struggles. It's not that he thinks you will fall in those struggles and temptations (for he already knows that you are determined to die rather than offend God mortally with your will). No, he does this to bring you to such a state of discouragement that you will abandon all your religious exercises, thinking you have sinned when you haven't sinned at all. But I don't want you to do that; one ought never to be discouraged because of any struggle one might experience, nor ever abandon any exercise or duty or anything else. If you can do nothing else, at least stand before the cross and say, "Jesus! Jesus! I entrust myself to our Lord Jesus Christ."[11]

You know that evil thoughts may come, but if the will does not consent—and would, in fact, rather die than consent—it is no sin. Only the

---

[8] The notion occurs a number of times in Catherine's letters from this period through 1378, as well as in *Dial.* 45, p. 93, where it is developed at some length. She seems to be taking it for granted that the monk's punishment is deserved, yet emphasizes that it is not, for all that, less identified with the sufferings of Christ.

[9] Gal. 5, 17.

[10] This is the only instance in which Catherine so refers to the devil.

[11] There is a parallel here with Let. T189/DT84 (in this volume).

will can sin. So find your encouragement in your good and holy will and don't worry about the evil thoughts. Realize that God's goodness allows the devil to torment us in order to make us humble ourselves and recognize his goodness, and to make us take refuge within his most tender wounds as a child takes refuge in its mother. For we will be kindly received by the gentle mother, charity. Realize that [God] does not want the sinner to die but to be converted and live.[12] It is such boundless love that moves him to give [us] troubles and permit temptations as well as consolation, since his will wants nothing else than that we be made holy.[13]

Keep living within the tender wounds of Christ,[i] and in God's holy love.

Textual Notes

a. S2: *Jesus Christ crucified / Christ.*

b. S2: [*My*].

c. *b*, S2: *his / God's.*

d. From *b*, S2; *a*: [*where*].

e. *b*, S2 add *dearest brother.*

f. S2: [*at . . . Son*] (*of God's Son* is there, but crossed out, with the text jumping forward).

g. *b*, S2: *death, we wouldn't evade them.*

h. *b*, S2: *Again, sometimes / sometimes.*

i. *b*, S2: *Jesus Christ / Christ.*

[12] Ez. 33, 11.
[13] 1 Thes. 4, 3.

LETTER T221/G152[1]
To Suor Bartolomea della Seta, nun of the Monastery of Santo Stefano in Pisa
Possibly late April to early May 1376

Bartolomea della Seta is identified by Tommasèo as a member of a noble Pisan family. It is not unlikely that Catherine made her acquaintance during her 1375 stay in Pisa, when she seems to have visited several monasteries in the city and its vicinity.

Given the nearness of the Monastery of Santo Stefano to Pisa,[2] it would not be surprising if the letter had been written shortly after Catherine's return from there. The linguistic evidence for placement of the letter is divided. Patterns which otherwise do not appear before mid-1377 might place it in 1377 or 1378. But because of other linguistic factors and because of its affinity to Let. T4 to an imprisoned Carthusian monk (with which it shares some significant themes), I would place it near the end of Catherine's time in Siena before her departure for Florence and Avignon, probably in early May.[3]

---

[1] MSS: Mo-*b*, F4, B, P2, T, R1, P5, F2, F1, P3, R2, Nd, V, S3, P4; translation based on Mo-*b* with special reference to F4, and to V for protocol only. Other relevant variants based on an unpublished transcription by A. Volpato.

[2] So the rubrics of several manuscripts identify it. Burlamacchi finds no record of the monastery, but says that it seems to have been outside the city, a convent of Vallombrosa, later transferred into the city to the monastery of San Benedetto, which belonged to the nuns of the order of Santo Stefano (*Cavalieresse*).

[3] The presence of a few non-standardized protocol elements (INVINIT, CRISTGES, TITUL, INVOCAT) would place this letter before 1377, but there is very little sharing with other letters that would incline me to place it before late 1375. Beyond this the linguistic evidence is divided. There are five letters which share fourteen or more of this letter's sixty-three analyzed patterns. Of these letters, one is dated in August 1375, one in June 1379, and the other four between April and December 1377. When one examines significant clusters within individual patterns, one is struck by the fact that while several begin in mid-1375 and end by mid-1376 (ANELLO, BEATITUD, DEGNINF, NATURDIV, PENREFRI, ROCCAAN—which does not occur at all after mid-1376—SCHIFPEN, SOLE, SPOSCONS), a good number also begin in early to mid-1377 and end in late 1377, the same period in which the four letters with the heaviest sharing of common patterns occur. Considerations in favor of earlier placement include a few non-standardized protocol elements which could place it before 1377, a single pattern (ROCCAAN) which otherwise occurs only from early 1375 to spring of 1376, and a striking paucity of sharing within individual patterns from mid- until late 1376. In favor of later placement are the notion of not wanting to gain heaven without suffering, which otherwise occurs only in 1377 and mid-1378, and several patterns which otherwise do not begin to appear before mid-1377 (PENREFRI, SENTGRAZ, TEMPCARO, TEMPTENE). Neither Fawtier nor Dupré Theseider attempt to date the letter.

§

In the name of Jesus Christ[a] and of gentle Mary.

Dearest daughter in Christ gentle Jesus,[b]

I Caterina, servant and slave of Jesus Christ,[c] am writing to you in his precious blood. I long to see you a true bride consecrated to the eternal bridegroom. A bride characteristically joins her will with that of her bridegroom. She is incapable of wanting more than he wants, and it seems she can think of nothing but him. Now reflect, my daughter, that you who are a bride of Christ crucified should not be thinking about or wanting[d] anything but him—I mean not consenting to such thoughts.[e] I'm not saying such thoughts won't come; neither you nor anyone else can prevent them. For the devil never sleeps, and God allows this in order to make his bride exercise[f] virtue and become perfectly reliable. This is why God sometimes permits her spirit to be dark and sterile and swamped[g] by all sorts of perverse imaginings, till it seems impossible to think about God—till she can scarcely remember God's name.[4]

When you sense this happening to you, be careful not to become depressed or unduly dismayed. And don't give up your exercise of prayer[h] because the devil says to you, "What good is this prayer to you, since you aren't praying with motivation or desire? It would be better for you not to do it at all!" Don't let that make you give up or become dejected. No, answer firmly,[i] "I would rather do my duty in pain, darkness, and struggle for Christ crucified than not do it and be at rest." And consider the fact that this is what characterizes the perfect bride of Christ:[j] that even if it were possible for her to enjoy herself in this life and still escape hell and have eternal life, she would not want it so. And what is her motivation? So much does it give her joy to be like Christ crucified that she would rather live by the way of the cross and of suffering than without suffering.[5]

Now what greater pleasure can a bride have than to be like her bridegroom, to be dressed in a garment like his? So because Christ crucified in his life chose nothing but the cross and suffering, and clothed himself in this garment, his bride considers herself blessed to see herself dressed in the same garment.[6] And because she sees that her bridegroom has loved her

---

[4] This is the only place Catherine refers to forgetting God's name. It may well reflect her own experience.

[5] If this letter is correctly placed between late April and early May of 1376, this is Catherine's earliest reference to the idea of not wanting to gain heaven without suffering. Interestingly, all of the near parallels in *The Dialogue* refer to our *not being able* to gain heaven without suffering.

[6] This is the garment of Christ's blood (which is identified with charity, the fire of the Spirit), the scarlet wedding garment which Catherine will later elaborate in so many con-

immeasurably much, she loves him and receives him with such love[7] and with so much desire that there are no words adequate to describe it.

This is why supreme eternal Goodness, in order to bring her to the most perfect love and to true humility, permits her all these struggles and this barrenness of spirit so that she will come to know herself and see that she is not.[8] For if she were anything at all she would relieve herself of the[k] suffering whenever she pleased. But because she is not, she cannot. Knowing herself, then, she humbles herself in her non-being and recognizes the goodness of God who through grace has given her being and every grace that is built upon being.

But you will say to me: "When I am experiencing so much pain and darkness and struggle I can see nothing but desperation, and I have no apparent grounds for hope at all, so miserable do I seem." I answer you, my daughter, that if you search you will find God in your good will. Even though you may be experiencing a good deal of struggle, you don't for all that feel your will deprived of wanting God. In fact, this is why you are sad and suffering: because you are afraid of offending God. So struggle ought to make you exultantly happy, not desperate, when you see that God sustains your good will and gives you displeasure over deadly sin.

I recall hearing once that gentle First Truth said the same to a servant of God when she was experiencing severe suffering and temptations.[9,l] Among other things, she was feeling so desperate that the devil said to her,

---

texts, for example, in Let. T54 to a nun of Sant'Agnesa in Montepulciano (in this volume): "You know, my dearest daughter, that the bride dresses up and adorns herself when she goes before her bridegroom. And to specially please her bridegroom she wears scarlet. This is what I want you to do; I want you to have within you the garment of charity, without which you could not go to the wedding. No, the same thing would be said to you as Christ said about the servant who went without a wedding garment: he commanded his servants to throw him out into the dark." Also Let. T102 to Raimondo da Capua (late 1379 or early 1380): "If we come to know and be espoused to this truth we will find grace in the blood, the wealth and life of grace. We will find our nakedness covered, find ourselves clothed in the wedding garment of charity's fire, fire mixed and kneaded together with the blood that was shed for love and made one with the Godhead."

[7] Catherine speaks of "receiving Christ" in only two other instances: in Let. T30/DT2 (vol. I) to the abbess and Suor Niccolosa of the monastery of Santa Marta in Siena, when she speaks of Martha as hostess receiving Christ, and in Let. T21 to an unnamed person (in this volume): "You were made to be a temple of God; you ought to be receiving Christ by grace, living virtuously, and sharing in the blood of the Lamb, in which our sins are washed away." So in this case she may or may not be making an oblique reference to sacramental communion.

[8] The allusion is to Catherine's early experience of God's telling her, "I am the one who is; you are the one who is not." (*Life*, I, x, 92, pp. 85–86)

[9] As is usually the case when Catherine begins a story in this way, the "servant of God" is herself. Raimondo da Capua recounts the present incident, or one very similar, in *Life*, I, xi, 110, pp. 101–102.

"What will you do, since you will spend your whole life in this sort of pain—and then have hell besides?" To this she responded fearlessly, with a brave heart and a holy contempt for herself: "I don't shrink from pain, for I have chosen suffering as my refreshment. And if God should give me hell in the end, that will not keep me from serving my Creator, since I am the one who deserves to live in hell because I have offended gentle First Truth. So if God should give me hell he will be doing me no injustice at all, because I am his."

Then our Savior, in the face of such true and lovely humility, relieved her of the darkness and the devils' torments. And suddenly there came the presence of our Savior—just as the sun is still there when the cloud passes. This made her melt into a river of tears in a sweet warm love, and she said, "Oh good gentle Jesus! And where were you when my soul was in such distress?" The gentle Jesus, spotless Lamb, answered: "I was with you. For I am unchanging. I never leave anyone who does not leave me first through deadly sin." And she entered into a sweet argument with him, saying, "If you were with me, why was I not conscious of you? How could I be next to the fire and not feel the warmth? And I *didn't* feel anything but freezing cold, sadness, and grief! It seemed to me I was filled with deadly sins."

And he graciously responded: "Do you want me to show you, my daughter, how you could struggle so and not fall into deadly sin, and how I was with you? Tell me, what is the source of deadly sin? Only the will. For sin lies in the consent of the will, as does virtue; there is no sin or virtue that is not voluntary. There was no such voluntariness [in your experience]. If there had been, you would have taken delight and pleasure in the devil's suggestions. But because your will was not there you were sad, and fear of sinning caused you pain. You see then how both sin and virtue lie in the will. So I am telling you not to let these struggles distress you unduly. No, I want you to glean the light of self-knowledge from this darkness, and in that knowledge learn the virtue of humility. Be exultantly happy, realizing that at times like this I am living within you in a hidden way. And your will is a sign to you that I am there, since I would not be within you by grace if you had an evil will.

"But do you know just how I am living within you by grace at these times? In the same way I was on the wood of the cross. I treat you in the same way my Father treated me. Reflect, my daughter, on how I was both blessed and sorrowful on the cross. I was blessed because of the union of the divine nature with the human, and yet my flesh suffered pain because the eternal Father withdrew his power into himself, leaving me to suffer pain. But he did not withdraw the union or ever cease being one with me. Consider, then, that this is the way I live within your soul. Often I withdraw into myself your feelings, but not grace, for grace is never lost except through deadly sin, as I've said. But do you know why I do this? Only to bring you to true perfection.

"You know that the soul cannot be perfected except on the two wings of charity and humility.[10] Now humility she learns through the self-knowledge to which she comes in times of darkness. And charity is gained by seeing that in love I have sustained a good and holy will in her. So the wise soul, I tell you, when she realizes that these times are the source of so much strength (and that is the only reason I allow the devil to tempt you), values them more than any other time.[m]

"Reflect, too, that you very much need these times for your salvation. For unless you were from time to time enticed by temptation, you would become very careless and give up the practice of continual desire and prayer. You are, after all, more alert during times of battle for fear of the enemy, and you secure the fortress[n] of your soul by running to me, your strength. This, of course, is not what the devil intends. I allow him to tempt you in order to bring you to virtue, and he tempts you to bring you to despair. Realize that the devil will tempt those who are determined to serve me not because he thinks they will actually fall into this or that particular sin (for he already sees that they would rather die than actually sin)—but what does he do? He tries to bring them to desperation by saying: 'Because of these thoughts and impulses that come to you,[o] nothing good will be of profit for you.' Now see how great is the devil's malice! Since he cannot win the first battle, he wins the second under the pretext of virtue. I don't want you, then, ever to follow his malicious will. No, I want you to take my will, as I've told you. And this is the rule I give you and want you to teach others[p] as the need arises."

So, my dearest daughter, that is just what I am telling you I want you to do. And be for me a mirror of virtue by following in the footsteps of Christ crucified. Bathe in the blood of Christ crucified. See that you don't look for or want anything but the crucified, as a true bride ransomed by the blood of Christ crucified—for that is my wish. You see very well that

---

[10] This up-and-down flight is elaborated under a somewhat different but related image in Let. T70 to Bartolomeo Dominici (vol. I): "*Oh blazing fire ever burning, you are indeed a fire!* This, it seems, is what the mouth of Truth said: 'I am fire and you are the sparks.' He says that fire always wants to return to its source, and so it always goes back up. *Oh charity, ineffable delight! How truly you speak, for we certainly are sparks! This is why you want us to humble ourselves.* Just as sparks receive their being from the fire, so let us acknowledge that our being comes from our first source. This is why he said, 'I am fire and you are a spark.' So let your soul not rise up in pride, but like a spark, let it first go up and *then* come back down. The first movement of our holy desire ought to be into the knowledge of God and his honor. Then let's come down to know our own poverty and indifference, but only after we have gone upward. Oh you who are asleep, wake up! There, when we find ourselves in the abyss of his charity—*there* will we be made humble! Oh gentle mother charity!"

you are a bride and that he has espoused you—you and everyone else—and not with a ring of silver[q] but with a ring of his own flesh.[11] Look at that tender little child who on the eighth day, when he was circumcised, gave up just so much flesh as to make a tiny circlet of a ring!

Oh measureless abyss and height of charity! How much you love this bride, the human race! Oh life by which everything lives! You rescued her from the hands of the devil, who had held her as his own possession; you rescued her from his hands by catching the devil on the hook of humanity, and you espoused her with your flesh. [At your circumcision] you gave your blood as a down payment, and in the end, when your body was slashed open, you paid in full. So drink up, my daughter! Don't become careless! No, get up with real eagerness and with this blood so break open your hard heart that it will never close up again—not because of any foolishness or indifference, not because of anything anyone may say.[12]

I'll say no more. Keep living in God's holy and tender love, finding your rest always on the wood of the most holy cross. Jesus, gentle Jesus! Jesus love! Amen. Amen.[r]

Textual Notes

a. From V; Mo-*b* has *Jesus Christ crucified / Jesus Christ.*

b. S7 [*Jesus*]; V, T, R1, R2, B, P2, P3, P5, F2, F4, Mo, S4: *Christ gentle Jesus.*

c. From V; Mo-*b* has *of the servants of Jesus Christ / Jesus Christ*; R2, Nd: *servant of the servants and slave of the servants.* S7: *Jesus Christ crucified / Jesus Christ.*

d. R3 [*nor wanting*]; P4 [*thinking about nor*].

e. R3 adds *apart from him.*

f. From R3; other Manuscripts have *grow in*; but, as Volpato notes, R3's reading is more consistent with parallel passages in *Dial.*

g. Bo2: *tormented* (*tormentata*) / *swamped* (*attorniata*).

h. S7, B, P2: *either the exercise or the act*; other Manuscripts have, literally, *exercise in the act*; V: *service / exercise.*

i. It. *virilmente.*

j. From R3; other Manuscripts have *those who are perfect.*

k. R3: *if she could have suffering / if she could relieve herself of the suffering.*

l. R3 adds *and desperation.*

---

[11] Cf. 1 Pt. 1, 18: "Realize that you were delivered . . . not by any diminishable sum of silver or gold, but by Christ's blood beyond all price: the blood of a spotless, unblemished lamb."

[12] There is an allusion here to the medieval belief that only hot blood could crack the hardness of a diamond. Cf. Vincent de Beauvais, *Speculum naturale*, L, VIII, ch. 39, which states that the fresh warm blood of a goat can shatter the diamond, which resists both iron and fire. For Catherine, however, the blood of Christ is also the fire of the Spirit.

m. P4, S4 have *The wise soul, I tell you, when she realizes that these times are the source of such strength, thereafter finds security in this. (And that is the only reason I allow the devil to tempt you.) And she values. . . .*
n. P5, F2: *ship / fortress.*
o. B, P2: *that you feel / that come to you.*
p. P5, F2: *follow and to teach others / teach others.*
q. F2, Bo2: *gold or silver / silver.*
r. Closing from R3; Mo-*b*: *Keep living in God's holy and tender love. Gentle Jesus! Jesus love!* R3: *Jesus, gentle Jesus! Amen. Deo gratias.* S7: *Jesus, gentle Jesus! Jesus love!* Bo2: *Jesus, gentle Jesus! Deo gratias!* V: *Jesus, gentle Jesus!* R2: *Deo gratias! Gentle Mary!* Nd: *Deo gratias! Jesus love!* B: *Jesus, gentle Jesus, etc.* P2: *May Christ gentle Jesus fill you with his holy love! Amen.* (to which S4 adds a second *Amen.*)

Part V:
To Florence and Avignon and Back
(May 1376 to December 1376)

Catherine, accompanied by Stefano Maconi, Bartolomeo Dominici, and a few other women and men, left Siena for Florence probably in early May of 1376. According to Raimondo da Capua, the journey was made at the behest of the same Florentine leaders who had commissioned him to go to Avignon in Catherine's name.[1] There she pursued her attempts to mediate a reconciliation between the Florentines and Pope Gregory XI. Apparently she wrote only one letter (T229/DT69 to the pope) during her brief stay in Florence—which would be understandable, given her focus at that point on a single mission.

If she had not already made her decision to travel to Avignon herself in the cause of unity, such a decision was made and solidified as she spoke with the Florentines. While she found the common folk trying desperately to live Christian lives even under the restrictions of the interdict imposed by Gregory XI on 31 March, Guelfs as well populists were determined to defend the civil rights of their republic even as they sued for peace.

It is uncertain whether Catherine's departure for the papal court was officially sanctioned by the Eight of War. Catherine seems to imply as much in her letter to Buonaccorso di Lapo Giovanni the following September (T234/DT82), and Raimondo da Capua states that the priors of the city met with her "in the neighborhood of Florence" and urged her "in the most pressing way" to go to Avignon to negotiate a reconciliation. But Florentine records mention neither the exchange nor the mandate. In any case, near the end of May she left Florence without written credentials and probably against the advice of some of her friends. With her on this stage of the journey were Stefano and Bartolomeo, Gherardo Buonconti of Pisa and his brothers Tommaso and Francesco, Alessa dei Saracini, Francesca (Cecca) di Clemente Gori, her sister-in-law Lisa, and a number of other disciples. Bartolomeo Dominici tells us that there were twenty-two persons

---

[1] *Life*, III, vi, 420, p. 381.

in her company in Avignon and that all were housed and fed at the pope's expense during their stay there.[2]

The group arrived in Avignon on 18 June. Two days later the pope granted her an audience and, with some hesitation, entrusted to her the negotiations with the promised Florentine ambassadors. When the latter arrived in early July, however, they refused to meet with her, asserting that they had no commission to do so. Though Catherine continued to plead the Florentine cause with Gregory, she began to devote more and more of her energy to the crusade, the return of the papacy to Rome, and the reform of the Church.

Gregory in fact departed for Rome on 13 September and arrived there in January. Catherine meanwhile returned to Siena with her own group, finally reaching there about the end of the year after stays in Varazze, Genoa, and Pisa.

[2] *Processo Castellano*, ed. Laurent, p. 317.

LETTER T229/G6/DT69[1]
To Pope Gregory XI, in Avignon
Mid-May 1376

By 18 April 1376 Pope Gregory XI had become so firm in his resolve to return to Rome that he asked for Venetian galleys to be ready for his embarkation on 1 September. In the present letter Catherine responds to an inquiry from the pope concerning his intent. She says she is "coming there soon," since it seems to her that "divine Goodness is about to turn the great wolves into lambs." This may very well be an indication that she is writing after her meeting with political leaders in Florence. Since she urges Gregory not to come "with an army," she has probably heard of his plan to send mercenary troops against the rebellious cities, a plan that was ready to proceed on 20 May 1376.[2] I would posit from these facts that Catherine is writing from Florence near the latter date, shortly before her departure for Avignon[3]

---

[1] MSS: Mo-*b*, S2, S4, P4; translation based on Mo-*b*. No relevant variants.

[2] The ambassador of Mantua to Avignon, Cristoforo da Piacenza, in his dispatch of 15 May 1376 (XX in A. Segre, "I dispacci di Cristofora da Piacenza, procuratore mantovano alla corte pontificale," *Archivio storico italiano*, ser. 5, xliii, 1909), says that 1500 lances and 8000 foot-soldiers are about to leave Avignon on 20 May. They actually set out on 27 May under the command of Cardinal Robert of Geneva, the same person the French cardinalate would elect as pope in opposition to Gregory XI two years hence .

[3] This placement is broadly supported by the linguistic data. Only one letter shares nine or more of this one's twenty-one analyzed patterns, Let. T218, also to Gregory XI, written just after Catherine's arrival in Avignon on 18 June. Two individual patterns show significant clusters from March to May 1376: PERDAMOR and PERDMED. Fawtier (II, pp. 144–145) places the letter in March or April 1377. Dupré Theseider places it in April, or possibly (with Burlamacchi) in May, after Catherine's meeting with the *priori* of Florence.

§

In the name of Christ crucified and of gentle Mary.

Revered father in Christ gentle Jesus,

I Caterina, your unworthy daughter, servant and slave of the servants of Jesus Christ, am writing to you in his precious blood. I long to see you a courageous man, free of slavish fear, learning from the good gentle Jesus, whose vicar you are. Such was his boundless love for us that he ran to the shameful death of the cross heedless of torment, shame, insult, and outrage. He suffered them all, totally free of fear, such was his hungry desire for the Father's honor and our salvation. For love had made him completely let go of himself, humanly speaking.

Now this is just what I want you to do, father. Let go of yourself wherever selfish love is concerned. Do not love yourself selfishly, nor others selfishly, but love yourself and your neighbors for God's sake and God for his own sake, since he is worthy of love, and since he is supreme eternal good. Take as your example this slain Lamb, for the blood of this Lamb will give you courage for every battle. In the blood you will lose all fear, and you will become a good shepherd who will lay down your life for your little sheep.

Up then, father; don't sit still any longer! Fire yourself with tremendous desire, expecting divine help and providence. For it seems to me that divine Goodness is about to turn the great wolves into lambs. This is why I am coming there soon, to lay them in your lap, humbled. I am certain that you, as their father, will receive them in spite of their persecution and injustice against you. You will learn from gentle First Truth, who says that the good shepherd, once he has found the little lost sheep, will put it on his shoulders and take it back to the fold.[4] So do that, father. Once your little lost sheep has been found, take it on love's shoulders and put it in the fold of holy Church. And right after that our gentle Savior wants and commands you to raise the standard of the most holy cross over the unbelievers, and let this whole war be picked up and directed against them. As for the soldiers you have hired to come here, hold them back and don't let them come, for they would ruin everything instead of setting things right.[5]

My dear father, you ask me about your coming.[6] I answer you in the

[4] Cf. Lk. 15, 5.

[5] Catherine must, therefore, have had some notice, perhaps from her disciples already in Avignon, of Gregory's military intentions. Since, however, the papal troops set out on 27 May, the deed would be done before Catherine's letter could reach the pope.

[6] None of Gregory's communications with Catherine is extant, but here as elsewhere

name of Christ crucified: come as soon as you can. If you can, come before September, and if you cannot come earlier, don't delay beyond the end of September. Pay no attention to any opposition, but like a courageous and fearless man, come! And, as you value your life, see that you don't come with an army, but with the cross in your hand, as a meek lamb. If you do, you will fulfill God's will. But if you come in any other way you will be violating that will rather than fulfilling it. Be glad, father! Be jubilant! Come! Come!

I'll say no more. Keep living in God's holy and tender love.

Gentle Jesus! Jesus love!

Pardon me, father. I humbly ask your dear blessing.

---

one can have some idea of their import from the tenor of Catherine's response. September is the date Gregory himself had set early in 1376 for his return to Rome. She wants him to come earlier, if possible.

Letter T255/G13/DT71[1]
To Pope Gregory XI, in Avignon
18 to 22 June 1376

The content of this letter makes it clear that Catherine is writing from Avignon. We know that she arrived there with her companions on 18 June 1376, having been preceded by Raimondo da Capua, Felice da Massa, Giovanni Tantucci, and Neri di Landoccio Pagliaresi. She was granted an audience with Gregory XI just two days later. The precision with which she outlines her concerns in this letter, and her statement that she will come to speak her mind in person whenever the pope wishes, could well indicate that this is a letter she has delivered to Gregory either upon her arrival or after her initial interview with him.[2]

§

In the name of Jesus Christ crucified and of gentle Mary.

Dearest, most holy father,

Your poor unworthy daughter in Christ gentle Jesus, Caterina, sends you her greetings in his precious blood. I long to see you a courageous man, free of any cowardice or selfish sensual love in regard to yourself or any of your relatives. For I see, when I ponder it in God's presence,[a] that nothing else will hinder your good holy desire or thwart God's honor and the reform and advancement of holy Church as much as this.[3] This is why I long, with boundless love, for God in his infinite mercy to free you from all halfheartedness and sentimentality, and make you a new man—I mean

---

[1] MSS: B, P2, A, H, P1, P3, S2, P4, S4; translation based on B as edited by Dupré Theseider, with reference to H. Other relevant variants based on Dupré Theseider.

[2] Though one can hardly expect the linguistic evidence to prove the letter's placement within days, it does strongly support it within a broader range. All four of the other letters sharing nine or more of this one's twenty analyzed patterns are dated between April 1376 and the beginning of 1377. Further, a remarkable number of significant clusters within individual patterns begin or end in this same period: ESALT, GIARDCHS, IMPEDDES, RICCPOV, RICHIAM, TIEPID, VOSTCAT. Dupré Theseider dates the letter to June or July. Fawtier (II, p. 149), interpreting her comment that she would be happy to go to the pope whenever it would please him, to speak with him in person, sees the letter as having been written before Catherine's first audience with Gregory.

[3] Dupré Theseider (n. 2 to this letter) agrees with Fawtier in identifying this "good holy desire" as Gregory's intention of returning to Rome. Ferretti holds that it is an allusion to the reform of the clergy, of which Catherine is also speaking here. Either may be right; no one was openly opposing reform, while many of Gregory's relatives were resisting his departure from Avignon.

transform you in burning, blazing desire—for there is no other way you can fulfill what God wills and his servants long for.

Oimé![b] My dearest *babbo*, forgive my presumption in saying what I've said—what I am compelled by gentle First Truth to say. This is his will, father; this is what he is asking of you. He is asking you to take just action against the multitudinous crimes of those who graze and feed in the garden of holy Church; he says that animals should not be eating what is meant for human beings.[4] Since he has given you authority and you have accepted it, you ought to be using the power and strength that is yours. If you don't intend to use it, it would be better and more to God's honor and the good of your soul to resign.

There is something else he wants and is asking of you. He wants you to make peace with all of Tuscany, with whom you are at war. Exact of each of your sinful rebellious children whatever each can yield, as far as possible without war. But do punish them, as a father must punish a child who has done wrong.

Finally, God's tender goodness is asking you to give full authorization to those who are asking to make the crusade; for what seems impossible to you *is* possible to the tender goodness of God,[c] who has commanded it and wants it to be. See to it, as you value your life, that you are not guilty of irresponsibility. Don't make light of the works of the Holy Spirit that are being asked of you. You can do them if you *want* to. You *can* see that justice is done. You *can* have peace, if you will put aside the world's perverse pretensions and pleasures[d] and keep only God's honor and what is really due holy Church. And you *have* the authority to give peace to those who ask you. You are not poor but rich—for you carry in your hand the keys to heaven, and it is opened to whomever you open it, and closed to whomever you close it[5]—and so if you fail to act, you will be severely rebuked by God. If I were in your place I would be afraid of incurring divine judgment. And so with all my heart I am begging you in the name of Christ crucified to be obedient to God's will (for I know you neither desire nor want to do anything but his will)—so as not to bring upon yourself that harsh rebuke, "Cursed be you, for time and power were entrusted to you and you did not use them!" I believe, father, because of God's goodness and because I find reason for hope in your holiness, that you will act in such a way that you will not incur that curse.

I'll say no more. Forgive me! Forgive me![e] My great love for your salvation, and my great pain when I see it threatened, makes me speak. I

---

[4] Cf. Mt. 15, 26: "It is not right to take the food of sons and daughters and throw it to the dogs."

[5] Cf. Mt. 16, 19. The imagery is further developed in *Dial.* 115, p. 215.

would gladly have said all this to you personally to unburden my conscience completely, and I shall be happy to come[f] whenever it pleases your holiness.[6] Don't make it necessary for me to complain about you to Christ crucified. (There is no one else I *can* complain to, since there is no one greater [than you] on earth.)

Keep living in God's holy and tender love. I humbly ask your blessing. Gentle Jesus! Jesus love!

Textual Notes

a. H: *dear presence / presence.*
b. H: *Oimé! Oimé! / Oimé!.*
c. From H; B has *him.*
d. P2: [*and pleasures*].
e. H: *come to you / come*
f. P2: [*Forgive me*].

[6] Fawtier deduces from this sentence that Catherine has not yet seen the pope when she writes this letter. If this is so, the letter would date to her first day or two in Avignon, since Raimondo (*Life*, III, vi, 159, p. 152) reports an audience "a few days" after her arrival there.

LETTER T230/G197/DT72[1]
To the Eight of War, in Florence
28 June 1376

The Eight of War were a special magistracy set up to take charge of the war between Florence and the papacy. In this letter, dated in the text as having been written on 28 June 1376, Catherine complains that the promised Florentine ambassadors have not yet arrived in Avignon.[2] Perhaps, however, she has never actually met with any of the Eight of War but only with members of the Guelf party, who were sympathetic to the papacy and among whom were some of her disciples. According to an anonymous chronicler, three ambassadors of the Eight left Florence on 2 June, though they were without power to treat of the affairs of the people and of the commune until 4 and 5 July.[3] Any knowledge on their part of Catherine's dealings with the Guelfs might well have been enough to make them spurn her attempts at mediation.

§

In the name of Jesus Christ crucified and of gentle Mary.

Dearest fathers and sons in Christ gentle Jesus,

I Caterina, servant and slave of the servants of Jesus Christ, am writing to you in his precious blood. I long to see you as true sons, so humble and obedient to our father that you will never turn back,[4] but will be truly and bitterly sorry for having wronged him. Those who do wrong, and then refuse to start over by being sorry, are undeserving of mercy. So I am inviting you to genuine heartfelt humility. Don't turn back. No, keep going forward, making good your initial holy resolution and growing stronger in it every day. If you want to be received into your father's arms, be like dead children begging for life, and I trust that in God's goodness you shall have it, if only you are willing to humble yourselves sincerely and admit that you have been at fault. But I am really displeased

---

[1] MSS: B, P2, H, P1, S1, P3, S3; translation based on S3, with reference to H. Variants from P2 based on Dupré Theseider.

[2] The date established by the text is broadly supported by the distribution of significant clusters within individual patterns, and more narrowly by UMILCUOR, which occurs only three times, between April and September 1376. While the six other letters which share six or more of this one's fifteen analyzed patterns range quite widely, all of them are dated later than this one.

[3] *Diario d'anonimo fiorentino*, ed. Gherardi, pp. 308–309.

[4] Cf. Lk. 9, 62.

with you if what is rumored here is true, that you have levied a tax on the clergy.[5] If it *is* true, it is a serious evil on two counts.

To begin with, you are offending God, since you cannot in good conscience levy such a tax. But it seems to me you are losing your conscience and everything else that is good! You seem to care for nothing but transitory material things that pass away like the wind—as if we didn't realize we are mortal and must die, and we don't know when. How stupid, then, to throw away the life of grace and be responsible for one's own death! I don't want you to go on like this any more. It is in fact turning back, and you know that to be worthy of glory it is not enough to begin; one must persevere to the finish.[6]

So I tell you, you will never achieve peace unless you persevere in humility and cease putting unjust obstacles in the way of the ministers and priests of God's Church. And here is the second thing I said is evil and pernicious in this. Besides the evil of offending God, I tell you, this [tax affair] is the ruination of your peace. For when the holy father finds out about it he will be even more angry with you. I'll tell you what certain cardinals have said—men who are seeking and really want peace. Now that they hear this they are saying, "It must not be true that they want to make peace. If they did, they would avoid every slightest action against the holy father's will and the practice of holy Church."[7] I think dear Christ on earth may say the same, and he has good reason to say it if he does. Please, dearest fathers, please don't try to block the grace the Holy Spirit is ready to give you,[a] and not because you deserve it but because of his clemency.

---

[5] Popular sentiment blamed the papacy for John Hawkwood's siege of Florence in June 1375, when the commune had paid the mercenary captain a handsome ransom for its freedom from harassment. Later the *Signoria* authorized the collection of funds through taxation or seizure of lands "from citizens and corporations" to reimburse the commune's treasury. Everyone, especially the curia in Avignon, saw this as aimed particularly at the clergy. Precisely on 28 June, the date of the present letter, the *Signoria* established a commission (the *Ufficiali de' preti*) with authority to levy forced loans on the clergy and to sequester their property. (R. Trexler, *Economic, Political, and Religious Effects of the Papal Interdict on Florence, 1376–1378: A Study of the Secular Penal Power of the Papacy in the Late Middle Ages*, Frankfurt am Main: Johann Wolfgang Goethe-Universität, 1964, p. 108; G. A. Brucker, *Florentine Politics and Society, 1343–1378*. Princeton: Princeton University Press, 1962, pp. 296–297. Brucker refutes the assertion that Hawkwood had been sent to conquer the city for the papacy.) Lay taxation of the clergy had been forbidden by a decree of the Fourth Lateran Council in 1215 (*Decretals* X 3.49.7) and by Pope Boniface VIII's decree *Clericis laicos* in 1296 (*Sext* 3.23.3).

[6] Cf. Mt. 10, 22: "But whoever holds out till the end will escape death." Lk. 9, 62: "Whoever puts a hand to the plow but keeps looking back is unfit for the reign of God."

[7] Dupré Theseider (n. 5 to this letter) believes that Catherine is probably referring to some conversation she has had with the Italian cardinals, particularly Iacopo Orsini, cardinal-protector of Siena, and Piero Corsini, cardinal-bishop of Florence, who had connections with the Guelfs, or better, the Albizzi, who had always favored loyalty to the pope.

Besides, you would be causing me embarrassment and dishonor, for only confusion and embarrassment could come from my telling the holy father one thing and your doing another. I beg you to stop it, and make an effort instead to show by what you say and do that you want peace, not war.

I have spoken with the holy father. He listened to me graciously, in God's goodness and his own, showing his enthusiastic love for peace. He was like a good father who looks not so much at the wrong his son has done him, as at whether the child is humbled, so that he can be completely merciful to him. Words can't describe how exceptionally happy he was! At the end of a good long conversation, he said that if things were with you as I had been telling him, he was ready to receive you as his children and to do about the matter whatever seemed best to me. I'll say no more here. The holy father thought he should give absolutely no other response until your ambassadors arrive.[8] I am surprised they still haven't come. When they do arrive I shall meet with them and then with the holy father, and I will write you my impression of the outcome. But you, with your new taxes, are destroying for me what has been sown! Stop it, for love of Christ crucified and for your own good! I'll say no more.

Keep living in God's holy and tender love.

Gentle Jesus! Jesus love!

Given in Avignon, the 28th day of June, 1376.[9]

Textual Notes

a. P2: *ad averla / a darvela.*

[8] Raimondo da Capua describes Catherine's meeting with the pope in *Life*, III, vi, 420–421, pp. 381–383: "He spoke Latin, and she expressed herself in the common Tuscan vernacular of Tuscany. I testify before God and humankind that the benevolent pontiff . . . left the peace-making in Catherine's hands. His words were: 'So that you may know clearly that I want peace, I leave it entirely in your hands. Remember, however, that the Church's honor is in your keeping. . . .' [He, however] had come to his own conclusions [regarding the ambassadors Florence had promise to send, and said]: 'Believe me, Catherine, they have deceived you and will continue to deceive you. They will send no ambassadors, or if they do, it will be a mission which will accomplish nothing.' "

[9] The closing of Let. T232/DT75 states that Catherine and her companions arrived in Avignon on 18 June.

LETTER T218/G3/DT74[1]
To Pope Gregory XI, in Avignon
28 June to 5 July 1376

We do not know how often Catherine actually met with Pope Gregory XI while she was in Avignon, but she did not hesitate besides to use letters to communicate with him, as well as the services of her male companions. She sends this letter to the papal court with Neri di Landoccio Pagliaresi, stating that she would prefer to say these things in person.

The reference to the pope's having been robbed of what is his may refer to the issue of taxation of the clergy, concerning which Catherine wrote Let. T230/DT72 to the Eight of War in Florence. This is probably the occasion for her focusing more strongly on the projected crusade, which she does in this letter. I would therefore place this letter shortly after 28 June 1376.[2]

§

In the name of Jesus Christ crucified and of gentle Mary,
mother of God's Son.

Very loved and reverend father in Christ Jesus,

I Caterina, servant and slave of the servants of Jesus Christ and your poor wretched unworthy daughter am writing to you in his precious blood. I long to see you the sort of[a] true gentle shepherd who takes an example from the shepherd Christ, whose place you hold. He laid down his life for his little sheep in spite of our ingratitude. The hounding, the wrongs, the scorn, the insults of the people he had created and so greatly blessed did not keep him from working out our salvation. No, as one in love with the Father's honor and our salvation he ignores his own suffering and conquers our malice with his wisdom and peace and kindness. Just so I am begging you, I am telling you, my dear *babbo*, in the name of Christ cruci-

---

[1] MSS: Mo, S2, P4, S4; translation based on Mo-*a*, corrected by *b*. No relevant variants.

[2] Such a placement is somewhat broadly but strongly supported by the linguistic evidence. The eight letters which share sixteen or more of this one's fifty-three analyzed patterns range from late 1375 to very early 1377. However, the strongest concentration of significant clusters within individual patterns falls between April and June 1376, with three clusters beginning in June (ARMCROC, LUMNFOND, UTILPROS), and seven ending there (DIVORANI, DOLCAMOR, EREDITA, MEMBPUTR, PORTNOME, PRIMAVERA, SUPERBPR). Both Fawtier (II, pp. 141–142) and Dupré Theseider place this letter sometime between June and September 1376.

fied, to conquer with kindness, with patience, with humility, with gentleness the wrongdoing and pride of your children who have rebelled against you their father.

You know that the devil is not cast out by the devil but by virtue.[3] Even though you have been seriously wronged—since they have insulted you and robbed you of what is yours[4]—still, father, I beg you to consider not their wrongdoing but your own kindness. Don't let this keep you from working out our salvation. And this will be their salvation: that you re-establish peace with them, for as long as a son is at war with his father he is dispossessed of his inheritance. Oimé! Father, peace, for love of God, so that all these children may not lose the inheritance of eternal life! For you know that God has placed in your hands the giving and the taking away of this inheritance as your kindness pleases. You hold the keys, and to whomever you open it is opened, and to whomever you close it is closed. This is what the good gentle Jesus said to Peter, whose place you take: "Whatever you shall loose on earth will be loosed in heaven, and whatever you shall bind on earth will be bound in heaven."[5]

So take a lesson from the true father and shepherd. For you see that now is the time to give your life for the little sheep who have left the flock. You must seek and win them back by using patience and war—by war I mean raising the standard of the sweet blazing cross and setting out against the unbelievers. So you must sleep no longer, but wake up and raise that standard courageously.

I am confident that by God's measureless goodness you will win back the unbelievers and [at the same time] correct the wrongdoing of Christians, because everyone will come running to the fragrance of the cross,[6] even those who have rebelled against you most. Oh what joy, if we were to see the Christian people giving the seasoning of faith to the unbelievers![7] For once these had received the light they would become perfect, like

---

[3] Cf. Mt. 12, 26–27.

[4] Dupré Theseider considers this a clear allusion to the revolt of the Italian cities, as a consequence of which the Church for a time effectively lost dominion over almost all of the papal territory (n. 3). It could, however, be a reference to the taxation of the clergy, an issue Catherine addresses in Let. T230/DT72 to the Eight of War in Florence, clearly dated 28 June 1376.

[5] Mt. 16, 19. Cf. *Dial.* 154, p. 328: "[Christ] left [the key of obedience] in the hands of his vicar, Christ on earth, whom you are all obliged to obey even to the point of death. Whoever refuses to obey him is . . . living in damnation."

[6] An echo of Sg. 1, 3: "Draw me! We shall run after you in the fragrance of your ointment." (Vulg.)

[7] She will develop this image of seasoning in *The Dialogue*, for example, 3, p. 29: "seasoned with loving charity"; 11, p. 44: "Discernment . . . seasons every virtue and virtuous deed." The basis for the image may be Mt. 5, 13 ("You are the salt of the earth.") or simply her own experience of cooking. The fact that Catherine is now turning her attention more

a new plant. And once the Holy Spirit's warmth and light had, through holy faith, displaced the chill of unbelief, they would produce the flowers and fruits of virtue in the mystic body of holy Church. So by the fragrance of their virtue they would help eliminate the vice and sin, the pride and filth that are rampant among the Christian people—especially among the prelates, pastors, and administrators of holy Church who have turned to eating and devouring souls, not converting them but devouring them![8]

And it all comes from their selfish love for themselves, from which pride is born, and greed and avarice and spiritual and bodily impurity. They see the infernal wolves carrying off their charges and it seems they don't care. Their care has been absorbed in piling up worldly pleasures and enjoyment, approval and praise. And all this comes from their selfish love for themselves. For if they loved themselves for God instead of selfishly, they would be concerned only about God's honor and not their own, for their neighbors' good and not their own self-indulgence.

Oimé! My dear *babbo*, see that you attend to these things! Look for good virtuous men, and put them in charge of the little sheep. Such men will feed in the mystic body of holy Church not as wolves but as lambs. It will be for our good and for your peace and consolation, and they will help you to carry the great burdens I know are yours. It seems to me, gracious father, that you are like a lamb among wolves. But take heart and don't be afraid, for God's providential help will always be with[b] you. Don't be surprised even though you see a great deal of opposition, and see that human help is failing us, and that those who should be helping us most disappoint us and act against us. Don't be afraid, but even more self-confident. Don't give up or restrain your sweet holy desire, but let it be more enkindled with each day that passes.

Up, father! Put into effect the resolution you have made concerning your return and the crusade.[9] You can see that the unbelievers are challenging you to this by coming as close as they can to take what is yours.

---

specifically to the calling of a crusade seems to reinforce the placement of this letter in relation to Let. T230/DT72.

[8] Here the image of the ravaging wolf has lent a negative sense to the "eating of souls" which is usually such a positive image in Catherine, for whom life in Christ means "eating souls at the table of the most holy cross." Note how she brings together the issues of church reform and the conversion of the Moslems, implying that the latter, with their newfound faith, will be a leaven for reform in the Church.

[9] It may be, as Dupré Theseider contends (n. 8 to this letter) that Catherine's words confirm that the return of the papacy to Rome and the crusade were already coupled in Gregory's intent and that the joining of the two projects did not come from Catherine's suggestion. On the other hand, it would not be unlike Catherine to assume that because she sees a relationship between the two, the pope does as well.

Up, to give your life for Christ! Isn't our body the only thing we have?[10] Why not give your life a thousand times, if necessary, for God's honor and the salvation of his creatures? That is what he did, and you, his vicar, ought to be carrying on his work. It is to be expected that as long as you are his vicar you will follow your Lord's ways and example.

So come, come! Delay no longer, so you may soon set up camp against the unbelievers, and so you will not be frustrated in the endeavor by these rotten members who are rebelling against you![11] I am asking you, and I want you to play a holy trick on them—I mean the kindness I've been telling you about.[12] This will be for them a fire of love, burning coals that you will heap on their heads.[13] In this way you will have gained both them and their material means to help you wage a real war against the unbelievers. This is what our gentle Savior did. By heaping such burning hot love on those who were rebelling against him, he succeeded little by little in making them his helpers, bearers of God's name. Take, for example, that dear preacher Paul.[14] He was a wolf, but he became a lamb, a gracious vessel of love[15]—and the fire with which Christ filled his vessel he carried through the whole world. He uprooted vice from Christians and planted virtue in them; unbelievers he drew away from error and unbelief, and offered them the light of faith. Now this is what gentle First Truth is telling you and wants you to do. What you have received, give.[16]

Peace! Peace! Peace, my dear *babbo*, and no more war! Let us set out against our enemies, wearing as armor the most holy cross and carrying the sword of God's sweet holy word.[17] Oimé! Feed your hungry servants who are waiting for you and for this time with tremendous blazing desire!

---

[10] Cf. Let. T183/DT56 (vol. I), where she urges Archbishop Iacopo da Itri: "Do we have anything [to give] but our one body? Well, let's give it in a hundred thousand deaths if need be."

[11] Catherine often refers in this way to the rebellious Italian cities.

[12] She has just a bit earlier advised Gregory to "conquer with kindness, with patience, with humility, with gentleness the wrongdoing and pride of your children who have rebelled against you their father."

[13] Cf. Rom. 12, 20, which cites Prv. 25, 21–22: "But 'if your enemy is hungry, feed him; if he is thirsty, give him something to drink; by doing this you will heap burning coals upon his head.' "

[14] It. *quello dolce di banditore*: the words evoke the image of a town crier, someone who shouts an urgent message in the streets.

[15] Here as elsewhere Catherine misquotes Acts 9, 15, which she would have heard in the Latin as *vas electionis*, "chosen vessel," or in the Tuscan vernacular as *vasello d'electione*; the latter she could easily have misheard as *vasello di dilectione*, which is what she uses.

[16] Cf. Jn. 17, 8: "The word you gave to me I gave to them." (Vulg.); Mt. 10, 8: "The gift you have received, give as a gift."

[17] Cf. Heb. 4, 12: "Indeed, God's word is living and true, sharper than any two-edged sword."

Take courage, take courage, father! Stay away from the bitterness that cripples, but take hold of the bitterness that strengthens[18]—bitterness at seeing God's name insulted, and strength in the trust that God will provide for your needs. I'll say no more, for if I followed my inclination I wouldn't stop as long as I had life in my body!

Forgive my presumption. Let my love and grief for God's honor and the advancement of holy Church be my excuse in the presence of your kindness. I would rather say it personally than in writing, for I think I would more completely unburden my soul. This is all I can do now. Have pity on the sweet loving desires being offered for you and holy Church in continual tears and prayers. Please don't treat them with indifference, but act on them vigorously, for it seems that spring is ready to burst into bloom, and soon the fruit will come, because the flowers are beginning to blossom. So have a courageous, absolutely fearless heart, as you follow the Lamb who was slain and consumed on the cross for us! Keep living in God's holy and tender love.

Please, reverend father, grant the request that Neri, the bearer of this letter, will communicate to you, if you find it possible and acceptable. Please listen to him and trust what he says.[19] Sometimes it is impossible to write about what we would like to; so if you want to send me any private message, entrust it to him by word of mouth, for you can do so with confidence. As for whatever I can do, I would gladly give my life if necessary for God's honor and the salvation of souls.

Gentle Jesus! Jesus!

Textual Notes

a. *the sort of* (*quello*) erased in the manuscript.

b. Literally: *be over.*

---

[18] Cf. *Dial.* 78, p. 147: "Their sadness is called not 'distressing sadness' that dries up the soul, but 'fattening sadness' that fattens the soul in loving charity, because sufferings increase and strengthen virtue, make it grow and prove it." Cf. also Let. T237/DT79 (in this volume): "Let your grief over what happened not be crippling; rather let it be the healing pain of a holy self-knowledge."

[19] Dupré Theseider speculates (n. 16 to this letter) that the pope has probably asked Catherine not to come to see him again, so as not to irritate too much those who are opposing his return to Rome. Catherine continues, however, to communicate with him through intermediaries, in this case Neri di Landoccio Pagliaresi.

LETTER T232/G244/DT75[1]
To Sano di Maco di Mazzacorno, in Siena
13 July 1376

This is the fourth of Catherine's eight extant letters to the Sienese wool-worker, Sano di Maco di Mazzacorno, through whom she often addressed the rest of her circle in Siena when she was away.[2] This letter is easily dated by a reference near the end to Catherine's having arrived in Avignon "twenty-six days ago," plus an addendum stating that that arrival was on 18 June 1376.[3]

§

In the name of Jesus Christ crucified and of gentle Mary.

Dearest brother and son in Christ gentle Jesus,

I Caterina, servant and slave of the servants of Jesus Christ, am writing to encourage you in his precious blood. I long to see you built up on the true foundation, Christ crucified, made one with him. He is the living rock, and every building founded on him is stable and secure. Without him nothing can have any firmness whatever.[a] This is what Paul, that man in love, said: "No one can be built securely on any other foundation than on the living rock, which is Christ crucified, for he is the one foundation God has laid."[4] And truly, dearest brother and son in Christ Jesus, it seems to me this is the truth.

For if we are truly built on Christ, no wind of pride or vainglory can blow us over, because our foundation is in deep humility, which sees how God stooped down to our humanity in order to save us.[5] So too, no matter how great the flood of greed or worldly and sensual pleasure, it cannot topple us if we are firmly stabilized on that rock who was never softened

---

[1] MSS: B, P2, R1, T, P5, F2, P3, S3; translation based on R1, with reference to T. Other variants based on Dupré Theseider.

[2] The earlier letters are T69/DT24, T147/DT25, and T142/DT26, all in vol. I.

[3] The date is in harmony with the linguistic evidence. Six letters sharing five or more of this one's fifteen analyzed patterns fall between mid-1375 and early 1377. More importantly, five significant clusters within individual patterns begin or end between late March and mid-July 1376 (GODPENA, INDOMNJC, INNAMOR, SCRIVCON, UMILTERR). Both Fawtier (II, p. 265) and Dupré Theseider place this letter on or very near 13 July 1376.

[4] Cf. 1 Cor. 3, 11 and Lk. 6, 48–49; the succeeding image of the flood is taken from the Lucan parable, as is Catherine's inclusion of "the living rock" in the passage from 1 Cor.

[5] Christ, therefore, is the personification of humility.

by bodily comfort or pleasure, and was utterly firm in suffering and pain. If we are in love with him we can hardly want to do otherwise than continually suffer shame and scorn, hunger and thirst, cold[b] and heat, injustice and slander with him,[c] and ultimately even[d] be delighted to lay down our bodily life for love of him. At that point we are actually glad to see ourselves made worthy to endure torment, ridicule, and mockery from the world for love of the good gentle Jesus. Our soul grows fat on such suffering. Thus we read of the apostles that they were glad when they began to be despised for the name[e] of Jesus.[6]

It is in this way that my soul longs to see us so built up on Christ crucified that neither the water of trial, nor the wind of temptation, nor even the devil with his wiles or the world with its allurements or the flesh with its impurity will ever be able to separate us from the love[f] of Christ and of our neighbors.[7] And don't let yourself be influenced by words the devil sows through other people in order to disquiet[g] your spirit or the spirits of my other dear sons and daughters in Christ Jesus. This is his old art of making the tongues of the wicked his instruments. And sometimes, by God's permission, he makes the tongues of God's servants his instruments in order to disquiet God's other servants.[8]

By the grace of our gentle Savior we arrived in Avignon twenty-six days ago. I have already spoken with the holy father and with several cardinals and other civil authorities. And the grace of our dear Savior has been much at work in the purposes for which we came here.[9] All of you, pray to God for Christ on earth and for peace. . . . Be happy, be joyful in

---

[6] Acts 5, 41.

[7] Cf. Rom. 8, 35–39: "Who will separate us from Christ? Trial, or distress, or persecution, or hunger, or nakedness, or danger, or the sword? . . . I am certain that neither life nor death, neither angels nor principalities, neither the present nor the future, nor powers, neither height nor depth nor any other creature, will be able to separate us from the love of God that comes to us in Christ Jesus, our Lord."

[8] Dupré Theseider (n. 5 to this letter) sees this as an allusion to the spiteful comments of certain Sienese concerning Catherine's journey to Florence and Avignon. Sano had perhaps complained of these in a letter which may have been waiting for her when she arrived in Avignon. The instrumentality of "the tongues of God's servants" could be a call in particular to the Company of the Virgin, of which confraternity Sano was a member. Cf. *Dial.* 36, p. 77: "The Holy Spirit is on [God's servants'] tongues to proclaim the truth, just as the devil is in the mouths of his servants." Also Filippo da Siena degli Agazzari, *Assempri*, p. 212: "There certainly is no place the devil so delights in dwelling as on the tongues of grumblers and detractors." (Perhaps from Augustine, *Enarratio in Ps. CXLIII*, 18—PL XXXVII, 1867: "You are holding converse . . . with those whose tongues have been put in the devil's hand.")

[9] Catherine will not be nearly so confident after the Florentine ambassadors, on their arrival, reject her mediation.

our Lord Jesus Christ. Encourage. ...[10] Keep living in God's holy and tender love.

Gentle Jesus! Jesus love!

We arrived in Avignon on the 18th[h] day of June 1376.[11]

Textual Notes

a. P2: [*whatever*].
b. *cold* supplied from P2, lacking in B.
c. P2: *for him and with him / with him.*
d. P2: [*even*].
e. B, P2: *honor / name.*
f. The text uses *carita* here.
g. *disquiet* supplied from R1; B, P2 have *attack.*
h. From T; R1: *28 / 18.*

[10] At this point the personal greetings and messages of Catherine and her companions must have followed.

[11] The date was probably appended by the scribe. It may well have been Stefano Maconi, since the letter is included only in the Maconian tradition of manuscripts and Caffarini's S3.

Letter T6/G166[1]
To Monna Lapa, her mother
July or August 1376

Lapa is certainly separated from Catherine at the time the latter writes this letter to her, exhorting her to patience and generosity in bearing her daughter's absence in God's service. She is probably writing in response to a letter of complaint from Lapa.

There are at least four periods we know that mother and daughter were separated: during Catherine's journey to Florence and Avignon (May to December 1376), until Lapa met the returning group at Pisa in December; during at least part of Catherine's sojourn at Rocca d'Orcia (August through December 1377), and possibly while Catherine was at Belcaro during April of that year; during Catherine's last mission to Florence (January to July 1378); and for the first month or two that Catherine was in Rome (November to December 1378). And Lapa probably did not go with Catherine on her first visit to Florence from mid-May to late June 1374.

The linguistic evidence favors placing this letter before 1377 but after spring of 1376.[2] I would therefore suggest that this is the first of Catherine's extant letters to her mother, probably written not too long after the saint's arrival in Avignon, but long enough for Lapa's complaints to have reached her, perhaps during July or August. It may have been sent with T232/DT75 (to Sano di Maco). Catherine will write her mother another letter in the same vein, T240/DT83, during the journey home, in October or November.[3]

---

[1] MSS: Mo, P4, S4; translation based on Mo-*a*, corrected by *b*. No relevant variants.

[2] Of the first four periods, all but the first can be excluded by the patterns INVINIT and PERMANE, neither of which occurs after 1376. Catherine's 1374 absence seems to be excluded as well, since even in its brevity this letter has little in common linguistically with letters of that time. Nor would such a short absence have been likely to provoke a strong remonstrance from Lapa. There are, on the other hand, two significant clusters within individual patterns which begin during the Avignon period, GODPENA and VESTVOLO. The three other letters which share five or more of this one's thirteen analyzed patterns are widely scattered.

[3] Tommasèo speculates from the tone of the letter that it is among the earliest, perhaps even earlier than 1371, during one of Catherine's journeys in the environs of Siena. Both Fawtier (II, p. 227) and Dupré Theseider (unpublished notes) consider the letter undatable.

§

In the name of Jesus Christ crucified and of gentle Mary.

Dearest mother in Christ Jesus,

I Caterina, servant and slave of the servants of Jesus Christ, am writing to you in his precious blood. I long to see you a true servant of Christ crucified, grounded in genuine patience, since without patience we cannot be pleasing to God. In patience we show our desire for God's honor and the salvation of souls. Besides, patience demonstrates that our soul is clothed in and conformed with God's sweet will, because it rejoices in everything and is content with whatever happens. So a person who is clothed in such a lovely garment is always at peace and is glad to suffer pain for the glory and praise of God's name.[4] And she gives herself and her children and all her possessions and her life for God's honor.

Now this is what I want you to do, dearest mother. I mean I want you to offer your whole will and me your poor undeserving daughter for God's service and honor and the salvation of souls with genuine good patience. Find your nourishment in the fruit of the most holy cross with the gentle humble loving Lamb. And in this way nothing will seem a hardship to you. Strip yourself of selfish sensual love, for it is time to give honor to God and our best efforts to our neighbors. Once you are stripped of selfish love, you will walk not laboriously but with delight.

I'll say no more. Keep living in God's holy and tender love.

Gentle Jesus! Jesus love!

---

[4] In Let. T104 to Raimondo da Capua (in this volume) Catherine expands on patience as a queen clothed in the sun: "Oh patience, how peaceable you are! Oh patience, what hope you give to those who possess you! Oh patience, you are a queen in control of and not possessed by anger! Oh patience, you serve sentence on selfish emotion when it would raise its head in anger! You carry a sword, double-edged with hate and love, to cut off and root out anger and pride and the impatience that is the pith of pride. Your clothing is the sun, alight with the true knowledge of God and warm with divine charity. The rays from [this sun] fall on those who do you wrong, heaping on their heads coals of fire ablaze with charity to burn up and consume the hatred in their hearts. You then, sweet patience grounded in charity, are the source of fruit for our neighbors and honor to God. This garment of yours is covered with stars, all the different virtues, for we can have no patience without the stars of all the virtues along with the night of self-knowledge, which is a sort of moonlight. And after this knowledge of ourselves comes the day, with the great light and warmth of the sun as a garment for patience. Who then would not fall in love with such a lovely thing as patience, with willingness to suffer for the sake of Christ crucified?"

LETTER T241/G354/DT73[1]
To Monna Giovanna di Corrado Maconi, in Siena
July or August 1376

Stefano Maconi, a relatively new disciple, was with Catherine from the first stages of her journey to Avignon in 1376. The young man's mother, Giovanna di Corrado Maconi, was apparently very attached to her son, and seems to have found a way to let Catherine know that she did not appreciate his being away from home! The rubric of T informs us that the present letter was written in that context.[2]

§

In the name of Jesus Christ crucified and of gentle Mary.

Dearest mother in Christ gentle Jesus,

I Caterina, servant and slave of the servants of Jesus Christ, am writing to you in his precious blood. I long to see you making your home in the cell of self-knowledge, so that you may attain perfect love, for I know that we cannot please our Creator unless we love him, because he *is* love and wants nothing but love. If we do know ourselves we find this love.[3] Why? Because we see our own nothingness, that our very existence is ours by grace and not because we have a right to it, and every grace beyond our existence as well—it is all given to us with boundless love. Then we discover so much of God's goodness poured out on us that words cannot describe it. And once we see ourselves so loved by God, we cannot help loving

---

[1] MSS: B, P2, T, R1, P5, F2, F1, P3; translation based on T, with reference to R1; variants from P2 based on Dupré Theseider.

[2] Though the linguistic evidence could incline me to associate this letter with a later context, I would accept the rubric as probably reflecting a trustworthy tradition. The letters which share a significant number of patterns with this one's fifty-one analyzed patterns are not in this case much help, since they are broadly scattered chronologically. There are a few significant clusters within individual patterns which begin or end in the early Rocca d'Orcia period, that is, August to October 1377: COGNAMA, COGNAMVR, COGNVERI, CUORANIM, DISORDAM, GIARDANI, PIACCREA, VERITDIL. Moreover, a significant number of patterns otherwise frequent and broad-ranging show a striking gap of non-occurrence during that period: ABITAZ, BONTADIO, DIOUMIL, NASCPIAG, PARTSENS, SPOGLCOR, UDIGRIDO. There are, however, also some significant clusters within individual patterns which could support placement fairly early in the Avignon period: UMILMANS, INTENDIM, COGNVERI. My placement concurs with that of Fawtier (II, p. 306) and Dupré Theseider.

[3] This is one of a few isolated early instances of Catherine's use of the image of "the cell of self-knowledge," an image she will begin to use more regularly in autumn of 1377.

him. And within ourselves we love God and our own rationality, and hate the sensuality that would take inordinate pleasure in the world.[4]

Some people delight in wealth or status, or would rather please creatures than the Creator. These build their foundation in worldly appearance, pleasure, and enjoyment. Then there are some who love their children or spouse or mother or father excessively, with too sensual a love. Such a love gets between their soul and God and keeps them from a clear knowledge of the truth of real heavenly love.[5] This is why gentle First Truth said, "Unless you leave father and mother, sisters and brothers, and your very self, you are not worthy of me."[6] God's true servants have always been very conscious of this, and quickly strip their heart, soul, and affection of the world and its pleasures and ostentation, and of loving anyone apart from God. Not that they don't love other people, but they love them only for God's sake, as creatures boundlessly loved by their Creator. But just as they hate in themselves the sensuality that rebels against God, so they hate this in their neighbors, for they see that it offends[a] supreme eternal Good.

Here is what I want you to do, dearest mother in Christ gentle Jesus. I want you to love God's goodness within yourself, and his immeasurable charity, which you will find in the cell of self-knowledge. In this cell you will find God. For just as God holds within himself everything that shares in being, so you will find within yourself memory, which holds and is well-suited to hold the treasure of God's blessing. There too you will find understanding, which makes us sharers in the wisdom of God's Son by understanding and knowing his will, a will that wants nothing but that we be made holy.[7] When we see this, our soul cannot be sad or shaken, no matter what happens, for we know that everything is done with God's providence and tremendous love.

I want you, I beg you for love of the slain Lamb, to use this knowledge to assuage the grief and heartache you have felt because of Stefano's departure. Be glad! Be happy! For this will surely make his soul and yours grow in grace. And by God's grace you will see him soon.

Getting back to self-knowledge: I tell you, you will also find there the gentle mercy of the Holy Spirit, the aspect of God that[b] gives and *is*[c] noth-

---

[4] Cf. Let. T245 to a Franciscan Tertiary (1378): "Because we see that sensual love deprives us of God, we hate our selfish sensuality and love reason. And therefore we do everything we do with the light of reason."

[5] This is a theme that is developed at great length in Let. T164/DT58 to Melina Barbani (in this volume).

[6] A fusion of Mt. 10, 37–39 and Lk. 14, 26.

[7] 1 Thes. 4, 3.

ing but love. Whatever the Spirit does is done because of love. And this movement of love you will find within your own soul, because our will is nothing but love, and its every affection and movement comes from nothing but love. It loves or hates whatever the eye of understanding has seen and understood. How true it is then, dearest mother, that within the cell of your soul you will find the whole of God. And he bestows such sweetness, refreshment, and consolation that no matter what may happen we cannot be shaken, because we have been made big enough to hold God's own will. How? By getting rid of all selfish love, by getting rid of everything that is not God's will.

Then right away our soul is transformed into a garden filled with fragrant blossoms of holy desire. And in the center of the garden is planted the tree of the most holy cross, the resting place of the spotless Lamb. He bathes and waters this glorious garden, irrigating it with his blood; and he himself bears the mature fruit of true solid virtues.[8] If you want patience, he is the bedrock of meekness, since not a murmur of complaint was heard from the Lamb.[9] He is the bedrock of deep humility, since God stooped down to humanity, and the Word stooped to the shameful death of the cross. If you want charity, he is that charity—and even more, for it was the power of love and charity that kept him nailed fast to the cross. The cross and nails could never have held the God-Man, had not the power of charity held him.

I'm not surprised that those who make of themselves a garden through self-knowledge are strong in the face of the whole world, for they are conformed and made one with supreme strength.[10] They truly begin in this life to have a foretaste of eternal life. They control the world by making light of it. The devils are afraid to get near a soul on fire with divine charity.[11] So up, dearest mother! I don't want you sleeping any more in irre-

---

[8] Cf. Prayer 17, pp. 148–149: "So you, eternal Word, watered this tree with your blood. With its warmth the blood makes the tree bear fruit." Also Let. T313 to Onorato Gaetano (1378): "With what is [the vineyard] watered? Not with water but with the precious blood shed with such blazing love, and that blood is there in the vessel of the heart." The imagery had been developed by Bernard de Clairvaux (*In Cantico sermo LXXV*, PL CLXXXIII, 1146): "The blood watered the arid land; the blood flooded the earth and watered it; the blood made peace for those in heaven and for those on earth."

[9] Cf. Is. 53, 7.

[10] The only other place Catherine speaks of self-knowledge as a garden is in Let. T113 to Bandeçça Salimbeni (in this volume): "The soil is true humility, as I've said, and the place you'll find it is the enclosed garden of self-knowledge. I say it is enclosed because if you dwell in the cell of self-knowledge, you are enclosed. You are not wide open, because you are not dissipated in worldly delights."

[11] Cf., among other places, Let. T172 to Frate Niccolò of Monteoliveto (in this volume): "[T]he devils run away from the heart and desire set ablaze in the fire of divine charity just as the fly retreats and doesn't land on a boiling pot—because he sees there his death, ready-

sponsibility and sensual love. No, with a boundless blazing love get up and take a bath in Christ's blood, hide in the wounds of Christ crucified.

I'll say no more. I'm sure that if you live in the cell I've been talking about you will discover none other than Christ crucified. And tell Corrado to do the same.[12] Keep living in God's holy and tender love.

Gentle Jesus! Jesus love!

Textual Notes

a. P2: *they are offending / it offends.*

b. Literally: *who is the part that. . . .*

c. P2: [*and is*].

---

made, in the scorching heat of the fire. But when the pot is lukewarm, [both fly and devil] hurry in, feeling right at home, and feed there."

[12] Giovanna's husband and Stefano's father.

LETTER T233/G8/DT76[1]
To Pope Gregory XI, in Avignon
About 14 August 1376

As Catherine writes this letter to the pope, it seems that Gregory is still wavering in his decision to return to Rome. This would make a likely date for the letter late July or the first weeks of August. If the reference to Gregory's request for Catherine's prayers at the end is the same as that referred to in Prayer 1, which seems probable, then the letter must have been written near 14 August, the date assigned to Prayer 1 by two of the manuscripts of the latter.[2]

§

In the name of Jesus Christ crucified and of gentle Mary.

Dear and gracious reverend[a] father in Christ gentle Jesus,

Your poor unworthy daughter Caterina, servant and slave of the servants of Jesus Christ, is writing to encourage you in his dear[b] blood. I long to see you free of all slavish fear, as I reflect how fear cuts off the vigor of holy resolution and wholesome desire.[c] So I have asked and will continue to ask[d] the good gentle Jesus to free you from all slavish fear, leaving you only holy fear.[3,e] May a blazing flame of charity so burn in you that you will not let yourself listen to the voice of incarnate devils, will not let yourself take the advice of evil counselors. Their foundation is in self-centeredness, and as I understand, they want to frighten you by saying you'll be killed. They say this to keep you from coming.[4] And I am

---

[1] MSS: Mo-*c*, B, P2, A, H, P1, P3, S2, P4, S4; translation based on Mo-*c*, with reference to H. Other variants based on Dupré Theseider.

[2] The linguistic evidence offers little support for (and none against) this dating of this short letter, except that the only other letter which shares six or more of its twelve analyzed patterns is from early September of 1376. Fawtier (II, p. 146) places the letter in July or early August, as does Dupré Theseider. Neither alludes to Prayer 1.

[3] Cf. Let. T133/DT32 to Giovanna d'Angiò (vol. I) for the contrast between "slavish" and "holy" fear The first is characteristic of slaves, who act out of fear of punishment; the second is characteristic of friends, spouses, and children, who fear only offending the one they love. Cf. *Dial.* 58, p. 112: "Slavish fear is not enough to win them eternal life. Love joined to holy fear, however, is enough. . . . The imperfectness of the fear of suffering was taken away by love, and what remained was the perfectness of holy fear, that is, fear simply of sinning, not because of personal damnation but because sin is an insult to me, supreme Goodness."

[4] In Let. T239/DT81 to Gregory XI (in this volume) Catherine will refer to a threat of poisoning. Given French resistance to the pope's return to Rome, however, there may well have been other threats on his life as well. Later in the letter she says that Raimondo da

telling you, in the name of Christ crucified, dearest most holy father, not to be afraid for any reason whatever.

Come confidently; entrust yourself to[f] Christ gentle Jesus. For if you do as you should, God will be on your side and no one will be against you.[5] Up, father, courageously! I tell you, you have no need to fear. But if you *don't* do as you should, you may well have reason to be afraid. It is your duty to come. So come! Come! Come trustingly, without any fear at all. And if anyone in your household should try to hinder you,[6] tell them boldly what Christ said to Saint Peter, who out of attachment to him wanted to keep him from going to his passion. Christ turned to him saying, "Get behind me, Satan! You are a stumbling block to me, because you are looking for human values rather than those that come from God. Don't you want me to fulfill my Father's will?"[7] Now you do the same, dearest father. As his vicar, follow his example. Be firm and decisive with yourself and with them, saying, "Though I should lose my life a thousand times, I want to fulfill my eternal[g] Father's will." (But let's admit it, you won't lose your life but rather gain the way and the means of continually winning the life of grace.[8]) So take heart, and don't be afraid, for you don't need to. Take up the weapon of the most holy cross, which is security and life for Christians. Let them say what they want. As for you, remain firm in your holy resolve.

My father Frate Raimondo told me on your behalf that I should pray to God, asking whether anything would stand in your way.[9] I had already prayed about it, before and after holy communion, and I saw neither death nor any danger at all. The dangers are made up by those who are advising you. Believe and entrust yourself to Christ gentle Jesus. I trust that God will not scorn so many prayers[h] made with such blazing desire and with so much sweat and tears. Forgive me, forgive me![i]

I'll say no more. Keep living in God's holy and tender love.[j]

Capua has asked her to pray and to seek some enlightenment from God on the matter.

[5] Rom. 8, 31.

[6] Gregory's father was particularly opposed to the projected return of the papal court to Rome.

[7] Mt. 16, 23.

[8] Cf. Mt. 10, 39: "Anyone who loses his or her life for my sake will find it." (Vulg.)

[9] Cf. the introductory caption of Prayer 1: "She made this prayer in Avignon just after Pope Gregory XI had commanded her to pray especially for him," to which early editors added that Gregory "had sent word for her to pray to God for him especially in the morning," perhaps taking a cue from Catherine's own reference to Holy Communion.

Textual Notes

a. B, P2: *Most holy and blessed / Dear . . . reverend.*
b. B, P2: *encourages you in his precious / is writing . . . dear*
c. P2: [*and wholesome desire*].
d. P2: [*and . . . ask*].
e. P2: *fear of God / fear.*
f. P2: *take courage in / entrust yourself to.*
g. P2: [*eternal*].
h. B, P2: *prayers of his servants / prayers.*
i. B, P2 transpose this sentence to after the next.
j. B, P2 add *Gentle Jesus! Jesus love!*

LETTER T231/G7/DT77[1]
To Pope Gregory XI, in Avignon
Mid-August 1376

The energy with which Catherine deals in this letter with the obstacles being placed in the way of the pope's return to Rome may well suggest that it follows closely on Let. T233/DT76. The rubric of B, in fact, states that the letter was written in response to a note from Gregory (possibly his answer to T233/DT76), and that it was this response that finally moved him to firm up his decision to leave Avignon.[2]

Several of the manuscripts have this letter in a Latin version which may well represent the letter as actually sent to the pope, who did not read Tuscan.[3] I am therefore following that version in the translation.

§

In the name of Jesus Christ crucified and of gentle Mary.

Most holy father in Christ gentle Jesus,

Your poor unworthy daughter Caterina sends you greetings in the precious blood of the Lamb of God.[a] I long to see you strong and firm as a rock in the good holy resolution you have already taken up,[b] so that all the contrary winds beating against you won't hurt you.[4] They come from human enemies, rising up out of malice through the devil's ministry and satanic furies,[c] who want to prevent all the good that will follow from your going [to Rome].

I understood from the note you sent me that you are being harassed by the enemies of all good, who never stop tempting you. And to persuade

---

[1] MSS: Mo (in Latin), B, P2, A, H, P1, S1, P3, S2, P4, S4 (text in Latin and Italian in the last three manuscripts). Translation based on Mo with reference to S2, and to H for protocol. Other variants based on Dupré Theseider.

[2] The dating of this very short letter is only very broadly supported by the linguistic data. Only two other letters share six or more of its mere twelve analyzed patterns, and these occur between September 1376 and January 1377. Of the critics, only Fawtier (II, p. 146) specifies the date of this letter to Pope Gregory XI as narrowly as August 1376; the others simply place it during the summer.

[3] There are also a few minor manuscripts which contain Latin versions of isolated letters: Let. T39 and T335, both to Carthusians, in G; Let. T221 to Bartolomea della Seta in Pa2; Let. T221 and T173 to a friar who has left his order in Va1.

[4] Cf. the parable of the house built on rock, Mt. 7, 24–25: "Anyone who hears my words and puts them into practice is like the wise man who built his house on rock. When the rainy season set in, the torrents came and the winds blew and buffeted the house. It did not collapse; it had been solidly set on rock."

you the more convincingly of the evil they want, they are claiming[d] that Pope Clement IV,[e] whenever he had to do anything, never wanted to act without the advice of his brother cardinals. True, he usually preferred their intentions and pronouncements to his own, even when he saw that his own were materially better, just as you yourself see what is right. Oimé! Most holy father, what malice and how much evil are arising because of the devil! These men cite Clement IV, plenty concerned about themselves and what is theirs, but much less concerned about the universal good to which everything else ought to be subordinate. Why don't these pious men also cite Pope Urban [V],[5,f] who sought the cardinals' advice when he was in doubt as to whether or not to act,[g] but who, when the matter was clear and obvious to him—as is your going [to Rome] to you, of which you are certain—didn't feel bound by their opinion even though they might all be against him.[6] Let your enemies direct your attention to *him*[7]—but they can't, because they are your enemies.

What sane person doesn't see that the holiest thing is for the lord of all the world to be seated on his proper throne? Surely, unless they are blind, they will admit this easily. And this is what the counsel of the good will always tell you.[h] It seems to me the advice of good people is concerned only with God's honor, the salvation of souls, and the reform of holy Church, and not with their own selfish love for themselves.[i] The advice of such people should be followed, I'm saying, but not the advice of those who love only their own life, honor, status, and pleasure—for their advice goes where their love is.

I beg you in the name of Christ crucified: let it please your holiness to hurry! Make use of a holy trick. I mean, let it look as if you are going to take a few more days, and then all of a sudden go! For the sooner you act, the sooner you will escape these tormenting anxieties. In fact, it seems to me their malice is becoming much more astute. Now they want to instruct you by giving you the example[j] of the wild animals who, once they escape

---

[5] The pope (as he will do in another case, cf. Let. T239/DT81 in this volume) has sent Catherine the text of a communication he has received, containing an allusion to Clement IV and his custom of turning to the cardinals for advice. In the Italian versions of this letter "the enemies of all good" are the cardinals: "I understood from the note you sent me that the cardinals are claiming that Pope Clement IV, whenever he had to do anything, never wanted to act without the advice of his brother cardinals. True, he often followed their opinion even though he thought his own was better. But (oimé!) most holy father, they cite Pope Clement IV for you, without ever mentioning Pope Urban V."

[6] Catherine replies to the allegation about Clement IV with an example even more pertinent because it is closer in time and very familiar to Gregory XI, who was on intimate terms with Urban V, his predecessor. This is the only time in her extant writings that Catherine mentions Urban V. It is clear from what she says that Gregory has already made up his mind to leave Avignon.

[7] That is, to Urban V.

from a trap, never go back to it![8] But I am begging you to follow with complete commitment [my] sound advice. The blessed God freed you once from their wicked counsel when they interrupted your journey last year. The devil had in fact laid a trap on their tongues. You were caught, and holy counsel was taken captive. Evil and harm followed because of it—indeed the worst evil and harm we have suffered until now![9,k] So now that you're the wiser, with the Holy Spirit's guidance you *won't* fall back into it.

Let's go quickly, my dear *babbo*,[l] and fearlessly! If God is for you, no one will be against you.[10] God himself will move you; God himself will be your guide, your helmsman, and your sailor.[11,m] So God *is* with you. Go quickly to your bride, who is all pale, and is waiting for you to bring back her color.[12] And the moment you arrive she will be more beautiful than any other.[n] I don't want to burden you with more words, for I would have much to say.

Keep living in God's holy and tender love. I am presumptuous: forgive me.[o] I humbly ask your blessing. . . .[13]

Gentle Jesus! Jesus love!

Textual Notes

a. B, P2: *in his precious blood / in . . . God.*

b. B, P2: *in the good, holy, and just resolution already begun / in . . . up.*

c. B, P2, H: *from worldly people through the deceitful, malicious mystery of the devils / from human enemies, rising up out of malice through the devil's ministry and satanic furies.*

d. B, P2: *The cardinals are claiming / that you are being harassed . . . claiming.*

e. *IV* supplied from P2.

---

8 The sense of the Latin seems to be that the cardinals are using the example of animals once trapped to convince the pope not to return to the "trap" of Rome.

9 This is probably what she had referred to in an earlier letter to Gregory (T185/DT54, vol. I): "Delay no longer, for your delaying has already been the cause of a lot of trouble."

10 Rom. 8, 31.

11 Latin *Iste dux auriga erit et nauta.* The line occurs only in Mo, and the triple image is unique here.

12 Cf. *Dial.* 132, p. 271 "[They] suck the blood of my bride, holy Church. By their sins they have left her pallid. The loving charity they ought to have had for this bride they have lavished on themselves." The image is somewhat different in *Dial.* 14, p. 50: "But look how my bride has disfigured her face! She is leprous with impurity and selfishness." Cf. also Prayer 3, p. 38: "You [Christ] are pallid because your creatures are constantly throwing your graces away, plundering your one bride."

13 The ellipses indicate that in the original there followed either something of a more private nature or simply the usual closing.

f. *True . . . better* from P3; B, P2: *he often followed their opinion even though he thought his own was better. But oimé, most holy father, they cite Pope Clement IV for you, without ever mentioning Pope Urban V / he usually . . . . Urban.*
g. P2: [*as to . . . act*].
h. B, P2: [*Let your enemies direct your attention to him—but they can't, because they are your enemies. What sane person doesn't see that the holiest thing is for the lord of all the world to be seated on his proper throne? Surely, unless they are blind, they will admit this easily. And this is what the counsel of the good will always tell you.*]
i. B, P2: [*for themselves*].
j. B, P2: *these point to the instructive example / their . . . example.*
k. B, P2: *Up to this point you've managed to escape from the trap of their advice, into which they made you fall once, when you postponed your departure. The devil made them lay this trap to accomplish precisely the harm and evil it did. / But I am begging you . . . . until now.*
l. From H; B, P2: *father.*
m. B, P2: *God is the one who is moving you / God himself . . . sailor.*
n. B, P2: [*And the moment . . . any other*].
o. Mo (Latin version) ends here. The rest of the letter is contained in the Italian version.

LETTER T235/G186/DT78[1]
To Charles V, King of France
August 1376

Sometime between 17 July and 27 August 1376, while Catherine was still in Avignon, Louis Duke of Anjou arrived there. Bartolomeo Dominici tells us in his testimony in the *Processo Castellano* that the duke's initial hesitations about Catherine soon gave way to admiration and respect. In fact, he invited her to come to his castle at Villeneuve, across the river from Avignon, where she spent three days.[2] Fawtier speculates, however, that Louis was using both the pope and Catherine to further his own ambitions for power, and that he asked the saint for this present letter to his brother, the king of France, only for that reason.[3] Very possibly the letter never reached Charles at all and perhaps was never even picked up by Louis or his servants for delivery. Still, it would not be her only attempt to influence the loyalties of France in regard to the papacy.

The historically supported placement of this letter in August 1376, shortly after Catherine's visit to Villeneuve, is broadly supported by the linguistic evidence.[4]

§

In the name of Jesus Christ crucified and of gentle Mary.

Dearest lord and father in Christ Jesus,[a]

I Caterina, servant and slave of the servants of Jesus Christ, am writing to you in his precious blood. I long to see you keeping God's dear holy commandments, for I know there is no other way we can share in the fruit of the blood of the spotless Lamb. This Lamb, the gentle Jesus, has taught us the way. He said so himself: "I am way and truth and life."[5] He is the dear Master who took the chair of the most holy cross to teach us.[6]

---

[1] MSS: B, P2, H, P1, P5, F2, P3, V; translation based on B as edited by Dupré Theseider, with reference to V, H. Other relevant variants based on Dupré Theseider.

[2] *Processo Castellano*, c. 1337.

[3] II, pp. 229–231.

[4] Only two other letters, both from 1376, share fifteen or more of its fifty analyzed patterns, and five of these patterns (PERDSCUS, PRESUMPR, RICCPOV, SERVEFIG, SOPRINFD) show significant clusters of occurrences during the same year. Fawtier (II, pp. 229–231) places the letter in late August or perhaps even early September. Dupré Theseider accepts Fawtier's placement.

[5] Jn. 14, 6.

[6] Cf. Augustine, *Sermo CCXXXIV* (PL XXXVIII, 1116): "That cross was a school,

Venerable father, look at the teaching and the way he is giving you. This is his way: pain, disgrace, insult, slander, and abuse. He endures hunger and thirst with true patience. He is saturated with disgrace, nailed fast to the cross for his Father's honor and our salvation. By his pain and shame he satisfied for the guilt and dishonor into which we had fallen through sin. He punished and made up for our wickedness in his own body, and he did it only for love and not because he had to.[7] This gentle Lamb who is our way made light of the world with all its pleasures and prestige. He hated vice and loved virtue. So as a son and servant faithful to Christ crucified, follow in his footsteps and in the way he teaches you. Bear patiently every pain, torment, and trial God permits the world to give you, for patience knows no defeat, but itself conquers the world. Do be a lover of virtue rooted in true holy justice, and despise vice.

There are three specific things I am asking you, in your position, to do for love of Christ crucified.

The first is to make light of the world and of yourself and of all earthly pleasures. Hold your kingdom as something lent to you, not as if it were your own. For you know well that life, health, wealth, honor, status, dominion—none of these belongs to you. If they did, you could own them in your own way. But just when we want to be healthy we are sick; just when we want to be alive we die; just when we want to be rich we are poor; just when we want to be in power we are made servants.[8,b] And all this because these things are not ours, and we can keep them only as much and as long as it pleases the one who has lent them to us. So it is really foolish to hold as if it were our own what belongs to another; it is, in fact, a thievery worthy of death. This is why I am asking you to act wisely, as a good steward, holding everything as lent to you who have been made God's steward.[9]

The second thing I am asking is that you uphold true holy justice. Let

---

where the teacher taught the thief. The wood on which he hung became a chair for teaching." Cavalca, *Specchio di croce, Prologo*, p. 2: "Christ . . . on the cross is like a teacher occupying his chair, for he teaches . . . every perfect doctrine."

[7] Cf. Let. T29/DT18, vol. I): "[Selfish love] so displeases him that he willed to work out vengeance and punishment for it upon his own body. He made himself an anvil, and on this anvil hammered out our sins."

[8] Cf. *Bestiario toscano secondo la lezione dei codici di Parigi e di Roma* . . . , p. 30: "Material things . . . are all like shadows: there is then nothing to hold on to. For the person who is rich today is poor tomorrow. The one who is healthy today is sick tomorrow. One day a person has children, only to lose them another day. And so it is with all earthly things."

[9] The themes of all things being ours only "on loan," and of those who have being stewards for those who have not, are quite frequently heard in Catherine's writings, but only here and in Let. T197, T247 (both in this volume), and T304 (1378) does she explicitly connect the two.

it not be adulterated by selfish love for yourself or by flattery or by human respect. And don't pretend not to see if your officials are inflicting[c] injustice for money, denying the poor their rights. No, be a father to the poor as a dispenser of what God has given you. And see to it that any wrongs in your kingdom are punished, and virtue honored. For all this is the work of divine justice.

The third thing is to follow the teaching given you by this Master on the cross, which is exactly what my soul most longs to see in you: friendship and love between you and your neighbor with whom you have been so long at war.[10] For you know well that without such love as its root the tree of your soul would not bear fruit. No, if you live in hatred this tree will dry up, not being able to drink in the moisture of divine grace. Oimé! Dearest father, this is what gentle First Truth is teaching you and leaving you as a commandment: to love God above all things and your neighbor as yourself. He gave you the example, hanging on the wood of the most holy cross. While the Jews cried, "Crucify him!" he cried out humbly, meekly: "Father, forgive those who are crucifying me,[d] because they don't know what they are doing!"[11] Look at his boundless charity! He not only forgives them, but excuses them before the Father. What an example! What a teaching! The just one, who never had the poison of sin in himself, suffers at the hands of the unjust to atone for our sin!

Oh how ashamed we should be to follow the teaching of the devil and sensuality,[e] more concerned about acquiring and keeping worldly riches—which are all empty and pass like the wind—than we are about our own and our neighbors' souls! For as long as we live in hatred for our neighbors we are hating our own selves, because hatred deprives us of divine charity. How stupidly blind not to see that with the sword of hatred for our neighbors we are killing ourselves![12]

So I am asking you and I want you to follow Christ crucified and be a lover of your neighbors' salvation. Show you are a follower of the Lamb, who in hunger for his Father's honor and the salvation of souls chose his own physical death. Do the same, my lord. Don't be concerned about losing[f] your earthly possessions, for the loss will be gain to you if only you can make peace with your brothers and sisters. I am surprised you aren't willing to sacrifice even your life if you could—to say nothing of material things—at the sight of all the physical and spiritual destruction there has been, and all the religious and women and children who have been abused and driven away by this war. No more, for love of Christ crucified! Don't

---

[10] The "neighbor" with whom France has been so long at war is England.

[11] Mk. 15, 13; Mt. 27, 22; Lk. 23, 21 and 34.

[12] The same thought will be repeated in Let. T258 to Ristoro Canigiani (1378); Let. T264 to Jacoma di Trincio de' Trinci (in this volume); and in *Dial.* 48, p. 99.

you realize that you are the cause of this evil if you don't do what you can? It is evil for Christians and unbelievers alike, for your squabbling has been and still is standing in the way of the mystery[g] of the holy crusade. Even if this last were the only evil coming from your warring, it seems to me we should be expecting divine judgment.

I beg you to stop being the agent of so much evil and the obstacle to such a good as the recovery[h] of the Holy Land and of all those poor souls who have no share in the blood of God's Son. You and the other Christian lords ought to be ashamed of such a thing. What a scandal, humanly speaking, and what an abomination before God, that you should be making war against your brother and leaving your enemy alone, and that you should be seizing what belongs to another and not get back what is yours![13] Enough of this stupid blindness! I am telling you in the name of Christ crucified to wait no longer to make this peace. Make peace! Make peace! Make peace, and turn the whole war against the unbelievers! Help promote and raise the standard of the most holy cross. God will hold you and the others responsible for this at the moment of your death, because of all the foolish apathy of which you have been and are guilty every day.

No more sleeping away the little time you have left, for love of Christ crucified and for your own good! Time is short and you must surely die, though you do not know when. May a fire of holy longing grow within you to follow this holy cross and make peace with your neighbor. This is how you will follow the way and teaching of the Lamb slain[i] on the cross and obey his commandments. You will follow his way by bearing patiently[j] the wrongs done you. You will follow his teaching by being reconciled with your neighbor for love of God. And you will prove this by following the most holy cross in the sweet holy crusade.

It seems to me that your brother, the lord duke of Anjou, is willing to dedicate himself to this holy work for love of Christ.[14] It ought to be a matter for repentance if so much good and such a sweet holy mystery were left undone because of you. This is your way now to follow in the footsteps of Christ crucified. This is how you will fulfill God's commandments and his will and mine—which is what I meant when I said I want to see you keeping God's holy commandments.

I'll say no more. Forgive my presumption. Keep living in God's holy and tender love.

Gentle Jesus! Jesus love![k]

---

[13] The reference is to the Holy Land, which Catherine with all of the medieval Church believes belongs by right to Christendom.

[14] Cf. Let. T237/DT79 and T238/DT80 (both in this volume), which also refer to the duke's intention.

Textual Notes

a. From V; others have *gentle Jesus / Jesus.*

b. H adds *and vassals.*

c. P2: *allow your officials to inflict / pretend ... inflicting.*

d. P2: *them / those ... me.*

e. H: curiosity / sensuality (*curiosità / sensualità*).

f. P2: *surprised if you lose / concerned about losing.*

g. P2: *business / mystery* (*mestiero / misterio*).

h. P2: *ransoming / recovery.*

i. H: *slain and abandoned / slain.*

j. *patiently* from P2; B: *with pain and patience.*

k. H adds *Mary!*

LETTER T237/G190/DT79[1]
To Louis, Duke of Anjou
End of August to early September 1376

This letter must have been written not too long after Let. T235/DT78 to King Charles V of France, and not long before the departure of Pope Gregory XI for Rome, therefore sometime between the end of August and the early days of September 1376. We are told by the rubric of B that the duke "had given a very sumptuous banquet the day before, and a wall had collapsed and killed several people." Catherine here uses the event to exhort the duke to repentance and to participation in the crusade.[2]

§

In the name of Jesus Christ crucified and of gentle Mary.

Dearest lord and brother in Christ gentle Jesus,

I Caterina, servant and slave of the servants of Jesus Christ, am writing to you in his precious blood. I long to see your heart nailed fast to the cross, to see your desire so grow that soon you will be ready and eager to raise the standard of the most holy cross against the unbelievers.[3] If you look at the Lamb slain and consumed with love on the cross to free you from death and give you the life of grace, I am certain this holy memory will fire you with longing to do it soon, and will curb any unruly pleasure and earthly vanity in your heart and soul. Such pleasure passes away like the wind and always leaves death in the souls of its possessors. Unless it is set in order it leads them at death into eternal death, for they have by their sin given up seeing God and have made themselves worthy of seeing and associating with the devils. And it is fitting that those who sin against God, the infinite Good, should suffer infinite punishment.[4]

---

[1] MSS: B, P2, H, P1; translation based on B as edited by Dupré Theseider, with reference to H. Other relevant variants based on Dupré Theseider.

[2] The dating of the letter is nicely supported by the linguistic data (though not as narrowly as by the historical evidence). Only one other letter, from August 1376, shares more than thirteen of this one's thirty-three analyzed patterns. Among those patterns, ABBRACC, AGNELCON, CONVERSD, MORTREQU, MORTDIST, NOZZDURA, PRESUMPR, SAZFATT, SOPRINFD, and VISIODIO cluster in concentrations around spring and summer of 1376. My placement of the letter concurs with that of Fawtier (II, p. 236) and Dupré Theseider.

[3] She is referring to the projected crusade. She has just written to Charles V, king of France (Let. T235/DT78): "It seems to me that your brother, the lord duke of Anjou, is willing to dedicate himself to this holy work for love of Christ."

[4] Cf. *Dial.* 3, p. 28: "Do you not know, my daughter, that all the sufferings the soul

I am talking about those who spend their whole lives in pleasure and in sumptuous living, looking for luxuries and for great honor at huge banquets. They spend everything they have on nothing but such things. The poor are dying of hunger, but they are busy looking for plenty of big meals, elegant dishes, expensive tables, and fine fancy clothes. They don't care that their wretched souls are dying of starvation because they deprive them of their food: holy virtue, holy confession, and God's holy Word—I mean the Word incarnate, God's only-begotten Son. We should by our affection and love be following in that Word's footsteps, loving what he loves, seeking what he sought. We should be loving virtue and despising vice. We should be seeking God's honor, and our own and our neighbors' salvation. This is why Christ said we do not live on bread alone but on God's Word.[5]

So I want you, dear lord and brother in Christ gentle Jesus, to follow this gracious Word, Christ crucified, in true virtue. Don't let yourself be deceived by the world or by the strength of your youth. For if we follow only the world, what Christ said of the Jews could be said of us: "They are like tombs, beautiful and whitened[a] on the outside, but inside full of the bones and stench of the dead."[6] Oh how well does gentle First Truth speak! It is indeed so, for on the outside they seem beautiful in all their finery, but their heart and affection are filled with these dead[b] transitory things that give off the disgusting stench of bodily and spiritual corruption.

But I trust that by God's goodness you will make such an effort to amend your life that those words will not apply to you. No, with tremendously blazing love you will take up the cross, where the death of deadly sin was spent and destroyed, where we won life. And here is what it will do for you: when you take up the cross, all your past sins against God will be taken away.[7] And then God will say to you, "Come, my beloved son. You have worked hard for me. Now I will relieve you; I will lead you to the wedding feast of everlasting life, where there is satiety without boredom, hunger without pain, pleasure without discord."[8] Earthly wedding

---

bears or can bear in this life are not enough to punish one smallest sin? For an offense against me, infinite Good, demands infinite satisfaction."

[5] Mt. 4, 4.

[6] Cf. Mt. 23, 27.

[7] Crusaders were granted a plenary indulgence for their participation.

[8] Cf. Pseudo-Augustine, *Meditatio* XXVII (PL XL, 921): "For [the blessed] shall have desire for the vision of God with satiety, and satiety with desire. Their desire shall not be a source of pain, nor their satiety a source of boredom." Also Cavalca, *Specchio di croce*, p. 184: "Sated, we shall be hungry, and hungering we shall be sated, but our satiety will be far from boredom, and our hunger far from pain." Cf. also Gregory, *Libri moralium*, XVIII, chap. LIV, 91 (PL LXXVI, 94), rendered as follows by Cavalca in *Descrizione de' dieci comandamenti*, p. 306: "We shall desire though we are sated, and we shall be sated even in our

feasts and banquets are not like this. They are costly, but we gain nothing from them, and the more we stuff ourselves at them, the more empty we become, and our enjoyment becomes a source of sadness.

You had a good example of that yesterday, when you gave a banquet that was so festive yet turned out to be such a great sorrow for you. God permitted this because of his very great love for your soul. He wanted to show you and the others who were there what sort of thing our empty revelry is. And God showed how little he liked what was going on—the words, the actions, the manners, the plottings. Oimé! I'm very much afraid, though, that our obtuseness is such that it doesn't even let us think about divine judgment! I'm telling you in the name of Christ crucified never to forget yesterday,[c] so that your affairs will always be conducted in good order, with virtue and fear of God, rather than with no fear of God. Take heart, take heart, for I trust that he in his goodness will do this for you. Let your grief over what happened not be crippling; rather let it be the healing pain of a holy self-knowledge.[9] Let it be a holy restraint to hold in check any disordered vanity in you—just as you do to your running horse when you pull in the reins to keep him on course.[10]

Up now, my dear son in Christ our gentle Jesus! Embrace the most holy cross. Answer God, who is using this cross to call you. This is how you will fulfill his will and my desire. And this is why I said I long to see your heart and your desire nailed fast to the cross. Before the holy father leaves, see that you reaffirm your holy desire by taking the holy cross in his holiness' presence, and the sooner the better, for the Christian people as well as for the unbelievers.[11] Be sure to do it soon; don't put it off any longer. Be willing to do without material things rather than lose the spiritual, especially in this dear holy work that God has put into your hands. He is making you worthy of what he in his goodness usually does for his great servants.

---

desiring. Yet satiety will not be a source of boredom, nor desire be accompanied by pain, as happens in this world."

[9] Cf. *Dial.* 78, p. 147: "Their sadness is called not 'distressing sadness' that dries up the soul, but 'fattening sadness' that fattens the soul in loving charity, because sufferings increase and strengthen virtue, make it grow and prove it."

[10] Cf. Let. T132/DT48 (vol. I), where the image of the tethered horse is used to illustrate the freedom of virtue rather than its restraining function: "When we are . . . stripped of our every wish and clothed in God's will, we are very pleasing to God. Like an untethered horse we run swiftly from grace to grace, from virtue to virtue. There is no tether to restrain us from running because we have cut ourselves loose from every disordered appetite and desire for our own will, which are the tethers and ties that keep the souls of spiritual persons from running free."

[11] In Let. T238/DT80 (in this volume) she will in fact tell the pope that the duke is willing to lead the crusade.

I'll say no more. Remember, my lord, that you will surely die, and you don't know when. Keep living in God's holy and tender love. Forgive my presumption.

Jesus, gentle Jesus![d]

Textual Notes

a. P2: [*and whitened*].

b. P2: [*dead*].

c. P2: *always hold yesterday reverently in your memory / never . . . yesterday.*

d. From H; B, P2: *Gentle Jesus! Jesus love.*

Letter T191/G221[1]
To Tommaso d'Alviano
Early September 1376, but possibly as late as January 1377

Tommaso d'Alviano, son of Ugolinaccio lord of Alviano, was born at the castle there in the early fourteenth century. In 1341 he entered the service of Matteo Orsini, and at some point became a mercenary fighter.[2] In 1366 he was elected Captain of the People in Florence, and in 1377 was appointed ecclesiastical administrator of Orvieto and commissary of Pierre d'Estaing, Cardinal of Ostia.[3]

Orvieto had been one of the few cities to stand firmly with Gregory XI after the republics of the Italian peninsula took up arms against the papacy in late 1375 in response to the call of the Eight of War of Florence. In this letter Catherine is asking Tommaso to come to the aid of the Church with his material possessions as well as his military service. References to his "company" and associated battle references seem to imply that he is at this point leader of a mercenary army.

It is not unlikely that Catherine came to know of Tommaso d'Alviano through Cardinal d'Estaing. If so, the letter would have to have been written after she had met the cardinal, which was most probably while she was in Avignon in the summer of 1376.[4] The known facts would seem to narrow the date to sometime between then and 1377. It seems implausible, however, that Catherine would so explicitly encourage fighting in the name of the papacy after February 3, 1377, when people on both sides of the struggle were incensed and scandalized over the brutality of papal troops against the innocent population of Cesena.[5] Also, it seems a bit unlikely that Tommaso would have been both mercenary leader and ecclesiastical administrator of a city at the same time.

The linguistic evidence would support placing this letter between the latter half of 1376 and very early 1377, when Tommaso is still a mercenary captain.[6] I am inclined to believe it is from early September 1376, shortly

---

[1] MSS: Mo, S3; translation based on Mo-*a*, corrected by *b*. No significant variants in S3.

[2] It was probably as such that in 1359 he had come into possession of the lands of one Giovanni da Vico.

[3] Note to the letters of Colluccio Salutati, I, 50; Pompeo Litta, *Famiglie celebre degli Italiani*, viii. Cf. also A. Theiner, *Codex diplomaticus dominii temporalis S. Sedis*, II, number 378, where Tommaso is said to have been, in 1359, in possession of landed properties belonging to Giovanni da Vico. All of the above cited by E. Seckendorff, *Politische Tätigkeit*, p. 75, n. 37.

[4] Perhaps she is even writing the letter at the behest of Cardinal d'Estaing.

[5] Cf. Gardner, *Saint Catherine of Siena*, pp. 205–207.

[6] She refers often between March and December of 1376 to "going against the unbelievers," a matter to which she does not allude again until late 1377 (though she does continue

before Catherine's departure from Avignon, with some possibility that it may have been written as late as January 1377.[7] She is here enlisting his service militarily in the papal cause.

There is one other extant letter to Tommaso d'Alviano, T259, which seems to have been written in the latter months of 1377.

§

In the name of Jesus Christ crucified and of gentle Mary.

Dearest brother in Jesus Christ,

I Caterina, servant and slave of the servants of Jesus Christ, am writing to you in his precious blood. I long to see you a faithful servant of holy Church, as a pillar and defender of this gentle bride of Christ.[8] For anyone who is found faithful will not see eternal punishment at the moment of death.[a] Every faithful Christian is obliged to be faithful and to serve holy Church, each according to his or her station in life.

God appoints those who will work in this glorious garden.[9] We are those workers, and there are three ways we must serve.

The first way belongs to all faithful Christians, who ought to work with holy humble prayers and true obedience. I mean they must be obedient and respectful to holy Church, the garden where Christians find pleasure and reap the life of grace—unless they spurn the blood [of Christ] through deadly sin and through disrespect and disobedience to holy Church.[10] But let us be like workers!

---

to speak of the crusade). Variations of the expression "advancement of the Church" (*esaltatione della chiesa*—ESALT) occur sixteen times up to mid-September of 1376, and not again, other than in *The Dialogue*, until late 1379. Furthermore, the strongest concentration of clustered occurrences of patterns is centered around September 1376 to January 1377.

[7] Fawtier (II, p. 259–260) places the letter possibly while the war between Florence and the papacy was dragging on but not too long before peace was negotiated, in 1377 or early 1378, or even at the beginning of Tommaso's term as administrator in Orvieto in 1377. Dupré Theseider (unpublished notes) declines to date it.

[8] While Catherine usually uses this title of "pillar" personally in reference to church hierarchy and clergy, she does apply it once to Queen Giovanna of Naples. So it could be appropriate here, even if Tommaso is still a mercenary captain, since Catherine assumes he is fighting in the name of the Church.

[9] Catherine often refers to the Church as a garden in which the fruitful tree is Christ the Lamb of God (Let. T145/DT40, vol. I). The garden is watered by the blood of Christ (*Dial.* 140) and of the martyrs and others who spend their lives for it (Prayer 9, Let. T344 and T373, written in 1379 and 1380 respectively). The faithful are both the plants (Let. T252/DT88, in this volume) and those who are feed in the garden (Let. T189/DT84, in this volume). Those who tend this garden must see that it is not allowed to become a wilderness (*Dial.* 122, 139), and are to uproot vice and plant virtue there (Let. T341, written in 1379).

[10] Cf. Let. T171/DT60 to Nicolò Soderini (in this volume): "How, then, can we be so

The second way belongs to those who are appointed to work in this garden as ministers, whose duty it is to administer the sacraments[b] of holy Church, to feed and nourish us spiritually, who must nourish us with [their] teaching and example. But if their example were no mirror of virtue, it does not diminish the life we derive from these sacraments so long as we receive them worthily. Nor should any fault or bad example of the shepherds lessen the respect we owe them, since the power of the sacrament is in no way impaired by any defect in them. So we ought to respect them in virtue of the sacrament and because they are God's anointed, called by the scriptures his christs.[11] No matter how good or evil they may be, God does not want the hand of seculars touching them. This is why this sin is very displeasing and abominable in God's sight. Wicked people, like members of the devil, want to set themselves up as judges by punishing their offenses. But they are persecuting holy mother Church as if they were blind.

It is because of this vile and unjustified persecution that God has provided the third way. Those in this third group work in this garden by helping the Church materially, serving her faithfully with their persons and with their possessions. It seems to me God has chosen you to be one of these, so that you may be a faithful servant of the Church now in her great need. This service is so pleasing to God that words cannot describe it, especially when one serves not so much for pleasure or self-interest as out of zeal for holy Church—zeal, that is, for the Church's growth and advancement. It is so pleasing to God that, even though many may lack the holy and upright motivation they ought to have, they will still be rewarded for every good service they render this sweet bride. God will be on the side of those who labor for the Church—and if God is on their side no one will be against them.[12]

So I am inviting you, dearest brother, to labor courageously, you and the others of your company, exerting yourselves with a good and holy intent for Christ's sweet bride.[13] This is the sweetest labor, more profitable than any other work in the world. This is a labor in which you win by losing. I mean that by losing your physical life you gain eternal life, since

---

brazen as to scorn this blood? And if you should say to me, 'I'm not scorning [Christ's] blood!' I say that is not so. Whoever scorns this gentle vicar is scorning the blood, because whoever acts against the one is acting against the other, since they are inseparable. How can you tell me that you can attack a body without attacking the blood within the body? Don't you know that this is a mystic body holding within itself the blood of Christ?"

[11] Cf. 1 Chr. 16, 22: "Touch not my anointed, and to my prophets do no harm." "Christ" comes from the Greek for "anointed."

[12] Rom. 8, 31: "If God is for us, who can be against us?"

[13] If Tommaso has a company, it would seem that he is still a mercenary leader. The references to shedding blood and winning by losing would also point to this military role.

in blood shed for holy Church every sin and evil one has committed is washed away.[14] And even if you should be victorious, you have already made the offering of your life before God by putting yourself in danger of death. And should you acquire any material goods, they are legitimately yours.[15]

Who then, dearest brother, would not want to submit to any pain or torment in order to be a faithful servant to this sweet bride? Those who are blinded, who spurn and persecute Christ's blood, will not put themselves in such a situation. They are in one blow killing both soul and body even while they are dissipating their temporal goods. Oh what a great favor God has done you and the others who serve the Church, to have made you not her persecutors but her helpers! I tell you, you could not repay such a favor even if you gave up your body to be burned![16]

I beg you, then, to respond with unspeakable love, to be a mirror of virtue in your station in life, so that you may act with a good and holy intent and be a solid pillar and a faithful servant, and so that the standard of the most holy cross may never leave your mind and heart. If you are not virtuous, if you do not cleanse your conscience in holy confession, you will not be a faithful servant to God or to God's Church, nor will you be a good worker in this holy[c] garden. This is why I said I long to see you a faithful servant of holy Church.

I beg you earnestly, you and the others, in the name of Christ crucified: do this. And always season the virtue of justice with mercy—for otherwise it would not be virtuous. Bathe yourselves in the blood of Christ crucified. Do what is yours to do with holy intent and with good care. And I will raise my spirit and my hands to heaven and pray continually for you and for the others, begging God to keep you safe from all evil and give you grace to make a sweet peace.

And once peace has come, let's all go together, as a lovely troop, against the unbelievers.[17] That will give me the greatest joy. But what gives me the greatest pain is to see that we have been brought to such a

---

[14] Those who fought in the papal armies, whether in a crusade or "at home," were promised a plenary indulgence for their participation. So Tommaso and his company are being invited to lend their services to the papal cause.

[15] Cf. Aquinas, *Summa Theologica*, II, q. 66, a. 8, reply to obj. 1: "If those who take spoils from the enemy are waging a just war, such things as they seize in the war become their own property. This is no robbery, so that they are not bound to restitution."

[16] Cf. 1 Cor. 13, 3.

[17] Clearly a reference to the crusade to regain the Holy Land, which Catherine has been promoting since early 1375. Those who will go with her to the Holy Land are here given that title Catherine uses of her disciples only in the context of the crusade: *una bella brigatta*.

pass that one Christian is fighting the other. And rebel children are fighting their father, persecuting the blood of Christ crucified!

I'll say no more to you. Keep living in God's holy and gentle love.

Gentle Jesus! Jesus love!

Textual Notes

a. The punctuation of Mo makes it clear that, in spite of the ambivalent word order in the original, *at the moment of death* modifies *see* rather than *is found faithful.*

b. S3: holy sacraments / sacraments.

c. *holy* inserted by *b.*

LETTER T238/G9/DT80[1]
To Pope Gregory XI, in Avignon
Early September 1376

It is clear from Catherine's remark toward the end of this letter that the pope has "already done the first thing by setting the wheels in motion for [his] departure" that it is being written after Gregory XI has definitively decided to leave Avignon. It must therefore be early September of 1376.[2]

The rubric of B names the scribe as Stefano Maconi.

§

In the name of Jesus Christ crucified and of gentle Mary.

Most holy father in Christ the gentle Savior,

Your poor unworthy daughter Caterina sends you her greetings in his precious blood. I long to see God's will and your desire fulfilled, and to see the standard of the most holy cross raised up high.[3] It seems it is God's gracious will that you do raise this sign, and I know, most holy father, that it is your own great desire. Since God wants it, and since you have the good will to do it, I am begging you and telling you, for love of Christ crucified, do not disappoint us. No, if the good gentle Jesus is sending you the way and the means of setting this holy work in motion, do it. If you do, God will favor his bride, and so you will go from war to peace with his divine help.

I know it was my understanding that you said, when I was with your holiness, that you had to have a prince who would be a good leader, and that otherwise you did not see how it could be done. I have your leader, holy father. The duke of Anjou is willing, out of love for Christ and reverence for the holy cross, to take on this task with loving and holy desire.[4] In his love for the holy crusade this seems light to him. And it will

---

[1] MSS: B, H, P1, P3, S2, P4, S4; translation based on S2, with reference to H. No relevant variants.

[2] The date is firmly supported by the linguistic data as well. The only other letter sharing eleven or more of this one's twenty-six analyzed patterns is from April 1376. Seven patterns (PASSTRET, VOSTCAT) or significant clusters within patterns (GIARDCHS, MONDCONF, PREZSANG, SOPRINFD, TEMMORTE) end by January 1377, and two clusters (MONDCONF, TEMMORTE) begin in September 1376. Fawtier (II, pp. 146–147) places the letter in late August or early September; Dupré Theseider places it in early September.

[3] Again, she is urging that the projected crusade be set in motion.

[4] Cf. Let. T235/DT78 and T237/DT79 (both in this volume), concerning the duke of

seem a real delight to him if only you, my most holy father, are willing to give it your attention. *Oimé! Dear God, Love, don't wait any longer to carry out your holy desire and gracious will!* May you know, may you know how to hold the treasures and gifts Christ is setting before you, now while you have time!

It seems divine Goodness is asking three things of you. For the first one I am [already] thanking God and your holiness. For he has strengthened and settled your heart, made you firm in the face of the opposition of those who want to keep you from going to take possession of your rightful place.[5] I am jubilantly happy about your wholesome perseverance so far in carrying out God's will and your own good desire.

Now I am asking you to be conscientious about fulfilling God's other two demands. When I prayed to our dear Savior for you, as you had asked,[6] and he revealed that I should tell you that you must go, I made excuses, considering myself unworthy to be the messenger of so great a mystery. I said, "My Lord, I beg you, if it is your will that he go, fire up his desire and make it grow stronger." And our dear Savior in his goodness said, "Tell him positively that I am giving him this one sure sign that I want him to go. Tell him the more opposition he encounters and the more people say he shouldn't go, the more he will feel a courage growing within him that no one can take away, though this is contrary to his natural bent.[7] And now I am telling you that I want him to raise the most holy cross against the unbelievers. And I want him to raise it as well against those in his care, those who graze and feed in the garden of holy Church, those who are ministers of my blood. I am saying I want him to raise the cross against these people by prosecuting their vices and sins."[8] Once vice has been rooted out, virtue is planted by putting this cross into the hands of good pastors and administrators for holy Church. And if in fact there aren't any such, he wants you to see that those who are chosen are good and virtuous people who are not afraid of physical death. God doesn't

---

Anjou, who has promised her he will go to offer his services to Gregory XI. Catherine had already in August 1375 suggested to Giovanna d'Angiò (Let. T143/DT39, vol. I) that if she would subscribe to the crusade, others would follow.

[5] That is, Rome. She believes, as do many of her day, that since Rome was the See of Peter, it should be the residence of every pope.

[6] So the pope has clearly seen Catherine as something of an oracle of the divine will, a role in which he cast Birgitta of Sweden while she was still alive.

[7] Dupré Theseider, *I papi di Avignone e la questione romana*, Firenze: Felice le Monnier, 1939, pp. 190–193, deals at some length with the character of Gregory XI, both his strengths and his shortcomings. Catherine here points out his irresoluteness, one of his chief weaknesses.

[8] Catherine's language shows that she sees the reform of the Church as a crusade as much needed as the crusade to regain the Holy Land.

want you to pay attention to their worldly status or grandeur or prestige (for Christ has nothing in common with such things). Be concerned only about the wealth and grandeur of their virtue.[9] In this way the good, by the power of the cross, will prosecute the vices of the wicked.

I beg you, most holy father, for love of the Lamb who was slain, consumed, and abandoned on the cross: as his vicar fulfill this holy will of his by doing what you can. Then you will be excused before him, and your conscience clear. But if you don't do what you can, God will really blame you. I trust in God's goodness and your holiness that you will do it. Just as you have already done the first thing by setting the wheels in motion for your departure,[10] so now you will see to the other two as well—the holy crusade, and the prosecution of the sins being committed in the body of holy Church.

I'll say no more. Forgive my presumption. His lordship the duke of Anjou will, I know, come with great eagerness to discuss with you the matter of the holy crusade, as I have told you. For love of God, make it worth his while and fulfill his sweet desire. I humbly ask your blessing.

Gentle Jesus! Jesus love!

---

[9] Also in Let. T109/DT51 (vol. I) she has outlined the qualities the pope should look for in those he would appoint to ecclesiastical offices: "And when the time comes to appoint pastors and cardinals, tell him they are to be appointed not for flattery or money or simony, but beg him as earnestly as you can to watch for virtue and a good holy reputation in the candidates. Let him not favor a nobleman more than a merchant, because it is virtue that makes a person noble and pleasing to God."

[10] Catherine seems to take for granted that Gregory will leave Avignon soon.

LETTER T210/G138[1]
To Matteo di Fazzio dei Cenni, in Siena
About September 1376

Matteo di Fazzio dei Cenni, lay rector of the Casa della Misericordia, a hospital near Siena's *Campo,* became Catherine's disciple quite early in her public life.[2] Since this letter is, according to the rubric, addressed to Matteo in Siena, one may quite safely assume that Catherine is elsewhere when she is writing. References to "members cut off" put it almost certainly after August 1375, when Florence joined the antipapal league. (That, in fact, is when Catherine first began to use the expression). It is also quite probable, since Matteo is a citizen of Siena, that Siena too has joined the antipapal league (which it did on 27 November 1375). Again, there are no references to lambs and wolves before late March 1376 and only one after October of that year, thus further narrowing the probabilities of when this letter was written. Other linguistic evidence seems to support its placement very near the end of Catherine's stay in Avignon.[3]

§

In the name of Jesus Christ crucified and of gentle Mary.

Very loved and dearest brother and son in Christ gentle[a] Jesus,

I Caterina, servant and slave of the servants of Jesus Christ, am writing to encourage you in the precious blood of God's Son. I long to see you immersed and drowned in the flowing tide of that blood of his. Remembrance of that blood restores warmth and light to cold and darkened souls. It gives generosity and frees from small-heartedness.[4] It frees from pride and pours in humility. It frees from cruelty and gives compassion.[5]

Oh boundless love, charity! I am not surprised that in your blood I discover the power of compassion, for I see it was through divine compassion and not

---

[1] MSS: Mo, R1, P5, P3, P4; translation based on Mo-*a*, corrected by *b*.

[2] Cf. introduction to Let. T137/DT45 (vol. I).

[3] SCRIVCON and PREZSANG occur only until September and November 1376 respectively, and ANSIET, FABBRIC, and SANGPIET do *not* occur otherwise until October 1376 or later. Four of the letters which share seven or more of this one's twenty-eight analyzed patterns range up to mid-1376, and three from 1378 to 1379. Neither Fawtier (II, p. 216) nor Dupré Theseider (unpublished notes) venture to date this letter, though Dupré Theseider considers several possible placements.

[4] Cf. Let. T205/DT5 to Bartolomeo Dominici (1378), where the idea is developed at length in reference to the crucified Christ but not specifically to his blood.

[5] It. *pietà*.

because you had to that you shed your blood and took vengeance on the consummately cruel cruelty we inflicted on ourselves when by sin we made ourselves worthy of death.[6]

I long, then, to see you immersed in this river so that you may absorb from it the kind of tender compassion and mercy you must constantly exercise in your way of life.[7] I do want to see you exercise this virtue for Christ's poor with your material possessions. But I am not satisfied with that. No, I am inviting you, as God invites my soul, to extend your fervent loving desires, with compassionately tearful eyes in the presence of divine compassion, to all the world.[8] And [Christ] teaches us very effectively. As one drunk with love, and out of his desire to do quickly what he has to do, he says, "Take the body of holy Church, its severed members as well as those still attached, and with tender compassion lay it on my body." On that body of his all[b] our sins were hammered out, for he was the one who in his pain captured the city of our soul, and the Father was the one who accepted the sacrifice.[9]

So let us eat, eat souls at this table, the body of God's dear Son.[10] Then, when anxiously painful desires and wearisome waiting have passed and have been replaced by sweetly and lovingly fulfilled desires in which our soul will find peace in seeing the accomplishment of what we have so long desired, we shall be able to cry out to the Father in the sweet and tender words of the Church: "Through Jesus Christ our Lord you have been merciful to us in ridding us of the wolves and planting the lambs."[11]

---

[6] Cf. Prayer 15 (pp. 127–136), all of which is a hymn to the paradox of compassion and cruelty.

[7] As rector of a hospital, Matteo would especially need these qualities.

[8] Perhaps Catherine is recalling her visionary experience of 1 April 1376, when Christ sent her to believers and unbelievers alike with the cross of redemption and the olive branch of peace. (Cf. Let. T219/DT65 to Raimondo da Capua and others, in this volume.)

[9] Note the close parallel with *Dial.* 140, pp. 288–289, where Elisha lays himself on the dead child, member for member, to revive him. Here that image is crossed, as it were, with the image of Christ's body as an anvil, an image which is first used in mid-1375.

[10] Catherine often speaks of "eating souls at the table of the cross," that is, finding one's nourishment in living and dying for the salvation of others along with the crucified Christ. Cf. Let. T208/DT6 to Bartolomeo Dominici (in this volume): "I want to see us at the table of the spotless Lamb, who is food, table, and waiter. The fruits on this table are the true solid virtues. No other table bears fruit, but this one's fruit is perfect, because this table is life-giving. This table has been furrowed, with channels everywhere flowing with blood. But among them all there is one channel flowing with blood and water mixed with fire, and to the eye that rests on this channel is revealed the secret of his heart. This blood is a wine on which our soul gets drunk. The more we drink, the more we would like to drink, and we are never fully satisfied, because his flesh and his blood are joined with the infinite God. Oh dearest son in Christ Jesus, let us eagerly run to this table!"

[11] She cites this prayer as if she is familiar with it from some liturgical source, but I have not found that source.

Oh father, brother, and son in Christ Jesus, let us then rise from the slumber of apathy, so that we may before long escape from the hands of the wolves and come to such bliss—not for our own sake but only for God's honor. This is the sort of compassionate strength I want us to have. And this is why I said that I long to see you drowned in the blood of God's Son, for it is the remembrance of his blood that nurtures the power of compassion and mercy in our soul.

I'll say no more. Keep living in God's holy and tender love.

Gentle Jesus! Jesus love!

Textual Notes

a. P3, T, R1: [*gentle*].

b. P3, R1: [*all*].

LETTER T234/G215/DT82[1]
To Buonaccorso di Lapo, in Florence
Early September 1376

Buonaccorso di Lapo came as Florentine ambassador to Siena in March of 1375. He was a member of the *Signoria* of Florence during March and April 1376, and may well have been the one who promised Catherine the city's support in her negotiations with the pope for peace. When the three Florentine negotiators arrived in Avignon in mid-July, Catherine asked to see them, and in Raimondo's presence reminded them of what the *Signoria* had promised her. She told them that the pope had entrusted her with the negotiations and that satisfactory terms would therefore be theirs if only they wanted them. The ambassadors insisted that Catherine had no credentials or authority in the matter; nor were they authorized to submit to what she asked.[2] The present letter is clearly written in reaction to that rebuff. Still, it must be quite near the pope's departure (and her own) from Avignon on 13 September, since she seems so certain of the pope's imminent departure. I would therefore place the letter in early September.[3]

§

In the name of Jesus Christ crucified and of gentle Mary.

Dearest brother in Christ gentle Jesus,

I Caterina, servant and slave of the servants of Jesus Christ, am writing to you in his precious blood. I long to see you and your other *signori* with heart and soul at peace in his very dear blood, where all hatred and war are quenched, and all human pride brought low. For in his blood we see how God stooped down to us by taking on our humanity, and how that humanity was nailed fast to the cross and opened up so wide that from the wounds in the body of Christ crucified that blood pours out and is administered to us by the ministers of holy Church. I beg you, for love of Christ crucified, to accept the treasure of the blood given you by Christ's bride.

---

[1] MSS: B, P2, T, P5, F2, P3; translation based on T, with relevant variants based on Dupré Theseider.

[2] Raimondo's account of this sequence of events is found in *Life*, III, vi, 420–421, pp. 380–382.

[3] This date is only very broadly supported by the linguistic data. All of the eight other letters which share six or more of this one's sixteen analyzed patterns occur before the end of summer 1377. And two significant clusters within specific patterns (PAROLOP, TENVILE) are concentrated within the first nine months of 1376. Fawtier (II, pp. 255–257) and Dupré Theseider place the letter near Gregory's departure from Avignon.

Be reconciled, be reconciled with her in that blood! Recognize your sins and offenses against her,[a] for those who recognize their guilt, and prove by their actions that they recognize it and are humbled, always receive mercy. But those never find mercy who offer words of repentance but fail to act accordingly.[4] I am saying this not so much for you as for others who might be guilty in this regard.

Oimé! Oimé! How heartsick I am, dearest brother, about the ways you have chosen to ask the most holy father for peace! For there has been more evidence of words than of action. I say this because when I came there to you and your *signori*, they seemed by their words to be repentant and willing to humble themselves by asking for the holy father's mercy. I told them, "Look, gentlemen, to the extent that you intend to speak and act with all humility, and are willing to have me offer you to your father as dead children,[5] I will work hard for your cause. Under no other conditions will I go." And they answered that they were satisfied.

Oimé! Oimé! Dearest brothers, this is the way and the door by which you must enter; there is no other. If you had followed this way in your actions as well as in your words, you would have had the most glorious peace anyone ever had. I am not saying this without foundation, because I know what the holy father's disposition was. But once we started getting off this path and following the scheming ways of the world, acting in fact differently from what was conveyed in what you said, the holy father has been given reason not for peace but for more consternation. For when your ambassadors came here they did not act as they should have, as they had been directed by the servants of God.[6] You went your own way, and I was never able to confer with them, in spite of what you told me when I asked for a letter of credentials. You said then that you would tell them we would confer together about everything. You said, "We do not believe this matter will ever be resolved except through the hands of the servants of God." And just the opposite has been done.

---

[4] Cf. Mt. 7, 21: "None of those who cry out 'Lord, Lord,' will enter the kingdom of God but only the one who does the will of my Father in heaven."

[5] She has used the same expression in an earlier letter to the Eight of War (T230/DT72, in this volume).

[6] When the three Florentine ambassadors (Pazzino Strozzi, Alessandro dell'Antella, and Michele Castellani) had finally arrived in Avignon in mid-July, they knew that the Eight of War were divided on the terms they would accept for reconciliation. At least some of them were unwilling to settle for anything less than a complete end to the Church's temporal power. At the same time, the *Signoria* elected on 1 July had commissioned the three "to make truce or peace with the pope or his commissary on whatever conditions they may see fit," and had written to Cardinals Orsini and Corsini asking for their intervention on behalf of a republic which had acted only in defense of its liberty. It is not surprising under these circumstances that the ambassadors were unwilling to deal with anyone other than "the pope or his commisary." (Cf. Gardner, *Saint Catherine of Siena*, pp. 178–181.)

All this is because we don't even have a true knowledge of our sins. I realize now that your humble words were prompted more by fear and necessity than by any motive of love or virtue. For had there in truth been any recognition of your guilt, your actions would have been consistent with what you had said. You would have put your needs and whatever you wanted from the holy father into the hands of the true[b] servants of God. And they would have so mediated your demands and those of the holy father that you would have come to a good understanding. But you failed to do that, and the offense to God and your own loss have been the source of great anguish for me. You do not realize how much evil and trouble come from your[c] stubborn insistence on your own direction.

Oimé! Oimé! Free yourselves from the bond of pride and bind yourselves to the humble Lamb. Do not insist on your scornful defiance of his vicar. No more of this, for love of Christ crucified! Do not hold his blood so cheap! What you failed to do in the past, do now. Do not be bitter or resentful if it seems to you that the holy father is demanding the hard or the impossible. He will not ask anything beyond your capability. He is only acting like a true father, who punishes his son when he does wrong. He scolds him severely in order to make him humble, to make him recognize his guilt. And a good son does not hold this against his father, for he knows that whatever his father does is done in love. The more his father rebuffs him, the more he returns, always asking for mercy.[7] So I am telling you in the name of Christ crucified: as often as you are spurned by your father, Christ on earth, run back to him. Let him do it, for he has his reasons.

Look, now he is coming back to his bride—I mean the place of Saint Peter and Saint Paul.[8] See that you run to him at once, with true humility of heart and repentance for your sins, following the holy principle on which you began. If you do, you will have spiritual and bodily peace. But if you don't we shall have troubles such as our ancestors never had; for we shall be calling down God's wrath upon ourselves, and shall have no more share in the blood of the Lamb.[9]

---

[7] She never tires of using this image of father and children in her attempts to persuade the rebellious republics to reconcile with the pope. (Cf. Let. T207/DT68, T255/DT71, T230/DT72, all in this volume.) Here she develops the imagery even further.

[8] Catherine is writing after the time of the pope's departure has been decided. Dupré Theseider (n. 7 to this letter) believes that she may even have entrusted the letter to the Florentine ambassadors themselves, who returned to Florence on 25 September and so were perhaps leaving Avignon during the first week of that month, not long before the pope and Catherine herself would leave.

[9] On 2 August 1375, Matteo Minucci had written in a letter: "If the Sienese will believe me that they should adhere to the Church, good for them; for there will be stranger things than have ever been seen in these parts" (Dupré Theseider, n. 8 to this letter). In fact, the

I'll say no more.

Be as diligent as you can, now that the holy father will be in Rome. I have done and will continue to do whatever I can, even to the point of death, for God's honor and your peace, and for the elimination of this obstacle to the sweet holy crusade. For even if this were the only evil to come of [our rebellion], we should be deserving of a thousand hells. Take heart in Christ our gentle Jesus, for I trust in his goodness that, if you act as you should, you will have a good peace. Keep living in God's holy and tender love.

Gentle Jesus! Jesus love!

Textual Notes

a. B, P2: [*in the blood. . . . her*].

b. P2: [*true*].

c. B, P2: *our / your*, as also in the next case.

curia was by late summer of 1376 threatening papal anathemas and the proclamation of a universal crusade against the Florentines.

LETTER T239/G10/DT81[1]
To Pope Gregory XI, in Avignon
Early September 1376

Under Catherine's strong influence, the vacillating Gregory XI had become firm in his resolve to leave Avignon and take the papacy back to Rome, when (according to the introductory rubric of B and P2) he received a letter purporting to be from a certain man well-known for his holiness. The communication, among other things, urged the pope to cancel his departure on the grounds that there was a plot in Rome to poison him. Gregory, as indicated by this reply, sent the letter on to Catherine for her assessment. The present letter was, then, written only shortly before 13 September 1376, when Gregory actually left Avignon for Rome.[2]

§

In the name of Jesus Christ crucified and of gentle Mary.

Dearest, gracious, most holy father in Christ gentle Jesus,

Your poor unworthy daughter Caterina, servant and slave of the servants of Jesus Christ, is writing to your holiness in his precious blood. I long to see you so strong and persevering in your good holy resolution that no contrary wind or devil, or anything or anyone else, can stand in your way. It seems [your enemies] want to come (as our dear Savior says in the holy gospel) in sheep's clothing, looking like lambs, though they are rapacious wolves.[3] Our Savior tells us to beware of them.

It seems to me, dear father, that they are already beginning to come to you in writing, and besides writing, this one announces that he will arrive at your door without warning.[4] He sounds humble, saying, "If you open to me I will come in and we will talk things over together."[5] He dresses

---

[1] MSS: Mo, B, P2, H, P1, P3, S2, S4, P4, V; translation based on Mo-*a*, corrected by *b*, with reference to V, H. Other relevant variants based on Dupré Theseider.

[2] The dating is strongly reinforced by the linguistic data, especially by significant clusters within individual patterns. Four of these (CARAVITA, COLTPARO, MADCHIES, MADRLATT) end by October 1376 and three others (QUIETAN, SOPRINFD, VOSTCAT) by January 1377. Further, two of these patterns (MANTELLO, QUIETAN) do not occur at all before September 1376. Both Fawtier (II, p. 147) and Dupré Theseider place this letter shortly before the departure from Avignon.

[3] Mt. 7, 15.

[4] Cf. Mk. 13, 35: "You do not know when the master of the house is coming."

[5] Cf. Rev. 3, 20: "Here I stand, knocking at the door. If anyone hears me calling and opens the door, I will enter the house and have supper with that person." Dupré Theseider (n. 5 to this letter) thinks it probable that the writer had opened his letter with this citation.

up in humility so you will trust him.

What a glorious virtue pride cloaks itself in![6] As I read it, he has dealt with your holiness in this letter as the devil often deals with people when, under the pretext of virtue and compassion, he injects poison into them. And he uses this device especially with God's servants, for he sees that he could never deceive them with naked vice. This, it seems to me, is what this devil incarnate is doing who has written to you under the guise of compassion and reputation for holiness. I mean, though it appears to come from a holy and just man, it comes in fact from evil men, counselors of the devil who cripple the common good of[a] the Christian congregation and the reform of holy Church, selfish people looking out only for their personal ends. But you can easily tell, father, whether it came from that[b] just man or not. It seems to me God's honor demands that you investigate it. In my opinion [the letter] is not [from] a servant of God, but seems a forgery. From anything I can see or understand from it, it doesn't sound to me like [the man he purports to be]. In fact, the forger doesn't seem to know his art very well. He should have gone to school first; he seems to know less than a toddler!

Look, most holy father, how he has appealed to what he knows is the weakest point, especially in those who are very tender and compassionate in their human love and easy on their bodies; for such people hold life more precious than anything else.[7] This is why he emphasizes this from his very first word. But I trust that in God's goodness and your own holiness this sort of fear will not affect you. You will be a rock set upon the living rock.[8] You will be more concerned about God's honor and the salvation of your sheep than about yourself—like a good shepherd who should lay down his life for his sheep.[9]

It seems to me this venomous man on the one hand endorses your return as good and holy; but on the other hand he says they are ready to poison you. He is, it seems, advising you to send some trustworthy people ahead, where they will find this poison on the counter-tops (in the shops, apparently). It seems people plan to administer it in small doses—over a

---

The identity of the purported author of the letter is unknown, but it must be someone noted for his holiness and known to Catherine. Tommasèo thinks it may be the Franciscan Pietro d'Aragona, who was in fact highly esteemed by Gregory XI, but it is impossible to identify him for certain.

[6] Cf. Bernard de Clairvaux, *De gradibus humilitatis et superbiae*, XVIII, n. 47 (PL CLXXXII, 967): "What a glorious thing humility is, that even pride wants to dress up in it!"

[7] In *Dial.* 84, p. 154, she speaks of "that natural tenderness which binds soul and body."

[8] Cf 1 Pt. 2, 4: "Come to him, a living stone. . . . You too are living stones, built as an edifice of spirit."

[9] Jn. 10, 11.

few days or a month or a year.[10] Well, I assume as much poison can as well be found on the counter-tops of Avignon or any other city as on those of Rome! And it can be had in small doses over a month or a year, or in bulk, however the purchaser might choose; one can find it anywhere!

And still he thinks you should send people ahead and so delay your return. In this way, he claims, you can wait for divine judgment to descend on these evil men who, according to him, are plotting your death. But if he were wise he would be waiting for divine judgment to descend on *him* for sowing the worst poison that has been sown in a long time in holy Church—since he is trying to keep you from doing what God is asking of you and what you ought to do.[11]

And do you know how this poison would be sown? If you sent [other people] instead of going yourself—as this good man advises—you would be the cause of scandal and revolt, both temporal and spiritual, when people discovered deception in you who take the place of Truth. Why? Because[c] people would be so scandalized and confused and bewildered if you decided and announced that you would return, and then did the opposite, failed to go.

So he is really telling the truth; he has the same gift of prophecy Caiaphas had when he said, "It is necessary for one man to die so the people may not perish."[12] He didn't know what he was saying, but the Holy Spirit, who was speaking the truth through his mouth, knew very well. Still, that wasn't the devil's intention! So this man may well be another Caiaphas. He is prophesying that if you send [people ahead] they will find the poison. This is, in fact, true. For if our[d] sins are so great that you stay here while your trusties go on ahead, they will find the poison being put into the shops of their own hearts and mouths, just as he said. And it would take not merely a day, but a month and a year, before they got rid of it!

I am really amazed at what this man says! He commends the endeavor as good and holy and spiritual, and then wants you to give up that holy endeavor[e] for fear of physical harm![13] The servants of God don't usually

---

[10] Cf. Bernardino da Siena, *Predicazioni*, VII, p. 67: "Do you know how a person acts who wants to poison someone? When he comes to administer the poison he doesn't give it to [the victim] straight, but mixed with something else . . . so the one who is taking it isn't aware of it."

[11] That is, Gregory's return to Rome.

[12] Cf. Jn. 11, 49–52. Also Franco Sacchetti, *Sposizioni di Vangeli*, XXXVIII: "Caiaphas didn't know what he was saying, and he prophesied the truth. So not every prophet is holy."

[13] Dupré Theseider (n. 11 to this letter) concludes from this remark that the writer of the letter was not advising against the pope's going but simply attempting to gain some time. Note, however, that Catherine does not say "postpone," but "give up," as if to say,

want to abandon the spiritual enterprise no matter what the physical or temporal cost, even if it should mean their lives. If they did, none of them would reach their goal, because it is perseverance in good holy desire, along with good works, that is crowned and deserves glory rather than confusion.[14]

This is why I told you, reverend father, that I long to see you immovably firm in your good resolution; for from this will follow peace with your rebellious children and the reform of holy Church. And I long for the fulfillment of the desire God's servants have to see you raise the standard of the most holy cross against the unbelievers.[15] Then you will be able to administer the blood of the Lamb to these poor unbelievers, for you are the cellarer[f] of this blood, and you hold the keys to it.

Oimé! Father, I beg you for love of Christ crucified to use your power soon, for without your power it cannot be done. I am not, for all that, advising you, dear father, to abandon your legitimate children, who feed at the breasts of Christ's bride, in favor of these bastard children who have not yet been legitimized through holy baptism. But I am hoping, by God's goodness, that if your legitimate children go to them with your authority, with the divine power of the sword of[g] the holy word, and with human power and force, these [unbelievers] will return to their mother, holy Church, and you will legitimize them.[16] It seems this would better serve God's honor, your own good, and the honor and exaltation of Christ's dear bride, than would following the foolish advice of this "just" man who suggests that it would be better for you and the other ministers of God's Church to live among unbelievers and Saracens than among the people of Rome and of Italy! I like his wholesome hunger for the salvation of the unbelievers, but I don't like his wanting to take the father away from his legitimate children, to take the shepherd away from the sheep gathered in the fold.

It seems to me he wants to treat you as a mother treats the child she

---

"The man says that, however good and holy it may be in itself to return the papacy to Rome, it would not be good to do it at the cost of your life."

[14] Cf. Mt. 10, 22: "Whoever perseveres to the end will be saved." (Vulg.)

[15] As always, Catherine sees peace, ecclesiastical reform, and the crusade, and the pope's return to Rome as interdependent.

[16] The chief goal of the crusade in Catherine's mind is the conversion of the unbelievers, who will be "legitimized" by baptism. (Christians are the legitimate children of Christ and his bride the Church, as also in Let. T168/DT53 [vol. I] and T101/DT23 [in this volume]. She sees the Moslems as "bastards," but nowhere does she say who she sees as their spiritual parents. The only implication in the label "illegitimate," then, seems to be that the unbelievers are *not yet* children of Christ and the Church.) Catherine says they will "return" to the Church, just as in Let. T218/DT74 (in this volume), she speaks of "winning back" the unbelievers. She probably, however, has no true understanding of the historical origins of Islam.

wishes to wean. She puts something bitter on her breasts, so the child will taste the bitterness before the milk; then out of fear of the bitterness the child gives up sucking,[h] for a child is more easily tricked by bitterness than by anything else.[17] This is what that man is trying to do to you. First he sets before you the bitterness of poisoning and persecution to trick the childishness of your tender sensual love, so that fear will make you give up the milk—I mean the milk of grace that will follow from your return.[18]

I beg you in the name of Christ crucified not to be a timid child but a courageous man. Open your mouth and swallow the bitter for the sake of the sweet. It would not be right for your holiness to give up the milk because of the bitterness. I trust in God's boundless, infinite goodness that, if you are willing, he will give you (and us) the grace of making you strong and firm, unmoved by any wind or demonic illusion or advice from any devil incarnate.[i] You will then follow God's will and your own good desire and the advice of the servants of Jesus Christ crucified.

I'll say no more.

I'll close by saying I do not believe the letter sent to you came from the servant of God who was named to you. Nor was it written from very far away. On the contrary, I think it came from quite near by, from the servants of the devil, who have little fear of God. For to the extent that I *might* believe it came from that man, I would not consider him a servant of God if *this* were all I saw!

Forgive me, father, for speaking so over-presumptuously. I humbly ask your pardon and your blessing. Keep living in God's holy and tender love. I beg his infinite goodness to give me the grace, for his honor, of seeing you soon putting your foot across the threshold, in peace, in quiet, in tranquility of soul and body.[j] I beg you, dear father, to grant me an audience whenever it might please your holiness, for I would like to see you before I leave. Time is short, so I would like it to be soon, if that should please you.[19]

Jesus, gentle Jesus!

---

[17] This comparison is found in a passage from Augustine, *Enarratio II in Ps. CXXX, sermo II* (PL XXXVI, 246): "This is what wet nurses do: they put something bitter on their breasts, and the children, put off by it, back away from the breast and want the table instead." The Dominican Tommaso da Siena (Caffarini) had in 1374 developed some of the same ideas in a letter to Catherine (Let. I, ed. Grottanelli) in which he was commenting on Ps. 131 (Vulg. 130); he had not, however, used the same imagery.

[18] In other contexts she uses the metaphor of Heb. 5, 12–13: "You need milk, not solid food. . . . Solid food is for those whose faculties are trained by practice to distinguish good from evil."

[19] Catherine requests one last audience, since she has decided to leave Avignon. Her departure must have taken place about the same time as the pope's, though she and her company took a separate route from that of the papal entourage.

Textual Notes

a. B, P2: *good and / good of.*

b. P2: *a / that.*

c. B, P2: *Truth, which would be much worse because / Truth. ... because.*

d. Mo: *your / our.*

e. P2: *to hinder it / you ... endeavor.*

f. B, P2: *administrator / cellarer.*

g. B: *and of / of.*

h. *b*: *the sweet / sucking.*

i. B, P2: [*or advice ... incarnate*].

j. B, P2 end here with *Gentle Jesus! Jesus love!*

LETTER T240/G169/DT83[1]
To Monna Lapa, her mother, in Siena
Late October 1376, or possibly early November

Catherine's mother was always extremely attached to her daughter and would, in fact, have liked to dominate her life far more than Catherine would allow. Catherine is on her way home from Avignon with her companions (by land, whereas the pope's entourage has gone by sea) when she writes this letter to reassure and, at the same time, chide the impatient Lapa. We know from the letter itself that Neri di Landoccio Pagliaresi and others have been very ill, which we know happens while the company is in Genoa for "a month or more" from October into early November.[2] When the group reaches Pisa, Monna Lapa will rush from Siena to join her daughter, so Catherine can hardly be writing this letter from Pisa, unless it is just after the group reaches there in mid-November. I would place it more likely in late October, before Catherine and the others leave Genoa.[3]

§

In the name of Jesus Christ crucified and of gentle Mary.

Dearest mother in Christ gentle Jesus,

Your poor unworthy daughter Caterina wants to comfort you in the precious blood of God's Son. How I have longed to see you truly the mother of my soul as well as of my body! For I know that if you love my soul more than you love my body, any excessive attachment you may have will die, and my physical absence won't be so wearing on you. No, it will even bring you consolation, and you will be ready to bear any burden for God's honor, knowing that I am being used for that same honor. So long as I am working for God's honor, my soul can't fail to grow in grace and in virtue; so really, dearest mother, if you do love my soul more than my body, you'll not be dejected, but consoled.

I want you to learn from that sweet mother Mary, who for God's hon-

---

[1] MSS: B, P2, R1, T, P5, F2, F1, P3, R2, Nd; translation based on T, R1. Relevant variants based on Dupré Theseider.

[2] *Life*, II, viii, 261–264, pp. 244–247.

[3] The clustering of four of the letter's fifteen patterns broadly reinforces this dating (DESIDDE, PENAFIN, PREZSANG, VOSTCAT). This placement agrees with Fawtier's (II, p. 221) and Dupré Theseider's.

or and our salvation gave us her Son, dead on the wood of the most holy cross. When Mary was left alone after Christ had ascended into heaven, she stayed with the holy disciples. And then she willingly agreed to *their* leaving, for her Son's glory and praise and for the good of the whole world, even though it was wrenching, since they had been a great consolation to each other. She chose the pain of their departure over the consolation of their staying, and this only because of her love for God's honor and our salvation.[4] Now it is from her I want you to learn, dearest mother. You know that I must follow God's will, and I know that you want me to follow it. It was God's will that I go away—and my going was not without mystery, nor without worthwhile results. It was also God's will that I remain away; it was no mere human decision, and whoever says anything else is lying. And so I must go in the future, following in his footsteps however and whenever it shall please his boundless goodness.[a]

You, my good sweet mother, ought to be happy rather than dejected over having to bear any burden for God's honor and for your salvation and mine. You were glad, I remember, for the sake of material gain when your sons left home to win temporal wealth. But now when it is a question of winning eternal life it seems to be so hard that you say you are going to go to pieces[5] if I don't answer you soon. All this because you love the part of me that I got from you (I mean your flesh, in which you clothed me)[6] more than you love the part of me that I got from God. Lift, lift up your heart and affection a bit to that dear most holy cross, where every burden becomes light. Be willing to put up with a little finite suffering to escape the infinite suffering we deserve for our sins.[7] Take heart now, for love of Christ crucified! And don't imagine that God has forsaken you, or I either. You will in fact be consoled, and that completely. However great the pain may have been, the joy will certainly be greater.

With God's grace, we will be coming home soon. We would be there

---

[4] In Let. T30/DT1 (vol. I) and T164/DT58 (in this volume) it is the disciples who are praised for their willingness to leave Mary for the sake of their preaching mission—not surprising, since there Catherine is addressing other disciples, and here she is speaking to her mother.

[5] The expression used (*dilequare*) echoes Lapa's earthy language, reflected also in the way Raimondo quotes her, for example, *Life*, XI, viii, 242, p. 230: "God must have put my soul crosswise in my body, so it can't get out!"

[6] The image is a common one, used also, for example, by Dante (*Inferno* XXXIII, 62–63) and by Cavalca (*Ammonimento a S. Paula*, p. 159). Catherine uses it in reference to the flesh of the incarnate Word (Let. T177/DT61, in this volume, and Prayers 1, 3, and 15) and in reference to human flesh "re-clothing" the soul at the final judgment (*Dial.* 41).

[7] Cf. 1 Cor. 11, 32: "It is the Lord who chastises us to keep us from being condemned with the rest of the world." (Vulg.)

already had we not been held up by Neri's being very ill.[8] Maestro Giovanni and Frate Bartolomeo have also been ill. ...[9]

I'll say no more. Give our greetings. ... Keep living in God's holy and tender love.

Gentle Jesus! Jesus love!

Textual Notes

a. P2: *charity and goodness / goodness.*

[8] Raimondo da Capua tells (*Life*, II, viii, 262, p. 245) of Neri's illness in Genoa, as well as Stefano Maconi's. Catherine here informs us that the Augustinian Giovanni (Terzo) Tantucci and the Dominican Bartolomeo Dominici have also been sick at this time. Perhaps Stefano's illness comes a bit later, or possibly the mention of it was in the portion of the sentence which has been lost (see the following note).

[9] This sentence and one in the following paragraph are left incomplete (with the deletions noted by *&c.*) in the manuscripts.

LETTER T246/G51/DT85[1]
To the prior of the Monastery of San Girolamo at Cervaia
October to November 1376

There is one other extant letter which Catherine wrote to the monks of Cervaia (T189/DT84, in this volume), which I have placed in early April of 1376. Nothing in the content of the present letter helps to date it. A number of linguistic patterns, however, place it clearly before 1377.[2] At the same time, two patterns which occur only after late 1376[3] incline me to place it very near the end of 1376. It is therefore not unlikely that it is being written while Catherine is still in Genoa (October to early November) during her journey from Avignon, since the monastery is not far from that city.

§

In the name of Jesus Christ crucified and of gentle Mary.

Dearest and very loved father,

I call you father in reverence for the sweetest of sacraments,[4] and I call you son in holy and true desire, the desire that gives birth to your soul before God in holy prayer as truly as a mother gives birth to her child. I Caterina, poor miserable servant and slave of the servants of Jesus Christ, encourage[a] you and send you my greetings in the precious blood of God's Son.[b] I long to see you with heart and affection consumed in his consumed and blazing love.

This love of his consumed and burned and destroyed all our sins on the wood of the most holy and venerable cross. And this sweet fire has never stopped and will never stop burning, because if his affection for us should ever cease, we would cease to be. Why? Because it would be the end of what gives us being, for only the fire of love moved him to draw us out of himself. And it seems God's boundless charity wanted to provide as well for our human weakness and poverty, always inclined and ready to offend

---

[1] MSS: Mo, S2, P4, Pa; translation based on Mo-*a*, corrected by *b*. No other relevant variants.

[2] CONSUMAM, OCCHINT, VOMICO as well as the non-standardized protocol patterns A-VOI and PREZSANG.

[3] MADORAZ, PERAMORE. Fawtier (II, p. 184) and Dupré Theseider place the letter as I do.

[4] She often so qualifies her address of priests as "father."

our Creator, for God saw to it that this medicine for our sickness would be kept for us.

The medicine for our sickness is none other than this fire of love, a love you can never exhaust.[5] This is what we receive as medicine when we see how the standard of the most holy cross is implanted in us. We were, in fact, the rock in which this cross was imbedded, for neither nails nor wood could have held this dear spotless Lamb unless love and affection had held him there.[6] So when we realize how sweet and dear a medicine we have within us, we must never lapse into indifference but must surely rise up in our affection and desire, and stretch out our hands in the self-contempt the sick person has who hates to be sick and loves the medicine the doctor gives.

Oh son and father in Christ Jesus, let's get up with burning blazing love, with self-contempt and deep humility, recognizing our own nothingness and laying our weaknesses before the doctor, Christ Jesus. Let's reach out our hand to receive the bitter medicines he gives us. These are the bitter things that come our way so often—all sorts of darkness, temptation, spiritual frustration, or other troubles that come from outside ourselves. At the time they do seem bitter to us. But if we act like wise patients, they will be really sweet to us. I mean we look at the affection of the gentle Jesus who is giving them to us, realizing he does it not out of hatred but out of amazing love, for he cannot want anything but that we be made holy.[7] Once we have seen his goodness, we see also our own need. We

---

[5] She has described this medicine more at length in her earlier letter (T189/DT84, in this volume) to the monks of this same monastery: "Our sin, or any diabolical illusion or temptation, however repulsive, filthy, and ugly it may be, need not make us falter; for our doctor has given us a medicine for any sickness we may have. I mean the baptism of blood and of fire in which the soul cleanses and washes away every sin, consumes and burns away every diabolical temptation and illusion—for the fire is steeped in blood, so it truly does burn. This fire is the love that is the Holy Spirit, for love was the hand that pierced God's Son and made him shed his blood."

[6] Cf. Let T223 to Cardinal Iacopo Orsini (in this volume): "Bit by bit, as we look within ourselves, we come to discover God's goodness, and we grow in such a fire of love that we can no longer love or desire anything but God alone, in whom we have found such boundless goodness. We see that within us is the stone that held up the standard of the most holy cross—for except for the force of God's love for us, the stone could never have held [the cross] nor could the nails have held [Christ] fast. I remember this being said once to one of his servants. She [Catherine] in her boundless desire said, 'Oh my Lord, what grace it would have been for me if I had been some of the stone or soil in which your cross was set, for I would have received some of your blood that flowed down from the cross!' Gentle First Truth answered, 'My dearest daughter, you *were* the stone that held me, you and everyone else—I mean my love for you—for nothing else could have held me.' " Catherine may have been, in part, echoing Cavalca, *Specchio di croce*, p. 41: "No bond of iron could have held Christ nailed or bound—only charity, the bond of perfection."

[7] 1 Thes. 4, 3.

really do need these things, because without them we would go from bad to worse. But they make us come to know ourselves. And they rouse us from the sleep of apathy and free us from ignorance, for they make us vomit up our pride.[8] And from this is born a justice, and a holy gentle patience that makes us willing to endure any pain and torment, considering ourselves undeserving of spiritual peace and quiet.

This is how people act who are in love with God, who have conceived within themselves an utter self-contempt. Once they have opened the eye of their understanding and contemplated God's boundless goodness and charity to them, sufferings seem so sweet and pleasant to them that they seem incapable of enjoying anything else. They are always thinking about how they might suffer for love of their God. This is the way my soul wants and longs to see you go, so that if God should lead us and give us the grace of laboring and of giving our lives for him if necessary, the ship of our soul will be provisioned with blood and with the fire of divine charity.[9] And these we will seek and obtain in the way I've described.

I'll say no more. Keep your eye on those in your charge, and never refuse to see for any reason. Keep living in God's holy and tender love.

Gentle Jesus! Jesus love!

Textual Notes

a. *b*: *am writing to encourage / encourage.*

b. *of God's Son* erased in manuscript.

[8] The image is often used of rejecting sin, whether in conversion or in sacramental confession.

[9] This could be a reference to the crusade, since Catherine often encouraged even monks to join that effort.

LETTER T247/G355/DT86[1]
To Monna Giovanna di Corrado Maconi, in Siena
About 15 November 1376

On 29 November 1376, Stefano Maconi sends a letter to Neri di Landoccio Pagliaresi, who is still in Pisa with Catherine and the other travelers, saying that he and his traveling companions have arrived back in Siena "the Friday before last" (that is, 21 November), "safe and sound" in spite of their fear of encountering bandits along the way.[2] He must, then, have left the group at Pisa to return home immediately on their arrival there from Avignon, perhaps at the renewed pleadings of his mother, Monna Giovanna. Catherine is surely sending this letter close on his heels, most probably with him as he leaves Pisa, since she both apologizes for having kept him so long and asks Giovanna to take good care of him for her, and since Stefano in his letter mentions having delivered the letters sent home with him. I would therefore place the letter about 15 November.[3]

§

In the name of Jesus Christ crucified and of gentle Mary.

Dearest sister and daughter in Christ Jesus,

I Caterina, servant and slave of the servants of Jesus Christ, am writing to you in his precious blood. I long to see you clothed in the wedding garment without which I know we cannot please our Creator or have a place at the wedding feast of everlasting life.[4] So I want you to dress up, and to make that more possible, I want you to take off all your selfish and sensual love for yourself, for your children, or for any created thing apart from God.

You must not love yourself or anything else apart from God, for it is impossible to serve two[a] masters. If you serve the one, the other despises

[1] MSS: Mo, B, P2, R1, T, P5, F2, F1, P3, R2, S3; translation based on Mo-*a*, corrected by *b*, with other relevant variants based on Dupré Theseider.

[2] Grottanelli, *Leggenda minore*, "*Lettere dei discepoli*," V.

[3] This placement is supported by the linguistic data, in that five significant clusters of the letter's forty-four analyzed patterns (A-VOI, ADORNVES, GENTIL, MONDCONF, UMILCUOR) end in the last months of 1376, and six begin there (ADORNVES, AFFETT, MONDCONF, NOZZDURA, UMILCUOR). Fawtier (II, p. 306) places the letter "perhaps" during Catherine's stay in Genoa after her departure from Avignon. Dupré Theseider places it about 29 November.

[4] This is the garment of charity, an image Catherine develops both in view of the parable of the wedding banquet in Mt. 22, 1–14 and within her own understanding of the blood of Christ.

you.[5] No one can serve God and the world, for they have nothing in common.[6] The world seeks honor, status, wealth, the promotion of its children to high rank,[7,b] nobility, pleasure, sensual enjoyment—all rooted in and built on evil pride. But God seeks and wills just the opposite. He wants freely chosen poverty, humility of heart, contempt of self and of every earthly joy and pleasure. He does not want [us seeking our][8] personal honor, but God's honor and our neighbors' salvation. He wants us seeking only how we can clothe ourselves in the fire of blazing charity, with adornments of sweet solid virtue, with true holy patience. So we will not be vindictive about any wrong our neighbors may do us, but bear everything patiently, and seek vengeance only on ourselves for having sinned against gentle First Truth. And whatever we love, we will love in God, and we will love nothing apart from God.

And if you should ask me, "How am I supposed to love?" my answer is that you must love your children and everything else for love of the one who created them, and not for love of yourself or the children. Nor must you ever offend God for their sake or for any other reason. I mean you must not love them for any good they might do you, nor as if they were your property, but as lent to you—because whatever is given us in this life is given for our use and on loan, and we are allowed to keep it just as long as it pleases the divine goodness that gave it to us.[9]

So you should use everything as one to whom Christ crucified has entrusted it for administration. This is true of your material possessions, of which you should give as much as you can to the poor, who stand in the place of God.[10] And it is true of your provision for your children, in that you must nurture and raise them always in the fear of God, and be willing

---

[5] Cf. Mt. 6, 24. As usual, Catherine reverses subject and object in the second clause.

[6] Cf. Rom. 12, 2: "Do not be conformed to this world." (Vulg.) This theme is picked up by Augustine in *Sermones*, CXXV (PL XXXVIII, 694): "It is impossible to love what is eternal without refraining from the love of what is temporal. . . . Those who love the world cannot love God, for their spirit is already occupied."

[7] Being from a well-placed family of Siena, Giovanna may be wishing just this for her son Stefano, who himself tells in the *Processo Castellano* of how his home-town friends taunted him as *Caterinato* ("be-Catherined") after he had become her disciple.

[8] At this point Catherine unconsciously switches the subject from God to the human person. I have had to take some liberties with the English in the rest of this paragraph to embody the shift.

[9] This is a thought on which Catherine often insists with regard to both material possessions and children.

[10] Cf. Giovanni dalle Celle, Let. XXV, ed. Sorio, p. 165: "I call you poor, and St. Gregory [*Homiliae in Evangelia II, homilia XL*, 10—PL LXXVI, 1310] calls you patrons. He says, 'They shouldn't be called poor, but patrons through whose hands our alms are borne into the presence of God, and through whose prayers we receive mercy.' " Catherine echoes this thought in Let. T177/DT61: "Reflect that the hands of the poor are helping you to offer and receive divine grace."

to have them die rather than offend their Creator. Sacrifice, sacrifice yourself and them to God! And if you see that God is calling them, do not resist his gentle will. Rather, if they [offer themselves] with one hand, you as a truly good mother bent on their salvation [should offer them] with both hands. Don't try to choose their state in life to suit yourself (for this would be a sign that you love them apart from God), but be satisfied with whatever state God calls them to.

For often a mother who loves her children in a perverse worldly way will say, "I'm happy to have my children serve God, but they can serve him in the world just as well as anywhere else!" But these foolish mothers, who so want to submerge their children in the world, often end up having them neither in the world nor in God. And it's only just that they should be deprived of them in body as well as in spirit, since they are so proud and ignorant that they would like to lay down the law to the Holy Spirit, who is calling these children of theirs. Such mothers love their children not in God, but with a selfish sensual love apart from God, for they love their bodies more than their souls.[11] Never, dearest sister and daughter in Christ gentle Jesus, can one be clothed in Christ crucified unless one is first stripped of this sort of love.[12]

I trust that in God's goodness this will not apply to you, but that, as a true and good mother, you will give yourself and them to the honor and glory of God's name, and so be clothed in the wedding garment. But to make this more possible for you, I want you to withdraw your desire and affection from the world and all that is worldly, and open your mind's eye to know God's love for you. For in love God has given you the Word, his only-begotten Son. And the Son has given you life with such burning love; he has opened up his body to make his blood a bath for us. How wretchedly foolish we are, who neither recognize nor love so great a gift! But all this is because our eyes are shut. If they were opened and intent upon Christ crucified, we would not disregard or be thankless for such a grace.

This is why I am telling you to keep your eyes open always. Fix them firmly on the Lamb, slain and consumed, so that you may never be guilty of such foolishness.

Up then, dearest daughter! Let's not wait any longer! Let's make up for lost time by loving truly, perfectly, so that having by grace put on during this life the garment I've described, we may rejoice and be happy at the wedding feast of everlasting life—you and your husband and your children. Find sweet comfort in Christ gentle Jesus. Be patient, and don't be dis-

---

[11] She chided her own mother with the same in Let. T240/DT83 (in this volume).

[12] Cf. Rom. 13, 14: "Put on the Lord Jesus Christ and make no provision for the desires of the flesh."

turbed that I've kept Stefano so long, for I've taken good care of him.[13] I've become one with you in love and affection, and so I've taken what belongs to you as if it were my own! I trust you haven't minded too much. I want to do all I can for you and for him, even to the point of death. You, his mother, gave birth to him once; now I want to give birth to him and to you and to your whole family in tears and in sweat, by my constant prayers and desire for your salvation.

I'll say no more. Give my greetings to Corrado,[14] and bless the rest of the family for me—especially my new plant who has just begun again to take root in the garden of holy Church.[15] See that you take care of him and nurture him in virtue for me, so that he may be a source of fragrance along with the other flowers.

May God fill you with his sweetest grace! Keep living in God's holy and tender love.

Gentle Jesus! Jesus!

Textual Notes

a. B, P2: *two opposing / two.*

b. B, P2: *children / the ... rank.*

---

[13] Cf. Let. T99/DT7 (vol. I), in which Catherine "pledges herself in the sight of God" to be responsible for another spiritual son, Neri di Landoccio Pagliaresi.

[14] Corrado is Giovanna's husband and Stefano's father.

[15] She is certainly referring to Stefano, who at his mother's insistence had returned home to Siena as soon as Catherine's party had arrived in Pisa. She often uses the image of the "new plant" for those new to a religious way of life (whether vowed or not) or to ecclesiastical office. She refers to Stefano's "again" taking root in the Church. As Stefano himself confesses in his testimony in the *Processo Castellano* (pp. 258–259), "I didn't at all want to get to know her [Catherine] at that time [before early 1376], since I was immersed in the whirlpools of worldly living. But eternal Goodness ... arranged through this virgin to free my soul from the gullet of hell."

LETTER T7/G23[1]
To Pierre d'Estaing, Cardinal of Ostia
5 to 15 December 1376

Pierre d'Estaing, descended from an illustrious French family, was a Benedictine. Having been archbishop of Bourges since 1368, he was made cardinal by Pope Urban V in June of 1370, and shortly thereafter appointed vicar general to the south of Italy, an appointment confirmed by Gregory XI at his accession to the papacy in January of 1371. During that year, Cardinal d'Estaing proposed to the pope that the territories of the Italian peninsula be joined under a single legate, himself, and that his authority be significantly increased, a proposal which M. Antonelli sees as indication of d'Estaing's political ambition.[2] None of d'Estaing's proposals was ever enacted. Instead, Gregory at the end of 1371 relieved him of his post in the south of Italy and appointed him his vicar general and legate to Bologna. In September of 1373 he was named cardinal bishop of Ostia, while still retaining the legation to Bologna until early 1374.

D'Estaing was in Avignon at the time of Catherine's stay there, and was delegated, along with Cardinal Giles Aycelin de Montaigu, to negotiate with the Florentine ambassadors after the latter had disavowed Catherine's authority to mediate their cause. He was the only French cardinal to support Gregory's return to Rome and on 21 December 1376 he, along with Cardinals Corsini and Tebaldeschi, would win the submission of Rome to Gregory. He died on 25 November 1377 at his titular church in Rome, Santa Maria in Trastevere.

The *Cronaca di Bologna* describes d'Estaing as "a very great and upright man ... [with] great legatorial powers, and more authority from the pope than had ever been given to any other representative of the Church."[3] Ammirato Scipione calls him "a man of large heart and great wisdom."[4] Gregory XI testifies to d'Estaing's nobility in a letter to the Florentines.[5] Gardner's assessment of his character is more nuanced: he "was a great-

---

[1] MSS: Mo, P3, P4, B, P2, P1, H, P5, F2, S4, S2; translation based on Mo-*a*, corrected by *b*, with variants based on an unpublished transcription by A. Volpato.

[2] M. Antonelli, "La dominazione pontificia nel Patrimonio negli ultimi venti anni del periodo avignonese," *Archivio della R. Società Romana di Storia Patria* XXX (1907), esp. pp. 129–140. Appendix III in XXXI, pp. 321–328, gives the text of d'Estaing's proposal.

[3] Della Pugliola, *Cronaca di Bologna*, in *Rerum Italicarum Scriptores*, ed. Muratori, XVIII, col. 491.

[4] *Istorie Fiorentine*, pt. 1, vol. ii, p. 680.

[5] Cited by Étienne Baluze, *Vitae Paparum Avenionensium*, col. 1039.

hearted and far-seeing man, of virtuous life and enlightened views, albeit of an aristocratic and somewhat overbearing disposition"[6]

The dating of Catherine's two letters to Pierre d'Estaing (this and Let. T11, in this volume, to be dealt with later) is of particular importance, and therefore merits a detailed discussion. If they were indeed written at the time of his appointment as legate to the south of Italy in 1370 (as Fawtier contends) or to Bologna in 1371 (as Burlamacchi, and after him Tommasèo, Gardner, Drane, and Seckendorff contend), Catherine's political activity must be understood to have begun already then. In his early notes, Dupré Theseider also seems to lean toward this opinion, but he eventually excludes both letters from his first volume and places this one in January 1377.[7]

The first question to be raised is that of the legation of Pierre d'Estaing. Burlamacchi had before him only manuscripts in which the rubric for this letter was simply, "To the cardinal of Ostia when he was made legate." Burlamacchi interpreted this to refer to d'Estaing's legation to Bologna in 1371, the only appointment to which he gives the title "legate," even though he annotates the word *legato* in the text of the letter in terms broad enough to apply to all of d'Estaing's appointments. Then, since d'Estaing was neither cardinal nor bishop of Ostia until 1373, he concludes that the use of that title in the rubric must be attributed to a later copyist. However, the rubric of P4, generally a "well-informed" manuscript according to Dupré Theseider, though comparatively late (after 1461), reads: "To the above-mentioned cardinal of Ostia, in Corneto, when he was there again (*nuovamente*) made legate by the holy father." If this rubric is correct, the legation in question could only be that of December 1376, made while Gregory was in Corneto on his way back to Rome. The term *nuovamente* could, it is true, mean either "again" or "newly." In the text of Catherine's letters it is used in both senses. For confirmation of a date we must, therefore, look to other questions.

Is it likely that Catherine knew Pierre d'Estaing or even knew of him in 1371? Drane speculates that d'Estaing may well have visited Siena during his years in the south of Italy. Seckendorff seconds this and adds that Catherine had probably heard of Gregory XI's bull of May 19, 1371, ap-

---

[6] *Saint Catherine of Siena*, p. 77.

[7] F. Burlamacchi's notes in Gigli's 1548 edition of the *Epistole e orationi* in *Opere*, I, pp. 166–172; Tommasèo's notes to Let. 7 in his 1860 edition of *Lettere*; Gardner, *Saint Catherine of Siena*, pp. 106–110; Drane, *History of St. Catherine of Siena*, vol. I, p. 280; Seckendorff, *Politische Tätigkeit*, pp. 26–30; Jorgensen, *Saint Catherine of Siena*, p. 162; Dupré Theseider, unpublished notes.

pointing him to Bologna.[8] This supposition seems just a bit gratuitous, since Catherine's activities before 1374 were, from all we know, still centered within a fairly small circle in Siena. She seems not to have become politically active beyond her own city before her relationship with Raimondo da Capua, which began in May of 1374. On the other hand, she certainly must have met d'Estaing while she was in Avignon, since he was one of the two cardinals delegated to meet with the Florentine delegation which had repudiated her mission in their regard. So a warm letter to him after that period would not be surprising. Nor would it be at all surprising that she would hear of his being sent to prepare Gregory's way in Rome, since she herself had been so intimately involved in the pope's return.

The linguistic evidence of the letter reinforces this judgment.[9]

While none of the linguistic clues by itself would substantiate the dating of this letter, taken together with the rest of the evidence they do speak strongly for associating this letter with d'Estaing's 1376 appointment.

If d'Estaing was in Corneto with Gregory XI as the rubric of P4 seems to imply, then it could not have been written before 5 December, when Gregory arrived in Corneto. Also, if d'Estaing and his companions managed to settle matters with the Romans on 21 December, it is not likely that he left Corneto later than 15 December. In any case, when Catherine writes the present letter, she has apparently heard only of the appointment, not of any departure for Rome, much less of any accomplishment of the mission. I would therefore date this letter between 5 and 15 December 1376.[10]

---

[8] *Archivio Vaticano, Reg. Vat. Gregorio XI*, vol. 274, fol. 41b, cited in Seckendorff, *Kirchenpolitische Tätigkeit*, p. 28.

[9] There are five themes which do not occur in any of Catherine's writings before 1376: Christ as book of life (LIBROVIT), Christ making or being made our way (FATTVIA), Christ's patient response to flattery and ingratitude (MUOVIMPA), Pilate's fear (PILATUCC), and being of service to one's neighbor (UTILPROS). Significant clusters within four individual patterns end in early 1377 (DIONINUOM, PERMANE, SERVEFIG, VITUPDIO). All three letters which share thirteen or more of this letter's forty-nine analyzed patterns are from 1377.

[10] Both Fawtier (II, pp. 161–162) and Dupré Theseider (unpublished notes) wonder whether Catherine's failure to apologize for her boldness (something she so often does when writing to members of the hierarchy and royalty) points to a time before d'Estaing was cardinal. However, a scan of all of Catherine's letters to hierarchy and royalty reveals that, while she invariably so apologized to the popes (except in the possibly incomplete Let. T371 to Urban VI in 1380), she did not always do so to other members of the hierarchy or to royalty.

§

In the name of Jesus Christ crucified and of gentle Mary.

Dearest reverend father in Christ gentle Jesus,

I Caterina, servant and slave of the servants of Jesus Christ, am writing to you in his precious blood, longing to see you bound with the bond of charity. I've heard you have been appointed legate[11] to Italy,[a] a fact that makes me particularly glad, since I think you will in this post be able to do much for God's honor and the good of holy church. But this legation of yours would by itself be useless without another sort of bonding. That is why I said I want you to be bound with the bond of charity. For you know that where grace is concerned we can be of no service either to ourselves or to our neighbors without charity.[12]

Charity is the sweet holy bond that binds the soul with its Creator. It bound God into humanity and humanity into God.[13] This charity beyond measure held the God-man nailed fast to the wood of the most holy cross.[14] It resolves disharmony, unites those who been separated.[15] It enriches those who are poor in regard to virtue, because it gives life to all the virtues. It gives peace and abolishes war. It lends patience, strength, and enduring perseverance to every good and holy endeavor. Neither pain nor torment nor insult nor derision nor abuse can weary it or make it stop

---

[11] The play on words here is lost in translation, the Italian *legato* being the past participle of two separate verbs which had in their evolution from the Latin come to have the same spelling: the one from *ligare*, having to do with "binding," and the other from *legare* (and *lex/legis*), having to do with legislation and appointment. Catherine almost certainly saw the two as a single linguistic entity. In any case, she uses the double meaning to call the new legate ("appointed") to a special depth of "binding" in charity by virtue of his new title.

[12] For a development of this theme, see *Dial.* 7, pp. 35–38.

[13] That is, in the incarnation of the Word. In Prayer 17 (pp. 146–153) and Prayer 24 (pp. 207–208) she expands on this "bonding" under the image of engrafting. There are two engraftings. The first is the union of God with humanity and of individual human persons with God in Christ, with charity as the band that wraps and holds the graft secure. The "second engrafting" is the "union," the inseparable identification of Christ with the cross, where charity is the "bond" that holds Christ fixed to the cross.

[14] Cf. Cavalca, *Specchio di croce*, p. 41: "No bond of iron could have held Christ nailed or bound—only charity, the bond of perfection." This is a concept Catherine refers to often in more expanded forms, for example, *Dial.* 14, p. 52; 77, p. 143; Let. T223 (in this volume); Prayer 24, p. 207.

[15] In the context of this letter Catherine almost certainly has in mind the rift between the Italians and the Avignon papacy, which she is hoping will be healed through Gregory's return to Rome. The next several sentences are one the most lyrical hymns to charity in all of Catherine's writings. Another is found in Let. T279, written in 1378. Compare these with her hymns to patience in *Dial.* 77, pp. 143–144, and Let. T104 (in this volume), and her ecstatic hymn to God as sea of peace in *Dial.* 167, pp. 364–366.

loving God and our neighbors. Unwillingness to suffer does not move it [to seek] pleasure; nor do any of the gratifications that the world with all its wiles could give move it to complacency.[16,b] Those who have charity are stable and persevering, because they are grounded on the living rock, Christ gentle Jesus.[17] I mean they have learned from him, by following in his footsteps, how to love their Creator. In him they have read the rule and the teaching they must keep to,[c] for he is way and truth and life,[18] and so those who read him, the book of life, hold to the straight way, concerned only for God's honor and the salvation of their neighbors.[19] This is how Christ gentle Jesus himself acted. Neither pain nor torments nor flattery nor our ingratitude made him take back this love for his Father's honor and our salvation. No, he endures to the end, till he has accomplished his desire, the task the Father has placed in his hands, to redeem the human race, and thus he achieves both the Father's honor and our salvation.[20]

In this bonding, then, and in this love I want you to follow and learn from gentle First Truth. He has built for you the road that gives you life;[21] he has given you the form[22] and the rule, and has taught you the

---

[16] The sentence is made a bit obscure by the presence of an apparently superfluous *né* in the original, but the sense is confirmed by a similar passage in Let. T252/DT88 to Pope Gregory XI (written about the same time if my dating of the present letter is correct): "For, if disordered pleasure or enjoyment or complacency about ourselves and the world were to make us turn toward material well-being, or if impatience were to make us turn away from difficulties and abuse, and if we were to let go of affection for virtue . . . , then we had better realize that virtue is acquired and made perfect only by means of its opposite."

[17] 1 Cor. 10, 4; Mt. 7, 24–27.

[18] Jn. 14, 6.

[19] Cf. Cavalca, *Specchio di croce*, p. 147: "Christ . . . is the book of life, in which every person, worldly, unlearned, or of any other condition, can see and read the law well summarized. For Christ on the cross observed all the commandments; he accomplished and interpreted all the prophecies and fulfilled all the promises made about him . . . ; he carried out what he had preached. And so whoever studies him well easily learns the whole bible." Catherine borrows from Cavalca's image of Christ as book in a number of places, most notably in Let. T69/DT24 and T225 (both in vol. I). She also refers elsewhere to our being written in the "book of life." But this is the first time she explicitly identifies this "book of life" with Christ, an identification she will repeat in Let. T242 (in this volume) and T316 (late 1378) and in *Dial.* 77, p. 142. She does not, however, develop the specific identity of Christ as the book of life from which we learn with Christ as the book of life in which we are written.

[20] Cf. Lk. 12, 49–50.

[21] Cf. *Dial.* 100, p. 188: "the straight way, cemented with my own blood." Whenever Catherine uses the image of mortar or cement, the lime is mixed with the blood of Christ, "the blood that unites and conforms the soul with God's gentle divine will and charity" (Let. GardI/DT52, vol. I). In this blood is the source of life for those who follow Christ, a concept borne out also in her interpretation here and elsewhere of Jn. 14, 6, which she always cites as "way and truth and life," without the definite articles.

[22] The sense here could be "example," though she otherwise uses the Italian *esemplo* for

doctrine of truth. So I want you, as a true son, as a servant ransomed by the blood of Christ crucified, to follow in his footsteps. With a brave heart and ready zeal never let pain or pleasure cut you short,[d] but persevere to the end in this and in every other task you undertake for Christ crucified. Be attentive to the wretched wickedness of the world[e] and of all the sins that are committed to insult God's name, and then do what you can to remedy such evil, as one hungry for God's honor and your neighbors' salvation. I am certain that if you are bound by the sweet bond of charity you will use the legation to which Christ's vicar has appointed you in just this way. But without being first bound by charity, your position as legate will be useless, nor will you be able to fill it as you ought. So I beg you to work hard at having this love in you. Bind yourself to Christ crucified, and follow in his footsteps with true solid virtue. And to your neighbors bind yourself in energetic love.[23]

I want us to reflect though, dearest father, that unless our motivation is stripped clean of all selfish love, of self-complacency and desire to please the world, it can never attain to this true and perfect love, this bond of charity.[24] For the one love is opposed to the other, so opposed that selfish love separates you from God and from your neighbors, while perfect love unites you to both.[25] The one love is death-dealing, while the other gives life. The one brings darkness, the other light; the one war, the other peace. Selfish love shrinks your heart till it has room neither for yourself nor for your neighbors, while divine charity so expands it that it can welcome friends and enemies alike—everyone, in fact—because it is clothed in Christ's love and so follows him.[26] Selfish love is wretched. It parts ways with justice and perpetrates injustices; it is characterized by a slavish fear

---

this meaning, and this would be the only instance in which the Italian *forma* would have that sense. Cf., however, Let. T166 to Colomba of Lucca (vol. I): "He did this to give us an example (*esemplo*), since he was our rule and way, which we must follow." (Elsewhere in her writings the term *forma* has the common meaning of "shape" or the philosophical meaning of that by which a thing exists as what it is, neither of which seems applicable here.)

[23] It. *affetto d'amore.* And in the following sentence, "motivation" is also *affetto.*

[24] The expression *piacere* (or *piacimento*) *di sè* in Catherine's writings is in this case, as in every other, ambivalent. It can connote both self-complacency and the desire to please oneself. As here, it is often associated with a desire to please others and/or the world.

[25] The theme is greatly expanded in Let. T164/DT58 to Melina Barbani (in this volume).

[26] Cf. Let. T204/DT5 to Bartolomeo Dominici (in this volume): "I want you to imitate this Word who is our rule, and the saints who followed him. Then you will become one with him and will have a share in his great-heartedness to replace [your own] small-heartedness. I tell you again, unless you rise up, open your eyes, and take as your model the boundless goodness and love God has shown to his creatures, you will never attain such perfect greatness of soul but will be so small-hearted that you will have no room either for yourself *or* for your neighbors." It is the *affetto* of Christ the cardinal is to be clothed in: his love, his motivation, his energy.

that keeps it from acting justly as it should, whether because of flattery or dread of losing prestige. This is the perverse servility[f] and fear that led Pilate to kill Christ.[27] Such people do no justice, but only injustice. They live neither justly nor virtuously, nor are they motivated by divine love. No, they live unjustly, viciously, in dark selfish love.

I want you to be completely freed from such selfish love and grounded[g] in true and perfect charity, loving God for God's sake, because he is worthy of love, since he is supreme eternal Goodness. And love yourself for God's sake, and your neighbors for God's sake and not for your own selfish advantage. So, my father, legate of our lord the pope, I want you to be bound[28] with the bond of true and blazing charity. This is what my soul longs to see in you.

I'll say no more. Take courage in Christ gentle Jesus. And be zealous, not irresponsible, in what you have to do. I will know that you are zealous if you are thus bound, and if you are hungry to see the standard of the most holy cross raised high.[29] Keep living in God's holy and tender love.

Gentle Jesus! Jesus love! Mary![h]

Textual Notes

a. *b* supplies *to Italy*.

b. B, P2, P3, H, P4: *Unwillingness to suffer does not move it either to pleasure or to the gratifications which the world with all its wiles could give.*

c. *they must keep to* supplied by *b*.

d. B, P2, P3, H, P4: *wear you out* (*straccandovi*) / *cut you short* (*staccandovi*).

e. *b*: *Give your attention to wiping out the wickedness of the world's wretchedness / Be . . . world.*

f. B: *unreadiness / servility*.

g. *grounded* written by *b* over erasure.

h. *Mary!* from H.

---

[27] Her references to Pilate (Let. T168/DT53 in vol. I; T196/DT64 and T123 in this volume; *Dial.* 116) all stress that for fear of losing his power he killed Christ. Cf. Cavalca, *Specchio dei peccati*, p. 90: "Pilate had him crucified, even though he knew he was blameless, for fear of losing the emperor's friendship, as the Jews were threatening, if he would let him go."

[28] Again, *legato*.

[29] The reference is to the mounting of a crusade, a cause Catherine promoted from her earliest letters to the end of her life, but most insistently during 1376.

Part VI:
Siena and Belcaro
(Late December 1376 through early Summer 1377)

After a three-month journey from Avignon, Catherine and her company reached Siena in late December 1377.

Catherine had already in early 1376 begun to plan for the establishment of a monastery for women.[1] Before leaving for Avignon that spring, she must have received at least the promise of a building, the ruined fortress of Belcaro just outside Siena, to be donated for the purpose by her disciple Nanni di Ser Vanni Savini.[2] While in Avignon she had obtained the necessary ecclesiastical permissions from Gregory XI.[3] On 25 January 1377 she appeared before the Defenders of the Commune of Siena to explain her project for the refurbishment of the fortress. On her assurance that she would not allow the property to be used for military purposes or to harbor "malafactors," the council voted to grant her petition, with "three hundred thirty-three white beans cast in favor, in spite of sixty-five black beans having been cast in opposition."[4]

---

[1] Cf. Let. T12 to the abbot of Sant'Antimo, Giovanni di Gano da Orvieto (vol. I).

[2] Raimondo's *Life* (II, vii, 235–238, pp. 223–226) tells that Nanni was sent to Catherine by persuasion of William Flete and then converted by Catherine in Raimondo's presence—who then remained Nanni's confessor "for several years." Raimondo puts an imprisonment of Nanni "a few days after he had made his confession," with his release "after a few days" with the loss of "a great deal of property." Then he cites the donation of Belcaro, but with no time reference. There is no indication in Raimondo's *Life* of when all this took place, except that Raimondo was already obviously Catherine's confessor and was in Siena with her (therefore after May 1374 and before his departure for Avignon in February 1376). Caffarini cites a papal document which he saw in Venice (since disappeared) as granting permission "to build a monastery of sisters from a certain fortress in the city of Siena . . . given to her for this purpose, . . . and to accept up to two thousand florins on the occasion of the building of that monastery, and this through the mediation of the abbot of the Monastery of Sant'Antimo." (Sources cited in Grottanelli's notes to *Leggenda minore*, pp. 219–222, and in C. Camaiori, "Memorie storiche di Belcaro," *Bullettino Senese di Storia Patria* 20, 1913, pp. 365–367.)

[3] *Leggenda minore*, ed. Grottanelli, p. 219.

[4] Such permission was needed for the conversion to civilian use of any military property, even a half-ruined one such as Belcaro. A document in the Archives of Siena records the

The next months found Catherine occupied with the beginnings of that monastery, which she named *Santa Maria degli Angeli* ("Saint Mary of the Angels"). That work, however, did not keep her from continuing to concern herself with larger church issues and the personal needs of her disciples.

council's vote regarding Catherine's petition for the conversion of the fortress, which Nanni "is ready to donate for the building of said monastery" (*Consiglio generale*, Reg. 186, fol. 69, transcribed in Laurent, *Fontes*, I, *Documenti*, pp. 41–43).

Letter T252/G11/DT88[1]
To Pope Gregory XI, at Corneto
Between 15 December 1376 and 13 January 1377

Pope Gregory had left Avignon with his entourage on 13 September 1376. He had then sailed from Marseilles on 2 October, while Catherine and her company had taken their own route toward home, mostly by land, delaying in Genoa for a month because of illness among them. The pope's voyage was not a pleasant one, beset as it was with storms as well as with rumors of trouble awaiting his disembarkment. A number of times he was ready to turn back, as, for example, when Catherine encountered him in Genoa in October.[2]

Gregory's spirits are still low when Catherine writes the present letter to him during his sojourn in the port city of Corneto (5 December 1376 to 13 January 1377) before the final lap of his journey back to Rome. She herself has probably returned to Siena, since she sends the letter with a Sienese who we have no reason to believe was with her in Pisa. Catherine also must have had time for word of the pope's vacillation to have reached her. From that point of view, her letter can hardly be earlier than about 10 December. And, since Stefano Maconi still addressed a letter to Pisa on 8 December with greetings for Catherine and her company,[3] this present letter to the pope is probably not earlier than at least 15 December.

The Sienese bearer of the letter is the Gesuato Tommaso di Guelfaccio,[4] who was perhaps either accompanying a Sienese delegation or himself making an initial approach to the returning pope on behalf of the Commune, both to welcome him and to plead the Sienese cause. The "children who have offended" the pope and whom she asks him to receive kindly may be the Sienese in particular or the representatives of all of the rebellious republics.[5]

---

[1] MSS: Mo, B, P2, R1, T, P5, F2, F1, P3, R2, Nd, S3; translation based on Mo-*a*, corrected by *b*, with reference to H. Other relevant variants based on Dupré Theseider.

[2] Cf. Prayer 3, which dates from this occasion.

[3] Stefano Maconi to Neri di Landoccio Pagliaresi, ed. Grottanelli, *Lettere dei discepoli*, VI.

[4] Specified in an addition at the end of S2 and S4.

[5] The linguistic evidence broadly supports the historically established date. Four of the six letters which share twelve or more of this letter's forty-one analyzed patterns fall between April 1376 and August 1377 (the other two in 1379). Three significant clusters within individual patterns (AMDIODDI, CREATURA, VIRNTIM) begin within a few months of the established date, and three end with this letter (GLORLOD, GLORTRIB, SOPRINFD). Fawtier (II, pp. 148–149) places the letter near the end of 1376, while Catherine is still in Pisa. Dupré Theseider simply places it between 5 December 1376 and 13 January 1377.

§

In the name of Jesus Christ crucified and of gentle Mary.

Most holy and most reverend father in Christ gentle Jesus,

Your poor unworthy daughter Caterina sends you her greetings in his precious blood. I long to see your heart firm, stable, and strengthened in true holy patience, for I believe that a heart weak and inconstant and unwilling to suffer will never succeed in doing the great deeds of God.

Every one of us who wants to serve God and be clothed in virtue must have this constancy and strength and patience. In no other way can we have God within our soul. For, if disordered pleasure or enjoyment or complacency about ourselves and the world were to make us turn toward material well-being, or if impatience were to make us turn away from difficulties and abuse,[a] and if we were to let go of affection for virtue (the virtues we had conceived through holy desire as well as those we still want to acquire), then we had better realize that virtue is acquired and made perfect only by means of its opposite.[6]

So it turns out that we are evading virtue if we shun its opposite—evading the very virtue with which we should be resisting and overthrowing virtue's opposite, vice. With humility we should be driving out pride; and with freely chosen poverty, driving out worldly wealth and pleasures and prestige. Let peace drive out and conquer war in our own soul and in the souls of our neighbors. Let patience master impatience through love for God's honor and for our own virtue. And through hatred[b] and contempt for ourselves, let us bear[c] courageously and patiently anguish, abuse, derision and insult, physical pain, and temporal loss. This is how we ought to be:[d] constant, firm, stable, and patient. Otherwise we could not be servants of Christ,[e] but would become servants and slaves of our own selfish sensuality—and that sensuality deprives us of constancy and makes us cowardly, weak and puny-hearted.

But that's not how we ought to act. No, we must take as our model gentle First Truth, who restored[f] our life by suffering, taking on the burden of our sins. Oh most holy father, my dearest *babbo*,[g] open your mind's eye; see and understand! If virtue is so necessary for every one of us, if each one of us individually needs it for the salvation of our own soul, how much more do you need this constancy and strength and patience—you who must feed and govern the mystic body of holy Church, your bride!

---

[6] This concept is more fully developed in *Dial.* 8, pp. 38–39, and 98, pp. 184–186. It is found also (a bit differently developed) in Cavalca, *Medicina del cuore*, p. 206: "The stronger opposition and the more provocation it has, the greater the virtue."

You know that when you entered as a new plant[7] into the garden of holy Church, you had to prepare yourself with virtue to resist the devil, the flesh, and the world, the three chief enemies who fight against us day and night and who never sleep. I trust in divine Goodness that he not only has made you resist these enemies but will make you resist all others, so that he will have in you what he created you for, that is, that you give glory and praise to his name and experience his goodness by receiving that eternal vision of him in which our blessedness consists.[8]

At this point you are Christ's vicar. You have taken this on in order to work and fight for God's honor and the salvation of souls and the reform of holy Church. These things, hard and painful for you, are given to you in particular over and above the common struggles given to every soul who would serve God, as I have said.[9] And because your burden is greater you need a more bold, courageous heart, fearful of nothing that might happen. For you know well, most holy father, that when you accepted holy Church as your bride you agreed also to work hard for her. You expected all these contrary winds of pain and difficulty to confront you in battle over her. So confront these dangerous winds like a brave man, with strength and patience and enduring perseverance. Never turn back because of pain or discouragement or slavish fear, but persevere, and rejoice in the storms and struggles. Let your heart rejoice, for in the many contrary things that have happened or will yet happen the deeds of God are surely being done, nor have they ever been done in any other way.[10] So we see that the Church's being persecuted, and every difficulty virtuous souls experience will end in peace, won through true patience and perseverance.[h] Perseverance emerges crowned with a crown of glory.[11]

So this is the answer. And this is why I said, most holy father, that I long to see you with a heart firm, stable, and strengthened in true holy patience. I want you to be a tree of love, engrafted into the Word who is love, Christ crucified—a tree with its roots in deep humility, for God's

---

[7] In Catherine's writings, the term "new plant" usually refers to novices in religion or in ecclesiastical office. Here the reference is most probably to Gregory's early days in clerical life.

[8] Cf. Aquinas, *Summa Theologica*, I–II, q. 3, a. 8: "There can be no final and perfect blessedness except in the vision of the divine Essence." Also *Summa Theologica, Supplementum*, q. 92.

[9] She makes this distinction elsewhere as well between the "common" calling of all Christians and more "particular" callings.

[10] In April (Let. T219/DT65, in this volume) Catherine recounted to Raimondo an experience in which Christ had "told and explained bit by bit the mystery of the persecution holy Church is now enduring, and of the renewal and exaltation to come. He said that what is happening now is being permitted to restore her to her original condition."

[11] Cf. Mt. 10, 22: "Whoever perseveres to the end will be saved." (Vulg.)

honor and for the salvation of your little sheep. If you are a tree of love so sweetly rooted, you will find the fruit of patience and strength at the tips of your branches, and crowned perseverance nested within you.[12] You will find peace and quiet and consolation in suffering when you see yourself conformed in that suffering with Christ crucified. And so, by enduring with Christ crucified, you will come with joy from much war[i] into much peace.

Peace! Peace, most holy father! May it please your holiness to receive your children who have offended you, their father. Let your kindness overcome their malice and pride. It will be no shame for you to bend down to placate your naughty child. Rather it will be the greatest of honors, and very advantageous for you before God and the people of the world. Oimé! No more war, my *babbo*! There is a way to have peace[k] without compromising your conscience. Let the war be directed against the unbelievers, where it belongs.[13] Follow the meekness and patience of the spotless Lamb, Christ gentle Jesus, whose representative you are.[l] I trust in our Lord Jesus Christ[14] that he will so work within you in this matter and the others that he will fulfill your desire and mine—for I have no other desire in this life than to see God's honor, your peace, and the reform of holy Church, and to see the life of grace in everyone.

You can be encouraged about the disposition of the people here: from what I've been given to understand, they simply want you as their father—especially this poor city that has always been your holiness' daughter, and was constrained by necessity to do things her people disliked doing.[15] To them it seemed they were forced to it. As for you, your holiness, excuse them, so as to catch them with the hook of love.[16]

I beg you, for love of Christ crucified, go as soon as you can to your own place, the place of the glorious apostles Peter and Paul. As for yourself, try to go confidently, and God for his part will provide you with everything you need for yourself and for his[m] bride's well-being. I'll say no more. Forgive my presumptuousness. Find encouragement and confidence

---

[12] The nearest Catherine will come to repeating this image will be in *Dial.* 77 (pp. 141–142): "These three glorious virtues—patience, courage, and perseverance—are rooted in true charity and have their place at the very top of that tree of charity which in turn is crowned with the light of most holy faith by which souls run without darkness along the way of truth."

[13] She will not speak of this directly again until a few letters written in fall of 1377.

[14] She uses the Latin: *in Domino nostro Iesu Christo.*

[15] "This poor city" is Siena if my reasoning in the introduction to this letter is correct. Siena had joined the antipapal league on 27 November 1375.

[16] Cf. Let. T196/DT64 (in this volume): "God, seeing that humankind is so quick to love, throws out to us right away the hook of love, giving us the Word, his only-begotten Son. He takes on our humanity to make a great peace."

in the true servants of God—I mean, in their prayers,[n] for they are praying and interceding much for you. I humbly ask for your blessing, and so do your other children. Keep living in God's holy and tender love.

Gentle Jesus! Jesus love![17]

Textual Notes

a. From H; B, P2: *turn to being difficult and abusive* (*dalle / o alle*).
b. P2: [*and for our . . . hatred*].
c. Lit: *to bear*; P2: *bear* (imperative).
d. *to be* conjectured by Dupré Theseider.
e. From H; B: *Jesus Christ*; P2: *God*.
f. B, P2: *demands / restored* (*richiede / rende*, but Dupré Theseider judges this to be a copyist's error).
g. P2: *father / babbo*.
h. P2: [*and perseverance*].
i. P2: [*from much war*].
j. From H: B, P2: *father*.
k. B, P2 have *se può avere la pace / si . . . pace*.
l. H: *whose voice you have / whose . . . are* (*voce / vece*).
m. From H: B, P2: *your / his*.
n. H: *in the prayers of God's true servants / in the true . . . prayers*.

[17] S2 and S4 add at this point: "Borne by Tommaso Guelfaccio."

LETTER T54/G160[1]
To a nun of the Monastery of Sant'Agnesa in Montepulciano
December 1376

The scribe of P4 comments that he has not discovered the identity of the nun to whom this letter is addressed. The theme makes it likely that the occasion is her profession. There is, however, nothing at all in the content of the letter to identify the addressee (other than her monastery) or to date the letter. The linguistic evidence persuades me that Catherine is writing in the last months of 1376, most probably in December after she has returned to Siena, where she would more easily hear of news from Montepulciano.[2]

§

In the name of Jesus Christ crucified and of gentle Mary.

My dearest and very loved daughter in Christ gentle Jesus,[a]

I Caterina, servant and slave of our Lord Jesus Christ and of his servants, encourage and bless you. I am writing to you in the precious blood of God's Son, longing for you to be a true bride consecrated to your bridegroom, dressed up and adorned with virtue.

You know, my dearest daughter, that a bride dresses up and adorns herself when she presents herself to her bridegroom. Specifically, she wears scarlet to please her bridegroom.[3] This is what I want you to do; I want you to have within you the garment of charity, without which you could not go to the wedding. No, the same thing would be said to you as was said about the servant who went without a wedding garment: [the king] commanded his servants to throw him out into the dark.[4] I don't want that to happen to you, my very loved daughter. If you are invited to go to the wedding I don't want you to be found without that lovely garment. In fact, I want you, and I command you, to decorate it for me with orna-

---

[1] MSS: B, P2, T, R1, P5, F2, F1, P3, P4; translation based on T, with variants from an unpublished transcription by A. Volpato.

[2] The letter contains two patterns which do not occur after 1376 (PREZSANG, SCRVCNBN). Further, ADORNVES occurs only in this letter and in Let. T247/DT86, the latter clearly dated in mid-November of 1376. A tight cluster of TEMMORTE is concentrated between September and December of that year. CUORDOPP, on the other hand, occurs only once before January 1377 other than in this letter, and from that point on occurs rather heavily. Both Fawtier (II, p. 227) and Dupré Theseider (unpublished notes) decline to date this letter.

[3] A Sienese bride's wedding dress was customarily scarlet. Thus Catherine's imagery of wedding garment and charity and Christ's redeeming blood come together.

[4] Cf. the parable of the wedding banquet in Mt. 22, 1–14.

ments. I mean [first of all] the ornament of true and holy obedience, by always being observant of your rule, submissive and obedient to milady[5] and even to the least one there. [Next] take the virtue of humility by being appreciative of the gifts and graces you have received from [your bridegroom]; this will nourish the virtue of holy[b] obedience in you.

See to it that you are a faithful bride. And do you know when you will be faithful to your bridegroom? When you love no one and nothing but him. So I want nothing to be found in your heart but God. Empty it of any selfish and sensual love for your relatives or for anything else at all. Without any fear of life or of death, but with a free heart and dressed in this holy garment, put yourself into the hands of your eternal bridegroom.[c] And place yourself within his will, so that he may make or unmake of you whatever may be for his honor and the best for you.[6]

I have no more to say to you.[d] Keep living in God's holy and tender love.[e]

Gentle Jesus and Mary love! May Christ gentle Jesus strengthen you. Amen.[f]

Textual Notes

a. *dearest* supplied from B, P2; *my* from R1.

b. P2: [*holy*].

c. P5, F2: *the Holy Spirit and your eternal bridegroom / your eternal bridegroom.*

d. *to you* supplied from R1, T, B, P2.

e. P3, F2: [*Keep ... love.*]. P3: *Keep living in the holy love of God's Son.*

f. From P3 and P5, F2. R1, T: *Gentle Jesus! Jesus love!* P4, P2: *Jesus, etc.* P3: *Gentle Jesus and Mary love!* P5, F2: *May Christ gentle Jesus strengthen you. Amen.* B: *Gentle Jesus! Jesus love! Gentle Mary!*

---

[5] That is, the prioress.

[6] Cf. Jer. 18, 1–6: "I went down to the potter's house and there he was, working at the wheel. Whenever the object of clay which he was making turned out badly in his hand, he tried again, making of the clay another object of whatever sort he pleased. Then the word of the Lord came to me: 'Can I not do to you ... as the potter has done?' " In Prayer 26 (p. 225) Catherine applies the image to herself: "You, good master, my sweet love—you are the master who breaks and refashions; you smash this vessel and put it back together again as it pleases your goodness."

Letter T130/G271[1]
To Ipolito degli Ubertini
Late December 1376 to very early 1377

The island of Gorgona, in the fourteenth century a full day's journey by boat from Pisa, had been a Benedictine monastery for all of the Middle Ages until 1373. In that year, discouraged by the constant depredations of pirates, the remaining members of the community with their abbot fled to Pisa. Gregory XI, learning of the fact, suppressed the Benedictine monastery and assigned all of its goods to the Carthusians, who promptly took possession. The founding prior of the new community was Bartolomeo Serafini da Ravenna, who at some point became a good friend of Catherine.[2] It was Bartolomeo who invited Catherine to the island in spring or summer of 1375. Gorgona became one of the monasteries Catherine encouraged men of her acquaintance to enter, Ipolito degli Ubertini of Florence among them.

This letter to Ipolito seems to imply that he has recently been widowed, since he has a "little girl" to look out for and yet is at liberty to join a religious order. (Catherine does not think he should let the girl's needs cause him to delay his move, but should rather find a good home for her.)

Clues within the content of this letter to Ipolito (in response to a letter from him) only begin to point a way to its dating. It is clear that Catherine already knows Niccolò Soderini, a relationship that almost certainly began during her stay in Florence in the spring of 1374.[3] If she did not meet Ipolito at that time, she could well have met him during her brief stay in Florence in May of 1376. She knows that the prior of Gorgona is coming to Florence, a bit of information she might have gleaned either during her 1375 visit to Gorgona or during her late 1376 stay in Pisa or through a letter from the prior.

The linguistic data would most strongly support placing this letter in late December 1376 or early 1377, shortly after Catherine's return from Avignon and Pisa.[4]

---

[1] MSS: B, P2, R1, P5, F2, P3; translation based on R1. No relevant variants.

[2] Cf. Gaetano Bonifacio, "Santa Caterina e l'isola di Gorgona," *Bollettino Storico Livornese* 4, 1940, pp. 136–140. Bonifacio cites Aristo Manghi's *La Certosa di Pisa* (F. Mariotti, 1911).

[3] Let. T171/DT61 (in this volume) was written to Niccolò earlier in 1376, before Catherine's second visit to Florence. That letter gives the impression that Catherine knew him well, since she sends greetings to his wife by name.

[4] While three of the five letters which share seven or more of this letter's twenty-four analyzed patterns are from 1377 and the other two earlier, significant clusters within individual patterns are more densely concentrated in late 1376 to early 1377, with three (AMDIODDI, CUORSPOG, TAGLSCIO) beginning there and IMPEDDES not occurring

§

In the name of Jesus Christ crucified and of gentle Mary.

Dearest brother in Christ gentle Jesus,

I, Caterina, servant and slave of the servants of Jesus Christ, am writing to you in his precious blood. I long to see you with a courageous heart, stripped of all sensual passion and attachment.[5] Attachment comes from selfish love; it stands in the way of every holy desire and perpetrates every sort of evil.

Those who are in love with themselves live in lukewarmness of heart. On the one hand, God calls to them by letting them see what a short time they have to live, how wretchedly weak the world is, how unstable and fickle. God lets them see that every least pleasure and concern people pursue excessively, apart from God, is punished miserably. So they begin to hate and despise the world and would gladly rise above it, realizing that those who abandon the world—I mean those who make light of the world's pleasures and status and ostentation—will possess the world.[6] They realize that every good is rewarded, and that they will receive in return a hundred times as much [as they have given up].[7] They are, therefore, ready to abandon the world completely.

But if selfish love is still alive in their heart, this desire becomes tepid. In their attachment they go on being attached [to the world] and procrastinating.[8]

This is not the way to act. We should kill all selfish love, reflecting that we are not sure we will have time.[9] If we were sure of it, we could say, "I'll get around to loosening this tie with the world, and once I am free, I'll go and bind myself to Christ crucified with the yoke of obedience." Dearest brother, since you are not sure of having time, throw off all selfish

---

at all before spring of 1376. The additional fact that TIEPID otherwise occurs only in the first seven months of 1376 (other than three occurrences in 1379) inclines me to put the later limits for the probable placement of this letter early in 1377 rather than later. Fawtier (II, p. 275) suggests 1375 as a possible date for the letter. Dupré Theseider (unpublished notes), concludes that the letter is not datable, though he thinks it must be after 1375.

[5] It. *tenerezza*, which for Catherine always implies undue attachment, whether to one's own comfort or to one's possessions or relationships.

[6] Cf. Mt. 5, 5: "Blessed are the lowly; they shall inherit the earth." (Vulg.)

[7] Mk. 19, 29: "All who have given up home, brothers or sisters, father or mother, wife or children or lands for the sake of my name will receive a hundred times as much, and will possess eternal life." (Vulg.)

[8] It. *si va pure attaccando, pigliando indugio di tempo.*

[9] Catherine often says in other letters, and also later in this letter, "Don't wait for time, because time won't wait for you."

love and sensual attachment. Think not of untying but rather of cutting. Take up in the hand of your free choice a knife that has two edges, hatred and love—love for virtue and hatred and contempt for vice and for the world and for your selfish sensuality. This is how you will prove you are a courageous person, not lukewarm or indifferent.

Respond, respond to God, who is calling you with good holy inspirations. The place is ready for you, a holy and pious place completely removed from the world, with a father, the prior of Gorgona, who is truly an angel,[10] a mirror of virtue with a good holy family. Don't put up resistance to the divine grace that is so benevolently asking you to let it live in your heart and will.[11]

I have the impression from the letter you sent me that your intention is good and holy, but you are putting it off too much by asking for two years. The devil is doing this because he regrets your good fortune. He makes you think there are things you have to do, so as to put obstacles in the way of your peace and tranquility. I really think you would do well to find a home for your little girl as soon as possible and get this load off your shoulders.[12] As for the other things, settle them quickly. These other affairs you have to attend to you could delegate to whatever proxy you see would do the right and proper thing for love of God and for you. But what concerns the little girl take care of yourself.

I beg you in the name of Christ crucified to hurry. Don't wait for time, because time won't wait for you! The prior of Gorgona is coming to see you.[13] Inform him fully of your intention, and make a true, firm, steadfast resolution. And if it should happen that you do decide to become a member of that holy and pious place (which will be the life of your soul), or if you should happen for any other reason to give your possessions to the poor, give some of them to this place, Gorgona. For the place must be well-supplied if it is to live according to the customs of the Carthusian Order.[14]

So up, courageously! For I trust in God's goodness that, if you bathe in the blood of Christ crucified, you will do this and everything else without putting it off.

---

[10] She is playing on the prior's name, Serafini.

[11] It. *affetto.*

[12] This seems to imply that Ipolito has recently been widowed and has a young daughter (It. *fanciulla*). Note that while Catherine thinks he should delegate his other affairs to someone else, she insists that he see personally to finding a home for his daughter.

[13] This is Don Bartolomeo Serafini.

[14] Even several years after its re-founding as a Carthusian monastery, Gorgona was heavily in debt and was still the target of pirate attacks. In 1378 Urban VI (possibly at Catherine's suggestion) will make generous donations to the monastery in view of the latter attacks. (Bonifacio, "S. Caterina e l'isola di Gorgona," p. 139.)

I'll say no more. Give my greetings to Leonardo and Niccolò Soderini, and also to Monna Antonia.[15] And bless all the rest of the family in Christ gentle Jesus. Keep living in God's holy and tender love.

Gentle Jesus! Jesus love!

---

[15] Leonardo and Monna Antonio are unidentified. Niccolò Soderini is a leading figure in the Guelf party of Florence; Catherine is often associated with him and follows his affairs closely.

Letter T17/G131[1]
To Frate Antonio da Nizza of the Order of Hermits of Saint Augustine at Selva di Lago, Lecceto[2]
Late December 1376 or very early 1377

While we know much about William Flete of Lecceto, we know very little about his friend and scribe, Antonio da Nizza (that is, from Nice). He is first mentioned in the closing of Let. T66/DT35 to William (vol. I), written probably in August or September of 1375. He was William's age, born about 1325. Even earlier than William he had left his native land to live in the ilex woods of Lecceto.[3]

Catherine will also write Let. T326 (December 1378) to Antonio da Nizza and William Flete, and T328 (early 1379) to Antonio alone. Of the dating of the present letter we are less certain. The linguistic evidence, however, would incline me to place it in very late 1376 or very early 1377, just after Catherine's return to Siena from Avignon.[4]

---

[1] MSS: Mo-*b*, T, R1, P5, F2, P3, V, P4; S3, Pa, S7; translation based on Mo-*b*, with reference to T, R1, P3, S7, S3 for protocols. Relevant variants based on an unpublished transcription by A. Volpato.

[2] Mo originally had "To whom I don't know," which is crossed out and replaced (in a fifteenth-century hand, according to Dupré Theseider, "Un codice inedito," p. 44, n. 1) with "Frate Antonio di Niçça." In S3 this letter is placed among those "to laypeople of honorable life," with the rubric, "To one who desired to live well according to God." In the edition of Aldo Manuzio it appears twice, under two different rubrics, one (number 130) to Antonio da Nizza, and the other (number 142): "Written to a devoted spiritual father of hers, about the devil's temptations concerning our selfish will, and how the will is often deceived." Gigli (*Opere*, I) concludes that the three versions actually represent a single letter, written to Antonio da Nizza. Other editors and commentators make no mention of this replication and discrepancy of rubrics. Since the judgment that the addressee is Antonio da Nizza is consistent with the manuscripts which preserve the more primitive protocol, it seems reasonable to trust it.

[3] William came to Lecceto in 1359. Both men died about 1390. (B. Hackett, *William Flete, O.S.A., and Catherine of Siena*, Villanova: Augustinian Press, 1992, p. 70)

[4] I would not place it later because of three patterns (A-VOI, PERMANE, PREZSANG) which do not otherwise occur (except in single isolated cases for two of them) beyond the end of 1376. And I would not place it earlier because of two patterns (INGANN, VOLSPIR) which do not otherwise occur before spring of 1377, and one (ELEGLUOG) which except for one early isolated instance does not otherwise occur before that same period. Also, all four letters which share eleven or more of this letter's forty-two analyzed patterns are from spring and summer of 1377. Both Fawtier (II, p. 214) and Dupré Theseider decline to date this letter.

§

In the name of Jesus Christ crucified and of gentle mother Mary.[a]

Dearest and very loved father and brother in Christ Jesus,

I, Caterina, servant and slave of the servants of Jesus Christ, am writing to commend myself to you in the precious blood of God's Son.[b] I long to see you engulfed, swallowed up in the furnace of divine charity, and your selfish will—the will that robs us of life and gives us death—itself burned and swallowed up there.[5]

But let's open our eyes, dearest brother. For we have *two* selfish wills: one that pursues sensual and bodily things, and a spiritual one that stands its ground, alive and unmortified, under the guise and pretext of virtue.[6,c] And how does the latter show itself? When it wants to choose times and places and consolations to its own liking. It says, "I would like this not for my own consolation but to please God more."[d]

But this is a great deception and illusion from the devil. He cannot fool God's servants by means of the first sort of will since they have already put that will to death as regards external sensual things, so he catches the second sort of will, our will regarding spiritual things.[e] So it often happens that we receive consolation from God and afterwards feel that it's been taken away from us. Later we may have another experience, one less comforting but more fruitful.[7] Because we are more enthusiastic about the experience that gives us more sweetness,[f] we are pained and disturbed when it is taken away. And why are we disturbed? Because our will is set on that sweetness and[g] doesn't want to be deprived of it. So we say, "It seems to me I possess and[h] love God more in the first sort of experience than in the second, since in the first I experience some fruitfulness, while in this I experience no fruit at all—nothing but pain and a lot of struggle—and I seem

---

[5] There is here a complex interplay of life and death in words which connote the phenomenon of drowning: the same fire of charity (which is also the blood of Christ, the water of life) enlivens one's best self as one is "drowned" in it, and in a like drowning kills one's selfishness.

[6] Catherine addresses this "spiritual self-will" also in *Dial.* 99, p. 187, and in several other letters.

[7] Cf. Let. T94 to Matteo Tolomei (in this volume): "Nor should we live merely for love of the fruit, the consolation we receive from our Lord, once we have become his friends. For such a love would not be strong, but would falter when we are deprived of the sweetness or consolation or spiritual joy. In fact, it would falter under any contrary wind of persecution or diabolical temptation or promptings of the flesh." Also Let. T346 to Urban VI (1378): "Let this tree bear the flower of conceiving virtue in your desire and giving birth to its fruit in hunger for God's honor and the salvation of your little sheep. When first we eat this fruit with the mouth of our holy desire, it seems bitter, but as we inwardly determine that we want to suffer for Christ crucified and for love of virtue even to the point of death, it becomes sweet."

to be offending God." I tell you, my son and brother in Christ Jesus, we are being deceived here by our selfish will, because we don't want to be deprived of this sweetness and the devil uses this bait to catch us.[8] And frequently we miss our opportunity because, by wanting time in our own way, we don't use the time we have except blindly and painfully.[i]

Our gentle Savior once said to one of his very beloved daughters:[9,j] "Do you know how these people act who want to fulfill my will [only] in consolation and sweetness and delight? When they are deprived of these they want to get away from my will, since that seems to them the best thing to do to avoid sinning. But hidden in this is a false sensuality, and by running away from pain they are falling into sin without even noticing it. If they were wise, however, and if they were enlightened within my will, they would look to the fruit and not to the sweetness.

"And what is the fruit? Contempt for self and love for me—contempt and love that come from self-knowledge. For this makes them recognize that they are sinful and that they are nothing; they see within themselves my goodness, in that I am maintaining their good will. They see also that I made them to serve me in greater perfection, and so they discern that I made them for the best and for their own good besides.[k] Then, dearest daughter, they don't want time in their own way, since they are humbled; because they know their own weakness they don't trust their own will but are faithful to me[l] and clothe themselves in my supreme eternal will. For they see that I neither give nor take away except to make them holy, and they see that love alone moves me to give you sweetness or take it away from you. This makes them incapable of being sad over any consolation that is taken away from them—whether interior or external, whether taken away by the devil or by other people—since they see that I would not permit it except for their own good.

"So[m] they are happy because they have light within and without. And they are so enlightened[n] that when the devil comes to confuse them with spiritual darkness and says, 'This is the result of your sins,' they reply as do those who do not shrink from pain: 'Thanks to my Creator who has remembered me in time of darkness by punishing me with suffering in finite time; this is great love, not to want to punish me in endless time.'[10]

---

[8] Cf. *Dial.* 69, pp. 130–132, for a more extended treatment of this theme.

[9] The reference is, of course, to herself in her usual style.

[10] Cf. Let. T13 to Marco Bindi (1378): "It is only sin that God hates in us, and this is why in this life he permits us to suffer all sorts of trials, whether in regard to our bodies or in regard to our material possessions, in whatever ways he sees we need such. As a good doctor he administers whatever medicine our weakness needs. And he does this either to punish our sins in this life (so that we may receive less punishment in the next life), or to test the virtue of patience in us as he did with Job. . . . [I]n spite of the fact that we deserve

"Oh, what spiritual tranquility these souls have because they have stripped themselves of the will that causes unrest! Not so with those whose will is alive within them, looking to have things their own way because they think they know better than I what they need. Often they say, 'It seems to me I am offending God. Take away my sin and do whatever you want.'[o]

"Here is the sign that your sin is taken away: when you see in yourself the good will not to want to sin, along with contempt for sin. You should take hope from this, for if all external works and all interior consolations were to fail, let but your good will remain and you are pleasing to me—and upon this rock grace is founded. And if you say, 'I don't think I have it,' I tell you this is untrue; for if you didn't have it you wouldn't be afraid of offending me. It is the devil who makes it seem so in order to bring you to confusion and uncalled-for sadness, and in order to make you hold on to your insistence on having consolations and times and places after your own liking. Don't believe him, dearest daughter, but always be ready to endure suffering in whatever way I may give it to you.[p] Otherwise you will be acting like a person standing in a doorway, lamp in hand, but holding his or her hand outside so that the lamp lights the outside while inside it is dark—in harmony with my will in external things by despising the world, but your spiritual [selfish] will alive within, veiled under the pretext of virtue."[11]

So did God speak to that servant of his whom I mentioned above. And this is why I said that I long for your will to be swallowed up and transformed[q] in him, so that we will be ready always to endure difficulty and pain in whatever way God wants to give them to us.[12] This is how we will be freed from darkness and come to possess the light.

Amen. Praised be Jesus Christ crucified and gentle Mary his mother![r]

Textual Notes

a. Taken from T, P3, and S7, which, according to A. Volpato ("Analisi diplomatistica," nn. 6, 7), are probably to be trusted in their preservation of an earlier version. The other manuscripts have *gentle Mary*.

b. Taken from R1. P3, V have *servants of Jesus Christ . . . in his precious blood*; Mo, S3

---

infinite punishment, he mercifully punishes us in this finite time. During this time, if we bear our trials with patience, we cancel our debt and we gain merit. This is not true of the punishments the soul suffers in the next life, for in the pain of purgatory one cancels debt but gains no merit." This contrast between punishment in time and punishment after death recurs in *The Dialogue* (2, 4, 45, 166) and in several other letters.

[11] The image of the lamp held outside the door is unique here.

[12] Note the shift to the inclusive "we."

have *servants of God ... in the precious blood of his Son*. S3 further omits *father* and *am writing to.*

c. P3, V: *We have two wills. The one is sensual and looks for sensual things. The other is spiritual, and under the guise and pretext of virtue it looks for spiritual things and holds its will firm. It demonstrates this when it wants to choose ..., and to say, "I would like this in order to have God more."* This version, however, contains internal contradictions.

e. P3: *he catches [them] the second time with spiritual things*; V: *he catches the second sort of will with spiritual things / he catches ... things.* V might well be better here.

f. V: *in love with what gives us sweetness / more enthusiastic ... sweetness.*

g. V: [*is set on that sweetness and*]

h. P3, V: [*possess and*].

i. V: [*except ... painfully*].

j. V: *The most beloved master once said to one of his own / Our ... daughters.*

k. P3, V: *And they see within themselves God's will when he sustains their good will, and he made them to live justly, humbling themselves before God, discerning that he made them for the best and for their own good / and they see ... besides.*

l. V: *they trust not their own will but entrust themselves to Christ / they don't trust ... me.*

m. P3, V: *In short / So.*

n. From V; others have *humbled (humiliato) / enlightened (illuminato).*

o. *Often ... want* from P3, V (the latter is missing *It seems ... God*); others have only *Take ... want*, which without reference to a speaker other than God is out of context here.

p. P3, V, T: *Let's not believe him, dearest brother, but always be ready to endure suffering in whatever way God may give it to us / Don't ... you.*

q. V: *to see you engulfed and swallowed up and transformed / for ... transformed.*

r. *Amen ... mother* from P3, T. (V: [*and ... his mother*]; Mo, S3: *I'll say no more. Keep living in God's holy and tender love.*

LETTER T45/G266[1]
To Francesco di Messer Vanni Malavolti
January 1377

Francesco Malavolti was a young nobleman of Siena who became Catherine's disciple at the instigation of his friend Neri di Landoccio Pagliaresi, probably early in 1374.[2] He was twenty-five at the time.[3] Like his friend Neri, he delighted in poetry, but was also "bold and hot-headed, lascivious and unrestrained." He first went to see Catherine only to please Neri, determined that if this woman should speak of things spiritual or so much as suggest confession, he would "answer her in such a way that she would never speak to me again." But like so many others, he was transformed in Catherine's presence and changed his ways, finding his pleasure now "in visiting churches and talking with the servants of God." He at some point married a girl of fifteen, "beautiful in body but even more so in spirit and virtue," and the two by mutual consent lived for a time "in the same house but not the same bed."

Francesco does, however, confess to at least two major lapses. He does not say when the first was except that it was considerably before Catherine's journey to Avignon. On that occasion he went to see Catherine as usual, as if nothing had happened, only to have her confront him with his guilt. The other lapse occurred while Catherine was away in Avignon, by which time Francesco already had children (apparently with the wife with whom he had lived or would later live celibately for a time). He says that on Catherine's return to Siena he went nevertheless to see her "at once, though not without great shame and fear." She, "sweet and kind mother that she was," received him graciously and bolstered him in his weakness. On a subsequent visit, one of Catherine's companions spoke "somewhat peevishly" about how fickle Francesco was. Catherine, "with a half-smile, said, 'Never mind, my sisters. This fellow can't escape my hands, no matter where he may choose to go! For just when he thinks I am far away, I shall throw such a noose or yoke around his neck that he will never be able to get out of it again!'.... At which the sisters, and I with them, burst into laughter."

---

[1] MSS: Mo, B, P2, P5, F2, P3, S3, T (the last two not listed by Fawtier in his chart of manuscripts); translation based on Mo-*a*, corrected by *b*, with reference to T. Gardner (p. 209) gives a full translation, which he says he bases on P5 because it is a better text than either Tommasèo or Gigli (*Opere*, II). I do not have access to P5, but have indicated in the notes wherever Gardner's English seems to show significant variation from Mo-*a*.

[2] This is the only extant letter of Catherine to Francesco.

[3] These facts of his life are found in Francesco's testimony in *Processo Castellano*, ed. Laurent, pp. 376–412.

The intent of the present letter is to get Francesco "back into the fold with your companions." She complains that he has not come to see her. Catherine would hardly have written asking Francesco to visit her either when she was on the road (all of 1375 and from May to December 1376), or when Francesco was actually in her company (as at Val d'Orcia in summer and autumn of 1377). Though such a letter might have been written after her return from Pisa and Lucca at the end of 1375, it seems far more likely that it is connected with the 1376 lapse described by Francesco himself (even though he seems to imply that he needed no encouragement to go see Catherine).

I would therefore place this letter in early 1377, surely before Catherine's time at Belcaro but most likely quite shortly after her return to Siena after the long absence of her journey to Avignon. For "certain women" of her *famiglia* in Siena quickly informed her of Francesco's wanderings, and she was surely quick to act on such news concerning one whose friendship and spiritual welfare she valued.[4]

§

In the name of Jesus Christ crucified and of gentle Mary.

Dearest and more than dearest son in Christ gentle Jesus,

I Caterina, servant and slave of the servants of Jesus Christ, am writing to you in his precious blood. I long to find you once again, little lost sheep! I long for this very deeply! And I long to put you back into the fold with your companions. But it seems to me the devil has so stolen you away as to make it impossible to find you again.[a] I your poor mother am going about looking for you, sending for you, because I would like to put you on the shoulders of my sorrow and my compassion for your soul.[5]

Open the eyes of your understanding, dearest son! Raise them above the darkness! Acknowledge your sin, not with spiritual dejection but with self-knowledge and trust in God's goodness.[6] Look at how wretchedly you

---

[4] Francesco himself (*Processo Castellano*, ed. Laurent, p. 376) tells of the women's report to Catherine. Gardner, *Saint Catherine of Siena* (p. 209), also connects this letter with Francesco's story of his lapse (therefore, early 1377). Both Fawtier (II, p. 289) and Dupré Theseider (unpublished notes) consider the letter undatable. In such a brief letter there is scant linguistic data from which to draw clues for chronological placement. However, the only letter which shares four or more of this one's six analyzed patterns is from autumn of 1377, and the pattern SUSTPADR occurs otherwise only in 1375 and 1376 (though only four times in all besides this).

[5] Cf. the parable of the lost sheep, Lk. 15, 3–7.

[6] Cf. *Dial.* 66, p. 124: "Now I do not want her to think about her sins individually, lest

have spent the fortune of grace your heavenly Father gave you.[7] Then do as that prodigal son did who had spent his fortune in evil living.[b] When he realized how destitute he had become, he acknowledged his failure and ran back to ask his father for mercy.[c] You do the same. For you are impoverished and destitute, and your soul is dying of hunger. So run back to ask your father for mercy.[d] He will help you and will not reject your desire, grounded in sorrow for the sin you have committed. No, he will lovingly fulfill that desire.

Oimé! Oimé! Where are your dear desires? Oh unhappy me! I've discovered that the devil has stolen away your soul and your holy desire! The world and its servants have set their traps, baited with their excessive pleasures and charms.

Get up! Take your medicine! No more sleeping! Comfort my soul, and don't be so callous about your salvation as to cheat me of a visit from you. Don't let the devil trick you with fear or embarrassment. Break this knot! Come! Come, dearest son! (I can well call you dear, so much have you cost me in tears and sweat and bitter grief.) Come now, and recuperate in your sheepfold.

I hold myself excused before God, because I can do no more. If you come, and if you stay, I'll ask no more of you than that you do God's will.[e]

Keep living in God's holy and tender love.

Gentle Jesus! Jesus love!

Textual Notes

a. Gardner has here: "the devil has so robbed me of thee that thou dost not let thyself be found," which would seem to indicate that P5 has a second-person rather than a third-person verb here.

b. *in evil living* added by *b.*

c. Gardner: *forgiveness / mercy.*

d. Gardner: *forgiveness / mercy.*

e. Gardner adds, presumably from P5: *May Christ Jesus console thee with thyself and me with thee!* He does not have the rest of the closing, which may or may not be in P5.

---

her mind be contaminated by the memory of her specific ugly sins. I mean that I do not want her to, nor should she, think about her sins either in general or specifically without calling to mind the blood and the greatness of my mercy. Otherwise she will only be frustrated. For if self-knowledge and the thought of sin are not seasoned with remembrance of the blood and hope for mercy, the result is bound to be confusion."

[7] Cf. the parable of the "prodigal" son, Lk. 15, 11–32.

Letter T285/G14[1]
To Pope Gregory XI
Late January 1377

The rubrics of H and P3 specify that this letter was written "after [the pope] had arrived in Rome," which would put it after 17 January 1377. In the course of the letter Catherine refers to the Sienese ambassadors who are coming to see Gregory. We know of such a delegation from several Sienese chroniclers. Like similar delegations from other republics, they are going to wish the pope well on his return to Rome. But the Sienese are going also to ask pardon for having sided with the antipapal league and, according to some, also to ask that the occupying papal troops leave the Sienese port of Talamone.[2] Neri di Donato says the ambassadors left Siena in January 1377, and though the date is missing from Neri's text it is surely toward the end of the month that they arrive.[3]

In Aldo Manuzio's first edition of the *Epistolario* we read that Catherine's letter is delivered by Tommaso Guelfaccio, a Sienese gentleman and friend of Catherine who had been converted by Giovanni Colombini and later joined his order of Gesuati. Guelfaccio is not named among the delegation by any of the chroniclers, but may have accompanied the group in Catherine's name. There is, however, no extant manuscript evidence for Manuzio's assertion.

We are told that Gregory received the delegation graciously "out of respect for Sister Caterina Benincasa, whose warm letter they had brought with them."[4] But none of the chroniclers tells us more specifically of the results of the mission.

Placement of the letter in early 1377 is supported by the linguistic data.[5] Because of the historical data I would place it in late January 1377.

---

[1] MSS: B, P2, A, S1, H, P1, S2, P4, S4; translation based on S2, with reference to H; variants based on unpublished notes of Dupré Theseider.

[2] Cf. Gardner, *Saint Catherine of Siena*, pp. 203–204, and Seckendorff, *Politische Tätigkeit*, pp. 137–139.

[3] *Cronaca Sanese*, in *Rerum italicarum scriptores*, ed. Muratori, vol. xv, col. 252: "These were the Sienese ambassadors who went to Rome to the pope: Messer' Andrea di Conte, Messer Joanni Vincenti, Ser Brizio Pavoli, Marino and Pietro Venturini; they all met and left on the . . . day of January, most honorable." O. Malavolti, *Historia de' fattie e guerre de' Sanesi*, 143v–144 names the same ambassadors. Seckendorff, *Politische Tätigkeit*, p. 138, n. 43, cites Giugurta Tommasi, *Storia di Siena*, as naming the ambassadors as Andrea Piccolomini, Niccolò Mara, and Domenico Placidi. Alessandro Gherardi, *La guerra dei Fiorentini con Papa Gregorio XI* (Firenze: Archivio storico italiano, 1868), doc. 321, says that the Sienese had already in November 1376 planned a delegation to Gregory but had been persuaded by the Florentines to desist.

[4] G. Tommasi, cited by Seckendorff, *Kirchenpolitische Tätigkeit*, p. 138, n. 43.

[5] Two significant clusters within individual patterns begin at that time (AMCACCOD,

§

In the name of Jesus Christ crucified and of gentle Mary.

Most reverend and most holy father in Christ gentle Jesus,

I Caterina, servant and slave of the servants of Jesus Christ and your unworthy daughter, am writing to you in his precious blood. I long to see you receive true and perfect peace from the return of your subjects and children to the yoke of holy obedience, so that you may be able to live in peaceful tranquility, body and soul. And may God in his boundless goodness and infinite charity grant me the grace to see you as the mediator who will reconcile souls with God after the war they have waged against him by their sins against his boundless goodness and your holiness. And I have no doubt that once this peace is made, all [the people] of Italy will be reconciled to one another.[6,a]

Oh how blessed my soul will be to see them bound to you in the bond of love when they return to obedience to you, and bound to one another in loving unity, through your holiness' mediation![b] Understand, holy father, that God did not join with humanity except in the bond of love, and love held him nailed fast to the cross[7]—because we who were made of love are not drawn in any other way but by love.[8,c] By the love of the Word, God's only-begotten Son, the war we waged by rebelling against God and submitting ourselves[d] to the mastery of the devil is abolished.

GIOGOBED) and four end there (CARBONI, DIOINUOM, QUIETAN, VIRTCACC). Both Fawtier (II, p. 150) and Dupré Theseider (unpublished notes) place the letter in late January 1377.

[6] Italy, of course, is not a single nation at this point. Catherine is referring to the peninsula.

[7] Cf Let. T253 to Trincio and Corrado de' Trinci da Fuligno (in this volume): "[Charity] is the bond that bound God with humanity and humanity with God in a union so perfectly made that it could not be broken by death or by anything else. *Oh true and sweet bond! So great is your power that you held the God-Man nailed fast to the wood of the most holy cross! For neither the nails nor any other iron could have held him had not love for his Father and our salvation held him.*"

[8] She has written to Gregory in very similar terms the previous spring (Let. T196/DT64, in this volume): "I am turning to you, our father and shepherd, begging you in the name of Christ crucified to learn from him who with such blazing love gave himself up to the shameful death of the most holy cross to save this little lost sheep, the human race, from the devils' hands. Because of its rebellion against God, here are the devils, holding this sheep as their own possession. Then along comes God's infinite goodness and sees the sheep's sorry state, its ruin and damnation. He knows he cannot use wrath or war to entice it away from them. Supreme eternal wisdom doesn't want to do it that way, even though the sheep has wronged him (for humankind, by its rebellion in disobedience, was deserving of infinite punishment). No, he finds a delightful way—the most sweet and loving way possible; for he sees that the human heart is drawn by love as by nothing else, since it is made of love."

And this is the way I see, most holy father, that you will abolish the war and the mastery the devil has gained in the city of your children's souls. For the devil is not driven out by the devil,[9] but you will drive him out with the power of your humility and kindness. The devil will not be able to stand this humility because he cannot; in fact, he is defeated by it. With your love and hunger for God's honor and the well-being of souls, you will learn from the Lamb who was slain and consumed, whose representative you are, and you will banish war and hatred from their hearts and heap coals of burning fire on the heads of these children—truly devils incarnate—who have rebelled against you, father.[10] With this sweet and gentle manner the devil and human pride will be conquered; for in no other way is so much good obtained as through humility. And war is conquered by patient suffering, by bearing and putting up with your children's shortcomings—not, however, foregoing correction, which must be given according to their capacity. Thus with merciful kindness and holy justice, and with love's gentle fire, the hatred in their souls will be consumed as water in a furnace. Extend your kindness to them, father, because everyone is more attracted by loving kindness than by anything else—especially our Italians here.[11] I fail to see any other way you can win them except by this. Do this and you will have from them whatever you want. And for this I am begging you, for love of Christ crucified, for the Church's welfare and benefit.

The Sienese[e] ambassadors are coming to your holiness. Now if there are any people in the world who can be won over by love, it is these. So please learn how to catch them with this hook.[12] Be a bit receptive to their apology for having done wrong, because they are sorry for it. It seems to them they have come to such a pass that they don't know what to do. Please, your holiness, my dear father,[f] if there is any acceptable way for them to act in your holiness' regard that would not leave them in a state of war against those with whom they are in league,[13] I beg you to

---

[9] Cf. Mt. 12, 26; Mk. 3, 23; Lk. 11, 18: "If Satan casts out Satan, he is divided against himself; how then will his kingdom stand?"

[10] Cf. Prv. 6, 28: "Can fire be carried in the bosom without burning one's clothes? Or can one walk on hot coals without scorching the feet?"; Prv. 25, 21–22: "If your enemies are hungry, give them bread to eat; and if they are thirsty, give them water to drink; for you will heap coals of fire on their head." The Proverbs passages are echoed in Rom. 12, 20: "No, 'if your enemies are hungry, feed them; if they are thirsty, give them something to drink; for by doing this you will heap burning coals on their heads.' " The idea, then, is that the example of love cannot but have an effect even on one's enemies.

[11] Gregory XI is French.

[12] She has used the same image in her letter to Gregory the previous March (Let. T196/DT64) and again just a few weeks before this (Let. T252/DT88).

[13] That is, the republic of Florence, leader of the antipapal league.

take it. Bear with them, for love of Christ crucified! If you do, I believe it will result in great good for holy Church and a lessening of evil.

Next I beg you to turn your attention to punishing the sins of the Church's pastors and officials when they are acting improperly. See to the appointment of good ones who are living virtuously and justly—which they must do for the honor of God, for their own salvation, and because it is their duty. Besides, layfolk are watching you very closely because they have seen all the trouble that has come of wrongs going unpunished.

I trust in God's supreme eternal goodness and in your holiness that you will do the first thing [I've spoken of] and every other good thing, as well as whatever must be worked out regarding this last matter.

I'll say no more. Forgive my presumption. I humbly ask your blessing. I commend to you the above-mentioned Sienese ambassadors.[g] Keep living in God's holy and tender love.

Gentle Jesus! Jesus love! Mary, gentle mother!

Textual Notes

a. P2, P3: [*to one another*]
b. P3, H, P4, S2 add *and kindness.*
c. P3, H, P4: *as well are we are / but.*
d. *submitting ourselves* supplied from a marginal gloss in S2.
e. P2, P3, H: [*Sienese*].
f. P3, H, P4: *babbo / father.*
g. B, P3, H: [*the above-mentioned Sienese ambassadors*]
h. B, P3, H: [*living . . . mother!*]; P4: [*Mary . . . mother!*]; P2: [*gentle . . . mother!*].

Letter T254/G84[1]
To Pietro di Missere Iacomo Attaghufi dei Tolomei
Late January 1377

Near the end of 1376, Queen Giovanna d'Angiò of Naples lent Pope Gregory XI a troop of four hundred lances to join the papal armies going to battle against Viterbo. The Florentines, under the prefect Francesco di Vico, went to Viterbo's aid. On 10 January 1377, news reached Florence that the prefect had scored a victory against the forces of the church, and that two hundred of the pope's soldiers had been taken prisoner.[2] In the present letter, Catherine is appealing to one of the prefect's friends, Pietro di Iacomo Attaghufi dei Tolomei, to intercede with Francesco di Vico on behalf of Luigi della Vigna da Capua, brother of Catherine's confessor Raimondo, who apparently was one of those captured.[3] Catherine says that Luigi was among the queen's troops. He is being held for a ransom of four thousand florins, which he is too poor to pay.

Since news of the battle did not reach Tuscany at all until 10 January, Catherine would not have known until after that of Luigi's plight. Since he was Raimondo's brother, however, and since Raimondo had so many connections with people in power, it was probably very near that date. Catherine would have been inclined to act quickly once she knew of the need of someone so close. I would therefore place this letter between 10 and 31 January 1377.[4]

---

[1] MSS: Mo, M, S5, S6, Ro; S3; translation based on Mo-*a*, corrected by *b*.

[2] *Diario d'Anonimo*, p. 328; Ammirato Scipione, *Libro XIII*.

[3] Fawtier II, p. 280, cites Calisse, *I Prefetti di Vico*, p. 558, doc. CLXXXVI, for the fact that Pietro Tolomei was a good friend of Francesco di Vico.

[4] This placement is strongly supported also by the linguistic evidence. All seven letters sharing fourteen or more of this letter's fifty-eight analyzed patterns are later than this one (April 1377 to late 1378 or early 1379). A number of significant clusters within individual patterns are more narrowly supportive, especially AMAINEST, ASPTMPSC, MANTELLO, PERSECU, QUIETAN, SERVPROS, SERVREGN, UTILDANN, UTILDIO. Both Fawtier (II, p. 280) and Dupré Theseider (unpublished notes) also place the letter here. Seckendorff does not deal with this letter.

§

In the name of Jesus Christ crucified and of gentle Mary.

Dearest and very loved brother in Christ gentle Jesus,

I Caterina, servant and slave of the servants of Jesus Christ, am writing to you in his precious blood. I long to see you a servant and lover of Christ crucified, because there is no other way we can be pleasing to God.

This is our duty. Everyone is bound and obliged to love Christ, since we have received nothing but service, joy, and pleasure from him. [God] loved us without our having loved him,[5] since when we did not exist he created us in his own image and likeness. And when we had lost grace because of Adam's disobedience he gave us the Word, his only-begotten Son, through love alone and not because he had received any service from us. We had in fact given him offense.

Because of our sin we had fallen into a state of war with God. Yet this very God we had offended gave us the Word, his Son, and made him our intermediary, our mediator, making peace out of our great war through the precious blood of the Lamb.[6] So his obedience conquered Adam's disobedience, and just as we had all contracted sin through disobedience, through the obedience of God's Son we all contracted grace.[7]

And the grace we have received through the mediation of this Word is infinite. For the mercy we receive when the blood is ministered to us in holy confession is as great as our sin, if only we turn to the blood of Christ with bitter sorrow for our guilt. When we vomit out the foulness of our sins through our mouth, that is, when we confess them well and conscientiously to the priest and he absolves us, he is giving us the blood of Christ, and in the blood the leprosy of our sins and shortcomings is

---

[5] Cf. 1 Jn. 4, 10. She has switched, by implication, from Christ to God as subject. (She simply continues to use the pronoun *he*.)

[6] Cf. Eph. 2, 13–14, where Paul is speaking of Jews and gentiles: "But now in Christ Jesus you who once were far off have been brought near by the blood of Christ. For he is our peace; in his flesh he has made the two into one and has broken down the wall, the hostility, that divided them." (Vulg.) Catherine, however, is applying the reference to humanity and God. Cf. also Col. 1, 20: "[Christ] reconciled all things in himself, making peace through the blood of his cross. . . . And you who once were aliens and enemies . . . he has now reconciled in the body of his flesh through his death." (Vulg.)

[7] Cf. *Dial.* 136, p. 280: "From his obedience you have all contracted grace, just as you had all contracted blame from disobedience." Cf. Rom. 5, 18–19: "Therefore just as one man's trespass led to condemnation for all, so one man's act of righteousness leads to justification and life for all. For just as by the one man's disobedience the many were made sinners, so by the one man's obedience the many will be made righteous." Catherine uses the language associated with disease: just as one contracts a disease (sin), so one also contracts health (grace) by association or parentage.

washed away.[8] All this God has given us through love and not because he owed it to us at all. So we certainly are obligated to love him, and must love him if we don't want eternal damnation.

But remember this one thing: those who act against this blood or side with those who are persecuting the blood (that is, persecuting the bride of Jesus Christ with their attacks and mockery and dishonor) will never share in the fruit of the blood unless they change their ways. Nor will they be excused because they take cover under the cloak of the sins of the ministers of the blood, saying, "It is the sins of wicked pastors that we are persecuting." We false Christians have come to the point of believing we are offering sacrifice to God by persecuting his bride![9] For even though the ministers may be devils incarnate full of wretchedness, we must not for all that be Christ's judges and executioners! These men are his anointed ones, and he wants it to remain his right or that of those to whom he has entrusted it to prosecute them. So temporal authorities or civil law cannot meddle in this without incurring spiritual death, because God does not want it so.[10] Such people are demonstrating not love for their Creator but hatred. They are truly ignorant and wretched who see themselves so loved, yet do not love. And great is God's patience in putting up with such evil!

Let us not, then, refuse to love and serve our Creator, because, as I've said, we are obliged to love him. And it is no shame to serve God, for to serve God is not to be a servant but to reign.[11] And the more perfect our service and the more we submit ourselves to him, the more free we are and the more we become masters of ourselves rather than being controlled by sin, the thing that has no being.[12] For we cannot bring a greater wretch-

---

[8] The image of vomiting for confession occurs often in Catherine's writings. She may well have read it (or heard it read) in Cavalca's *Trattato della mondizia del cuore.*

[9] Cf. Jn. 16, 2: "Indeed, an hour is coming when those who kill you will think that by doing so they are offering worship to God."

[10] Cf. *Dial.* 115, p. 215: "Because [the pope] has sent [the clergy] out as his helpers, it is his task to correct them for their faults, and it is my [God's] will that he do so. For by the dignity and authority I have bestowed on them I have freed them from slavery, that is, from submission to the authority of temporal rulers. Civil law has no power whatever to punish them; this right belongs solely to the one who has been appointed to rule and serve according to divine law. They are my anointed ones, and therefore it has been said through Scripture: 'Dare not to touch my christs.' Therefore, a person can do no worse violence than to assume the right to punish my ministers."

[11] Catherine's reference is probably to Augustine, *Meditatio XXXII* (PL XL, 925): "To serve God is to reign." Let. T29/DT18 (vol. I) is Catherine's only previous reference to this line from Augustine; she will use it several times within the next few months.

[12] Cf. Let. T30/DT1 to the nuns of the Monastery of Santa Marta (vol. I): "*You alone are the one who is good. You are the peaceful sea from which come all things that have being.* But that which has no being—sin, I mean—is not in him. Here is what supreme Truth said to a useless servant of his: 'I want you to be a lover of all things, because they are all good, perfect, and worthy of love. I, supreme Goodness, made them all—all but sin. Sin is not in me, dearest daughter, because if it were, it would be worthy of love. *Oh boundless charity!*

edness on ourselves than to become the servants and slaves of sin, since we thereby lose the being that is grace. We serve nothingness and we become nothings.

What wretchedness, that people who are blind and stupid and have no light at all should so lower themselves as to refuse to serve their Creator, and to serve the devil and the world with its pleasures (which have no stability) and their own selfish sensuality! They give up serving infinite Goodness, who loves them so immeasurably,[13] such a glorious and gentle Lord, who has ransomed us not with gold or silver but with the precious blood of his only-begotten Son.[14] No one can resist him.[15] We have [already] been sold,[16] and we cannot resell ourselves to the devil or to anyone else by serving creatures apart from God. We are, it is true, bound and obligated to serve our neighbors, but not with any service that would be contrary to God's will.[17]

Oh how glorious is the mastery we win by serving our Creator! For we rule over the whole world and make light of its customs and manners. And we rule over ourselves rather than being ruled by anger or impurity or any other vice; instead we rule over all the vices with loving affection for virtue. There are many who rule over cities and fortresses, yet have no control over themselves. But without this any mastery is poor and unenduring. Besides, their mastery is always imperfect, with little rationality and less justice. They pass judgment and sentence according to their selfish sensuality and according to human pleasure and will. It is, therefore, not justice but injustice, since justice cannot be contaminated with selfish love or bribery or flattery or human respect. So those who love God would rather die than offend him in this matter or any other. These are the faithful servants, and they are made masters of themselves, who control their selfish sensuality and their free choice with reason.

You want us to hate ourselves [only] because of our perverse will, the source of that which does not exist in you.' "

[13] This is Catherine's earliest reference to God's love as "immeasurable" (*inestimabile*).

[14] 1 Pet. 1, 18–19.

[15] It. *ricalcitrare*, literally, "kick against." The allusion is to Acts 26, 14, where Jesus chides Paul for his futile attempts to "kick against the goad" of grace. This is Catherine's earliest use of the expression in her extant writings.

[16] That is, sold to God when Christ bought us back from the devil.

[17] Cf. Aquinas, *Summa Theologica*, II–II, q. 26, a. 4, reply to obj. 2, "In spiritual matters . . . a person must not suffer injury by sinning in order to free a neighbor from sin." Also *Dial.* 11, p. 44: "The light of discernment, which is born of charity, gives order to your love for your neighbors. It would not permit you to bring the guilt of sin on yourself to benefit your neighbor. For that love would indeed be disordered and lacking in discernment which would commit even a single sin to redeem the whole world from hell or to achieve one great virtue. No, neither the greatest of virtues nor any service to your neighbor may be bought at the price of sin."

Since it is, then, such a dignity and so essential for our salvation to love and serve God, and since the opposite is so dangerous and wretched, I want and beg you, dearest brother, to serve God with all your heart and all your will. And don't wait for time, because you are not sure you will have it—for we are condemned to die and don't know when. So we must not lose the present time for that which we aren't sure of having.

We've said that we are bound to love God. Those who love must serve and be of some use to the one they love. But I see that we cannot be of any use to God, since we do not profit him by our good or hurt him by our evil.[18] So what should we do? We must give glory and praise to God's name and live lives full of virtue. And our effort and the fruit we must give to our neighbors, serving them in whatever is according to God, and enduring and putting up with their shortcomings in true and well-ordered charity. It would be disordered love to commit sin in order to please or save our neighbors. It must not be so, for a well-ordered love in God is unwilling to give up our soul even to save the whole world. Even if it were possible to send everyone to eternal life by committing a single sin, we must not do it. We ought, though, to give up our bodily life for the soul of a neighbor, and our material possessions to save someone physically.

This, then, is how we have to love God, with our neighbors as intermediary, and this is how we demonstrate that we love him.[19] You know how Christ said to Saint Peter: "Peter, do you love me?" When Peter answered that Jesus knew very well that he loved him, and this three times, he said, "If you love me, feed my little sheep."[20] It is as if he were saying, "Here is how I will know whether you love me: if, since you cannot be of any service to me, you come to the aid of your neighbors, nurturing them and giving them your best efforts in true holy teaching."

So we must come to our neighbors' aid according to our ability, some of us by teaching, some by praying, some with our possessions. And those of us who cannot help with possessions must help through our friends. We must always have charity for our neighbors, then, and be of service to them in the way God has appointed for us.

This is why I am turning to you for a merciful favor, proclaiming to you Christ's word: "Peter, do you love your Creator and me? Then serve

---

[18] Aquinas, *Summa Theologica*, I–II, q. 73, a. 8, reply to obj. 2: "Human beings can do God no harm in God's substance, though they can try to do so in things which concern God, for example, by destroying faith." Catherine expresses this idea only here and in Let. T35 to several monks of Monteoliveto Maggiore (late 1377 or early 1378).

[19] While there have been earlier scattered references to serving God in the person of our neighbors, this letter represents the beginning of Catherine's full development of this theme which becomes so central to her spirituality and teaching.

[20] Jn. 21, 15–18. Note that the person Catherine is addressing is named Peter also.

me in your neighbors who are in need, to the extent that you can; but always put God's honor first, never offending him." I've heard that Luigi della Vigna da Capua, Frate Raimondo's brother (who was with the queen's people), has been arrested by the prefect's people, and that they have fined him four thousand florins.[21] It is impossible for him to pay this sum, because he is poor.

So I am begging you, and I urge you in that blazing charity that God has shown you and everyone else in the blood of his Son, to intercede with the prefect (for I've heard that this is within his power). Ask him for pity's sake to do us the favor and mercy, for love of Christ crucified, of letting Luigi go free without demanding of him what he cannot do. Tell him this is an alms, and convince him that through this God is giving him time to put his life in order and turn to real virtue,[22] to peace and tranquility of soul and body, and especially to reverence and obedience as a faithful Christian servant to holy Church.[23] The consequence of this will be everlasting life for him, where he will have life without death and light without darkness, satiety without boredom and hunger without pain.[24] And I pledge to him and you that I will offer continual prayers, tears, and longing for your salvation for as long as I live, as divine grace will grant me. I have nothing else to give you.

Treat [Luigi] as you would me, for love of Christ crucified and to show your love for him and for me and for Frate Raimondo, who is my spiritual father.

Give my regards to the prefect and tell him to follow in the footsteps of Christ crucified, to immerse himself in the blood of Christ crucified.

I'll say no more. Keep living in God's holy and tender love.

Gentle Jesus! Jesus love!

Textual Notes

a. Mo-*b*: *Now I say that those / Those.*

---

[21] "The queen's people" are the troops sent by Queen Giovanna d'Angiò of Naples to aid the cause of Pope Gregory XI. The prefect is Francesco di Vico.

[22] Cf. *Dial.* 93, p. 172: "Sometimes I [God] lend such persons time . . . , giving them an opportunity to correct themselves."

[23] Because the prefect is party to the Florentine rebellion against the papacy, he is with the rest of that city under interdict.

[24] Cf. Pseudo-Augustine, *Meditatio XXVII* (PL XL, 921): "For [the blessed] shall have desire for the vision of God with satiety, and satiety with desire. Their desire shall not be a source of pain, nor their satiety a source of boredom." Catherine probably knew the passage, whether by reading or hearing, from Cavalca's *Descrizione de' dieci comandamenti* (p. 306): "We shall desire though we are sated, and we shall be sated even in our desiring. Yet satiety will not be a source of boredom, nor desire be accompanied by pain, as happens in this world."

LETTER T209/G2[1]
To Pope Gregory XI
Shortly after 17 January 1377, perhaps just after 3 February

The rubrics of H and P3 specify that this letter was written after Gregory had arrived in Rome, therefore sometime between 17 January 1377 and Gregory's death on 27 March 1378. The tone of the letter would certainly fit Gregory's early days back in Rome; such a placement is strongly supported by the linguistic data.[2]

I would therefore place this letter not long after 17 January 1377. In fact, the reference to "paying so much attention to temporal authority and possessions that we lose sight of the great slaughter of souls and dishonor to God that comes from war" could well be a reference to the scandal of 3 February, when more than four thousand innocent inhabitants of Cesena were slaughtered by papal troops in the name of firmness of policy.[3]

§

In the name of Jesus Christ crucified and of gentle Mary.

Most holy and most reverend father in Christ gentle Jesus,

Your unworthy[a] daughter Caterina, servant and slave of the servants of Jesus Christ, is writing to you in his precious blood, longing to see you at peace—with yourself and with your children. God is asking this peace of you and wants you to do whatever you can about it.

Oimé! It does not seem God wants us paying so much attention to temporal authority and possessions that we lose sight of the great slaughter of souls and dishonor to God that comes from war![4] It seems rather that

---

[1] MSS: Mo, B, P2, P1, H, P3, S2, S4, P4; translation based on Mo-*a*, corrected by *b*, with relevant variants based on an unpublished transcription by A. Volpato.

[2] All six letters which share thirteen or more of this letter's forty-five analyzed patterns are dated in the first eight months of 1376. There are two patterns (FOGLVENT, LAVFACCI) which do not occur at all before early 1377, but frequently thereafter. And QUIETAN begins to appear only in September 1376. To support the placement of this letter very soon after Gregory's return to Rome there are four significant clusters which end in January 1377 (COLONCHS, PASTRETT, QUIETAN, VIRTCACC). Dupré Theseider (unpublished notes) places the letter shortly after Gregory's arrival in Rome, and Fawtier (II, pp. 140–141) within the first quarter of 1377. Seckendorff (*Politische Tätigkeit*, p. 131) places it with the arrival of the Florentine delegation in Rome at the end of January 1377, though the letter makes no mention of this event.

[3] Cf. Gardner, *Saint Catherine of Siena*, pp. 205–206.

[4] She reiterates the same message in Let. T11 to Cardinal Pierre d'Estaing (in this volume): "What an incomprehensible thing to imagine and actually to see, that we should be

God wants you to open your mind's eye to the beauty of souls and to the blood of his Son in which he washed our soul's face.[5] And you are minister of this blood. So he is inviting you to be hungry to have souls as your food. For those who are hungry for God's honor and the salvation of his little sheep, to find them and snatch them from the devils' hands, are ready to let go not only of their possessions but of their physical life as well.

You could say though, holy father: "I am bound in conscience to protect and regain what belongs to holy Church." Oimé! I must admit that is the truth, but it seems to me one ought to take even better care of what is more dear. The Church's treasure is the blood of Christ given in payment for souls.[6] The treasure of the blood was paid not for temporal possessions but for the salvation of the human race. So even though you have the responsibility to conquer and protect and rule over the treasure of the cities[7] the Church has lost, you are much more obligated to regain all these little sheep, who are a treasure within the Church. She is ever so impoverished because of their loss. Not that she is intrinsically impoverished—for the blood of Christ cannot diminish—yet she loses a certain adornment of glory that she receives from those who are virtuous and obedient and submissive to her.[8] So it is better to let go of the mud of temporal things than the gold of the spiritual. Do whatever can be done, and once you have done that you are excused before God and before the people of the world.

---

at war with God because of all these sins of both the pastors and their subordinates, and because of this rebellion against holy Church! And at war physically yet! Wherever there is war, every faithful Christian ought to be ready to redirect it against the unbelievers, but these traitorous Christians are waging war against each other! ... Peace! Peace! Peace, dearest father! Be concerned, you and the others, more about the loss of souls than about the loss of cities, and make the holy father see this, for God wants souls more than cities."

[5] This is the first reference in Catherine's extant writings to the blood of Christ washing the soul's face, though she has written often before of bathing in Christ's blood.

[6] The only other reference to this concept in Catherine's extant writings is in *Dial.* 120, p. 230, where she speaks of "the great treasures of the Church's sacraments." Note, however, that just after this she also calls people the treasure of the Church. She may well be reflecting the remark of Saint Lawrence. According to tradition, when his persecutors demanded that Lawrence surrender the Church's treasure, he gathered before them the poor and the lame. The story is retold in Jacopo da Voragine's *Legenda aurea*, with which Catherine was familiar.

[7] In the Italian, the article is plural but the participle is singular (the noun *città* has the same form for singular or plural). The emphasis could be on Florence, at this time still under interdict, but Florence is in any case not the only city at stake. The reference could, in fact, be Cesena (on which see the introductory notes).

[8] She repeats here a point she makes elsewhere in other terms: that the blood—the life—of Christ and the life of the redeemed have become inextricably one in the mystery of the cross. It is the parable of the vine and the branches (Jn. 15, 1–8; Let. T313 and T321, both written in autumn of 1378), of the double engrafting of the Word into humanity and onto the cross (Prayer 17, pp. 147–153), of the vessel of the human heart holding the blood of Christ (Let. T153).

You will conquer more people with the staff of kindness, love, and peace, than with the club of war, and you will besides have back what is yours both spiritually and temporally.

When my soul draws close to God, very hungry for our salvation and the reform of holy Church and the good of the whole world, God seems to reveal no other remedy (nor do I see any other in him) than that of peace.[9] Peace! Peace, for love of Christ crucified! Overlook your children's ignorance and blindness and pride. With peace you will deliver them from war, division, and hostility, and unite them. With virtue you will cast out the devil.[10]

Open[b] wide the eye of your understanding, with hunger and longing for the salvation of souls, and look at these two evils: the evil of the temporal grandeur, lordship, and possessions you think you are obligated to regain;[11] and the evil of seeing souls lose grace and the obedience they owe your holiness. Then you will see[c] how much more you are obligated to regain those souls! Once your mind's eye has seen and discerned which is the lesser evil, you, most holy father, who are caught between two such great evils, ought to choose the lesser of them. If you do choose the lesser in order to avoid the greater, you will in fact avoid both evils and both will turn to good. I mean that in peace you will have won back your children and you will have what is your due.

Forgive me![12] I am not saying this to lecture you. I am compelled by gentle First Truth and by my desire, my dear *babbo*,[e] to see you at peace, at rest, body and soul. For I don't see how, with these disastrous wars, you can have a single hour of good. What belongs to the poor is being eaten up to pay soldiers, who in turn devour people as if they were meat![13] And I can see that it is standing in the way of your holy desire for the reform of your spouse.[f]

Reform her, I say, with good pastors and administrators. And you

---

[9] Recall the themes of reform and peace in Catherine's petitions in *Dial.* 1, p. 26: "The second was for the reform of holy Church. The third was for the whole world in general, and in particular for the peace of Christians who are rebelling against holy Church."

[10] In other more extended passages Catherine's source in the gospel is clear, for example, in Let. T218/DT74 (in this volume): "You know that the devil is not cast out by the devil but by virtue." Cf Mt. 12, 24–32, and parallel texts in Mk. and Lk., where Jesus is accused of casting out devils by the power of Beelzebul. There is a hidden play on the word *virtù* here, which is etymologically "power." In the longer Catherinian texts, the *virtù* that casts out the devil is variously patience and humility (Let. T261, vol. I), humility and kindness (Let. T285, in this volume), and the blood of Christ (*Dial.* 129, p. 259).

[11] That is, the evil of having lost these things.

[12] The Italian is *Mia colpa!*, as in the *Confiteor* (in its older form) at the beginning of Mass: *Mea culpa, mea culpa, mea maxima culpa*, usually translated, "Through my fault, through my fault, through my most grievous fault!"

[13] Cf. Rev. 9, 3–10: "With their iron jaws they eat and devour the poor of the earth."

know you can hardly do that with war, since as long as you think you need princes and lords, you will consider yourself obligated to appoint pastors in their way rather than your own. That, however, is the worst of reasoning: to appoint in the Church—no matter what the apparent need—pastors or any others who are not virtuous but self-seeking. They should rather be seeking themselves for God's sake by pursuing the glory and praise of his name. And they must not be bloated with pride, nor impure as pigs, nor leaves that whirl about in the winds of worldly ostentation and vanity and wealth.[14]

Oimé! Not so, for love of Jesus Christ and the salvation of your own[g] soul! Do whatever you can to remove the reason for war so that you will not be put into this position of having to appoint them according to human dictates rather than according to God's will and your own desire. It is the help of Christ crucified you need; so direct your desire and affection to him and not to human beings and human help. No, to Christ gentle Jesus whose place you hold—for it seems he wants the Church to return to its original lovely state![15] Oh how happy will be your soul and mine when I see you as the initiator of so great a good that what God is now permitting to be done by force may at your hands be done by love! The way you will do it is with peace and with pastors who are true, virtuous, humble servants of God. And you will find such if your holiness[h] will take the trouble to look for them.

For there are two things that have made and are still making the Church lose her temporal goods: war and dearth of virtue. For where there is no virtue there is always war against our Creator. War, therefore, is the cause of all this. Now I am telling you that if you want to regain what is lost there is no other remedy except to use the opposite of what has caused the loss. I mean using peace and virtue to regain it, as I've said. In this way, too, you will realize your other holy desire and the desire of the servants of God and of poor wretched me, that is, to win back the poor souls of the unbelievers who are not sharing in the blood of the slain, consumed Lamb.[16]

Now you see, most holy father, what a good is being impeded and how great is the consequent evil. I trust in God's goodness and your holiness that you will do everything in your power to apply this remedy, holy

---

[14] Catherine's first use in her writings of wind-blown leaves as an image of fickleness or instability.

[15] Cf. Let. T206/DT63 (in this volume), in which she refers to "those holy early days" when the Church was "poor, humble, and meek." Cf. *Dial.* 149–151, pp. 313–324.

[16] The reference is to the crusade. Her emphasis, however, has shifted away from avenging the wrongs the "unbelievers" have done to the Church and toward their conversion to Christ.

peace. This is God's will. And I am telling you in his most gracious name to seek the advice of the true servants of God in this and in whatever else you have to do, for they will counsel you in truth. Find your joy in them, because you need them. And it will, therefore, be good as well as very necessary for you to keep them at your side and set them up as pillars in the mystic body of holy Church.[17]

I believe that Frate Iacomo da Padova,[18,i] the bearer of this letter, is a true and dear servant of God, and I commend him to you. I ask you too: let it please your holiness later on always to be willing to see him and the others close to you. I'll say no more. Keep living in God's holy and tender love. Forgive my presumptuousness. I humbly ask your blessing.

Gentle Jesus! Jesus love!

Textual Notes

a. B, P2: *poor unworthy / unworthy.*
b. *b*: *Open, open / Open.*
c. *you will see* supplied by *b* in the margin.
d. B, P2: [*and discerns*].
e. B, P2: *father / babbo.*
f. B adds *holy Church.*
g. P3: *our / your own.*
h. H: *lordship / holiness.*
i. Supplied by H, P3; others have simply *F. J. da P.*

[17] Dupré Theseider (unpublished notes) sees in this an apparent allusion to a new creation of cardinals, among whom she wishes to see a number of "servants of God," that is, reformers. However, while Catherine often uses the expression "pillars in the Church" to refer to cardinals, she also uses it of others who play a supportive role in the Church. So perhaps this is a first indication of her dream of a "council of the servants of God," which she will pursue, though without much success, under Urban VI. On this, cf. Let. T322, T323, T326, T327, T328 (all written to this purpose in late 1378 and very early 1379), and Urban's bull of 13 December 1378 inviting individuals to such a councel (Laurent, *Fontes*, I, *Documenti*, pp. 53–55).

[18] Giacomo da Padova was an Olivetan monk. See the notes to Let. T32, addressed to him. Perhaps Catherine gave Iacomo the letter to deliver during a visit to Monteoliveto.

Letter T155/G320[1]

To Niera, wife of Gherardo Gambacorta, in Pisa
Early 1377, or possibly later

Catherine had grown close to Monna Niera's family as well as that of Gherardo's brother Piero during her stay in Pisa in 1375.[2] It had in fact been Pietro Gambacorta who had first invited her to that city.[3] The present letter could have been written in response to a communication from Niera, or shortly after Catherine had actually seen the couple and observed the things she is so eager for Gherardo to repent of and confess.

The linguistic evidence is not overwhelming. Still, there is very little support to place it earlier than 1376.[4] Catherine would have been near Niera during her 1375 stay in Pisa and very likely saw her again during her brief stay in Pisa on the return journey from Avignon (late 1376). It would not be surprising if Catherine would write to her not very long after that visit, feeling she had not had sufficient time to talk with her in person. I am placing the letter, then, with another to Pisa from early 1377 simply as one logical possibility, but it may actually have been written later.

§

In the name of Jesus Christ crucified and of gentle Mary.

Dearest daughter in Christ gentle Jesus,

I Caterina, servant and slave of the servants of Jesus Christ, am writing to you in his precious blood. I long to see you so clothed in the garment of divine charity, in true and perfect love, that every other love will leave your heart and affection. For our soul cannot be clothed in two different loves at the same time. If our soul is clothed in the world, it cannot be clothed in God; the two are quite opposed to one another. When we set our love and affection on the world, we love ourselves with a sensual love. We are always seeking after honors, status, and wealth, for pleasure, en-

---

[1] MSS: B, P2, R1, P5, F2, F1, P3, R2, Nd; translation based on R1, with reference to R2. No relevant variants.

[2] Piero's daughter Tora would become Suor (Sister) Chiara in 1382, when she became a Dominican nun. She would be beatified in 1830.

[3] Cf. Let. T149/DT22 (vol. I), for Catherine's initial response to his invitation.

[4] The three letters which share nine or more of this one's twenty-four analyzed patterns range from late 1376 to early 1378. Three significant clusters within individual patterns begin in the last months of 1376 (NOZZDURA, OGGETOCC, SPREGSEC). There is no real linguistic evidence on which to base a late limit to placement of the letter. Both Fawtier (II, p. 309) and Dupré Theseider (unpublished notes) consider the letter undatable.

joyment, and sensual comforts—pleasures that lead souls to eternal death. For those who love the world and its pleasures excessively are invariably rooted in pride, and from pride all the vices are born.[5]

Oh what misery such hearts reap! They are totally immersed in perverse worldly concerns. The result is that they lose the life of grace and win death; they lose the light and enter the darkness. They fall into the vile servitude of sin, and so become servants and slaves of what is not. And a worse fate there could not be. Such souls literally take themselves and put themselves into their enemies' hands!

Now I don't want this for you, dearest daughter (nor for my son Gherardo)! I want you with a true holy diligence to strip your heart and affection of this perverse love and clothe it in love for Christ crucified, with perfect blazing charity, living always in love and affection for your neighbors. Such love is full of joy and gladness and is thoroughly pleasant. It fills and fattens the soul with virtue. It opens the eye of understanding and makes it gaze steadily upon Christ crucified and his indescribable love for us. So by loving we are filled with love and take to following in the footsteps of the one we love. And because it is Christ we love, we follow in the footsteps of Christ, finding continual delight in virtue. We conform ourselves with him in difficult times by being patient. And when we are prospering and enjoying worldly gratification and prestige and fame, we conform ourselves with him in our disdain for these things. That is, just as Christ disdained worldly pleasures, so we too disdain them with true and holy diligence when we are clothed in love.

This is what holy and divine love does. This is the wedding garment we must have if we are to be invited to the wedding feast of everlasting life.[6] And this is why I said that I long to see you clothed in true and perfect love, so that you may fully realize God's will—and my desire—that neither wants nor seeks anything but that you be made holy.[7]

Bathe in the blood of Christ crucified. In the blood you will discover the fire of love.[8] In the blood our iniquities are washed away. Christ's representative does this when we confess and he absolves our soul. What he

[5] Cf. Sir. 10, 15: "Pride is the source of all sin." (Vulg.)

[6] Cf. the parable of the guest expelled from the wedding feast for lack of a proper garment, Mt. 22, 1–14.

[7] 1 Thes. 4, 3.

[8] Elsewhere she explicitly makes the blood of Christ the scarlet wedding garment, for example, in Let. T102 to Raimondo da Capua (late 1379 or early 1380): "If we come to know and be espoused to this truth we will find grace in the blood, the wealth and life of grace. We will find our nakedness covered, find ourselves clothed in the wedding garment of charity's fire, fire mixed and kneaded together with the blood that was shed for love and made one with the Godhead."

is doing is simply pouring Christ's blood over our head.[9] Tell Gherardo that now is the acceptable time, while he is still alive, not to disdain this blood. For he has no certainty about when he must die or how long he will live. Let him go and vomit out the filth of his sins through his mouth by confessing conscientiously and well, for otherwise it will be impossible for him to share in divine grace.

I beg you, my daughter and my son, for love of Christ crucified, do not let love for your children or selfish love for yourselves or worldly pleasure pull you away from what you are duty-bound to do.

I'll say no more. Keep living in God's holy and tender love.

Gentle Jesus! Jesus love!

---

[9] Cf. Prayer 25, p. 215, where Catherine prays, "Today you have again given my soul remission of my sins through your vicar." The present text (where the Italian is also *vicario*) may be a confirmation that in that prayer she is referring not to the pope but to another confessor, since surely Gherardo's confessor would not be the pope.

Letter T158/G48[1]
To Nino da Spazzavento, a Pisan priest
Perhaps early 1377, with the possibility that it was written as late as 1379

Nino,[2] chaplain of the cathedral in Pisa, was the son of the Pisan Puccetto da Spazzavento. A generous man, he gave to the Pisan Carthusians his inheritances from his father and his merchant brother-in-law, Pietro Mirante Virginis. The money helped to build the beautiful monastery of Calci just outside the city. In 1381 he gave the monks there everything he owned and established the Company of the Stigmata in honor of St. Francis and perhaps also in honor of Catherine of Siena, who had died the previous year.[3]

Catherine almost certainly did not meet this priest until her 1375 stay in Pisa, nor is there any linguistic grounds for placing the letter before the end of that period. In fact, this letter has very little in common linguistically with other letters before 1377.[4]

One might infer from the theme of the letter than Nino is dejected about his growing old. We do not know when he died, though we do know he was still living in 1381. It is not inconceivable, however, that he felt the effects of aging for some years. There is no really strong evidence (only a single pattern, and that not absolutely) for not placing this letter even as late as the last months of Catherine's life (when Nino also would have been closer to death). It is therefore with reservation that I place it in the first months of 1377, after Catherine's return from Avignon and Pisa.

---

[1] MSS: Mo, P4, S4, Pa; translation based on Mo-*a*, corrected by *b*. No relevant variants.

[2] Short for Giovannino, or "little Giovanni."

[3] Burlamacchi, note to the letter in Gigli, *Opere*, I, p. 336.

[4] Of the six letters which share nine or more of this one's twenty analyzed patterns, three are from 1377 (with one other earlier, two later). Also, Catherine in this letter relates *affetto* ("affection, will, motivation") with *intelletto* ("intellect, understanding"), which she does not otherwise do at all before late 1376, and does very frequently (forty-two times) thereafter. On the other hand, the expression *Dio-e-uomo* ("God and human" or "God-man") occurs very frequently (thirty-three times) up to late 1377, and only four times thereafter. Also the theme of the Trinity as power, wisdom, and mercy, though it does appear once in early 1376, begins to appear very frequently only from summer 1376 onward. Both Fawtier (II, p. 180) and Dupré Theseider (unpublished notes) consider the letter undatable.

§

In the name of Jesus Christ crucified and of gentle Mary.

Dearest father in Christ gentle Jesus,

I Caterina, servant and slave of the servants of Jesus Christ, am writing to you in his precious blood. I long to see you bathed, immersed in the blood of Christ crucified, and hidden in his open side. In the blood you will discover fire (because it was shed for love), and in his open side you will find hearty love.[5] For Christ shows that everything that he does in us is done with just such hearty love. Then your soul will be set ablaze with a fire of holy desire, a desire that is an impulse of love.[6] Those who clothe themselves in it[7] never grow old but are constantly rejuvenated. It makes them fresh with virtue; it strengthens and enlightens them and unites them with their Creator. For in Christ crucified they find the Father and share in his power. And they find the wisdom of God's only-begotten Son, who enlightens their understanding. They see and experience the mercy of the Holy Spirit when they discover the fond love with which Christ gave us the gift of his Passion, making his blood a bath in which our iniquities are washed away, and making his open side a refuge and a dwelling where our soul rests, where we discover and experience God-and-humanity.[8]

Now this is what I want us to do, dearest father. Then our understanding's eye will never close but will constantly keep watch, contemplating how much God loves us—with a love he has demonstrated through his Son. Our will will love always and never stop loving. Neither pleasure nor pain nor anything else that is said or done to us will ever slacken our love for our Creator. Even if all our other works and all our physical activity should fail, our love must never fail.

I'll say no more. Keep living in God's holy and tender love.

Gentle Jesus! Jesus love!

---

[5] It. *amore corale.*

[6] It. *affetto d'amore.*

[7] The pronouns could allow that it is desire we are to be clothed in, but reading the antecedent as Christ's blood is more consistent with what Catherine writes elsewhere. Only in one instance is desire imaged as a garment (Let. T144/DT34 to Monna Pavola da Siena, vol. I), and then it is the garment Christ wears.

[8] That is, divinity and humanity united in the person of Christ.

Letter T184/G143[1]
To the prior and brothers of the Company of the Virgin Mary in Siena
Near Holy Week of 1377

The men to whom this letter is addressed are members of the lay confraternity serving La Scala Hospital in Siena.

The confraternity's origins, according to Burlamacchi, date to the early fourth century, when the first Christians of Siena gathered to pray in certain grottos not far from the tower in which their apostle, Sant'Ansano, had been imprisoned and from which he had been led to his martyrdom. Above these grottos in the ninth century was erected La Scala Hospital, one of the oldest of Europe, named according to some accounts for three stairs of an ancient temple of Diana discovered in the excavation made for its foundation. The confraternity's church and quarters were located beneath the hospital. Its coat of arms bore an image of the virgin, a cross, and a discipline, symbol of the brothers' life of asceticism. Their ministry was to shelter the poor; to serve the hospitals both within and outside the city; to aid needy girls, pregnant women, pilgrims, and prisoners; and to educate young men. Within their quarters Catherine was given a tiny room in which she could join the brothers in prayer without being seen and where she could rest when she had been working at the hospital beyond the curfew.[2]

References to the paschal sacrifice of Christ and to Easter communion place the present letter in Lent, and most probably near the end of Lent. But in what year? Neither historical fact (the war of the Florentines against the papacy) nor the linguistic evidence would allow placing it before 1376. So it must be near Holy Week of 1376, 1377, or 1378. By Holy Week of 1376 Gregory XI had just placed Florence under interdict (31 March), and Catherine was still in Siena, with Raimondo having already gone to Florence en route to Avignon.[3] During Holy Week of 1377 Catherine still may have been in Siena or perhaps already at Belcaro, where her monas-

---

[1] MSS: T, R1, R2, P3, P5, F2, Nd; translation based on R1, with relevant variants based on an unpublished transcription by A. Volpato.

[2] Cf. Emiliano Lucchesi, "Santa Caterina da Siena e le sue relazioni con i Monaci di Vallombrosa," *Memorie Domenicane* 65 (1948), p. 216: "Because of [Catherine's] encouragement, it seems that [Giovanni dalle Celle] had joined the famous *Compagnia della Madonna sotto le volte dell'ospedale di S. Maria della Scala* in Siena, to which many other prominent people also belonged, including Iacopone da Todi, Giovanni Colombini, S. Bernardino da Siena, Catherine herself, and most of her disciples." (Lucchesi cites Cividali's edition of Giovanni dalle Celle, p. 20.) Catherine, of course, could be called a member of the confraternity only by association, since all true members were men.

[3] Dupré Theseider (unpublished notes) thinks the letter must have been written from Siena, but this does not seem to be a necessary conclusion from the data.

tery was consecrated in April. During Holy Week of 1378 she was almost certainly in Florence.

The linguistic evidence leads me to exclude 1378, but the choice between 1376 and 1377 depends on other clues.[4] At both times Catherine would have had good reason to be concerned about the situation in Florence. ("Pray especially for our city[5] that God may send us true and perfect unity, and that we may renounce every sin we have committed against our Savior and holy Church. And pray earnestly that God in his compassion may convert into true peace the devastation that has come of the Florentines' war with the holy father on account of our sins.") Gardner says that Siena joined the antipapal league "promptly" at the end of 1375,[6] so Catherine would have reason already in 1376 to speak of the sins of Siena against the Church. Still, she would probably not have reason to refer to the *devastation* caused by the Florentine war until considerably later. I would therefore favor 1377 over 1376 for this letter, placing it near Holy Week of that year because of Catherine's exhortation to the brothers to prepare for their Easter communion. ("Let your hearts be softened now in this holy season that puts before us this spotless Lamb roasted on the cross over the fire of blazing charity, who at Easter will tenderly give himself to you as food.") The possibility of Catherine's being at Belcaro at this time could explain her writing rather than speaking with the brothers in person.

---

[4] With eighty patterns analyzed, both the paucity of pattern sharing with other letters and the lack of clusters of occurrence within individual patterns around Easter of 1378 would lead me to eliminate that year from consideration. There are, however, strong concentrations of both horizontal and vertical sharing around Easter in both 1376 and 1377. Fawtier (II, p. 216) places the letter in March of 1378.

[5] That is, Siena.

[6] *Siena*, p. 54.

§

In the name of Jesus Christ crucified and of gentle Mary.

Dearest, very[a] loved sons in Christ Jesus,[b]

I Caterina, servant and slave of the servants of Jesus Christ, am writing to you in his precious blood. I long to see you bound in the sweet bond of charity, the bond that held the God-man nailed fast to the wood of the most holy cross. You know that if charity had not held him, neither nails nor cross could have.[7] Charity is the sweet, pleasant bond that joined human nature with the divine. And for what reason? Only love. It was love that drew us forth from God, creating us in God's image and likeness. And when we lost grace, and God wanted to give us back what we had lost because of our guilt and sins,[c] in love he sent us the Word, his only-begotten Son. He wanted us to have grace once again through his blood. And this obedient Son of his ran to the shameful death of the cross as one in love with our salvation.

So everything God has done and continues to do for us is done for love. This is why, when we contemplate this boundless and indescribable love, we are opening the eye of our understanding and knowledge to the blood of Christ crucified, the blood in which, more than anywhere else, the vastness of indescribable charity is set before us. And he said as much: that one can show no greater love than to give one's life for a friend.[8] *Oh boundless love!*[d] *If you praise the love that gives one's life for a friend as being the greatest love there can be, how much more deserving of praise is your love for us, for we had become your enemies, and you gave your life, paid the price of your blood, for us! This goes far beyond all other love. Oh gentle and loving Word, God's Son, you became our mediator. By your death you reconciled us with God!*[9] For the nails became for us the key that unlocked eternal life, so opened it up that it cannot be closed to anyone who does not so choose, because we cannot be forced to sin at all against our will.[10]

Sin is what closes the door to us and deprives us of the destiny for

[7] Cf. Cavalca, *Specchio di croce*, p. 41: "No bond of iron could have held Christ nailed or bound—only charity, the bond of perfection."

[8] Jn. 15, 13.

[9] Cf. Rom. 5, 8–10: "It is precisely in this that God proves his love for us: that while we were still sinners, Christ died for us. Now that we have been justified by his blood, it is all the more certain that we shall be saved by him from God's wrath. For if, when we were God's enemies, we were reconciled to him by the death of his Son, it is all the more certain that we who have been reconciled will be saved by his life."

[10] These two ideas, of the nails being made keys to open heaven, and of human freedom, are brought together in only two other places, Let. T112 (from this same period) and T159 (earlier in this volume).

which we were created. Sin robs us of life and gives us death. It robs us of light and gives us darkness, because it dims the mind's eye and keeps it from seeing either the sun or the dark. I mean here the dark of self-knowledge, in which we discover and see the dark sensuality that is always rebelling and fighting against our Creator.[11] And if we do not see our own darkness we cannot know the love and light of divine goodness.[12]

I said that when we contemplate this boundless love we conceive indescribable love. We have made our will conform[e] with God's.[13] We see and discern clearly that God wants nothing else but that we be made holy,[14] and that whatever he gives or permits us—trials or consolations or persecution or distress or derision or abuse—everything is given so that we may be made holy in him.[15] For there can be no holiness without virtue, and we can have virtue only by means of what opposes it.[16] So once we know this love we cannot be disturbed or saddened by anything at all that happens, from whatever source. If we did, we would be grieving over our own good and over the goodness of God who permits it for us. The sensual part of us does indeed feel it when something goes against us, but reason takes control of those feelings and keeps them in their proper place. And how will we keep these feelings in their place, so that they don't rebel against our Creator? I'll tell you.

Pleasure as well as distress is kept in check by the sweet and holy remembrance of God, that is, by the continual consideration of death that comes with self-knowledge. We see, dearest sons and brothers in Christ gentle Jesus, that we are all mortal. The moment we are created in our mother's womb we are condemned to death and will surely die, and we know neither when nor how. And who of us will not check and cut off any unwarranted pleasure that comes from empty and foolish worldly joys, if we consider that our life is so short that we can expect death any day? (For our life is no bigger than the point of a needle!) We will, I tell you, keep ourselves in check and not pursue honor or prestige or great-

---

[11] Cf. Rom. 7, 18–24. This is the only instance in which Catherine uses the expression, "the dark of self-knowledge." It is clear from the context and from other references, however, that she means the dark one can see only in the light of self-knowledge.

[12] Cf. *Dial.* 8, pp. 8–9, for an analogous juxtaposition of opposites—sin and virtue—to which Catherine will in fact allude in the next paragraph.

[13] Literally, "We have made and conformed our will with God's." The sense of our "making" our will is not clear; perhaps it is a scribal error, since nowhere else does Catherine use this expression. Tommasèo saw it as a reference to our role, as rational creatures, in "creating" ourselves by our actions, but his reasoning seems a bit stretched.

[14] Cf. 1 Thes. 4, 3.

[15] 1 Cor. 1, 2.

[16] That is, as she says so often elsewhere, virtue (and each specific virtue) is tested and proved and strengthened only by one's dealing with what opposes it.

ness; nor will we be avaricious in our possession of wealth. In fact, if we do have wealth we will become Christ's stewards of it for the poor.[17] We will not want to have or keep that wealth in pride, but in deep and sincere humility, seeing and realizing that in this dark life nothing is stable or enduring but all passes away like the wind. As for trials, we bear them patiently because we see that every difficulty we can suffer in this life is small. Why small? Because our time is small. The pain that is past you don't have, and what is yet to come you aren't certain of having because you don't know whether death will come to you and free you from all pain. All you have, then, is this point of time that is present to you. So the thought of death frees you from impatience in trial and from undue pleasure in consolation.

It isn't, though, a matter simply of the thought of death. That would only lead to frustration. The thought of death has to be accompanied by well-ordered love and fear of God—I mean the avoidance of sin and vice so as not to offend our Creator. Sin doesn't exist in God, and so it is unworthy of being loved[f] or desired by us who are God's children, created in God's image and likeness.[18] We ought to love what he loves and hate what he hates. If we do, our mind's eye is opened and we see how advantageous it is to despise vice and love virtue, and how harmful the contrary is. For if death comes upon us suddenly (for we have no certainty!) and we are sleeping in vice and sin, it will bring us eternal damnation with no further escape.

But living virtuously always brings us joy, and peace with God and with our neighbors.[g] Once we have risen above rancor we feel a familial charity, and so we love our neighbors as we love ourselves. And we should therefore love both friends and enemies and desire their salvation in so far as they are rational creatures. We should try as hard as we can to be tolerant and put up with their shortcomings, hating the vice that may be there but not hating the person. We rejoice with God's servants who are rejoicing. We weep with the wicked who are living in a time of weeping, in the compassion and sorrow we bear because of their offense against God.[19] And we willingly surrender ourselves to every kind of pain and torment in order to bring the wicked back to the condition of those who are rejoicing, who are living as lovers of lovely, royal virtue.

---

[17] Cf. *Dial.* 151, p. 319, where she says that those who possess wealth "are not so much possessors of it as distributors for the poor."

[18] Cf. *Dial.* 18, p. 56: "I am the Creator of everything that has any share in being. But sin is not of my making, for sin is non-being. Sin is unworthy of any love, then, because it has no part in me."

[19] Rom. 12, 15 (Vulg.): "Weep with those who are weeping, and rejoice with those who are rejoicing."

In this way we are living in unity and keeping God's commandment, since for love of him we are loving our neighbors. This is the sign Christ gave us for our recognition as his children and disciples, and this is what he said to his disciples: "Love, love one another. For by this it will be known that you are my disciples!"[20] If we travel along this sweet and pleasant way[h] we are living in grace, and in the end we will find ourselves in the eternal vision of God.

But of all the things I ask of you, my sons, I beg you more than anything else to love one another. We must engraft our heart and affection into the love of Christ crucified. And since we see that he has loved us supremely, we must take that love of his and bind ourselves so closely with our neighbors that nothing will ever be able to loosen or undo this bond of love—neither the devil, nor any injury these very neighbors may do us, nor our own selfishness. I know that in any other way we are living in damnation, and that is why I said I long to see you bound in the bond of charity.

You have every reason to be so united. You were all created by God, and redeemed by the same blood. Besides, there is the sweet holy community you have made in the dear name of Mary, who is your[i] advocate, the mother of grace and of mercy.[21] She is not wanting in gratitude to those who serve her; no, she is grateful and appreciative. She is the intermediary, a real chariot of fire, who in conceiving within herself the Word, God's only-begotten Son, brought and gave [to us] the fire of love—for he is love itself.[22] Serve her, then, with all your heart and all your will, because she is your most gracious mother.

I beg you also to hate and despise the sin of impurity and every other sin, for it would be unbecoming to serve in impurity Mary who is supreme purity.

Sleep no longer, dearest fathers, brothers, sons! Rouse yourselves with love for virtue and with hatred and disgust for sin. See how abominable sin is to God, who allowed his Son, on account of it, to suffer his passion and death. And with what love he bore pain, ridicule, derision, and abuse, and in the end the shameful death of the cross! Bathe yourselves in the blood of Christ crucified. Under the impulse of love hide yourselves in his wounds. A friend cannot show greater love than to give his life for his friend, and he has given his life for you and to you, with his body slain

---

[20] Jn. 13, 35

[21] Recall that she is writing to the Confraternity of the Virgin.

[22] Cf. Prayer 18, p. 156: "O Mary, chariot of fire, your bore the fire hidden and veiled under the ashes of your humanness." The image is that of the embers banked up and protected by the ashes so that when fire is needed, the ashes can be blown away to free the flames.

and split open![23] Let your hearts be softened now in this holy season that puts before us this spotless Lamb roasted on the cross over the fire of blazing charity, who at Easter[24] will tenderly give[j] himself to you as food.[25] I ask you all, then, to prepare yourselves for holy communion—unless there is some impediment that cannot be rescinded without recourse to Rome.[26]

I'll say no more.

Love, love one another! Keep living in God's holy and tender love. I your unworthy servant commend myself to your prayers, though I'm sure you do pray for me. And I beg you, I urge you in the name of Christ crucified, in all your prayers and in all the holy works[k] God allows you to do, to offer them in sacrifice to God for the reform of Christ's sweet bride, holy Church, and for the peace and unity of all Christians.

Pray especially for our city[27] that God may send us true and perfect unity, and that we may renounce every sin we have committed against our Savior and holy Church. And pray earnestly that God in his compassion may convert into true peace the devastation that has come of the Florentines' war with the holy father on account of our sins.[l] For I'm telling you that unless we help ourselves with continual prayer and crying out to divine mercy, we are in a worse state both materially and spiritually than we ever have been. Let's knock at the door of God's mercy with prayer and desire for peace. He is kind and so will not despise the voice of the people that cries out to him. Listen to the good gentle Jesus, who teaches that we should knock and call out to him, enlightened by faith that we will be heard; otherwise our prayer will be worthless. Gentle First Truth says: "Knock and it shall be opened to you; ask and it shall be given you; call and you shall be answered."[28] Since he teaches us how, let us give ourselves to it in good holy earnestness, in perfect and enduring persever-

---

[23] Cf. Prayer 19, p. 172: "It was in this Word's Passion that souls came, by your light, to a perfect knowledge of your charity's affection. For then the fire hidden under our ashes began to show itself completely and generously by splitting open his most holy body on the wood of the cross. And it was to draw the soul's affection to high things, and to bring the mind's eye to gaze into the fire, that your eternal Word wanted to be lifted up high."

[24] It. *nella Pasqua.* It could also be "at Passover," or "on the feast," but given the context, it is almost certainly Easter.

[25] In Let. T52 to Jeronimo da Siena (in this volume) she explicitly images the cross as the spit on which the Lamb of God is roasted.

[26] The members of the confraternity may or may not have a dispensation from the interdict which at the time is barring the Sienese from the sacraments; this is probably what Catherine is referring to. The obligation to receive holy communion during the Easter season (the "Easter duty" mandated since the early thirteenth century) was generally assumed to include the obligation of sacramental confession as well.

[27] That is, Siena.

[28] Mt. 7, 7–8; Lk. 11, 9–10.

ance. For, as he himself says, if he won't grant [what we ask] for any other reason, he will grant it because of [our] persistent pestering.[29]

I'll say no more.

Gentle Jesus! Jesus love! Mary![m]

Textual Notes

a. R2, T, Nd: [*very*].

b. P5, F2: *gentle Jesus / Jesus.*

c. Other Manuscripts: *sin / sins.*

d. P5, P2: *charity and love / love.*

e. From T, P5; other Manuscripts have *confirmed our will.*

f. R2, Nd: *loved in us /* [loved].

g. R2, Nd: *joy with God and peace with our neighbors / joy . . . neighbors.*

h. Nd: *life / way* (*vita / via*).

i. P3: *our / your.*

j. R2, Nd: *in holy communion gives / at Easter . . . give.*

k. T, R2, P3, P5, Nd: *devotions and in all the holy prayers / prayers . . . works.*

l. R2, Nd: *of the war that we are seeing planned / that has come . . . father.*

m. R2, P3: [*Mary!*]; P5: *Keep living in Christ gentle Jesus. Amen*; Nd: *Jesus love! Gentle Jesus! Jesus love! finis — di sancta Caterina.*

[29] Cf. Lk. 11, 5–8.

Letter T260/G309[1]
To the prisoners in Siena
26 March 1377 (Holy Thursday)

Catherine's biographers and other commentators have traditionally assumed that this letter is addressed to all of the prisoners of Siena simply as prisoners. However, in July 1376 at least one of the Knights Hospitalers was taken prisoner by the Sienese after the battles in the lands of the Alberese. He was not released until the following April.[2] Given Catherine's interest in the Hospitalers as key players for the projected crusade, as well as the knight imagery in the letter and the fact that this letter has a good deal in common with her letter addressed about this same time to the prior of the Pisan Hospitalers (T256), Catherine may well be addressing herself primarily to this Hospitaler and others taken in the same battle. If this is the case, the letter illustrates Catherine's involvement in ecclesiastical politics as much as it does her interest in the oppressed as such. She does, however, seem to assume that the letter will be read to all of the prisoners, since she advises "those who can" to prepare for their Easter confession and communion.

The linguistic evidence is supportive of the date provided by the manuscripts, Holy Thursday, 26 March 1377.[3]

§

In the name of Jesus Christ crucified and of gentle Mary.

Dearest sons in Christ gentle Jesus,

I Caterina, servant and slave of the servants of Jesus Christ, am writing to you in his precious blood. I long to see you bathed in the blood of Christ crucified with holy desire. Keep that blood before your mind's eye. If you do, you will learn a true willingness to suffer. For Christ's blood sets be-

---

[1] MSS: B, P2, T, R1, P3, P5, F2, R2, Nd; translation based on T, R1. No relevant variants.

[2] Neri di Donato, *Chronache Senesi*, ed. A. Lisini and F. Iacometti, in *Rerum Italicarum Scriptores*, n.s. xv, part vi (Bologna, 1932–1937), 661–662, 667. I am grateful to Thomas Luongo for having first pointed out the probable relationship of this source to the present letter (private correspondence, 1996).

[3] Two of the three letters sharing ten or more of this one's thirty-six analyzed patterns are from March to April 1377. The patterns CAGIMORT, FIELACET, PECCCAG, and SANGMANI also show significant clusters concentrated at that time. Dupré Theseider (unpublished notes) places the letter on 26 March 1378, noting that the rubric he has consulted has *mcclxviij*. Both R1 and B, however, clearly have *mcclxvij*. Also, Holy Thursday was on 26 March in 1377 but not in 1378.

fore us our God's infinite mercy and charity as well as our own sinfulness, and that brings us to hate and despise our sins and shortcomings and to love virtue.

You might ask me, dearest sons, why we see our sins and God's mercy more clearly in the blood. I answer that it is because the death of God's Son was offered to God for our sins.[4] Sin was the cause of Christ's death. God's Son had no need to go the way of the cross to enter into his glory, since the poison of sin was not in him, and eternal life belonged to him. But a huge war had broken out between God and us because we wretched people had lost eternal life through our sins. Humankind was weakened and sick in its rebellion against its Creator, but could not take the bitter medicine that was the consequence of its sin. We needed God to give us the Word, his only-begotten Son. And so, in his boundless charity, he brought about a union of the divine nature with the human; the infinite joined himself with our poor limited flesh.

He came as a doctor who was weak, as our knight who was also a doctor.[5] I tell you, with his blood he healed our sinfulness. And he gave us his flesh as food and his blood as drink.[6] This blood is so sweet and mild and so strong that it heals every weakness, and brings life out of death. It dispels darkness and gives light.

Why does deadly sin make us fall into all these evils? Because sin robs us of grace and life and gives us death. It dims the light of understanding and makes us the devil's servants and slaves. It takes away our true security and gives us unwarranted fear (since sin is always fearful). Those who let themselves be controlled by sin have lost control.[7]

Oimé! Oimé! How many evils follow upon sin! How much trouble, anxiety, and weariness God lets us experience simply because of sin! And all these sins and evils are annihilated in the blood of Christ crucified, because in the blood we are cleansed of our iniquities when we go to holy confession. In the blood we learn patience, for when we reflect on the offenses we have committed against God and the remedy he has set up to give us the life of grace, we come to a genuine willingness to suffer. So it really is true that he is a doctor, since he has given us his blood as medicine.

I said that he is weak as well. I mean that he has taken on our weak-

---

[4] The theme reflects the Last Supper event commemorated on Holy Thursday, when Jesus said, "This is my blood, the blood of the covenant, to be poured out in behalf of many for the forgiveness of sins." (Mt. 26, 28)

[5] It is not surprising that Catherine would add the image of Christ as knight if it is indeed the imprisoned Knight Hospitaler, and possibly some of his fellow soldiers as well, that she is addressing.

[6] Jn. 6, 56.

[7] It. *signoria*, literally, "lordship."

ness[8] by taking on our mortality, our mortal flesh, and he took out the punishment for our sins on this flesh in his own wonderful body. He acted like a wet-nurse who is nursing a baby. When the baby is sick she takes the medicine for it because the baby is tiny and weak and wouldn't be able to tolerate the bitterness since it drinks nothing but milk. *Oh dearest Love, Jesus! You are the wet-nurse who took the bitter medicine by enduring pain, disgrace, agony, insults. You were bound, beaten, scourged at the pillar, nailed fast to the cross. You were saturated with scorn and shame, tormented and consumed by thirst without any relief. They gave you vinegar mixed with gall and utter reproach. And you bore it patiently, praying for those who had crucified you. Oh immeasurable love! You not only pray for those who are crucifying you but you excuse them, saying, "Father, forgive them, because they do not know what they are doing."*[9] *Oh patience exceeding all patience! Now has there ever been anyone who was harassed, beaten, mocked, and killed, yet pardoned and prayed for the perpetrators? Only you, my Lord! So it really is true that you took the bitter medicine for us weak, sick babies, and through your death give us life. And with the bitterness you give us sweetness. You hold us to your breast like a wet-nurse, and have given us the milk of divine grace. You took the bitterness, and in this way we receive health.*

So you see, he is weak for us!

I say that he is a knight. He came onto this battlefield and fought and conquered the devil. Saint Augustine says, "With unarmed hand this knight of ours defeated our enemies when he rode out on horseback on the wood of the most holy cross."[10] The crown of thorns was his helmet. His scourged flesh was his breastplate. His nailed hands were his gloves of mail. The lance at his side was the sword that cut off our death. His fastened-down feet were his spurs. Look how wonderfully this knight of ours is armed! Surely we ought to follow him and be encouraged in our every difficulty, in every adversity!

This is why I said that Christ's blood shows us our sins as well as the remedy and the overflowing divine mercy we have received in his blood. Bathe yourselves in the blood of Christ crucified, for there is no other way we can share in his grace or have the destiny we were created for. And there is no other way you would be able to endure your troubles patiently. For in the thought of the blood everything bitter becomes sweet and every heavy burden light.

---

[8] Is. 53, 4: "It was our weaknesses he bore." (Vulg.)

[9] Lk. 23, 34.

[10] Cf. Cavalca, *Specchio di croce*, pp. 132–133: "He mounted the cross as his horse. . . . With unarmed hand, nailed to the cross, he conquered the enemy." However, Cavalca attributes only the reference to Christ as unarmed to Augustine. The continuation of Catherine's imagery here is also very close to the same long passage from Cavalca.

I'll say no more to you because I have very little time. Keep living in God's holy and tender love. And remember that you will surely die, and you don't know when. Those of you who can, see that you get ready for confession and holy communion, so that you may be resurrected in grace with Christ Jesus.[11]

Gentle Jesus! Jesus love!

---

[11] Since it is Holy Week, the time has come for the confession and communion during the Easter season, an obligation established since the thirteenth century. If all of the prisoners Catherine is addressing are in fact Hospitalers, one wonders why any of them would not be able to fulfill this obligation. So this may be an indication that she intends her letter to be read by or to all of the prisoners.

LETTER T256/G42[1]
To Niccolò dei Strozzi, prior of the Pisan Knights Hospitalers of St. John
March to early April 1377

Niccolò dei Strozzi had been commander of the Paduan Hospitalers (Knights of St. John) when this religious order of knights had gathered in assembly in Avignon in November 1373.[2] The rubric of the present letter states that it was written when, as prior of the Tuscan Hospitalers, he had gone to Venice to arrange matters for the crusade about to begin. The Knights of St. John had agreed to meet in Venice in March of 1377, and there is documentation of a decision of the Venetian Senate taken on 19 April to refuse the prior the ships he had requested.[3] So this letter must have been written in March or early April. A year later Niccolò would be in Vonitza, a town on the Gulf of Arta, apparently believing that the crusade was imminent.[4] Niccolò may have died in Epirus during 1378, for he is not heard of again from that point on.

The linguistic evidence strongly supports the placement of this letter in March to early April 1377.[5]

---

[1] MSS: B, P2, T, R1, P3, P5, F2, Pa; translation based on R1, with relevant variants from B as noted in Dupré Theseider, unpublished notes.

[2] Malta, cod. 347, fol. 51–51v, cited by Anthony Luttrell in "Gregory XI and the Turks: 1370–1378," *Orientalia Christiana Periodica* 46 (1980), p. 416. All of the following information is based on that same article. Burlamacchi identifies the addressee of this letter with the unnamed Hospitaler who seized the Alberese and Talamone from Siena in 1376 and April 1377, but this, in Luttrell's opinion, is almost impossible. (Cf. *Chronache Senesi*, ed. A. Lisini and F. Iacometti, in *Rerum Italicarum Scriptores*, ns. xv, part vi, Bologna, 1932–1937, 661–662, 667.)

[3] *Archivio di Stato di Venezia, Misti del Senato*, xxxvi, fol. 5v, cited in Luttrell, "Gregory XI and the Turks: 1370–1378". The record does not name the prior, but Luttrell concludes from other records of the same period that "the Pisan prior" must be Niccolò.

[4] He is at Vonitza on 24 April 1378, when he appears as *nicolaccius de ystorchiis de floren' pisarum prior*. (Malta, cod. 48, fols. 168b–169, cited by Luttrell, "Gregory XI and the Turks: 1370–1378," p. 416.)

[5] Three of the four letters sharing nineteen or more of this one's sixty-eight analyzed patterns are from March to September 1377. There is, further a concentration of significant clusters within individual patterns in this period, especially CAMPOBAT, CAPITANO, CROCEDES, FOGLVENT, FUMO, MANGGUST, MORTDES, PIETRCRO, SPALLE, TORNIELL, VENTMOND, VITTOR. Fawtier (II, p. 179) places the letter probably in March 1377, when the Hospitalers had agreed to meet in Venice. Dupré Theseider places it before that date.

§

In the name of Jesus Christ crucified and of gentle Mary.

Dearest son in Christ gentle Jesus,

I Caterina, servant and slave of the servants of Jesus Christ, am writing to you in his precious blood. I long to see you a courageous knight, stripped of selfish self-centeredness and clothed in divine love. For a knight who is put on the battlefield to fight should be armed with the weapon of love, the strongest weapon there is. It wouldn't be enough only to be armored in breastplate and mail.[6] Unless he had the weapon of love, and a desire and craving for honor, and the determination to know what he was fighting for, as soon as he saw the enemy he would often as not become fearful and retreat. Just so, I tell you, when we begin to enter the battlefield to fight against vice and against the world, the devil, and our selfish sensuality, unless we are armored in virtue and carry in our hand the knife of hatred and of a true holy sense of conscience grounded in divine love,[7] we fall back without even fighting. Like irresponsible people armed with selfish sensuality, we lie down and fall asleep in sin and vice.

This is the glorious armor that rescues us from eternal death and gives us light and delivers us from darkness. It lifts us from being beasts to being human. For those who live in vice and sin and impurity take on the form and ways of beasts. Just as beasts have no reasoning power, and act according to their instincts, so those who have become like beasts have lost the light of reason and let themselves be guided by fleshly impulse and by whatever other disordered desires come upon them. All their desire is set on nothing but indecency, in eating and drinking plenty, in delicacies, pleasure, prestige, and worldly honor—all of which are as passing as the wind. Such people are not true knights and are in no condition to sustain an attack, because they have put on the armor of death and made themselves as good as beasts.

I don't want this to be true of you. No, I want you to be really and courageously human. But I want you to be more than simply human. Once you have fought against vice and are growing in virtue you will be angelic, you and your company, as God has called you to be. For you know that the [ordinary] human[a] state is marriage. But you and your

---

[6] It. *corazze e panziere.* In medieval armor the former was the breastplate; the latter was the plate or mail piece extending down from the lower edge of the breastplate to protect the abdomen. Bernardino da Siena (*Prediche,* X, ed. Bargellini), shortly after Catherine, describes it as "a shirt of iron."

[7] This is the only instance in which Catherine makes the second edge of the knife not love itself but "a sense of conscience (It. *coscienza*) grounded in love."

religious order (like other religious), whom God has appointed to a state of continence, belong to the angelic state.[8] It wouldn't be right—in fact, it would be displeasing to God and abominable to the world—if you who are called and are on your way to greater perfection would end up as beasts. For you are appointed not only to the human or angelic state but to that of the glorious martyrs, appointed to give your lives for Christ crucified.[9] It would be really disgusting to mix [such a] great treasure with ugly miserable mud![10]

So up, courageously and without any slavish fear, to the two battles into which God has sent you! The first is the ordinary battle everyone is given to fight, since, as soon as we have come of age to discern vice from virtue, we are surrounded by our enemies. That is, the devil and our own flesh and perverse sensuality that are always fighting against the spirit.[11] Fight them, though, with love for virtue and hatred for vice.

The other battle is assigned to you[b] in particular by grace, and not everyone has been made worthy of it.[12] To this battle you have to go armed not only with material weapons but with spiritual ones. For if you didn't have the weapons of love for God's honor and desire to win over the city of these poor unbelieving souls who have no share in the blood of the Lamb, you would win little success[13] with your material weapons. So I want you, dearest father and son, you and your whole company, to take Christ crucified as your focus (I mean his wonderful precious blood that was shed with such blazing love to free us from death and give us life) so that your purpose in going may be realized fully and completely, and that you may receive the greatest success of all, the success of grace and life (for it is by grace that we come to everlasting life).

Learn from this slain, consumed Lamb, who with delight in the food of his Father's honor and our salvation set himself to eating it at the table of the shameful cross, paying no attention to his weariness and grief. As one in love with the eternal Father's honor and the salvation of the human race, he was firm and constant. He was unmoved by weariness or agony or derision or abuse. Nor was he moved by our ingratitude, as he saw that he

---

[8] The Knights Hospitalers were a religious order, though their mission was military in character.

[9] A clear reference to Catherine's hope for a crusade, in which these knights would certainly be involved.

[10] Catherine frequently uses mud as an image for the filth of impurity. In this case it refers to violation of the knights' vow of chastity.

[11] Gal. 5, 17.

[12] Niccolò is, as the rubric of R1 states, at Venice for the purpose of getting things in order for the crusade.

[13] It. *frutto*, which in view of succeeding uses of the word, Catherine might intend to signify booty.

was giving his life for people who would be neither grateful nor appreciative of such a great gift.

Our King behaves like a true knight who perseveres in battle until the enemies are defeated. Once he had eaten this food,[14] with his scourged flesh he conquered our enemy the flesh. With true humility, he, God, stooped down to our humanity in suffering and shame, and conquered pride and worldly pleasure and prestige. And with his wisdom he conquered the malice of the devil. So with unarmed hand, nailed fast to the cross, he defeated the prince of the world, with the wood of the holy cross as his mount.[15] This knight of ours came armed with the breastplate of Mary's flesh, flesh that bore the blows to make up for our wickedness.[16] The helmet on his head is the painful crown of thorns, driven right into his brain. The sword at his side is the wound in his side, revealing to us the secret of his heart; it is a sword with a point of light that ought to pierce our inmost heart with the force of love.[17] The staff in his hand is there in mockery.[18] And the gloves on his hands and the spurs on his feet are the scarlet wounds in the hands and feet of this gentle loving Word. What armed him? Love. What held him nailed firm and fast to the cross?

---

[14] That is, the love for God's honor and the longing for human salvation which motivated and nourished him.

[15] Cf. Cavalca, *Specchio di croce*, pp. 136–137: "Because Christ came to free the soul, his spouse, from the hands of the devil, who was holding her as an adulteress, we might say that he came armed as a knight for battle—just as two lovers sometimes duel over one they both love. So he mounted the cross as his horse. His spurs were the nails in his feet. The lance was the staff he held in his hand. His scarlet vest was his bloodied flesh. The well-wrought helmet on his head was the crown of thorns pressed down into his skull. The sword at his side was the wound in his side. The gloves on his hands were the wounds in his hands. This is how our Savior came armed to seize the mastery the devil had over humankind."

[16] Each time Catherine uses the image of the breastplate (*corazza*) it has a different meaning: charity embodied in Christ's blood (Let. T128, in this volume), humility (Let. T159, in this volume), or the human will (Let. T183, vol. I). Here it is Christ's flesh, which she sees as Mary's. While elsewhere she refers to the Word being engrafted into flesh in Mary, this identification of Jesus' flesh with Mary's is unique. What is particularly interesting in this is that she sees Mary's flesh as Christ's armor, protecting him from the blows of the enemy.

[17] Cf. Cavalca, *Specchio di croce*, pp. 132–133: "Christ let his side be opened up to show us his heart. So Saint Bernard says that through the opening up of his side he revealed the secret of his heart, and one can see the kindness of Christ's heart." The image of the two-edged sword is one that Catherine uses very frequently, but this is the only time she gives that sword a "point of light." It is, however, very consonant with the two-edged sword of Heb. 4, 12, which "penetrates and divides soul and spirit, joints and marrow, and judges the reflections and thoughts of the heart."

[18] For Cavalca the staff is the lance that pierced Christ's side. Catherine may be forgetting or simply ignoring Cavalca's metaphor here. Her own version is somewhat inconsistent with the rest of her imagery as she continues. Cf. Mt. 27, 29: "Weaving a crown out of thorns they fixed it on his head, and stuck a reed in his right hand. Then they began to mock him by dropping to their knees before him, saying, 'All hail, king of the Jews!' "

Neither the nails nor the cross, which were not capable of holding the God-Man, but the bond of love for the Father's honor and our salvation. Love for us was the stone that held him upright.[19]

Who is so vile-hearted as not to be roused from weak-heartedness to become courageous against any enemy at the sight of this knight and captain at the same time done to death and victorious? No one! This is why I told you to take Christ crucified as your focus.

Dye your cloak in the blood of Christ crucified, and with this you will defeat the first enemies—I mean those in the first battle I spoke of. For Christ has already defeated them for us and has made us free by rescuing us from perverse servitude to the devil. And if the devil should ever try to attack us, let's have recourse at once to the weapons and armor[20] of God's Son.

Once your vices are dead, you will take as your food and begin to eat and savor God's honor and the salvation of your neighbors. Hungry for this food, you will follow the Lamb so as to be able to have this sweet spoil, which in love's affection you must imagine as [already] yours. Neither pain nor death nor anything else that could happen will make you abandon him or turn back. Oh how glorious is this battle! When we are conquered we win, and we are never losers again—not unless we were so base as to turn our backs. But if we persevere we will always win. We will do as God's Son did. He jousted with death on the cross, and life conquered death and death life. By giving his physical life he destroyed the death of sin; with death he conquered death. And death also conquered life, since sin was the cause of the death of God's Son.

Oh what a sweet joust and tournament he fought! And you who are chosen for this same tournament on the cross of desire for God's honor and the ransom of unbelieving souls must play the life of the light of faith against the death of unbelief. Should you end up dead, that is the best part, for death will be the conqueror of death. Thus we see that the blood of the martyrs gave life to the unbelievers and to wicked tyrants. And if I am conquered without bloodshed, I am still victorious. I mean that if God would not permit me to die,[21] this is no less a victory, and is therefore good and glorious.

But it would not be glorious for those naive and crazy people who go

---

[19] Cf. Cavalca, *Specchio di croce*, p. 41: "No bond of iron could have held Christ nailed or bound—only charity, the bond of perfection." In Let. T29/DT18 (vol. I); T82, T223, T246/DT85 (in this volume), and T366 (1379) the stone which holds up the cross is the (redeemed) soul.

[20] It. *arme*, which includes both weapons and armor. Catherine's imagery above also includes both.

[21] Literally, "if God should not permit it, if I should remain alive."

merely for the sake of vanity or their own sentimental purposes. They would accomplish little, and would be paying a great price for small merchandise, for they would be paying the price of their lives for pitiful worldly vanity. Such people receive their reward in this finite life. Their armor is the garment of selfish self-centeredness. They are people not of deeds but of wind, and as such they whirl about like leaves with no stability or firmness because they are not focused on Christ crucified and they have not taken up the weapons of life.

It is my desire that you should be a true knight, you and the others of your company. This is why I said that I long to see you a courageous knight sent onto this glorious field. I hope that by God's infinite goodness you will fulfill his will (for that is what he is requiring of you) as well as my desire.

I'll say no more. Bathe yourself in the blood of Christ crucified and hide yourself in his wonderful wounds. And take up the most holy cross as your shield. Keep living in God's holy and tender love.

Gentle Jesus! Jesus love! Mary!

Textual Notes

a. B: [*human*].

b. B: *everyone / you.*

c. B: [*Mary!*].

LETTER T257/G223/DT50[1]

To Conte di Monna Agnola and to his companions, in Florence
March to April 1377

We know nothing apart from what this letter reveals of this Conte, son of one Monna Agnola. Since the rubric of B specifies that the letter is being sent to him and his companions in Florence, and since he is apparently in touch with Giovanni dalle Celle, the renowned hermit of Vallombrosa and Catherine's disciple, we can conclude that he is probably a Florentine.[2] The tenor of Catherine's letter to him seems to indicate that he is young and that he and his companions have some thought of joining the crusade. Catherine seems to suggest that, in consultation with Giovanni dalle Celle, they attach themselves to the Hospitalers in this venture.

The expedition of the Hospitalers envisioned in the papal bull of 8 December 1375 was delayed throughout 1376 by a number of causes, including the fact that the Hospitalers' master, Fr. Juan Fernández de Heredia, was commander of the papal fleet which brought Gregory XI back from Avignon. After Gregory's return to Rome in January 1377, plans for the expedition were being reactivated, with financial preparations being made during February and March.[3] Luttrell believes that, while the present letter could have been written as early as December 1375, it is more probable that it was written closer to the time a crusade expedition was actually due to depart. In fact, a number of Florentines did take part in this minor crusade, and the city of Vonitza, to which the Hospitalers acquired a title in 1377, was held by the Florentine Maddalena Buondelmonti.[4] And the men to whom this letter was addressed seem to have been Florentines.

Luttrell gives no more precise date for the actual beginnings of the expedition but seems to indicate that it had to be after mid-April, when Pisa refused a request of the Hospitalers for ships.[5]

Given the strong linguistic evidence and the above reasoning, I would agree with Luttrell's placement of this letter.[6] There are, besides, many par-

---

[1] MSS: B, P2, T, P3, P5, F2; translation based on T, with relevant variants from Dupré Theseider.

[2] Burlamacchi (note A to this letter) speculates that he is the Conte de Ser Conte to whom Let. T83/G237 is addressed. The arguments against this supposition will be addressed in my notes to that letter.

[3] Cf. Anthony Luttrell, "Gregory XI and the Turks: 1370–1378," p. 412.

[4] "Gregory XI and the Turks: 1370–1378," p. 415.

[5] "Gregory XI and the Turks: 1370–1378," p. 416.

[6] Three letters share thirteen or more of this one's thirty-seven analyzed patterns; two of these are from spring of 1377, the other from April 1376. Also, the distribution of the patterns CAPITANO, ESCADIMO, IPSOFACT, SAETTA, and SANGFORT supports 1377 against 1375, while no patterns would support the placement of Dupré Theseider and

allels with Let. T256 to Niccolò dei Strozzi, prior of the Pisan Hospitalers.

§

In the name of Jesus Christ crucified and of gentle Mary.

Dearest sons in Christ gentle Jesus,

I Caterina, servant and slave of the servants of Jesus Christ, am writing to you in his precious blood. I long to see you such true knights that you will lay down your lives for Christ crucified. You have been put on the battlefield of this darksome life, where we are in continual struggle with our enemies. The world pursues us with wealth and status and honor, and would have us believe that these are lasting; but they fade and pass like the wind. The devil assails us with many trying things—making people do us wrong—often taking away what is ours, and only to pull us away from love for our neighbors; for once we have lost love we have lost life. The flesh annoys us with excitement and great weakness in order to take away our purity, for when we are deprived of purity we are deprived of God, since God is supreme and eternal Purity.

Our enemies never sleep, but are always on the watch to harass us. God permits this to give us constant opportunity for merit, and to rouse us from the sleep of carelessness. You know that when a man senses he is going to be attacked by his enemies, he is careful to take precautions to defend himself from them. He is well aware that if he should fall asleep, he would be in mortal danger. This is why God lets us experience these things, so that we will wake up and seize the weapons of hatred and of love. Hatred shuts the door of consent[a] against the vices by resisting them with the greatest possible displeasure, and we open the door to the virtues by reaching out the arms of love to receive them within our soul with tremendous desire and affection. So you see, it is good, very good, that our enemies should rise up against us.

We must not be afraid—nor can we be afraid[b]—if we are decisive. Rather we should find strength in saying, "We can do everything through Christ crucified."[7] And of what should we be afraid if we trust in our Creator? We see that our captain on this battlefield is Christ Jesus, and he has defeated our enemies with his blood. He has defeated the world's pleasures and riches with lowliness and voluntary poverty, by enduring hunger, thirst, and persecution. He has routed the devil and his malice by his wis-

Fawtier. Dupré Theseider places the letter in December 1375, and Fawtier (II, pp. 260–261) places it in late 1375 or very early 1376.

[7] Cf. Phil 4, 13.

dom, catching him with the bait and hook of our humanity through the union of the divine nature with the human.[8] Our flesh has been conquered by his flesh scourged, macerated, saturated with disgrace on the wood of the most holy cross, and in the end raised above all the choirs of angels in the resurrection of God's Son.[9] There is no body or spirit so corrupt that the sight of our humanity so perfectly united with the divine nature would not make it purify itself and rather die than spiritually defile itself.

We have discovered what we have to do: Christ our captain has defeated these enemies for us and has so weakened and bound them that they cannot overcome us unless we so choose.[10] So we must not be afraid but fight courageously. We must mark ourselves with the sign of the most holy cross, set before our eyes the blood of the spotless Lamb, and take up the sword of hatred and of love to strike out at our enemies. This is the common battle in which everyone must engage who is born and reaches maturity.[11]

It seems to me that God's boundless goodness has chosen you as knights to fight effectively against vice and sin, in order to win the treasure and wealth of virtue. And it seems to me now that he is inviting you to grow to genuine maturity by letting yourselves be lured on by hunger for the salvation of the unbelievers. And it seems that he wants you to be the first warriors to go out against them, for now the crusade is about to begin. The holy father is sending out against them the *frieri* and whoever is willing to follow them.[12] Now I am asking you to consult with Don Giovanni,[13] and talk over with him what these young men, including

---

[8] In most instances when Catherine uses this image she specifies that the bait is humanity, the hook divinity.

[9] Cf. *Dial.* 42, p. 86: "to see their own nature, this clay of Adam, exalted above all the choirs of angels." Also *Dial.* 126, p. 245; 110, p. 205: "You attained such excellence because of the union I effected between my Godhead and human nature that your excellence and dignity is greater than that of the angels. For it was your nature I assumed, not that of the angels. So . . . I, God, became a man and humanity became God through the union of my divine nature with your human nature." Cavalca, *Specchio di croce*, p. 124, places this greater dignity simply in the incarnation of Christ rather than specifically in the resurrection, as Catherine does in the present letter.

[10] Perhaps a paraphrase of a passage from Cavalca, *Trenta stoltizie*, p. 21: "The enemy is weak and cannot conquer anyone who does not want to be conquered." Also *Dial.* 14, p. 53: "But such is the freedom of your humanity, and so strong have you been made by the power of this glorious blood, that neither the devil nor any other creature can force you to the least sin unless you want it."

[11] Catherine distinguishes, here and elsewhere (for example, in Let. T252/DT88 in this volume), between "common" battles (or struggles) and the "particular" or "special" struggles experienced by the more perfect. In her letter to Niccolò dei Strozzi, prior of the Pisan Hospitalers (T256, in this volume), she has explicitly identified the "particular battle" in this case with the crusade. This is what she is addressing here also, though she does not use the contrasting term "particular battle."

[12] In Tuscany the Hospitalers were known as the *frieri*.

[13] This could be Giovanni dalle Celle, Catherine's friend and disciple who lived at Val-

Leonardo, will be conveying to you by word of mouth.[14] Do what the Holy Spirit inspires you to do with the advice of Don Giovanni.

For I believe our Savior is making this beginning in order to get the whole thing going later on.

Without any fear, my dear sons, put on the mail[15] of blood, of our blood thoroughly fused with the blood of the Lamb. Oh what a sweet lovely armature that will be, fit to resist every blow! With the sword of hatred and of love you will strike and defeat your enemies; with the armature of blood you will endure. Oh dearest sons, think of how much delight this armor affords: in enduring, it conquers; in being struck, it strikes.[16] For within it are arrows that shoot out unseen. But though they are unseen they produce visible effects because their blows generate flowers and fruits—flowers of praise and glory to God's name, which with their fragrance overpower the stench of unbelief; and after the flower the fruit: that we receive merit for our labors here, that we live and grow in grace and in the end live in the eternal vision of God.

Don't be indifferent; no, be zealous! Don't forego the fruit because of a little hard work. There is no other way you can be courageous knights. This is why I told you that I long to see you as courageous knights stationed on the battlefield. And this is why I am begging you, so that you may fulfill God's will and my desire: immerse yourselves, drown yourselves, get drunk in the blood of Christ crucified, for in the blood is the heart made strong.

I'll say no more. Keep living in God's holy and tender love.

Gentle Jesus! Jesus love!

Textual Notes

a. P2: *knowledge / consent.*

b. P2: [*nor . . . afraid*].

l'Ombrosa near Florence, or it could be (as Burlamacchi, and after him Tommasèo with some doubt, and Ferretti without hesitation suggest) the grand master of the Knights Hospitalers, Fernández de Heredia. But why Catherine would refer to the latter as "Giovanni" would be a mystery. It seems more probable that the reference is indeed to Giovanni dalle Celle, especially since it is advice Catherine wants the young men to seek from him.

[14] Dupré Theseider surmises (n. 9 to this letter) that Leonardo is certainly a Florentine, perhaps of the Soderini or Frescobaldi family. Catherine's letter has been entrusted to a group of young men who are to further explain Catherine's intentions and wishes.

[15] The word Catherine uses is *pantiera,* which was the plate or mail piece in medieval armor extending down from the lower edge of the breastplate to protect the abdomen. Bernardino da Siena (*Prediche,* X ed. Bargellini) describes it as "a shirt of iron" (Dupré Theseider, n. 11 to this letter).

[16] In *Dial.* 117 (p. 219) God says, "I am like the rock that is not hurt by what is thrown at it, but glances it back at the one who threw it." In *Dial.* 78, p. 146, the imagery is, as in the present case, implicitly of armor: "The arrow that finds nowhere to enter returns to the one who shot it. . . . So the arrow poisoned with sin returns to the one who shot it."

LETTER T72/G301[1]

To Romano, a flax dresser of the Company of the Bigallo in Florence
January to August 1377, with more probability of March or April

The guild of the flax workers to which the addressee of this letter belonged was the ninth of the fourteen corporations of the "Minor Arts" in Florence. The Company of the Bigallo was a confraternity founded in the thirteenth century by the Dominican Peter of Verona. Its original purpose had been the combating of the Cathar movement (a cause in which its founder was assassinated),[2] but by Catherine's day it had redirected its efforts toward the care of the sick, and had been entrusted particularly with a ministry to the Hospital of Santa Maria del Bigallo, some five miles south of Florence on the road to Arezzo.[3]

The only possible clue within the text to the letter's date is that Catherine is wondering what Romano has done about his resolution to enter religious life, a resolution he had confided to her before he left her. She does not say whether they had met while she was in Florence or somewhere else. If she had seen him when she was in Florence on her way to Avignon, it would not be unlike her to write, once she had returned home, to encourage the gentleman to follow through. It could well be that Catherine's work with her monastery at Belcaro reminded her of Romano and prompted this letter. Linguistically, the letter does in fact seem to fit best in the first months of 1377.[4] I would therefore place this letter surely in the first eight months of 1377, but most probably around March or April.

---

[1] MSS: B, P2, P5, F2, P3, R2, Nd; translation based on R2.

[2] Catharism was a religious movement which seems to have existed alongside the Christian Church from near apostolic times. Basing their philosophy and theology on a variant interpretation of Jn. 1, 3, the Cathars (popularly though erroneously called Albigensians) professed a dualistic doctrine which denied the goodness of all things material. The Dominicans had from the time of their foundation been engaged in preaching against them.

[3] Tommasèo, introductory note to the letter.

[4] There are four letters which share eleven or more of its forty-one analyzed patterns. Two of these fall in spring and summer of 1377. The other two fall in 1378 and 1379, where there is no concentration of significant clusters within individual patterns. Many such clusters, however, begin in the first three months of 1377 and several end by summer of that year (ARATO, ASPTMPSC, FERRO, NAVICREL, REALVEST, SANTPROP, SCIOGLLG, SPIRCLEM, SPREGSEC, STOLTMAT, TAGLSCIO, VIRTCOMI).

§

In the name of Jesus Christ crucified and of gentle Mary.

Dearest son in Christ gentle Jesus,

I Caterina, servant and slave of the servants of Jesus Christ, am writing to you in his precious blood. I long to see that you are persevering in virtue, and not turning back to look at what you have already plowed.[5] For you know that only perseverance is crowned.[6]

You have been called and invited[a] by Christ to the wedding feast of eternal life. But no one should go to that feast not [properly] dressed. So you should be wearing the wedding garment; otherwise you will be expelled from the wedding feast as a wicked servant.[7] It seems to me that gentle First Truth has sent messengers to announce the wedding to you and to bring you the garment. These messengers are the good holy inspirations and sweet desires given you by the Holy Spirit's mercy, the holy thoughts that make you avoid vice and repudiate the world and all its pleasures, and bring you to the wedding feast of true solid virtue. Let your soul be clothed in love, and with that love you will enter everlasting life. You see, God's holy inspirations bring you the garment of virtue. They make you love it, and so you put it on, and then you are invited into the wedding feast of eternal life. How so? The garment of virtue and of blazing charity brings grace, and grace brings the vision of God that constitutes our blessedness.

So I beg you, for love of Christ crucified, respond courageously and don't be remiss. Remember that simply beginning, putting one's hand to the plow, is nothing, as I've said. Holy thoughts begin the plowing, and perseverance in virtue finishes it. And the Holy Spirit turns over the soil of our perverse sensual will just as a person who plows turns over the soil.

Often people who fall in love with this wonderful invitation and this lovely garment look to see if there is a really sharp blade with which they can turn over the soil more effectively in order better to break it open. They come to the realization that there is nothing more perfect for cutting open and breaking up and getting the weeds out of our will than the iron [blade] and yoke of holy obedience. Once they have discovered this, they learn from the obedient Word, God's Son, and for love of him they want to be obedient even to the point of death. They offer no resistance. They

---

[5] Lk. 9, 62: "Anyone who puts a hand to the plow but keeps looking back is unfit for the reign of God."

[6] Cf. 1 Cor. 9, 24: "You know that while all the runners in the stadium take part in the race, the award goes only to one."

[7] Mt. 22, 1–14. Catherine is, however, confusing the parable with Mt. 18, 32 (Vulg.) when she refers to the guest as a "wicked servant."

act wisely in wanting to row not with their own arms but with another's, that is, the rule.[8]

I recall that when you left me, you had the holy desire and determination to respond to God, who was calling you, and to give yourself to holy obedience. I don't know how you are doing in this regard. I beg you to do well and diligently and with healthy determination whatever you still have not done. May you learn[9] how to hurry and cut yourself off from the world. Don't wait for time, because you can't be sure you'll have time. What stupidity and insanity to lose what you have for the sake of what you don't have!

Bathe in the blood of Christ crucified and hide in his open side, and there you will see the secret of his heart. Gentle First Truth shows that whatever he does in us is done with heartfelt love.[10] Respond to him with love. He is our dear God who wants only love. And those who love will never offend the one they love.

So up, my son! Sleep no longer in the slumber of apathy! Go soon to your father the abbot, with your will dead, not alive. For if you should go with a live will, I'd say you shouldn't put your foot inside the door, since it would do neither you nor him any good. I trust, in God's goodness, that you will follow in the footsteps of Christ crucified. Don't bother untying the bonds of the world, but take out the knife of hatred and love and cut them—quickly!

I'll say no more. Keep living in God's holy and tender love.

Gentle Jesus! Jesus love!

Textual Notes

a. From other Manuscripts R2: *married / invited*, which is surely a scribal error.

---

[8] Cf. Let. T36 to several Monteolivetan novices in Bologna (in this volume): "But I call your attention to the fact that divine providence has put you in a ship, so that you will not sink in the stormy sea of this darksome life. That ship is genuine and holy religious life. It is maneuvered under the yoke of sincere and holy obedience. Just think of how great a favor God has done you because he knows how weak your arms are! For those who are in the world navigate this sea on their own power, but those in religious life navigate on the power of others. When we are truly obedient we are not accountable for ourselves; rather the order is accountable for us—if we have been obedient to our superiors. I will know that you are following the slain Lamb if you are obedient."

[9] It. *sappitene.*

[10] Cf. Let. T189/DT84 to the monks of Cervaia and to several monks of Monteoliveto Maggiore (in this volume): "I remember in this regard what First Truth once said to one of his servants. She asked, 'Once you were dead, why did you want your side to be opened and to pour out such a torrent of blood?' And he said, 'There are many reasons, but I will tell you two important ones. First of all, I wanted this because by having my side opened I showed you the secret of my heart. For my heart held more love for humankind than any external physical act could show. The other reason was the baptism that was given to the human race because of the merits of my blood.' "

LETTER T112/G329[1]
To the Countess Bandeçça Salimbeni of Siena
Near April 1377

While Catherine was in Avignon, she obtained permission from Pope Gregory XI to establish a monastery for women. She had earlier asked her friend Giovanni di Gano da Orvieto, abbot of Sant'Antimo, to be on the lookout for a good property and especially for some good prospective leaders.[2] Before leaving Siena for Avignon she had received from one of her converts, Nanni di Ser Vanni Savini, the promise of an abandoned fortress named Belcaro some three miles southwest of Siena. Because it had been a military installation, she needed the approval of the Defenders of the Commune of Siena to put it to a non-military use. This approval she gained from the *Consiglio generale* on 25 January 1377.[3] Raimondo da Capua tells us that the monastery was founded "for ladies of the upper classes,"[4] among whom Catherine had many disciples.

In the present letter Catherine invites Bandeçça, daughter of the deceased Giovanni d'Agnolino Salimbeni and sister of the younger Agnolino, living in exile at the family fortress at Rocca d'Orcia, to join the community to be formed at Belcaro.[5] She says that "the work is really getting on." When Catherine writes Let. T270 on 16 April, the place will be habitable and in fact occupied. So she must be writing the present letter sometime after the end of January but still before April and probably even close to April. This historically established placement is strongly supported by the linguistic evidence.[6]

---

[1] MSS: Mo-*b*, B, P2, F1, T, R1, P5, P3, F2, S3; translation based on Mo-*b*, with variants from unpublished notes of Dupré Theseider.

[2] Cf. Let. T12/DT66 (vol. I): "So I would like the two of you [the abbot and Monna Moranda di Francesco di Monte Alcino] to get together and if you can, locate a suitable place for establishing a really good monastery, and put a few good leaders there—for as far as *members* are concerned, we have plenty."

[3] The original account of Catherine's meeting with the Defenders of Siena and of their response to her petition is preserved in the *Archivio di Stato di Siena, Consiglio generale*, 187 (formerly 190), fol. 9r–v. It is transcribed in various places, including Laurent, *Fontes*, I, *Documenti*, pp. 41–43. The vote was three hundred thirty-three white beans in favor versus sixty-five black (opposed).

[4] *Life*, II, vii, 238, p. 226. There are references also in *Processo Castellano*, pp. 52, 428, 441.

[5] Bandeçça is a nickname for Benedetta.

[6] In particular, significant clusters within the patterns CREATURA, FOGLVENT, FUGVELEN, LARGCUOR, PIACC, PIACCREA, PICCOL, PIEDAFFE, SERVREGN, STOLTMAT are concentrated in this period. This placement agrees with that of Fawtier (II, p. 300) and Dupré Theseider (unpublished notes).

§

In the name of Jesus Christ crucified and of gentle Mary.

Dearest daughter in Christ gentle Jesus,

I Caterina, servant and slave of the servants of Jesus Christ, am writing to you in his precious blood. I long to see you a servant and spouse of Christ crucified, since to serve God is not to be a servant, but to reign.[7] It is not like sinful service to the world, which is demeaning and makes us servants and slaves of the devil. Sin, because it is nothingness, makes us nothings.[8]

So[a] understand, dearest beloved daughter, that if we serve wealth and other people apart from God—I mean if we have an excessive desire and appetite for worldly wealth and pleasure, or are vain and self-complacent—we plunge into death. We lower ourselves, because we are subjecting ourselves to things that are less than we are. These things are all empty, as lacking in constancy and stability as a leaf whirling in the wind.[9] All created things were made to serve us, and we were made to serve our Creator.[10] So we are deluded. The more we desire these passing things, the more we lose the lovely mastery that serving our Creator gives us, and subject ourselves to what is not. For when our love is out of order and apart from God, we sin against God. So it really is true that by serving the world[b] we become nothings.[c]

Oh how stupid and foolish to devote oneself to serving one who rules[d] over nothing except what is nothingness—I mean sin! The devil rules over no one except those who do evil. And how does he rule over them? By punishing them with torture in eternal damnation. And the world, too. I mean our disordered love for the world, for the things of the world are good in themselves. But the evil will of those who use these things makes them bad, because they want and take them with no fear of God. This is why I call them agents that bind us to the devil in torment. I tell you, this

---

[7] Catherine's reference is probably to Augustine, *Meditatio XXXII* (PL XL, 925): "To serve God is to reign."

[8] Cf. Augustine *Soliloquia*, V (PL XL, 868): "Evil is nothing but the privation of good, just as blindness is nothing but the privation of light. So evil is nothing, for it was made without the Word, without whom nothing is made. . . . Therefore, since all things were made through the Word, evil was not made through him. It remains, therefore, that whatever was not made is not good . . . and therefore evil things are not, for they were not made, and so they are nothing, for without the Word nothing was made."

[9] Cf. *Dial.* 128, p. 252, and often elsewhere in the letters. Also Giordano da Rivalto, *Prediche inedite*, ed. Narducci, p. 360: "The will is the most fickle thing there is, more fickle that a leaf, constantly changing." Also Cavalca, *Specchio di croce*, p. 31: "They should be rooted and grounded in charity, that is, they should not be moved by every wind."

[10] The idea recurs often, for example, in *Dial.* 150, p. 317; 47, p. 96; Prayer 15, p. 135.

servitude to death deprives us of the light of reason and leaves us darkness; it steals the riches of grace and leaves us the poverty of vice.

I don't want you, my daughter—because it is so dangerous—to give yourself to this sinful service of the world. No, I want you to be a true servant of Christ crucified, who ransomed you with his precious blood. He is our gracious God, who created us in his own image and likeness. He gave us the Word, his only-begotten Son, to free us from death and give us life.[11] With his blood he delivered us from the slavery of sin and made us free by rescuing us from the power of the devil, who was holding us as his own. Even more, the blood has made us strong and put us in possession of eternal life. For his nails were made into keys for us, a key that unlocked the gate that had been closed because of sin.[12] This gentle Word mounted the wood of the most holy cross as if it were his horse and he the true knight, and he routed the enemy and put us so securely in possession of everlasting life that neither the devil nor anyone else can take it from us against our will.[13]

Service to him, then, is indeed sweet; without it we cannot share in divine grace. This is why I said that I long to see you a servant and spouse of Christ crucified. Once you become his servant (for to serve God is to reign), little by little you become his spouse. I want you to be a faithful spouse. I don't want you ever to leave your bridegroom by loving or wanting anything apart from God. Love this gracious and glorious bridegroom who has given you life, and who will never die. Other husbands die and pass away like the wind—and often they are the cause of death to us. You have experienced how constant they are,[e] for in a short time the world has

---

[11] An interesting ambivalence here, on Catherine's part, concerning Christ as God and as Word.

[12] There is a play on words in the Italian: *e' chiovi ci sono facti chiave*, a pun used also by Dante, Petrarca, and others. (Tommasèo, note to the letter) Cf. Let. T184 to the Prior and Brothers of the Company of the Virgin Mary in Siena (in this volume): "For the nails became for us the key that unlocked eternal life, so opened it up that it cannot be closed to anyone who does not so choose, because we cannot be forced to sin at all against our will. Sin is what closes the door to us and deprives us of the destiny for which we were created." The only other place, besides these two letters, where Catherine joins the nail/key image with the idea of human freedom is Let. T256 to Niccolò dei Strozzi (in this volume).

[13] Cf. Cavalca, *Specchio di croce*, pp. 136–137: "Because Christ came to free the soul, his spouse, from the hands of the devil, who was holding her as an adulteress, we might say that he came armed as a knight for battle—just as two lovers sometimes duel over one they both love. So he mounted the cross as his horse. His spurs were the nails in his feet. The lance was the staff he held in his hand. His scarlet vest was his bloodied flesh. The well-wrought helmet on his head was the crown of thorns pressed down into his skull. The sword at his side was the wound in his side. The gloves on his hands were the wounds in his hands. This is how our Savior came armed to seize the mastery the devil had over humankind."

kicked you twice, and divine Goodness permitted this to make you run from the world and run to him as your father and bridegroom.[14]

Run away, then, from the world's poison, which it offers you in a flower. It shows itself as a child, when it really is old. It pretends that life is long, when it really is short. It seems to have some stability, when in reality it is as changeable as a leaf whirling in the wind. You have seen clearly that it has no stability in your regard, so realize that if you trust it again it will do the same thing to you. The next one will be as mortal as the first.

So rouse yourself from any softness or selfishness, and enter into the wounds of Christ crucified, where there is true and complete security. He is that lovely place where the bride fills the lamp of her heart. The heart really is a lamp. Like a lamp, it should be narrow at the bottom and wide at the top.[15] I mean your desire and affection should be restricted where the world is concerned, while your heart's affection in Christ crucified should be expansive, loving him and holding on to him with true and holy determination.[16] Then you will fill this lamp at the open side of Christ crucified. There you will find the fire of divine charity revealed to you in Christ's wounds, and his open side will show you the secret of his heart, that what he has given and done for us he has done in simple[f] love. This is where you will find deep and sincere humility, which is the oil that feeds the flame and light in the heart of Christ's bride. What more generous love[g] could you find than to see that he laid down his life for you?[17] And what greater lowliness can be seen or found than to see God stooped down to humanity? Or the God-Man running to the shameful death of the cross?[h] Such humility confounds all the world's pride, pleasure, and grandeur. This is the little virtue that is nurse and governess of charity.[18]

---

[14] The countess has lost first her husband to death, and then her fiancé. The image is later used by Bernardino da Siena as well, in reference to a widow: "She has experienced the world's kicks."

[15] Catherine here expands on the gospel parable of the wise virgin (Mt. 25, 1–13). The comparison between the heart and the lamp is found also in Let. I of Giovanni Colombini, but not in the same detail. An analogous image is used by Franco Sacchetti (*Sermo IV*): "Just as a boat is closed at the bottom, toward the earth, and open toward the sky, so should a good person be closed toward the earth, and open in spirit and will toward heaven." There is also a comparison of virginity to the lamp, narrow and closed below and open and lighted above, in Girolamo da Siena, *Soccorso de' poveri*, p. 49, but he may have borrowed it from Catherine.

[16] I have here followed P2, P3, and S3 (*tenendolo con vera e santa sollecitudine*), since this version fits the context better than Mo's text (*temendolo . . .*, "respecting him. . . .")

[17] Cf. Lk. 14, 26; Mt. 10, 37.

[18] Cf. Let. T33 to the Abbot General of Monteoliveto Maggiore (1378): "Charity's wet-nurse is deep humility. And what food does this nurse give her? The food of light and of self-knowledge, and by this light [the soul] has come to know her poverty and the frail

Next the bride is welcomed by her bridegroom and led into the room where table, food, and waiter are found. The room is the divine essence, where the real connoisseurs[19] are fed. There we experience the eternal Father as table, the Son as food, and the Holy Spirit as the one who waits on us. And so the soul experiences and is in truth filled with the eternal vision of God.

So sleep no more, but rouse yourself from the slumber of worldly delights and follow Christ as your delight. Don't wait for time, because you are not sure of having it; it will disappoint you. For just when we think we are living, death comes to take time away from us. So if you are wise you will not lose the time you have for the sake of the time you don't have. Respond, then, with a firm and steady[i] heart to God who is calling you. Don't put your faith in anyone who would stop you—mother, sister, brother, or any creature's body. You know that in this case we are not to obey them. This is what our Savior said: "Unless you renounce father and mother, sisters and brothers, and even yourself, you are not worthy of me." So we have to renounce the whole world and ourselves too, and follow the standard of the most holy cross.[20]

I'll say no more. Keep living in God's holy and tender love.

Gentle Jesus! Jesus love![j]

I'm telling you, my daughter, if you want to be a true spouse of your Creator, leave your father's house. Be prepared to come whenever the place is ready. It is already begun, and the work is really getting on—I mean the monastery of Santa Maria degli Angeli at Belcaro.[21] If you come, you'll be coming to the land of promise!

I'll say no more. May God fill you with his sweetest grace!

Textual Notes

a. All manuscripts except Mo: [*So*].

b. F1, P5, F2: *the devil and the world* / *the world*.

c. F1, P5, F2: *less than nothing* / *nothings*.

d. B, P2: *loves to rule* / *rules*.

---

sensuality that is the cause of all such poverty. In this knowledge she humbles herself and conceives a contempt for herself with which she nurtures in herself the fire of divine charity, coming to know God's unspeakable goodness, the goodness that is the beginning and end of all her knowing."

[19] It. *i veri gustatori*. Elsewhere I have usually translated this as "the truly joyful," but here the more literal translation seems fully in place.

[20] Cf. Mt. 10, 37–39.

[21] This is the name of the monastery Catherine is in the process of founding in the old fortress of Belcaro.

e. Literally, *he is.*
f. B, P2, R1, P3, T, F1, P5, F2: *simple and pure / simple.*
g. P2: *greatness of heart / generous love.*
h. B, P2, R1, P3, T, F1, P5, F2 add *for us.*
i. B, P2, R1, P3, T, F1, P5: [*and steady*].
j. F1: *Gentle Jesus! Amen.* P5, F2: *Be encouraged in Christ gentle Jesus. Amen.*

LETTER T114/G267[1]
To Agnolino di Giovanni dei Salimbeni da Siena
About April 1377

The noble Salimbeni family of Siena were alternately in and out of favor with their city. Agnolino Salimbeni became effectively the head of his family when his father Giovanni died in 1368, so it was he who had control of his sister Benedetta's[2] future. In spring of 1377 Catherine was trying to convince Benedetta to enter the monastery at Belcaro as soon as it should be finished (Let. T112, in this volume), and in the present letter she is urging Agnolino not to stand in the way of his sister's desire, in spite of family resistance. Since the matter of family resistance is not mentioned in Catherine's letter to Benedetta on this subject (T112), I would guess that Catherine was perhaps informed of this in a communication from the countess after that letter was received. I would therefore place the present letter to the countess' brother a bit later than Let. T112, but still before Catherine's going to the Salimbeni fortress at Rocca d'Orcia in August of 1377.[3]

§

In the name of Jesus Christ crucified and of gentle Mary.

Dearest son in Christ gentle Jesus,

I Caterina, servant and slave of the servants of Jesus Christ, am writing to you in his precious blood. I long to see you a real fighter, like a true knight never running to escape being struck. That is how renegades behave.

My dear son, we have been put on this battlefield and we must fight persistently, everywhere and always. We have our enemies who attack the city of our soul: the flesh with its disordered sensual pleasure, the world with its honors and delights, and the devil with his malice.[4] The latter, to

---

[1] MSS: Mo, M, S5, S6, Ro, S3; translation based on Mo-*a*, corrected by *b*. No relevant variants.

[2] Familiarly called Bandeçça.

[3] This placement is supported also by the linguistic evidence. While four of the five letters sharing twelve or more of this one's fifty analyzed patterns are from before 1377, several significant clusters within individual patterns are concentrated in the first months of that year (CAPITANO, FUMO, SAZMENO, SPIRCHIA). Besides, there are several patterns which occur only once or not at all before spring of 1377 (ABBAI, CANECONS, FUMO, SAZMENO, SPIRCHIAM). Fawtier (II, p. 274) places the letter in the second half of 1377. Dupré Theseider (unpublished notes) places it either in the spring of that year, relating it to Let. T112, or possibly in September.

[4] That is, the three classic enemies usually grouped as the devil, the world, and the flesh.

get in the way of our holy desire, sets snares either by himself or by sitting on his servants' tongues making up speeches, fawning, flattering, threatening, criticizing, slandering—all to discourage us and make us weary of our good and holy deeds. But we like brave knights must resist him and keep our city safe by locking the gates of uncontrolled feeling.

Put the watchdog of conscience there to bark at any enemy who passes, and to rouse the mind's eye to see whether it is an enemy or friend, vice or virtue.[5] You have to give this dog food and drink—blood to drink and fire to eat. That will rouse him from the chill of lethargy and make him alert. I'm telling you, my son Agnolino, give this dog of yours, your conscience, the fire of blazing charity to eat, and for drink give him the blood of the spotless Lamb, who was opened up on the cross and shed his blood from every part of his body. We have to give him this drink, and if we do he will be completely reinvigorated, and you will be a real fighter.

Next take the sword of hatred and of love, of hatred and disgust for vice and of love for virtue, and with this sword kill our enemy the flesh, the worst and most perfidious enemy we could have, along with its pleasures. Your conscience will make your mind's eye see how dangerous an enemy this carnal pleasure is when it passes through your soul, so that you may kill it. Look too at the scourged flesh of Christ crucified, so that you may be ashamed to indulge your body in excessive pleasure and gratification. With the virtue of true humility confound the devil with his malice and the snares he has set to capture souls. Let this dog, your conscience, bark and rouse your mind's eye to see how dangerous it is to be taken in by his tricks. Turn within and recognize your humanity; recognize that you have no being [of yourself], lest you yield to pride. For it is humility that breaks all the devil's snares.

We should really be ashamed to be proud when we see that we are not (that we have our being from God and not from ourselves), and when we see God stoop down to us. For with profound humility supreme Exaltedness came down to something so lowly as our flesh. This gentle loving Lamb, the Word incarnate, gives us strength, because he is the source of all strength. He came as our captain, and with unarmed hand, nailed fast to the cross, he confounded our enemies.[6] And his blood has been left on the battlefield to energize us, his knights, to fight courageously and fearlessly. The devil has become powerless because of the blood of this Lamb, for he can do to us only as much as God allows, and God does not allow us to be

---

[5] Cf. *Dial.* 129, p. 257, and 131, p. 263, where this same imagery is developed.

[6] Cavalca (*Medicina del cuore*, p. 109), quoting Bernard de Clairvaux, also calls Christ our captain.

loaded with more than we can carry.[7] Our flesh was confounded by Christ's scourging and torture; the world by the shame, scorn, insult, and abuse Christ crucified bore; and wealth by his voluntary poverty. For supreme wealth is so poor that he has nowhere to lay his head when he is on the wood of the most holy cross.[8]

So, my son, when this enemy, worldly honor and prestige, wants to come in, make your dog (your conscience) bark and wake the guard (your understanding) to see that no worldly honor and prestige—no matter what its source—has any stability or constancy at all. You know, since you've seen and experienced it.[9] I want you to see then that shame rather than honor comes from giving oneself too much to these transitory things that pass away like the wind. It is a case of subjecting ourselves to something less than we are. We who are infinite (in the sense that our existence never ends) serve these finite things. (But we can end our existence as far as grace is concerned by sinning mortally.)

So if we want honor and rest and fulfillment, we had better love and serve something greater than ourselves. God is our redeemer, lord, and father, supreme and eternal goodness, worthy of our love and service. In fact, we owe him this if we want to share in divine grace. He is supreme power and fulfillment. It is he who fills and satisfies us and strengthens our every weakness to make us dwell in peace and quiet, in fulfillment and security. There is no one and nothing else that can satisfy us. And the reason is that every other created thing is less than we are. To put little value on the world, therefore, is wealth and honor for us. But foolish and stupid people don't recognize this as true honor, and consider it quite the contrary. You, though, rise above your sensual feelings like a real fighter and acknowledge this truth.

Don't be so willing to believe these wicked and treacherous people, for the devil is talking through their mouths, trying to stand in the way of your life and salvation, to provoke you to wrath and to contradict God's will. So don't believe these councilors of the devil. Rather believe and respond to the Holy Spirit, who is calling you. Pull out the discipline of boldness and answer them with a courageous heart. Tell them you are not willing to resist God—for you wouldn't be able to.

I know that many evil things have been and will be said about the countess by members of your own household and by others because she

---

[7] Cf. 1 Cor. 10, 13: "God will not let you be tested beyond your strength."

[8] Cf. Mt. 8, 20.

[9] The Salimbeni have had bloody feuds with the Tolomei, and several of them have perished in wars involving the entire Republic of Siena. At the time this letter is being written they are in fact living in exile, banished by the Republic to their fortress, Rocca d'Orcia, about fifty miles from Siena. (See the introduction to the following group of letters.)

wants to be a servant and spouse of Christ.[10,a] These wicked people, to hinder her and you, will put before you their fears and suspicions. They will present as disgrace and debasement what is the greatest honor you could possibly have. Not only is it a present honor, but your honor and memory will live before God and in the world forever, beyond that of all of your ancestors. How foolish and stupid we are to want to put our affection and care and hope into a straw fire! There was indeed a great flare-up the first time you gave her in marriage, but that quickly faded and left nothing but the smoke of mourning. The second time the material for a fire seemed to be there, but the wind of death came and carried him away.[11] So she as well as you would be really simple-minded if she would not respond now that the Holy Spirit is calling her. She has seen that the world is rejecting her and is pushing her toward Christ crucified.

By divine goodness I am sure that you will not be one to put yourself at variance with God's will on account of anything that may be said. Nor will what the world says either carry you off or make you run. *Shut*[12] the mouths of those in your charge so they won't talk so much! Confront them! I have no doubt that you will—unless both your mind's eye and your dog (conscience) are indeed asleep! If you don't, you are no courageous fighter but will prove yourself an utter coward.[b] And I want to see you courageous! This is why I said that I long to see you a true fighter on this battlefield, especially in this new battle you now have on your hands concerning the fate of the countess. The devil knows he is the loser, and that's why he's making people give you so much trouble. So take courage, and kill off all worldly thinking. And may Christ crucified live in you.

I'll say no more. Keep living in God's holy and tender love.

Gentle Jesus! Jesus love!

Textual Notes

a. *b*: *Jesus Christ / Christ.*

b. There follows an erasure of two or three very short words in Mo.

---

[10] This is Agnolino's sister, the countess Benedetta (Bandeçça), to whom Catherine has written (Let. T112) about this very matter, urging her to join the monastic community about to be formed at Belcaro.

[11] Benedetta's first husband had died. She then became engaged to another man, but he died before they could even be married. Cf. Let. T294 to Sano di Maco and others (in this volume): "You go up in smoke like a straw fire which, when no one is present, is put out by any little wind or rain—so that nothing remains but the black smoke of a darkened conscience."

[12] In the original, Catherine actually repeats the verb for emphasis.

LETTER T270/G12[1]
To Pope Gregory XI
16 April 1377

This letter to Gregory XI is precisely dated in nearly all of the manuscripts, a date that is broadly supported by the linguistic evidence.[2] From its closing we know that Catherine is writing from her new monastery of Santa Maria degli Angeli at Belcaro, where Raimondo da Capua and the Lecceto Augustinian Giovanni Tantucci are with her. She is sending as courier a certain Anibaldo.

The letter reiterates many of the themes on which Catherine has already addressed the pope. Her expressed desire to go to Rome is very significant, since when Urban VI later orders her to come she will demur because of people's gossip about her travels and activities.

§

In the name of Jesus Christ crucified and of gentle Mary.

Dearest and most holy father in Christ Jesus,

I your poor unworthy daughter Caterina, servant and slave of the servants of Jesus Christ, am writing to you in his precious blood. I desire, as I have long desired, to see you a courageous and fearless doorkeeper. You are the doorkeeper of God's wine cellar, the doorkeeper of the blood of his only-begotten Son, whose representative you are on earth. From no hands but yours can we have the blood of Christ.[3] You feed and nurture faithful Christians. You are the mother who nurses us at the breasts of divine charity,[a] giving us neither blood without fire nor fire without blood, since the blood was shed with blazing love.[4]

---

[1] MSS: Mo-*c*; B, P2, P1, H, P3, P5, F2, S2, P4, S4; translation based on Mo-*c*, corrected by *b*, with reference to H; variants based on unpublished notes of Dupré Theseider.

[2] Five of the seven letters which share eleven or more of this one's thirty-six analyzed patterns fall between April 1376 and October 1377. Several significant clusters within individual patterns are concentrated around the early months of 1377, most markedly CONDESCE, RIMEDIO, and SPINROSA.

[3] Cf *Dial.* 115, p. 215: "You know that I set before you the mystic body of holy Church under the image of a wine cellar. In this wine cellar was the blood of my only-begotten Son. . . . Christ on earth stood at the door of this wine cellar. He had been commissioned to administer the blood."

[4] This is the only instance in which Catherine images the pope as a nursing mother in relation to the blood of Christ. Most often the mother is charity (Let. T161 and T165/DT59 in this volume; T108/DT49 and T322, written in 1378; T356, written in late 1378 or early 1379; T357, written in 1379). Once she is the Holy Spirit (*Dial.* 141), and twice the

Oh you who govern us! I say that I have long desired to see you a courageous and fearless man, learning from the gentle Word, so in love, who courageously ran to his shameful death on the most holy cross in order to accomplish his Father's will and our salvation. This gentle Word brings us peace, because he was the mediator between God and us.[5] Neither our ingratitude, nor insult, nor torment, nor abuse keeps this gentle loving Word from running to this shameful death on the cross—as one in love with our salvation—for there is no other way we could have reached the peace that was the effect [of his death].

Oh our most holy father! I beg you, for love of Christ crucified, follow in his footsteps. Oimé! Peace! Peace,[b] for love of God! Do not look at our wretchedness and ingratitude and foolishness, nor at your rebellious children's harassment. Oimé! Let your kindness and patience conquer their malice and pride! Have mercy on so many who are perishing, body and soul!

Oh shepherd and doorkeeper of the blood of the Lamb! Don't be held back by any suffering or shame or abuse you think is being directed at you, nor by slavish fear, nor by the devil's perverse counselors who counsel only for war and misery.[6] Most holy father, don't let all of this keep you from running to the shameful death of the cross, as his vicar following Christ. By suffering pain and torment and disgrace and insult, carry the cross of holy desire, desire for God's honor and the salvation of your children. Be hungry, hungry, and with the eye of your understanding climb up onto the cross of desire and consider how many evils result from this perverse war, and how great is the good that follows on peace.

Oimé, my *babbo*![c] How unfortunate my soul, since my sins are the cause of all evil! It seems the devil has taken control of the world—not by himself, because he is nothing, but because we have turned it over to him. Everywhere I turn I see people handing him the keys of free choice, with perverse willingness: layfolk, religious, clerics are running pridefully to worldly enjoyment, prestige, and riches full of wretched filth!

---

crucified Christ (Let. T85, written in late 1378 or early 1379; T165, written in 1379). Sometimes she is the Church (Let. T138/DT41, vol. I; T317, written in late 1378 or early 1379), and sometimes she is prayer (Let. T67, written in 1378; T150, written in late 1378 or early 1379). And once Catherine refers to herself by this image (Let. T105/DT8, vol. I).

[5] Cf. 1 Tim. 2, 5: "One is the mediator between God and humankind, the man Jesus." And Eph. 2, 14: "It is he who is our peace." This is a favorite theme of Catherine's, for example, in Let. T3 to the Curate of Casole and others (vol. I): "This Lamb is the mediator who on the cross made atonement for the offense against the Father and gave us the life of grace. Only through this mediator is the greatest peace made out of great war."

[6] Burlamacchi in his note to the letter (Gigli, *Opere*, I) suggests that these counselors were the French cardinals who, as Pius III would say, later broke with Urban VI because he did not instigate war in Italy.

But more than all the other things I see as so abominable to God are the flowers who are planted in the mystic body of holy Church.[7] They ought to be fragrant, and their lives a mirror of virtue. They ought to love and savor[d] God's honor and the salvation of souls; yet they spread the stench of every sort of wretchedness. Lovers of themselves, they join their own sins with those of the others, especially in persecuting Christ's dear bride and your holiness. Oimé! Here we are, condemned to death, and we have declared war on God![8]

Oh my *babbo*,[e] you have been given to us as mediator to make this peace.[9] But I don't see how it can be done unless you carry the cross of holy desire, as I've said. We are at war with God, and your rebellious children are at war with God and your holiness. God wants and is demanding that you, to the extent of your power, take the control from the devils' hands. Put your hand to removing[f] the stench of holy Church's ministers; pull up the stinking weeds and plant fragrant flowers, virtuous men who fear God.

After that I beg your holiness, please, to condescend to grant peace. Accept it in whatever way it can be had without violating this dear Church or your conscience. God wants you to attend more to souls, and more to spiritual affairs than to the temporal. Act courageously, because God is on your side. Work fearlessly.[g] Don't be afraid when you see all these trials and troubles; take heart in Christ gentle Jesus. For the rose is being born among the thorns, and from among all these persecutions will come the reform of holy Church, light to relieve Christians of darkness, life for the unbelievers, and the raising of the holy[h] cross.[10]

You, as our intermediary and [God's] instrument, do whatever you can,

---

[7] That is, evil clerics. Cf. Let. T206/DT63 to Gregory XI (earlier in this volume): "You are in charge of the garden of holy Church. So [first of all] uproot from that garden the stinking weeds full of impurity and avarice, and bloated with pride (I mean the evil pastors and administrators who poison and corrupt the garden). Oimé! *Use* your authority, you who are in charge of us! Uproot these weeds and throw them out where they will have nothing to administer! Tell them to tend to administering themselves by a good holy life. Plant fragrant flowers in this garden for us, pastors and administrators who will be true servants of Jesus Christ crucified, who will seek only God's honor and the salvation of souls, who will be fathers to the poor."

[8] Cf. Let. T207/DT68 to the *Signori* of Florence (in this volume): "[W]hoever like a gangrenous limb rebels against holy Church and against our father, Christ on earth, has fallen under the sentence of death, because whatever we do to him we are doing to Christ in heaven, whether it is reverence or dishonor."

[9] Again she puts the pope, as "Christ-on-earth," rather astonishingly, in the place of Christ. Cf. 1 Tim. 2, 5: "One is the mediator between God and humankind, the man Jesus Christ." (Vulg.)

[10] That is, the crusade. Here again one sees Catherine's motives for so passionately promoting a crusade.

zealously and without indifference or fear. In this way you will be a true minister, and you will fulfill God's will and the desire of his servants who are dying of grief yet cannot die, seeing their Creator so offended and the blood of God's Son so maligned.

I cannot [go on] any more! Forgive me, most holy father, for my presumption; let my love and my grief be my excuse to you. I'll say no more. Give your life for Christ crucified. Uproot vice and plant virtue. Take heart, and don't be afraid.

Keep living in God's holy and tender love.[i]

I truly long to be in your holiness' presence again. I have many things to discuss with you. My reason for not having come is all the good and useful things we've had to do for the Church.[11]

Peace! Peace, for love of Christ crucified, and no more war! There is no other solution.

I commend to you Anibaldo, our[j] faithful servant.[12]

This letter is written at our[k] new monastery for which you gave me permission; it is called Santa Maria degli Angeli.[13] I humbly ask your blessing. Your negligent sons, Maestro Giovanni and Frate Raimondo, commend themselves to your holiness.[14,l]

Textual Notes

a. P5: *at your breasts, that is, at the breasts of holy Church / at ... charity.*
b. P3: *father, peace / Peace! peace!*
c. B, P2, P5: *my dear father / my babbo*; P3, H, P4: *my dear babbo / my babbo*; S2: *babbo / my babbo.*
d. P5: *savor and feed on / love and savor.*
e. B, P2, P5: *father / babbo.*
f. B, P2: *cleansing / removing.*

---

[11] Tommasèo thinks Gregory must have invited her to Rome, as Urban VI would later. It could, however, simply be Catherine's way of hinting that she would like to be so invited. In any case, it is an indication of her longing to go to Rome.

[12] There was in Rome at this time, according to Tommasèo, a nephew of Cardinal Tebaldeschi by this name, but it is unlikely she is referring to him. It seems much more plausible that Anibaldo is the bearer of the letter.

[13] Formerly a villa of the Savini and a fortress, it had been donated to Catherine by one of her converts, Nanni di Ser Vanni Savini. With Gregory's permission (obtained while she was in Avignon), and with the consent of the rulers of Siena (obtained 25 January 1377), she had converted it into a monastery for some women of her circle. Cf. Let. T112, T114 (both in this volume).

[14] Giovanni (Terzo) Tantucci (an Augustinian hermit of Lecceto) and Raimondo da Capua had been Catherine's companions in Avignon and were, therefore, known to the pope. One of them may have been the writer for Catherine here, as the self-abasing qualifier "negligent" probably indicates.

g. From H, P4, P5, B, P2; Mo, P3: *God works fearlessly.*
h. H, P4, B, P2, P3: *most holy / holy.*
i. H closes the letter here with: *Gentle Jesus! Jesus love! Written at . . . blessing.*
j. Only Mo has *our*; all others have *your.*
k. Only Mo has *our*; all others have *your.*
l. B, P2 [and others? Not H] insert: *May Jesus Christ crucified be with you. Gentle Jesus! Jesus love!*

Letter Fawtier 16[1]
To Iacomo di Viva, at the Costarda dei Barbieri in Siena[2]
29 April 1377

Iacomo di Viva is known to us only from this letter. He may be a relative of the Carthusian Pietro di Giovanni di Viva of the monastery at Maggiano near Siena.[3] The letter is dated, "From the Carthusian monastery, 29 April."[4]

From which monastery is Catherine writing, and in what year? We can assume from the address to which the letter is sent that Iacomo is in Siena, and that the monastery in question is close enough to the city that she can write only his street address on the letter. It cannot, therefore, be 1378, when Catherine was in Florence on 29 April; nor can it be 1379, when she was in Rome. Nor could it have been in 1375, when she was in Pisa. 1376 would be a possibility, since she probably did not leave Siena for Florence until early May, but it does not seem too likely that she would have made another trip so soon before that one when she was surely in the midst of her preparations for a major journey. That leaves 1377 to be considered.

Raimondo mentions in very vague terms a visit with Catherine and others to "certain servants of God outside the city" after their return from Avignon, a trip from which he says they returned to Siena "on the feast of Saint Mark the Evangelist," that is, on 25 April 1377.[5] Catherine could, then, have made another trip the short distance to one of the Carthusian monasteries near the city by 29 April. The possibilities are Maggiano, Pontignano, and Belriguardo. Given Pietro di Giovanni di Vivo's affliation with Maggiano, it may well be from the monastery at Maggiano that Catherine is writing, and it may well be Pietro who has brought Iacomo's message to her.

---

[1] MS: Original at Oxford, St. Aloysius Church. Edited and published by Fawtier (as number 16) in his *Catheriniana*, *Mélanges d'archéologie et d'histoire* XXXIV (1914), pp. 31–32. Translation based on photograph of original in *St. Peter's* article cited below (photocopy acquired through the kindness of Anselm Nye of London). Spender's translation is not as accurate at Fawtier says it is, nor does it always reflect a correct reading of the manuscript.

[2] This is the Costarella dei Barbieri, the steep alleyway leading from Via di Città down into the Campo opposite Via dei Pellegrini.

[3] Let. T287a (in this volume) is addressed to Pietro.

[4] Jorgensen, *Saint Catherine of Siena*, p. 402, speculates that this line may actually have been written at the time the manuscript was given to one of its later possessors. But Fawtier insists, and I would have to agree, that the date line is in the same hand as the rest of the letter. Jorgensen also says that the scribe is Barduccio Canigiani, but while the hand is fairly close to that of Casanatense 292 (C), which is certainly Canigiani's, it does not seem close enough to justify that assumption. Besides, Barduccio did not even become part of Catherine's circle until early 1378.

[5] *Life*, II, xii, 315, p. 292.

Iacomo has, according to the letter, sent word to Catherine that a certain Frate Antonio has gone to Bologna, leaving nothing behind.[6] Catherine asks Iacomo to try to find out more and promises to write to "our Frate Tommaso" about the matter. She could be doing the latter either because Tommaso is in Bologna and could therefore intervene, or simply because Tommaso would have an interest in Antonio. The fact that she will *write* to him, however, makes it more likely that he is not in Siena. This Tommaso could be either Tommaso dalla Fonte or Tommaso Caffarini, but is more probably the latter. Caffarini was certainly in Bologna at the time of Catherine's death in 1380,[7] and he may well have been there in 1377, since there is no other reference to him at that period, other than his own indication that he was with Catherine at Rocca d'Orcia for at least some of her time there.[8]

Catherine also asks Iacomo to deliver a message to a certain Monna Bartolomea, who is apparently going to Rome. This must be Bartolomea di Domenico, to whom Let. T278 is addressed when Bartolomea is actually in Rome.[9] (But this affords no clue as to the year in which the letter was written.)

I therefore place this letter quite confidently on 29 April 1377.[10]

This is one of the eight letters of Catherine which we possess in the original, that is, the letter as it was actually sent by Catherine to the addressee. It was donated by Hartwell de la Garde Grissell to the Jesuit Church of St. Aloysius at Oxford and first published in photograph by Arthur F. Spender "Siena," *St. Peter's, an illustrated magazine*, London, in-8°, vol. IV, Sept. 1899–Feb. 1900, pp. 21–31.[11] It does not occur in any

---

[6] This could be the Augustinian Antonio da Nizza of Lecceto, to whom Catherine does refer as *frate*, but it could also be some other Antonio.

[7] *Libellus de Supplemento*, II, vii, iii, p. 180.

[8] *Processo Castellano*, p. 49.

[9] Let. T278 is follows the present letter in this volume.

[10] The linguistic data yields next to no clues for the dating of this brief letter, since every one of its twelve analyzed patterns is chronologically broadly spread. Only two letters share six or more of these, and they are from late 1375 and from April 1376. This, plus the lack of the usual opening invocation, might incline me toward 1376 were it not for the very close proximity of Catherine's impending journey to Florence and Avignon that year—unless perhaps the monastery in question is Pontignano and the letter was written on a stop there on the way to Florence. However, this seems a very tenuous possibility, since Catherine does not tell Iacomo where to send whatever news he might learn concerning Antonio, something one would think she would have done if she were planning to be anywhere but in Siena in the very near future. Both Fawtier (II, pp. 275–277) and Dupré Theseider (unpublished notes) assign the letter to 1377.

[11] The article also includes a somewhat inaccurate English translation of the letter. Fawtier (*Catheriniana*, pp. 31–32) gives the information that the letter is written on a sheet of paper 201mm by 176mm, with the address on the reverse. The writing, he says, is very close to that of the letter preserved at the Confraternity of Santa Lucia in Siena (T192), and

collection of Catherine's letters.

What is puzzling about the letter (besides the fact that it appears in none of the collections) is that it is in so many ways different in style and expression from Catherine's other writings. Is it not authentic? Or could it have been written not at direct dictation but simply with a general direction from Catherine as to content? I would not presume to exclude it on the grounds of such questions, but have indicated several of the letter's unusual characteristics in the notes. What follows assumes that the letter is indeed authentic.

§

Dearest son in Christ gentle Jesus,[12]

I Caterina, servant and slave of the servants of Jesus Christ, am writing to you in his precious blood, to encourage you to persevere in his grace and in most holy fear of God.[13] This fear is a hindrance to doing evil as well as an inexhaustible fountain of all good. Remember that those who scorn earthly human weakness win the grace and love of the gentle Jesus, and those who abandon the world are on the road to the eternal blessedness of paradise to enjoy him. Remember that his most precious [blood] washed away all sin and rescued us from that enemy, the devil, who defiled us with his malice and indecency and led us to our souls' eternal death. Humility makes our flesh rise to the heights and abandon forever the wealth that is a greater hindrance to good than anything else, that leads us more easily than anything else to the devil.

So choose the shortest way, the way of poverty,[14] to come to that holy spotless Lamb, Jesus, who for love of us was crucified. It is the thought that there is no better way for us to be saved that leads me to encourage you so to follow [the way] of good. Then you will have that infinite mercy of being like one of the guests at the wedding feast of eternal life.[15] You will be stripped of the sensual love that corrupts our soul and entices us to what is not good for us, and will have the wedding garment of charity that Jesus welcomes.

I tell you once again, what you propose to do gives me great joy.[16] I

---

is neither the hand of Neri di Landoccio Pagliaresi, nor, probably, of Stefano Maconi.

[12] The letter bears no invocation in the manuscript.

[13] She does not use her usual formula, "I long to see you. . . ."

[14] It is unusual for Catherine to speak simply of poverty rather than "voluntary poverty" when she is referring to poverty as a virtue.

[15] Cf. the parable of the wedding banquet, Mt. 22, 1–14.

[16] From the context, it would seem that Antonio has decided to enter a religious order.

beg you for love of Christ Jesus crucified to do it, to gain spiritual peace and serenity, and so that you will not be deluded by darkness and your flesh will not be inclined to sin. Those who have abandoned the filth of the world truly love their Creator and seek only the love of Christ. They throw away for good[17] all worldly and temporal things. They crush and dispel all carnal immorality[18] and give themselves completely to charity, to that blazing charity that held Christ bound and nailed on the cross.

You sent me word that Frate Antonio has gone to Bologna and hasn't left anything behind. Try to get news of him, and I will write to our Frate Tommaso about it.

Encourage Monna Bartolomea and tell her to ask the glorious apostles Peter and Paul to give me and our other poor folks grace, for our peace and the salvation of our souls.[19]

I'll say no more. May God fill you with his sweetest grace and divine goodness.

Gentle Jesus! Jesus love!

From the Carthusian monastery, 29 April.[20]

---

[17] Literally: "throw far away from themselves."

[18] It. *distrugie et dissolve omne difetto carnale.*

[19] Monna Bartolomea is almost certainly Bartolomea di Domenico, to whom Let. T278 is addressed in Rome, since the context here suggests that she is going to Rome soon.

[20] This line is in Latin in the original: *Ex Carthusia iij kal-maij.*

Letter T278/G357[1]
To Bartolomea di Domenico, in Rome
May 1377 (shortly after Fawtier 16)

The woman to whom this letter is addressed is almost certainly the Monna Bartolomea to whom Catherine asked Iacomo di Viva to deliver a message when she was about to leave for Rome.[2] One can safely assume, then, that she, like Iacomo, is from Siena.[3] And, since Catherine admonishes her about "excessive love for our children," one can assume that she is a mother.

Though the rubric places Bartolomea already in Rome, the letter seems to treat mainly of issues facing a person about to leave on a pilgrimage rather than one who has already arrived. Or perhaps she has only just arrived. Catherine's reference to Bartolomea's "going to the pardons" seems to indicate a specific indulgenced occasion, but I know of no record of such occasions.

There is little clue in the linguistic data for dating this letter.[4]

All one can guess, then, is that this letter was written at least a bit after Fawtier 16 and almost certainly before the end of 1377—therefore sometime between May and December of 1377. From the tone of the letter, it would seem most probable that it was written while Bartolomea's Roman pilgrimage was in its earliest stages, that is, in May.

§

In the name of Jesus Christ crucified and of gentle Mary.

Dearest mother and daughter in Christ gentle Jesus,

I Caterina, servant and slave of the servants of Jesus Christ, am writing to you in his precious blood. I long to see you a good sincere pilgrim, acting as sincere pilgrims do on their journey[a] in this life. We are continually[b] running on toward our end in death, and so I want you courageously to

---

[1] MSS: B, P2, R1, P5, F2, F1, P3; translation based on R1, with variants from unpublished notes of Dupré Theseider.

[2] Cf. Let. Fawtier 16, the letter preceding this one, addressed to Iacomo.

[3] There is no Bartolomea di Domenico in the various published lists of *Mantellate*.

[4] The four letters which share five or more of its fifteen analyzed patterns are scattered between 1376 and 1378. The only individual pattern which gives any clue at all is AGNELCON, which shows only a single isolated occurrence after 1377. Fawtier (II, p. 309) says only that the letter must be prior to Catherine's own journey to Rome in November 1378. Dupré Theseider (unpublished notes) considers it undatable.

do as wise pilgrims do who are never concerned about either the weariness or the pleasure they may experience along the way. No, they look only to the final[c] goal they want to reach. Nor should we pilgrims pay attention to our troubles or to anything harmful or disgraceful that is said or done to us. Don't turn back because of your unwillingness to suffer, but [go on] in true holy patience, like someone who has no reason to stay here. What I am saying is that we, too, shouldn't let our cravings or excessive enjoyment make us turn to pleasure or comfort, but should bravely walk on, not allowing our delight in them to make us stop.

On this journey we should have a staff in our hand so that we can defend ourselves against the wild animals and against our enemies. Let this staff, my dearest mother and daughter, be the most holy cross. On this staff you will find the Lamb, slain and consumed with love, who defends us against our enemy, our sensuality.[5] For when we contemplate such a fire of love, we mortify and kill our perverse willfulness. I say that he defends us against the animals, by which I mean the devil's evil suggestions, the world's false flatterings, and our excessive love for our children or anyone else. Oh how sweet is this glorious wood which is our soul's support! It helps us run on and reach our goal! And our end and goal is eternal life. This is the objective I want you to set before your mind's eye, and then you will be a true pilgrim and will reach the port of salvation.

Bathe, bathe, in the blood of Christ crucified! Go on lapping up the blood of Christ crucified[d] through these pardons.[6] For when people go to the pardons they are doing nothing less than harvesting the blood, since the pardon is granted us because of the blood of the spotless Lamb.

Keep living in God's holy and tender love.

Gentle Jesus! Jesus love! Mary![e]

Textual Notes

a. B, P2: [*on their journey*].

[5] Like the bronze serpent Moses raised up on a staff, so that those who looked at it would be saved from the bites of the poisonous snakes that plagued the journeying Israelites. (Nm. 21, 9)

[6] Indulgences, initially granted in the late eleventh century to crusaders in remission of other penitential obligations upon their crusading vow and confession, were gradually extended in more limited forms to the entire Christian populace. One such indulgence was attached to attending a preaching event, so that such occasions became very popular. Though some preachers ("pardoners") abused the system for personal gain, in its purer form it did not involve a monetary exchange but simply allowed Christians to substitute more lenient penances for earlier more severe ones. Catherine refers to the indulgence as an occasion to "lap up Christ's blood," that is, to drink in with abandon the fruits of Christ's gift of himself.

b. B, P2: [*continually*].
c. B, P2: [*final*].
d. *Walk . . . crucified* from B, P2; R1 jumps from *crucified* to *crucified*, omitting this.
e. *Mary!* from B, P2; R2 has simply: *Jesus, etc.*

LETTER T8/G82[1]
To Frate Giusto, prior of Monteoliveto Maggiore
May to June 1377

Frate Giusto di Giovanni da Volterra is known to have been prior of Sant' Andrea in Volterra from 1378 to 1380, prior of San Giovanni sul Venda from 1380 to 1381, and again prior of Sant'Andrea from 1381 to 1383, at which monastery he died in 1384.[2] His tenure as prior of Monteoliveto must therefore have ended before whatever date in 1378 marked the beginning of his appointment to Volterra.

Catherine had known the Benedictine monks at Monteoliveto near Siena certainly by early 1376, when she recommended that a certain priest be taken there to "settle his affairs."[3] Over the years, she referred a number of her young disciples to the Olivetan Benedictines and followed them with her correspondence.[4] The present letter concerns a young man born out of wedlock who has been refused admittance to Monteoliveto Maggiore by Frate Giusto, presumably because of the circumstances of his birth, even after an apparent first intervention by Catherine through the mediation of the prior of San Benedetto in Siena. Catherine is not happy with that decision, nor with the thinking she suspects has motivated it.

Catherine's apparent reference to the prior of San Benedetto would seem to imply that she is writing the letter from Siena and that the young man in question is Sienese.[5]

The linguistic evidence in general inclines me to place the letter in the first eight months of 1377. Now Catherine was in Siena from January through March and from May probably until early July in 1377. Particulars of the linguistic evidence,[6] in combination with the references in the

---

[1] MSS: B, P2, P1, H, P3, P5, F2, P4, Pa; translation based on P4, with protocol from H.

[2] This information is from P. Lugano, "L'istituzione di Montoliveto nella seconda metà del Trecento" and "Santa Caterina da Siena e i monaci di Montoliveto." He cites archival records from Monteoliveto, which unfortunately do not begin in detail until 1379.

[3] Cf. Let. T208/DT6 (in this volume), written to Bartolomeo Dominici at Asciano probably during Holy Week of 1376.

[4] Thirteen of her letters to Olivetan monks and novices survive.

[5] Lugano believes there is good reason to suppose the disciple in question here is Giovanni di Bindo di Doccio, to whom Let. T76 and T189/DT84 (both in this volume) are directed. If this is true, this letter would have to have been written before 1373, when we know that Giovanni was already a member of the monastic chapter at Monteoliveto Maggiore. The linguistic evidence, however, does not at all support such an early date. Umberto Meattini (*Epistolario*, p. 1474) says that the young man seems to be the son of Catherine's friend Nanni di Ser Vanni, who donated the fortress of Belcaro for the establishment of her monastery. If he is right, a placement of this letter near the time of the founding of Santa Maria degli Angeli would be even more logical.

[6] All three letters sharing fifteen or more of this one's forty-four analyzed patterns fall

text of the letter, lead me to place this letter during the second of these periods, that is, between her month at Belcaro (April) and her departure for the Val d'Orcia in early July.

§

In the name of Jesus Christ.[a]

Dearest father in Christ gentle Jesus,

I Caterina, servant and slave of the servants of Jesus Christ, am writing to you in his precious blood. I long to see you eating and savoring souls. Take your lesson from gentle First Truth, who in his restlessly yearning hunger and thirst for our salvation cried out from the wood of the most holy cross, "I thirst!"[7] It is as if he were saying: "I am more longingly thirsty for your salvation than I can show you through this finite suffering." Yes, he is tortured with physical thirst, but that suffering is finite. It is the pain of holy desire, shown us in his thirst for the human race, that is infinite.[8] *Oh good and gentle Jesus, you let us know you are thirsty, and at the same time you ask for a drink. When do you ask us for a drink? When you show us your loving charity, my Lord.*[9]

---

between August 1377 and July 1378, but there is a very marked concentration of significant clusters within individual patterns between January and August 1377 (ACCETDES, AFFETT, AMORPRSN, FIELACET, GIARDREL, GRANBASS, MANGGUST, MATRIMON, ORAZVIG, PADMANIF, PENADES, PENAFIN, PROSMEZZ, SANGMANI, SERVPROS). Three of these patterns in particular (ACCETDES, FIELACET, PADMANIF) incline me to place the letter closer to August than to January. Both Fawtier (II, p. 193) and Dupré Theseider (unpublished notes) decline to date the letter.

[7] Jn. 19, 28. Catherine uses the Latin *Sitio.*

[8] Cf. *Dial.* 75, p. 139, where she expands upon the redemptive power of Christ's infinite desire. Her source is almost certainly Cavalca, *Specchio di croce*, p. 136: "We must, of course, believe that [Christ] suffered physical thirst, but he was even more thirsty and desirous for our salvation. This is why he said, 'I am thirsty'—that is, I am longing for human salvation. By this he wanted to let us know that he loved us more than he could show. For even though he showed us the most perfect love he could in dying for us, that deed was finite, and the infinite could not be shown by a finite deed. And this is why he said, 'I am thirsty.' It was as if he said, I have more ardor, warmth, and desire in my heart that can be shown by what I do."

[9] A more expanded parallel to this theme of giving Christ a drink occurs in Let. T148/DT36 to Bishop Angelo Ricasoli (vol. I): "There you find the slain Lamb, feeding on the Father's glory and our salvation—for his love is so great that he could not express it in [mere] physical suffering. *Oh sweetest, boundless, beloved charity! It was your infinite hunger and thirst for our salvation that made you cry out that you were thirsty! Though your agony there caused you intense physical thirst, your thirst for our salvation was even greater. Oimé! Oimé! There is no one to give you anything to drink except the bitterness of sin upon sin! How few there are who give you a drink freely and with pure loving affection!* . . . You may say to me, 'My daughter, I have nothing to give him.' But I have already told you how I desire

You can easily see, dearest father, how his blood reveals his boundless love.[10] For he gave his blood out of love, and it is with this love that he asks us for a drink. I mean that [Jesus], who loves, is asking to be loved and served. It is only right that the one who loves ought to be loved. This is how we give our Creator a drink: when we give him love for love. But we cannot give it to him through any service we can render him; no, we must give it to him in the person of our neighbor.[11]

This is why we so eagerly turn our attention to giving our neighbors the sort of service we know most pleases God, and to this we dedicate ourselves. And the service that pleases our Savior more than any other is that of rescuing souls from the devil's hands, snatching them from their worldly condition, from the jaws of worldly vanity, and bringing them into the holy state of religious life. It's not just a matter of not ignoring or evading them when they come with such desire; no, you must be ready to die in order to rescue them. This is the holy drink God's Son is asking for on the cross, and we mustn't be slow to give it to him, but eager—for you can see very well that he is dying of this thirst. And we must not do as the Jews did, who gave him sour wine and gall.[12]

When does he get sour wine and gall from us? When we live in a sensual sort of selfishness, in a deep-seated apathy, in a readiness to accommodate the world out of human respect, with scant watching and prayer, with little hunger for God's honor or the salvation of souls. This is indeed a sour wine, a gall mixed with terrible bitterness. [Jesus] gets the unpleasantness (because he does not like it), but the bitterness and harm come back to us.[13]

---

and long for you to be nailed fast to the cross, where we find the slain Lamb. . . . So we cannot say that we have nothing to give him. No, we should take the wine of his indescribably thirsty desire for our salvation, and give it back to him in the person of our neighbor."

[10] Christ's blood, for Catherine is revelatory of the whole "truth" of God: justice, mercy, and "boundless love."

[11] Catherine expounds often on the concept of serving God in the person of one's neighbors, but nowhere more succinctly than in *Dial.* 64, p. 121: "I ask you to love me with the same love with which I love you. But for me you cannot do this, for I have loved you without being loved. Whatever love you have for me you owe me, so you love me not gratuitously but out of duty, while I love you not out of duty but gratuitously. So you cannot give me the kind of love I ask of you. This is why I have put you among your neighbors: so that you can do for them what you cannot do for me—that is, love them without any concern for thanks and without looking for any profit for yourself. And whatever you do for them I will consider done for me."

[12] Jn. 19, 29; Mt. 27, 48; Mk. 15, 36. Catherine's use of the term "Jews" here seems to betray at least a latent version of the antisemitic bias that so characterized the Middle Ages.

[13] Cf. *Dial.* 117, p. 219: "Not that I myself can be harmed or persecuted by them, for I am like the rock that is not hurt by what is thrown at it, but glances back at the one who threw it."

What then do we need so as not to give him this sort of drink? Nothing is needed but love. And love cannot be had except from love. When it is enlightened, love rises up to draw love into itself. This is what I mean: with loving desire we must raise the eye of our understanding and focus on Christ crucified. This is what has revealed to us the eternal Father's will and the love that made him create us for one purpose only, that we should have eternal life. It is the blood of the Word, God's only-begotten Son, that reveals this love to us, this purpose for which we were created. Once our desire[b] has opened the eye of our understanding and focused on the desire of Christ crucified, we draw love into ourselves and find ourselves loving what God loves and hating what God hates. And because sin has no part in God, we so hate and despise it that we not only find no pleasure in it but would give a thousand physical lives (if we had so many) to rescue souls from deadly sin.

Give him a drink for me, dearest father! For you see with what love he is asking you for one. Let me see your good holy desire grow for this wonderful food.[14] Don't ever be swayed by eminence, by greatness or lowliness, by legitimacy or illegitimacy of birth. God's Son, whose example we must follow, never despised (nor now despises) anyone, whatever his or her position or parentage, whether just or sinner. No, he receives with love anyone who is determined to get up out of the filth of deadly sin, out of the emptiness of the world, and return to grace. This is the teaching he gave, and although he gave it to everyone, much more is it given to you and to the others who govern and administer the order. So when good plants[15] come into your hands, and they come with hunger and desire for the order and are leaving the world out of love for virtue and running to the yoke of obedience, you must not despise or shun them for any reason, no matter how they were born. God doesn't despise the soul of one conceived in deadly sin any more than one conceived in wedlock. What our God looks for is good holy desires. So I want you and I beg you to receive in charity this new plant whom the prior has sent with the request that he be received into the order.[16] He has a good holy will. His natural condition is good, too.[17] He has lovingly set his heart on religious life, and the

---

[14] That is, souls, as she imaged at the beginning of the letter.

[15] She often refers to novices in religious life and to persons new in any church office as "new plants."

[16] Lugano concludes from this remark that Catherine had appealed to the prior of San Benedetto in Siena, who must, according to what follows, have sent a messenger to Monteoliveto Maggiore and that the messenger must have returned with a negative response. ("L'istituzione de Montoliveto nella seconda metà del Trecento," p. 68, n. 50)

[17] The expression Catherine uses is *condizione naturale*, an expression she uses nowhere else. Perhaps she is referring to his health, perhaps to his personality.

Holy Spirit is calling him specifically to your order. You must not—and I know that you don't want to—resist the Holy Spirit.

I am very surprised that your answer was no—really astonished! Maybe it was the fault of the messenger; maybe he didn't know any better. Not that what he did was wrong, but he didn't know how to do more. I'm begging you now for love of Christ crucified to be utterly disposed to accept [this young man], for he will be an honor to God and to the order. Don't send him back to me.[18] He is a good young man, and if he were not good, I wouldn't be sending him to you. I am asking you this as a favor, but according to the rule of charity it is your *duty* to do it. Don't be stingy with the one who comes to you asking for a drink: give it to him. This is how I will know that you are on the cross:[19] if you give a drink to the thirsty one who is asking you for a drink.[20] I don't see how we can be pleasing to God otherwise. And this is why I said that I long to see you hungrily eating and savoring souls for God's honor.

I'll say no more. Keep living in God's holy and tender love.

Gentle Jesus! Jesus love!

Textual Notes

a. From H; P4: *In the name of Jesus Christ crucified and of gentle Mary.*

b. It. *affetto.*

[18] It. *non mel lassate.* The sense could also be, somewhat colloquially: "Don't let him go on me."

[19] The meaning is clearly that she wants the prior to be nailed to the cross with Christ. Thus a mutuality in the "giving to drink" is introduced.

[20] The one who is asking for a drink is both the young man and God.

Part VII: The Mission to the Val D'Orcia (July to December 1377)

In 1369 the Reformers in Siena brought back to the city several exiled families, including the Tolomei, the Malavolti, the Piccolomini, and the Saracini—all names which figure among Catherine's disciples. Then, in 1374, after a series of uprisings, they exiled the Salimbeni, who occupied a number of fortesses in the Orcia Valley (the Val d'Orcia), fortresses which had in fact been granted to the Salimbeni in 1274 by a grateful Commune after they had saved it from bankruptcy. From the valley, which was part of Siena's territory, they began a relentless campaign against the Commune. The family of Agnolino Salimbeni occupied the fortress overlooking Bagno Vignoni, the Rocca d'Orcia. His cousin Cione di Sandro Salimbeni lived in Castiglioncello di Trinoro, about ten miles to the east as the crow flies, but at least twice that distance by road.

In the summer of 1377, Catherine made a journey to the Val d'Orcia to reconcile Agnolino and Cione, who were feuding over a castle to which both laid claim. Francesco Malavolti, Tommaso dalla Fonte, Raimondo da Capua, Neri di Landoccio Pagliaresi, Gabriele de' Piccolomini, "and many others" are documented as being with her,[1] as well as Pietro di Giovanni Ventura,[2] Giovanni Tantucci,[3] and Tommaso Caffarini, who himself says he joined Catherine at the Rocca (probably after her return from Sant'Antimo).[4] Catherine herself in her own letters mentions the presence of her sister-in-law Lisa, Alessa dei Saracini (for part of the time), Bruna, Tomma,[5] the hermit Fra Santi, Matteo Tolomei, and Bartolomeo Dominici. Gardner and Drane also include Stefano Maconi.[6]

---

[1] Testimony of Francesco Malavolti, *Processo Castellano*, pp. 391–400, especially p. 396.

[2] Testimony of Francesco Malavolti, *Processo Castellano*, p. 425.

[3] According to a letter of Giovanni dalle Celle (Let. VI, ed. Cividali, p. 442), written during this period.

[4] *Processo Castellano*, p. 49.

[5] The last two unidentified.

[6] Gardner, *Saint Catherine of Siena*, p. 213; Drane, *History of St. Catherine of Siena*, vol.

The most complete account of Catherine's mission to the Val d'Orcia comes to us in the testimony of Francesco Malavolti in the *Processo Castellano*.[7] He tells us that she stopped first at Montepulciano, a journey of about forty miles. If Eugenio Lazzareschi is right, and I am inclined to believe he is, she spent a fair amount of time in Montepulciano dealing with, among other things, the reconciliation of the Spinelli and the sons of a certain Lorenzo[8] and converting Giacomo de' Cavalieri del Pecora.[9] When Catherine and her company continued on their way, they left Francesca (Cecca) di Clemente Gori and Catherine's mother Lapa at the Monastery of Sant'Agnesa, where Cecca's daughter Giustina was a novice.

Francesco Malavolti tells us that from Montepulciano the company went to Castiglioncello di Trinoro, about twenty miles by winding road to the south of Montepulciano. There they would spend some time with Cione di Sandro Salimbeni and his wife Stricca.

From there the group traveled another thirty-seven miles, by roads that wound first to the southwest to Radicofani, then northwest to Bagno Vignoni, and finally a bit south to Rocca d'Orcia, the home of Agnolino, his sisters Bandeçça and Isa, and their mother Biancina. At some point after that, while Raimondo was still with her, Catherine and at least some of her company traveled thirteen miles or so to the west to the Abbey of Sant'Antimo, where her friend Giovanni di Gano da Orvieto (the same who had presided at the consecration of Belcaro in early April) hosted them for perhaps a week or so.[10]

They had been at or in the environs of the Rocca "for several weeks" when Catherine sent Raimondo to Rome "with certain proposals which, if only people had understood, would have been for the advantage of the

---

II, p. 59. I have not, however, found documentation for this in the primary sources; nor do Gardner and Drane name their source. Perhaps they draw their conclusion from Raimondo's remark (*Life*, III, i, 342, pp. 317–318) that Stefano "left his father and mother and his three brothers, as well as his own native place, and followed her wherever she went." On the other hand, Caffarini in his *Libellus de Supplemento* says that Stefano "was the first to whom she wrote in her own hand after she had miraculously learned to write and to read." That letter is in any case not extant, but if Caffarini is right, it would have to have been written from Rocca d'Orcia, probably in October. However, Caffarini also says that Stefano was with Catherine "the whole time" in Rome, which is clearly contradicted by evidence in Catherine's letters and in Stefano's own testimony.

[7] Pp. 391–400.

[8] Cf. Let. T123 (in this volume).

[9] *S. Caterina da Siena in Val d'Orcia*, Firenze: Tip. Domenicana, 1915, p. 25, citing P. Bartoli, *Istoria di S. Agnesa di Montepulciano con delle memorie della medesima città e suoi uomini illustri*, Siena: Rossi, 1779, p. 116.

[10] Francesco Malavolti in his testimony in the *Processo Castellano* (p. 405) says she was there "for a time" (*per aliquale temporis spatium*), and speaks of the crowds who came "over several days in succession" (*quampluribus diebus continuis*) to hear her.

holy Church of God."[11] While there, he was elected prior of the Dominican community at the Church of Santa Maria sopra Minerva in Rome, and so did not return to Catherine. Not long after his departure Catherine had the mystical experience which prompted her to begin work on her book, *The Dialogue*. By then it was early October.

When, then, did this Val d'Orcia period begin? Raimondo speaks of spending "several weeks" at the Rocca with Catherine. He has to have been in Rome by early October for Catherine to have received the letter from him to which she refers in Let. T272. It would surely have taken him more than a week to reach Rome from the Rocca (after a meeting with Niccolò Soderini in Siena), a journey of about two hundred miles. Then it would have taken another week or more for a letter to reach Catherine, even if he had written it immediately after his arrival. But she also mentions in Let. T272 having received a letter from the pope, which must add at least another few days. So, backing up from Catherine's receipt of the letters, one might estimate that they had been sent near the end of September, with Raimondo arriving in Rome about the last week of that month. He must, then, have left the Rocca in mid-September at the latest. If he had been in the latter place for "several weeks," he and the rest of Catherine's company must have arrived at the Rocca by early August. The visit to Castiglioncello di Trinoro (considering travel time), would then be about the last week or so of July, and the visit to Montepulciano would perhaps begin the second week of July. This would have Catherine and her party leaving Siena in early July at the very latest. The very earliest she could have left would be early May, since the sources tell us that she spent most of April with the new community at Belcaro.

The many letters Catherine wrote during these five or six months seem to build up to a watershed, a sort of "continental divide," as themes accumulate which will be developed very similarly in *The Dialogue*.

---

[11] *Life*, II, ix, 274, p. 255, and III, vi, 422, p. 382.

Letter T153/G170[1]
To Monna Catarina, Baccemea, Orsola, and other women of Pisa
June to October 1377

The Catarina to whom this letter is addressed is not identified in any manuscript. She may be the niece of Nella and Niccolò Buonconti and wife of Gherardo Buonconti, in whose home Catherine has stayed during her months in Pisa in 1375.[2] As for Baccemea and Orsola, we do not meet them anywhere else in what is written by or about Catherine.[3] Because the letter is addressed to these two women jointly along with the "other women," it seems safe to assume that they have some common bond, if only as friends and followers of Catherine.[4]

There is nothing in the content of the letter to lend a clue as to when it was written, though it is the sort of letter that might well have been written not long after one of Catherine's departures from Pisa to reinforce things she had said to the women while with them. That could place it either in early 1376 or in early to mid-1377. The linguistic evidence does not at all support placing the letter during the first of these periods, but points strongly toward the summer or early autumn of 1377.[5] So it could have been written from Siena or Belcaro or, more probably, Rocca d'Orcia. There is no way of being more precise.

---

[1] MSS: Mo-*a*, P4, S4; translation based on Mo-*a*. There are no relevant variants.

[2] Meattini (*Epistolario*, p. 620) in fact assumes that it is Catarina Buonconti.

[3] Baccemea is named only in the rubric of Mo, where Catarina is not named.

[4] Fawtier, II, p. 227, assumes that the women are *Mantellate*. However, it is not likely that Catarina Buonconti would have been a *Mantellata* while her husband was still living.

[5] All eleven letters which share ten or more of this one's thirty-five analyzed patterns are dated from spring of 1377 onward. Further, eight of these eleven are dated between August 1377 and January 1378, and there is no concentration of clusters within individual patterns before June of 1377 or after early 1378. One of these patterns (VASESANG) does not occur at all before August of 1377. Two (PRUDENT, SANGINTR) show only two or three isolated instances each before that date, and DIOINUOM does not occur at all after October of that year. Neither Fawtier nor Dupré Theseider (unpublished notes) ventures a date.

§

In the name of Jesus Christ crucified and of gentle Mary.

Dearest daughters in Christ gentle Jesus,

I Caterina, servant and slave of the servants of Jesus Christ, am writing to you in his precious blood. I long to see you immersed and bathed in the blood of the slain Lamb, considering that it is in this blood that we have life.

So I want you, my very loved daughters, to open the eyes of your understanding to gaze within the vessel of self-knowledge.[6] In this knowledge you will discover that you are a vessel into which this glorious and precious blood is received. The divine nature is fused into the blood with the fire of charity.[7] When you gaze into the vessel of self-knowledge you discover this blood which God has given through his Son.[8] And since the blood was shed only because of sin, you discover in it the knowledge of yourself. And when you see that you are sinful, you see also divine justice in the blood, since [Christ] shed his blood to bring sin to justice. Then you know that God's eternal will wants nothing other than that we be made holy;[9] for [Christ] would not have given his life if he had wanted anything other than our good. So gaze into the blood that you discover within the vessel of your very selves.

Open, open the eyes of your understanding onto Power, the eternal Father, whom you find in this blood because of the union of the divine

---

[6] This is the only place Catherine develops the image of self-knowledge as a vessel. Also unique here is her treatment of the human heart as a vessel holding the blood of Christ. Though the latter image occurs elsewhere (but nowhere before 1377), it is not drawn out in such detail anywhere else. Here she joins the image of the heart as vessel with that of Christ's blood as a reflecting pool or mirror in which one can come to know oneself as well as God within oneself.

[7] The "fusion" of the fire of the Holy Spirit and the blood of Christ is explained in Let. T189/DT84, written both to the monks of San Girolamo at Cervaia and to several monks of Monteoliveto Maggiore (in this volume): "Our sin, or any diabolical illusion or temptation, however repulsive, filthy, and ugly it may be, need not make us falter; for our doctor has given us a medicine for any sickness we may have. I mean the baptism of blood and of fire in which the soul cleanses and washes away every sin, consumes and burns away every diabolical temptation and illusion—for the fire is steeped in blood, so it truly does burn. This fire is the love that is the Holy Spirit, for love was the hand that pierced God's Son and made him shed his blood. [The fire and the blood] became one, and so perfect was their uniting that we cannot have fire without blood, nor blood without fire."

[8] Cf. Let. T82 to three women of Florence (in this volume): "Now we are the vessel that has received this blood. And we are the rock into which the standard of the most holy cross was set."

[9] 1 Thes. 4, 3.

nature with human nature.[10] And you will find Wisdom, the Son. And in that Wisdom you will recognize God's supreme eternal goodness as well as our own poverty when you discover Mercy, the Holy Spirit, who was the bond that joined God with humanity and humanity with God, and who held this Word fixed and nailed to the wood of the most holy cross.[11] So your will will be filled and will reach out to love, and you will bind yourselves so tightly with Christ crucified that neither the devil nor anyone else will ever be able to separate you from him.[12] In fact, anything that may act against you will only serve to strengthen your union with God and with your neighbors. For virtue is tested by what opposes it,[13] and the more virtue is tested in us, the more perfect our union with our Creator becomes.

Though it may sometimes seem to you that difficulties are a cause of separating you from union with God and from virtue, this is not the case. In fact, difficulties intensify our virtue and our union [with God], because if we are wise and are clothed in the blood of Christ crucified, the more we see ourselves hounded and kicked around by the world, the more we raise our affections above the world. And if the devil is the source of the assaults, it makes us humble ourselves, makes us get up from the sleep of carelessness and be utterly alert.

If you would be wise and prudent, let go of all ignorance. Then you will conceive a light and a knowledge, and you will receive grace in such measure that not only will it be a source of light within you but it will give light beyond you to others. You will be an example and mirror of

---

[10] She begins here to develop the Augustinian Trinitarian analogy of God the Father as power, the Son as wisdom, and the Spirit as mercy, to which she barely alluded in Let. T181/DT55 to Nicola da Osimo in early 1376 (vol. I). Here as elsewhere, she stresses that where one is, the others are also. Cf. Prayer 10, p. 78: "But did your wisdom come into the world alone? No. For wisdom was not separate from power, nor was power without mercy. You, wisdom, did not come alone then, but the whole Trinity was there."

[11] Cf. Let. T129/DT29 to Bartolomeo Dominici (vol. I): "The Holy Spirit is the light that banishes all darkness, the hand that upholds the whole world. In that vein I recall his saying not long ago, 'I am the One who upholds and sustains the whole world. It was through me that the divine and human natures were brought together. I am the mighty hand that holds up the standard of the cross; of that cross I made a bed and held the God-Man nailed fast to it.' "

[12] Cf. Rom. 8, 38: "I am certain that neither death nor life, neither angels nor principalities, neither the present nor the future, nor powers, nor height nor depth nor any other creature, will be able to separate us from the love of God that comes to us in Christ Jesus, our Lord."

[13] Cf. Let. T213 to Daniela of Orvieto (1378): "[I]n illness the virtue of patience is proved; in struggles and in the devils' provocations, courage and steady perseverance are proved; and in the troubles we suffer at the hands of others our humility and patience and charity are proved. And in the same way, God allows all our other virtues to be proved by what opposes them."

virtue. And so you will fulfill what our Savior said, that we should be shining lamps who give light, not darkness.[14]

Up, then, dearest daughters! Let me not hear that you are still sleeping, or see you darkened with selfish love.[15] Let me see you rather with an indescribable love, a love in which you seek yourselves for God's sake, your neighbors for God's sake, and God for God's sake. For God is eternal Goodness and deserves to be loved, not offended, by us.

I'll say no more. Love, love each other, my dearest and very loved daughters! Bind yourselves in the bond of true and blazing charity. Keep living in God's holy and tender love.

Gentle Jesus! Jesus love!

---

[14] Mt. 5, 16.

[15] Cf. Prayer 19, p. 179: "Grant that we may not be foolish, blind, or cold, or see so darkly that we do not see ourselves, but give us the gift of knowing your will."

LETTER T115/G332[1]
To Madonna Isa Salimbeni
June or early July 1377

Madonna Isa,[2] daughter of Giovanni d'Agnolino Salimbeni, was a widow, like her sister the Countess Benedetta (Bandeçça). Catherine has already seemed determined to have the latter enter her newly-founded monastery at Belcaro.[3] Now she is urging Isa as well to take the habit, either as a tertiary or perhaps also at Belcaro. Though social mores of the times assumed that a woman's marriage or other place in life would be arbitrated by her parents or older brothers, Catherine not only urges Isa to speak out concerning her own future, but even says it would be wrong for her not to do so. Surely she is voicing her own experience within her own family.

Since Catherine already knows she is coming to Rocca d'Orcia, the home of Isa's exiled family ("before I come there"), the letter must be close to that time, that is, near early August 1377. It was, however, probably written before Catherine left Siena, which would place it some time in June or early July.[4] This historically established date is supported by the linguistic evidence.[5]

§

In the name of Jesus Christ crucified and of gentle Mary.

Dearest daughter in Christ gentle Jesus,

I Caterina, servant and slave of the servants of Jesus Christ, am writing to you in his precious blood. I long to see you a steadfast and faithful spouse, not whirling about in the wind like a leaf.[6] I don't want your soul or your holy desire to be tossed about by any contrary wind of trouble or persecu-

---

[1] MSS: Mo-*b*, S3; translation based on Mo-*b*, with variants from S3.

[2] Isa (or Lisa) is a diminutive of Elisabetta.

[3] See Let. T112 and T114, both in this volume.

[4] Fawtier (II, pp. 300–301) places Catherine's journey to Rocca d'Orcia in October, and therefore places this letter slightly before that date. Dupré Theseider (unpublished notes) places it variously in summer or mid-September of 1377. Raimondo says in *Life* II, ix, 274, p. 255, that he had been at the Rocca for "several weeks" before Catherine sent him to Rome sometime in September 1377. So Fawtier cannot be right in placing Catherine's arrival at the Rocca in October.

[5] All four letters sharing five or more of this one's fifteen analyzed patterns fall between March and October 1377. Further, there are significant clusters at that point within the individual patterns AGNELCON, FOGLVENT, POTERE, and SCEM. FOGLVENT is particularly significant in that it occurs eight times within the first ten months of 1377 and not again until late 1378.

[6] This is one of Catherine's favorite images for fickleness and instability.

tion the world or the devil may send. No, withstand them all courageously with love for virtue and for constancy, remembering the blood of Christ crucified. Don't let your desire be swayed by anything anyone might say when they come with their speeches and their wicked advice.[7]

If you are a steadfast and faithful spouse, with a firm footing on the living rock, Christ gentle Jesus,[8] your strength will not falter, nor will words fail you. No, they will be given to you.[9] For power and boldness ought to grow, not diminish, in one who really desires to acquire virtue. As I recall, you have made yourself feared by the world, and have trampled underfoot all human respect and opinion—and this you've done just for the wretched world. Virtue, then, ought to find you no less vigorous. Where you had one tongue before, you ought now to have a dozen, and answer boldly the speeches of the devil, who would stand in the way of your being saved. If you maintain your silence you will be reproached on the last day. It will be said to you, "Cursed be you who remained silent!" So don't wait for that harsh reprimand. If you are willing to follow the Lamb abandoned and consumed on the cross on his path of suffering, torment, disgrace, and insult, I am certain that you will not keep silent.

I want you then to follow Christ your spouse, and join this new battle with a bold and holy desire to fight persistently even to the point of death, saying, "Through Christ crucified I can do anything; he is in me who strengthens me."[10] In the beginning now you feel the thorns, but afterward you will have the fruit of it, and receive the glory of being praised by God.[11] So up courageously, with true holy persistence! Don't hesitate at all!

Concerning the habit, it seems to me you should follow what the Holy Spirit has asked through your own mouth,[12] without being influenced by

---

[7] Cf. Let. T114 to Isa's brother Agnolino, in which Catherine alludes to the family's loud resistance to their sister Bandeçça's becoming a nun.

[8] 1 Cor. 3, 11: "No one can lay a foundation other than the one that has been laid, namely Jesus Christ." And 1 Pet. 2, 4–5: "Come to him, a living stone. . . . You too are living stones, built as an edifice of spirit."

[9] Cf. Mt. 10, 19–20: "When they hand you over, do not worry about what you will say or how you will say it. When the hour comes, you will be given what you are to say. You yourselves will not be the speakers; the Spirit of your Father will be speaking in you."

[10] Cf. Phil. 4, 13.

[11] Cf. *Dial.* 44, p. 90: "Beforehand, this decision is a thorn bush they seem to encounter when they follow the way of truth. Conscience always pulls in one direction, and sensuality in the other. But as soon as they decide courageously, despising themselves, and say, 'I want to follow Christ crucified,' the thorn bush is broken and they discover my immeasurable tenderness."

[12] It. *mi pare che sia da seguitare quello che lo Spirito Santo per la vostra bocca domandó.* Perhaps Catherine means that Isa, in asking for the habit, is giving evidence of the Spirit's will. (Cf. again Mt. 10, 20: "You yourselves will not be the speakers; the Spirit of your

anybody. Let them prattle on as they will! This will not diminish your devotion to your glorious father Saint Francis; on the contrary, it will increase it.[13] Still, you are free—though it would very probably be wrong for you to turn back on what you have begun.[14]

So far as the countess is concerned, it seems to me it would be good if it could be arranged for her to go to the Rocca before I come there. After that we will do whatever the Holy Spirit will have us do.[15]

I'll say no more. Keep living in God's holy and tender love.[a] Bathe in the blood of Christ crucified.

Gentle Jesus! Jesus love!

Textual Notes

a. S3 adds *Gentle Jesus! Jesus love!*

Father will be speaking in you.") By "the habit" Catherine could mean either the religious habit of monastic life or the habit of the lay "third orders," since at that time members of the latter (such as Catherine herself) wore the habit of their respective orders even though they were not living in monasteries.

[13] Burlamacchi supposes that Isa has been married to Paolo Trinci, one of the lords of Fuligno. The Trinci family had a great devotion to Saint Francis. One of their relatives, a certain Fra Paolo, had a few years earlier worked for a reinvigoration of the Franciscan rule, which had fallen into laxity. It would seem logical to conclude from Catherine's remarks here that Isa is perhaps thinking she should become a Franciscan, either a nun or a tertiary. She will in fact eventually be received as one of the Dominican *Mantellate*. Her name occurs in the list of women received at San Domenico in Siena in April 1378. (Laurent, *Fontes* I, *Documenti*, p. 49)

[14] Catherine often admonishes her correspondents about "turning back," a theme she develops in Let. T126 (to Cecca di Clemente Gori and Allesa dei Saracini, in this volume) in a way particularly relevant to Isa's situation: "[N]ever look back to see what you have already plowed. I mean this in two senses. The first is when a person has left behind worldly corruptions and later mentally looks back at them with selfish pleasure. . . . But unless [our selfishness] has been completely uprooted both materially and spiritually we will in time be guilty of the second way of looking back. And do you know what this second way is? It is not a turning back to worldly pleasures, but happens when we have begun to put our hand to the 'plowing' of becoming very perfect. The perfection I mean consists most of all in completely smothering and drowning our own will, and this even more in spiritual things than in temporal (since we have already become detached from the temporal, but are now preoccupied with the spiritual). . . . What I am saying is that unless we have completely uprooted our self-centered love we will turn back a second time and sin against our being made perfect."

[15] The countess is Isa's sister Bandeçça. This is almost certainly a reference to the matter of whether Bandeçça should enter the monastery at Belcaro. (Cf. Let. T112 and T114 in this volume.)

Letter T123/G202[1]
To the Defenders of the Commune of Siena
About mid- to late July 1377

Under the government of the Reformers (the *Riformatori*), who had come to power in 1368, the fifteen Lord Defenders (*Signori Difensori*) with the Captain of the People at their head formed the supreme magistracy of Siena.[2]

This letter to the Defenders includes a number of allusions which must be taken into account for its chronological placement. They have sent Catherine a communication by way of Tommaso di Guelfuccio,[3] asking her to serve "as mediator" for the reconciliation between them and their "fellow-citizens," presumably the Salimbeni. She is also very aware of the gossip concerning her activities, but her comments do not seem to reflect the sort of tension with the Defenders that will be so evident in her later communications with them.[4]

She mentions also that she has some obligation to fulfill in regard to the Monastery of Sant'Agnesa in Montepulciano and in the same breath says that she has "to be with Messer Spinello's nephews in regard to the reconciliation of Lorenzo's sons." Lorenzo has not been identified. Verdiani Bandi includes Spinello Tolomei among the leading citizens of Montepulciano who were "enemies of the Sienese government" even as late as 1384.[5] However, they were also at odds with the Salimbeni. Lazzareschi cites "the chronicler" as reporting that Spinello and Agnolino and Cione de' Salimbeni had in 1377 "renewed their old enmities."[6] He assumes from the tone of Catherine's remarks that she is writing this letter while she is still at Montepulciano, before she has even arrived at Rocca d'Orcia. I am inclined to agree with him, placing the letter probably about mid- to late July.[7]

---

[1] MSS: Mo-*b*; translation based on Mo-*b*.

[2] For details of this rise of the Reformers and the structure of their government, cf. Gardner, *The Story of Siena and San Gimignano*, London: J. M. Dent, 1902, pp. 30–37.

[3] Tommaso has also served as Catherine's courier to carry Let. T252/DT88 to Gregory XI at Corneto.

[4] Let. T121 in this volume and T311 and T367, both written in 1379.

[5] *I Castelli della Val d'Orcia e la Repubblica di Siena*, Siena: Tip. Turbanti, 1976, p. 88. It is not clear who is being reconciled with whom.

[6] *S. Caterina in Val d'Orcia*, p. 25, citing Orlando Malavolti, *Historia de' fatti e guerre de' Sanesi*, Venice, 1599, II, pp. 144v–145.

[7] Gardner, *Saint Catherine of Siena*, pp. 213–214, notes that Catherine's 1377 attempt at mediation was only partially successful. The following spring, in spite of the intervention of the new bishop of Siena, Luca Bertini, Spinello would attack the lands of the Salimbeni, renewing the hostilities between the two clans. In spite of this association with Montepul-

The linguistic evidence clearly reinforces the placement of this letter in the Val d'Orcia period, a placement already necessitated by the allusions mentioned above.[8]

§

In the name of Jesus Christ crucified and of gentle Mary.

Dearest sons and [my] temporal lords in Christ gentle Jesus,

I Caterina, servant and slave of the servants of Jesus Christ, am writing to you in his precious blood. I long to see you governing courageously and fearlessly both your own city and the city lent to you.[9] For I know that slavish fear degrades and obstructs[10] the heart. It makes us live and work not like rational people but like witless animals, because slavish fear comes from self-centeredness.

We can see in rulers and subjects, in religious and laity, in people of every class, just how dangerous this self-centeredness is. They have no concern for anyone or anything but themselves. If they are lay subjects they never observe or obey what is imposed on them by their rulers. If they are rulers they never pass judgment reasonably but in their concupiscence are guilty of all sorts of injustice, some for their own advantage and some out of human respect, judging not according to truth but according to what others want. And some act out of fear that if they displease others they may be put out of office. Such people are blindly afraid and suspicious of everything—afraid when they should not be so, but not when they should be.[11]

Oh selfish love and slavish fear! You blind the eye of understanding

---

ciano, Gardner (p. 217) seems to imply that he would place the letter further into the Val d'Orcia period.

[8] The eleven letters which share a significant number of patterns with this letter's fifty-one analyzed patterns are all dated from about August 1377 onward. While a number of significant clusters within individual patterns are concentrated in the Val d'Orcia period, several are very strikingly marked as beginning and/or ending between August and October 1377: ALLUMVER, AMORVERD, CIECAMOR, INCOMPOR, OMBRPAUR, SOMETVER, TIMORRIV, VIRNTIM, VOLONTA. Fawtier (II, p. 248) in his commentary places the letter before 1374, reasoning that Catherine would hardly be reconciling a Tolomei feud from Salimbeni territory (p. 249), but in his chronological chart on p. 313 he places it in August or September 1377. Dupré Theseider places the letter in November 1377.

[9] Later in this same letter she will explain that God lends authority to human beings for a time "according to local manners and customs" but that the loan is only temporary.

[10] It. *impedisce et avvilisce.*

[11] She is obviously directing her theme toward the gossip she refers to at the end of the letter, the suspicions about the activities of her company in the Val d'Orcia.

and keep it from knowing the truth! You take away the life of grace, the control of one's own city as well as of the city one has been lent. You make people insupportable to themselves because they want what they cannot have, and what they do have they possess in anxiety because they are afraid of losing it.[12] So they suffer constantly, either from lack of possessions or from fear, because their own will is not being fulfilled. So even in this life they are experiencing hell.

Oh blindness of selfish love! Oh misplaced fear! You become so blind that you not only condemn ordinary people along with the wicked (who could be justly condemned and their treachery feared), but you give in to your fear of the wicked and condemn the just. You presume to despise God's poor servants who are seeking God's honor and the salvation of souls as well as peace and tranquillity for the cities, never ceasing to offer their sweet desires and continual prayer, tears, and sweat in the presence of divine goodness. Oh selfish love and slavish fear! How can you tolerate fearing and passing judgment on those who are ready to die for your welfare and for your republic's preservation and growth in peace and tranquillity? But truly, dearest brothers, this is the perverse fear, the perverted love, that killed Christ. For Pilate, out of fear of losing his authority, was blinded and failed to recognize the truth, and so he killed Christ. Yet the very thing he feared happened to him; for later, when it pleased God (not that Pilate's sin pleased him), Pilate lost soul and body as well as his authority.[13]

Now it seems to me the whole world is full of these Pilates who in blind fear think nothing of persecuting God's servants, stoning them with words of slander and harassment. So great is their blindness that they consider neither whom they are persecuting nor how. No, like beasts they let themselves be guided by their selfish sensuality, applying to [God's servants] the same laws and perspectives one would apply to people whose sole concern is this world. I tell you in truth, every time we so judge as to slander and condemn the works, the actions, the ways, and the associations of God's servants (oimé!) we have reason to fear divine judgment ourselves. For God considers what is done to his servants as done to himself.[14] So we would only be calling down God's wrath upon ourselves.

---

[12] The notion of being insupportable even to oneself begins to occur only at this point in Catherine's writings.

[13] Cf. Cavalca, *Specchio de' peccati*, p. 90: "Pilate had [Christ] crucified even though he knew he was innocent, because he was afraid of losing the emperor's friendship—if he would have lost it as the Jews were threatening. . . . [He] didn't consider what a poor exchange he was making—for fear of temporal troubles going to eternal troubles."

[14] Cf. Mt. 25, 40 (Vulg.): "As often as you did it to the least of my sisters or brothers, you did it to me."

Dearest brothers and lords, we need to approach God—and God's servants as well—with holy fear. Don't be tearing them apart with rumors and unwarranted suspicions. Let them stay or go as pilgrims as the Holy Spirit guides them, to seek and work for God's honor, for the salvation of souls and their rescue from the devils' hands, and for your well-being and peace and tranquillity. Let none of you be so foolish as to want to lay down rules for either the Holy Spirit or his servants.[15] It seems to me that Christ was more tolerant when he himself was wronged than when his apostle Saint Thomas was. For he didn't stand up for his own rights but responded gently to the one who had struck him: "If I have spoken evil, attest to the evil; but if I have spoken well, why do you strike me?"[16] This is not how he acted in Thomas' case. No, when Thomas was struck in the face while at table, [Christ] avenged the act before he got up by letting the offender be strangled by a beast which afterward tore off the offending hand and put it on the table in front of Saint Thomas.[17] So he will put up with everything else from us before this.[18] No matter how great the sins we might commit, this would be the one for which we could expect the greatest punishment.[19] And all this blindness comes from selfish love and slavish fear. That is why I said I long to see you courageous and fearless men.

But my soul does want to see you grounded in holy and sincere fear of God. This is the kind of fear that nourishes divine love within us. This is the holy fear that keeps God before our eyes so that we would rather die than offend God or harm our neighbor, rather die than do an injustice—or even do something just without looking first to all the circumstances. So

---

[15] Cf. Let. T294 to Sano di Maco and others (in this volume): "Let it not try to make rules for the Holy Spirit, who is himself both rule and giver of the rule."

[16] Jn. 18, 23.

[17] According to the account in the *Legenda aurea* for the feast of St. Thomas, the apostle and the provost of the king of India were once at a banquet. A Jewish flutist there recognized Thomas as a Jew and sang a Hebrew song in praise of the God of the Hebrews. When Thomas asked her to sing again, a steward struck him on the cheek. Thomas said to him, "It is better for you to be punished at once with a punishment which will quickly be over, and to be pardoned in the life to come. Know then that before I leave this table the hand that struck me will be carried away by dogs." The steward later went to get water, when he was attacked and killed by a lion. Dogs tore his body to shreds, and one of them carried his right hand into the banquet hall. The author of the *Legenda aurea* himself says, "This act of vengeance is condemned by Saint Augustine in his book, *Contra Faustum*, and the story is declared apocryphal."

[18] That is, laying down rules for God's servants.

[19] Cf. Mk. 3, 29: "Every sin will be forgiven. . . . but whoever blasphemes against the Holy Spirit will never be forgiven." If Catherine has this passage in mind, she is indeed laying a heavy burden on those who try to lay down rules for God's servants.

you need this holy fear, and with it you will keep possession of both your own city and the city lent to you, nor will the devil or anyone else be able to rob you of it.

Our own city is the city of our soul. We possess it in holy fear based on familial charity, on peace and unity with God and with our neighbors in true solid virtue. But those who live in hatred and rancor and discord, those filled with selfish love, those who live in filthy lust so that there is no difference between them and the pigs, are not in possession of their soul.[20] They have no control over their own city, but are rather controlled by sin and vice. They have so degraded themselves as to be ruled by what is not; they have lost their dignity, that is, grace. They have no appreciation for Christ's blood, the price that was paid for us and that shows us divine mercy and supreme eternal Truth, indescribable love—love that created us and bought us back not with silver but with blood,[21] and revealed to us our own greatness and nobility. Blind indeed are those who do not see such blazing love and how great is the poverty into which they are led when they fall into the darkness of deadly sin.

These people will hardly be in possession of what is lent to them if they don't first of all rule and control themselves. By authority that is lent I mean authority over cities or any other temporal authority that is lent to you and to other people of the world. These are lent for a time, as it pleases divine Goodness and also according to local manners and customs. Either life or death can make them pass away. In any case, they are only lent. Those who are in control of themselves will hold them in holy fear, with well-ordered and not excessive love, as something not their own but on loan. They will guard this loan of authority that is given them with fear and reverence of the one who gave it.

You have this authority from God alone, so that when the Lord asks to have back what was loaned it can be given back without danger of eternal death. I want you, then, to hold it with sincere and holy fear. I tell you, people of the world have no recourse but to live virtuously if they want to preserve their spiritual and their temporal status, for our sin and guilt are our only downfall. So get rid of guilt, and you will be relieved of

---

[20] Cf. Let. T59 to Pietro, priest of Semignano (vol. I): "These days we are seeing the exact opposite of the purity God requires! Not only are they not God's temples carrying the fire of God's word, but they have become stalls, lodgings for pigs and other animals! They carry within the house of their souls the fire of anger, hatred, animosity, and ill will. For they harbor pigs, a filthiness that is incessantly rolling about within them like a pig in the mud!"

[21] Cf. 1 Pt. 1, 18 (Vulg.): "You were bought back . . . not with corruptible gold or silver, but with the precious blood of Christ as a spotless, unblemished lamb."

fear. You will have a heart strong and fearless, and won't be afraid of your own shadow.[22]

I'll say no more. Forgive my presumptuousness. Let my love for you and for all my fellow citizens, and my sadness over your ways and habits (hardly in good order in relation to God!), be my excuse before God and before you. I feel like weeping over our blindness, since it seems we are bereft of light. May God in his infinite goodness and mercy free you from all the darkness of ignorance and enlighten the eye of your understanding to know and discern the truth. That way you will not be able to go astray. I'll say no more here, though I would have much to say.

Dearest brothers and lords, I am responding to the letter I received from Tommaso di Guelfuccio in your name. I thank you for the charity I see you have toward your fellow citizens in seeking their peace and tranquillity, and your charity for poor me, undeserving as I am that you should want me to come or that you should ask me to be a mediator for this reconciliation, since I am inadequate to that task or to any other, no matter how small.[23] I shall, however, let God's adequacy work,[24] and I will bow my head to obey you in so far as the Holy Spirit allows me, to go or to stay according to your pleasure—yet always putting God's will ahead of any human will—for I am certain that with any conscience at all you would not want me to violate God's will in order to do that of human beings. I don't see, therefore, how I could come right now, today.

There is something I must do for the monastery of Sant'Agnesa, and besides, I have to be with Messer Spinello's nephews in regard to the reconciliation of Lorenzo's sons.[25] You know that you began to arrange for this a long time ago already, and it has never been brought to a conclusion. I wouldn't want it to remain unfinished now because of my irresponsibility or my sudden departure; I would be afraid God would reprove me. I will hurry as much as I can, though, as God gives me grace. As for you and the others, be patient, and don't let your minds and hearts be filled with all sorts of fantastic notions, all of which come from the devil, who is trying to impede God's honor and the salvation of souls as well as your own peace and tranquillity.

---

[22] This expression begins to appear only now in Catherine's writings.

[23] The remark seems to imply that they have written to ask her, since she is with the Salimbeni, to serve as mediator in reconciling the Salimbeni with the Commune. (But it also seems they want her to return to Siena, and immediately, for this purpose.) This would, of course, be to the Commune's advantage, since the Salimbeni are in constant conflict with the city, having taken several towns in the territory over the past months, and no attempt on the city's part to retake the fortress in the Val d'Orcia has succeeded.

[24] Cf. 2 Cor. 12, 9 (Vulg.): "My grace is adequate for you, for power is made perfect in weakness."

[25] See the introduction to this letter.

I'm sorry about the energy and effort my fellow citizens are spending in worrying and wagging their tongues over me. It seems they have nothing else to do but speak ill of me and the company that is with me. They are right about me, because I am full of faults; but they are not right about the others. Nevertheless, in suffering we shall win out, for patience is never defeated, but always wins out and remains in command. I'm sorry, because the blows always fall back on the heads of those who deal them, since it is often they who are left with the guilt and suffering.

I'll say no more. Keep living in God's holy and tender love.

Gentle Jesus! Jesus love!

LETTER T294/G245[1]
To Sano di Maco and all her other children in Siena
Mid-August 1377

We have already seen a good number of Catherine's letters addressed to her circle in Siena through the wool-worker Sano di Maco.[2]

The fact that Catherine refers in this letter to others' apparent concern over her having left the community at Belcaro on its own would seem to indicate that she has, in some of her disciples' estimation, been away too long from this monastery which she established in April 1377. Clearly she is also away from Siena, since the letter is addressed to her disciples there. The conclusion must be that she is almost certainly at the Salimbeni fortress, Rocca d'Orcia. Her emphasis on not passing judgment on the servants of God may well be prompted by the rumors of subversive plots which began to rumble in Siena while she was there. She refers to having "begun" to accomplish God's work, which would seem to indicate that she has not been at the Rocca very long. Since she probably arrived there around early August, I would place this letter about mid-August 1377.[3]

§

In the name of Jesus Christ crucified and of gentle Mary.

Dearest children in Christ gentle Jesus,

I Caterina, servant and slave of the servants of Jesus Christ, am writing to you in his precious blood. I long to see you strong and persevering[a] until the end of your life, for I believe that without perseverance none of us can please God or receive the crown as prize. Those who persevere are always[b] strong, and strength makes them persevere.

We really need the gift of strength, for we are besieged by many enemies. There is the world with its pleasures[c] and deceits. There is the devil

---

[1] MSS: Mo-*b*, B, P2, T, R1, R2, P3, P5, F2, S3, Nd; translation and variants based on unpublished notes by Dupré Theseider and A. Volpato.

[2] They are Let. T69/DT24, T147/DT25, T142/DT26 in vol. I and T232/DT75 in this volume.

[3] This placement is strongly supported by the linguistic evidence. All seven letters which share thirteen or more of this one's forty-six analyzed patterns are from July 1377 and later. A number of clusters within individual patterns begin and/or end between August and October of that year: CARITFRT, FALSGIUD, FOGLVENT, FUMO, MANTELLO, ODIOSANT, ORAZVIG, PONLEGGE. Dupré Theseider (unpublished notes) places the letter in 1377, after April. Fawtier (II, pp. 265–266) places it "very probably" while Catherine was at the Rocca, and certainly after the founding of Belcaro.

with all his harassment[d] and temptations. Sometimes he sits on people's tongues to make them speak viciously and grumble, and often he makes them take what is ours, but he does so only to draw us away from love and charity for our neighbors.[4] And the flesh rises up with selfish sensuality, wanting to fight against the spirit. All these enemies of ours have besieged us, but we need have no slavish fear, for they have been conquered by the blood of the spotless Lamb.[5]

To the world we must respond daringly and resist it by despising its pleasures[e] and prestige, discerning that it is neither stable nor enduring. It shows us a long life with flowering youth and great wealth[f]; yet it is clear that these are completely empty.[6] For from life we go to death, from youth to old age, from wealth to poverty, thus always running toward our end in death. We have to open our mind's eye to see how wretched they are who put their trust in the world. In this way we shall begin to despise and hate what we formerly loved.

As for the devil, we must respond to his deceit courageously, seeing that he is weak and can conquer only those who want to be conquered. So let's answer with lively faith and hope, and with a holy self-contempt. This self-contempt will make us patient in the face of every worldly[g] temptation and trying harassment. From whatever source they may come, we shall bear them all with true patience if we hate our selfish sensuality and love being on the cross with Christ crucified.

From living faith we shall draw a will in accord with God's, and we shall extinguish every human judgment from our mind and heart and discern only the will of God,[7] who seeks and wants nothing but that we be

---

[4] Cf. *Dial.* 36, p. 77, where Catherine speaks of the Holy Spirit being on the tongues of God's servants, and Let. T114 to Agnolino Salimbeni (in this volume), where the devil sits "on his servants' tongues making up speeches, fawning, flattering, threatening, criticizing, slandering—all to discourage us and make us weary of our good and holy deeds." Cf. also Filippo degli Agazzari, *Gli assempri, leggende del secolo xiv,* ed. C. F. Carpellini, Siena: I. Gati, 1864, p. 212: "There is certainly no place the devil so likes to be and to dwell as on the tongues of gossipers and detractors."

[5] Again she is basing her message on the three classic enemies: the devil, the world, and the flesh.

[6] Cf. Let. T262 to Tora Gambacorta (1378): "The world once showed itself to you beautiful and pleasurable. Now it has shown that all its joys and pleasures are vain, ephemeral. They bring bitter sadness to those who are excessively attached to them. They rob us of the life of grace and give death, leaving us in the greatest misery and poverty. It is good, then, to flee from the world and to hate our selfish sensuality and all worldly pleasure, despising them with all our heart and soul, and to serve only our wonderful Creator."

[7] Cf. Mt. 16, 23; Rom. 12, 2. Catherine seems to be drawing on the sense of both passages here and elsewhere when she speaks of discerning God's will, often in contrast with judging by human standards, for example, in *Dial.* 100, pp. 187–192, where she dedicates an entire chapter to the theme.

made holy.[8] In this way we do not find our neighbors a stumbling block; we don't complain about them or pass judgment on those who talk about us unfavorably. We condemn only ourselves, seeing that it is God's will that permits them to harass us for our own good.

Oh how blessed are they who clothe themselves in so sweet a discernment![i] They do not condemn the world's servants who wrong them. They pass no judgment on the servants of God by wanting to make them do as they would, as do many proud and presumptuous people who under the cloak of God's honor and the salvation of souls find scandal in God's servants. Under cover of this cloak they take to grumbling and say, "I don't like how they live." Thus they upset themselves, and with their words they upset others, making it appear that what they say is motivated by love—and so it seems to them. But if they open their eyes[h] they will discover the worm[j] of opinionated presumption. They let this perverse opinionatedness sit as judge, passing judgment by their own standards and not according to God's mysteries and all the holy ways he works in his creatures. Let human pride be ashamed, and let it be willing to see that in the eternal Father's house there are many dwellings.[9] Let it not try to make rules for the Holy Spirit, who is himself both rule and giver of the rule.[10] Nor let it set limits for the one who cannot be limited.

God's true servants, clothed in his supreme eternal will, will not do this. They will in fact reverence the ways and actions and habits of his servants because they discern that they are not a human affair but God's. Though we may not like some things and though they may not go as we are accustomed to having them go, we should assume and believe that they are pleasing to God. For we must not and cannot pass judgment on anything except what is plainly and expressly seen to be sinful. And those who are in love with God and have lost themselves don't see even this in

---

[8] 1 Thes. 4, 3.

[9] Jn. 14, 2. Cf. Let. T64 to William Flete (1378): "They do not sit in judgment on God's servants or anyone else, but rejoice in every situation and every way of living they see, saying, 'Thanks to you, eternal Father, that you have so many rooms in your house!' And they are happier with the many different ways they see than if they were to see everyone walking the same way, because this way they see the greatness of God's goodness more fully revealed."

[10] Cf. Let T50 to Caterina di Ghetto (in this volume): "See that you don't act like those stupid and senseless people who want to appoint themselves as both investigators and judges of what God's servants do and how they live. Such people are deserving of severe reproach. Realize that wanting to make God's servants walk the same way we do is nothing less than an attempt to regulate and legislate for the Holy Spirit—which is absolutely impossible." Also Let. T247 to Giovanna di Corrado Maconi and Let. T123 to the Defenders of Siena (both in this volume); and *Dial.* 68, pp. 129–130.

a judgmental way but in displeasure for the sin and offense against God, and with great compassion for the soul of the sinner, for whose salvation they would gladly give themselves over to any torment.[11]

Now this is the perfection I am inviting you to, dearest children. Try with all true and holy eagerness to acquire it. And reflect that such true and holy discernment will give you every perfection without any scandal[k] or pain. Rash judgment, on the other hand, causes every sort of pain and guilt and grumbling and ruinous disloyalty toward God's servants. All of this comes from selfish passion and deep-rooted pride that takes to judging people's intentions. Those who do this are always turning back.[l] They don't persevere in loving their neighbors, nor do they ever have a strong and enduring love. Theirs is, in fact, like the imperfect love Christ's disciples had before his passion.[12] Because his presence gave them so much pleasure, they loved him. But because their love was not grounded in truth but in their pleasure and enjoyment, it failed when he was no longer present. They didn't know how to suffer with Christ, but fled in fear. Look out, look out, lest this be true of you! You very much enjoy a person's presence, but in that person's absence you go up in smoke like a straw fire which, when no one is present, is put out by any little wind or rain—so that nothing remains but the black smoke of a darkened conscience.[13]

All this happens because we have become judges of other people's intentions and of the ways and habits of God's servants, rather than discerning God's gentle will. No more of this now, for love of Christ crucified! Be faithful children, strong and persevering in Christ gentle Jesus, and so you will conquer the devil's temptations and the words he speaks by sitting on people's tongues.[14]

As for our last enemy, the poor flesh with its sensual desires, let it be conquered with the flesh of Christ, scourged and nailed to the wood of the

---

[11] Cf. *Dial.* 100, p. 191: "When you cannot see clearly and openly whether the sin is deadly, you must not pass judgment on it in your mind, but be concerned only about my will for that person. And if you do see it, you must respond not with judgment but with holy compassion."

[12] Mt. 26, 56. Cf. Let. T94 to Matteo di Francesco Tolomei (in this volume), where she develops at greater length this theme of the imperfection of Peter's love for Christ.

[13] The only other instance in which she uses the contrast of straw fire and smoke is in Let. T114 to Agnolino Salimbeni. There, however, the image refers to the excitement over Agnolino's sister Bandeçça's marriage and its aftermath. Note, however, that the two letters are quite close in time.

[14] Since it is her disciples she is chiding for rash judgment here, the judgment in question may be something other than Catherine's activities, or it may be that even some of her disciples are uneasy about her association with the Salimbeni.

most holy cross.[15] Tame it with fasting, vigils, and continual prayer, and with sweet blazing and loving desire.

This, then, is the gentle way we shall defeat and vanquish our enemies with the power of Christ's blood. This is how you will fulfill his will and my desire, which suffers when it considers how imperfect we are.[16] I trust in God's infinite goodness that he will assuage my desire in your regard. So I beg you not to be indifferent, but conscientious. Don't be leaves whirling in the wind. No, be firm, stable, and constant, loving one another with a true familial charity, bearing and putting up with each others' faults. By this I will know whether you love God, and me as well, who desire nothing but to see you truly united.

Love, love one another! Immerse yourselves in the blood of Christ crucified and hide yourselves in his wonderful wounds. I'll say no more.

I commend to you the monastery of Santa Maria degli Angeli.[17] Don't be surprised that I'm not there, for good children do more when their mother is away than when she is there, because they want to show their love for her and get more into her good graces.

I'll say no more. Keep living in God's holy and tender love.

Gentle Jesus! Jesus love![m]

Please, Sano, read this letter to all my children. And all of you pray to God for us, so that he will allow us to accomplish what is for his honor (as we have begun to do) and the salvation of souls. We want to have no other desire, no other work, despite those who wanted and still want to prevent it.[18,n]

May God fill you with his sweetest grace![o]

Textual Notes

a. R2, Nd: *constant / persevering.*

b. R2, Nd: [*always*]

---

[15] Cf. Let. T257/DT50 to Conte di Monna Agnola and companions (in this volume): "Our flesh has been conquered by his flesh scourged, macerated, saturated with disgrace on the wood of the most holy cross, and in the end raised above all the choirs of angels in the resurrection of God's Son."

[16] It is not clear whether she means that Christ's will suffers, or her own desire. The next sentence would seem to point to the latter.

[17] The monastery for nuns that Catherine has just established in the former fortress at Belcaro, given her by Nanni di Ser Vanni.

[18] This is probably a reference to the objections the Sienese government was raising to her being in the Val d'Orcia, a concern which may also be reflected in her dwelling in this letter on rash judgment.

c. R2, Nd: *wealth / pleasures.*
d. B, P2: *adversity*; R2, Nd: *malice / harassment.*
e. R2, Nd: *wealth / pleasures.*
f. R2, Nd: *pleasures and wealth / wealth.*
g. P5, F2: [*worldly*].
h. B, P2, R1, T, R2, P5, P3, Nd, F2: *mind's eye / eyes.*
i. B, P2, T, R2, Nd, F2: [*Oh . . . discernment!*]
j. P5, F2: *light / worm.*
k. P2: *doubt / scandal*; B: [*scandal or*].
l. R2, Nd: *turning the time / turning back* (probably a scribal error).
m. Only Mo has *I'll say. . . . Jesus love!*
n. B, P2, R1, T, P5, P3 add: *Keep living, etc.*; R2, Nd end: *Keep living in God's holy and tender love, and may he fill you with his sweetest grace! Gentle Jesus! Jesus love!*; Nd adds besides: *Amen. Amen.*
o. B, P2, R1, T, P3: *Gentle Jesus! Jesus love!*; F2: *Keep living in Christ gentle Jesus. Amen.*; S3 (in margin): *This monastery [Belcaro] is mentioned in ch. xii of the deposition of Fra Tommaso d'Antonio, etc.*

Letter T250/G65[1]

To Fra Giovanni di Gano da Orvieto, abbot of Sant'Antimo
Late August 1377

Catherine has supported Giovanni di Gano da Orvieto in the reform of his monastery, located about thirteen miles west of Rocca d'Orcia.[2] He in turn has assisted her in the foundation of her convent at Belcaro. Now she has apparently promised to come to Sant'Antimo.

Both her references to complaints about her activities and the fact that Raimondo will accompany her to Sant'Antimo would place this letter during Catherine's early days at Rocca d'Orcia, before Raimondo's mid-September departure for Rome. Such a placement is supported by the linguistic evidence .[3]

§

In the name of Jesus Christ crucified and of gentle Mary.

Dearest father in Christ gentle Jesus,

I Caterina, servant and slave of the servants of Jesus Christ, am writing to you in his precious blood. I long to see you enlightened with the true and wonderful[a] light our souls need. I mean, I want you to open your mind's eye to see and contemplate God's supreme eternal will within us, and to use that will as your standard of judgment.[4]

This is the dear vision that makes us wise, no longer ignorant. It makes us careful, not thoughtlessly[b] passing judgment on other people's intentions (as God's servants in their zealous love often do under pretext of virtue). This light makes us virtuous, no longer fearful. We discern God's will for us with due reverence. That is, we see that whatever God permits, whether persecution or consolation, whether from human or diabolic

---

[1] MSS: Mo-*b*, B, P2, R1, P3, P5, F2, S2, P4; translation based on Mo-*b*, with variants based on an unpublished transcription by Dupré Theseider.

[2] Cf. Let. T12 (vol. I).

[3] All but one of the letters which share heavily with this one are very long and are spread from September 1377 through 1379. (The one which is nearer this one in length is from September 1377.) A number of significant clusters within individual patterns, however, point fairly strongly to the Val d'Orcia period: FALSGIUD, GIUDICVO, LABORE, PRUDENT, SPECUL, VOLONTA. Fawtier (II, p. 189) places the letter near mid-1377 "with the necessary reservations." Dupré Theseider (unpublished notes) places it at Rocca d'Orcia, "where she has been at least two months." Meattini (*Epistolario*, p. 1484) believes it was sent from Genoa, as Catherine was returning from Avignon in September 1376.

[4] Cf. Mt. 16, 23 (Vulg.): "You are judging by human standards, not by God's."

sources, it is all done to make us holy.[5] So we rejoice in God's boundless charity and trust his providence to provide for our every need. God's giving is always well measured, and if he increases the measure he increases our strength. This we see and know when our mind's eye is enlightened and we come to recognize God's will, and are therefore made lovers of that will.

I tell you, this light does not pass judgment on the intentions of God's servants or anyone else. No, it discerns and reverences the fact that the Holy Spirit is guiding them. Therefore it isn't so bold as to grumble that they are being influenced by other people. No, it assumes they are being guided by God alone.

Still, we could ask, "Is there any servant of God so enlightened that no one could possibly see more than that person?" No. In fact, it is necessary that God's servants share with each other the light and the gifts and graces they receive from God in order to display God's magnificence and maintain the order of charity, and to show that the light and magnificence of gentle Truth himself is not limited but infinite. It also makes us humble ourselves and recognize God's light and grace in his servants. God sets his servants up as fountains, this one with one sort of water and that one with another. They are put in this life both to give themselves life and for the comfort and refreshment of God's other servants who are thirsty for these sorts of water, that is, all the different gifts and graces God puts into his servants.[6] This is how God meets our needs.

So it is true that no one is so enlightened as not to need light from others—and often. On the other hand, those who are truly enlightened by this gentle will of God's give light by the light of faith. They don't grumblingly pass judgment on or find a stumbling block in those they would counsel. Neither their giving of counsel nor its results cause them pain.[7] What I mean is that if the other accepts their advice they are glad, but if he or she doesn't accept it, they quietly discern that it is not without mystery[8] and necessity and providence and God's will. And so they remain peaceful and calm and without pain. For they are clothed in God's will. Nor do they wear themselves out talking, peddling their view of things to others. Instead they try to restrain their own views and immerse them in God's sweet view of things, offering to God any doubt or fear they might

---

[5] 1 Thes. 4, 3.

[6] This image is unique here. By "giving themselves life" she presumably means that one drinks also from the fountain of divine life within oneself. Cf. Jn. 4, 14 (Vulg.): "Whoever drinks the water I give will never be thirsty. No, the water I give will become a fountain within that person, leaping up to provide eternal life."

[7] It. *ma per sì facto modo che sta e rimane sença pena.*

[8] It. *misterio,* which for Catherine always connotes divine action.

have about them. They generously surrender themselves to God along with their doubts about their neighbors. This, then is the gentle wisdom in which those who are enlightened by this true light move or stay where they are, and so they enjoy eternal life [even] in this life.

It is just the opposite with those who are foolish, even though they are serving God. They are really serving only themselves with their judgments and opinions disguised as virtue and loving zeal. And this frequently leads to serious sin and grumbling and scandal. This is why we need the true unadulterated light. But I don't see how we can really have it except by getting rid of our own clouded darkness, by toppling our own opinions rather than holding on to them.

Oh glorious light! Oh you who are immersed in the light! You are lost in it, because you see yourself not for yourself, but see only the light within you. And in that light you see and judge your neighbors. So you see and love your neighbors and respect them in the light, and not according to your own view or any rash judgment passed under the guise of loving zeal.

It is good, then, to look at things with our mind's eye open and our will immersed and lost [in the light]. This is how, by the light of true love and in reverence for God's will and that of his servants, we will acquire the light and achieve true and perfect purity, and no longer find a stumbling block in God's servants. For we will not set ourselves up as their judges. Rather we will find encouragement in them, and will be happy with whatever they do, whether they move or stay where they are, because we will have discerned and seen God's will in them.

So up, dearest father and son! Let's put our mouths to the breast of divine charity and there taste this sweet pleasant milk that will bring us to the perfection of the saints and make us follow the Lamb's rule and example. Then we will be freed from fear. We will throw ourselves into thorns and difficulties and not evade hardship.[9] Instead we shall grieve over the sin of the grumblers and over human scandal, and shall carry these into God's presence with great compassion. And we shall pursue the holy works we have begun for God's honor and the salvation of souls, and in his gentle will we shall complete them. I won't say any more about this affair, except this. Let's immerse ourselves in the blood of Christ crucified without any fear whatever, knowing that if God is for us no one can be against us.[10]

---

[9] Cf. *Dial.* 44, p. 90, where she calls the will's decision a thorn bush. "Beforehand, this decision is a thorn bush they seem to encounter when they follow the way of truth. Conscience always pulls in one direction, and sensuality in the other. But as soon as they decide courageously, despising themselves, and say, 'I want to follow Christ crucified,' the thorn bush is broken and they discover my immeasurable tenderness."

[10] Rom. 8, 31

I don't know when I will be able to come; I have no way of knowing how long I will stay here.[11] I will hurry as much as I can, but my staying or moving on will always be dictated not by human will but by God's gentle will. I want you to realize, you and the others who let your hearts be burdened with so much pain and so many imaginings, that I with all my infirmities neither stay put nor go about wearing myself out at my own whim, but only as I am driven by God for his honor and the salvation of souls.[12] So if weak hearts choose to find evil in good, there is nothing I can do about it. It mustn't make me turn back and give up the plowing.[13] If I did it would seem that we were plowing at some human behest, and then the weeds would come up and choke the grain.[14]

I'll say no more. Keep living in God's holy and tender love.

Gentle Jesus! Jesus love!

Textual Notes

a. P5 adds *and most perfect.*

b. P3 adds *or carelessly.*

---

[11] It seems Catherine's plans for her work at Rocca d'Orcia are still open-ended.

[12] These remarks would seem to indicate that Giovanni himself has not been totally supportive of Catherine's mission to the Val d'Orcia.

[13] Lk. 9, 62.

[14] Mt. 13, 25.

Letter T118/G175[1]
To Caterina dello Spedaluccio and Giovanna di Capo, in Siena
Mid-August to early September 1377

Caterina dello Spedaluccio and Giovanna di Capo are both members of the Sienese *Mantellate* and disciples of Catherine.[2] As Catherine writes this letter to them, she has been at the Rocca at least long enough for the Dominicans Bartolomeo Dominici and Matteo Tolomei to have spent some time at Montepulciano (or perhaps at Siena) and for Alessa dei Saracini and a certain Bruna to have gone on to Montegiovi with the countess Benedetta (Bandeçça) Salimbeni and her sister Isa. Yet, the fact that Raimondo is still with Catherine has to place it almost certainly before mid-September, by which time he will have left for Rome. This placement is broadly supported by the linguistic data.[3]

§

In the name of Jesus Christ crucified and of gentle Mary.

Dearest daughters in Christ gentle Jesus,

I Caterina, servant and slave of the servants of Jesus Christ, am writing to you in his precious blood. I long to see you obedient daughters, one in true and perfect charity. This obedience and love will make all pain and darkness melt away for you. For obedience frees us from the source of pain, our perverse selfish will, which holy[a] obedience drowns and kills.[4] And darkness is dispersed and consumed by the force of unitive charity, because God is true charity and supreme eternal light.[b] This is why I want you, dearest daughters, to work hard at letting go of your own will and having this light, because it is so necessary.

This, as I still remember, is the teaching you were given—though you haven't learned it very well. I beg you, dearest daughters, to do what you

---

[1] MSS: B, P2, R1, T, P5, F2, F1, P3; translation based on R1, with variants based on an unpublished galley by Dupré Theseider, as proofread against B by A. Volpato.

[2] She will write Let. T214 (in this volume) to these same two women a bit later.

[3] Only one other letter shares five of this one's thirteen analyzed patterns, and it (Let. T101) is from early 1376. However, significant clusters beginning and/or ending in autumn of 1377 (DIMIAMOR, OBEDPENT, VOLONTA) reinforce placement of the letter at that time. Dupré Theseider (unpublished notes) places the letter in mid-September 1377, assuming that Catherine did not reach Rocca d'Orcia until near that time. Fawtier (II, p. 224) places the letter between October and December 1377.

[4] This theme is developed in *Dial.* 45, pp. 91 94. It occurs also in Bernard de Clairvaux, *In tempo Resurrectionis sermo III*, 3 (PL CLXXXIII, 290): "Let selfish will cease and there will be no hell. For where else does that fire rage but in the selfish will?"

haven't done. Unless you do, you will be in continual pain, and you will bring the same on wretched me, who deserve every sort of pain. We should be acting for God's honor, as did the holy apostles. After they had received the Holy Spirit, they left one another as well as that gentle mother Mary.[5] Though they would have been very happy to stay together, they let go of their selfish pleasure to seek God's honor and the salvation of souls. And they didn't think, because Mary sent them away, that her love was for all that diminished or that they no longer had her affection. This is the rule we have to take for ourselves.

I know my presence is a great comfort to you. Still, you as obedient women should for God's honor and the salvation of souls give up the pursuit of your own selfish comfort. Don't yield to the devil, who makes it seem you have been deprived of my loving affection for you, body and soul. Otherwise [your love] would not have its foundation in God.[c] I am certain of this, that I love you only for God's sake. And why are you suffering so inordinately over things that really have to be done? What ever will we do when we have to do great things, if we fall so far short in little ones? We will have to be sometimes together, sometimes apart, according to circumstances. Right now our gentle Savior allows us and in fact wants us to be apart for his honor.

You are in Siena; Cecca and Grandma are at Montepulciano;[6] Frate Bartolomeo and Frate Matteo have been there and will be there again.[7] Alessa and Monna Bruna are at Montegiovi, eighteen miles from Montepulciano. They are with the Countess and Madonna Isa.[8] Frate Raimondo, Frate Tommaso, Monna Tomma, Lisa and I are at the Rocca among the

---

[5] This is a comparison frequently invoked by Catherine when she is preaching detachment from those one loves. Cf. especially Let. T164/DT58 to Melina Barbani (in this volume).

[6] Just as Catherine's disciples called her "Mamma," so they often called Lapa "Grandma" (*Nonna*). Let. T117 to Lapa (in this volume), also documents the presence of the two women at the Monastery of Sant'Agnesa in Montepulciano, where they have apparently stayed while Catherine has gone on to the Rocca.

[7] Bartolomeo Dominici and Matteo Tolomei have been with Catherine at Rocca d'Orcia, and she apparently is aware that they have been at Montepulciano and will be going there again—unless "there" is Siena, which it could be if Matteo has indeed gone to visit his sick sister as his mother has begged in the message to which Catherine responds with Let. T120 (in this volume).

[8] The identity of Monna Bruna is unknown; she is not listed among the *Mantellate* in 1378. Montegiovi is on Monte Amiata, thirty miles from Siena. Catherine thinks it useful to specify its distance from Montepulciano, as if she thinks her Sienese friends may not know where it is. E. Lazzareschi, *S. Caterina da Siena in Val d'Orcia*, p. 42, deduces from a mutilated passage at the end of Let. T119 (to Alessa, in this volume) that the object of the mission to Montegiovi was the conversion of the unnamed woman mentioned in that passage.

scoundrels,[9] and so many demons incarnate are being eaten up that Frate Tommaso says he has a stomach ache! And with all this they aren't satisfied; they have an appetite for more, and are finding work here at good wages![10,d] Beg divine goodness to give them huge bittersweet mouthfuls. You can imagine how sweet it is to see God being honored and souls being saved! You should neither want nor desire anything else. There is nothing you could do that would be more pleasing to God's supreme eternal will and mine.

So up, my daughters! Begin to make a sacrifice of your will to God! Don't be satisfied to keep living on milk forever; we have to get the teeth of our desire ready to chew on bread that is hard and moldy, if necessary.[11]

I'll say no more. Bind yourselves in the sweet bond of charity; that's the only way you will prove that you are daughters. Take heart in Christ gentle Jesus. And encourage all my other daughters. . . .[12] We'll be back as soon as we can—as it pleases divine goodness.[13] Keep living in God's holy and tender love. . . .[e]

Textual Notes

a. B: *true holy / holy.*
b. B, P2 skip from the first occurrence of *charity* to the second.
c. P3: *you / God.*
d. P2, T: [*pezzo*]; P3: *peso / prezzo.*
e. B has the usual ending. T adds *Mary*! P3: *Gentle Jesus! Jesus and Mary, love*! F1: *I'll say no more. Keep living in Christ gentle Jesus.* F2: *I'll say no more. Keep living in Christ gentle Jesus, love.*

---

[9] With Catherine at Rocca d'Orcia, then, are Raimondo da Capua, Tommaso dalla Fonte (as Francesco Malavolti also testifies in the *Processo Castellano*), Catherine's sister-in-law Lisa, and a certain Monna Tomma (that is, Tommasa—though F1 and F2 call her Antonia) whose identity is unknown. The "scoundrels" (It. *mascalzoni*, an expression she uses only here) may be the Salimbeni men, in whose feuds Catherine has had to intervene, or they may be the crowds who are coming for confession. It is clear from what follows that she is being quite playful about the situation.

[10] A rather humorous version of Catherine's much-used image of "eating souls." Raimondo (*Life* II, vii, 239, p. 227) and Francesco Malavolti (*Processo Castellano*, ed. Laurent, pp. 384–390) speak of the crowds who gathered to hear Catherine preach, so that the priests who accompanied her to hear confessions were kept more than busy.

[11] Cf. 1 Cor. 3, 1–2; Heb. 5, 13–14. Cf. also Let. T296 to Giovanni dalle Celle (in this volume), where she says we "cannot eat [this food] in truth without suffering a great deal."

[12] At this point there were probably specific greetings and possibly other personal notes, omitted by editors who were compiling the letters for purposes of spiritual edification.

[13] Back, that is, in Siena. The presence of Raimondo indicates that Catherine and her company have not been at the Rocca for more than the "several weeks" Raimondo says he spent there before going to Rome. At least at this point Catherine seems to have no long-range plans for staying in the Val d'Orcia.

Letter T122/G304[1]
To the goldsmith Salvi di Messer Pietro, in Siena
Late August to early September 1377

Salvi di Pietro was a member of the Company of the Virgin at Santa Maria della Scala in Siena,[2] as were a number of Catherine's other disciples. This letter indicates that rumors are continuing to fly in Siena concerning Catherine's activities "in the lands of the Salimbeni" and that Catherine has already had some communication with her disciples on this matter. It is also clear that Raimondo da Capua is still with the company in the Val d'Orcia, a fact that would place the letter after Catherine's arrival there but before Raimondo's departure for Rome. I would therefore place this letter a bit later than the one in which Catherine has complained to Sano di Maco and the others about these rumors (Let. T294) but before mid-September, when Raimondo will no longer be with Catherine's company.[3]

§

In the name of Jesus Christ crucified and of gentle Mary.

Dearest son in Christ gentle Jesus,

I Caterina, servant and slave of the servants of Jesus Christ, am writing to you in his precious blood. I long to see you a truly faithful servant of Christ crucified. I want neither prosperity nor adversity ever to make you turn back. No, [go on] courageously in living faith, for you know that faith without deeds is dead.[4] And faith is put into action in our conceiving the virtues within us through love's impulse, and in our giving birth to their fruits in true patience. We do this through the mediation of our neighbors, when we mutually put up with and share the burden of each others' shortcomings.[5]

---

[1] MSS: Mo-*b*, T, R1, P3, S3, B, P2, P5, F2; translation based on Mo-*b*, with variants based on unpublished notes by A. Volpato.

[2] E. Lucchesi, in "Santa Caterina da Siena e le sue relazioni con i Monaci di Vallombrosa," *Memorie Domenicane* 65 (1948): pp. 197–227, says that it seems that Salvi di Pietro joined the confraternity at Catherine's urging.

[3] This placement is supported by the linguistic evidence. All but one of the fourteen letters which share eighteen or more of this one's seventy analyzed patterns are from September 1377 or later. More telling, however, are the significant clusters within individual patterns which begin and/or end between September and December 1377: AMORFEDE, COGNDIFT, LUMEVEST, PAZZPROV, PERDAMOR, PROSPER, PRUDENT, RICRGRAZ, SERVFEDE, VERITCRE.

[4] Jas. 2, 17.

[5] Cf. *Dial.* 74, pp. 136–137: "I gave her a share in this love, which is the Holy Spirit,

It would not be enough for us and for our salvation to have received just the form of faith and divine grace when we received holy baptism.[6] True, this is enough for the little child who dies very young[a] and receives eternal life purely through the mediation of the blood of the Lamb.[7] Once we have reached maturity, though, merely having been baptized is not enough. We must also make use of the light of faith in love. Compare it with physical sight. Though we may have eyes, and those eyes may be clear[b] and healthy enough for seeing, unless we freely choose for love of the light to open them (for we can), one might say that even though we have eyes, in a sense we do not.[8] We have eyes because of our Creator's goodness, but we don't have their power because in our sinful self-will we don't open them. In that sense we can say that our eyes are dead and ineffectual.

So, dearest son, God in his infinite goodness has given us our mind's eye, and fills that eye by giving us the light of faith in holy baptism. Besides, he gives us back our freedom of choice by freeing [our will] from the bonds of original sin. Then, once we have reached the age of reason, he asks us to use our free choice, in love for the light, to choose freely to open this eye that he has given us.

Once we see, then, that we have eyes to see, we ought to open them to our Creator. And by what light should we set about seeing in God? Love alone. For nothing can be done, either spiritually or materially, without love. So if I want to love the things of sense, that is where my eye settles to find its pleasure. And if I want to love and serve God, my mind's eye opens and focuses on God.

Love attracts love. That is, when I see that God loves me supremely, I can't help loving him in return. Seeing that I am created in God's image

---

within her will by making her will strong to endure suffering and to leave her house in my name to give birth to the virtues for her neighbors. Not that she abandons the house of self-knowledge, but the virtues conceived by the impulse of love come forth from that house."

[6] "Form" here has the philosophical sense of the principle which determines and gives coherence to all of the observable characteristics of a given entity. Cf. *Dial.* 98, p. 185: "In baptism, through the power of my only-begotten Son's blood, you received the form of faith."

[7] Cf. Aquinas, *Summa Theologica*, III, q. 69, a. 6: "Some of the early writers held that children do not receive grace and virtues in baptism, but that they receive the imprint of the character of Christ, by the power of which they receive grace and virtue when they arrive at the perfect age. But this is evidently false, for two reasons. First, children like adults are made members of Christ in baptism, so they must necessarily receive an outpouring of grace and virtue from their Head. Secondly, if this were not true, children who die after baptism would not enter eternal life."

[8] Cf. Cavalca, *Specchio di croce*, p. 215: "Understanding is an eye for the soul, and if it is not clear and clean, the soul cannot see. This is why St. Bernard says, 'Pure truth can be seen only with a pure eye.' "

and likeness and created anew to grace by the blood of God's only-begotten Son makes me let go of my sensual love and conceive a true love. My eye has found the light, and the light itself has made me love the light. And so I never let up trying to hate and flee from whatever would deprive me of the light, and to love and desire whatever will give it to me. So I rise up with living faith and conceive the virtues as my children, longing to clothe myself in God's supreme eternal will, since this eye and the light of faith have shown my appetite God's will, which wants only that we be made holy.[9]

And who reveals this to us most clearly? The Word, God's Son, who came in the chariot of our humanness, filled with love's fire, and with his blood showed us the Father's will so that it might be realized in us.[10] For that sweet will with which God had created us to give us eternal life was not being realized in us because of our sin; we had lost it. And so God sent us the Son to show it to us, to make it clear, when he gave him up to the shameful death of the cross. And whatever he gives us or permits us is for this purpose only, that we may share in his supreme eternal beauty.

If we are wise, then, once we have opened our eyes by the light of faith, we pick up a holy sense of judgment, discerning not by human standards but in terms of God's holy will, which wants only our good.[11]

Do you know what comes from this light? A water peaceful, clear, and unpolluted; a water undisturbed by impatience in adversity, or by the devil's harassment, or by injury, persecution, or other people's grumbling.[12] We are never moved; we remain still, because we have seen that God permits these things for our good, to give us the destiny for which we were created. This is the way; there is no other for us. So we have to pass through all sorts of thorns and briars, following Christ crucified because he

---

[9] 1 Thes. 4, 3.

[10] Cf. *Dial.* 58, p. 112: "The fiery chariot of my only-begotten Son came bringing the fire of my charity to your humanity with such overflowing mercy that the penalty for sins people commit was taken away." Also Prayer 18, p. 156: "O Mary, chariot of fire, you bore the fire hidden and veiled under the ashes of your humanness." The comparison is to the biblical chariot in which Elijah was taken up to heaven (2 Kg. 2, 11), from whence he was expected to return. Thus, in Jn. 1, 21, John the Baptist is asked whether he is Elijah and in Mt. 16, 14, when Jesus asks his disciples who people say he is, they respond that some think he is Elijah.

[11] Cf. Mt. 16, 23; Rm. 12, 2. Catherine seems to be drawing on the sense of both passages here and elsewhere when she speaks of judging in terms of God's will, often in contrast with judging by human standards, for example, in *Dial.* 100, pp. 187–192, where she dedicates an entire chapter to the theme.

[12] Cf. *Dial.* 167, p. 365: "Truly this light [of faith] is a sea, for it nourishes the soul in you, peaceful sea, eternal Trinity. Its water is not sluggish; so the soul is not afraid because she knows the truth. It distills, revealing hidden things, so that here, where the most abundant light of your faith abounds, the soul has, as it were, a guarantee of what she believes."

is the way. He told us so: that he is way and truth and life.[13] So those who keep to this way are indeed following the truth, for in them is realized the will of the Father, who is leading us to the destiny for which we were created. If there had been any other way for us, he would have said that no one could come to the Father except through the Father. But he did not say that, because the Father cannot suffer. The Son can. And since we have to travel the way of suffering, we have to follow Christ crucified.[14,c] And I tell you, we will not be disturbed by inordinate affection and desire in worldly prosperity, but will trample it underfoot. We will treat it with scorn when we see by the light of faith that these are transitory things that pass like the wind, and those who desire and possess them with undue attachment are cheated by them of both the way and the light of grace.

If we act as I have described, we give birth in living faith to living children[15] for God's honor and our neighbors' salvation. For it is through our neighbors that our love for God is proved. Why? Because our love can be of no service to God, but God wants us to do him service through the intermediary he has given us, our neighbors, by bearing with their shortcomings, by carrying them before God in compassion, by enduring with patience the wrongs they do us, and by treating God's servants with due reverence.[16] If we act in any other way, we may say that[d] our faith is dead, never put into action.

I am not, for all that, saying that our sensuality will not often feel contradicted, but such contradiction doesn't detract from our perfection. In fact, it contributes to our being granted perfection, because we become more aware of our shortcomings, and more aware of God's goodness in keeping our will from turning back and consenting to our sensual feelings by taking pleasure in them, but rather [prompting us to] set these feelings right through our self-contempt.[17] Thus through self-knowledge we reap the virtue of humility from these feelings, and through knowledge of God's goodness to us we reap charity. This is why I said that I long to see you grounded in the light of living faith, because I know it is so wonderful and so necessary that without it we cannot have the life of grace. And that

---

[13] Cf. Jn. 14, 6: "I am way and truth and life. No one comes to the Father except through me." In *Dial.* 44, p. 90, Catherine compares the thorn bush to the decision to follow Christ crucified. Once the decision is made, once one has passed through the thorns to enter upon the bridge that is Christ, one experiences God's care and tenderness.

[14] So also *Dial.* 96, pp. 179–182, as well as 53, p. 106.

[15] That is, the virtues.

[16] For the concept that we cannot be of any service to God directly but must serve God in our neighbors, cf. *Dial.* 64, p. 161.

[17] This is the concept of the "good and holy will" Catherine so often speaks of as a sure sign that God is within the soul even when it is besieged by temptation.

is why I said that I long to see you a faithful servant, never unfaithful to Christ crucified. So I beg you, rouse yourself from the slumber of apathy and get up, truly and perfectly conscientious. Open your mind's eye to God's love for you so that you may realize God's will and my desire for you. I'll say no more here.

Here is my answer, dearest son, to the letter[e] you sent me. I was especially happy when I saw there a little bit of what God has revealed to a servant of his.[18] I mean that those who call themselves [my] children have taken scandal because of the tricks of the devils who were lurking within them to steal the seed the Holy Spirit had sown in them. Unwise as they were and not firmly grounded on the living rock, they put up no resistance. Instead they have sown in others the same scandal they were feeling, and all under the pretext of virtue and love! So now I'm telling you emphatically:[f] it is God's will that I stay here.[19] All the rumors and suspicions heaped on both me and my father Frate Raimondo had made me fear that I was offending God by my staying. But to satisfy my tremendous desire, that Truth who cannot lie clarified the matter for same servant of his. "Continue to eat at the table where I have put you," he said. "I have put you at the table of the cross to eat—in your[g] pain, with all these grumblings—to seek and savor my honor and the salvation of souls. I have put these souls, in this place, into your hands so that they may be rescued from the devils' hands and be reconciled with me and with their neighbors. You are not to leave them until what has been begun is finished. The devil is sowing all this evil just to prevent all this good. Go back then, and don't be afraid; I will be on your side."[20]

Because of what was said to this servant of God my soul was at peace. I am trying to do whatever good I can, though that may be less than perfect, for God's honor, the salvation of souls, and the welfare of our city.[21] And I am happy to be following in the footsteps of my Creator, and to be treated badly for the good I do. In return for my doing them honor they disgrace me; for giving them life they want to do me to death. But what they consider death is life to us, and to us what they consider disgrace is honor. Those who are guilty of sin are the ones who are disgraced. But where there is no guilt there is neither disgrace nor fear of punishment. My trust is not in human beings but *in Domino nostro Jesu*

---

[18] Catherine is referring to herself in the third person, as she so often does where God's revelation to her is concerned. She goes on to say that this is how she knows of her disciples' collusion in the gossip about her.

[19] The emphasis may indicate that this letter is a bit later than T294 to Sano di Maco and the others, in which she has complained about the same "rumor-mongering."

[20] Cf. Rom. 8, 31: "If God is for us, who can be against us?"

[21] That is, Siena.

Christo.[22] Here is what I shall do. They give me slander and persecution,[h] and I will give tears and continual prayer as much as God gives me grace. Whether the devils want it or not, I will do my best to use[i] my life for God's honor and the salvation of souls throughout the whole world, and especially for my city.

The citizens of Siena are acting shamefully in believing or imagining that we are about to be contriving plots in the lands of the Salimbeni or anywhere else in the world. They are afraid of God's servants but not of wicked people. Yet the latter are prophesying and they are unaware of it. They are prophesying as Caiphas did when he prophesied that one man should die for the people so that they[j] would not perish. He didn't know what he was saying—but the Holy Spirit knew well, for the Spirit was prophesying through Caiphas' mouth.[23] That's how it is with my fellow citizens. They believe that plots are being devised by me or by my companions. They are telling the truth without knowing it. They are prophesying. For there is nothing I want to do, or want those with me to do, except to plot to defeat the devil and snatch from him the control over people that he has seized because of deadly sin, and to plot to take hatred from their hearts and reconcile them with Christ crucified and with their neighbors. These are the plots we are about, and I want all who are with me to be about these plots. I am sorry we are so remiss that we do it only halfheartedly. So I'm begging you, my dear son, and tell all the others too, to pray to God that I may be really zealous about doing this and every holy deed for God's honor and the salvation of souls.[24]

I'll say no more—since I would have a lot more to say! The disciples of Christ won't be recognized by the fact that they say, "Lord! Lord!" but by their following in the Lord's footsteps.[25] Encourage Francesco in Jesus Christ.[26] Frate Raimondo, poor slandered man, sends you greetings and asks you to pray to God for him that he may be good and patient.[27] Keep living in God's holy and tender love.

Gentle Jesus! Jesus love![k]

---

[22] Catherine several times cites this biblical expression ("in our Lord Jesus Christ") in Latin. Her enumeration of contrasts between herself and her persecutors echoes Phil. 1, 18–26.

[23] Jn. 11, 49–52. Cf. Franco Sacchetti, *Sposizioni di Vangeli*, XXXVIII: "Caiaphas didn't know what he was saying, and he prophesied the truth. So not every prophet is holy."

[24] By "the others" Catherine means especially the members the Company of the Virgin at Santa Maria della Scala, Salvi di Pietro's confraternity, but she probably has in mind as well all of her disciples in Siena.

[25] Mt. 7, 21.

[26] Francesco is unidentified.

[27] Raimondo da Capua was even more a target of rumor in Siena because of his known political interest where the church was concerned.

Textual Notes

a. P3, S3: *in purity / very young* (*in puritia / in pueritia*).
b. B, P3, R1, T: *full / clear* (*pieno / puro*).
c. B, P2, P3, R1, T add *who is our way and our rule.*
d. B, P2: *I say / we . . . say that.*
e. B, P2, R1, T: *letters / letter.*
f. Mo has *se* ("if") for *che* ("that"), a probable copyist error.
g. P2: *true / your* (*vera / vostra*).
h. B, P2: [*and persecution*].
i. P3: *exalt / use* (probable copyist error: *exaltare / exercitare*).
j. B, P2: *all the rest / they.*
k. R1, T add *Mary!*

LETTER T110/G346[1]
To Monna Stricca, wife of Cione di Sandro Salimbeni
Between August and October 1377

The principal object of Catherine's journey to the Val d'Orcia was to resolve the feud between Cione di Sandro Salimbeni, lord of Castiglioncello di Trinoro, and his cousin Agnolino di Giovanni Salimbeni, lord of Rocca d'Orcia.[2] The object of their contention was a certain castle to which both were laying claim. Francesco Malavolti, who was with Catherine during the entire Val d'Orcia mission ("four months and more," according to him), says that after her time in Montepulciano she went "next to Castiglioncello, where Cione di Sandro was in residence, and after that she went up to the fortress where the other [cousin], Agnolino, lived."[3] This was probably about late July.

Cione's wife Stricca may well have been as responsible as Agnolino's mother Biancina for Catherine's coming on this mission of reconciliation.[4] This letter to her must have been written before February 1379, the date of Cione's death, since Stricca is not referred to in the rubric as a widow. E. Lazzareschi,[5] and Gardner after him,[6] assume that the letter predates Catherine's visit to Stricca's home. While this is possible, the linguistic data point far more strongly to the period following that visit, some time between August and October.[7]

---

[1] MSS: Mo-*a*, M, S5, S6, Ro, F3; translation based on Mo-*a*. No relevant variants.

[2] See the introduction to this section.

[3] Testimony of Francesco Malavolti, *Processo Castellano*, pp. 391–392. We owe to him the most complete account of this period.

[4] Francesco Malavolti says simply (p. 391) that she was "led by the Spirit." Raimondo (*Life*, II, ix, 274, p. 256) says no more than that she was there, "as arranged, to conclude the business of peace."

[5] *S. Caterina in Val d'Orcia*, p. 27.

[6] *Saint Catherine of Siena*, p. 212. Gardner follows Lazzareschi very closely in nearly everything related to this period.

[7] Five of the eight letters sharing ten or more of this one's thirty-eight analyzed patterns are from August to October 1377. One is from November and the other two are later. While many of the analyzed patterns occur very frequently over a very broad time span, a few show significant clusters beginning and/or ending in this same period: AUGUSTIN, DAFIGLIO, FEDEOPER, PERAMORE, PUNTA, SAZFAST. The letter has, on the other hand, very little in common with letters before 1377 or after late 1377.

§

In the name of Jesus Christ crucified and of gentle Mary.

Dearest daughter in Christ gentle Jesus,

I Caterina, servant and slave of the servants of Jesus Christ, am writing to you in his precious blood. I long to see you a faithful servant of your Creator, grounded in true perfect patience. Reflect that there is no other way you can please God.

We are pilgrim travelers in this life, running on toward our ending in death; we have no permanence in time.[8] So we have to have the light of most holy faith if we would reach our goal without the darkness getting in our way. But it must be a living faith, that is, a faith accompanied by good deeds, since the saints say that faith without deeds is dead.[9]

We have believed that God is God; that he created us in his own image and likeness; that he gave us the Word, his only-begotten Son; that [this Word] was born from Mary's dear womb and died on the wood of the most holy cross to free us from death and give us the life of grace that we had lost because of Adam's disobedience; that because of the Word's obedience we all contracted grace just as in the beginning we had all contracted death because of the first sin.[10] And to give us hope for our resurrection on the final day of judgment, he revealed to us his own resurrection.[11] So as soon as we have so sweetly acquired the light of faith and seen how unspeakably much God loves us, we fall in love with this great light, this wonderful love God has for us.

With this same vision we begin to see that God wants only that we be made holy.[12] Whatever he gives or permits in this life he gives for this purpose: trial as well as consolation, hurt and mockery and abuse, the world's harassments and the devil's temptations, hunger and thirst; illness and poverty as well as pleasure and prosperity. God permits all of these for our good. He permits us to have wealth so that we may be its administrators for the poor.[13] [He gives us] worldly pleasure and prosperity not

---

[8] It. *stantia di tempo*, an expression Catherine uses nowhere else. Cf. Heb. 13, 14: "We have here no lasting city, but look to the future."

[9] Jas. 2, 26.

[10] Cf. Rom. 5, 12–19, where Christ is compared with Adam.

[11] Cf. 1 Cor. 15, 16 and 20: "If the dead are not raised, then Christ was not raised; and if Christ was not raised, your faith is worthless. . . . Christ is now raised from the dead, the first fruits of those who have fallen asleep."

[12] 1 Thes. 4, 3.

[13] Cf. Let. T247/DT86 to Giovanna di Corrado Maconi (in this volume): "So you should use everything as one to whom Christ crucified has entrusted it for administration. This is true of your material possessions, of which you should give as much as you can to

to make us lift up our heads in pride, but rather that we should humble ourselves all the more in holy thanksgiving for divine goodness. He gives us trials (no matter what their source) and poverty to lead us to true and perfect patience, and so that we may realize how fickle and unreliable the world is. This makes us detach our affection and desire from the world and set it on God alone by means of true solid virtue. In this way we will receive the fruit of our hardships. For every hardship we endure for love of God is rewarded. Its fruit is kept for us in everlasting life, where there is life without death, light without darkness, satiety without boredom, and hunger without pain. This is what Saint Augustine says: "Satiety is far from boredom, and hunger is far from pain."[14] In the other life every good is rewarded and every sin is punished.

So those who have this living faith give birth to true and holy deeds. They are genuinely patient in suffering any pain or hardship for God and for the remission of their sins.[15] In fact, they hold all suffering in reverence, reflecting who it is that gives it, and why, and to whom.

Who is the giver of suffering? It is God, supreme eternal Goodness, and God does it not out of hatred but out of a special love. So [Christ] said to his disciples, "It is not hatred but a special love that makes me send you out to be persecuted and martyred by the world. I love you with the same love with which my Father has loved me, and because he loved me with a special love he sent me to suffer the shameful pain of the most holy cross."[16]

And why, I ask, does God give us [suffering]? Out of love, as I've said, and for our sanctification, so that we may be made holy in him.

And who are we to whom these hardships are given? We are the ones who are not. Because of our sins we are deserving of a hundred thousand hells if we could receive so many. For, because we are offending the infinite Good, the consequence ought to be an infinite punishment. But God

---

the poor, who stand in the place of God." Also Let. T304 to Lodovica di Granello (1378): "Do your duty well, because in whatever you can do you must be a steward [of your possessions] for the poor, you and anyone else who has [any means]. For the poor, along with the loving charity of the one who is giving the alms, are the hands that lead us to eternal life."

[14] Cf. Cavalca, *Descrizione de' dieci comandamenti*, p. 306: "We shall desire though we are sated, and we shall be sated even in our desiring. Yet satiety will not be a source of boredom, nor desire be accompanied by pain, as happens in this world."

[15] This is the only instance in which Catherine explicitly connects the remission of sin with virtue or good deeds. She does, however, often say that it is better to bear the punishment for one's sins in this life through finite pain than in the next life through "infinite" pain—as in fact she says just a bit later in this very letter.

[16] *b* corrects the clause to read, "Although he loved me . . . , he sent me. . . ." That reading, however, is not consistent with the reasoning Catherine presents in the first part of this very free rendering of Jn. 15, 9 and 18–20.

mercifully punishes us in finite time by giving us finite punishment. Hardship in this life lasts only as long as time and no longer, and so the shortness of time makes even great hardship small. Our time, say the saints, is no greater than the point of a needle; human life is so small as to be nothing. Past hardship we no longer have. As for what is still to come, we don't know for certain whether we shall ever have it, since we aren't sure we will have the time. So we have only this present moment and no more.

So up, dearest daughter! Rouse yourself from slumber; sleep no more! Rather follow in Christ's footsteps with living faith, with true holy patience. Bathe yourself in the blood of Christ crucified.

I'll say no more. Keep living in God's holy and tender love.

Gentle Jesus! Jesus love!

LETTER T71/G358[1]
To Monna Bartolomea d'Andrea Mei da Siena
Late August to October 1377

We know nothing of Bartolomea d'Andrea Mei other than that she was of the Buoninsegna family.[2] There is no hint in this letter as to the occasion for Catherine's writing. Only the linguistic evidence serves to place it chronologically in the first months of Catherine's stay at Rocca d'Orcia, probably very near Let. T103, with which it has much in common.[3]

There are a number of passages in this letter in which sentences seem to stumble over each other out of sequence, perhaps in the form of parenthetical afterthoughts inserted just as they occurred to Catherine. (Or perhaps Catherine was in a particularly harried mood when she dictated the letter.) In these cases I have taken the liberty to shift these parenthetical clauses to their most logical position.

§

In the name of Jesus Christ crucified and of gentle Mary.

Dearest mother and daughter in Christ gentle Jesus,

I Caterina, servant and slave of the servants of Jesus Christ, am writing to you in his precious blood. I long to see you grounded in true solid virtue, for without virtue as intermediary we cannot be pleasing to our Creator.[4]

God has always willed to give the life of grace through an intermediary. You know well that after the first human being, Adam, had fallen into sin through disobedience, the consequence of which sin was eternal death, when God wanted to restore him to grace and give him eternal life, he did it using his only-begotten Son as intermediary. He gave him the charge of killing our disobedience by means of his obedience, of consuming and destroying our death and restoring life to us by means of his death. And the

---

1 MSS: Mo-*a*, *b*, M, S5, S6, Ro; translation based on Mo-*a*. No relevant variants.

2 Meattini, *Epistolario*, p. 618.

3 Three of the four letters which share sixteen or more of this one's sixty-six analyzed patterns are from the last five months of 1377; the fourth is from April of that year. Even more strikingly, a number of significant clusters within individual patterns begin and/or end between August and October 1377: CONCEPPR, ELEGLUOG, GIACMORT, INGANN, OFFEND, PAZPROV, PROPVOL, PRUDENT, SDEGN, SERVFEDE, SERVMERC, TRIBCONS. Neither Fawtier (II, p. 309) nor Dupré Theseider (unpublished notes) ventures a date for this letter.

4 Only in this letter, T103, T213, T369, and *Dial.* 7 (p. 36) does Catherine speak of virtue as intermediary or means.

Son truly did this. On the wood of the cross this gentle loving Word jousted in a tournament with death, and by means of death he defeated death even while death killed his life. What I mean is that the death that is our sin killed God's Son on the wood of the most holy cross, so that by means of his death he freed us from death and gave us perfect life again. So life emerged a free lady, and she defeated the infernal devil who had held and possessed lordship over humankind in spite of the fact that humankind should have no lord but God.[5]

It is this [lordship of the devil] that brings us into that original death,[6] so that we lose the life we have through the blood of Christ. This happens when we choose to serve our selfish sensuality by inordinate desire, whether for prestige or wealth or children or any other created person or thing in any way that is not directed to and grounded in God.

And sometimes we become spiritually enslaved to our selfish will under the pretext of spirituality and of wanting to possess God more than we do.[7] This happens when we long to have consolation or trial and diabolic temptation or times and places in our own way. Sometimes we say, "I'd like to have my trials in some other way, because it seems this way is making me lose God. I would endure the former patiently, but I can't manage this way. If I weren't offending God, I'd be willing, but I feel bad because it seems this is making me sin." Dearest mother, if you open your mind's eye you will see that this is selfish sensual will cloaked in the spiritual. If we were wise, we wouldn't act this way. No, with lively faith we would believe that God doesn't permit more than we can bear, nor does he permit it unless it is necessary for our salvation. For he is our God, and he wants nothing other than that we be made holy.[8]

We frequently do the same with selfish spiritual consolations. If we don't experience these when we'd like, if we don't get times and places as we'd like them but instead experience struggles and annoyances and a sterile and dried-up spirit,[9] we become hurt and embittered, anxious and deeply depressed. Often the devil deceitfully makes us think that what we are saying and doing is neither pleasing nor acceptable to God. He says, in

---

[5] Cf. Let. T36 to several Olivetan novices (in this volume), where the soul is the free lady: "Get drunk on the blood of this gentle Lamb, who has made the fortress of your soul strong, who has delivered it from slavery to the devil's perverse tyranny and given it back to you a free woman."

[6] It. *prima morte*, literally, "first death." This is an expression Catherine uses nowhere else, but the context of the entire letter seems to indicate that she is referring to our entering into the death brought on by Adam's sin. I have therefore translated it as "original death" as being parallel to "original sin."

[7] This is the first instance of Catherine's use of the term "selfish will" (*propria volontà*).

[8] 1 Thes. 4, 3.

[9] It. *mente*.

effect, "Why isn't God pleased? Because you are so wicked! Let it be for now. Perhaps at another time you'll feel better and be able to make your prayer." The devil does this so that we'll give up the physical and spiritual practice of actual holy prayer, both vocal and mental.[10] Why? Because once we have lost the weapon with which God's servants defend themselves against the blows of the devil, the flesh, and the world, he would have what he wants from us. Then the city of our soul would be surrendered to him and he would enter it as lord. That's the only way it can go once we have lost the weapon and the power of prayer.[11]

Prayer in its turn gives us the weapons of true humility and blazing charity, because holy prayer gives us perfect knowledge of ourselves and our own weakness and of God's infinite charity and goodness. And we come to know both ourselves and God better in times of struggle and when our spirit is all dried up. We learn more perfect humility and conscientiousness from these [experiences].

So if we are wise enough not to serve our own selfish will in the guise of consolation and not to believe the devil, but with holy hatred [of our selfishness] persevere in prayer in whatever way God grants it to us—whether with feelings of sweetness or with a sense of bitterness—we gain more (as I've described) in the bitterness and pain, no matter in what form God sends it, than in the sweetness. Why? Because in our need we run to our benefactor completely humbled and conscientious, knowing that by ourselves we can do nothing. God is the only one in whom we trust, the only one who can and wants to come to our aid.

If we want to attain true virtue, then, we must attain it by suffering with true and sincere patience these spiritual ordeals as well as whatever vexation people deal out to us in the form of abuse or other sorts of stumbling blocks. For without patience as intermediary we cannot attain

---

[10] In *Dial.* 66, pp. 123–127, Catherine develops more at length the different kinds of prayer and some of the temptations associated with them.

[11] Catherine describes this surrender quite graphically in a number of places, for example, Let. T169a to the Carthusian Niccoloso di Francia (early 1378): "So it really is good to be happy in times of struggle and never let them dishearten us. For sometimes, when the devil fails to trick us with the hook of pleasure, he tries to catch us on the hook of discouragement. He would like to make us believe in these times of struggle that God is reproaching us and that our prayer and our other holy exercises are doing us no good. He says within our mind: 'What you're doing is worthless. You should be praying and doing these other things with a sincere heart and a calm spirit, not with all sorts of indecent thoughts. In this case it would be better for you to put it aside.' The devil does all this so that we will throw off our holy exercises and humble prayer, the very weapon with which we defend ourselves—or let's say, the bond that binds us to God and so fortifies our will and increases our strength with the blazing charity with which we resist the blows, as I've described. This is why the devil tries, with this hook [of discouragement], to make us throw off prayer, for once we have lost this [weapon], he can eventually get from us whatever he wants."

proven virtue. We might well conceive it, but these trials are the means to our giving birth to it.[12]

Virtue is proved in difficulty just as gold is proved in fire.[13] For if in difficulties we were to give no genuine proof of patience but try to avoid the difficulty (in the ways I've described above or in any other possible way), this would be a clear sign that we were not serving our Creator, that we were not letting ourselves be governed by him in accepting humbly and with love whatever our Lord gives us. It would not give evidence of faith that we are loved by our Lord. For if we truly believed this, we could never find a stumbling block in anything. We would value and reverence the hand [that offers] the bitterness of adversity as much as the hand [that offers] prosperity and consolation, because we would see that everything is done out of love. The very fact of our not seeing this would demonstrate that we had become servants of our selfish sensuality and spiritual self-will[14] and that we had made these our lord and were therefore letting ourselves be governed by them.

Since this servitude to the world and to our spiritually selfish will is deadly, we must flee from it. It gets in the way of perfection, keeps us from being free servants of God. It makes us want to serve God in our own way rather than God's—which is not right and makes our service mercenary. So much evil comes of this![15]

I tell you, then, we must follow this way and teaching that he has given us. God wants to do everything by using intermediaries.[16] We see clearly that we were not created by ourselves but that God himself made his charity an intermediary. By means of his pure love he created us in his image and likeness so that we might share in and enjoy the eternal sight of him. But we lost this through the selfish love and sin of our first father. So to give us back what we had lost, God gave us his Son as intermediary, and this mediator took on the blows [in our place]—since the war [between us

---

[12] The clauses in this paragraph in the original are in a rather haphazard order, as if Catherine were putting the logic together as she dictated, adding parenthetical afterthoughts as it developed. I have tried to reconstruct the logical sequence intended in the thought.

[13] Cf. Job, 23, 10: "If God proved me, I should come forth as gold." And Zeph. 13, 9: "I will test them as gold is tested." Ps. 66, 10: "For you have tried us as silver is tried by fire."

[14] At this point the text has the clause, "or from whatever source it comes, as has been said" which seems to make no sense at all in the context, since nowhere has she indicated that this selfishness can come from different sources.

[15] This is the first time Catherine introduces the contrast between mercenary and free or faithful service. She will develop it further in *Dial.* 60, pp.113–116, where she writes of the stages of love.

[16] This is one of those passages where parenthetical clauses seem to be inserted as afterthoughts. "So much evil comes of this!" actually occurs in the text just after "I tell you . . . ," and "God wants . . ." follows immediately after that.

and God] had been so great that there was no other way this peace could have been made.[17] Why? Because the infinite God had been offended, and finite humankind who had sinned could never, by any suffering they might have borne, have made satisfaction to the dear infinite God. So the blazing depths of God's charity found a way to make this peace.

In order for justice to be satisfied, the eternal Godhead, divine in nature, joined himself with human nature. Once the infinite God was united with finite humanity, the human Christ's suffering on the wood of the most holy cross was sufficient to make atonement to his Father and to appease the wrath that had come upon humankind.[18] This gentle Word struck a single blow on the wood of the cross. But in that single blow he worked mercy for humankind and gave us the grace we had lost, thus satisfying mercy; and he satisfied justice, which required that sin be avenged. He took this vengeance on his own body, in the same nature that had sinned, since Christ's flesh was made from Adam's clay.[19]

Yet we, ungrateful and unappreciative as we are, often lose grace by our own sins and declare war on God. Sometimes it is a matter of mortal combat. At other times it is a matter of vexation between friends.

The combat is mortal when we die the death of mortal sin by making a god of the world, of our flesh, and of wretched pleasures. In this case we have lost life completely. True, we can regain it through confession and the mediation of Christ's blood so long as we are living. But take note that without this mediation we cannot be alive in grace or reach everlasting life.

"Vexation between friends" concerns men and women[20] who are serving God without sinning mortally. They are living in grace and want to be true servants of God. But often they would foolishly like to choose times and places, consolation and trial and temptation, in their own way.[21] This foolishness comes of their spiritually selfish will's having set itself up as lord, and it takes them a bit away from the truth. Not that they have abandoned the truth; that would constitute mortal sin. But it does offend against the perfection to which in truth they aspire. Then God is vexed with these people who are his friends, because it seems to him they are not

---

[17] Cf. Rom. 5,1: "Now that we have been justified by faith, we are at peace with God through our Lord Jesus Christ."

[18] Catherine here espouses the traditional theology of redemption, that because sin is an offense against an infinite God it demands an infinite atonement, which only a divine being can provide. However, because sin was committed by humankind, justice also demanded that the atonement be made by a human being.

[19] In Prayer 18, pp. 159–160, she unfolds the drama of the debate between justice and mercy in the "great eternal council" of God.

[20] This is one of the rare instances in which Catherine specifies both genders explicitly.

[21] Again, there is a series of clauses tumbling one upon another, this time with no main verb. I believe the translation "But often . . . they aspire" conveys the sense.

acting and have not acted with the unadulterated freedom with which they ought to act. So God has established an intermediary for us, and he requires that we use it if we want to assuage his indignation and displeasure, and if we don't want to impede our progress toward sweet perfection. He requires that we deny our selfish will; that we neither seek nor want anything but Christ crucified; that all our joy be in resting in Christ's humiliations by giving birth to the virtues we have conceived through holy desire in truly humble charity toward our neighbors.

Through this intermediary of suffering with true and holy patience whatever pain or hardship or spiritual sterility God sends us, we will be grounded in true solid virtue. We will be adults in our power and knowledge, not children who don't want to do anything or go anywhere except in their own way. I don't see that there is any other way we can go! And this is why I told you that I long to see you grounded in true solid virtue. Also, I want your soul to be united with God through effective love, and this can't happen without virtue as intermediary. For, as I've said, God wants to do everything through intermediaries.

I'm certain that, by God's infinite goodness, you will fulfill his will and my desire.

I'll say no more. Keep living in God's holy and tender love.

Gentle Jesus! Jesus love!

Letter T40/G372[1]
To certain of her daughters in Siena
August to October 1377

This brief letter, at least in its extant form, is quite generic in its content and therefore a bit difficult to place chronologically. One can guess first of all that it is almost certainly from a period when Catherine is away from Siena for some time. The linguistic evidence does not at all support placing it during Catherine's stays in Pisa (1375) or Avignon (1376) or even during her month at Belcaro (April 1377). Nor does this letter have much in common with others written during her times in Florence (1378) or Rome (1378 to 1380). This leaves the Val d'Orcia period, when in fact there is at least fairly convincing support for placing the letter most probably in the early months of her stay, that is, between August and October.[2]

§

In the name of Jesus Christ crucified and of gentle Mary.

Dearest daughters in Christ gentle Jesus,

I Caterina, servant and slave of the servants of Jesus Christ, am writing to you in his precious blood. I long to see you faithful servants of our Creator. I want to see you persevering, never letting anything at all—neither excessive joy at prosperity nor impatience and bitterness over adversity—make you turn back. I want and beg you not to let anything whatever obstruct or take away your holy desire.

To make holy desire grow in you and not flag, I want you to open your mind's eye and come to know God's unspeakable love for you. In love he gave you his only-begotten Son, and that Son gave his life for you in such blazing love that it should melt the hardness of any hard heart.[3]

---

[1] MSS: B, P2, R1, P5, F2, F1, P3, Pa; translation based on R1. (I have indicated in the textual notes where Tommasèo differs from R1.)

[2] All three letters which share nine or more of this one's twenty-seven analyzed patterns are dated between August and December 1377. There are, however, a few significant clusters within individual patterns which begin and/or end between August and October: DAFIGLIO, FEDELINF, IMPEDDES, LAVFACCI, UTILDIO. Neither Fawtier (II, p. 309) nor Dupré Theseider (unpublished notes) assigns a date to this letter.

[3] Cf. Let. T248 to Bartalo and Orsa Usimbardi, and to Francesco di Pipino and his wife Agnesa (1378): "Oh boundless love! Oh immense charity! Oh fire of divine charity! What heart could see that it is loved with such blazing love and not melt with love and be totally transformed in it? A heart would have to be exceedingly hard, harder really than diamond, not to be warmed by such a fire! So I want you . . . to rouse yourselves from the sleep of indifference; get up and, with your mind's eye, look at this great fire of love." Also *Dial.*

Here focus your mind's eye, considering and pondering the price [paid for you], God's Son. In his blood wash your soul's face.

Wake up and rouse yourselves from the slumber of apathy! And once you've washed,[a] be sure you put on the white of purity and the color[b] of blazing charity, both[c] of which you will find in the blood of the Lamb.[4] I want you to consider, my daughters, that you[d] cannot have this purity of mind and body if you are doing a lot of socializing with other people and setting your love and desire on them or on created things apart from God's will.[5] Nor is it compatible with selfish love or physical self-indulgence. No, it is won with very earnest watching and prayer, and with continual remembrance of your Creator and constant acknowledgment of God's unspeakable love for you.

After you have acquired purity in the way I've described, you will see that there is no service you can do for God, and so you will extend your love to your neighbors, doing for them the service you cannot do for God. You will visit the sick, help the poor, and console those who are troubled. You will weep with those who weep and rejoice with those who rejoice.[6] I mean you will weep with those who are grieving in deadly sin by being compassionate and by offering continual prayers for them in God's presence. And you will rejoice with those who are glad because they are true servants of Jesus[e] Christ crucified, always happy to be in their company.

I beg you, my daughters, to do this. This is how you will be faithful rather than faithless servants. And this is what my heart longs to see in you.

I'll say no more. Keep living in God's holy and tender love.

Gentle Jesus! Jesus love!

4, pp. 31–32: "They have, with the hand of free choice, encrusted their heart in a diamond rock that can never be shattered except by blood. Still, . . . let them . . . seek the blood of my Son and with that same hand let them pour it over the hardness of their heart. It will shatter the diamond and they will know the fruit of the blood which was paid out for them." Medieval sources such as Vincent de Beauvais, *Speculum naturale*, state that the fresh warm blood of a goat has power to shatter diamonds, which resist both iron and fire.

[4] Cf. Let. T81 to Francesca Tolomei (1378): "With the fire of his charity he cleansed her of sin, washing her in the water of holy baptism, which has power for us because of the blood. The blood gave the soul her color. Her face had been completely pale because of Adam's sin, and the blood made it ruddy. All this was done for love. So you see how the blood shows you God's love for you. . . . He is supreme purity—so pure that the nearer the soul his bride comes to him, the more pure and cleansed of sin she becomes."

[5] On the other hand, in Let. T217 (in this volume), sent separately to monasteries in Monteluce and Perugia, Catherine says that such purity is *fostered* by association with God's servants. Note also her comment in this regard later in the present letter.

[6] Rom. 12, 15.

Textual Notes

a. Tommasèo: *you are up* (*levata*) / *you've washed* (*lavata*).
b. Tommasèo: *heart* (*cuore*) / *color* (*colore*).
c. Tommasèo: [*both*].
d. Through this sentence and the next, Tommasèo has the first person plural.
e. Tommasèo: [*Jesus*].

LETTER T1/G168[1]
To Monna Lapa, her mother
Late August or early September 1377

Catherine and her company had visited the monastery of Sant'Agnesa in Montepulciano in the first weeks of their stay in the Val d'Orcia. There Lapa had stayed (or been left) with Francesca (Cecca) di Clemente Gori, whose daughter Giustina was a novice in that community. The two were still there in October, according to Let. T117 and T118, and, judging from Let. T117, it is probably intended that they will remain there until Catherine's return journey to Siena.

As in all of Catherine's extant letters to Monna Lapa, the matter under discussion is patience, with which Lapa is evidently not richly endowed. Possibly Lapa has again been complaining of her daughter's absence, as she clearly did while Catherine was on her mission to Avignon.[2] Perhaps the "little things" that seem so big to Lapa are the restrictions inherent in living at the monastery. In any case, if I am right in placing this letter in this general period, it does not seem unreasonable to conjecture that it might have been written some time before T117, in which Catherine deals explicitly with the length of her absence, as she had in the letter toward the end of her Avignon journey.

Of the four periods during which we know that Catherine was away from her mother, the linguistic evidenceindicates that this letter was probably written between September and December 1377.[3] But the probable relationship of this letter and Let. T117 leads me to speculate that this one may have been written in late August or early September.

---

[1] MSS: Mo-*a*, B, P2, P1, P5, F2, P3, P4, S4; translation based on Mo-*a*. No relevant variants.

[2] Cf. Let. T240/DT83 (in this volume).

[3] While there are seventeen other letters which share five or more of this short letter's fifteen analyzed patterns, seven of these have been placed between September 1377 and late December or possibly very early 1378, while the rest are broadly scattered. As for individual patterns, significant clusters of FRUTFADI, GRATCOGN, PARTECVT, PAZPROV, and VEROCOGN begin and/or end between September and December 1377. Though P4 (as opposed to Mo) includes the non-standardized protocol elements CRISTGES, PREZSANG, it is possible that these could be accounted for by Catherine's employment for this letter of the scribal services of one of the women, perhaps Alessa.

§

In the name of Jesus Christ crucified and of gentle Mary.

Dearest Mother in Christ gentle Jesus,

I Caterina, servant and slave of the servants of Jesus Christ, am writing to you in his precious blood. I long to see you possessed of true knowledge of yourself and of God's goodness within you, for without this true knowledge you would be unable to share in the life of grace. This is why you should try with a genuine and holy eagerness to realize that you are not, and to acknowledge that your existence is from God, along with whatever gifts and graces you have received and continue to receive from him every day. This will make you grateful and appreciative. You will achieve true holy patience, and won't be seeing little things as so big. In fact, it will seem a small thing to suffer great things for Christ crucified.

A knight is no good unless tested on the battlefield. In the same way your soul has to be tested in the battle through a good many trials. Then, when you are seen to give good proof of patience—when you don't turn back in unwillingness to suffer and in taking offense at what God permits—you can rejoice and be glad and look forward with perfect joy to everlasting life. For then you are finding your rest in the cross, your consolation in the pains and disgrace of Christ crucified. Then you can with good reason look forward to seeing God for all eternity, for Christ promised it.[4] For those who are persecuted and tried in this life are later consoled and satisfied and illuminated in the eternal vision of God, experiencing God's sweetness fully and without intermediary.[5] Even in this life God begins to console those who labor for him. But without knowledge of ourselves and of God we could never reach this great good. So I beg you as earnestly as I know how, as earnestly as I can, to try to have this knowledge, so that we won't lose the fruit of our efforts.

I'll say no more. Keep living in God's holy and tender love.

Gentle Jesus! Jesus love!

---

[4] The text adds *to them*, perhaps a case of Catherine's losing track of her antecedents, just as in the preceding sentences in the original she has alternated between *you* and *she* (the soul) as subject, but the meaning is clear.

[5] In these few sentences Catherine combines elements from several of the beatitudes: the sorrowing shall be consoled; those who hunger and thirst shall be satisfied; those who are persecuted shall possess the reign of God in joy (Mt. 5, 3–12).

LETTER T121/G201[1]
To the Lord Defenders of the City of Siena
Late August to early September 1377

The rubric in the manuscripts specifies that Catherine wrote this letter while she was at Sant'Antimo. The date, therefore, is settled once one has established when she was there. This, if my reasoning in the introduction to this group of letters is correct, was some time between late August and early September of 1377, when Raimondo da Capua was still with Catherine.[2]

Within a broad but pointed discussion of justice, the letter addresses two chief issues. The first is the complaints being leveled against the activities of Catherine and her company in the Val d'Orcia. Fawtier observes that by this time Catherine's friend and supporter Pietro de' Marchesi di Monte Santa Maria has left office as senator. The man who has taken his place, Filippo da Brescia, is described by Neri di Donato as "of slight wisdom, a military type, effeminate, and not very honorable,"[3] and so would not be likely to counter the accusations against this woman who, with her followers, presumes to meddle with enemies of the Commune.

The second issue is the campaign by the archpriest of Montalcino against Giovanni di Gano da Orvieto, abbot of Sant'Antimo. Giulio Prunai details and documents the story.[4] Montalcino was under the jurisdiction of the diocese of Arezzo, but because of its location within the territory of Siena, the archpriest of its church of San Salvatore came under the spiritual authority of the abbot of nearby Sant'Antimo, an authority he resented. As Catherine states in this letter, he would use any pretext to malign the abbot and anyone associated with him. He would later, in fact, physically attack the abbot on the occasion of a visitation, for which he would be relieved of his benefice. In retaliation he would expel his successor at sword-point and install a man of his own choice and continue his

---

[1] MSS: Mo-*b*, R1, T, P3, P5, S3, F2; translation based on Mo-*b*; variants based on unpublished notes by A. Volpato.

[2] The linguistic data is not very helpful, since the few significant clusters within individual patterns are only broadly centered around the Val d'Orcia period. Fawtier (II, pp. 247; 194–196) places the letter between August and 4 October 1377. Dupré Theseider (unpublished notes) reasons that if Catherine went to Sant'Antimo *after* having been with the Salimbeni, complaints and denunciations in Siena would be understandable, but not if she went there first. He therefore places the letter in November or December. But he does not account for Raimondo's presence.

[3] Neri di Donato, *Annales Senensis* (*Rerum Italicarum Scriptores*, ed. Muratori, XV, cc. 250, 256).

[4] "L'assoluzione dell'arciprete di Montalcino in un documento del diplomatico fiorentino del 1379," *S. Caterina da Siena*, n.s. 17 (1966, n. 1): pp. 11–15.

persecution of the abbot and even make an attempt on his life. That deed would win him imprisonment on the abbot's order. However, he would escape, violently evict the Williamite monk who has been put in charge of San Salvatore, and resume his post. July 1379 would again find him in prison, but on 1 October of that year he would be granted a pontifical pardon because of his ill health and repentance.

Gardner assumes that Pietro is Pietro di Giovanni Venture.[5]

§

In the name of Jesus Christ crucified and of gentle Mary.[a]

Dearest lords in Christ gentle Jesus,

I Caterina, servant and slave of the servants of Jesus Christ, am writing to you in his precious blood. I long to see you true lords, with courageous hearts. I mean, I want you to be masters of your selfish sensuality, truly and solidly virtuous, followers of your Creator. Otherwise you could not in justice hold on to the temporal lordship God in his grace has granted you. Those who have to rule and govern others must rule and govern themselves first. How could the blind see to guide others?[6] How can the dead bury the dead,[7] the sick care for the sick, or the poor come to the aid of the poor? Impossible!

Truly, dearest sirs, those who are blind and have darkened their mind's eye with deadly sin have no knowledge either of themselves or of God. Hardly, then, can they see or correct the sins of their subjects. And if they do correct[b], their correcting is as unenlightened and flawed as they themselves are. I have often seen and continue to see guilt punished where there is no guilt, while those who are wicked and evil and deserving of a thousand deaths go unpunished. Scant light does not permit discernment of the truth and puts slander where there is no slander. It generates suspicion of those who are worthy of trust and confidence.[c] (I mean God's servants, who are giving these same people birth in tears and sweat and in continual holy prayer; who are exposing themselves to every sort of danger, pain, and torture for God's honor and the salvation of these people and the whole world.) Yet at the same time it trusts those who are rooted in selfish love for themselves and who are swayed by every wind. This is all the result of scant light and darksome sin. So you have to have light.

I say that the dead cannot bury the dead. I mean that those who are

---

[5] Page 216.
[6] Cf. Mt. 15, 14.
[7] Cf. Mt. 8, 22.

dead to grace have neither the courage nor the strength to bury the dead (their neighbors' sin), because they know that they are as dead as their neighbors. For this reason they neither know how to nor want to correct [the sins of their subjects]. They see that they themselves have the very same illness but they are unconcerned. They have no concern for those in their charge, though they see their illness. And so serious is the illness of mortal sin that they cannot cure it unless they first cure themselves. By the very fact that they are living in deadly sin they have become poor and have lost the wealth of true solid virtue because they have not followed in the footsteps of Christ crucified. So they cannot come to the aid of the poor, deprived as they themselves are of the wealth of divine grace.

Because of the darkness they have lost the light, for they do not see sin where it is. And so their acts are unjust rather than just. Because of their illness they lose the strength of holy and sincere desire, the desire for God's honor and their neighbors' salvation. And their illness will get worse and worse unless they seek out the doctor, Christ crucified, and vomit out their corruption through their mouth in holy confession. If they do this, they receive life and health. If not, they receive death—and as I said, the dead cannot bury the dead. And what greater poverty can there be than to be deprived of the light, of life and health? I do not know what could be worse.

Those who do not govern themselves, then, are not good or even fit to govern others. So you have to have the things I have spoken of, and this is why I said I want to see you true lords. But I am convinced that it is impossible to be a true lord unless one is in control of oneself, that is, is governing one's selfish sensuality with reason. This is why I am telling you in what serious trouble they are who, instead of ruling themselves, let themselves be ruled by their own wretchedness. I want you to be careful not to fall into this.

So try, try to open your mind's eye, and do not be blinded by such misplaced fear! Make up your mind to believe and trust in God's servants rather than in the wicked servants of the devil, who to conceal their wickedness make you see what is not there. Do not be wanting to put God's servants in opposition to yourselves; for it seems God puts up with anything else more than he puts up with abuse, scandal, and defamation directed against his servants. What you do to them, you do to Christ. Doing them ill would be disastrous. Dearest brothers and lords, do not allow either yourselves or others to do this. Rather cut off the tongue of the rumor-monger! I mean, reprove the gossipers and put no faith in them. In this way you will be practicing virtue and will avert many scandals. But it seems our sins hardly deserve so much. It seems just the opposite is happening. It is the wicked who are listened to, while the good are unheeded.

I have heard that either the archpriest of Montalcino or someone else has roused suspicion among you. He does this to conceal his own evil deeds against the abbot of Sant'Antimo, who is as great and perfect a servant of God as has lived in these parts in a very long time. If you had the least bit of light, not only would you not have suspected the abbot, but you would have given him the respect he deserves. I beg you, then, for love of Christ crucified, please[d] do not stand in his way,[e] but come to his aid and help him with what he needs. Every day you are complaining that priests and other clerics are not being corrected, and now when you find those who are willing to correct them, you stand in their way and complain.[8]

As for my coming here with my family,[9] I am told that people are suspicious and are grumbling to you about it. I do not know, however, whether this is true. But if you valued yourselves as much as they and I value you, you and all the other citizens would not so lightly harbor such thoughts and feelings. You would stop your ears so as not to hear. The others and I have sought and continually are seeking your spiritual and material welfare. We have spared no effort, offering to God sweet and loving desires along with floods of tears and sweat, to make reparation so that we may not incur the divine judgment we deserve for our sins. I am not so virtuous as to know how to do anything but imperfectly. The others, who are perfect and who attend only to God's honor and the salvation of souls, are the ones who are doing it. But neither the ingratitude nor the foolishness of my fellow citizens will keep us from working even to the point of death for your welfare. We shall learn from that gentle lover Paul, who says, "The world curses us, and we bless; the world persecutes us and hounds us, and we bear it patiently."[10] And we shall do the same; we shall follow his rule. It will be the truth that sets us free.[11]

I love you more than you love yourselves. And I love peace and your security[f] as much as you do. So do not believe that I or any of the others of my family would do otherwise. We are put here to sow God's word and to gather in the harvest of souls. Every one of us should be about our own business, and the business God has appointed us to is this. So we have to be about it, and not bury our talent, for if we did we would be deserving of great blame.[12] No, we have to use it always and everywhere and for everyone. God is not partial to the who and the where,[13] but to holy and

---

[8] Giovanni di Gano da Orvieto had been commissioned to reform the Sant'Antimo community in the wake of the plagues of 1348 and 1374.

[9] Catherine's favorite name for her followers (*la famiglia*).

[10] 1 Cor. 4, 12.

[11] Cf. Jn. 8, 32.

[12] Cf. Mt. 25, 14–30.

[13] Cf. Acts 10, 34: "God shows no partiality."

sincere desire. So it is with this [sincere and holy desire] that we have to work.

I see that the devil is unhappy about the loss he has sustained and will continue to sustain by our coming here, by God's goodness. I came for nothing but to eat and savor souls, and to rescue them from the hands of the devils. I want to lay down my life for this, even if I had a thousand lives to lay down. For this reason I will go and stay as the Holy Spirit makes me.[14]

Pietro[15] will tell you in person my chief reason for coming here and for staying.

I'll say no more. Bathe in the blood of Christ crucified if you want life. Otherwise we shall fall into eternal death. Do not be angry at what you read and hear, but endure it patiently. My love and sorrow make me say so much—love, I tell you, for your welfare and sorrow for our foolishness. May God in divine judgment not take from us the light to know the truth!

I'll say nothing more. Keep living in God's holy and tender love.

Gentle Jesus! Jesus love![g]

Textual Notes

a. R1: *gentle Mother Mary / gentle Mary.*
b. P5, F2: *know / do correct.*
c. R1, T, P3: [*and confidence*]; P5, F2: [*trust and*].
d. R1, T, P3, P5: [*please*].
e. P3 adds *by what you say.*
f. P5, F2: *company / security* (*conversazione / conservazione*)—but F2 corrects to *conservazione* in the margin.
g. R1, T add *Mary!* P5, F2 have only *Keep living in Christ gentle Jesus. Amen.*

---

[14] Raimondo da Capua (*Life* II, vii, 239, p. 227) writes of this period at Sant'Antimo: "I myself, more than once, have seen a crowd of a thousand or more men and women, as if rallied by the sound of an unseen trumpet, crowding in from the mountains and the country districts around Siena, just to see her and hear her. And when they heard her, or even only had sight of her, their hearts were pierced by sorrow for their evil deeds. Weeping and grieving for their sins they ran in search of confessors—of whom I myself was one—and then confessed their sins with a deep contrition which showed how mighty a flood of heaven's grace had been poured out within their hearts. Such scenes I witnessed myself, as I said, not once or twice, but over and over again."

[15] This is very probably Pietro di Giovanni Venture, who has been with Catherine during this period.

Letter T103/G195[1]

To Benuccio di Piero and Bernardo di Uberto de' Belforti of Volterra
Late August to October 1377

The Belforti had been lords of Volterra until they were deposed from power by the Inghirami family during a revolution in 1361.[2] Benuccio di Piero de' Belforti was distantly related to the Salimbeni family of Rocca d'Orcia, his mother being Angiola[3] Salimbeni, daughter of Benuccio di Sozzo di Francesco Salimbeni.[4] Eugenio Lazzareschi suggests, therefore, that it may well be Biancina Salimbeni who has asked Catherine to address the still-smoldering hatred of the Belforti as she has the hostility of Biancina's feuding relatives.[5] If this is the case, the present letter is almost certainly being written during Catherine's stay at Rocca d'Orcia. Dupré Theseider also cites a contract and promise of peace concluded by the Belforti on 27 January 1377, and supposes that the present letter must almost certainly post-date that event.[6] The linguistic evidence, too, would support placement during the first months of Catherine's stay at Rocca d'Orcia.[7]

§

In the name of Jesus Christ crucified and of gentle Mary.

Dearest sons in Christ gentle Jesus,

I Caterina, servant and slave of the servants of Jesus Christ, am writing to

---

[1] MSS: Mo-*a*, *b*, S3; translation based on Mo-*a*.

[2] Catherine will write Let. T68 to Bandeçça di Bocchino de' Belforti, whose husband was killed in the 1361 uprising.

[3] Or Angela.

[4] *Istoria genealogica delle famiglie Salimbeni di Siena*, ed. Idlefonso di San Luigi in *Delizie degli Eruditi toscani*, appendix to vol. XXIII, Florence, 1786, p. 80 (cited in Fawtier II, p. 241, n. 1).

[5] *S. Caterina da Siena in Val d'Orcia*, pp. 12–13. Lazzareschi corrects errors of fact here in the accounts of Drane and Gardner.

[6] Dupré Theseider, unpublished notes. He gives as his source "not. Salerno di Giammino."

[7] While the letter has much in common with Let. T3 (vol. I), dated late January to early May 1376, the latter also concerns the theme of reconciliation. The only other letter sharing fifteen or more of this one's thirty-five analyzed patterns, T71 (in this volume), treats of other themes and was almost surely written from the Rocca. Also, a number of fairly significant clusters within individual patterns point to that period rather than earlier in 1377 (CUORANIM, MEZZVIRT, PUNICORP). Several clusters make it all but certain that the letter was written before November 1377 (AGNELCON, CUORANIM, GUERRDIO, TRAMEZZA). I would therefore concur with Lazzareschi's hypothesis, placing this letter probably during Catherine's first few months at Rocca d'Orcia.

you in his precious blood. I long to see you reconciled, heart and soul and energy, with Christ crucified.[8] There is no other way you can share in divine grace. You know, my sons, that sin is the only thing that puts us at war with our Creator. How then can we bring about this peace, since our sins have brought us into deadly war and we are damned to eternal punishment unless we make peace?

I certainly[a] want us to search out the way, because we have fallen into such danger and harm, both spiritually and physically. And I don't see that we have any other way but one—I mean the holy way God dealt with us when the sin of Adam brought the whole human race into war with God. In that case God's mercy wanted to make peace with us, and yet our sin had to be atoned for. So he sent the Word, his only-begotten Son, to be our mediator and our peace. And God's Son took our sins and punished them in his own body, mediator and peace that he was for us.[9] And where did he punish them? In his sad, painful, and shameful death by crucifixion.[10]

So you see how God has made peace with us through his Son. That peace is so perfect and complete that to provide even for our falling again into war through sin and failure, he left us his blood. We receive this blood in holy confession, and we can make use of it every day and have as much of it as we want.[11] Since we have received so much grace and mercy from God, I don't want us to be unappreciative or ungrateful. No, I want us to follow in the footsteps of Christ crucified, so that we can in that way be reconciled with him. Otherwise we would be living in continual damnation.

---

[8] Cf. Mk. 12, 30: "You shall love the Lord your God with all your heart, with all your soul, with all your mind, and with all your strength." On the basis of this parallel, I translate *affetto* here as "energy."

[9] Is. 53, 6; Eph. 2, 14.

[10] Cf. Let. T3 to the Curate of Casole and others (vol. I): "I long to see you following the Lamb, slain for us on the wood of the most holy cross. He was our peace and our mediator, because he intervened between God and humankind. He made the greatest peace out of our great war, looking not at our sins but at his own boundless goodness."

[11] Cf. *Dial.* 75, pp. 138–139: "There is a second way the soul receives this baptism of blood, figuratively speaking. This my divine charity provided because I know how people sin because of their weakness. Not that weakness or anything else can force them to sin if they do not want to, but being weak they do fall into deadly sin and lose the grace they had drawn from the power of the blood in holy baptism. So my divine charity had to leave them an ongoing baptism of blood accessible by heartfelt contrition and a holy confession as soon as they can confess to my ministers who hold the key to the blood. ... But if they cannot confess, heartfelt contrition is enough for the hand of my mercy to give them the fruit of this precious blood. ... So you see, this baptism is ongoing, and the soul ought to be baptized in it right up to the end. ... In this baptism you experience that though my act of suffering on the cross was finite, the fruit of that suffering which you have received through me is infinite."

I have said that God by means of his Son (and his Son by means of his blood) has delivered us from war and given us peace. And now I am telling you the same. You must stop your warring and escape eternal damnation by means of virtue. Otherwise you will be confounded both in this life and in the next.

But I want you to understand that we can neither love God nor be virtuous without the mediation of our neighbors, because it is in our neighbors that we find love and virtue. How so? I'll tell you. I can't show my Creator my love for him directly, because I can be of no service to God. So I have to use God's creatures as intermediaries, and do for them the service I cannot do for God.[12] So it was when Christ asked Peter, "Peter, do you love me?" When Peter said, "Yes," Christ responded, "Feed my little sheep. In the love you bear me you can do me no service; so do it for your neighbors."[13] So you see, we need an intermediary in order to make peace of the great war we are waging against God.[14] It is by using this intermediary that you will acquire the other means, virtue, which I told you was the sweet glorious means of delivering us from all war and darkness. But keep in mind that this virtue is discovered and acquired in love for our neighbors, by loving friends and enemies alike for the sake of Christ crucified, by putting out the fire of anger and hatred we have harbored against our brothers and sisters.

The virtues of charity and humility are discovered and acquired only in loving our neighbors for God's sake, because those who are humble and peaceable banish anger and hatred for their enemies from their heart. And charity will banish self-centeredness and expand their hearts in a familial charity that loves enemies and friends alike as they love themselves, for the sake of the Lamb who was consumed and slain. It will give them patience in the face of any injurious word or deed, and gentle strength to know how to endure and bear with their neighbor's shortcomings.

Those, then, who have so pleasantly acquired virtue by following in the footsteps of their Savior take all the hatred they had for their neighbors and turn it against themselves by hating their own sins and wrongs and

---

[12] Cf. *Dial.* 64, p. 121: "I ask you to love me with the same love with which I love you. But for me you cannot do this, for I loved you without being loved. Whatever love you have for me you owe me, so you love me not gratuitously but out of duty, while I love you not out of duty but gratuitously. So you cannot give me the kind of love I ask of you. This is why I have put you among your neighbors: so that you can do for them what you cannot do for me—that is, love them without any concern for thanks and without looking for any profit for yourself. And whatever you do for them I will consider done for me."

[13] Cf. Jn. 21, 15–17.

[14] Note that she makes a distinction here between Christ as mediator and our neighbors as intermediary or means (*mezzo*). This letter and Let. T71 show Catherine's earliest development of the theme that virtue is acquired by means of one's neighbors.

vices against their Creator, who is infinite Goodness. And so they want to take revenge on themselves and punish those offenses in their own sensual selves. When they were living by feeling and worldly standards they were hungry for hatred and revenge toward their neighbors. Now their reason, ruled by true and perfect charity, wants to do the opposite, wants to love those neighbors and make peace with them. And every vice in the same way has virtue for its opposite. This is the virtue that reconciles us with God, and so[b] by means of virtue we make up for the harm we have done.

This is why I told you that my desire is to see you reconciled with your Creator, [with all your] heart and energy. This is the true way and there is no other for us. In my desire for your salvation then, my sons, I want you to get rid of the sword of hatred. Don't be like those stupid fools who, in striking out at others, strike themselves. They are the first to die. For those who live in deadly hatred, wanting to kill their enemies, drive the sword first into their own breast. The point of their hatred runs through their own heart and so they are dead to grace. No more war, then, for love of Christ crucified! Don't insist on keeping yourself in physical and spiritual torment. Fear the divine judgment that hangs over us[c] always.

I don't want to say any more. I'll speak to you in person about this and about other matters having to do with your salvation. But for now I am urging and begging two things in the name of Christ crucified. The first is that I want you to make peace with God and with your enemies. For you cannot make peace with gentle First Truth unless you have first made peace with your neighbors. The other thing I ask is that you not consider it too much to come to me for a while as soon as you can. If it weren't so difficult, I would come to you.[15]

I'll say no more. Keep living in God's holy and tender love.

Gentle Jesus! Jesus love!

Textual Notes

a. *certainly* supplied by *b* over erasure.

b. *and so* supplied by *b.*

c. S3: *you / us.*

[15] Volterra is about thirty-five miles west of Siena, and Catherine, if she is indeed at Rocca d'Orcia, is about thirty miles southeast of Siena.

Letter T253/G194[1]

To Messere Trincio de' Trinci da Fuligno and to his brother Corrado
Mid-September 1377

Trincio de' Trinci was lord of Fuligno and a *gonfaloniere* (standard-bearer) of the Church.[2] Though he and his brother Corrado were, in Gardner's words, "ferocious despots," they were in the service of the Church. And Catherine had an additional motive for following their affairs because they were brothers of Biancina Salimbeni, her hostess at Rocca d'Orcia.

In the present letter, certainly written from the Rocca, Catherine commends the two for their loyalty to the Church in spite of ingratitude on the part of the pope and the cardinal of Geneva, but she also urges them to conversion. Trincio had already been warned by the Franciscan tertiary Tommaso Unzio (whom Trincio had threatened to burn alive) that he would live only as long as the great bell of Fuligno remained intact. The prophecy would be fulfilled when on 28 September 1377 the enemies of the Trinci would rise against them. The great bell would crack as it sounded the signal to the conspirators for the assault on Trincio's palace. Trincio would be stabbed to death and his body hurled from the balcony into the piazza below, where it would remain for several days unburied.

Shortly after Trincio's death, Catherine will write a letter of condolence and encouragement to his widow, Jacoma d'Este (Let. T264).

The linguistic evidence strongly supports placing the letter not only during Catherine's time at Rocca d'Orcia, but even more precisely in September. Since Catherine was probably away from the Rocca at Sant'Antimo in early September, I would place the letter most probably in mid-September (after Catherine's return from Sant'Antimo) and surely before Trincio's death on 28 September.[3]

The rubric of Mo specifies that this letter was dictated in a state of ecstasy.[4]

---

[1] MSS: Mo-*a*, M, S5, S6, Ro, S3; translation based on Mo-*a*.

[2] This background information is based on Gardner, *Saint Catherine of Siena*, pp. 221–222.

[3] The only letter sharing twenty or more of this one's seventy analyzed patterns is also from the Val d'Orcia period. More narrowly, however, a number of significant clusters within individual patterns begin and/or end in September or October 1377: CARINCRE, CAVERNA, COGNANIM, DIOINUOM, PADMANIF, PARTECVT, VERVOL. Gardner, because of the letter's theme of the cross, places the letter on 14 September, the feast of the Triumph of the Cross. Fawtier (II, p. 240) places it simply sometime before the catastrophe of 28 September. Dupré Theseider, even more generally (unpublished notes), places it in September or October, apparently incognizant of the date of Trincio's death.

[4] This annotation is added to the rubrics for a number of Catherine's letters, especially during this period of her life. Her contemporaries relate that she would often lapse into a state of trance or ecstasy (It. *astrazione*) while praying or dictating. The letters bearing this

§

In the name of Jesus Christ crucified and of gentle Mary.

Dearest brothers in Christ gentle Jesus,

I Caterina, servant and slave of the servants of Jesus Christ, am writing to you in his precious blood. I long to see you true servants of Christ crucified, bound with the sweet bond of charity. This is the bond that bound God with humanity and humanity with God in a union so perfectly made that it could not be broken by death or by anything else.

Oh true and sweet bond! So great is your power that you held the God-Man nailed fast to the wood of the most holy cross! For neither the nails nor any other iron could have held him had not love for his Father and our salvation held him. So strong was this love, dearest brothers, and so constant, that neither the devil nor anyone else could dampen its perseverance. It was not dampened by the wrongs people did him then, nor is it dampened by the wrongs we do him now. It is not dampened by our ingratitude or theirs, or by the devils either. For we cannot by our maltreatment keep him from loving us or make him forsake his obedience to his eternal Father. No, he persevered even to the point of death on a cross. This gentle loving Word, God's only-begotten Son, by his steady perseverance revealed to us the eternal Father's will and sweet truth. His will is that we be made holy.[5] This is the truth, and for this destiny God created us, that we might be made holy in him for the glory and praise of his name[6] and might experience and enjoy the sight of him for ever.

Oh dearest, very loved brothers, I want you to contemplate the overflowing depths of his charity in choosing to stoop down to our humanity because our sin had blinded us and made us ignorant of this sweet truth and gentle will of his! Oh wretched pride! How ashamed we should be to be proud while God is humbled, and has given us the Word clothed and veiled in our humanity!

Now who can even see well enough to see God's exaltedness descending to such lowliness and binding himself with humanity and humanity with himself? Open, open your mind's eye, and you will see the blood of God's Son overflowing! For that splitting open of his body has made it clear to us that God loves us without measure and wants nothing other than our good. If he had wanted anything else he would never have given us such a Redeemer.

---

annotation are sometimes marked by rambling sentences and unusual grammatical structures.

[5] 1 Thes. 4, 3.

[6] Cf. Eph. 1, 12.

Oh sweetest boundless charity! The ashes have burst open (I mean your body) from the burning heat of love for our salvation![7] *You, God eternal, have let yourself be seen, and have made the price [of our redemption] visible, so that the lowliness of our understanding can have no excuse not to be lifted up. You have made yourself lowly, and at the same time joined lowliness with exaltedness. By love's coercion, then, let our human understanding and will be lifted up to know the exaltedness and magnificence of your charity, God eternal, as we recognize in you the lowliness of your humility. This is what you said, gentle loving Word: "If I am raised up high I will draw everything to myself."*[8]

It is as if this gentle eternal Truth wanted to say, "If I am brought low in the humiliation of the shameful death of the cross, I will draw your hearts to the height of the divinity, uncreated charity." So we can say that when the human heart is drawn, all the soul's powers and affection are drawn, along with everything we do, whether spiritual or temporal. And since everything created was made to serve us, when we are drawn, everything else is drawn as well. This is why he said, "If I am raised up high I will draw everything to myself."[9]

It is good to open our mind's eye and contemplate our Creator's affection. So I want you, dearest brothers, to remember that when your mind's eye is clouded over with selfish sensual love it is impossible to know this truth. Eyes that are weak, covered with dust or cataracts,[10] cannot see the light of the sun. And the mind's eye cannot see if it is covered with the dust of disordered love and affection for the world (with these transitory things, I mean, that pass away like the wind), or if fleshly affection covers it with dishonorable living, with wallowing in the mire of wretched carnality, which makes people brute beasts and deprives them of light and knowledge. Such people, I tell you, cannot know this truth. They have, in fact, become lovers of falsehood and are following in the footsteps of their father the devil, who is the father of lies.

So I want you to raise your mind's eye and your love above these transitory things and above all fleshly vice, and cleanse your soul through holy confession. I'm not for all that telling you to leave where you are unless

---

[7] In the days before matches and easy fire, ashes were used to preserve the fire for further use, an image often reflected in Catherine's writings. Here, however, one is reminded of the heat of the earth's core splitting through the ashes covering a volcano or of embers that suddenly burst into flame.

[8] Jn. 12, 32. It is probably these references which lead Gardner to state, quite categorically (p. 222) that Catherine is writing on the feast of the Triumph of the Cross. The passage from Jn. 12 was, in fact, the gospel reading for that feast.

[9] The theme of the soul's three powers "and everything else" being drawn to Christ is developed at length in Let. T259 to Tommaso d'Alviano (in this volume).

[10] It. *carne,* "flesh"—which is significant for what follows.

the Holy Spirit should so inspire you. But I do want you to hold your positions in holy fear of God, being courageous, like virtuous men and not like animals.[a] Treat those under you with justice and kindness.

Honor[11] the state of holy matrimony by not defiling it, not violating it with any disordered appetite. No, restrain your feelings with the thought of Christ's blood and of the union of the divine nature with our human nature. That will make your miserable flesh ashamed to stoop to such wretchedness. With this holy meditation your flesh will sense the perfume of purity and you will live in holy matrimony with reverence and fear of God. Respect also the days commanded by holy Church.[12]

If you live in this way, you will be fruitful trees, and the fruit you produce will be good and will praise and glorify God's name. And you will be engrafted into the tree of life, Christ gentle Jesus, who will bind you with the same strong bond of love that held him nailed fast to the cross.[13] When you are bound with God and your neighbors by this gentle bond you will so share in its strength that neither the devil nor anyone else will be able to pull you away from being strong and constant even to the point of death. Your love will not relax because of ingratitude or lack of appreciation on the part of the people you serve, nor because of all the different imaginings the devil may put into your heart to make you hate or despise your neighbors.[14] You will not lose your strength, because you are bound and joined with the bond of charity, as I've said. You will indeed be true servants of Christ crucified within your state of life. There is no other way you can share in the life of grace. And this is why I said that I long to see you true servants of Christ crucified, bound with the gentle bond of charity.

I hope in God's goodness that you will fulfill his will and my desire, and this will be because of his goodness and the service you are doing his dear bride. For he is our God, appreciative and grateful to those who serve him. Everything we do for him is very pleasing to him, but most of all

---

[11] Literally, "keep."

[12] Though the Church in earlier centuries had expected married couples to abstain from sexual intercourse on all great feasts and on fast days as well as during the woman's menstruation, pregnancy, and lactation, these expectations had largely become, by Catherine's day, a matter of counsel. They were, however, always dependent on the husband's will. For example, Hedwig of Silesia (d. 1243) is commended by her hagiographer for observing continence "every year through Lent and all of Advent, all of the Ember Days and Fridays, on the vigils of the saints and their solemnities, and on the Lord's days." (*Acta Sanctorum*, 8 October, cited in Dyan Elliott, *Spiritual Marriage: Sexual Abstinence in Medieval Wedlock*, p. 225.) Yet Catherine does refer here to "days commanded."

[13] This imagery of engrafting is developed in detail in Prayer 17, pp. 147–153.

[14] Gardner (p. 222, n. 1) sees in this a reference to the pope's lack of appreciation and the alleged treachery of the cardinal of Geneva, for which he cites *Anonimo Fiorentino*, pp. 337–338, and D. M. Manni, *Cronichetta d'Incerto* (in *Cronichette antiche di vari scrittori del buon secolo della lingua toscana*, Florence, 1733, p. 213).

what we do in service to holy Church, no matter how or in what state of life we are serving. It is true that the more we serve with a sincere heart and without partiality, the more we are pleasing to God. Nevertheless, everyone's pleasingness is measured by the standard of love. But just as God rewards service, he punishes offense. And just as those who serve more are rewarded more, so those who offend more are punished more. Why? Because we are serving the blood of Christ or refusing to serve the blood of Christ. That is why the reward or the punishment is greater.

So, dearest brothers in Christ gentle Jesus, be for me faithful servants of Christ crucified and of his dear bride. In this way you will experience and know God's eternal will, which wants nothing other than that we be made holy. He has revealed this will to us, as I've said, by his humility [in taking on] our humanness,[15] and by the dear blood he shed for us in such blazing love. Bathe yourselves, then, in the blood of Christ crucified in faith and trust. And nurture your families on this teaching.

I'll say no more. Keep living in God's holy and tender love.

Gentle Jesus! Jesus love!

Textual Notes

a. M: *stupid people or animals / animals.*

[15] It. *con la baççezza della nostra humanità.*

LETTER T197/G268[1]
To Matteo di Tomuccio of Orvieto
In or near September 1377

The person to whom this letter is addressed has not been identified. Nor is there any clue in the content of the letter as to when it might have been written. The linguistic evidence, however, strongly excludes any date before summer of 1377 and points most convincingly to autumn of that year. Because of the letter's specific similarities with Let. T220 and T294, I am inclined to place it near those letters, in or near September 1377.[2] The point of the present letter, however, is clearly the personal conversion of the addressee and does not seem to be at all related to opposition to Catherine's activities.

§

In the name of Jesus Christ crucified and of gentle Mary.

Dearest brother and son in Christ gentle Jesus,

I Caterina, servant and slave of the servants of Jesus Christ, am writing to you in his precious blood. I long to see you a solid rock, not a leaf that turns with every wind.[3] For those who do not have their foundation on the living rock, Christ gentle Jesus (that is, those whose desire and affection are fixed on the fleeting things of the world which pass away like the wind, rather than God alone) come to nothing because they are deprived of grace.[4]

---

[1] MSS: Mo-*a*, M, S5, S6, Ro, S1; translation based on Mo-*a*. No relevant variants.

[2] Three of the four letters sharing twenty or more of this one's ninety-two analyzed patterns fall between August and October 1377, where there is also a striking concentration of significant clusters within individual patterns, especially ASPTMPSC, CIECAMOR, COGNDIFT, CONDESC, CORPVOL, COSTANT (no other occurrence before August 1377), DOPPIO (no other occurrence before September 1377), FALSGIUD, FOGLVENT, FONDPAZ, FUMO (only two isolated occurrences after October 1377, and none before March 1377), GUASTGUS (no other pre-*Dial.* occurrence), LEGGCUOR, LORDFACC (no other occurrence before September 1377), LUMEPERF, MATRIMON, MUT, NAVICREL, ORAZVIG (only three isolated occurrences before August 1377), PIETRCRO (only one isolated occurrence after late 1377), REPUTAZ (earliest other occurrence in September 1377), SOSPETT (latest occurrence in *Dial.*), and SPINROSA. Both Fawtier (II, p. 289) and Dupré Theseider (unpublished notes) consider this letter undatable.

[3] Catherine may be thinking of Matteo's city, Orvieto, which is built on a high rocky plateau and is therefore much exposed to the wind.

[4] Cf. 1 Pt. 2, 1: "Come to him, a living stone. . . . You too are living stones, built into an edifice of spirit." She surely also has in mind the parable of the house built on sand, Mt. 7, 24–27, as is evident from the allusions that follow.

This grace sustains us, is the source of our life. It gives us perfect light and frees us from darkness, grounding us in true holy fear of God and in perfect humility and familial love for our neighbors. The wind of trouble does not move it to impatience, nor does the wind of consolation move it to excessive delight. And the wind of wealth and the smoke of worldly honor do not puff it up with pride. All this comes of our being stable, with Christ crucified as our foundation.

Though the three principal winds may blow, the winds that are the source of every other wind, they do not bother us.

The first wind is the devil,[5] from whose mouth comes the wind of all sorts of evil thoughts and temptations. Sometimes it is the temptation to vanity, which makes our heart flighty and immature, and feeds our desire and appetite for worldly prestige. But sometimes the temptation comes under the pretext of virtue, and this temptation is more difficult than any other to recognize as such. Only the humble recognize it and cannot be deceived by it.

And here is the pretext of virtue that the devil presents. Suppose he finds us ignorant and lacking in the virtue of humility or true self-knowledge, still imperfect and not knowing ourselves sufficiently—even though we may have begun to desire God and show signs of virtue. He lets us see things about our neighbors, spiritually as well as materially (that is, in matters spiritual and material), and then the devil blows with the wind of rash judgment.[6] We wickedly pass judgment on our neighbors and on God's servants and on the servants of the world, and we aren't even aware of it. We would steal the right of judgment from God's hand—for only God has the right to judge. And why aren't we aware of it? Because the devil has cloaked this judgment in the mantle of virtue so that we think we are doing good. Our vision is so blurred that often we think we are offering sacrifice to God.[7] But we are deluded by the pride within us. If we were truly humble, grounded in true self-knowledge, we would be ashamed to see ourselves being so judgmental, because we would see that it is tantamount to wanting to make rules for God. For we are trying to make rules

---

[5] The text has simply, "That is, the devil ...," But Catherine goes on to develop at length each of the "three principal winds," the devil, the world, and the flesh, the three classical enemies of the spirit. There is an implied imaging of these enemies as winds in Let. T36, T94 (both in this volume), T275 (1378), and *Dial.* 36, and it is explicit in Let. T232 (in this volume), but nowhere else does she develop the imagery in the detail she gives it here.

[6] Cf. *Dial.* 101, p. 193: "You would think you were judging rightly when in fact you were judging wrongly by following what you saw, for often the devil would make you see too much of the truth in order to lead you into falsehood." This theme of rash judgment is also developed at length in Let. T62 and T294 to Sano di Maco and others.

[7] Cf. Jn. 16, 2 (Vulg.): "An hour is coming when all who kill you will think they are offering sacrifice to God."

for God when we take scandal in God's servants by wanting to direct people in our way rather than as God calls them.[8]

Those who are grounded on Christ the living rock will resist such impulses and not give in to them. With true humility they will try to be glad and give glory to God for the ways and practices of his servants. And they will try to be compassionate to those who fail, asking divine Goodness to look on them with mercy, drawing them away from sin and leading them back to virtue. In this way they pick the rose from among the thorns.[9] And they keep their mind sincere. They don't go around fantasizing, filling their memory with all sorts of imaginings about the spiritual and material things they think they are perceiving. That is how stupid and idiotic and presumptuous people act. They have no perception yet of themselves, and still they want to investigate the affairs of others under the pretext of doing good! They are allowing themselves to be blown about by this perverse wind that is so dangerous. Oh cursed mouth! How you have poisoned the world with your stench![10] (I am referring to people in the world as well as people who have abandoned the world, as I've said.[11]) And after they have passed judgment in their heart, they belch out the stench of their grumbling, leaving their minds empty and scandalized over God and their neighbors. So it really is good to avoid this with true holy diligence.

The second evil and dangerous wind is the world, which delights in excessive and selfish love for self and looks for selfish pleasure and comfort. When we set our sights on these things,[12] the world puts a cover of beauty over its darkness and wretchedness and fickle instability, making itself appear lovely and attractive. And so it deceives us.[13] It tells us that life is long, when it is short. It makes us think that all its pleasures and comforts and riches are solid and that they are ours, when they are [really] changeable and are only lent to us to use as we need them. For inevitably either they are taken away from us, or we are taken away from them. They are

---

[8] She makes this same association between self-knowledge and judgment in *Dial.* 99, p. 186.

[9] The same image is used in Let. T29 to Regina della Scala and in *Dial.* 100, p. 190, and 143, p. 297.

[10] Cf. Jas. 3, 1–12, on the evils that can be worked by the tongue. Note that Catherine mixes from here on the metaphors of the wind (or breath) from the devil's mouth and the breath from the mouth of the one who is influenced by the world, the devil, and the flesh.

[11] It. *in quelli che sono nel secolo e fuore del secolo, come decto è.*

[12] The subjects of the verbs are confusing in these sentences. I have interpreted them in their logical sense in the context, which makes "the world" the subject.

[13] Cf. *Dial.* 46, p. 96: "The goods of the world, all its delights and pleasures, if they are got and had apart from me with selfish and disordered love, are just like scorpions. I showed you this image in your early days . . . and I told you that these scorpions carry gold in front of them and venom in their tails. The venom does not come without the gold, nor the gold without the venom—but the gold is what one sees first."

taken away from us sometimes because we lose them, sometimes because someone steals them, sometimes because one circumstance or another causes them to fail or be used up. And we are taken away from them, I tell you, when gentle First Truth calls us, separating our soul from our body. Then we leave behind our body as well as the world with all its pleasures, and there is no one who can ward off this separation with riches or honors.

So weak and blinded people who have not removed the dirt of the world from their eyes, but have in fact kept it there, keep whirling around like leaves on a tree in the wind of disordered selfish love for themselves and for the world. From their[14] cursed mouth comes a whining, self-conceited envy of their neighbors, frequently resulting in hatred and rancor toward their neighbors. Often they claim for themselves what belongs to others, and to obtain these things they make use of oaths and perjury and lying testimony. It gets so bad that they even wish for their neighbors' death! Because of it, they end up devouring the possessions and flesh of those they ought to love as they love themselves!

Such people have no stability at all. They begin things with enthusiasm but rarely finish them. They are grounded on sand, where no structure can be built without having it soon crumble.[15] They are bereft of the life of grace and have lost the light of reason. They go about not like rational creatures but like animals.

So we really must be grounded on the living rock. Those who have set their mind's eye there, and have set their affection there in holy desire, cannot be—do not allow themselves to be—blown over by this evil wind. No, they resist it. They defend themselves with contempt for the world and its vanity and pleasures. They batter down pride with deep humility and by longing for voluntary poverty. Those who have wealth or prestige do indeed possess these, but they possess them not with excessive love or in disregard for God's will but with love and holy fear. They act as Christ's administrators, assisting the poor and supporting God's servants, reverencing them because they are continually offering prayers and burning desires and sweat and tears before God for everyone's salvation.[16]

---

[14] Literally, "this."

[15] Cf. Mt. 7, 26–27: "Everyone who hears these words of mine and does not act on them will be like a foolish man who build his house on sand. The rain fell, and the floods came, and the winds blew and beat against that house, and it fell—and great was its fall!"

[16] Cf. Let. T304 to Lodovica di Granello: "I thank divine Goodness and you for the alms you've given and seem to want to give to God's religious servants, who for this finite temporal sustenance give us prayer, a source of infinite good for us. Do your duty well, because in whatever you can do you must be a steward [of these things] for the poor, you and anyone else who has [any means]. For the poor, along with the loving charity of the one who is giving the alms, are the hands that lead us to eternal life."

Such people are happy no matter what their circumstances of time or status, because they are free of the bitterness of a disordered will that is grounded in selfish love. Since this foundation, then, is so wonderful, we should waste no time in securing it—for we are not sure we will have time.

The third principal wind, I tell you, is the flesh, which belches out such an awful stench that it is not only repulsive to God, but even to the devils. It actually makes beasts of human beings, because it has about as much shame as animals have. Such people are like pigs wallowing in the muck, as they wallow in the mud of indecency. They destroy themselves, no matter what their state in life. If they are married, they defile their state with disordered love. Though they ought to approach that sacrament with fear of God, they approach it without restraint,[17] hardly decently. The wretches don't consider to what dignity our human nature attained by God's union with our poor flesh, for if they opened their mind's eye to consider it, they would sooner die than give themselves to such wretchedness.

And do you know what stench comes from this mouth to poison anyone they come near? Their heart becomes suspicious, and their tongue grumbles and curses, believing that what is in themselves is also in the other person. They are like sick people whose stomachs are sour, and because they are sick, food doesn't seem good to them—not only regular food, but even the special food the doctor has prescribed for them to eat. When they see people eating whose sense of taste is healthy, they find it difficult to believe that it doesn't taste the same to them. So it is with the stupid people who give themselves up to carnal pleasures. They have so soured their appetite that they not only see evil in the common herd, that is, in those we commonly see sinning in this way, but they even find scandal in the healthy.[18] They even find scandal in their "special food," that is, their spouses, whom God has given them in consideration of their fragile infirmity.[19] So this food harms them, too, since they are unrestrained, as I've said. And often they become suspicious and jealous, judging this good thing evil, and dislike and hatred set in where there ought to be love. Their perception is distorted because their eye is sick. If their eye were healthy it would not be so.

Oh how many wretched wrongs and sins come from this wretched

---

[17] It. *disordinato.*

[18] It. *non tanto della communità, cioè di che communemente si veggono in questo defecto e' n piglino male, ma ne' sani si scandalizzano.*

[19] Aquinas (*Summa Theologica, Supplement*, q. 42, a. 3) cites Augustine as saying that "marriage affords a remedy for the sick." Aquinas elaborates: "But it is not a remedy except to the extent that it is somehow effective. Therefore it has some efficacy for the repression of concupiscence." Cf. 1 Cor. 7, 9: "It is better to marry than to burn."

wind! These people are always being eaten up inside. And after they belch out this stench from their mouth, they take to passing judgment on their spouses. And this gives birth to another wrong. For if by divine inspiration the desire should come to them to rise above this and live perfectly within their state of life, the worm of suspicion that has already entered their body squelches the fragrance of virtue and they return to their original filth, and they come to dislike what had at first attracted them.[20] Nor are they constant or persevering in virtue. No, they turn back to look at what they have already plowed instead of looking at themselves to get to know their sinfulness and weakness.

All this happens because they did not build their foundation on the living rock. So this evil wind has battered them and knocked them down. We must, then, rise above this wretched foundation, this putrid flesh, and make our foundation on the living rock, Christ. Then when the wind comes it will not be able to harm us. Instead we will resist with the true virtue of continence and purity, controlling our unrestrained will with the discipline of reason and of holy fear of God. We will say to ourselves: "Shame on you, my soul, for wanting to dirty your face and defile your body through impurity! You are made in God's image and likeness. And you, flesh: because of the union the divine nature effected with you, human nature, you attained such dignity that you have been exalted above all the choirs of angels!" Then we will sense the fragrance of purity and a desire to correct this vice by means of prayer and watchfulness, hatred and disgust. And we will make use of other instruments, physical and external instruments. We will punish our body with penance whenever it wants to rebel against the spirit. And above all other remedies against this vice stands humble prayer, with watchfulness and perfect self-knowledge. Nothing can ever be a match for this when the spirit is surrounded by the sense of strong evil thoughts and impulses. No, we think of taking the remedies, and the very thought of the remedy chases away the thoughts and imaginings.[21] It will be a water to quench the fire of disordered impulses.

So don't be afraid! Courageously take up the standard of the most holy cross. Those who have their foundation on this living rock lean on this standard and use it to sail onward, with the remedies I've spoken of, even

[20] That is, by renouncing intercourse and entering into so-called "spiritual marriage." Their "original filth" is unrestrained pleasure in marriage; "what had at first attracted them" is the inclination to complete abstinence.

[21] This is the only instance in which she says that the very thought of the remedy is effective.

to the point of death.[22] For they see clearly that only perseverance is crowned, not simply beginning.

So, dearest brother and son, I want you to rise above your lack of perseverance and begin to enter within yourself. For it seems to me, from what I see in the presence of divine Goodness, that you've already wandered a good way outside yourself! And all this is because your principle and foundation have not really been in truth, have not been built on the living rock. There is no other reason God's servants do not persevere except that they are imperfectly grounded. And because they are weak, when the strong winds come (I mean the devil, the world, and the flesh) and find them without strength and without any support of virtue, they fail. I've been thinking of the remedies for your fall and your need to take them and make a more perfect beginning with deeper humility and contempt for yourself. And this is why I said that I long to see you a solid rock, with your foundation on the living rock, Christ gentle Jesus—and not on sand. I trust in God's infinite goodness that, if you are willing to humble yourself and get to know yourself, you will accomplish God's will and my desire. And you will win the life of grace. You will be freed from darkness and will have perfect light.

I'll say no more. Keep living in God's holy and tender love.

Gentle Jesus! Jesus love!

---

[22] Cf. Let. T220 to Suor Maddalena di Alessa: "Reflect that if you were to crash on the reef of disobedience because of your selfish love, your ship would be wrecked. You would drown, and you would lose the treasure, that is, the fruit of the holy intention you had when you promised obedience at your profession. So rouse yourself from this selfishness so that you won't perish. Courageously, like a true bride raise the tree of the humble spotless Lamb, your Bridegroom, on your ship—I mean the most holy cross, with the sail of his obedience. For you see, he spread this sail of obedience to his Father and ran on the speedy wind of love and of hatred for sin and for this sensual love, right up to the shameful death of the most holy cross." Note that Catherine usually uses this image of the cross as mast only in reference to religious obedience.

Letter T126/G176[1]
To Monna Alessa dei Saracini and Monna Cecca di Clemente Gori
Late September 1377

References to gossip about Catherine in Siena and to her "little boat" being emptied of all but God suggest that this letter was written not very long after Raimondo's departure for Rome about mid-September 1377, a placement which is strongly supported by the linguistic evidence.[2]

§

In the name of Jesus Christ crucified and of gentle Mary.

Dearest daughters in Christ gentle Jesus,

I Caterina, servant and slave of the servants of Jesus Christ, am writing to you in his precious blood. I long to see you so persistently constant in virtue that you will never look back to see what you have already plowed.[3] I mean this in two senses.

The first is when a person has left behind worldly corruptions and later mentally looks back at them with selfish pleasure. People like this never go forward but instead turn back to eat what they had once vomited out.[4] This is why Christ said that no one ought to turn back to look at what has already been plowed. That is, we shouldn't turn around to look at former pleasures or to admire this or that accomplishment of ours, but should give divine goodness the credit for such things. We should be going forward in persistent virtue, turning not backward but within, in self-knowledge, where we discover how generous is God's goodness. This sort of knowl-

---

[1] MSS: Mo-*a*, corrected by *b*, S5, S6, Ro, P4, S4; translation based on Mo-*a*. No relevant variants other than *b*'s.

[2] This placement is strongly supported by the linguistic evidence. Six of the eight letters which share eleven or more of this one's thirty-two analyzed patterns fall between October and December of 1377. A number of significant clusters within individual patterns occur seldom or not at all before late August (AMAINVER, CAPOVOL, CONSENZ, COSTANT, ODIOSANT, OFFEND, VOLSPIR). Most convincing, however, is PERFCOM, which occurs only in October 1377 and then once more in 1378. Fawtier (II, p. 228) declines to date this letter. Dupré Theseider places it immediately after T125, in October or November 1377.

[3] Lk. 9, 62.

[4] Cf. 2 Pt. 2, 20–22: "When people have fled a polluted world by recognizing the Lord and Savior Jesus Christ, and then are caught up and overcome in pollution once more, their last condition is worse than their first. It would have been better for them not to have recognized the road to holiness than to have turned their backs on the holy law handed on to them, once they had known it. How well the proverb fits them: 'The dog returns to its vomit.' "

edge strips us of selfish love and clothes us in holy hatred and a divine love so that we seek only Christ crucified—not other people, not created things, not ourselves on a sensual level, but only Christ crucified, loving and desiring [a share in] his humiliation. If we practice this and have torn out selfish love by its roots we will go forward and will not look back. But unless [our selfishness] has been completely uprooted both materially and spiritually we will in time be guilty of the second way of looking back.

And do you know what this second way is? It is not a turning back to worldly pleasures, but happens when we have begun to put our hand to the "plowing" of becoming very perfect. The perfection I mean consists most of all in completely smothering and drowning our own will, and this even more in spiritual things than in temporal (since we have already become detached from the temporal, but are now preoccupied with the spiritual). In this sort of perfection we love our Creator in truth, and his creatures for his sake—more or less, in proportion to their love. What I am saying is that unless we have completely uprooted our self-centered love we will turn back a second time and sin against our being made perfect. We may offend by loving creatures without measure (for it is only God we should love without measure, while we should love creatures with moderation, in reference to the Creator). Or we become lax about our love for someone we love with a special love.[5] Such laxity, even if it is not an offense against the one we love, cannot but slacken our love for God. (But if we are motivated by rumor or scandal, or by the fact that the one we love is far away, or by the absence of selfish consolation, we are not without fault.) So those who become careless in their charity for their neighbors are in fact turning back.

That, then, is not the way. Perseverance is the way. This is why I said that I long to see you persistently constant in virtue. I was thinking of how you've been walking among the wolves of gossip, and how it seems none of you is so strong as not to weaken. For[a] I've seen some turn back[b] who I thought had built such defenses that no wind could ever harm them, even to the point of death. I hadn't thought they would *ever* turn their faces back, nor for that matter even a glance. This truly is a sign that the root has not been torn out, for if it had, we would be doing as God's true servants do who are not turned back by thorns or difficulties, by gossip, by people's advice or threats, or by fear of their relatives. No, we would in truth be following Christ crucified; we would follow him to prison and to death.[6] And we would follow his example. I don't mean independently

---

[5] Cf. *Dial.* 144, pp. 302–303, for an expansion of this theme of friendship.

[6] Cf. Lk. 22, 33: "[Peter] said to him, 'Lord, I am ready to go with you to prison and to death.' "

of true and holy obedience to the rule. (For even if *he* wanted that, I would not.[7])

But apart from this, I'm sorry for the spiritual harm that is being done—yet not for myself, because they are doing me a favor. For he and the others are giving me occasion to know my foolishness and ingratitude in not having recognized even up to now my time[8] or the graces I have received from my Creator. So they are making me grow in virtue. Still, I have decided not to be silent, because a mother is responsible for telling her children what they need to hear. He and the others were given birth with plenty of tears and sweat, and I will continue to give them birth until I die, as God grants me grace in this sweet time of solitude that gentle First Truth has given to me and to this poor little family.[9] And it seems he wants my soul's little boat to be fitted out once more, filled only by my Creator—filled with the exercise of seeking and knowing the sweet truth, with continual groans and prayers in God's presence for the salvation of the whole world. May God give us grace, you and me and everyone else, to do this very conscientiously!

Commend us to Teopento's prayers, now that he has time in his cell.[10] For we are pilgrim travelers in this life, destined to experience both the milk and the thorns of Christ crucified. And tell him to read this letter. Let whoever has ears, hear; and whoever has eyes, see; and whoever has feet, get going.[11]

Don't turn back, but go forward, following Christ crucified, and with your hands do holy, true, and good works grounded in Christ crucified.

I'll say no more. Keep living in God's holy and tender love.

Gentle Jesus! Jesus love!

Textual Notes

a. *For* added by *b.*

b. *turn back* inserted by *b.*

---

[7] There is no expressed antecedent to "he," but the reference must have been clear to Alessa and Cecca. (It can hardly be God, since Catherine would never say that she did not want something even though God wanted it! And she continues to refer to this unnamed person in the next paragraph.) See, however, the final full paragraph of the letter and the note there.

[8] Cf. Lk. 19, 44: "You failed to recognize the time of your visitation." (Vulg.)

[9] This "time of solitude" could be her respite at Sant'Antimo in September or her later time at Rocca d'Orcia. I would guess, however, that it is the latter, after Raimondo's departure for Rome, since she goes on to refer to the emptying of her "little boat" and its being filled with God alone.

[10] Teopento is not identified in any Catherinian text. Possibly he is the unnamed person referred to in the preceding paragraph; this paragraph could then follow as a slightly sardonic challenge directed to him.

[11] Cf. Mt. 11, 15; 13, 9, and parallel passages in Mk. and Lk. (Vulg.)

LETTER T120/G344[1]
To Monna Rabe, wife of Francesco de' Tolomei
Late September 1377

At Rocca d'Orcia, Catherine is the guest of the Salimbeni family, yet she continues to associate also with members of the Tolomei family, though the two clans were constant rivals. In fact, one of the Tolomei, the Dominican Matteo, has accompanied her first to Montepulciano and now to the Rocca (see Let. T117 in this volume). Monna Rabe (short for Orrabile, from Onorabile) degli Agazzari, wife of Francesco di Tato Tolomei, is the mother of three of Catherine's disciples: the *Mantellate* Francesca and Ghinoccia, and the friar Matteo. The occasion of the present letter is the illness of Francesca Tolomei[2] because of which Rabe has ordered Matteo to return at once to Siena "no excuse accepted."

When Catherine writes this letter, the only friars with her must be Matteo and Bartolomeo Dominici, since she says that if Matteo were to leave, "his companion" (by process of elimination, Bartolomeo) would be left alone at the Rocca. So Raimondo da Capua must have already left for Rome. As for Tommaso dalla Fonte, who we know is with Catherine for most of her time in the Orcia Valley, he may be away on one of those brief missions for which Catherine seems to have used various of her disciples during this period. The letter must therefore be later than mid-September, the probable date of Raimondo's departure. It must also be before Matteo joins Raimondo in Rome, and we know from Let. T272 that he is there when that letter is written near mid-October.[3] On the basis of these facts, and supported by the linguistic evidence, I would place this letter to Monna Rabe in late September 1377.[4]

---

[1] MSS: B, P2, R1, T, P5, F2, F1, P3; translation based on R1, with variants from an unpublished transcription of B by Dupré Theseider.

[2] Francesca will die on 3 January 1379, having in the meantime received the habit (perhaps in a monastery—cf. Let. T81, written to her on that occasion) during her illness.

[3] The only other possibility would seem to be if there was a time earlier when Raimondo and Tommaso had gone off on a brief mission from the Rocca, for example, when Raimondo met with Niccolò Soderini in Siena before his departure for Rome. That would have to have been between mid-August and mid-September. There was a letter of Catherine apparently intended for S6 but never actually copied beyond the following description, a letter "to Fra Matteo Tolomei and Fra Jacomo of the Friars Preachers; the letter is preserved at Lecceto in the sacristy, among the relics, and was copied by Fra Ambrogio of Siena, Olivetan, in 1520." For this letter "preserved at Lecceto in the sacristy," not only has the original been lost, but there is no copy of a letter to the friars Matteo Tolomei and Jacomo in any manuscript. If we had that letter, it might shed light on the sequence of events here.

[4] Two of the three letters sharing ten or more of this one's thirty analyzed patterns are dated between August and October 1377. (The third is a very long letter from late 1378.) Besides, the most dense concentration of significant clusters within individual patterns

§

In the name of Jesus Christ crucified and of gentle Mary.

Dearest daughter in Christ gentle Jesus,

I Caterina, servant and slave of the servants of Jesus Christ, am writing to you in his precious blood. I long to see you living dead to your selfish sensuality, because this is the only way you can share in the life of grace. So I want you with tremendous energy and desire to make an effort to lift yourself above worldly weakness, for it is not fitting that we who are made to enjoy a home[a] in heaven,[5] nourished by virtue as our food,[b] should be finding dirt[6] tasteful and feeding on our sensual selfishness, the source of all the vices. No, we ought to be getting up and climbing to the high place of the virtues as we open our mind's eye to gaze upon the wood of the cross, where we find the Lamb, the tree of life, who has made a stairway of his body.[7]

The first stair he has taught us to climb is his feet, that is, affection. For just as the feet carry the body, so affection carries the soul. Once you have climbed this first stair, that is, once your feet are nailed fast to the cross, you will find your affection stripped of its disordered love.[8] When you reach the second stair, the open side of Christ crucified, you will see the secret of his heart, with what indescribable love he has made his blood a bath for you.[9] At the first stair your affection gets up and strips itself

---

occurs in this same period, with BOCCDESI, PACEBOCC, PARTECVT especially significant. Dupré Theseider (unpublished notes) places the letter in autumn of 1377, perhaps in early September. Fawtier (II, p. 303) holds that it is in no way certain that the letter is from the Rocca d'Orcia period, since nowhere is it stated that Matteo is with Bartolomeo.

[5] This is Catherine's only explicit reference to heaven as "home" (It. *abitazione*).

[6] It. *la terra*, which could be either "dirt" or "the earth." Parallel passages would suggest the former, for example, *Dial.* 33, p. 74: "These are the greedy misers who act like the mole who feeds on dirt right up to the end." And Let. T88 to Bishop Angelo Ricasoli (vol. I): "[T]heir eyes and their desire were fed not on dirt but on God's honor and other people's salvation."

[7] The development of the stair analogy here is clearly parallel with *Dial.* 26 and 59–76. She has begun to develop this imagery earlier in Let. T74 (vol. I, early 1376). It will occur again in Let. T75 (in this volume), but nowhere else. This imagery is used also by Giordano da Rivalto (ed. Narducci, pp. 1–2 and 240–243). Only here and in Let. T220 and T355 does she call "the Lamb" the "tree of life." In Let. T113, T171, T346, T354, and Prayer 17, Christ crucified is the tree of life. Elsewhere, the cross is the tree (but not the "tree of life"), and the Lamb is the fruit on that tree.

[8] In *Dial.* 49 the image becomes clearer: the first step on the stairway that is the body of Jesus crucified is his nailed feet, to which the soul climbs by means of its "feet," its affection (that is, desire, will, motivation). And joined with the crucified, the soul's affection is stripped of all disordered love.

[9] Again, the image is developed in *Dial.* 26 and 59–76. Cf. also Let. T189/DT84, sent separately to the monks of Cervaia and to several Olivetan monks (in this volume): "No wonder the memory of the blood lives on in the hearts of God's servants, for it is mixed

clean; at the second you experience the love you find in Christ's open heart. When you see the third stair, I mean when you reach the mouth of God's Son, you are nourished in peace. For once our soul has been stripped of perverted sensual love (the source of war) and clothed in the love of Christ crucified, we discover patience.[10,c] Then all bitterness[d] seems sweet to us; in fact, we rejoice in the world's persecution and harassment, from whatever direction God permits it, because we have discovered the peace of his mouth.[11] The giver of peace unites himself with the one to whom he gives it. So once we are clothed in virtue we experience God in the movement of love, and we join the mouth of our holy desire with God's desire and so are united [with him] in peace and tranquillity.[12]

So you see how Christ has made a stairway of his body so that we may climb up to the height of heaven, everlasting life. There there is life without death, light without darkness, satiety without boredom, hunger without pain—for, as Saint Augustine says, boredom is a stranger to satiety, and pain a stranger to hunger, because the citizens of eternal life are satisfied in the eternal sight of God with all they desire and hunger for.[13] How wretchedly foolish are we if through our sin we lose such a good and make ourselves deserving of great evil!

Up, then, dearest daughter, and don't wait for the time you don't have! No, with a great thrust of love lift yourself above[e] the perversity of your sensual love, which deprives you of the light of reason and makes you love the world and your children all out of proportion. There is no other way you can reach the destination for which you were created. This is why I said I long to see you living dead to your selfish will and selfish love—

---

with fire! I remember in this regard what First Truth once said to one of his servants. She asked, 'Once you were dead, why did you want your side to be opened and to pour out such a torrent of blood?' And he said, 'There are many reasons, but I will tell you two important ones. First of all, I wanted this because by having my side opened I showed you the secret of my heart. For my heart held more love for humankind than any external physical act could show. The other reason was the baptism that was given to the human race because of the merits of my blood.'"

[10] That is, a willingness to suffer.

[11] A kiss of peace was solemnly exchanged to seal a reconciliation between two warring parties, a kiss that was given on the lips. Also, liturgical rubrics included at some points a kiss of peace, this given in the form of an embrace.

[12] This is the only place she explicitly associates union with arriving at the mouth of the crucified, the "kiss of peace." The association is, however, implicit, in *Dial.* 76, pp. 140–141.

[13] Cf. Pseudo-Augustine, *Meditatio XXVII* (PL XL, 921): "For [the blessed] shall have desire for the vision of God with satiety, and satiety with desire. Their desire shall not be a source of pain, nor their satiety a source of boredom." The idea is repeated by Cavalca, (*Specchio di croce*, p. 184): "Sated, we shall be hungry, and hungering we shall be sated, but our satiety will be far from boredom, and our hunger far from pain." Also in *Descrizione de' dieci comandamenti*, p. 306: "We shall desire though we are sated, and we shall be sated even in our desiring. Yet satiety will not be a source of boredom, nor desire be accompanied by pain, as happens in this world."

because it seems to me you are still too alive to these. I noticed this in the letter you wrote, that blind love was making you move away from ordering your priorities in terms of God.

You wrote that Francesca was very ill, and so you wanted Frate Matteo to come—no excuse accepted—and that if he didn't come you would put your curse on him! If he couldn't do otherwise, you said, let him take a peasant as companion![14] You can't, I tell you, deny your ridiculous foolishness. Never mind that it was not as God would have it; if you had even the little bit of sense nature endows us with, you wouldn't have acted so. If you wanted or still want Frate Matteo to come, or if that's needed to make your daughter happy, you would have sent a couple of friars, so that the one might come back there with Matteo and the other stay here—since you know very well that he can't come alone, and his companion can't stay here alone. But no, you carry on as if your emotions have run away with you, like a person whose ears are buzzing with gossip.[15] And all this because you haven't lifted your face from the ground, haven't climbed even the first stair, [Christ's] feet. If you had, you would be wanting only that your son pursue God's honor and the salvation of souls. Driven by that desire, you and the others would plug your ears and lop off your tongues so as not to hear what's being said to you and not to say it yourself. So no more of that!

Bathe yourself in the blood of Christ crucified. Lift yourself out of this consorting with the dead and associate with the living, in true and solid virtue.

I'll say no more. Comfort Francesca. . . .[16] Keep living in God's holy and tender love.

Gentle Jesus! Jesus love! Gentle Mary![f]

Textual Notes

a. P5, F1: *blessedness / a home* (*beatitudine / abitazione*).

b. P2: [*as our food*].

c. P5, F1: *peace / patience.*

d. P5, F1, F2: *love and all bitterness / all bitterness.*

e. P5, F2, F2: *above the world and / above.*

f. P5, F1, F2: *Keep living in Christ gentle Jesus. Amen.* Only B has *Gentle Mary!*

---

[14] Members of the mendicant orders never traveled without a companion. The rule was rigorously applied; cf. the Acts of the Provincial Chapter of Pisa, 1340: "Let it be decreed that no one is to go out alone for any reason or pretext whatever . . . , and if anyone should do so, let him be held in suspicion." (Cited in I. Taurisano, *I Domenicani in Lucca*.)

[15] Since Rabe belonged by marriage to the Tolomei family, it is not surprising that she would be influenced by rumors that Catherine and her disciples (including all of her own children!) were involved in political mischief among the Salimbeni.

[16] The ellipses probably indicate the deletion of additional personal notes.

LETTER T117/G167[1]
To Monna Lapa, her mother,
at the Monastery of Sant'Agnesa in Montepulciano[2]
Late September 1377

The rubric in the manuscripts specifies that Catherine wrote this letter while she was at Rocca d'Orcia. She must have been there at least long enough for word to have arrived from Lapa, who has been left at the monastery, about her distress. Since Catherine mentions "staying longer," one can conclude that there has been a change of plans since she wrote to Caterina dello Spedaluccio and Giovanna di Capo (Let. T118) that she would be returning to Siena as soon as she could. In fact, one gets the impression that once Catherine has arrived at the Salimbeni fortress her plans are being formed one project at a time with no preconceived end point.

There is no hint as to what "great scandal" Catherine is attempting to resolve that "has nothing to do with the countess." She originally went to settle the feud between the countess' brother Agnolino and their cousin Cione, which would certainly have something to do with the countess. Perhaps it is the conflict between the abbot of Sant'Antimo and the archpriest of Montalcino, in which case she may have just returned from her journey to the abbey. In any case, I would place this letter at least a bit later than Let. T118, but after T1, possibly in late September.[3]

§

In the name of Jesus Christ crucified and of gentle Mary.

Dearest mother and daughter in Christ gentle Jesus,[4]

I Caterina, servant and slave of the servants of Jesus Christ, am writing to you in his precious blood. I long to see you so clothed in the fire of divine

---

[1] MSS: Mo-*b*, P4, S4; translation based on Mo-*b*, with variants based on unpublished notes by A. Volpato.

[2] The rubric includes Monna Cecca (di Clemente Gori) as addressee. Cecca, however, is simply greeted in the context of the letter. The letter itself is clearly directly to Catherine's mother.

[3] In such a short letter, with only thirteen patterns to analyze, the linguistic evidence is not much help. The nine letters which share five or more of these patterns are quite widely spread chronologically, as are most individual patterns. MARIAMAD, however, occurs in only five isolated cases after October 1377. Fawtier (II, p. 221) simply places the letter, based on the rubric, during Catherine's stay at the Rocca. Dupré Theseider (unpublished notes) places it more precisely in October.

[4] Note, from the address, that Catherine is treating her mother as a disciple, something she has not done in earlier letters to her (T6, T240/DT83, both in this volume).

charity that you will bear with true patience every pain and torment, hunger and thirst, harassment and injury, derision, slander, abuse—and anything else.

Learn from the slain and consumed Lamb, who ran with such blazing love to the shameful death of the cross. And live in the company of the most gracious mother Mary, who though she loved the holy disciples tremendously, consented to their leaving her so that they might pursue God's honor and the salvation of souls by following in the footsteps of her dear Son. And she remained all but alone, a guest and a pilgrim. As for the disciples, though they loved her immensely, they left with joy and put up with every sort of suffering for God's honor. They went before tyrants and submitted to every sort of persecution. And if you had asked them, "Why are you leaving Mary, and why are you suffering so joyfully?" they would have answered, "Because we have let go of ourselves and are in love with God's honor and the salvation of souls."[5]

This, dearest mother and daughter, is the way I want you to act. If you haven't been so up to now, I want you to be set ablaze in the fire of divine charity, seeking always God's honor and the salvation of souls. Otherwise you would really be in pain and in trouble, and you'd have me in the same state. Understand, dearest mother, that I your poor daughter have been put on this earth for no other purpose; this is what my Creator has chosen me for. I know you are happy to have me obey him. If you think I am staying here longer than you would like, I beg you to be content, because I cannot do otherwise. I believe that if you knew the circumstances you yourself would be sending me here. I am staying to resolve a great scandal, if I can. It has nothing to do with the countess, however.[6] So beg God and the glorious virgin, all of you, to grant us a good outcome.

As for you, Cecca and Giustina,[7] drown yourselves in the blood of Christ crucified, for now is the time to prove your virtue. May God give you all his sweet eternal benediction.

I'll say no more. Keep living in God's holy and tender love.

Gentle Jesus! Jesus love!

---

[5] She follows here as elsewhere the popular version of the dispersion of the disciples of Christ after the Ascension. Note that she sees Mary as the "guest" of the beloved disciple, John.

[6] P4 has *difecto / de' fatti*, thus yielding: "It is not the countess' fault, though." The countess is Benedetta (Bandeçça) Salimbeni.

[7] Cecca di Clemente Gori, who has stayed at Montepulciano with Lapa, and her daughter Giustina, who is one of the nuns there. The fact that Catherine's niece Eugenia is not mentioned would seem to indicate that the latter has not yet joined the community at Sant' Agnesa.

LETTER T125/G161[1]
To Monna Nera, prioress of the *Mantellate* of Siena
Late September or October 1377

Catherine, it will be remembered, was a member of the Sienese *Mantellate*. Since the appointment of Raimondo da Capua as her confessor, however, she was subject to no one but him within the Dominican Order, a provision that did not always sit well with her sisters in the *Mantellate*, possibly even their prioress.[2] If so, the frankness with which Catherine addresses this woman so much her senior is quite remarkable.

Since the rubric of Mo specifies that the letter was written "while she was at the fortress of Agnolino," it has to be from between September and December 1377.[3] Its tone and content seem to reflect Catherine's concerns during the early part of that period, when she was contending with criticism from Siena. Such a placement is strikingly supported by the linguistic evidence. I would therefore place the letter in September or October of 1377, with other letters in which Catherine addresses the same concerns.[4]

§

In the name of Jesus Christ crucified and of gentle Mary.

Dearest mother in Christ gentle Jesus,

I Caterina, servant and slave of the servants of Jesus Christ, am writing to you in his precious blood. I long to see you doing as does the good Shepherd, who gives his life for his little sheep. This, dearest mother, is what you should be doing: attending to God's honor and to the well-being of the little sheep he has put in your charge. Don't be careless about it, be-

---

[1] MSS: Mo-*b*, P4, S4; translation based on Mo-*b*. No relevant variants.

[2] In April 1378 the latter office was held by Monna Caterina di Ranuccio Saracini, who had been a member of the group at least since 1352, so it may be to her that the present letter is addressed, even though the name in the rubric is Monna Nera. Dupré Theseider (unpublished notes) states that the prioress to whom this letter is addressed "must be Nera ser Michelis from the list of *Mantellate*, among the oldest by entrance even from the end of 1352, because she is in group A." Nera is not, however, designated as prioress in the 1353 list; the title is given rather to the first name (illegible) on that list (Laurent, *Fontes*, I, *Documenti*, pp. 23, 47).

[3] This is where both Fawtier (II, p. 220) and Dupré Theseider (unpublished notes) place it.

[4] Though this brief letter provides only ten patterns to analyze, all but one of the six letters which share four or more of these patterns fall between April and October 1377 with three in September and October. Besides, CONFITTO occurs only very sporadically after October, and there is a tight concentration of occurrences of CORRGIUS in October.

cause for that God would reproach you. No, be genuinely concerned, setting aside all selfishness and human respect.

You know, dearest mother, that a superior who is too in love with herself never gives correction, because she is always afraid. And if she does correct, her correction is often dictated not by the truth but by what people will think, or by her own selfish opinion, her own dislike for certain people's ways. This is not right, since God has many ways with his servants and leads them along many paths. For us it is enough to see their desire to follow Christ crucified. If your correcting is dictated by your own opinion it is more likely to be unfair rather than just. You ought simply to correct according to the faults you see, gently raising your own will to God's honor and looking with understanding at those in your charge, giving each one what she needs. So you have to treat those who are less perfect in one way, those who are more perfect in another, knowing how to adapt to their needs but always firm in correcting the faults you see and never for any reason letting them go uncorrected. I hope in God's boundless and infinite charity that you will do this.

Open your mind's eye and look at what motivated the spotless Lamb, nailed fast to the cross. You will see that this true master laid down his life for his little sheep, and how lovingly and devotedly he lived among us, carrying and putting up with us poor things, always perfectly attentive to the Father's honor and our well-being. Neither our ingratitude nor people's grumbling nor the devils' malice kept him from accomplishing our salvation. This, by his goodness, dearest mother, is the way I hope you will act. Don't hesitate because we your wretched daughters and our whole community are ungrateful, or because of people's talk and grumbling, or because of the malice of the devil, who to hinder God's honor and the salvation of souls is sitting on their tongues so that they say things they shouldn't be saying.

So do what you can, and withstand all these things without any fear at all. Let your mind and your affection never deviate from the truth, since there is nothing else you want to desire except that God be honored and that your daughters be mirrors of virtue. Then God will fulfill your desire, and you will find consolation in yourself as well as in them. For whenever others do something virtuous there is always joy and consolation in it. Act in this way, then, for love of Jesus Christ crucified.

I'll say no more. Keep living in God's holy and tender love.

Gentle Jesus! Jesus love!

LETTER T220/G155[1]
To Suor Maddalena di Alessa,
nun of the Monastery of Santa Bonda near Siena.
September or October 1377

We have met the nuns of Santa Bonda in Catherine's letter to Suor Costanza (T73, vol. I). The nun to whom the present letter is addressed has not been identified beyond the detail given in the rubric of Mo that her mother's name is Alessa.

Reference to the complaints in Siena about Catherine's activities, unexpected parallels with Let. T294 and T197 (in this volume), and the linguistic evidence lead me to place this letter in September or October of 1377.[2]

The first part of the present letter is repeated in Let. T182 to Suor Bartolomea della Seta. I believe that, of the two letters, the ending of T220 seems more integrated with the beginning, and so would place it before T182; but then again, the scribe of Mo is one of Catherine's own secretaries, Neri di Landoccio Pagliaresi, and he calls the ending of T220 an "addition," so it could be that T182 is the prototype.[3]

It is interesting to note that this letter, like some others of the Rocca d'Orcia period, is filled with awkward clause sequences, as well as some of the same inconsistency of pronouns.

---

[1] MSS: Mo-*a*, M, S5, S6, B, P2, R1, P5, F2, F1, P3, P4, S4; translation based on Mo-*a*. No relevant variants.

[2] Fourteen other letters share sixteen or more of this one's seventy-three analyzed patterns. Nine of these are from the last five months of 1377 (and five are later). The probable placement of this letter is further narrowed by a number of significant clusters within individual patterns which begin and/or end between August and November of 1377: AMODCRIS, BENEFATT, CARNRIB, CIECAMOR, COGNAM, INCOMPOR, MARETEMP, NAVICREL, NUDITA, OBEDPENT, ODIOAMPR, PERAMORE, RADSUPER, REALVEST, SANTPROP, SCHIFPEN, VENTVELA. Dupré Theseider (unpublished notes) speculates that the letter may be from the Rocca d'Orcia period. Fawtier (II, p. 227) declines to date it.

[3] Note that Mo simply places the section unique to Let. T220 immediately *after* Let. T182 and at its end notes that it belongs to a letter sent to Suor Maddalena, daughter of Monna Alessa, and identifies her monastery as Santa Bonda. The scribe places a cross-hatch in the margin of Let. T182 at the point at which the ending of Let. T220 begins.

§

In the name of Jesus Christ crucified and of gentle Mary.

Dearest daughter in Christ gentle Jesus,

I Caterina, servant and slave of the servants of Jesus Christ, am writing to you in his precious blood. I long to see you dressed in a royal garment, the garment of blazing charity. This is the garment that covers your nakedness, hides your shame, and warms and consumes your coldness.

When I say that it covers your nakedness, I mean that a soul created in God's image and likeness, if it had being without divine grace, would not attain the end for which it was created. So we must from the very beginning have the garment of grace, and we receive it in baptism, through the mediation of Christ's blood.[4] With this garment, infants who die in childhood have eternal life.[5] But we spouses have had a bit more time, and if knowledge of our eternal Bridegroom's boundless charity hasn't clothed us in a garment of love for him, we might say that the grace we received in baptism is naked. So we must lift up our affection and desire in true knowledge of ourselves, open our mind's eye, and come to know within ourselves God's goodness and his boundless love for us. For once our understanding sees and knows, our will[6] cannot but love its benefactor, and our memory cannot but embrace him.[7] And so by loving we attract love, and we find ourselves clothed, our nakedness covered.

I say that [this garment] hides our shame, and it does this in two ways.

The first is that it despises sin and so throws off its shame. How? The shame we bring upon ourselves when we offend our Creator is replaced by the garment of love for virtue, and we begin to be fruitful and to give honor to God. (For from everything we do God wants the flower of hon-

---

[4] Here the garment of grace, or of charity, is not quite equated with Christ's blood as it is elsewhere. Rather, Christ's blood is the means by which one acquires this garment.

[5] Cf. Aquinas, *Summa Theologica*, III, q. 69, a. 6: "Some of the early writers held that children do not receive grace and virtues in baptism, but that they receive the imprint of the character of Christ, by the power of which they receive grace and virtue when they arrive at the perfect age. But this is evidently false, for two reasons. First, children like adults are made members of Christ in baptism, so they must necessarily receive an outpouring of grace and virtue from their Head. Secondly, if this were not true, children who die after baptism would not enter eternal life."

[6] It. *affetto*, "affection."

[7] It. *ritenga* reflects the Augustinian concept of the memory's "holding" what is presented by understanding. Usually Catherine speaks of memory holding not our benefactor, but the blessings we have received.

or but leaves the fruit for us.[8]) So you see how [this garment] hides the shame of sin.

But I say that it also relieves us of another sort of shame. Once our will is dead to selfishness and to all transitory things, we do not see as shameful the things that sensuality (because of its selfish love and worldly perception) is ashamed of. In fact, we delight in shame, torment, mockery, abuse, and reproach. We consider ourselves well off to the extent that we are trampled on by the world. So we are happy, for the sake of God's honor, if the world hounds us with all sorts of abuse, and the devil with all sorts of harassment and temptation, and the flesh with its hankering to rebel against the spirit. We rejoice in all this, [wanting] in self-hatred to take vengeance on ourselves in order to be conformed with Christ crucified, and regarding ourselves as undeserving of spiritual peace and calm. We are not ashamed to be mocked and ridiculed by all three of these enemies (the world, the flesh, and the devil), because our sensual will is dead, clothed in the garment of the supreme eternal will of God. No, we reverence all of this, as we should, because God permits it not out of hatred but out of

---

[8] It might seem from this image, also found elsewhere, that Catherine was unaware of the relationship between blossom and fruit, since there is no fruit without the loss of the blossom, but in Let. T144/DT34 to Monna Pavola, Christ is blossom become fruit: "[Mary] was the field wherein was sown the seed of the incarnate Word, God's Son. Truly, . . . in that lovely blessed field the Word was engrafted into Mary's flesh as a seed is sown in the earth. In the sun's warmth it sprouts and blossoms and bears fruit, while the seed's husk remains in the ground." And in Let. T113 to Bandeçça Salimbeni, Catherine carries the image to its logical development: "[D]on't you see that we are a tree of love, because we were made for love? And this tree is so well made that no one can keep it from growing or take its fruit without the tree's consent. And God has given this tree a worker to tend it as it pleases, and this worker is free choice. . . . [I]f this worker, free choice, plants the tree where it ought to be planted, that is, in the soil of true humility (for it should not put it on the mountain of pride, but in the valley of humility), then it will produce fragrant blossoms of virtue, especially that topmost blossom of glory and praise for God's name. And all the other sweet blossoms and fruits, its virtuous deeds, will receive fragrance from that topmost blossom. This is the blossom, dearest daughter, that makes our virtues flower; it is the blossom God wants for himself. The fruit he wants to be ours. . . . He has no need of our fruit, because he lacks nothing. . . . Supreme eternal Goodness saw that human beings cannot live on blossoms but only on fruit. (If we eat blossoms we die, but on fruit we live.) That is why God took the blossom for himself and gives the fruit to us. And if we foolish people want to feed on the blossom—that is, give ourselves the glory and praise that ought to be God's—it robs us of the life of grace and gives us eternal death if we die without changing our ways to keep just the fruit for ourselves and give the blossom, the glory, to God. . . . Once a tree is full-grown it stretches out its branches and offers fruit to its neighbors—I mean the fruit of holy, humble, continual prayer and the example of a good holy life. And it stretches out its branches to them, too, whenever it can, by offering them material help with a great and generous heart, sincere and unfeigned." So it is precisely in bearing fruit and sharing it with our neighbors, rather than trying to hold on to the beauty of the blossom, that we surrender the blossom of glory to God.

love. We accept it with the same love with which we see it is given. So it is a lovely thing to desire the shame that casts out shame.[9]

Oh how blessed we are to be so sweetly enlightened! For we hate these passions of ours and those that are aroused in us by others, but we love the suffering these passions cause us. By our own passions I mean our selfish sensuality. By the passions aroused in us by others I mean [our resentment of] the world's harassment.[10]

So consider yourself deserving of the pain, dearest daughter, but undeserving of the fruit that issues from the pain. These things will be the ornaments you will wear on your royal garment. You know very well that [our] eternal Bridegroom did the same, for he adorned his garment with all sorts of sufferings: scourging, torments, mockery, abuse, and finally the shameful death of the cross.[11]

I say also that [this garment of charity] warms us and consumes our coldness. We are warmed, I say, by the fire of blazing charity, and we show it in our passionate desire for God's honor in our neighbors' salvation,[12] by bearing with and sharing the burden[13] of their shortcomings. We rejoice with God's servants who are rejoicing, and we weep with the wicked who are living in a time of weeping, in the compassion and sorrow we bear because of their offense against God.[14] And we willingly surrender ourselves to every kind of pain and torment in order to bring the wicked back to the condition of those who are rejoicing, who are living as lovers of lovely, royal virtue.

When I say that [this garment] consumes our coldness, I am referring to the coldness of selfish love for ourselves. This sort of love blinds us, keeping us from knowing either ourselves or God. It robs us of the life of

---

[9] Literally, "It is, then, lovely to desire shame, for with it shame is cast out."

[10] It. *Però che insiememente e hodiare i movimenti nostri e gli altrui, e amare le pene che per essi movimenti sosteniamo. Movimento nostro è la propria sensualità, ma movimenti altrui sono le persecutioni del mondo.* B adds what appears to be a gloss: *cioè la colpa odiare di colui che perseguita.* This seems at first blush to be an unusual use of *movimento*, which in Catherine's writings, when it does not have the literally cognate sense of "movement," refers to the movement of passion. However, the added comment of B does seem to clarify the sense, which I have tried to convey in a rather expansive translation.

[11] Nowhere else except in these twin letters (T182, T220) does she speak of Christ putting ornaments on his garment of charity.

[12] Usually Catherine speaks of God's honor *and* one's neighbors' salvation, but here and in Let. T98, T63, T72, T96, T105, T157 (all of which date from the time of the composition of *The Dialogue* or later), and in *The Dialogue* itself, ch. 19 and 23, she refines the expression to God's honor *in* one's neighbors' salvation, reflecting her conviction that one honors God precisely in working for one's neighbors' salvation. We have seen the same idea in the image of the flower and the fruit, above.

[13] It. *portando e sopportando.*

[14] Cf. Rom. 12, 15: "Rejoice with those who rejoice; weep with those who weep." Catherine's interpretation, however, is slightly different from Paul's.

grace. It gives birth to impatience as the root of pride sends out its branches. In our misplaced love we become offensive to God and to our neighbors, and unbearable to ourselves. We are constantly rebelling against [God's] commands. And all of this is the result of selfish self-love.[15]

So I want you, dearest and very much loved daughter, to get rid of all selfish love for your selfish sensuality (for it isn't good for Christ's bride to be loving what her Spouse doesn't love). I want you, by the light of reason, to embrace virtue.[16] The only way you can navigate this stormy sea, this darksome life, is on the ship of holy obedience you have boarded. Without this ship, dearest daughter, you would never get to the port of everlasting life to be united with the eternal Bridegroom.

Reflect that if you were to crash on the reef of disobedience because of your selfish love, your ship would be wrecked. You would drown, and you would lose the treasure, that is, the fruit of the holy intention you had when you promised obedience at your profession. So rouse yourself from this selfishness so that you won't perish. Courageously, like a true bride, raise the tree of the humble spotless Lamb, your Bridegroom, on your ship—I mean the most holy cross, with the sail of his obedience. For you see, he spread this sail of obedience to his Father and ran on the speedy wind of love and of hatred for sin and for this sensual love, right up to the shameful death of the most holy cross. Now you do the same.[17]

In ready obedience and true humility, with love for God and for your neighbors, love and bear with your sisters in charity. No thought of taking scandal in spiritual matters,[18] no rumor-mongering! Be tolerant and sympathetic regarding what you see or hear about your neighbors. Whenever you are reproached accept it with reverence, presuming that these things are said not in hatred but in love—even if they should offend you.[19] In this way you will free yourself of the indignation and of all the pain. You will have affection for virtue and contempt for vice and for selfish and misplaced love. You will have learned from the good gentle Jesus, who is rule, way, and teaching to you. He teaches us this rule and lesson by his obedience. He does not avoid suffering but perfects it on the wood of the most holy cross in shame, in mockery and abuse, in insult and ignominy.

---

[15] Here the part common to Let. T220 and T182 ends.

[16] This is corrected from the Tommasèo text; Mo has "with the weapons of reason." The latter is probably an error, though in Let. T332 (1379) Catherine speaks of reason arming itself with the knife of hatred and love. However, she has not spoken of this pairing of hatred and love in the present letter, either in general or under the image of the knife.

[17] The same imagery is used in Let. T197 to Matteo di Tomuccio (in this volume).

[18] It. *scandalo di mente.*

[19] The manuscripts actually have *ti facessero* ("should make you"), which seems to be a scribal error. The translation is therefore conjectural.

He is your way, for just as he walked the way of the cross, so you and everyone else must follow him, suffering every sort of pain, torment, and vexation for love of him, spreading your sail on this tree, Christ crucified—I mean the sail of love and the power of desire with constant prayer. This prayer is a deliverer and a fetcher.[20] It delivers our desires, filled with the self-contempt and love for virtue that is proved in our charity toward our neighbors. And it fetches back God's desire and will, and having fetched it, puts it on its back with the hands of good holy deeds.[21]

Then [if you do all this], you will find yourself stripped of your selfish love and clothed in the wedding garment. If not, you will not be a true bride. Nor will you be strong against all this grumbling about us—of which I know you are hearing, and which I know has caused you pain.[22] But I don't want you having any more pain [over it], because this is the path God's true servants must walk! I've been reflecting that those who do all that I've been talking about are completely freed from pain and stay peaceful and calm, and this is why I told you that I long to see you stripped of selfish sensual love and clothed in this royal garment, in the abyss of the eternal King's charity.[23] Then you will be freed from the pain of obedience as well as from the pain this grumbling is causing you. And you will live in peace and calm, experiencing God through grace, so that in the end you may receive the eternal vision of God. There all pain is finished. There we receive the fruit of virtue, the fruit that issues from [our] labors.

May God grant you and the others his sweet eternal benediction! Keep living in God's holy and tender love.

Gentle Jesus! Jesus love!

---

[20] Cf. Let. T30/DT1 to the Abbess and Suor Niccolosa (vol. I), where the "deliverer and fetcher" is Catherine herself, praying for her correspondents.

[21] Cf. Let. T35 to several Olivetan monks (late 1377 or early 1378): "You have the rudder of holy obedience, and for mast, the tree of the most holy cross. Spread the sail of his blazing charity, and use that sail to reach the port of salvation. You have only to breathe the wind of holy desire, with self-contempt, with humble and obedient and constant prayer, and this favorable wind, with perseverance, will bring you to the port of eternal life." Only here, however, does she introduce the image of prayer as a wind "delivering" our desire and "fetching" God's desire, evoking perhaps the image of a ship taking a cargo in one direction and then bringing another cargo back in exchange.

[22] The reference has to be to the complaints in Siena about Catherine's activities in the Val d'Orcia. The nuns, though cloistered in their monastery, could well be hearing news of these rumors from others of Catherine's disciples.

[23] This last phrase, found in Mo but not in the Tommasèo text, is echoed in the closing of Let. T182. Cf. Ps. 103, 6: "The abyss is like a garment in which he (or it) is clothed." (Vulg., following the Septuagint; in the Hebrew it is clearly the earth which is clothed in the deep; in the Vulgate translation from the Septuagint it could be either God or the earth.)

LETTER T182/G151[1]
To Suor Bartolomea della Seta of the Monastery of Santo Stefano in Pisa
September or October 1377

Catherine has already written one letter (T221) to Bartolomea. The present letter simply repeats a good part of the preceding one (Let. T220), also addressed to a nun, and then adds its own ending. The chronological placement in this case rests entirely on this letter's relationship with T220, though that placement is broadly supported by the linguistic evidence within this much shorter letter.[2]

§

In the name of Jesus Christ crucified and of gentle Mary.

Dearest daughter in Christ gentle Jesus,

I Caterina, servant and slave of the servants of Jesus Christ, am writing to you in his precious blood. I long to see you dressed in a royal garment, the garment of blazing charity. This is the garment that covers your nakedness, hides your shame, and warms and consumes your coldness.

When I say that it covers your nakedness, I mean that a soul created in God's image and likeness, if it had being without divine grace, would not attain the end for which it was created. So we must from the very beginning have the garment of grace, and we receive it in baptism, through the mediation of Christ's blood.[3] With this garment, infants who die in childhood have eternal life.[4] But we spouses have had a bit more time, and if knowledge of our eternal Bridegroom's boundless charity hasn't clothed us

---

[1] MSS: Mo-*a*, M, S5, S6, Ro, B, P2, R1, P5, F2, F1, P3, P4, S4; translation based on Mo-*a*. No relevant variants.

[2] Four other letters share seven or more of this one's twenty-one analyzed patterns. Two of these are from the last five months of 1377; two are very long letters in late 1378. A few significant clusters within individual patterns begin and/or end between August and November of 1377: CIECAMOR, INCOMPOR, RADSUPER, REALVEST, SAZFAST. Dupré Theseider (unpublished notes) speculates that the letter may be from the Rocca d'Orcia period. Fawtier (II, p. 227) declines to date it.

[3] Here the garment of grace, or of charity, is not quite equated with Christ's blood as it is elsewhere. Rather, Christ's blood is the means by which one acquires this garment.

[4] Cf. Aquinas, *Summa Theologica*, III, q. 69, a. 6: "Some of the early writers held that children do not receive grace and virtues in baptism, but that they receive the imprint of the character of Christ, by the power of which they receive grace and virtue when they arrive at the perfect age. But this is evidently false, for two reasons. First, children like adults are made members of Christ in baptism, so they must necessarily receive an outpouring of grace and virtue from their Head. Secondly, if this were not true, children who die after baptism would not enter eternal life."

in a garment of love for him, we might say that the grace we received in baptism is naked. So we must lift up our affection and desire in true knowledge of ourselves, open our mind's eye, and come to know within ourselves God's goodness and his boundless love for us. For once our understanding sees and knows, our will[5] cannot but love its benefactor, and our memory cannot but embrace him.[6] And so by loving we attract love, and we find ourselves clothed, our nakedness covered.

I say that [this garment] hides our shame, and it does this in two ways.

The first is that it despises sin and so throws off its shame. How? The shame we bring upon ourselves when we offend our Creator is replaced by the garment of love for virtue, and we begin to be fruitful and to give honor to God. (For from everything we do God wants the flower of honor but leaves the fruit for us.[7]) So you see how [this garment] hides the shame of sin.

But I say that it also relieves us of another sort of shame. Once our will is dead to selfishness and to all transitory things, we do not see as shameful

---

[5] It. *affetto*, "affection."

[6] It. *ritenga* reflects the Augustinian concept of the memory's "holding" what is presented by understanding. Usually Catherine speaks of memory holding not our benefactor, but the blessings we have received.

[7] This image, also found elsewhere, seems to indicate that Catherine was unaware of the relationship between blossom and fruit, since there is no fruit without the loss of the blossom. However, in Let. T144/DT34 to Monna Pavola (vol. I), Christ is blossom become fruit: "[Mary] was the field wherein was sown the seed of the incarnate Word, God's Son. Truly, . . . in that lovely blessed field the Word was engrafted into Mary's flesh as a seed is sown in the earth. In the sun's warmth it sprouts and blossoms and bears fruit, while the seed's husk remains in the ground." And in Let. T113 to Bandeçça Salimbeni (in this volume), Catherine carries the image to its logical development: "[D]on't you see that we are a tree of love, because we were made for love? . . . God has given this tree a worker to tend it as it pleases, and this worker is free choice. . . . [I]f this worker, free choice, plants the tree where it ought to be planted, that is, in the soil of true humility . . . , then it will produce fragrant blossoms of virtue, especially that topmost blossom of glory and praise for God's name. And all the other sweet blossoms and fruits, its virtuous deeds, will receive fragrance from that topmost blossom. This is the blossom, dearest daughter, that makes our virtues flower; it is the blossom God wants for himself. The fruit he wants to be ours. . . . He has no need of our fruit, because he lacks nothing. . . . Supreme eternal Goodness saw that human beings cannot live on blossoms but only on fruit. (If we eat blossoms we die, but on fruit we live.) That is why God took the blossom for himself and gives the fruit to us. And if we foolish people want to feed on the blossom—that is, give ourselves the glory and praise that ought to be God's—it robs us of the life of grace and gives us eternal death if we die without changing our ways to keep just the fruit for ourselves and give the blossom, the glory, to God. . . . Once a tree is full-grown it stretches out its branches and offers fruit to its neighbors—I mean the fruit of holy, humble, continual prayer and the example of a good holy life. And it stretches out its branches to them, too, whenever it can, by offering them material help with a great and generous heart, sincere and unfeigned." So it is precisely in bearing fruit and sharing it with one's neighbors, rather than trying to hold on to the beauty of the blossom, that one surrenders the blossom of glory to God.

the things that sensuality (because of its selfish love and worldly perception) is ashamed of. In fact, we delight in shame, torment, mockery, abuse, and reproach. We consider ourselves well off to the extent that we are trampled on by the world. So we are happy, for the sake of God's honor, if the world hounds us with all sorts of abuse, and the devil with all sorts of harassment and temptation, and the flesh with its hankering to rebel against the spirit. We rejoice in all this, [wanting] in self-hatred to take vengeance on ourselves in order to be conformed with Christ crucified, and regarding ourselves as undeserving of spiritual peace and calm. We are not ashamed to be mocked and ridiculed by all three of these enemies (the world, the flesh, and the devil), because our sensual will is dead, clothed in the garment of the supreme eternal will of God. No, we reverence all of this, as we should, because God permits it not out of hatred but out of love. We accept it with the same love with which we see it is given. So it is a lovely thing to desire the shame that casts out shame.[8]

Oh how blessed we are to be so sweetly enlightened! For we hate these passions of ours and those that are aroused in us by others, but we love the suffering these passions cause us. By our own passions I mean our selfish sensuality. By the passions aroused in us by others I mean [our resentment of] the world's harassment.[9]

So consider yourself deserving of the pain, dearest daughter, but undeserving of the fruit that issues from the pain. These things will be the ornaments you will wear on your royal garment. You know very well that [our] eternal Bridegroom did the same, for he adorned his garment with all sorts of sufferings: scourging, torments, mockery, abuse, and finally the shameful death of the cross.[10]

I say also that [this garment of charity] warms us and consumes our coldness. We are warmed, I say, by the fire of blazing charity, and we show it in our passionate desire for God's honor in our neighbors' salvation,[11] by bearing with and sharing the burden[12] of their shortcomings.

---

[8] Literally, "It is, then, lovely to desire shame, for with it shame is cast out."

[9] It.: *Però che insiememente e hodiare i movimenti nostri e gli altrui, e amare le pene che per essi movimenti sosteniamo. Movimento nostro è la propria sensualità, ma movimenti altrui sono le persecutioni del mondo.* B adds what appears to be a gloss: *cioè la colpa odiare di colui che perseguita.* This seems at first blush to be an unusual use of *movimento*, which in Catherine's writings, when it does not have the literally cognate sense of "movement," refers to the movement of passion. However, the added comment of B does seem to clarify the sense, which I have tried to convey in a rather expansive translation.

[10] Nowhere else except in these twin letters (T182, T220) does she speak of Christ putting ornaments on his garment of charity.

[11] Usually Catherine speaks of God's honor *and* one's neighbors' salvation, but here and in Let. T98, T63, T72, T96, T105, T157 (all of which date from the time of the composition of *The Dialogue* or later), and in *The Dialogue* itself, ch. 19 and 23, she refines the expression to God's honor *in* one's neighbors' salvation, reflecting her conviction that one honors God

We rejoice with God's servants who are rejoicing, and we weep with the wicked who are living in a time of weeping, in the compassion and sorrow we bear because of their offense against God.[13] And we willingly surrender ourselves to every kind of pain and torment in order to bring the wicked back to the condition of those who are rejoicing, who are living as lovers of lovely, royal virtue.

When I say that [this garment] consumes our coldness, I am referring to the coldness of selfish love for ourselves. This sort of love blinds us, keeping us from knowing either ourselves or God. It robs us of the life of grace. It gives birth to impatience as the root of pride sends out its branches. In our misplaced love we become offensive to God and to our neighbors, and unbearable to ourselves. We are constantly rebelling against [God's] commands. And all of this is the result of selfish self-love.[14]

But the true garment I've described consumes it all and rids us of it. It leaves us in the light of divine grace, so that we are [no longer] walking in the dark. No, we walk in truth along the way of the consumed spotless Lamb, and through Christ crucified, the gate, we enter into the eternal Father's wedding feast.[15] There we are established firmly in God, and have no more fear that the world or the flesh or the devil can separate us from him. There we find life without death, satiety without boredom, and hunger without pain.[16]

No more, then! Carry on! Carry on! Make your shoulders like those of a porter, and don't refuse any load if you really want to keep earning right up to the end![17] It would be really unbecoming for the bride to travel a path different from her Bridegroom's. And there is no other way for us to carry on except by being clothed in the way I've described. This is why I

---

precisely in working for one's neighbors' salvation. We have seen the same idea in the image of the flower and the fruit, above.

[12] It. *portando e sopportando.*

[13] Cf. Rom. 12, 15: "Rejoice with those who rejoice; weep with those who weep." However, Catherine's interpretation is slightly different from Paul's.

[14] Up to this point, this letter has been identical with Let. T220; from here on, the two letters differ.

[15] The imagery reflects the parable of the wedding banquet from Mt. 22, 1–14.

[16] Cf. Cavalca, *Specchio di croce*, p. 184, paraphrasing Pseudo-Augustine (*Meditatio* XXVII, PL XL, 921): "Sated, we shall be hungry, and hungering we shall be sated, but our satiety will be far from boredom, and our hunger far from pain."

[17] The image is unique here, related perhaps marginally to the thought expressed in Let. T217, to two different monasteries (written in this same period): "You will bear with and share the burden of your neighbors' shortcomings. You will be united with God in love and with your neighbors in God. You will be tolerant of any physical pain or inconvenience your neighbors may cause you, if only you can win your own soul." (Cf. Mk. 8, 36, Vulg.: "What profit does a person have who gains the whole world and loses his or her own soul?")

said that I long to see you dressed in [this] royal garment, in the abyss of the eternal King's charity.[18]

I'll say no more. Hide yourself in the open side of Christ crucified. Bathe and drown yourself in his wonderful blood. Keep living in God's holy and tender love.

Gentle Jesus! Jesus love!

[18] Cf. Ps. 103, 6: "The abyss is like a garment in which he (or it) is clothed." (Vulg., following the Septuagint; in the Hebrew it is clearly the earth which is clothed in the deep; in the Vulgate translation from the Septuagint it could be either God or the earth.)

LETTER T151a/G338[1]
To Nella Buonconti
September to November 1377

Nella Buonconti, wife of Niccolò, was the mother of Catherine's 1375 Pisan host Gherardo, and of his brothers Francesco and Tommaso. Catherine has already written to her at least once (Let. T161), in March or April of 1376. In that letter she spoke of the inconstancy of the world and the need to be wary of losing time. The occasion of the present letter is apparently some trial Nella is undergoing, and its chief message is an exhortation to patience; but Catherine also advises her about thinking ill of others, especially those closest to her.

The linguistic evidence strongly supports placement of this letter during Catherine's stay at Rocca d'Orcia, most probably between September and November.[2]

§

In the name of Jesus Christ crucified.[a]

Dearest mother in Christ gentle Jesus,[b]

I Caterina, servant and slave of the servants of Jesus Christ, am writing to you in his precious blood. I long to see you grounded in true perfect patience, since there is no other way we can be pleasing to God. Without patience, we experience [even] in this life the earnest[3] of hell.

Oh true, oh lovely patience! You are the virtue that is never overcome. No, it is you who triumph. You give us hope for glory.[c] *You dissolve hatred and animosity in the heart and liberate us from contempt for our neighbors.*[d] *You free our soul from pain. You make the heavy weight of hardships light, and be-*

---

[1] MSS: R2, Mo-*a*, S3, M, S5, S6, Ro; translation based on R2 as transcribed (unpublished) by A. Volpato, with variants based on Volpato's transcription. (Note that R2 leaves six lines blank at the head of the letter, lines which no rubricist ever filled in with information as to the addressee.)

[2] Three of the four letters which share fifteen or more of this one's sixty-two analyzed patterns are from these same months. (The fourth is from 1378.) The letter with which this one shares by far the most patterns (twenty-one of its eighty-six) is T264 to Jacoma di Trincio da Fuligno, from November 1377. Both letters are about patience (with Let. T264 far more detailed), but with very different accents. The most overwhelming support for a September to November placement, however, lies in the striking concentration of significant clusters within individual patterns between September and November of 1377. A full twenty-three of this letter's patterns show significant clusters in that period, with ten of these particularly confined there: ARRA, ASPTMPSC, CONCEPPR, DIOPRDIO, INNAMOR, LEGGCUOR, MAREONDE, MONDSAZZ, REALPAZ, SAZMENO. Fawtier (II, p. 309) and Dupré Theseider (unpublished notes) both decline to date this letter.

[3] That is, "guarantee" or "down payment."

cause of you bitter things[e] *become sweet. In you, patience, royal*[f] *virtue learned in calling to mind the blood of Christ crucified, we discover life.*[4]

Oh dearest mother, this is the most essential of all the virtues, because we cannot cross[g] this sea without troubles assaulting us no matter where we turn. This sea batters us with its waves, and the devil with all his temptations. And more: what the devil can't do himself he does by using other people.[5] He takes up his position on the tongues and in the hearts of his servants and before their mind's eye. He makes them see what doesn't exist.[6] So they conceive within their hearts all sorts of evil thoughts and resentments regarding their neighbors—often regarding those they most love. Once they have conceived these things within, the devil takes up his position on their tongue and causes them to give birth to them in words. Words lead to actions,[h] and this is how he divides those who love each other.[i] This is the source of the impatience and antipathy and hatred that deprive people of the unity of love.[j]

We mustn't believe the devil. No, we must mount the bench of our conscience to pass judgment. We must defend ourselves against this dangerous wave with hatred and contempt for ourselves, opening our mind's eye to know God and God's goodness, to know his eternal will, which neither wants nor seeks anything but that we be made holy.[7] He allows the devil to cause others to torment and harass us only to prove the virtues of love and true patience within us,[k] and so that our imperfect love may become perfect. For the virtue of love[l] is proved and strengthened in interaction with[m] our neighbors.[8]

---

[4] Later in this same year, in a letter to Raimondo da Capua (T104), she will sing an even more elaborate hymn to patience: "*Oh patience, how peaceable you are! Oh patience, what hope you give to those who possess you! Oh patience, you are a queen in control of and not possessed by anger! Oh patience, you serve sentence on selfish emotion when it would raise its head in anger! You carry a sword, double-edged with hate and love, to cut off and root out anger and pride and the impatience that is the pith of pride. Your clothing is the sun, alight with true knowledge of God and warm with divine charity. The rays from [this sun] fall on those who do you wrong, heaping on their heads coals of fire ablaze with charity to burn up and consume the hatred in their hearts. You then, sweet patience grounded in charity, are the source of fruit for our neighbors and honor to God. This garment of yours is covered with stars, all the different virtues, for we can have no patience without the stars of all the virtues along with the night of self-knowledge, which is a sort of moonlight.*"

[5] She often speaks of people "taking on the function of the devils" by luring others away from God.

[6] She expresses an analogous thought in *Dial.* 102 (pp. 193–194): "Often the devil would make you see too much of the truth in order to lead you into falsehood. He would do this in order to make you set yourself up as judge of other people's spirits and intentions, something of which, as I [God] told you, I alone am judge. . . . For the devil would like to [make] you pass judgment on something that is not there in your neighbors."

[7] 1 Thes. 4, 3.

[8] Cf. *Dial.* 8, p. 38: "Your neighbors are the channel through which all your virtues are

This[n] teaches us to love God for God's sake, because God is supreme eternal goodness and so deserves to be loved. It teaches us to love ourselves for God's sake. It teaches us to love our neighbors for God's sake, not for our own profit or for the joy or pleasure we may find in them but because God created them and loves them. It teaches us to serve our neighbors and help them in a way we cannot serve God. Since we can be of no use to God, we must be of service to our neighbors. This is how the perfection of our love is proved. When it is this perfect, no injury or unpleasantness that is inflicted on us, nothing in our neighbors that displeases us, will make us stop loving or serving[o] them, because we will be concerned only with pleasing God.

So this is why God grants all the hardships we experience. The devil, on the other hand, does it for the opposite reason, to lure us away from the impetus of charity. As for us, let's be wise in the face of the devil's intentions[p] and follow God's gentle will.

The world sets[q] about using all its power to hound us with all sorts of scourges: with its lack of firmness and stability, with its poverty. It is so poor that it cannot satisfy our desires. For all the things of the world are less than we; they were all made to serve us, and we were made for God alone.[r] So let us serve God alone, with all our heart and all our energy, for God is the good who fills our heart and gives it peace.[9]

Because this patience is so useful and essential, we must acquire it. And how shall we get it? By means of the light, by opening our mind's eye and learning to know that we are not, acknowledging that our existence[10] is the gift of God's boundless charity. This is how we know God's goodness: from the fact that we exist and from every gift we have been given over and above our existence. Once we have seen that we are loved by God, we see that it is out of love that God has given us the Word, his only-begotten Son. And the Son has given his life for us.

Now, since the Son has given his life for us with such blazing love, we ought to be convinced that every burden that is laid on us, whether agreeable or disagreeable, from whatever source it may come, is given us out of love and not out of hatred. It is given only for our good, so that we may achieve the end for which we were created. And we should realize that our burdens are no greater or smaller than time—and time[s] is as small as the point of a needle. In breadth and in length our burdens are nothing at all.

---

tested and come to birth, just as the evil give birth to all their vices through their neighbors."

[9] So sings Augustine in his *Confessions* (Bk. I, 1): "Our hearts are restless till they rest in you."

[10] Literally, "our being" (and the same in the following references to existence).

So they are tiny, finite. The burdens of the past we no longer have, since time has fled. The burdens of the future we don't have either, because we don't know for sure whether we will have that time.

Once we have seen how short time is, we should realize how useful [patience] is. Ask that dear apostle[t] and lover Paul about it. He says, "The sufferings of this life are not worth comparing with the future glory that God has prepared for those who reverence him and who with good patience endure the holy discipline imposed on them by divine Goodness."[11] In their patience, these people are experiencing even in this life the earnest of eternal life.

And if, in our weakness and impatience, we should lift up our head against our Creator and be unwilling to suffer, let us look within and consider where impatience leads.[12] The earnest of hell begins even in this life, and in the end we come to eternal damnation. I have never seen a single burden relieved by impatience. In fact, impatience increases the burden because things are as burdensome as our will makes them. So get rid of your selfish sensual will and clothe yourself in the gentle will of God, and the burden will be relieved![13]

This, then, is how to attain true and perfect patience. I beg you, for love of the gentle Jesus Christ crucified, not to evade these dear sweet means for attaining the virtue of patience, for I know that you like everyone else need it very much. It is because I know this need that I said I long to see you grounded in true holy[u] patience.[v] I urge you, dearest mother, if you want to be relieved of your burdens and temporal infirmities, keep your eyes on the slain, consumed Lamb, so that the fire of his charity may warm your heart and soul to love for patience and consume all the cold and damp of selfish sensual love and passion and self-pity.[14] Then you will attain perfect knowledge of God's goodness, which has allowed this neediness and infirmity for your good and to make you holy, so that the

---

[11] Cf. Rom. 8, 18, on which Catherine quite freely amplifies here.

[12] Here it is clear that the deepest meaning of "patience" for Catherine is "willingness to suffer."

[13] Cf. Let. T264 to Jacoma di Trincio da Fuligno: "People often say, 'I can't bear it and I don't want to bear it!' But they have to bear it none the less. And their unwillingness piles weight upon weight because of their selfish will. For our selfish will is the ground of all suffering, and so our burden is as great as our will makes it. Take away my [selfish] will and the burden is lifted."

[14] Cf. Let. T30/DT1 to the nuns of the Monastery of Santa Marta (vol. I): "Now may our hearts remain stubborn no longer. I beg you in the name of Christ crucified: let this stone be melted in the hot overflowing blood of God's Son, in that blood whose warmth is enough to melt the hardness and frigidity of any heart! How does it make us melt? Only in the way we've been talking about—with hatred and love. This is what the Holy Spirit does when he enters the soul."

past in which we[15] have so offended God may be purged and atoned for in this finite time. God does this in his mercy in order to absolve us from infinite punishment by means of the finite pain we accept with great love and sincere patience.

You will discover this holy knowledge in the crucified love of the spotless Lamb. His blood will be for you an anointing that will refresh and comfort your soul in your infirmities. I tell you, your soul will find such sweetness there that not only will you not try to evade hardships, but will consider it a hardship to be deprived of them.[16]

Since [patience], then, is so attractive and so essential to our salvation, let's not wait for time, because we aren't certain we will have time. No, let us with true holy solicitude lift our desire above selfish sensuality and set it on the blessed gentle Jesus, the crucified Christ, who is our rule and our way.

I'll say no more. Keep living in God's holy and tender love.

Gentle Jesus! Jesus love!

Textual Notes

a. Mo, S3, M, S5, S6 add *and of gentle Mary*; in Mo, M, S5, S6 the invocation precedes the inscription.

b. R2 had first written: *Dearest mother in Christ crucified* but then begins again without erasing the first version.

c. Mo, S3, M, S5, S6 all have *grace / glory* (*gratia / gloria*).

d. R2 had first written but then canceled out *pain / neighbors* (*pena / prossimo*).

e. Mo, S3, M, S5, S6: *the bitter / bitter things.*

f. *reale* can have the sense of "royal" or "solid."

g. From As; others have *possiamo / passiamo* (*can / cross*).

h. S3, M, S5: *affetto / effetto*, though S3 corrects it to *effetto*. Only the latter makes sense here.

i. S3, M, S5: *diviene / divide*, giving *this is how the one loving becomes the one loved*, which in the context makes no sense.

j. From Mo, S3, S5. R2: *humility of love*; S6: *life of love*. Also, R2 has as the main

[15] As she so often does, Catherine deliberately switches to the first person plural to include herself when she is speaking of another's sin.

[16] Cf. Let. T38 to Agnesa Malavolti (in this volume): "[Christ] suffered with such patience that no cry of complaint was heard from him. . . . This, I tell you, is what these souls experience. This is why they do not want to find joy except with Christ crucified. For if it were possible to acquire virtue and avoid hell and have eternal life with consolation both spiritual and temporal in this world, and without suffering, they would not want it so. They would rather have eternal life by suffering even to the point of death than to have it in this other way, if only they can be like Christ crucified and be clothed in his humiliation and pain."

verb here *veggiamo* ("we see"), which does not make as much sense in the context as the version given by Mo, S3, M, S5, S6, As, which I have chosen to follow.

k. R2 adds: *and so forth*, which makes no sense in the context, and which Mo, Se, M, S5, S6, As do not have.

l. S3, M, S5: *love for virtue / virtue of love.*

m. Literally, *by means of.*

n. It is not clear whether the subject of *teaches* is meant to be simply this course of events or God.

o. From Mo, S3, M, S5, S6; R2 has *respect* (*osservare / servire*).

p. S3: *temptation / intentions* (*i[n] te[m]ptacione / intenzione*).

q. Mo, S3, M., S5, S6: *And let's counteract the world, which sets ... / The world sets ....*

r. Mo, S3, M, S5, S6: [*alone*].

s. Mo, S3, M, S5, S6: *our time / time.*

t. Mo, Se, M, S5, S6: [*apostle*].

u. Mo, S3, M, S5, S6: *perfect / holy.*

v. The text from this point on, except for *I'll say no more. ... tender love*, is contained only in R2.

Letter T151b[1]
To Frate . . . .
September to November 1377

This letter to a religious brother is an only slightly edited version of that addressed to Nella Buonconti (T151a). The brother was apparently originally identified in the rubric of the manuscript, but his name has been so overwritten as to be illegible.

The only basis for the chronological placement of the letter lies in the linguistic evidence.[2]

§

In the name of Jesus Christ crucified and of gentle Mary.

Dearest son in Christ gentle Jesus,

I Caterina, servant and slave of the servants of Jesus Christ, am writing to you in his precious blood. I long to see you grounded in true perfect patience, since there is no other way we can be pleasing to God. Without it, we experience [even] in this life the earnest[3] of hell.

Oh true, oh lovely patience! You are the virtue that is never overcome. No, it is you who triumph. You give us hope for glory.[a] *You dissolve hatred and animosity in the heart and free us from contempt for our neighbors. You free our soul from pain. You make the heavy weight of hardships light, and because*

---

[1] MSS: As; translation based on an unpublished transcription of the letter in As by A. Volpato. In the manuscript T151a is converted to masculine forms. (It is the only text in As.) Volpato treats the version in As as a separate entity from the principal redaction. He points out that Dupré Theseider (*Epistolario*, p. LVII) was misled by identical *incipits* to identify the As version of this letter with T39 to Giacomo, Carthusian of Pontignano, though Fawtier II, p. 78, clearly identifies that letter with T151. As has as inscription: To Fra . . . (with the rest overwritten and illegible).

[2] Three of the four letters which share fifteen or more of this one's sixty-two analyzed patterns are from these same months. (The fourth is from 1378.) The letter with which this one shares by far the most patterns (twenty-one of its eighty-six) is T264 to Jacoma di Trincio da Fuligno, from November 1377. Both letters are about patience (with Let. T264 far more detailed), but with very different accents. The most overwhelming support for a September to November placement, however, lies in the striking concentration of significant clusters within individual patterns between September and November of 1377. A full twenty-three of this letter's patterns show significant clusters in that period, with ten of these particularly confined there: ARRA, ASPTMPSC, CONCEPPR, DIOPRDIO, INNAMOR, LEGGCUOR, MAREONDE, MONDSAZZ, REALPAZ, SAZMENO. Fawtier (II, p. 78) and Dupré Theseider (unpublished notes) both decline to date this letter.

[3] That is, "guarantee" or "down payment."

of you the bitter becomes sweet. In you, patience, royal[b] *virtue learned in calling to mind the blood of Christ crucified, we discover life.*[4]

Oh dearest son, this is the most essential of all the virtues, because we cannot cross this sea without troubles assaulting us no matter where we turn. This sea batters us with its waves, and the devil with all his temptations. And more: what the devil can't do himself he does by using other people.[5] He takes up his position on the tongues and in the hearts of his servants and before their mind's eye. He makes them see what doesn't exist.[6] So they conceive within their hearts all sorts of evil thoughts and resentments regarding their neighbors—often regarding those they most love. Once they have conceived these things within, the devil takes up his position on their tongue and causes them to give birth to them in words. Words lead to actions.[c] This is the source of the impatience and antipathy and hatred that deprive people of love's unity with those they love.[d]

We mustn't believe the devil. No, we must mount the bench of our conscience to pass judgment. We must defend ourselves against this dangerous wave with hatred and contempt for ourselves, opening our mind's eye to know God and God's goodness, to know his eternal will, which neither wants nor seeks anything but that we be made holy.[7] He allows the devil to cause others to torment and harass us only to prove the virtues of love and true patience within us, and so that our imperfect love may become perfect. For the virtue of love[l] is proved and strengthened in interaction with our neighbors.[8]

---

[4] Later in this same year, in a letter to Raimondo da Capua (T104), she will sing an even more elaborate hymn to patience: "*Oh patience, how peaceable you are! Oh patience, what hope you give to those who possess you! Oh patience, you are a queen in control of and not possessed by anger! Oh patience, you serve sentence on selfish emotion when it would raise its head in anger! You carry a sword, double-edged with hate and love, to cut off and root out anger and pride and the impatience that is the pith of pride. Your clothing is the sun, alight with true knowledge of God and warm with divine charity. The rays from [this sun] fall on those who do you wrong, heaping on their heads coals of fire ablaze with charity to burn up and consume the hatred in their hearts. You then, sweet patience grounded in charity, are the source of fruit for our neighbors and honor to God. This garment of yours is covered with stars, all the different virtues, for we can have no patience without the stars of all the virtues along with the night of self-knowledge, which is a sort of moonlight.*"

[5] She often speaks of people "taking on the function of the devils" by luring others away from God.

[6] She expresses an analogous thought in *Dial.* 102 (pp. 193–194): "Often the devil would make you see too much of the truth in order to lead you into falsehood. He would do this in order to make you set yourself up as judge of other people's spirits and intentions, something of which, as I [God] told you, I alone am judge. . . . For the devil would like to [make] you pass judgment on something that is not there in your neighbors."

[7] 1 Thes. 4, 3.

[8] Cf. *Dial.* 8, p. 38: "Your neighbors are the channel through which all your virtues are tested and come to birth, just as the evil give birth to all their vices through their neighbors."

This[f] teaches us to love God for God's sake, because he is supreme eternal goodness and so deserves to be loved. It teaches us to love ourselves for God's sake. It teaches us to love our neighbors for God's sake, not for our own profit or for the joy or pleasure we may find in them but because God created them and loves them. It teaches us to serve our neighbors and help them in a way we cannot serve or help[g] God. Since we can be of no use to God, we must be of service to our neighbors. This is how the perfection of our love is proved. When it is this perfect, no injury or unpleasantness that is inflicted on us, nothing in our neighbors that displeases us, will make us stop loving or serving them, because we will be concerned only with pleasing God.

So this is why God grants all the hardships we experience. The devil, on the other hand, does it for the opposite reason, to lure us away from the impetus of charity. As for us, let's be wise in the face of the devil's intentions and follow God's gentle will.

And let's counteract the world,[9] which sets about using all its power to hound us with all sorts of scourges: with its lack of firmness and stability, with its poverty. It is so poor that it cannot satisfy our desires. For all the things of the world are less than we; they were all made to serve us, and we were made for God. So let us serve God alone, with all our heart and all our energy, for God is the good who fills our heart and gives it peace.[10]

Because this patience is so useful and essential, we must acquire it. And how shall we get it? By means of the light, by opening our mind's eye and learning to know that we are not, acknowledging that our existence is the gift of God's boundless charity.[11] This is how we know God's goodness: from the fact that we exist and from every gift we have been given over and above our existence. Once we have seen that we are loved by God, we see that it is out of love that God has given us the Word, his only-begotten Son. And the Son has given his life for us.

Now, since the Son has given his life for us with such blazing love, we ought to be convinced that every burden that is laid on us, whether agreeable or disagreeable, from whatever source it may come, is given us out of love and not out of hatred; it is given only for our good, so that we may achieve the end for which we were created. And we should realize that our burdens are no greater or smaller than time—and our time is as small as the point of a needle. In breadth and in length they are nothing at all. So

---

[9] This is a clause which does not occur in the version to Nella Buonconti.

[10] So sings Augustine in his *Confessions* (Bk. I, 1): "Our hearts are restless till they rest in you."

[11] Literally, "our being" (and the same in the following references to existence).

our burdens are tiny, finite. The burdens of the past we no longer have, since time has fled. The burdens of the future we don't have either, because we don't know for sure whether we will have that time.

Once we have seen how short time is, we should realize how useful [patience] is. Ask Saint Paul about it. He says, "The sufferings of this life are not worth comparing with the future glory that God has prepared for those who reverence him and who with good patience endure the holy discipline imposed on them by divine Goodness."[12] In their patience, these people are experiencing even in this world the earnest of eternal life.

And if we should in our weakness and impatience lift up our head against our Creator and be unwilling to suffer, let us look within and consider where impatience leads.[13] The earnest of hell begins even in this life, and in the end we come to eternal damnation. As for myself, I have never seen a single burden relieved by impatience. In fact, impatience increases the burden because things are as burdensome as our will makes them. So get rid of your selfish sensual will and clothe yourself in the gentle will of God, and the burden will be relieved![14]

Textual Notes

a. *grace / glory* (*gratia / gloria*). Mo, S3, M, S5, S6 all have the same error!

b. *reale* can have the sense of "royal" or "solid."

c. *affetto / effetto*; only the latter makes sense here, however, and this is what most of the manuscripts of T151a have. The manuscript for T151b does not have the following clause, found in all of the manuscripts for T151a: *and this is how he divides those who love each other.*

d. Here As varies from the manuscripts of T151a, which do not have *with those we love* (*con la cosa amata*).

e. Literally, *by means of.*

f. It is not clear whether the subject of *teaches* is meant to be simply this course of events or God.

g. As differs from the manuscripts of T151a in adding *or help.*

---

[12] Cf. Rom. 8, 18, on which Catherine quite freely amplifies here.

[13] Here it is clear that the deepest meaning of "patience" for Catherine is "willingness to suffer."

[14] Cf. Let. T264 to Jacoma di Trincio da Fuligno: "People often say, 'I can't bear it and I don't want to bear it!' But they have to bear it none the less. And their unwillingness piles weight upon weight because of their selfish will. For our selfish will is the ground of all suffering, and so our burden is as great as our will makes it. Take away my [selfish] will and the burden is lifted." At this point As ends the letter with *etc.*, perhaps an indication that the present letter was copied from the letter to Nella Buonconti (T151a). It is impossible to know whether the copy actually sent to the brother included the rest of the content of Let. T151a or not.

Letter T55/G53[1]
To Dom Guillaume Rainaud, Prior General of the Carthusians
September to November 1377

Guillaume Rainaud was prior general of the Carthusians from 1367 until his death in 1402.[2] Tommasèo notes that upon his election Guillaume refused the title of abbot general offered him by the pope, as well as the rank of cardinal and the dispensation of his monks from abstinence from meat in case of illness.

At the time of the schism of 1378 he transferred his loyalty from Urban VI to the Clementine papacy. The loyalties of religious in this matter, however, tended to follow political lines, and so the order was split. Stefano Maconi, in a letter of 1402 to the monks of the Grande Chartreuse, alludes to a letter Catherine sent to Guillaume at that time, attempting to persuade him to remain loyal to Urban.[3] "You knew of this from the letter which this virgin sent to your father general Guillaume, with me writing as she dictated orally."

However, the present letter was certainly not written in that context, since it has only encouragement for the prior general as he prepares for a chapter.

The period from December 1378 is excluded by the events of the schism, but more broadly, this letter shares little with others of 1378 and 1379 beyond patterns which are quite common at least from 1377 on. I would also exclude from consideration the period before August 1377, since this letter contains so many patterns which appear either not at all or in very isolated cases up to that point.[4] We are brought, then to the general period of Catherine's stay in the Val d'Orcia; but more narrowly within that period, a few patterns would lead me to place it sometime between September and November 1377.[5]

---

[1] MSS: B, P2, H, P1, P3, R2, P4, Pa; translation based on R2, consulting H.

[2] Laurent, in the Introduction to his edition of the *Processo Castellano* (p. xviii), citing F. A. Lefébure, *S. Bruno e l'ordre des Chartreux*, Paris, 1883, vol. I, pp. 208–209.

[3] Laurent, *S. Bruno e l'ordre des Chartreux*, pp. 256–257, n. 1, reproduces the relevant segment of Stefano Maconi's letter. The letter of Catherine to Guillaume to which Stefano refers is not extant, even in the Maconian codices.

[4] COGNVERI, GIARDREL, INCOMPOR, LABORE, NAVICRIS, NUVOLPR, ORAZVIG, RAGUARD, VASESANG, VOLCONSU.

[5] These specific patterns are CIECAMOR, NAVICRIS, RAGUARD. Fawtier (II, p. 185) places this letter either at the time of Guillaume's election in 1367 or in 1377 before the schism. Dupré Theseider (unpublished notes) sees the same two possibilities. Meattini (*Epistolario*, p. 1476) is certainly mistaken in claiming that Guillaume "did not submit to the schism (*non si sottomise allo scisma*).

§

In the name of Jesus Christ crucified and of gentle Mary.

Dearest reverend father in Christ gentle Jesus,

I Caterina, servant and slave of the servants of Jesus Christ, am writing to you in his precious blood. I long to see you immersed and bathed in the blood of God's Son. I reflect that when our memory is filled with the blood of Christ crucified, our understanding is irresistibly drawn to gaze into our memory, where it finds the blood. There it sees the fire of divine charity, boundless love, blended and kneaded together with the blood, since the blood was shed and given to us out of love.[6]

Then at once our will follows our understanding, loving and longing for what the eye of our understanding has seen. So our will lifts up its energy[7] and love in the love of Christ crucified, the love it has discovered in the blood, as I've said. Then we immerse ourselves in this blood; I mean, we drown to death all our perverse sensual will, which often rebels against its Creator. And we throw out all selfish self-love and clothe ourselves in God's eternal will, the will that we have discovered and experienced in the blood. For the blood reveals that God wants nothing else but that we be made holy,[8] since if God had wanted anything different, he would never have given us the Word, his only-begotten Son.

So we see plainly that whatever God permits for us in this life, he permits for no other purpose. We see that everything that has being comes from God. Nothing, therefore, that happens to us—trouble or temptation or injury or torment or slander or anything else that could possibly happen to us—can or will disturb us. Rather, we are content and hold these things in reverence, reflecting that they come from God and are given to us as good favors, not out of hatred but out of love.

---

[6] In Let. T153 to Catarina Buonconti and Orsola and other women of Pisa (in this volume) Catherine expands upon the idea that the mystery of the blood of Christ is to be discovered within oneself: "So I want you, my very loved daughters, to open the eyes of your understanding to gaze within the vessel of self-knowledge. In this knowledge you will discover that you are a vessel into which this glorious and precious blood is received. The divine nature is fused into the blood with the fire of charity. When you gaze into the vessel of self-knowledge you discover this blood which God has given through his Son. And since the blood was shed only because of sin, you discover in it the knowledge of yourself. And when you see that you are sinful, you see also divine justice in the blood, since [Christ] shed his blood to bring sin to justice. Then you know that God's eternal will wants nothing other than that we be made holy; for [Christ] would not have given his life if he had wanted anything other than our good. So gaze into the blood that you discover within the vessel of your very selves."

[7] It. *affetto*.

[8] 1 Thes. 4, 3.

So we neither can nor should complain, because we would be complaining about our own good. And souls who are clothed in God's gentle will are not in the habit of complaining about anything that could possibly happen to them. The only exception is sin against God. About sin we grieve and ought to grieve, because we see that it is contrary to God's will. Sin, then, is worthy of hatred because it is not from God and therefore is nothingness. Everything else, everything that has being, is from God, and so those who are in love with Christ love it and hold it in reverence.

Such souls see themselves not for themselves but for God. And they see God for God, because God is supreme eternal Goodness, worthy of being loved. And they see their neighbors for God rather than in terms of their own advantage.[9] They do not choose time and circumstance or comfort or weariness in their own way but accept with affectionate love whatever pleases divine Goodness. They find joy in everything because those who love cannot find pain distressing.

They rejoice in struggle. If they are hounded by the world they are happy. If they are subordinates they bear the yoke of obedience with great joy and patience. If they are in authority they tolerate and endure their subordinates' shortcomings, that is, whatever ingratitude or abuse they may suffer at their hands. As good gardeners they would risk death to root out the brambles of vice and plant the virtues in their souls.[10] They mete out an honorable justice, seasoned with mercy. They are unconcerned about their own pain. They do not evade hard work but bear it joyfully.

They do not want to lose the time they have for what they do not have. Not that the tempting thought doesn't sometimes occur to them, "If you didn't have this burden and anxiety of authority, you might be more able to possess God in your peace and quiet." But the devil does this, suggesting to them the time of peace in order to keep them in a continual state of war.[11] For those whose will is not at peace in the situation God has put them in are constantly in pain. They become unbearable to themselves and so lose both the one time and the other. The time of their authority they do not use, and the time of quiet they don't have, and so they give up both the present and the future!

---

[9] Cf. Let. T62 to Sano di Maco and others: "We have sought ourselves not selfishly but for God, because God is supreme eternal Goodness and deserves our love and service. And it has sought our neighbors for God's sake, with no regard for self-interest."

[10] That is, in the souls of their subordinates.

[11] Cf. Let. T30/DT1 to the Abbess of Santa Marta in Siena: "If you tell me about the great concern you must have over temporal things, [I answer that] things are only as temporal as we make them. I've already told you that all things come from the highest Goodness; so everything is good and perfect. I don't want you evading hard work under the plea that these things are temporal."

So we must not believe the devil's cunning. No, take up with vigor what you have. This is how souls clothed in God's will act, as I've said above. They sail on in any kind of weather, in times of weariness as in times of serenity.[12] For they have been stripped of selfish self-love and of all the sensual passion and self-indulgence that are the source of all evil and pain.

One source of suffering is not having what one wants. But when we are clothed in God's eternal will in place of our own we are made one with God. Then, impelled by love, we begin to judge according to God's eternal will; we see and conclude and are convinced that God wants only that we be made holy.[13] This is why God created us in his own image and likeness, so that we might be made holy in him and experience and enjoy the sight of him forever. The eye of our understanding has seen and known this in the blood of Christ crucified; it is the blood that has shown us the eternal Father's truth. *Oh glorious blood! You give us life. You make the invisible visible to us. You show us divine mercy by washing away the sin of disobedience with the obedience of the Word from which the blood came.*

Up, for love of Christ! Bathe, bathe, and live in continual watching, and prayer,[a] dearest father! If you gaze into the blood with the eye of your understanding, you will be keeping watch over those in your charge out of hunger and concern for God's honor and the salvation of souls. In this way you will have continual prayer, that is, continual holy desire. You need this to preserve your own salvation in the position you are in. Since God has appointed you to a position of authority, you must not be timid or negligent, or go about with your eyes closed so that you know nothing.

I am begging you, then, to be hungry! Learn from the Lamb, opened up and so consumed for you that he ran to his shameful death on the cross with joyous hunger for God's honor and our salvation. You have good reason, then, to let go of all fear and negligence and unknowing blindness, since God has plainly set before you the Word, his only-begotten Son, and the blood. And if you say, "I am ignorant; I don't even know myself well, let alone what I should be doing for those in my charge," here is my answer. If you are hungry for God's honor, though you may not be able to do it by yourself, God will work in you whatever is necessary for the salvation of those in your charge. Only have hunger and desire.

But I don't see how your can have this hunger except through the blood. And this is why I said that I long to see you immersed and bathed in the blood of Christ crucified. For in the blood we lose our love for our own lives and for that perverse selfishness we have in regard to ourselves.

---

[12] Note that the Italian *tempo* is the word both for "weather" and for "time."

[13] 1 Thes. 4, 3.

That selfish love keeps us from acting justly, whether out of fear of losing our position or because we would indulge and please other people rather than God. It makes those in authority follow human respect and opinion rather than God's will and good conscience. This is what has destroyed the order in the past and continues to destroy it—as is happening for lack of correction and for having superiors who are not upright but degenerate[14] and indiscreet. For just as good superiors revitalize those in their charge, bad superiors destroy them. And all of this comes from selfishness.

In the blood of Christ we let go of this selfish love. And we gain an ineffable love when we see how he has given his life out of love to buy back this adopted child, the human race. When we see such love, love is drawn by love, and our desire is lifted up to love what God loves and to hate what God hates. And because we see that God loves human beings most of all, we conceive a seemingly insatiable love for the salvation of souls. We hate sin and vice because they are not in God, and we love the virtues in others for God's honor. We let go of our indifference concerning them and become conscientious. We let go of our love for our body, and would be willing to die a thousand deaths if so much were needed. We let go of blindness and recover the light, because the cloud of selfish love has been removed and now the sun of divine love, blazing charity, shines, burning away all our unknowing.[15] And all of this we have drawn from the blood.

Oh glorious and precious blood of the humble spotless Lamb! Who of us will be so hardened and foolish as not to take the vessel of our heart and, impelled by love, carry it to the side of the crucified Christ, which holds and pours out blood in torrents? There, within, we discover God, that is, the divine nature joined with our human nature. We discover the fire of love that reveals to us the secret of his heart through his open side, showing us how impossible it was for him to show by these finite sufferings a love as great as his desire and will. For there is no comparison between his finite pain and infinite love.[16]

Well, dearest father, let's not wait any longer! In this bit of time that God has kept for you, and especially now that the time for chapter is coming when faults are more conspicuous, be conscientious about punishing them, so that the spoiled and rotten member may not spoil the healthy. But administer justice always with mercy. And don't take action lightly; rather take care to use wise persons of good conscience to search out and probe the truth. Whatever you have to do, do it always with divine coun-

---

[14] It. *incorretti*, literally, "uncorrected."

[15] It. *ignorazia*.

[16] She will expand on this in *Dial.* 75.

sel, with holy prayer; and use as well the human counsel of God's dear and good servants—which is also divine. Always try to have at your side persons who are a mirror of religious life.[17]

And more urgent than all the other things I am begging you to attend to is the matter of appointing good priors, virtuous persons capable of governing. For there are many who are personally good but are not good at governing. This is how religious orders are destroyed. They are revitalized by the opposite. When you find good ones, keep them.[18]

No fear, for love of Christ crucified! I am certain that if, impelled by love, you bathe in his blood and drown all selfish love there by letting it be burned away in God's eternal will (which you will discover in the blood), you will accomplish this and anything else you and they need.

I'll say no more. Forgive my foolishness. Keep living in God's holy and tender love.

Gentle Jesus! Jesus love!

Textual Notes

a. So H; others have *Bathe, bathe, and live in continual watching and prayer, dearest father, keeping watch with the eye of your understanding in the blood.* H actually has *continentia* ("continence") rather than *continua* ("continual"), but the context makes clear that this is a scribal error.

[17] The gathering of representatives of the order at chapter was a time in which faults against the rule were confessed and punished, the business of the order was attended to, and superiors were elected and/or appointed.

[18] Recall that when she was planning for her own monastic foundation (eventually Belcaro), she wrote to the abbot of Sant'Antimo (Let. T12/DT66, vol. I), "I would like the two of you to get together and if you can, locate a suitable place for establishing a really good monastery, and put a few good leaders there—for as far as *members* are concerned, we have plenty."

LETTER T267/G91[1]
To Frate Raimondo da Capua
Very early October 1377

Raimondo da Capua apparently left for Rome about the middle of September. Catherine's remarks in this letter to him indicate that she knows Pope Gregory XI is displeased with her activities in the Val d'Orcia, but this is something of which she may have been aware already when she sent Raimondo to Rome. In fact, the pope's displeasure may have been the reason for her sending him "with certain proposals which, if only people had understood, would have been for the advantage of the holy Church of God."[2] Or it may have been these very proposals which angered Gregory XI.

The letter includes a message for the pope, which Raimondo should deliver if he sees the latter. I would therefore guess that this letter was written not very long after Raimondo's departure, early enough, in fact, for a response from him to have reached her before she writes her next letter to him (T272), which I would place about 10 October or shortly thereafter.[3]

§

In the name of Jesus Christ crucified and of gentle Mary.

Dearest and very loved father in Christ gentle Jesus,

I Caterina, servant and slave of the servants of Jesus Christ, am writing to you in his precious blood. I long to see you really fighting against the devil's insidious temptations, against human malice and persecution, and against your own sensual love.[4] Unless you use virtue and holy hatred to

---

[1] MSS: Mo-*a*, corrected by *b*; P4, S2, M, S5, S6, Ro; translation based on Mo-*a*, with variants from *b*, and noted also where Tommasèo's text differs. The letter is characterized by many structural difficulties, apparent missing elements, and vocabulary strange for Catherine.

[2] *Life*, II, ix, 274, p. 255, and III, vi, 422, p. 382.

[3] The linguistic evidence is helpful only in so far as it reinforces the placement of the letter during the Val d'Orcia period, and more narrowly near October, because of significant clusters within individual patterns which begin and/or end at that time: GONFCROC, LABORE, LUMNFOND, PETCHIES, SALUPERF, SERVEFIG, SOPRINFD, VERCOMBA. Fawtier (II, p. 200) places this letter at the end of September 1377, before Let. T272, near Raimondo's arrival in Rome. Dupré Theseider in his unpublished notes for this letter, after reviewing the opinions of Gigli (*Opere*, I), Gardner (*Saint Catherine of Siena*, pp. 224–226), and Fawtier, leaves the sequence of Let. T267 and T272 unresolved, simply placing this one in September or October 1377. In his notes for Let. T272, however, he implies that he has concluded that Let. T267 is indeed prior to Let. T272.

[4] Another version of the three classic enemies, the devil, the world, and the flesh.

expel this last enemy, you will never be strong against the other struggles we face every day. Selfish love weakens us, and so we must use the power of virtue to get rid of it. And we shall acquire virtue in the indescribable love God has shown us in the blood of his only-begotten Son.[5] This love, drawn from divine love, gives us light and life. It gives us light to know the truth and how essential it is for our salvation, for reaching great perfection, and for suffering with genuine patience and courage even to the point of death. And it is by means of this courage, learned by the light that lets us know the truth, that we acquire the life of divine grace.[6]

Get drunk, then, on the blood of the spotless Lamb. And be a faithful servant of your Creator, not an unfaithful one. Don't let any struggle or darkness you may encounter make you doubt or turn back. No, persevere faithfully until death, because you know very well that perseverance will yield you the fruit of your efforts.

I've heard from a servant of God who constantly holds you before God in prayer,[7] that you have been experiencing tremendous struggles and that your spirit has been overtaken by darkness because of the devil's illusions and deceits. He wants to make you see the crooked as straight and the straight as crooked, and he does this to make you stumble along the way so you won't reach your goal. But take heart. God has provided and will continue to provide for you, and his providence will not fail you. See that in everything you turn to Mary as you embrace the cross. And don't ever give in to spiritual discouragement, but navigate the stormy sea on the ship of divine mercy.

I know that you are not about to fight back if you have suffered or had been suffering any persecution at the hands of religious and layfolk (even within the mystic body of holy Church), or if you have endured or had

---

[5] Cf. Let. T181 to Nicola da Osimo (vol. I): "[K]nowing that water was not good enough for tempering the mortar he would use to secure the stones (I mean the stones of sweet solid virtues), [God] gave us the blood of his only-begotten Son. Before the coming of God's Son, you know, no virtue had the power of giving us the life we had lost because of sin."

[6] Cf. Let. T169 to Niccoloso di Francia (early 1378): "For when the devil finds our soul armed with courage in the face of his assaults, he sees that we put up with those assaults gladly because of our holy hatred for ourselves and our desire to be conformed with Christ crucified and to endure pain and weariness for love of him. He sees that we fend off his assaults with a loving decision in favor of our Creator, that is, we do not consent with our will to any of his illusions. So this courage that the devil discovers and sees in us gives him pain, and he finds himself vanquished, while we are left filled with divine grace, all ablaze with love and inspired for battle, inspired to fight for Christ crucified." Elsewhere (Let. T28/DT17 in vol. I and T309 in this volume) she speaks of "the courage (or strength) of grace."

[7] She is referring to herself. She seems to imply that she knows of his grief through her own prayer, of which she will be even more explicit in Let. T272.

been enduring displeasure or indignation from Christ's vicar (whether on your own account or because of my being with all these people).[8] No, bear it patiently. Get away quickly and go to your cell to get to know yourself in holy meditation on the fact that God considers you worthy of suffering for love of truth, worthy of being persecuted for his name.[9] In genuine humility consider yourself deserving of the suffering but unworthy of its fruit.

Do everything you have to do with prudence, keeping your attention on God. Whatever you have to do or say, rehearse it first between God and yourself in holy prayer.[10] The teacher you will find there is the Holy Spirit, who is mercy. He will pour into you a light of wisdom that will make you discern and choose what will honor God. This is the lesson given you by gentle First Truth, who provides for your needs with boundless love.

If you should happen, dearest father, to come before his holiness the vicar of Christ, our dearest most holy father, humbly remember me to him. To his holiness I confess that I have been guilty of great foolishness and negligence against God. I have disobeyed my Creator, who had invited me to cry out in restless desire, to cry out before him in prayer, and to be near his vicar with my presence and my words.[11] In every possible way I have sinned outrageously. And I believe it is because of my great wickedness that he and holy Church have suffered these persecutions. So if he complains about me, he has reason to do so, and to punish me for my sins. But tell him I will do my best to correct my faults and to obey him more perfectly.

So I trust that divine Goodness will turn the eye of his mercy toward me by freeing me from my sins and ignorance, and toward Christ's bride

---

[8] The intent of this last sentence is not clear. (*So che dagli huomini religiosi o secolari, et anco nel corpo mistico della sancta chiesa, se riceveste o aveste ricevuto alcuna persecutione o dispiacimento o indegnatione dal vicario di Cristo, o per voi, o aveste sostenuto o sosteneste per me, con tutte queste creature non state a contastare.*) Dupré Theseider (in his unpublished notes) wondered whether perhaps a line of the original had been omitted in the manuscripts, while Arrigo Levasti, in a note to Dupré Theseider, wondered whether *se riceveste* should be *ne riceveste* ("I know that you *have* received. . . .) with *ma* ("but") understood before *non state a contastare*. My translation is therefore a bit conjectural; however, it assumes no missing text.

[9] Cf. Acts 5, 41 (Vulg.), where the apostles were "full of joy that they had been considered worthy of suffering ill-treatment for the name of Jesus."

[10] *Ditelo e fatelo inançi tra Dio e voi, col meçço della sanctissima oratione.* Tommasèo text: *ditelo e fatelo dinanzi a Dio e a voi* ("say and do it first before God and yourself"). Catherine writes a number of times about prudence in word and action, but this seems to be the only place in which she speaks of "rehearsing" in prayer what one intends to say or do.

[11] She seems to imply here that she feels she should have gone to Rome.

by giving her refreshing peace and renewal—with great suffering, since nothing but hard work will succeed in pulling out the brambles of all the sins that are choking the garden of holy Church. And he will grant [his vicar] grace, whenever he is willing, to be a courageous man and not turn back because of any burden or persecution inflicted on him by his wicked children. But let him be constant and persevering and not shun hard work. Let him throw himself like a lamb into the midst of the wolves, hungrily desiring God's honor and the salvation of souls, and abandoning his care for temporal things to attend to the spiritual. If he does this (and divine Goodness is asking it of him), the lamb will take control of the wolves and the wolves will return to being lambs. Thus we shall see the glory and praise of God's name and the good and peace of holy Church. There is no other way. It will be done not with war but with peace and kindness, and with that holy spiritual punishment a father must give a guilty child.

Oimé, Oimé, Oimé, most holy father![12] Had you only done it the very day you got back to where you belong![13] I trust in God's goodness and in your holiness that you will do what has not yet been done. This is the way to regain both the temporal and the spiritual. You know (for you were told) that this is what you were asked to do: to see to the reform of holy Church; to attend to the punishment of sins and the planting of virtuous pastors; and to grasp the opportunity for holy peace with your wicked children in the best way possible and in the manner most pleasing to God, so that afterwards[a] you might set things right [by marching] against the unbelievers with the standard of the most holy cross as your weapon.

We must use peace and kindness, not cruelty and war. Those who have sinned must be punished not as much as they deserve (for they would not be able to bear that much), but as much as sick people can tolerate. I believe that our negligence, our failure to do what was possible, is perhaps the reason such devastation and harm and disrespect have befallen holy Church and her ministers. If we do not take measures to do what has not yet been done, I fear that our sins will make us deserving of even greater troubles—I mean such as would give us an even harder thrashing than the loss of temporal things. And I, because of my scant virtue and my great disobedience, am the wretched cause of all these evils and of all your suffering!

Most holy father, soften[b] your displeasure toward me in the light of reason and truth—not the punishment, but only your displeasure. To whom shall I go if you abandon me? Who would help me? Where would

---

[12] She suddenly begins to address the pope directly, as if wanting to convey the message in her own words through Raimondo.

[13] That is, to Rome.

I seek refuge if you were to cast me out? My persecutors pursue me and I run to you and to God's other children and servants. And if you in your displeasure and indignation[c] should abandon me, I will hide in the wounds of Christ crucified, whose vicar you are. I know he will receive me, because he does not want sinners to die.[14] And if I am received by him, you *will* not cast me out. In fact, we shall stand in your[d] place to fight courageously for Christ's dear bride, armed with virtue. In her I want to end my life with tears and sweat and sighs, and give my blood and the marrow of my bones for her. And I won't care if the whole world rejects me, because I will be resting with weeping and great suffering on the breast of this dear bride. Forgive me, most holy father, for all my foolish offense against God and against your holiness. Let truth, eternal Truth, be my excuse and my liberator.[15] I humbly ask your blessing.

To you, dearest father, I have this to say.[16] Stand before his holiness with as brave a heart as you can muster,[e] free of any slavish pain or fear. But first stand before Mary and the most holy cross in your cell in most holy and humble prayer, in true knowledge of yourself and with lively faith and a willingness to suffer. Then go confidently and do whatever you can for God's honor and the salvation of souls, even to the point of death. Give to him the message I've written in this letter in whatever way the Holy Spirit prompts you.

I'll say no more. Keep living in God's holy and tender love.

Gentle Jesus! Jesus love!

Textual Notes

a. *afterwards* supplied by *b*.
b. Tommasèo: *regard* (*mirate*) / *soften* (*miticate*).
c. *b* adds *toward me*.
d. Tommasèo: *our* / *your*.
e. Tommasèo: *Stand . . . whenever you can* / *Stand . . . muster* (*quando* / *quanto*).

---

[14] Cf. Ez. 33, 11.

[15] Cf. Jn. 8, 32: "You will know the truth, and the truth will set you free." While Catherine often speaks of the truth as freeing, this is the only place she uses truth as her "excuse."

[16] She is now addressing Raimondo again.

LETTER T264/G324[1]

To Madonna Jacoma, widow of Messer Trincio de' Trinci da Fuligno
Early to mid-October 1377

Trincio de' Trinci, as we have seen, was lord of Fuligno and *gonfaloniere* (standard-bearer) of the Church. (See introduction to Let. T253, addressed to him shortly before his death.) His wife Jacoma d'Este was the daughter of the Marquis of Ferrara. Trincio was assassinated on 28 September 1377 by his political enemies within his own city.

Trincio's brother Corrado was at Anagni at the time, but returned to Fuligno on 6 December at the invitation of the people to become lord of the city. Having massacred the rebels who had killed his brother, he ruled until 1386, when he died childless. He was succeeded first by Trincio's son Ugolino, and later by Trincio's widow, Jacoma.

In the present letter, Catherine expresses her condolences to Jacoma on the tragic death of her husband, who had in fact confessed his sins before dying, as Catherine says, "in the service of the Church." Her remarks about God's reestablishing Jacoma once more in her earthly home would imply that Corrado has not yet returned to power, which would place the letter certainly before the date of that event, 6 December. I would guess that Catherine is writing not long after Trincio's assassination.[2]

§

In the name of Jesus Christ crucified and of gentle Mary.

Dearest sister in Christ gentle Jesus,

I Caterina, servant and slave of the servants of Jesus Christ, am writing to you in his precious blood. I long to see you grounded in true and perfect patience, without which I believe we cannot be pleasing to God or remain in his grace. For by the very fact that we are unwilling to suffer[3] we are deprived of God's [presence] in grace, since unwillingness to suffer comes from selfish love for ourselves. We are clothed in our selfish sensual will,

---

[1] MSS: Mo-*a*, *b*, M, S5, S6, Ro, S3; translation based on Mo-*a*.

[2] The linguistic data support the placement within the historically established period, especially significant clusters within the patterns AMARDOLC, MARINFER, DISCIPLI, FINITPUN, IMPAZPRI, JERUSAL, MONDCONT, MORTIMMO, OGGIDOM, PAZPROV, PENSAM, REALPAZ,VISIOPAC. Fawtier (II, pp. 297–298) places the letter between Trincio's death and Corrado's return to power on 6 December. Dupré Theseider (unpublished notes) narrows his placement to November.

[3] It. *impazienti*.

and in God there is neither selfish love nor selfish sensuality.[4] So you can see why those who are unwilling to suffer are deprived of God.

It is impossible, says Christ, to serve two masters, for if we serve the one, we will hate the other, since they are opposed to one another.[5] The world and God have nothing in common, and that is why the world's servants are so different from God's. Those who love the world delight in nothing but selfishly and excessively loving pleasure, wealth, prestige, honor, and power—all of which are as fleeting as the wind, for they have in themselves no stability or endurance. Such people have an inordinate desire for a long life (though life is short) and for health (though we must often be ill). Worldly enjoyments or consolations are so unenduring that they are inevitably either taken from us or we from them. Thus God sometimes permits them to be taken from us, as when we lose earthly goods or even the physical life of those we love. Or it happens that we leave them, as when God calls us from this life through physical death. What I am saying is that because of their disordered love for themselves and everyone else—children, spouse, siblings, father and mother—as well as for worldly pleasures, the world's servants suffer intolerable pain if they lose them. They are impatient. They become unbearable to themselves. And this is not surprising, since our grief is in proportion to the love with which we possess. Even in this life these people experience an earnest of hell,[6] and they will indeed end up in eternal damnation unless they protect themselves from it by acknowledging their sins and by suffering with true patience, reflecting that God has permitted these things for our own good.

Oh, dearest sisters and daughters,[7] how foolish people are to devote their love to the miserable mastery of the world! It is faithless and full of deceit, and those who put their faith in it are deluded. The world makes a show of being beautiful but is filthy; it would like to appear stable and solid but it changes. How clearly we see this! For today we are rich and tomorrow poor; today lords and ladies, tomorrow vassals; today alive, tomorrow dead. So we see how unstable the world is. This seems to be what the glorious Paul meant when he said to those who presume to trust in themselves and in the world: "Be careful, for just when you think you are really standing you will fall."[8] And that is the truth.

---

[4] Nowhere else does she state this so directly, though she does speak elsewhere of sensuality rebelling against God. (Tommasèo has: "neither selfish love nor selfish sensuality is God.")

[5] Mt. 6, 24.

[6] In the sense of a "first installment," with the guarantee of more to follow.

[7] Perhaps she is addressing Jacoma's sister-in-law, Corrado's wife, as well, since she had earlier addressed a letter (T253, in this volume) to both men.

[8] 1 Cor. 10, 12.

We must, therefore, rise above the love and confidence we are putting in the world, because no matter where we turn, its gift is the evil of sin and pain. The things of the world[a] are stumbling blocks and trouble for those who possess them apart from God. So we must love what we love in God and for the glory and praise of God's name.

I wouldn't for all that[b] want you to think that God doesn't want us to love. He does want us to love, for everything that was made by God is worthy of love, since God who is supreme Goodness has made all things good and cannot do anything but good. Things are made evil and sinful only when we don't love them by God's standards and with genuine humility, acknowledging that they are from God. It is this sin, then, this misplaced desire of ours, that is unworthy of love. In fact, it deserves hatred and punishment because it is not in God.

The world, this wretched master, is truly very much at odds with God. God wants virtue and the world wants vice. In God is all patience,[9] while the world is unwilling to suffer. In Christ crucified is all mercy; he is solid and stable and immutable.[10] Christ's promises never fail, because he is life and from him we have life.[11] Christ is truth, for he keeps his promises, rewarding every good and punishing every sin.[12] He is light, the source of our light.[13] Christ is our hope, our provider, our strength.[14] Christ never fails anyone who trusts in him, for we are provided for in proportion to our trust in our Creator. Christ frees us from weakness and strengthens the heart of the troubled who with genuine humility and confidence ask his help. We have only to turn our mind's eye, enlightened by true light, to his boundless charity, and we shall acquire this light from its source, the blood of Christ crucified. Without the light we could never see what a pitiable thing it is to love the world, nor how good and beneficial it is to love and fear God, and without this vision it would be impossible to love the one who is worthy of love or to despise vice and sin,[c] which are deserving of hatred.

This, then, is the gentle Master I want you to serve with true patience. You have experienced how painful slavery to the world is, and what pain there is when it suddenly fails you. So draw near to Christ crucified and begin to serve him with all your heart and with all your soul. Begin to

---

[9] Cf. Ps. 103, 8: "Merciful and gracious is the Lord, slow to anger and abounding in kindness."

[10] Cf. Jas. 1, 17: "the Father of the heavenly luminaries, who cannot change and who is never shadowed over."

[11] Jn. 1, 3–4.

[12] Jn. 14, 6.

[13] Jn. 1, 4.

[14] 1 Tim. 1, 1.

bear with true patience the holy discipline to which God has subjected you—not because he hates you but because of his great love for [your husband's] salvation.[15] He was so merciful as to let him die in the service of holy Church. For had he died in any other way he would have had much to do[16] for all his idle entanglements with the world and all his worrying about his friends and relatives (things that easily get in the way of our salvation). God loved him with a special love and wanted to provide for his salvation, and this is why he let him come to such a pass. For his soul it was sweet. And you ought to be a lover more of his soul than of his body, since the body is finite and mortal, while the soul is immortal and infinite. So you see how supreme Providence has seen to his salvation, and for you he has provided some trials to bear so as to have something to reward you for in eternal life.

We have already said that every good is rewarded and every sin punished. By this I mean that every pain and trial that is borne with patience [is rewarded], and every unwillingness to suffer, every complaint and hatred against God and our neighbors and ourselves [is punished]. In fact, the good gentle Jesus wanted you to know what sort of thing the world is, how pitiable it is to make a god of one's children or spouse or social position or anything else.

And if you say to me, "The burden is too great for me to bear," I answer you, dearest sister, that it is a small burden and quite bearable. I say it is small because time is so small and short. For our burden is only as great as time is long. Once we have left this life our burdens are gone. And how long is our time? The saints say it is like the point of a needle, whose height and breadth are nothing. So it is with our physical life, for it lasts only until it pleases divine Goodness to take us from this life.

I tell you again,[d] it *is* bearable, for none of us can relieve ourselves of it by our unwillingness to suffer! People often say, "I can't bear it, and I don't *want* to bear it!" But they have to bear it none the less. And their unwillingness piles weight upon weight because of their selfish will. For our selfish will is the ground of all suffering, and so our burden is as great as our will makes it. Take away my [selfish] will and the burden is lifted.

And what takes away this [selfish] will? The remembrance of the blood of Christ crucified. This blood is so wonderful that in the remembrance of it every bitterness becomes sweet and every heavy burden light. For in Christ's blood we discover the inexpressible love with which he loves us. Because of his love he gave us life and restored to us the grace we had lost

---

[15] The text has simply "his," but the referent is clear.

[16] Presumably she means that Trincio would have had much to atone for, and thus would have had much to suffer in eternity.

because of sin. In his blood we discover the generosity of his mercy, and there we see that God wants nothing other than our good. Oh sweet blood, on which our soul gets drunk! It is the blood that gives us patience and clothes us in the wedding garment we need to enter eternal life. This is the garment of charity, without which we would be thrown out of the banquet of eternal life.[17]

Truly, dearest sister, in the remembrance of this blood we find every delight, relief from our every burden and trial. This is why I told you that the remembrance of this blood strips us of the sensual will that makes us unwilling to suffer. And remembrance of the blood clothes us in God's will, in which we suffer so patiently that nothing that happens to us can trouble us. In fact, we grieve more when we sense that we are rebelling against God in our grief over these burdens than we do over the burdens themselves. This is how I want you to act. Be sorry that you *are* grieving in an emotional way.[18] In this way you will put to death the vices of anger and impatience and will attain perfect virtue.

Consider within yourself how much suffering Christ has borne for you. Consider with what love he has granted you this [suffering of yours], only so that you might be made holy in him.[19] And consider how small the burden is because of the brevity of time, as I've said. Consider how our every effort will be rewarded, how good God is, and how his goodness cannot want anything but our total good.[20] I'm saying that if you keep this holy thought in mind, it will make everything easy to bear.[21] It will make you bear every trial with true knowledge of our sins,[22] knowledge that we deserve every sort of burden, and knowledge of God's goodness to us, in which we find such great mercy. For our sins we would deserve infinite punishment, but God punishes us with these finite sufferings while at the same time counting the sin atoned for. And what is more, by his grace we who serve him by suffering with true patience merit eternal life. He is so kind that to serve him is more to reign than to be a servant.[23] God makes all his servants kings and queens, free lords and ladies, for he has

---

[17] Cf. the parable of the wedding banquet, Mt. 22, 11–13.

[18] In Catherine's view, one should be ashamed to give in to grief or to anything else on an emotional level. One's responses should be grounded solely in God's will.

[19] Cf. 2 Cor. 5, 12: "For our sakes God made him who did not know sin, to be sin, so that in him we might become the very holiness of God."

[20] It. *tutto nostro bene.*

[21] Cf. Mt. 11, 29: "My yoke is easy and my burden light."

[22] As she so often does, Catherine switches to the first person plural (thus including herself) when she speaks of sinfulness.

[23] Cf. Augustine, *Meditatio XXXII* (PL XL, 925): "To serve God is to reign."

freed them from slavery to the devil and from blind servitude to the perverse tyranny of the world.

Up then, dearest daughters![24] We mustn't waste any more time, since service and disordered love of the world and creatures and ourselves is so bitter, and since it is so sweet to serve and fear our gentle Savior, our natural Lord,[25] who in his infinite charity loved us before we even existed! Let's serve him with all our heart and all our energy and all our strength, with royal patience full of sweetness,[26] trusting by the true light, living faith, that he will help us in our every need. This virtue [of patience] is always in control, is always victorious and never vanquished, because she never lets anger dominate or possess her. Whoever has her never sees eternal death, but even in this life experiences the earnest of eternal life. Without her we live in death, deprived of the good of earth as well as that of heaven.

This is why I said[e] that I long to see you grounded in true and perfect patience. I see how great the danger is, and I sense that because of what has happened to you, you need it if you are not to lose the fruit of your efforts. And this is how you must act, so that when gentle First Truth calls you to account at the moment of your death you will be able to say, "My Lord, I have run the race and have finished this life in the faith and trust I had in you,[27] enduring with patience the burdens you granted me for my own good. Now I ask you as a favor, through the merits of your blood, to grant me yourself, who are life without death, light without darkness, satiety without boredom, and sweet hunger without any pain.[28] You are so filled with every good that words can never describe nor the heart imagine nor the eye see how great is the good you have prepared for me and for the others who willingly bear every sort of burden for love of you."[29]

I assure you, dearest sister, if you do this God will reestablish you once more in your earthly home, and in the end you will return to your true homeland, Jerusalem, vision of peace. It was the same with Job, who proved his patience. He lost all he had—his children dead, his possessions

---

[24] This plural may be an error, or Catherine may have both Jacoma and her sister-in-law in mind.

[25] This reference to Christ as our "natural Lord" is unique here.

[26] It. *reale*, which can have the sense simply of "real" or "solid," but in some cases Catherine speaks of patience as queen. Given the references to royalty above, she may well intend the connotation of royalty here.

[27] Cf. 2 Tim. 4, 7 (Vulg.): "I have finished the race; I have kept faith."

[28] Cf. Cavalca, *Descrizione de' dieci comandamenti*, p. 306: "We shall desire though we are sated, and we shall be sated even in our desiring. Yet satiety will not be a source of boredom, nor desire be accompanied by pain, as happens in this world."

[29] Cf. 1 Cor. 2, 9.

gone, his health so destroyed that his flesh crawled with vermin. (But he still had his wife to goad him with her constant nagging!) And in all these things Job didn't complain, but said, "God gave them to me and God has taken them away from me. May his name be glorified in everything." And God, seeing such patience in Job, gave him back double for all he had had, giving him his grace here, and in the end, eternal life.[30]

Now that is what you must do. And don't let your feelings or the world or the devil or anything anyone may say deceive you. Guard your heart against hatred toward your neighbors, for that is the worst leprosy there is. Hatred makes us like the man who wants to kill his enemy but instead turns the point of the knife on himself and kills himself before he can kill his enemy. That's the way it is with hatred, because the knife of hatred kills us before it kills the other person. I hope in God's goodness that you will guard yourself against this. And so that you'll be better able, get into the habit of going to confession often. Keep company willingly with God's servants. And find your pleasure in prayer, where you will come to a better knowledge of both yourself and God. Bathe yourself in the blood of Christ crucified.

I'll say no more. Keep living in God's holy and tender love.

Gentle Jesus! Jesus love!

Textual Notes

a. *The things of the world* supplied by *b.*
b. *for all that* supplied by *b.*
c. *sin* written over erasure by *b.*
d. *again* supplied by *b.*
e. *b* inserts above the line: *and say.*

[30] Jb. 42.

LETTER T314/G343[1]
To Costanza, wife of Niccolò Soderini[2]
and
To certain devoted children of hers
Mid-October 1377

Raimondo da Capua tells us that, shortly before Catherine sent him to Rome "with certain proposals which, if only people had understood, would have been for the advantage of the holy Church of God," he met with Niccolò Soderini in Siena.[3] Perhaps he gleaned information about Costanza's fears during that visit and conveyed the word to Catherine, who then wrote this letter.

The rubrics of R1 and T add *essendo tornata a firenze* ("having returned to Florence"). This could mean either that Costanza has returned to Florence or that Catherine has returned there. If the reference is to Costanza, it could simply mean that the latter has been in Siena with her husband and has now returned home. (Catherine sends greetings to Niccolò and to their daughter.) If the reference is to Catherine, the letter would probably have to be placed in early 1378, when Catherine went to that city at the behest of Pope Gregory XI. However, this is the less likely possibility, since Catherine, being on such close terms with the Soderini family, would hardly have communicated with them by letter when she was in the same city. Also, the linguistic data would support the first scenario. In fact, since this letter includes four patterns which occur nowhere else except in *The Dialogue*, I am inclined to place it in October, when Catherine was beginning to work on her book.[4]

The letter to Costanza is closely duplicated twice in the manuscript S7, addressed there simply to "Dear children" and without the closing personal greetings of the letter to Costanza. The second version (S7*b*) is incomplete.

---

[1] MSS: Mo-*a*, *b*, B, P2, S3, T, R1, P3, P5, F2, F1, S7; translation based on Mo-*a* for Costanza, with reference to S7*a* for anonymous disciples, with variants based on an unpublished transcription by A. Volpato.

[2] S3 describes Costanza as *donna che fu di Niccolò Soderini*, which would make her a widow, but this has to mean simply that Costanza was widowed at the time the manuscript was being transcribed, since in the letter Catherine sends greetings to Niccolò.

[3] *Life*, II, ix, 274, p. 255, and III, vi, 422, p. 382.

[4] The patterns which occur otherwise only in *The Dialogue* are CORPLASS, ESSERCON, MISPECC and TIMSERVC. Other significant clusters within individual patterns are ABBRACC, FURROBB, MARETEMP, PENAMENT, SCHIFPEN, SCIOGLEG, SONNCORP, and VISIOPAC. Both Fawtier (II, p. 309) and Dupré Theseider (unpublished notes) speculate about 1378 as a possible date, but both conclude that the clues are too vague to permit placement of the letter.

§

In the name of Jesus Christ crucified[a] and of gentle Mary.

Dearest daughter[b] in Christ gentle Jesus,

I Caterina, servant and slave of the servants of Jesus Christ, am writing to you in his precious blood. I long to see your heart and affection so divested of wretched love for the world that you will come to loathe and detest every contemptible thing.[c] Then you will say with the dear apostle Paul, "I long to be freed from my body and to be with Christ."[5]

Paul knew that physical life was a great obstacle between himself and God, and this in two ways. The first is that the body is always rebelling against the spirit, and in rebelling against the spirit it is rebelling against its Creator. The other is that our physical life keeps us from seeing God until our soul is freed from this bondage.[6] This is why Paul and God's other servants are impatient of life and long for death.

But remember that there are two deaths we must die before we attain to life. The first is death to all perverse selfishness. This sensual will leads those who do not kill it to eternal death. So we must rise above [this selfishness]. We must take up[d] the knife of hatred and love (that is, of hatred for sin and love for virtue) as we wait for the second death, our physical death, which puts an end to all struggle and darkness and brings us to the light of the vision of our[e] God. Reflect, my daughter,[f] that unless we have lived with our will dead in the way I've described, our physical death will not be so glorious. Indeed, it will be very painful.

So I want you to pursue true solid virtue, fleeing the world and its pleasures and drawing near to God. Then you will receive utter joy and happiness and confidence. You will lose all slavish fear. You will conceive a living faith, and in that faith you will contemplate divine mercy and discover that God neither wants nor seeks[g] anything other than that we[h] be made holy.[7] And in order that we might be made holy in him, he gave us the Word, his only-begotten Son, and willed that that Son should die the shameful death of the cross. There is such immense mercy in this that no

---

[5] Phil. 1, 23. The only other place Catherine refers to this passage is in *Dial.* 84, p. 154: "They long for death, and so they say, 'Who will free me from my body? I long to be set free from my body and to be with Christ.' And such as these say with Paul, 'Death for me is in longing, and life in patience.' "

[6] Cf. *Dial.* 79, p. 149: "So it seemed to Paul that his sense of sight was fighting against his spiritual vision. In other words, his human feeling of his body's bulk was a block to the eye of his understanding and was keeping him from seeing me face to face." This contrast is expressed only in this letter and in two places in *The Dialogue* (the second being ch. 45, p. 92).

[7] 1 Thes. 4, 3.

human heart or language can possibly describe or even imagine it. Mercy, therefore, relieves us of fear and pain.

Sometimes people suffer a great deal from fear of death and because of their self-indulgence. The first is a delusion the devil puts in their minds. He says, "You see that you are going to die, and you haven't done[i] a bit of good! So do you know where you're going? Your deeds have earned only hell!" On the other hand, he makes them feel sorry for themselves by saying, "Just think! Your body is so pampered now with worldly pleasures, but soon you will die and be uglier than any animal!" The devil[j] in his perversity puts these thoughts and suggestions in their heart only to lead them to discouragement and despair. He wants them to see only their shortcomings and sins, and to hide the divine mercy from them.

We have to counter the devil's great malice by responding to these interior suggestions of his. Turning our gaze to our Creator, we should say, "I acknowledge[k] that I am mortal, but this is a tremendous grace for me, since death will bring me to my goal, to God who is my life. I acknowledge, too, that my life and deeds deserve only hell. But I have faith and trust in my Creator, in the blood of the Lamb who was slain and consumed,[8] that he will pardon my sins and grant me grace. I will try in this present time to amend my life. But if death should overtake me before I have amended my life—that is, before I have yet done penance for my sins—I [still] say that I trust *in Domino nostro Jesu Christo*,[9,l] because[m] I see that there is no comparison between my sins and divine mercy.[10] Even if all the sins that could possibly be committed were gathered together in one person, it would be like[n] a drop of vinegar in the sea."

This is how sins compare with divine mercy, if only we are willing to come back and receive it with a true and holy disposition, with a contempt for our sin that cancels out our fondness for our body and for all created things. In this way we gain confidence. We grow in love for our goal. We lose the slavish fear of discouragement. With immense gladness we rejoice with Christ crucified our joy, looking forward with the greatest happiness and serenity to the hour of death. We not only look forward to it; we long to see ourselves lifted up from the world to be with Christ.[11]

Up then, my dear daughter![o] No more fear! Live this bit of time in joy, with a desire for virtue. Bear patiently whatever physical or spiritual suf-

---

[8] All manuscripts except Mo-*a* and F1 add *and* before *in the blood* . . . , which gives less emphatic expression to Catherine's Christology, in which trust in the Creator is precisely *in* the blood of Christ. I have therefore kept Mo-*a*'s reading.

[9] She cites the Pauline expression, as elsewhere, in Latin.

[10] Again, the concept occurs elsewhere only in *The Dialogue*, as in ch. 132, p. 268, where God says that his "mercy is incomparably greater than all the sins anyone could commit."

[11] Phil. 1, 23.

fering God sends you, whether in the form of illness or in any other[p] form. Don't let me see you evading suffering,[q] but reach out to embrace the cross and suffering. For every pain you suffer is given you by God for your good, because he wants to reward you when you come in from the stormy sea of this darksome life and arrive at the place of rest, your true city, Jerusalem, vision of peace. There all our willingness to suffer, every good deed we have done in this life, is rewarded.

Oh how stupid and insane would be the merchant into whose hands the treasure has been placed that he might invest it for profit, and who would in fear of pain bury it in the earth! He would certainly deserve great reproach and [even] the forfeiture of his life! We are merchants to whom the treasure of time has been entrusted along with freedom of choice—the free will God has given and entrusted to us so that we might make a profit. So as long as we have time we can either gain or lose, just as our will chooses. We would be stupid, then, if we were to let apprehension or fear of pain make us bury the time and will we have been given for gaining eternal life by living virtuously (and not for buying hell by living in vice). For we *are* living in vice when we bury time and will in the earth—that is, in inordinate earthly attachments and desires that are divorced from God.

And this is why I said that I long to see your heart and affection divested of slavish fear and of all worldly love and attachments. I want[r] you to be clothed only in Christ crucified. There put your faith and your trust. Then the devil will not be able to trick you into inordinate fear of death. No, choose with longing to return to your goal.[12]

I'll say no more.[s] Bathe in the blood of Christ crucified.

Bless your little girl[t] in Christ gentle[u] Jesus. Remember me to Monna Nera and to Niccolò. Tell them to learn how to steal time and spend it in true holy desire while they have it.[13]

Keep living in God's holy and tender love.

Gentle Jesus! Jesus love!

Textual Notes

a. S7*a*: [*crucified*].

b. S7*a*: *children*.

c. S7*a, b* add *about it* (*sua*).

[12] We come from God, and we *return* there as our goal. Cf. Prayer 4, p. 42, where Catherine addresses St. Paul: "You, wonderful Paul, pondered this well, and so you truly knew where you had come from and where you were going—and not only where you were going but even the road you were traveling, for you had come to know your origin and your goal."

[13] The letter to the anonymous disciples (S7*a*) does not have *Bless. . . . have it.*

d. Mo-*b*, S3: *cut it with* / *take up* (having written *tagli col* over *tolga*).
e. P5, F2: [*our*].
f. S7*a*: *children* / *daughter*.
g. S7*a*, *b*: [*nor seeks*].
h. S7*a*, *b*: *you* / *we*.
i. At this point the microfilm of S7 ends, in the midst of its second version of the letter. (The next folio on the microfilm is numbered 7, but is blank, and folio following that is numbered 10, and begins a transcription of *The Dialogue*.)
j. Mo-*b*, S3 add *so in this way* at the head of the sentence.
k. S7*a*: *know* / *acknowledge*.
l. P5, F2 have the formula in Italian, with *my* / *our*.
m. *because* supplied from Mo-*b*, S3.
n. Mo-*b*, S3: *less than* / *like*.
o. S7*a*: *my dear children*.
p. P3, S3: [*other*].
q. It. *non mi schifate pene*.
r. T, P3, P5, F2, Mo-*b* introduce the sentence with *But*.
s. P5, F2 add *to you*.
t. P5, F2: *daughter* / *little girl*.
u. S3: [*gentle*].

LETTER T82/G367[1]
To three women of Florence
Mid-October 1377

There is no indication in either text or rubric as to who these Florentine women might be. References to withdrawal from the world, the wish to be perfect, and the obligation of prayer at specified times would make it likely that these women have recently joined a Third Order ("tertiary") group, perhaps the *Mantellate*.

Catherine seems often to have written exhortatory letters such as this shortly after being with those to whom they are addressed. In this case, however, the linguistic evidence points away from any such period. In fact, the linguistic evidence lends strong support for placing it during Catherine's stay in the Val d'Orcia, most probably between September and December.

Perhaps the letter was written at the same time as another to a Florentine woman, Costanza Soderini (Let. T314, written most probably about mid-October 1377). That letter, like this one, speaks of detachment from the world. We know that Raimondo da Capua met with Niccolò Soderini shortly before he left for Rome about mid-September. Though that visit took place in Siena, Niccolò could have brought news or letters from the women, which Raimondo could then have brought to Catherine.[2] I am therefore placing this letter with Let. T314 in mid-October 1377.[3]

The letter is designated in both manuscripts as one of those dictated in ecstasy.[4]

---

[1] MSS: Mo-*a*, F3; translation based on Mo-*a*.

[2] Raimondo's own account (*Life*, III, vi, 422, p. 382) implies that he returned to Rocca d'Orcia once more after his journey to Siena.

[3] The letter has very little in common with letters written before summer of 1377 and shares most heavily with letters written between August and December of that year. Of the six letters which share fourteen or more of this one's sixty-five analyzed patterns, four are concentrated in those months. More narrowly still, a number of significant clusters within individual patterns begin and/or end between October and December 1377: CUORDOPP, CUORLIBE, CUORMESC, OPERCONG, PARTSENS, PIETRCRO, PRESUMSE, SONNCORP. Both Fawtier (II, p. 309) and Dupré Theseider (unpublished notes) consider the letter undatable.

[4] Rubric in Mo: "*Una doctrina a tre donne di Firenze. In abstractione facta.*" F3 has just the latter designation.

§

In the name of Jesus Christ crucified and of gentle Mary.[a]

Dearest daughters in Christ gentle Jesus,[b]

Since God has taken you away from the filth of the world,[5] don't turn back to look at what you've plowed.[6] No, always look to what you have to do to keep up the holy resolution and beginning you've made.

What must we see and do in order to keep up our good will? I'll tell you. You must always live in the cell of self-knowledge. You must come to know that you are not, that you have your being from God.[7] You must come to know your sins. You must come to know how short time is. (Time is precious for us, because in time we can gain everlasting life or lose it, as we please, and once time has passed we can do no good.[8]) And you must come to know God's great goodness within you, and his indescribable love for you, revealed through the Word, his only-begotten Son. And this gentle loving Word revealed it to you through his blood.

Now we are the vessel that has received this blood. And we are the rock into which the standard of the most holy cross was set. For neither cross nor nails nor earth could have held this humble loving Word if love had not held him.[9] But his love for us held him and made him stay on the

---

[5] The letter in both manuscripts begins thus abruptly, without the customary opening protocol.

[6] Lk. 9, 62.

[7] That is, though you have being, it is completely dependent on God, from whom it comes.

[8] Cf. Let. T314 to Costanza Soderini (in this volume), where this theme is developed: "Oh how stupid and insane would be the merchant into whose hands the treasure has been placed that he might invest it for profit, and who would in fear of pain bury it in the earth! He would certainly deserve great reproach and [even] the forfeiture of his life! We are merchants to whom the treasure of time has been entrusted along with freedom of choice—the free will God has given and entrusted to us so that we might make a profit. So as long as we have time we can either gain or lose, just as our will chooses. We would be stupid, then, if we were to let apprehension or fear of pain make us bury the time and will we have been given for gaining eternal life by living virtuously (and not for buying hell by living in vice). For we *are* living in vice when we bury time and will in the earth—that is, in inordinate earthly attachments and desires that are divorced from God."

[9] In Let. T223 to Cardinal Iacopo Orsini (in this volume) she relates these ideas to a personal experience: "We see that within us is the stone that held up the standard of the most holy cross—for except for the force of God's love for us, the stone could never have held [the cross] nor could the nails have held [Christ] fast. I remember this being said once to one of his servants. She in her boundless desire said, 'Oh my Lord, what grace it would have been for me if I had been some of the stone or soil in which your cross was set, for I would have received some of your blood that flowed down from the cross!' Gentle First Truth answered, 'My dearest daughter, you *were* the stone that held me, you and everyone else—I mean my love for you—for nothing else could have held me.' "

tree of the cross. So our heart and affection must be engrafted into him in love if we want to share in the fruit of his blood.[10]

Once we have so wonderfully come to know God, we love what we know of God's goodness and hate what we know of the sensual aspect of ourselves. This is for us the source of true humility, and humility is the nurse and governess of charity.[11] This makes us move forward without turning back. We grow from virtue to virtue,[12] exercising ourselves in vigils and in continual humble prayer, in constant holy desire and in good holy actions. Such is the "continual prayer" every person should practice beyond the specific prayer prayed at the regular obligatory times.[13] One should omit the latter only for obedience or for charity, and never because of difficulties or because of physical or spiritual sleepiness. In the latter case, one should wake up one's body with physical activity or by making prostrations[14] or with other exercises likely to dispel sleep once it has had its due.

As for spiritual sleepiness, it has to be dispelled with hatred and contempt for oneself. With a holy aggressiveness mount the bench of your conscience and reproach yourself, saying, "So you're sleeping, my soul? You sleep, and divine Goodness is watching over you—but time is passing and not waiting for you. Do you want the judge to find you asleep when he calls you to account for your time, for how you've spent it, and for how you've been grateful for the gift of his blood?" Then your spirit will wake up! Even though it may not have felt like waking up, it is waked up anyway, and dispels selfish love from your soul.

This is how one goes forward, advancing from perfection to perfection. And you do apparently want to achieve this perfection. For love does not

---

[10] In Let. T185/DT54 to Gregory XI (vol. I) Catherine develops at length the image of our being engrafted into Christ, the tree of life. Elsewhere (for example, in Let. T27 in vol. I and T172 in this volume) she speaks of the Word engrafting himself first into our humanity and then onto the wood of the cross.

[11] Cf. Let. T33 to the Abbot General of Monteoliveto (1378): "Charity's wet-nurse is deep humility. And what food does this nurse give her? The food of light and of self-knowledge, and by this light [the soul] has come to know her poverty and the frail sensuality that is the cause of all such poverty. In this knowledge she humbles herself and conceives a contempt for herself with which she nurtures in herself the fire of divine charity, coming to know God's unspeakable goodness, the goodness that is the beginning and end of all her knowing."

[12] Cf. Ps. 83, 8 (Vulg.): "They go from strength to strength; they shall see the God of gods in Zion." Note that in Catherine's Tuscan as in the biblical text, "virtue" and "strength" are the same word.

[13] If these three women are indeed tertiaries, they are obligated to certain prayers daily.

[14] The manuscript bears a gloss in the margin: "not physical prostrations," but Catherine very probably does mean physical prostrations (the symbolic gesture for begging mercy and forgiveness), since the intent is to wake oneself up physically.

live lazily but is always doing great things. If you do this, you will clothe yourself not just in the outward act of virtue but in its pith, and you will savor the virtue of patience, which is in turn the pith of charity.[15] You will rejoice in suffering, if only you can be like Christ crucified, and bearing his pains and humiliation will seem a pleasure to you. You will avoid socializing and delight in solitude. You will not presumptuously trust yourself but will have confidence in Christ crucified. Your spirit will be filled not with fantasies but with true solid virtue. Your love for God will be sincere, not feigned; single-hearted, not two-faced. You will love him in truth above all things, and will love your neighbors as you love yourself.[16] Neither the devil's tormenting you with evil and ugly thoughts, nor the weakness of your flesh, nor the harassments of other people will weary or discourage you. Rather you will say with the apostle Paul, with lively faith: "I can do all things through Christ crucified, who is in me and who gives me strength."[17] You will in humility consider yourself deserving of suffering but undeserving of its reward.

Love, love each other in Christ gentle Jesus with a sisterly love[18] drawn from the depths of his own charity! I'll say no more. May God fill you with his most holy grace!

One thing I beg of you: don't go looking for all sorts of advice. Take one counselor who will advise you sincerely, and follow that counselor. For following the advice of many is a dangerous affair. Not that any advice that has its foundation in God isn't good. But just as God's servants have different ways even though they are all motivated by charity, so they teach differently. So when people look to too many of them, they find themselves wanting to model themselves on all of them, and then in the end you find they have nothing from any one of them! So it is better, and even essential, that you settle on one, and try to be perfect in [following] that one, even though you may like the teaching of every one of them. I don't mean you should go searching for the sake of searching. Still, you should be pleased about the different and varied ways God has with his creatures

---

[15] *Dial.* 95, p. 178: "All of the virtues can at times simulate perfection when they are really imperfect, but they cannot deceive patience. For if this gentle patience, the very heart (pith) of charity, is present in the soul, she shows that all the virtues are alive and perfect. But if she is absent, it is clear that all the virtues are imperfect and have not yet arrived at the table of the most holy cross. For it is here that patience was conceived in knowledge of self and of my goodness, and brought to birth through holy contempt, and anointed with true humility."

[16] Mt. 19, 19.

[17] Cf. Phil. 4, 13.

[18] It. *con una carità fraterna.*

and hold them in reverence, when you realize that there are so many dwelling places in our Father's house.[19]

Now immerse yourselves in the blood of Christ crucified, gentle love, and bathe there. Keep living in God's holy and tender love.

Gentle Jesus! Jesus love!

Textual Notes

a. The invocation is not in F3.

b. F3: [*in Christ gentle Jesus*].

---

[19] Jn. 14, 2. Also *Dial.* 100, pp. 189–190: "They find joy in everything. They do not sit in judgment on my servants or anyone else, but rejoice in every situation and every way of living they see, saying, 'Thanks to you, eternal Father, that in your house there are so many dwelling places!' And they are happier to see many different ways than if they were to see everyone walking the same way, because this way they see the greatness of my goodness more fully revealed."

Letter T272/G90[1]
To Frate Raimondo da Capua, at Rome
10 October 1377, or shortly thereafter

Catherine refers near the beginning of this letter to the sense she had had of Raimondo's grief on the feast of Saint Francis (4 October). She also says that her concern has been relieved by letters she has received from both him and the pope. This letter must therefore be not only after 4 October, but it must also be after the following Saturday (10 October) or a succeeding Saturday, when she describes at great length her having taken four particular petitions to prayer.[2]

This letter clearly serves as a framework a bit later when *The Dialogue* is elaborated. I have noted the parallels as they occur without reproducing the passages. In many cases a sentence or two of the letter serves as the beginning of a "chapter" in the book. Interesting to note are the many embellishments to the *Dialogue* rendition of the bridge that are not present here: roof, walls, shops, etc. This may well indicate that that section of *The Dialogue* was written or at least elaborated while Catherine was in Florence in 1378, with the *Ponte Vecchio* only a short walk from the house where she was staying.

---

[1] MSS: Mo-*a*, P4 (partial), M, S5, S6, Pa, S2; translation based on Mo-*a*, with variants based on unpublished notes of Dupré Theseider. In P4 this letter is the first of those written to Dominicans, with a miniature at the head of the group.

[2] While the linguistic evidence strongly supports the placement of this letter during the Val d'Orcia period, and even more narrowly in October or November, it does not suffice to prove conclusively when the letter was written in relation to Let. T267. A good number of significant clusters within individual patterns do, however, begin and/or end between October and November 1377: ALLENT, AMASERVE, GERMTRIB, LAVFACCI, LEGGEPER, LUMNFOND, MARIAMAD, MENSDESI, MUOIO, NONPUO, PONSED, PROPVOL, SPOSVERI, VERITCMP. (For ease of management, a number of wide-ranging and very frequent or redundant patterns have been deleted from the chart and from analysis for this very long letter: PERMANE, PERODISS, CIEC, DESVEDER, GESUCRST, ONORSAL, SOMETER, SVSCHIAV, GUERPHYS, FIOR.) The critics are in disagreement on the placement of this letter. Fawtier (II, p. 198) places it before Let. T226 (which he dates 14 April 1378), perhaps on 10 or 11 October 1377, given Catherine's reference to the eve of Mary's day, that is, Saturday. Dupré Theseider (unpublished notes) places it in early October 1377. Gardner (*Saint Catherine of Siena*, p. 226) would put the letter later, since Pope Gregory returned to Rome from Anagni only on 7 November (but it is not said when Gregory went there).

§

In the name of Jesus Christ crucified and of gentle Mary.

Dearest and very loved father in Christ gentle Jesus,

I Caterina, servant and slave of the servants of Jesus Christ, am writing to you in his precious blood. I long to see you a follower and lover of truth, so that you may be a true son of Christ crucified (who is Truth itself) and a fragrant flower in our holy order and in the mystic body of holy Church. And this you must be. You mustn't let the thorns of persecution make you give up or turn back, because it would be absurd to give up the rose for fear of the thorns. I long to see you courageous, not afraid of anyone at all. And I'm certain that God in his infinite goodness will fulfill my desire.

Take heart, dearest father, where Christ's dear bride is concerned, for the more bitter troubles she experiences, the more divine Truth promises to make her overflow with sweet consolation.[3] And this will be her sweetness: reform by means of good holy pastors who are flowers of glory, who give God glory and the fragrance of virtue.[a] This reform concerns the flowers [only], her ministers and pastors.[b] The *fruit* of this bride has no need of reform, because this is never diminished or spoiled by the sins of her ministers.[4] So be happy about the bitterness, since Truth[c] has promised to give us relief.

I experienced both bitterness[d] and consolation when I received dear *Babbo*'s letter and your own—bitterness for the harm done to holy Church and for your own bitterness, which I had sensed very intimately on the feast of Saint Francis; and happiness because you relieved me of my great concern.[5] After I had read the letters and understood everything, I asked a servant of God to offer tears and sweat in God's presence for this bride and for *Babbo's* weakness.[6] At once, by divine grace, there welled up in her a desire and joy beyond all measuring. She waited for morning, in

[3] This passage parallels *Dial.* 12, p. 47.

[4] Aquinas, *Summa Theologica,* III, q. 64, a. 6, says that so long as a priest has not been suspended from his ministry or excommunicated, those who receive the sacraments from him, even though he may be in sin, do not share in his sin, but rather "in the Church, from whom he has his ministry."

[5] This is very probably the experience in prayer to which she referred in her earlier letter to Raimondo (Let. T267, in this volume): "I've heard from a servant of God who constantly holds you before God in prayer, that you have been experiencing tremendous struggles and that your spirit has been overtaken by darkness because of the devil's illusions and deceits."

[6] The "servant of God" is, as usual in these narrations of personal experience, herself. *Babbo* ("Papa") is Pope Gregory XI.

order to have Mass. (It was Mary's day.[7]) When it was time for Mass she took her place with true knowledge of herself, ashamed of her imperfection in God's presence. And rising above herself with restless desire and gazing with her mind's eye on eternal Truth,[e] she made four petitions as she held herself and her father in the presence of Truth, her Spouse.[8]

First [she asked] for the reform of holy Church.[9] Then God, letting himself be compelled by her tears and bound by the cord of her desire, said, "My dearest daughter, look how [the Church] has dirtied her face with impurity and selfish love, with bloated pride and with the avarice of those who nurse at her breasts.[10,f] But draw sweat and tears from the fountain of my divine charity; take them and wash her face.[11] For I assure you, her beauty will be restored not with the sword, nor with war or cruelty, but with peace, with continual humble prayer, sweat, and tears shed with restless desire by my servants. So I shall fulfill your desire with much suffering, and my providence will never fail you."

Although this prayer included the salvation of all the world, still she went on with a more specific petition for the whole world. Then God showed with what great love he had created humankind, saying, "Look now how everyone is attacking me.[12] See, daughter, with how many different sins they attack me, especially with their wretched and abominable self-centeredness. This is the source of all the evil with which they have poisoned the entire world. Now you, my servants, come before me with many prayers and so you will soften the wrath of divine justice.

"Understand that no one can escape from my hands. Open your mind's eye and look into my hand"[13] Raising her mind's eye, she saw the whole world enclosed in God's hand. Then God said, "I want you to understand that no one can be taken away from me. Everyone is here either for justice or for mercy, so everyone is mine. And because everyone came forth from me, I love everyone indescribably much,[g] and I will be merciful to them through the mediation of my servants."

Then, with the fire of desire growing, she was at once joyful and sad and gave thanks to divine Goodness as if she knew that God had shown her people's sins in order to compel her to rise up with more concern and

---

[7] That is, Saturday, traditionally dedicated to Mary.

[8] Cf. *Dial.* 1, p. 26, where this experience forms the beginning framework for Catherine's book.

[9] For parallel passage, cf. *Dial.* 14, p. 50.

[10] The reference is not only to the clergy, but to all Christians.

[11] The parallel with *Dial.* continues at 15, p. 54.

[12] For parallel passage, cf. *Dial.* 17, p. 55.

[13] For parallel passage, cf. *Dial.* 18, p. 56.

greater desire.[14] This holy and loving fire grew to such an extent that in her desire to see her body sweat blood, she thought nothing of the watery sweat she was pouring out. She said to herself, "My soul, you have frittered your whole life away, and this is why all these evils, great and small, general and particular, have come upon the world and holy Church! So[h] I want you to heal them now with a sweat of blood." Then this soul, spurred on by holy desire, rose with greater effort, opened her mind's eye, and looked at herself in the mirror of divine charity. There she saw and experienced how much we are bound and obligated to seek the glory and praise of God's name in the salvation of souls.[15]

And this is what eternal Truth chose you for and called you to when he responded to the third petition, which was her hunger for your salvation.[16] He said, "Daughter, I want him to seek this very conscientiously. But neither he nor you nor anyone else could have this without all these persecutions, in whatever way I choose to send them to you. Tell him that, since he longs to see[i] my honor in holy Church, he must conceive enough love to be willing to suffer with true patience. And by this I will know that he and my other servants are in truth seeking my honor. Then he will be my dearest son, and will rest on the breast of my only-begotten Son,[17] of whom I have made a bridge so that you may all achieve the realization and enjoyment of the fruit of your labors.

"Understand, my children, that the road had been so broken up by Adam's sin and disobedience that none of you could reach your destination.[18] And so my truth was not being realized, the truth that I had created you in my own image and likeness so that you would have eternal life, sharing in and enjoying me, supreme eternal Goodness. This sin sprouted thorns and brambles in the form of many difficulties, along with a river continually dashing with its waves. And that is why I have given you[j] my Son as a bridge, so that you won't drown while crossing the river. But open your mind's eye, and see how this bridge reaches from heaven down to earth. Certainly, if it were of the earth it could never be made long enough to span the river and give you life.[19] So [my Son] joined the height of heaven, the divine nature, with the earth of your human nature. You must, therefore, keep to this bridge by seeking the glory of my name

---

[14] For parallel passage, cf. *Dial.* 19, p. 57.

[15] For parallel passage, cf. *Dial.* 20, pp. 57–58.

[16] The reference here is to Raimondo. "This" is "the glory and praise of God's name in the salvation of souls" just referred to.

[17] Cf. Jn. 13, 23 (Vulg.): "One of his disciples, the one whom Jesus loved especially, was resting on Jesus' breast."

[18] For parallel passage, cf. *Dial.* 21, p. 58.

[19] For parallel passage, cf. *Dial.* 22, p. 59.

in the salvation of souls,[20] by enduring all your labors and pain, by following in the footsteps of this gentle loving Word. You are my workers, whom I have set to work in the vineyard of holy Church because I want to be merciful to the world.[21]

"But beware of taking the way down below, because it is not the way of truth.[22] Do you know who they are who cross the river below the bridge? They are the wicked sinners for whom I am asking you to pray to me, and for whom I am asking your sweat and tears because they are lying in the darkness of deadly sin. They are making their way through the river, and unless they take up my yoke and put it on,[k] they will come to eternal damnation.

"There are some who, because they are afraid of suffering, climb up from the river bank and leave deadly sin behind. They feel the thorns of difficulty, and that is why they come up out of the river. If they are not careless and don't fall asleep in self-centeredness, they set foot on the bridge and begin to climb by loving virtue. But if they persist in their selfish love and carelessness, everything hurts them and they don't persevere. One contrary wind is enough to make them return to their vomit."[23]

When she had seen in how many different ways people were drowning, [God] said, "Look at those who are walking by way of the bridge of Christ crucified." And she saw many of them running along without any pain at all, because they weren't carrying the weight of their selfish will. These were [God's] true children. They had left themselves behind and with restless desire were on a single-minded search for God's honor and the salvation of souls. On the feet of their affection they were following Christ crucified, who was the bridge. The water was running on down below them, and the thorns were being crushed by their feet and so did them no harm.[24] That is, in their love they thought nothing of the thorns

---

[20] She often speaks of seeking God's honor *and* the salvation of souls. This is one of several places where she makes it clear that God's honor is realized *in* the salvation of souls.

[21] For parallel passage, cf. *Dial.* 23, p. 60.

[22] For parallel passage, cf. *Dial.* 29, p. 71.

[23] Prov. 26, 11: "As dogs return to their vomit, so fools repeat their folly." Also 2 Pt. 2, 20–22: "When people have fled a polluted world by recognizing the Lord and Savior Jesus Christ, and then are caught up and overcome in pollution once more, their last condition is worse than their first. It would have been better for them not to have recognized the road to holiness than to have turned their backs on the holy law handed on to them, once they had known it. How well the proverb fits them: 'The dog returns to its vomit,' and 'A sow bathes by wallowing in the mire.'" Cf. Let. T266 to Ristoro Canigiani (1378): "We act like filthy animals who think nothing of alighting on something rotten after leaving the sweetest honey. . . . For after sharing in the sweetness of [God's] charity we think nothing of settling into our own wretchedness by returning to the vomit of the world's corruption."

[24] For parallel passage, cf. *Dial.* 45, p. 93.

of persecution, and they carried in true patience the worldly successes that are cruel and deadly thorns to souls who possess them with inordinate love. They despised these things as if they were poison. They were taken up with nothing but the delight of being on the cross with Christ, because he was their focus.

There were others who were going along slowly.[25] And why? Because they had their mind's eye not on Christ crucified but on the consolations they derived from Christ crucified. These consolations produced in them an imperfect love. They often hesitated in their walking, as Peter did before the Passion when he had kept before him only the pleasure of associating with Christ.[26] That is why he fell short when he was deprived of this consolation. But when did he become strong? After he had let go of himself and wanted to know and seek nothing but Christ crucified. In the same way these people are weak, and they slacken the pace of holy desire when they see their spirit deprived of the pleasure and selfish consolation that were their focus. Then later, when the prickings of temptation come, whether from the devil or from other people or from themselves because of their spiritual softness, and they see themselves deprived of what they loved, they become weak and stumble along the way of Christ crucified. For though they were in Christ crucified, they wanted to follow the Father—since the Father cannot suffer—and [so] experience the sweetness of all those consolations.[27] But the Son can suffer. This is why I said they were following the Father. But it is clear that there is no remedy for their weakness except if they follow the Son.

This is why eternal Truth said, "I say that no one can come to me except by means of my only-begotten Son; for he is the one who made the way you must follow. He is way, truth, and life.[28] Those who go by this way come to know and experience the truth. In the sufferings he bore for them they taste my ineffable love for them.[l] You know well that if I hadn't loved you I would not have given you such a redeemer. But because I loved you eternally, I gave up this only-begotten Son of mine to the shameful death of the cross. And he by his obedience and his death[m] destroyed Adam's sin and the death of the human race.[29]

"So they know my truth, and once they know the truth they follow the truth. And so they receive everlasting life, because they have kept to the way of Christ crucified. They have reached the gate[n] of truth and

---

[25] For parallel passage, cf. *Dial.* 60, pp. 113–115.

[26] Cf. the account of the Transfiguration (Mt. 17, 1–8), where Peter wants to build three tents to prolong the joy of the experience.

[27] For parallel passage, cf. *Dial.* 75, p. 137.

[28] Cf. Jn. 14, 6.

[29] For parallel passage, cf. *Dial.* 4, p. 29.

passed through it to find themselves in the peaceful sea with those who are truly joyful.[30]

"And so you see, my daughter, that there is no other way for these [weak people] to become strong. Nor is there any other way except this for them to be capable of union with my Truth as their Spouse or to reach the perfection for which I have chosen them. Every other way but this is painful and imperfect, because the only source of pain is selfish will, whether spiritual or temporal. So those who don't have this selfish will are relieved of all crippling pain. The only pain they still feel is the unbearable pain of [seeing] me offended, [but even that pain] is ordered and moderated because it is seasoned with the charity that makes the soul wise, so that no suffering disturbs its harmony with my gentle will."

There were others who had begun to climb.[31] They were beginning to recognize their sinfulness; yet they were abandoning sin only for fear of the punishment that follows upon sin, and fear of punishment is imperfect. She[32] saw many of these running from imperfect to perfect fear, and these were going eagerly through the second stage and on to the last. But there were many who because of this slavish fear were sitting down apathetically at the entrance to the bridge. They had begun so spasmodically and so halfheartedly that they remained in their lukewarmness, without adding a spark to the fire of knowing themselves and God's goodness to them.°

Gentle Truth said of these: "See, daughter, how impossible it would be for those who don't go forward by practicing virtue to keep from going backward. And this is why. You cannot live without love, and whatever you love you try to know and serve better. In knowing yourself, you will come to know better the overflowing generosity of my charity. But if you make no effort to know yourself, [you won't know me]. Because you don't know me, you won't love me. And because you don't love me, you won't serve me. As soon as you are deprived of me, you automatically return to your wretched selfish love for yourself, since you cannot live without love. People like this act like dogs that, after they have eaten, vomit, and later on because of their filthiness, when their eye lights on the vomit, they eat it, thus nourishing themselves on filth.

"So it is with these careless halfhearted people. In fear of the punishment they have vomited up the filth of their sins in holy confession and have begun to be just a bit willing to enter on the way of truth. But because they don't move forward they necessarily go backward. Turning

[30] It. *i veri gustatori*. Note the somewhat paradoxical imagery both here and in *The Dialogue*: at the end of the bridge over the stormy river is the peaceful sea.

[31] For parallel passage, cf. *Dial.* 49, p. 100.

[32] That is, Catherine, still speaking of herself in the third person.

their mind's eye back to their vomit from before, they have shunned the sight of the pain and have turned back to look at sensual pleasure, and that is why they have ceased to be afraid. So they eat up the vomit again, nourishing their affections and desires on their own filth. They are, therefore, much more to be reproached, much more deserving of punishment than the others.

"This is how viciously I am offended by my creatures! This is why, my dearest children, I want you to increase, not diminish, your desires by nourishing yourselves at the table of holy desire. Let my true servants rise up and learn from me, the Word, to put the little lost sheep on their shoulders and carry them with pain and many vigils and prayers.[33] This is how you will pass over by way of me, the bridge, as I have said, and you will be spouses and children of my truth. And I will pour into you a wisdom and a light of faith that will give you perfect knowledge of the truth, from which you will acquire all perfection."

Since it pleased God's kindness and compassion to reveal himself and his secrets, desire goes on living in such restlessness that all our soul's powers shout out in unison their longing to leave the earth, filled as it is with such imperfection. (In the presence of such things, dearest father, language fails us. Understanding seems to be darkened, so weak is its vision.) Our soul's powers strain to reach their destination so as to experience the supreme eternal Trinity with the true citizens. There one can see God given glory and praise. There shine the virtues and the hunger and desire of true ministers and perfect religious who in this life were like lamps set on the lamp stand of holy Church to give light to all the world.[34]

Oimé, *Babbo*! What a difference between them and the ministers and religious of today![35] Of these [God] complained with truly just passion: "These people have descended to the level of the fly, such an ugly insect that it alights on something sweet and fragrant and then, after leaving it, thinks nothing of landing on disgusting and filthy things.[36] In the same way these wicked people are allowed to taste the sweetness of my blood, but they don't care. They abandon the table of the altar. They abandon the administration and guardianship of my body and the other sacraments

---

[33] She has subtly changed the speaker from God (the Father) to the incarnate Word, alluding here to the parable of the good shepherd (Jn. 10).

[34] Cf. Mt. 5, 15: "You are the light of the world. . . . People do not light a lamp and then put it under a bushel basket. They set it on a stand where it gives light to all in the house."

[35] For parallel passage, cf. *Dial.* 110, p. 205.

[36] This is the only place in which Catherine uses the image of the fly in this way. In every other instance, the reference is to the devil, who avoids the zealous soul as a fly avoids a boiling pot.

of holy Church, which are so fragrant and full of sweetness and mellowness that they give life to souls who taste them in truth. In fact, the soul cannot live without them. They leave all this, and then[p] think nothing of wallowing in all the filth their minds and bodies do wallow in. Not only does such iniquity stink to me, but even the devils find this wretched sin repugnant."

After divine Goodness had responded to the first three petitions in the way I've described, dearest father, he responded to the fourth.[37] This petition asked God's help and providence to take care of something that had happened to a person I cannot name in writing but whose name I will tell you in person—unless God would do me such a merciful favor as to let my soul leave this wretched body before I see you.[38] This body is a perverse law that is always fighting against the spirit.[39] And you know very well that I am telling the truth. So it would be a grace for me to be freed from it.

I said, and I say again, that eternal Truth deigned to respond to the fourth petition and to the restless desire that was asking. He said, "Daughter, my providence will never fail those who are willing to receive it, and those who are willing to trust in me perfectly. They are the ones who call on me in truth, not only with words but with love and in the light of most holy faith. Those will never experience me or my providence who call on me only with the sound of words: 'Lord! Lord!'[40] For unless they ask me with another sort of motivation I will not know them; they will be known to me not in my mercy but in my justice. So I am telling you that my providence will not fail people if they are willing to trust in me. But I want you to see with what great patience I have to put up with them and with others of my creatures whom I created in my own image and likeness with such tender love."

So, opening her mind's eye in obedience to his command, she saw in the abyss of his charity that he was supreme eternal Goodness, and how for love alone he had created all people and redeemed them with the blood of his Son. And with this very same love he has given whatever he has

---

[37] For parallel passage, cf. *Dial.* 139, pp. 285–286.

[38] One can only guess who this person is. From what follows later, it is clear that he is someone who has been executed or assassinated. It could be Trincio da Fuligno, who was assassinated on 28 September 1377 and to whom Catherine had written just a few weeks earlier (Let. T253), encouraging him to conversion.

[39] Rom. 7, 22–23: "My inner self agrees with the law of God, but I see in my body's members another law at war with the law of my mind; this makes me the prisoner of the law of sin in my members."

[40] Cf. Mt. 7, 21: "None of those who cry out, 'Lord, Lord,' will enter the kingdom of God, but only the one who does the will of my Father in heaven."

given, difficulties as well as consolation. Everything is given for love and to provide for our salvation, and for no other reason.

And he said, "The blood shed for you demonstrates that this is the truth. But those who are blinded by their self-centeredness and great unwillingness to suffer are scandalized. What I do for love and for their good, to save them from eternal suffering and to give them the wages of eternal life, they perceive as evil and hateful, harmful and ruinous. So why do they grumble about me and hate what they ought to reverence, and why do they want to pass judgment on my hidden judgments, all of which are just?[41] They act like blind people who want to judge good and evil by their limited and inadequate knowledge, by the touch of the hand or sometimes by taste or the sound of a voice. They don't want to lean on someone who has a light, but foolishly want to walk by feeling about with their hands.[42] Their sense of touch is deceived because it has no light to discern color. Taste too is deceived because it doesn't see the filthy insect that has alighted on the food. And their ear is deceived in its enjoyment of sound because it doesn't see the singer who, with that sound, can kill one who because of the enjoyment is off-guard.

"That is how these people act, as if they were blind. Having lost the light of reason, they touch worldly pleasure with the hands of sensual emotion, and think it is good. But because they don't see, they don't realize that it is a fabric with many thorns and the misery of anxiety woven into it, so that the heart possessing it becomes unbearable even to itself. It is the same with the mouth of desire that inordinately loves worldly pleasure. This pleasure seems exquisitely sweet when eaten, but there on top of it is the filthy insect of all the deadly sins that make the soul filthy. Unless [those who have eaten it] go by the light of faith to be purified in the blood, it will cause eternal death. What they hear is self-centeredness, and it sounds so sweet to them[q] that they run after this love for their selfish sensuality. But because they don't see, they are deceived by the sound and discover that they have been led into the ditch, bound with the bond of sin in the hands of their enemies. For they are, as it were, blinded by their selfish love, and because they have put their trust in their own love and knowledge, they don't lean on me, their way and their guide, their life and their light.

"Those who follow me cannot be deceived or walk in darkness.[43] [But these people] do not trust me, though I want nothing other than that they

---

[41] Ps. 118, 137 (Vulg.): "Just is the Lord, and right the Lord's judgments."

[42] Mt. 15, 14 (Lk. 6, 39): "Let them go their way. They are blind leaders of the blind. If one blind person leads another, both will end up in the ditch."

[43] Jn. 8, 12: "I am the light of the world. No follower of mine shall ever walk in darkness."

be made holy.[44] I give and permit everything out of love, and they are constantly scandalized in me. Yet I patiently endure and put up with them because I loved them without their having loved me.[45] They are always harassing me with impatience, hatred, complaints, and with all sorts of infidelity. They want to set themselves up to investigate with their own blind sight and opinion my hidden judgments, which are all made justly and lovingly. They don't yet know themselves, and so they see falsely. For those who do not know themselves cannot know me or my judgments in truth. Daughter, do you want me to show you how greatly the world is deceived regarding my mysteries? Then open your mind's eye and look at me."

She gazed with restless desire as he showed her the condemnation of the one whose case she had prayed for. And he said, "I want you to know that to save him from eternal damnation (where he was, as you see), I allowed this to happen to him, so that with his blood in my blood he might have life. For I had not forgotten his reverence and love for my dearest mother Mary. So I did for him in mercy what the ignorant consider cruelty.

"All of this happens to people because of their self-centeredness, which robs them of light so that they do not know the truth. But if they chose to remove the cloud, they would know the truth and love it.[46] Then they would hold everything in reverence, and at harvest time they would gather in the fruit.

"But in everything, in this as well as in every other thing, my children, I will fulfill your desire, along with much suffering. My providence will be more or less near people in proportion to the measure of their confidence in me. And whatever I provide over and above what their measure holds, I do so to fulfill the desire of my servants who are praying to me for them. For I am not one to spurn those who humbly ask me, whether for themselves or for others. That is why I am inviting you to ask me for mercy for these and for the entire world. Conceive, my children, and give birth to this child, the human race, with hatred and sorrow for sin and with blazing and yearning love."[47]

---

[44] 1 Thes. 4, 3.

[45] 1 Jn. 4, 19: "We for our part love God because God loved us first." The verb is in the past tense in the original ("I loved them"), implying that the first movement of God's love for the soul is not prompted by any love on the part of the soul.

[46] Cf. Let. T301 to Ristoro di Pietro Canigiani (1378 or 1379): "But you will say to me, 'If this knowledge is within us, how is it that we become attached also to what works against our salvation?' I answer you that this comes from the selfish love that has covered over this light, just as a cloud sometimes covers over the light of the sun. So our error isn't the light's fault, but the cloud's. Then our free will blindly chooses what is harmful to the soul rather than what is useful. The soul naturally always desires the good, but its error lies in this, that it doesn't look for the good where it is, because the darkness of selfish love has deprived it of light."

[47] Cf. Let. T259 to Tommaso d'Alviano: "Christ, then, wanted to show that the eternal

Oh dearest and sweetest father, when I saw and heard so much then from[r] gentle First Truth, my heart felt as if it would break in two! I am dying and cannot die! Have compassion on your poor daughter, who is living in such torment because God is so offended, and who has no one to whom she can unburden herself—except that the Holy Spirit has provided for me interiorly by his mercy, and outwardly has provided me a diversion in writing.[48]

Let's all take heart in Christ gentle Jesus, and let suffering be our refreshment. And let's eagerly and without hesitation accept the sweet invitation, dear father. Rejoice, because you have been called so sweetly. Suffer with great joy and patience, without being crippled by pain, if you want to be a spouse of Truth and comforter of my soul. In no other way could you have grace, and that would deeply sadden me. That is why I said I long to see you a follower and lover of truth.

I'll say no more. Keep living in God's holy and tender love.

Bless Frate Matteo in Christ gentle Jesus.[49]

This letter and another I sent you I've written with my own hand on the Isola della Rocca,[50] with so many sighs and tears that I couldn't see even when I was seeing. But I was filled with wonder at myself and God's goodness when I thought of his mercy toward his human creatures and his overflowing providence toward me. He provided for my refreshment by giving me the ability to write—a consolation I've never known because of my ignorance—so that when I come down from the heights I might have a little something to vent my heart, lest it burst. Because he didn't want to take me yet from this dark life, he fixed it in my mind in a marvelous manner, the way a teacher does when he gives his pupil a model. Shortly after you left me, I began to learn in my sleep, with the glorious evangelist John[s] and Thomas Aquinas.[51]

Father had given him the task of conceiving this child, the human race, through the impulse of love, and to give it birth on the wood of the most holy cross in true obedience."

[48] She will shortly describe—though in rather obscure terms—how she has come to know how to write.

[49] Matteo Tolomei, a Dominican. Catherine a bit earlier wrote Let. T120 to his mother Rabe, chiding her for demanding that her son return to Siena because his sister Francesca was ill. At that time he was apparently the only friar besides Bartolomeo Dominici with Catherine at the Rocca. Perhaps he had accompanied Raimondo to Rome.

[50] The Salimbeni fortress, where Catherine is a guest at this time. A modern resident of the town and guide at the fortress (now a historic monument) says that it is called the *Isola*, or "island," because its top levels are so often above the haze that rises from the valley below, like an island in a sea of clouds.

[51] The Italian is not entirely unambiguous: *Unde subito che fuste partito da me col glorioso evangelista Johanne e Thomaso d'Aquino, così dormendo cominciai a imparare*. She seems to be describing a dream-like experience. Fawtier ("whatever one might say for or against [the letter's] authenticity") is not convinced that the ending of the letter implies that Catherine

Forgive me for writing so much, but my hands and tongue run along with my heart.

Gentle Jesus! Jesus love!

Textual Notes

a. P4, M: *the fragrance and glory of virtue /glory . . . virtue.*
b. *and pastors* inserted by Mo-*b* above the line.
c. *Truth* (*Verità*) written by *b* over an erasure of four letters.
d. I have followed Mo here; other manuscripts break the sentence after *bitterness,* yielding "refreshment after bitterness."
e. P4: *Life / Truth* (*vita / verità*).
f. S2: *and is bloated with the pride / with . . . pride.*
g. M, S2: *faithfully / indescribably much* (*fedelmente / ineffabilemente*).
h. *So* added in Mo by *b.*
i. M: *longs for my honor / longs to see my honor.*
j. M, S2: *have told you about / have given you* (*detto / dato*).
k. S1, S2, M: *unless I put it on them / and put it on.*
l. S2: *and taste the ineffable love I showed them in the sufferings he bore for them / and . . . for them.*
m. M, S2: *love / death* (*amore / morte*).
n. M, S2: *way / gate.*
o. *them* (*loro*) written by *b* over an erasure of two words.
p. *b* adds *I say.*
q. The text has: *Hearing and self-centeredness sound sweet* (*L'udire et l'amore proprio di sé che gli fà uno dolce suono*). Other manuscripts have *What they hear is selfish love, and it sounds sweet to them* (*L'udire è l'amore proprio. . . .),* which in fact corresponds with the parallel passage in the *Dialogue.* This latter syntax makes more sense, so it is what I have followed.
r. *b* corrects *la* ("the") to *dalla* ("from the").
s. *John* is inserted above the line by *b.*

---

has learned miraculously to read. Grion (*Dottrina e Fonti,* pp. 165–166) agrees with Fawtier and with Hurtaud (*Dialogue de Sainte Catherine de Sienne,* Paris: Lethellieux, 1931) in rejecting this postscript (about Catherine's learning to write) as not being authentic. Dupré Theseider ("Sono autentiche le Lettere di S. Caterina?" p. 244) accepts it as authentic, but Grion finds Dupré Theseider's arguments inconclusive. Personally I believe there is sufficient anecdotal evidence in the sources to indicate that Catherine did at this time in some fashion (miraculous or otherwise) learn to write in at least an elementary sort of way. She is said to have written (in her own hand) Prayer 6 as well as Let. T367, which the Sienese scholar Celso Cittadini says he copied out from "a letter in St. Catherine's own hand given to me by Signore Hippolito Agustini, Knight Commander of Siena, and preserved today at Santa Lucia in Siena." Although there are originals of Let. T192 and T365 at Santa Lucia, the original of Let. T267 referred to by Cittadini is no longer extant.

Letter T173/G134[1]
To a brother who has left his order
In or near October 1377

The tone of this letter suggests that the friar to whom it is addressed is someone Catherine knows well. She says, "If I were nearby . . . ," but this would be a clue to her whereabouts only if one knew where the brother is to whom she is writing.

The linguistic data would seem to place the letter in the Val d'Orcia period, most probably near October. Further, a number of themes are here developed much as they are in *The Dialogue*.[2]

§

In the name of Jesus Christ crucified and of gentle Mary.

Dearest son in Christ gentle Jesus,

I Caterina, servant and slave of the servants of Jesus Christ, am writing to you in his precious blood. I long to see you enlightened by truth, so that knowing it, you will be able to love it. When you love the truth, you will clothe yourself in it and will hate all that is contrary to it and rebels against it. And what is within the truth, as well as whatever truth loves, you will love.

Oh dearest son, how we need this light! In it is our salvation. But I see no way for us to have this lovely light for our understanding without the pupil of most holy faith which is within this eye.[3] And if this light is clouded over or darkened by selfish love for ourselves, our eyes have no light and therefore cannot see. And if we do not see, we do not know the truth. So you have to get rid of this cloud for your vision to remain clear. But what can we use to dissipate and get rid of this cloud? Holy hatred of ourselves [that comes from] knowing our sins and knowing how generously divine Goodness deals with us.

---

[1] MSS: Mo-*a*, M, S5, Ro, P4, Pa, Va, Bo2; translation based on Mo-*a*.

[2] All six letters sharing twenty-three or more of this one's one hundred six analyzed patterns are from October 1377 or later. Most convincing, however, are the significant clusters within individual patterns which begin and/or end in or very near October 1377: AMARVERI, ANDLUCE, ASPTMPSC, ATTPORT, COGNFOND, JERUSAL, MARETEMP, NUVOLPR, OBEDLUNG, PUPILFED, SPECUL, VISIOPAC, VITUPDIO. Both Fawtier (II, p. 214) and Dupré Theseider (unpublished notes) decline to date this letter.

[3] For medieval physiology, the pupil *is* the light within the eye, not merely an opening which lets in the light.

In this knowledge the virtue of patience is learned, since those who know their sinfulness and the sensual law that fights against the spirit hate themselves.[4] They are content to have not only other people but even the animals take vengeance on them. They grow fat on injury, derision, vilification, and reproach. They take delight in suffering and all kinds of persecution, considering them refreshing.

This knowledge of ourselves gives birth to profound humility, so that we do not lift up our head in pride but humble ourselves more and more. And the knowledge of God's goodness within us nourishes us and makes us grow in vigorous charity.

This charity, nurtured by humility, has at her side a child, true discernment.[5] So we wisely pay our debt to God by giving glory and praise to his name. To ourselves we pay the debt of hatred and contempt for our selfish sensuality. And to our neighbors we give the kindness of loving them as we should, with a familial charity generous and well-ordered, not feigned or out of proportion. For the virtue of discernment has its root in charity and is nothing else but a true knowledge of ourselves and of God. So it pays what is due to each and everyone—but not without the light. For if discernment did not have the light, its every principle and work would be imperfect. And we cannot have the light without true knowledge of ourselves (from which we draw hatred) and of God's goodness within us (from which we draw love).

But when people have [the light], they become true servants of their Creator. Though they are living in the night of this darksome life they walk with the light, and though they are on the stormy sea they receive and experience interior peace. They are always running on toward perfection, constant and persevering right up to the moment of their death. They bravely endure the assaults of the devils and never collapse in battle, no matter what their state in life may be. If they are laypersons, they are good laypersons.

And if they are religious, they are perfect religious and navigate in the ship of true obedience, never leaving it. The mirror in which they look to see themselves is the rule with its customs and observances, and they are constantly trying to realize these in themselves. They don't give in to the devil when he tries to take them on with slavish fear by saying, "You can't put up with the hardships of the rule and the hounding of your brothers, or with the penances that will be imposed on you, or with difficult com-

---

[4] Cf. Rom. 7, 21: "My inner self agrees with the law of God, but I see in my body's members another law at war with the law of my mind."

[5] Cf. *Dial.* 10, p. 42: "So the tree of charity is nurtured in humility and branches out in true discernment."

mands!" No, those who have the light laugh in the face of all this. They respond as people dead to their selfish will and enlightened by the light of most holy faith, "I can do anything through Christ crucified,[6] for I know truly that he does not lay a heavier load on his creatures than they can bear.[7] So I want to leave the measuring up to him and, for my part, bear these things with true patience. For in truth I know the truth. And I know that whatever God grants or permits, he does it for my good, so that I may be made holy in him."[8]

Oh how blessed are those who have come to such a light of perfection through sweet knowledge of the truth! For they see and surrender to the knowledge that whatever God permits, he does it out of special love. For God who is love itself cannot but love his human creatures. He loved us before we even existed because he wanted us to share in his supreme eternal good. So whatever he gives us is given for this purpose.

But the wretched people who are without this light of holy faith do not know the truth. And why do the wretches not know this truth? Because they haven't got rid of the cloud of selfish love. So they don't know themselves and therefore don't hate themselves. And they don't know divine Goodness and therefore don't love him. If they do love at all, their love is imperfect, because they love God only to the extent that they see themselves getting pleasure and consolation from him, and they love their neighbors only to the extent that it is to their own advantage. So they are neither strong nor persevering in what they have begun, since as soon as their mouth is deprived of the milk of intense consolation they falter and turn back to look at what they have already plowed.[9] But if in truth they had known the truth, it would not turn out that way.

Yet even if they are imperfect and happen to turn back, they still have reason after their fall to do what they had failed to do, that is, hate themselves by the light of faith. And do it they should, for God is more displeased with perseverance in sin than with the sin itself. It is human to sin, but perseverance in sin is an affair of the devil! So we shouldn't be throwing ourselves in with the dead as long as we still have time. We shouldn't be insensitive to the prick of conscience, which is calling us by continually gnawing at us. We shouldn't say, "I'm still waiting. Maybe this sour pear isn't ripe yet." Oh how stupid and insane, to wait for the time we don't have while we aren't responding in the time we do have! We are

[6] Phil. 4, 13: "I can do all things in him who strengthens me."

[7] Cf. 1 Cor. 10, 13: "God will not let you be tested beyond what you can bear." (Vulg.)

[8] 1 Thes. 4, 3.

[9] Cf. Lk. 9, 62: "Anyone who puts a hand to the plow but keeps looking back is unfit for the reign of God."

acting just as if we were sure of having time! How painful it is, how cutting, for God's servants to see them being so insane! What evil they are doing! They are offending God, supreme eternal Truth. They are harming themselves with their guilt. And they are grieving God's servants, who are famished for the honor of their Creator and for the salvation of [their] souls.

Oh dearest son, turn your memory back a bit.[10] Open your mind's eye to recognize your sins in hope for mercy! See, see the truth! Return to your fold! There is no other way you can know the truth, since you cannot know it when you are in sin. Outside your fold you are not living free of deadly sin, and you are burdened with excommunication; so you cannot know this truth.[11] But if you return to the fold, you will know the truth, since then you will be free of sin. Stretch out your will to love and long for your Creator and for your ark, holy religion.[12]

Don't you give a thought to the fact that in this situation you are among the most pitiable of people? Externally you seemed to have a great sense and knowledge of God. You seemed to find supreme joy in tasting the milk of prayer and in offering up sweet loving desires. But in fact and in truth you seem not to have been grounded on the living rock, Christ gentle Jesus. I mean, you seem not to have been loving him without regard to your own consolation. You seem not to have been unadulterated by human respect and the need to please others. For if your foundation had in truth been in Christ crucified and in self-knowledge, as I've described, you would never have fallen or come to such a sorry pass. We fall only when our foundation is not dug deeply into the valley of humility and grounded on the living rock, Christ gentle Jesus,[13] when we have no wish to follow in his footsteps, when we want to choose times and places according to our own liking rather than solely as eternal Truth pleases.

Oh dearest son, I want you to do what you have not done, and to do it not in spiritual dejection or despair but in true hope, with the light of most holy faith. By that light you will in truth come to know [God's] mercy, and in this mercy you will find relief from the terrible dejection that seems to have come from seeing yourself fallen from the heights of heaven into profound and total misery. Get up, then, with a holy hatred that considers yourself deserving of shame and dishonor and undeserving of the fruit of grace. Hide yourself under the wings of God's mercy, for he

---

[10] It. *tornivi un poco la memoria in capo.*

[11] A religious who left his or her order without a formal dispensation was automatically excommunicated and was presumed to be living in mortal sin.

[12] She compares the state of religious life to the ark in which Noah, his family, and other creatures were saved from the flood.

[13] Cf. 1 Pt. 2, 4: "Come to him, a living stone. . . . You too, as living stones are built into an edifice of spirit." Also the parable of the house built on rock, Mt. 7, 24–27.

is more ready to pardon than you are to sin. Immerse yourself in the blood of Christ, where your soul will grow fat on hope.

Don't wait any more for time, because time is not waiting for you! No, be forceful and even violent with yourself and say, "My soul, acknowledge your Creator and his great mercy which has kept some time for you. He is lending you that time, mercifully waiting for you to return to your fold."

Oh gentlest love! How well this mercy suits you!

Take a good look! What kept God from ordering the earth to swallow us up and the animals to devour us after our first fall?[14] Instead he lent us time and waited patiently for us. What explains our having received such favor? Our non-existent virtues? No! Only God's infinite mercy! So now that he is treating us so mercifully when we are lying in the darkness of deadly sin, we should be so much more hopeful in lively confidence that he will do the same if we acknowledge our sins and return to the ark, to the yoke of obedience.[15] There let us trample underfoot and kill our selfish will and sleep no longer.[16]

Oimé! Oimé! I believe my sins are the reason for yours!

I beg you, don't insist on staying where you are! Don't continue to harm yourself and insult God! Don't continue to grieve your brothers! No, take on once again the yoke of obedience and the key of Christ's blood which you have thrown into the deep well.[17] You cannot have or

---

[14] Cf. Nm. 16, 31, where the earth opens to swallow up the rebellious Israelites.

[15] Cf. Let. T36 to several Olivetan novices (in this volume): "[D]ivine providence has put you in a ship, so that you will not sink in the stormy sea of this darksome life. That ship is genuine and holy religious life. It is maneuvered under the yoke of sincere and holy obedience. Just think of how great a favor God has done you because he knows how weak your arms are! For those who are in the world navigate this sea on their own power, but those in religious life navigate on the power of others. When we are truly obedient we are not accountable for ourselves; rather the order is accountable for us." The original both in Let. T36 and in the present letter is a bit problematic, since *giogo* can refer either to a yoke as for oxen or to one of the banks of oars in a galley. In T287 Catherine describes the *giogo* with which a religious sails as *dolce e soave*, echoing the gospel reference to the yoke of Christ (Mt. 11, 29–30). It is therefore probable that, in the context of the ship image, she is thinking not so much of the oars themselves as of the chains which bind the rowers of the Mediterranean galleys, who in her day are usually slaves or prisoners. (This interpretation would be borne out by the reference to weak arms.) She does not, however, anywhere speak of religious as slaves or prisoners, but only as servants. Except for naming herself "servant and slave," she reserves the term *slavery* for servitude to sin.

[16] As she so often does when she speaks of others' sins, Catherine switches deliberately to the first person plural, including herself. Here this intent is reinforced by what follows.

[17] In various places (for example, *Dial.* 27, 66, 77; Let. T83, T30), Catherine speaks of Christ opening the gates of heaven with his blood, shed in obedience. In *Dial.* 115 the key is explicitly related to the key entrusted to St. Peter. Then, in *Dial.* 154–156, she speaks of Christ's having taken up the key of obedience, which Adam had thrown into the mud. "Not until the Word my only-begotten Son came was this key of obedience picked up

use this key without sin, since you have left the garden of holy religion, in which you had been planted to be a fragrant flower, strong and truly persevering until your death. So take up again [the yoke and the key] with heartfelt contrition, with contempt for the sin you have committed, with hatred for your sensuality, and with lively faith. Gaze into supreme eternal Truth, and take hold of the firm confidence that God and the order will mercifully welcome you and pardon you the sin you have committed. And the eternal Father will come to meet you with the overflowing fullness of his grace.[18]

May this, then, be the true Jerusalem to which you aspire and to which you choose to journey. I mean holy religion. Then you will find Jerusalem, the vision of peace, for there your conscience will be at peace.

Go into the tomb of self-knowledge, and with Magdalen ask, "Who will roll back the stone from the tomb for me? For the stone (that is, the guilt of sin) is so heavy that I can't budge it." And as soon as you have acknowledged and confessed how imperfect and heavy you are, you will see two angels, who will roll this stone away. I mean that divine help will send you the angel of holy love and reverence for God (a love that is never alone but gives us the company of love for our neighbors), and the angel of hatred (accompanied by true humility and patience), to roll this stone away.[19] So, with true hope and lively faith, never leave the tomb of self-knowledge.[20] Persevere in staying there until you find Christ risen in your soul by grace. Once you have found him, go and proclaim it to your brothers—and your brothers are the true, solid, lovely virtues with whom

---

again. He purified it in the fire of divine charity after he had picked it out of the mire (*loto*) and washed it with his blood. With the knife of justice he straightened it and on the anvil of his body he hammered out your iniquities. He repaired it so perfectly that no matter how you might damage it with your free choice, by your same free choice you can, with the help of my grace and using these same instruments, repair it again." (pp. 328, 330–331) In the present context we have both the concept of obedience and the image of the "key of the blood." The key, in the sense that her addressee (who must be a priest) cannot use it without sin so long as he remains outside his order, is clearly the authority to dispense Christ's blood. Yet the close connection here with the discussion of obedience leads me to think that Catherine has in mind the full complexity of the image. So, while the word *puzza* is not used in the *Dialogue* passage as it is here, and while the manuscripts I have been able to consult (only Mo and P4), both have *pozzo* ("well"), I strongly suspect that Catherine actually had the key being thrown not into "the well," but into the "filth" (*puzza*). Nowhere else is the well a negative image. In Let. T41 it is the monastic cell, and in Let. T343 it is the well of humility, from the dark depths of which one can look up and see the stars of God's goodness and beauty.

[18] Cf. the parable of the prodigal son, Lk. 15, 11–31.

[19] Cf. Mk. 16, 3–5.

[20] She suddenly switches for a few sentences to third person singular, but I have continued to use the second person singular, since it is clear that she is continuing to address the brother.

you want to and do take up your residence. Then, Christ lets you touch him in continual humble prayer by appearing to your soul in a way you can feel.[21] This is the way; there is no other.

I am certain that if you have the light of most holy faith and know the truth in truth as I've described, you will keep to these ways without negligence. You will not dally, but will conscientiously seize the bit of time that is yours. Otherwise you would be living always in the dark, because you would be far away from the light. And you would be living in sadness, because the joy of grace would not be within you. You would be a limb cut off from the mystic body of holy Church. And this is why I said—because there is no other way—that I long to see you enlightened by the truth by means of the light of most holy faith, which is the pupil of the mind's eye through which we come to know the truth. So I am begging you, for love of Christ crucified and for your own salvation, to fulfill my longing.

I'll say no more. Keep living in God's holy and tender love.

If I were near you, I would know what demon it is that has snatched away my little sheep, and what sort of bondage it is that is keeping him bound so that he isn't returning to the flock with the others. But I will do my best to see it in continual prayer, and with this knife I will cut the bonds that are holding him. And then my soul will be happy!

Gentle Jesus! Jesus love!

[21] She is mixing elements from different resurrection stories. Cf. Jn. 20, 16, where the risen Christ says to Mary Magdalen, "Do not touch me." (Vulg.)

LETTER T75/G146/DT62[1]
To the nuns of San Gaggio near Florence
and
To the nuns of Monte San Savino
In or near October 1377

The main body of this letter was sent to the Augustinian nuns of San Gaggio about a mile from Florence and, in another copy, to the Benedictine nuns of a small monastery near Monte San Savino eighteen miles east of Siena, founded in 1336.[2] This is the only extant letter to either monastery. The fact that the version sent to San Gaggio (the only address given in the rubric of Mo) names Monna Ghita as abbess would seem to place the letter not too long after her predecessor Monna Nera's death on 3 February 1376 and Monna Ghita's succession in March.[3] The linguistic evidence, however, points strongly toward October 1377.[4] Further, there are close and even exact parallels with *The Dialogue* in the passage concerning the stairway of Christ's crucified body.

Placing the letter to San Gaggio in late 1377 would, of course, imply more than a year's delay in Catherine's receiving word of or responding to Monna Nera's death. But given the location of the monastery in Florence and the fact that we know nothing other than this letter of Catherine's association with the nuns there, this may not be surprising. One might speculate that Niccolò Soderini had relayed the nuns' distress to Raimondo da Capua when the two men met in Siena (probably in September), and that Raimondo had in turn informed Catherine upon his return to Rocca d'Orcia. In any case, it seems hard to imagine that a letter which has so

---

[1] MSS: Mo-*c*, corrected by *a*, *b*; B, P2, T, R1, P5, F2, P3, P4, S4; translation based on Mo-*c*, with reference to T and R1; other variants based on Dupré Theseider.

[2] Burlamacchi, notes to the letter in Gigli, *Opere*, I, p. 832.

[3] Dates given by Dupré Theseider, with reference to his *Notes* (unpublished notes to which I have not had access).

[4] Two of the four letters which share fifteen or more of this one's fifty-eight analyzed patterns are from October 1377. (These two are both to women's monasteries; the other two, both very long letters not to nuns, are from 1375 and late 1378.) More importantly, the only strong concentration of significant clusters within individual patterns is centered in late 1377, with two of these patterns having no other occurrence before then (SUPERBOB, VOLONTA) and several others only one or two isolated occurrences (ADULTER, BOCCDESI, NATIVITA, OBEDPENT, PACEBOCC, PIEDAFFE, PIEDCOST, PROSPER, SEGNAMOR). There are, further, several clusters which end in October 1377: ADULTER, BOCCDESI, OBEDPENT, PACEBOCC, PIEDCOST. On the other hand, the letter does have two non-standardized protocol elements in R1 and V: CRISGESU and a non-standardized final invocation (both of which do, however, occur sporadically after 1376). Fawtier (II, p. 227) declines to date this letter. Dupré Theseider places it probably in March 1376.

little in common linguistically with others of early 1376, and so much in common with others of late 1377, could have been written at the earlier date.

There is nothing to indicate whether the letter to Monte San Savino was written earlier or later, but most probably the two were written about the same time. I would therefore place the letter (to both monasteries) in or near October 1377.

§

In the name of Jesus Christ crucified and of gentle Mary.

Dearest mother and daughters in Christ Jesus,[a]

I Caterina, servant and slave of the servants of Jesus Christ, am writing to you in his precious blood. I long to see you hidden and enclosed in the side of Christ crucified. Otherwise it would be useless to be enclosed within [convent] walls; in fact, it would be like being in prison. So just as you are enclosed physically, let your affection and desire be securely enclosed, turned away from worldly ambition and pleasure to follow your Bridegroom, Christ gentle Jesus. I have no doubt that if you are lovers of the eternal Bridegroom, you will follow in his footsteps.

Do you know what path your Bridegroom walked? One of freely chosen poverty and obedience. Out of humility, supreme exaltedness descended to the lowliness of our humanity. Because of that humility and his ineffable love for us he gave up his humanity to the shameful death of the cross, choosing the way of torment,[b] scourging, torture, and insult. You are to imitate that humility. But know that it cannot be achieved except through genuine self-knowledge and by contemplating the deep humility and meekness of the Lamb who was slain in such blazing love. I said that he walked the way of true poverty. He was so poor that he had nowhere to lay his head. At his birth the gentle Mary didn't even have a little blanket in which to wrap her Son.[5]

So you, his spouses, must follow such a way of poverty. You know you have promised to live such poverty until you die, and I beg you, for

---

[5] Here, as in *Dial.* 151, p. 320, Catherine follows a tradition well documented but nevertheless at variance with Lk. 2, 7: "and wrapped him in swaddling clothes." Cf. Bonaventure, *Meditationes*, p. 52: "Our Lady had no clothes to swaddle him in"; Bianco da Siena, *Lauda XIII*, 9: "Oh poor Jesus, for no other reason than to enrich us with infinite wealth—oh dear nursling—your exaltedness had nothing to be covered with!" Bernardino da Siena, *Predicatio* XIX, says that the Virgin had "neither swaddling clothes nor blankets" for Jesus.

love of Christ crucified, to keep that promise.[6] Otherwise you would be adulteresses rather than spouses, since you would be giving your love to something apart from God—just as a wife is called an adulteress if she loves another man more than she loves her husband. And how does a wife show her love? By obeying her husband.

So it is that obedience follows close upon poverty and humility. The more a spouse [of Christ] freely embraces poverty of spirit, and the more she renounces worldly riches and ambition, the more humble she is. And the more humble she is, the more obedient she is. Proud people are never obedient because their pride makes them unwilling to bend or submit to anyone. I want you, then, to be humble, despoiled in heart and affection until death. You, mother abbess, must be obedient to the rule, and the rest of you must be obedient to the rule and to your abbess. Learn a lesson, do, from your[c] Bridegroom, the good gentle Jesus, who was obedient even to the point of death.[7] Realize that you cannot share in the blood of the Lamb without obedience. What is a religious woman without the yoke of obedience? She is dead, a devil incarnate really.[d] She is breaking the rule, not keeping it. Breaking God's holy commandments, and beyond this, breaking the promise[e] she made in profession, has brought her to the sentence of death. Oh dearest sisters and daughters in Christ! I don't want you to fall into this trap.[f] I want you to be conscientious and not to break the rule in even the slightest matter.

Do you want to find happiness with your Bridegroom? Then kill your disordered will and never rebel against true obedience. Genuine obedience, you know, never questions the superior's will but bows at once and carries it out.[8] Fall in love with this truly royal[g] virtue! Do you want to have peace and tranquility? Then renounce your own will, because a selfish will is the source of all suffering.[9] Put on the sweet eternal will of God. If you do, you will experience eternal life and will be called earthly angels even in this life.[10]

---

[6] Cf. *Dial.* 164, p. 356: "[They] have given it by contract in profession, when they renounced their very selves into the hands of their superiors and promised to observe obedience, continence, and voluntary poverty. And their superiors promised, if they would observe it until death, to give them eternal life."

[7] Phil. 2, 8: "He was humbler yet, even to accepting death, death on a cross."

[8] Cf. *Dial.* 159, p. 343: "[The obedient] have no wish to question or judge their superiors' will, but by the light of faith they discern my will in them, believing in truth that my mercy makes them command or not command as is necessary for their salvation."

[9] Cf. Let. T118 to Caterina dello Spedaluccio and Giovanna di Capo (in this volume): "This obedience and love will make all pain and darkness melt away for you. For obedience frees us from the source of pain, our perverse selfish will, which holy obedience drowns and kills." The theme is developed in *Dial.* 45, pp. 91–94.

[10] "Earthly angels" is an expression Catherine uses often in her letters to religious. It is

Conform yourselves to[h] gentle First Truth. You can never do this, though, unless you open your mind's eye to gaze into the fire of divine charity that God has enkindled in his rational creatures. Mother and daughters, realize that you are under a much greater obligation than others.[i] God has given to you in particular more love than he has given other people, since he has taken you out of the ugliness, the murky fetid worldly[j] life that reeks of corruption and shame, and has chosen and set you apart for himself. So you must never be careless, but look for all the ways, all the places and things in which you can please him most.

And if you ask, "What is the way?" I will tell you it is the way he chose, the way of disgrace, suffering, torment, and scourging. "And how?" Through genuine humility and blazing charity, an indescribable love by which we renounce all worldly riches and ambition. And from humility we progress to obedience, as I have said. Upon such obedience follows peace, since obedience frees us from all suffering and gives us every joy—for the selfish will, the source of suffering, has been done away with.

To make it possible for us to climb to this perfection, Christ[k] actually made for us a staircase of his body.[11]

If you look at his feet, you see that they are nailed fast to the cross to form the first stair. This is because we have first to rid ourselves of all selfish will. For just as the feet carry the body, desire carries the soul. Reflect that we can never have any virtue at all if we don't climb this first stair. Once you have climbed it, you arrive at deep and genuine humility.

Climb the next stair without delay and you come to the open side of God's Son. There you find the fiery abyss of divine charity. At this second stair, his open side, you find a storehouse filled with fragrant spices.[12] There you find the God-Man. There your soul is so sated and drunk that you lose all self-consciousness, just like a drunkard intoxicated with wine; you see nothing but his blood, shed with such blazing love.

Then, aflame with desire, you get up and climb to the next stair, his mouth. There you find rest in quiet calm; there you taste the peace of obedience. A person who is really completely drunk, good and full, falls

---

explained in *Dial.* 113, p. 212, in relation to priesthood: "No angel has this dignity, but I have given it to those men whom I have chosen to be my ministers. I have sent them like angels, and they ought to be earthly angels in this life." In Prayer 2 also, p. 26, the expression refers to priests. Other writers of the time also used the expression in similar ways.

[11] Her only earlier use of the stairway image has been in Let. T74 to Niccolò da Montalcino (vol. I). It will later figure prominently in *The Dialogue* (especially ch. 26). The sentence near the start of that chapter, "For just as the feet carry the body, the affections carry the soul," is identical to one in the following paragraph.

[12] The *botiga* is a shop or business place that specializes in one sort of work or merchandise, or a storehouse. In *The Dialogue* it is usually translated as "hostelry," since the *botiga* along the bridge (ch. 27) is a shop where pilgrims can stop to eat, drink, and rest.

asleep, and in that sleep feels neither pleasure nor pain.[13] So too the spouse of Christ, sated with love, falls asleep in the peace of her Bridegroom. Her feelings too are asleep so that, even if all sorts of troubles befall her, they don't disturb her at all. If she is materially well off she feels no disproportionate pleasure, because she has already stripped herself of all that at the first stair.[l] This, then, is where she finds herself conformed with Christ crucified, united with him.

Run on courageously then, because you have the path, the way, and the place where you can find the bed on which to rest, the table where you may find enjoyment, and the food with which you can satisfy yourselves. For he has made himself our table, our food, and our servant.[14] You would really be deserving of reproof if in your carelessness you did not seek rest, or if you foolishly stayed away from food. I want you, I beg you in the name of Christ crucified, to warm and bathe yourselves in the blood of Christ crucified. So that you may become one with him, do not evade hard work.[m] The work is light, and the reward great. I'll say no more[n] about this.

I hear that your very dear mother and mine, Monna Nera, has found her place at the table of everlasting life, where she is enjoying the food of life.[15] She has found the spotless Lamb as her reward. Just as I told you before that he is table and food and servant, so I am telling you now that she, as a true servant of Christ crucified, has found the eternal Father as her table and her bed. For in the eternal Father she is finding her every need fulfilled. All[o] our work, all our moving about from place to place, is to get food and a place of rest.

I'm saying that Monna Nera has found supreme eternal Goodness, God eternal, so[p] she has no need to move about in search of any of these things. The place where she is is a firm and stable place, where she finds as her bed of rest the supreme eternal Godhead. The Father is her table. The Son is her food, for through the mediation of the incarnate Word, God's Son, we can all reach the port of salvation if we so desire. The Holy Spirit waits

---

[13] Cf. Let. T29/DT18 to Regina della Scala (vol. I): "We will be like a heavy drinker, who thinks not of herself but only of the wine she has drunk and of what she still has left to drink. Get drunk on the blood of Christ crucified! Don't let yourself die of thirst when you have it right there before you! And don't take just a little, but enough to make you so drunk that you will lose yourself."

[14] This triple image of table, food, and servant is usually Trinitarian in Catherine's works. Here it is applied to Christ, though with Trinitarian implications, as the following paragraphs make clear.

[15] Nera de' Manieri was the foundress and first abbess of the monastery of San Gaggio, and the rest of the letter is only in the copy addressed to that monastery (Dupré Theseider, n. 11). We do not know for certain how the version sent to Monte San Savino ended, unless the ending of B and P2 (see Textual Notes) is from that version.

on her, for it was through love[16] that the Father gave us his Son as food, and through love the Son gave us life while taking death for himself so that by his death we might share in everlasting life. We who are pilgrim travelers[17] in this life receive this reward only imperfectly, but she has received it in its entirety, and nothing can take it from her. You, as her true daughters, ought to be happy for your mother's reward and happiness. This ought to give you a true and holy willingness to suffer—first of all out of respect for the one who has done it, who has taken her presence from you, for you should not be quarreling with God's eternal will. Secondly, it is to her advantage to have escaped all the toil and pain that were her lot for so long a time, and to have gone to a place of rest.[18] But I beg you, as her true daughters, to follow her example, her teaching, and the holy practices in which she nourished you.

Don't be afraid, though it may seem you've been left orphans, or as sheep without a shepherd, for you are not orphans. God will provide for you, and she is offering her good holy prayers for you in God's presence. You still have Monna Ghita.[19] I ask you to obey her in all that is commanded according to God and religious life. As for you, Monna Ghita, I ask you as earnestly as I can to take good care of this family by maintaining it and providing for its growth in good works. Don't be careless, because God will demand an account from you.

I'll say no more.

Keep living in God's holy and tender love.

Jesus, gentle Jesus![q]

Textual Notes

a. From T, R1, P2; B, Mo: *gentle Jesus / Jesus.*

b. P2: *shame / torment.*

c. Mo: *your eternal / your.*

d. P2: *She is really dead, and a devil incarnate / She . . . really.*

e. Mo-*a, b*: *promise and vow / promise.*

f. P2: *error / trap.*

g. P2: [*truly royal*]. (*Reale* could also be translated as "real" or "solid.")

h. Mo: *Take courage in / Conform . . . to* (*Confortatevi / Conformatevi*).

i. Mo-*b*: *many others / others.*

---

[16] Catherine consistently identifies the Holy Spirit as love and mercy.

[17] Cf. 1 Pt. 2, 11: "I urge you, while you are strangers and pilgrims." (Vulg.)

[18] Nera, dying in 1376 at seventy-two years of age, had governed the monastery for a good thirty-two years (Dupré Theseider, n. 13 to this letter).

[19] Ghita degli Albizzi, widow of Tommaso Corsini and second abbess of the monastery (Dupré Theseider, n. 14 to this letter).

j. Mo: [*worldly*].
k. Mo: *Christ our Savior / Christ.*
l. Literally, *through the first affection.*
m. Mo adds *but take delight in these labors.*
n. B, P2 continue, ending the letter here: *Hide yourselves in Christ crucified. Keep living. ...*
o. Mo-*b*: *Dearest, all / All.*
p. All manuscripts except Mo-*b*: *where / so.*
q. From T, R1; B, P2: *Gentle Jesus! Jesus love! / Jesus, gentle Jesus!*

Letter T11/G24/DT23[1]
To Pierre d'Estaing, Cardinal of Ostia
October 1377

There is nothing in its content to date this second of Catherine's two extant letters to Pierre d'Estaing, cardinal of Ostia and titular cardinal of Santa Maria in Trastevere in Rome. It is clear, however, from the linguistic evidence, that the letter must be placed in October 1377 or shortly thereafter.[2] And it must be prior to the cardinal's death on 25 November of the same year.

Also, Let. T242 to Bishop Angelo Ricasoli repeats all but verbatim about two thirds of the present letter, and is almost certainly copying this letter rather than vice versa.[3] Historical facts place Let. T242 in October of 1377. We cannot know for certain how much time elapsed between these two letters, since we do not know whether such copying was ever done from retained drafts or whether it was always done from a letter just dictated. Catherine's spontaneous style would make the former scenario unlikely, even if we assume that some sort of file of earlier letters was being kept. I would therefore guess that the present letter was written very shortly before Let. T242, most probably during October 1377.

§

In the name of Jesus Christ crucified and of gentle Mary.

Dearest reverend father in Christ gentle Jesus,

I Caterina, servant and slave of the servants of Jesus Christ, am writing to you in his precious blood. I long to see you a courageous and fearless man, so that you may serve Christ's dear bride bravely, and work for God's honor in matters both spiritual and temporal, in the way this dear bride

---

[1] MSS: Mo-*a* (no corrections by *b*), M, S5, S6, Ro, S2, S4, P4; translation based on Mo-*a*, with S2 checked for variants. Other manuscripts are not textually significant.

[2] Dupré Theseider places this letter (as DT23) late in 1374. Fawtier (II, p. 164) places it in October 1370. All of those who date Let. T7 to the time of d'Estaing's early papal appointments (1370–1372) date this one to the same period. (Cf. Introduction to Let. T7.) The letter has very little in common, however, with any letters written before autumn of 1377. A number of significant clusters within individual patterns, moreover, begin and/or end precisely in October of that year: AMORVERD, CORRGIUS, CROCDESI, CROCEDES, LUMEVEST, MAESTRVE, ONORAMOR, ONORFADP, PERFCOM, PETCHIES, RADSUPER, SOPRINFD, SUPERBOB, TEMMORTE, UOMONUOV, VESTVECC, VIRNTIM.

[3] See n. 19.

needs in these times. I am certain that if you raise your mind's eye to see her need, you will act zealously and not out of any fear or indifference.

None of our actions is effective if we act out of slavish fear. No matter what our position, we will fail in small things as well as great, and will never finish what we have begun. Oh how dangerous such fear is! It cuts off the arms of holy desire.[4] It blinds us and keeps us from seeing or knowing the truth, because the source of this fear is the blindness of self-centeredness. For as soon as we love ourselves selfishly and merely on the level of feeling,[5] we become fearful. Why? Because we have set our love and trust in something weak, something completely unstable and inconstant, something as passing as the wind.[6]

Oh perversion of love! What harm you bring both to those with power (temporal or spiritual) and to those who are subject to power! Those who are in church offices never correct people because they are afraid of losing their positions of authority, afraid of displeasing their subordinates. And you harm subordinates as well, because there is no humility in those who love themselves so perversely. In fact, there is in such love a deeply rooted pride, and the proud are never obedient.[7] Those who are temporal lords do not promote justice, but are again and again guilty of evil and deceitful injustice, because they act to please themselves or other people. So for lack of correction and punishment their subordinates become more wicked still, because they are being encouraged in their vices and wrongdoing.[8]

Since selfish and inordinately fearful love is so dangerous, you must run away from it. You must focus your mind's eye on the spotless Lamb. He is our rule and our instruction, and him we must follow.[9] He is love and

---

[4] Cf. Let. T129/DT29 to Bartolomeo Dominici (vol. I), where it is stinginess, "doing the bare minimum," that cuts off the arms of holy desire. In either case, it is such holy desire that leads one to the greatness of soul that does the work of God.

[5] The original is *amore proprio sensitivo*. Neither adjective ever has a positive connotation in Catherine's writings.

[6] This refrain runs through Catherine's writings from beginning to end, but occurs more frequently in the last three years of her life.

[7] Cf. Let. T75/DT62, addressed to two different monasteries of nuns (in this volume), for one summary of the intimate relationship Catherine sees among obedience, humility, and charity. It is a frequent theme in her writings. Cf. especially Let. T36, T38, T95, T217 (in this volume) and Let. T35 (late 1377 or early 1378), T67 (1378), T84 (1379), most of which are written to religious; and *Dial.* 154–165, pp. 327–360.

[8] Cf. Let. T123 to the Defenders of Siena (in this volume): "Oh blindness of selfish love! Oh misplaced fear! You become so blind that you not only condemn ordinary people along with the wicked (who could be justly condemned and their treachery feared), but you give in to your fear of the wicked and condemn the just!"

[9] Here and in Let. T242 (in this volume) and *Dial.* 75, p. 137, Christ himself is "our rule and instruction." Elsewhere, as in Let. T220 in this volume; Let. T243 (1377), T64 (1378); and various places in *The Dialogue*, he gives his disciples the example of his obedience and self-sacrifice as rule and instruction.

truth itself.[10] He sought nothing but his Father's honor and our salvation. He feared neither the Jews and their persecution, nor the devils' malice, nor ignominy nor scorn nor abuse. He did not in the end fear even the shameful death of crucifixion. And we are his students in this dear and agreeable school.[11]

So, dearest most gracious father, I want you in sweet wisdom and with the greatest zeal to keep your mind's eye on this book of life, which affords you such gentle and agreeable instruction. Be concerned only about God's honor and the salvation of souls, about serving Christ's dear bride.[12] In this light[13] you will shed your self-centeredness and be clothed in divine love. You will seek God because of his infinite goodness and because he is worthy of our seeking and our love. For God's sake you will love yourself and virtue, and you will hate sin. And with this same love you will love your neighbors.

You know very well that divine Goodness has set you within the mystic body of holy Church and nourished you at the breast of this dear bride[14] only to have you eat the food of God's honor and the salvation of souls at the table of the most holy cross. It is his will that this food be eaten only on the cross,[15] that is, by bearing physical difficulties with constant restless desire.[16] This is what God's Son did. As he endured torments in his body he endured also the pain of desire, and the cross of desire was greater than the physical cross. And this was his desire: hunger for our redemption in fulfillment of his eternal Father's commission—and he suffered until he saw this accomplished.[17] Also, since he is the eternal

---

[10] As inseparable as love and truth are in Catherine's thought, both in God and in human virtue, this is one of only five instances of God/Christ being *identified* as "truth and love" together. The others are Let. T123, T242, T259 (all in this volume), and Prayer 17.

[11] Cf. Augustine, *Sermo CCXXXIV* (PL XXXVIII, 1116): "That cross was a school, where the teacher taught the thief. The wood on which he hung became a chair for teaching." Also Cavalca, *Specchio di croce, Prologo*, p. 2: "Christ . . . on the cross is like a teacher occupying his chair, for he teaches . . . every perfect doctrine."

[12] A. Volpato, "L'onore di Dio e la salute delle anime in S. Caterina" (*Atti del simposio internazionale Cateriniano-Bernardiniano*, Siena: Accademia Senese degli Intronati, 1982), develops at length the integration of Catherine's theology of "the honor of God and the salvation of souls" and of conformity with Christ in his redemptive role, an integration Volpato sees as an element of "profound originality" in Catherine's writings (p. 304).

[13] "This light," judging from similar passages, must be the light of knowledge and faith that comes from the teaching of Christ.

[14] This is the earliest extant reference in Catherine's works to the Church as a nursing mother. It occurs twenty-one more times in later letters and in *The Dialogue*.

[15] The meaning is both "at" the cross as at a table, and "on" the cross, since eating at this table implies that one is crucified with Christ. Again we see Catherine's interpretation of conformity with Christ identified with a sharing in his redemptive role.

[16] It. *molti anxietati desiderii*.

[17] Cf. Prayer 18, pp. 162–163: "I see that this Word, once written in you, [Mary,] was

Father's wisdom, he saw those who would share in his blood as well as those who through their own fault would not. Because his blood was given to all, he grieved for the foolishness of those who would be unwilling to share in it.[18] This was the crucified desire he bore from beginning to end. And when he had given his life the cross of desire ended, but not desire itself.

This is what you and every other person ought to be doing: offering both physical effort and the effort of desire, grieving at the offense done to God and the harm done to all the souls we see perishing. It seems to me it is time, dearest father, to be giving honor to God and our best efforts to our neighbors.[19] We must not, then, regard ourselves selfishly or merely on the level of feeling, nor with slavish fear. No, we must act with true love and holy fear of God.[20]

You are now in a position of both spiritual and temporal power.[21] So I beg you for love of Christ crucified to act courageously. Secure God's honor whenever and wherever you can, counseling and helping toward the

---

never without the cross of holy desire. Even as he was conceived within you, desire to die for the salvation of humankind was engrafted and bound into him. This is why he had been made flesh. So it was a great cross for him to carry for such a long time that desire, when he would have liked to see it realized at once." Also Let. T16 to a great prelate (in this volume).

[18] Cf. Let. T12/DT66 to Giovanni di Gano da Orvieto (vol. I), in which she relates this vision of Christ to his cry of "I thirst!" Though here the reference is to not sharing by deliberate choice, she elsewhere includes those who do not share in the blood because of ignorance, that is, the unbelievers (Let. T133/DT32 in vol. I; T209, T256 in this volume; Prayer 1).

[19] In Let. T104 to Raimondo da Capua, written in late 1377 (in this volume), she will place this admonition in the context of a discussion on the use of time, and attribute it to an experience she has had in prayer: "In our concern for [souls] we steal time from ourselves—time, that is, that we might have had for our comfort, any comfort, new or old—and we give that time to our neighbors. This is why, when that servant of God asked, 'My Lord, what do you want me to do?' he answered, 'Give honor to me, and your best efforts to your neighbors.' " "Best efforts" translates *fadiga*, which always conveys the connotations of its English cognate, *fatigue*, within the effort or labor.

[20] Up to this point, Let. T242 is identical with this one except for a few details which could well be ascribed to scribal differences and have no bearing on the meaning of the text or its translation. It is the continuing elaboration of themes in this letter, in contrast with the rather compact summarizing conclusion of Let. T242, which leads me to suspect that this is the earlier of the two letters.

[21] *Voi sete posto ora. . . .* The *ora* ("now") complicates the problem of dating this letter. Is it to be interpreted as a reference to a recent appointment? If so, which one? If my placement of the letter in October 1377 is correct, it could be the continuation of d'Estaing's mission to the Romans in December 1376. In this case, "now" must be interpreted to imply that d'Estaing's particular responsibilities to the Romans continued even after the agreements of 21 December 1376 had been concluded (cf. Introduction to Let. T7 in this volume). In any case, d'Estaing's position as cardinal would give him both spiritual and temporal power.

wiping out of vice and the promotion of virtue. A holy attitude makes temporal actions spiritual;[22] so act courageously, as far as you are able bringing about the peace and unity of the whole country.[23] If for this holy work it should be necessary to give your bodily life, let it be given—even a thousand times, if possible! How incomprehensible to imagine, and actually to see, that we should be at war with God because of all these sins on the part of pastors and subordinates alike, and because of this rebellion against holy Church! And at war physically yet! Wherever there is war, every faithful Christian ought to be ready to redirect it against the unbelievers, but these traitorous Christians are waging war against each other![24] So God's servants are bursting with bitter grief because of the tremendous sin against God and because of the harm being done to those who are perishing because of it. And the devils are happy because they are seeing what they want to see.

It is good, then, to give up[a] our lives after the example of the teacher of Truth, indifferent both to honor and to the disgrace the world wants to bring upon us through painful punishment and physical death.[25] I am certain that you will do this with eagerness if you are stripped of your old self, your selfish sensuality, and clothed with the new self, Christ gentle Jesus,[26] because then you will be free of slavish fear. Otherwise you will never do it at all. In fact, you will fall into all the sins I spoke of earlier.

I was thinking about the fact that because you have been placed by God in an office that requires no fear except holy fear, you need to be a courageous and fearless man, stripped of self-centeredness, and that is why I said that I long to see you a courageous and fearless man. I trust that divine Goodness will be gracious to you and to me, and fulfill what is his

---

[22] Cf. Let. T30/DT1 to the abbess of Santa Marta in Siena (vol. I): "If you tell me about the great concern you must have over temporal things, [I answer that] things are only as temporal as we make them. I've already told you that all things come from the highest Goodness, so everything is good and perfect. I don't want you evading hard work under the plea that these things are temporal. I want you to be conscientiously concerned, with your attention directed as God would have it."

[23] It. *paese*. If the letter is correctly dated in October 1377, she is probably referring to all of the republics involved in the tensions surrounding the antipapal revolt and the return of Gregory XI to Rome.

[24] One of Catherine's reasons for supporting the idea of a crusade was that it would unite Christians who were warring against each other, and most especially against the papacy, in a common external cause. From other references to this cause, it is clear that Catherine believed that the chief effects of a crusade would be the conversion of the unbelievers and the possible martyrdom of the Christian participants. She certainly had no idea of the outrages committed in the name of crusading.

[25] Perhaps d'Estaing was being threatened, or possibly Catherine is interpreting an illness as being a direct result of his efforts with the Romans. He will in fact die on 25 November 1377.

[26] Eph. 4, 22–24.

will as well as your desire and mine. Peace! Peace! Peace, dearest father! Be concerned, you and the others, more about the loss of souls than about the loss of cities, and make the holy father see this, for God demands of us souls more than cities.[27]

I'll say no more. Keep living in God's holy and tender love.

Gentle Jesus! Jesus love!

Textual Notes

a. The manuscripts have *darci*, but this can only be a copyist error for *dare*, since there is no parallel usage of the reflexive anywhere in Catherine's writings, and no reason for its use in this context.

[27] There is an echo here of Let. T209 to Gregory XI (in this volume): "You could say though, holy father: 'I am bound in conscience to protect and regain what belongs to holy Church.' Oimé! I must admit that is the truth, but it seems to me one ought to take even better care of what is more dear. The Church's treasure is the blood of Christ given in payment for souls. The treasure of the blood was paid not for temporal possessions but for the salvation of the human race. So even though you have the responsibility to conquer and protect and rule over the treasure of the cities the Church has lost, you are much more obligated to regain all these little sheep, who are a treasure within the Church."

LETTER T242/G37[1]
To Bishop Angelo Ricasoli
October 1377

The rubric of T and P5 specifies the occasion of the present letter as Ricasoli's leaving his episcopal city in order to respect the interdict. The bishop had in fact left his see in Florence in May 1376 for this reason. Then, in October 1377, when the republics which had been placed under interdict demanded that their bishops return, under pain of fine, Ricasoli refused the order and fled instead to Siena. This last "leaving" seems to be the more likely context of Catherine's letter, since she is encouraging him to persevere in what he has begun, an exhortation not found in the longer letter addressed to Cardinal Pierre d'Estaing (T11) from which most of this one is copied.[2]

§

In the name of Jesus Christ crucified and of gentle Mary.

Reverend and dearest father in Christ gentle Jesus,

I Caterina, servant and slave of the servants of Jesus Christ, am writing to you in his precious blood. I long to see you a courageous and fearless man, so that you may serve Christ's dear bride bravely, and work for God's honor in matters both spiritual and temporal, in the way this dear bride needs in these times. I am certain that if you raise your mind's eye to see her need, you will act zealously and not out of any fear or indifference.

None of our actions is effective if we act out of slavish fear. No matter what our position, we will fail in small things as well as great, and will never finish what we have begun. Oh how dangerous such fear is! It cuts off the arms of holy desire.[3] It blinds us and keeps us from seeing or knowing the truth, because the source of this fear is the blindness of self-

---

[1] MSS: B, P2, T, R1, P5, F2, P4; translation based on T and R1, with variants based on an unpublished transcription by A. Volpato.

[2] Fawtier (II, p. 172) places the letter in either May 1376 or October 1377. Dupré Theseider (unpublished notes) places it in October 1377. This is strongly supported by the linguistic data. A number of significant clusters within individual patterns, moreover, begin and/or end precisely in October of that year: AMORVERD, CORRGIUS, CROCDESI, CROCEDES, LUMEVEST, ONORAMOR, ONORFADP, PERFCOM, PETCHIES, RADSUPER, SUPERBOB, TEMMORTE, VIRNTIM.

[3] Cf. Let. T129/DT29 to Bartolomeo Dominici, where it is stinginess, "doing the bare minimum," that cuts off the arms of holy desire. In either case, it is such desire that leads one to the greatness of soul that does the work of God.

centeredness. For as soon as we love ourselves selfishly and merely on the level of feeling,[4] we become fearful. Why? Because we have set our love and trust in something weak, something completely unstable and inconstant, something as passing as the wind.[5]

Oh perversion of love! What harm you bring both to those with power (temporal or spiritual) and to those who are subject to power! Those who are in church offices never correct people because they are afraid of losing their positions of authority, afraid of displeasing their subordinates. And you harm subordinates as well, because there is no humility in those who love themselves so perversely. In fact, there is in such love a deeply rooted pride, and the proud are never obedient.[6] Those who are temporal lords do not promote justice, but are again and again guilty of evil and deceitful injustice, because they act to please themselves or other people. So for lack of correction and punishment their subordinates become more wicked still, because they are being encouraged in their vices and wrongdoing.[7]

Since selfish and inordinately fearful love is so dangerous, you must run away from it. You must focus your mind's eye on the spotless Lamb. He is our rule and our instruction, and him we must follow.[8] He is love and truth itself.[9] He sought nothing but his Father's honor and our salvation. He feared neither the Jews and their persecution, nor the devils' malice, nor ignominy nor scorn nor abuse. He did not in the end fear even the shameful death of crucifixion. And we are his students in this dear and agreeable school.[10]

---

[4] The original is *amore proprio sensitivo*. Neither adjective ever has a positive connotation in Catherine's writings.

[5] This refrain runs through Catherine's writings from beginning to end, but occurs more frequently in the last three years of her life.

[6] Cf. Let. T75/DT62, addressed to two different monasteries of nuns (in this volume), for one summary of the intimate relationship Catherine sees among obedience, humility, and charity. It is a frequent theme in her writings. Cf. especially Let. T36, T38, T95, T217 (in this volume) and Let. T35 (late 1377 or early 1378), T67 (1378), T84 (1379), most of which are written to religious; and *Dial.* 154–165, pp. 327–360.

[7] Cf. Let. T123 to the Defenders of Siena (in this volume): "Oh blindness of selfish love! Oh misplaced fear! You become so blind that you not only condemn ordinary people along with the wicked (who could be justly condemned and their treachery feared), but you give in to your fear of the wicked and condemn the just!"

[8] Here and in Let. T242 (in this volume) and *Dial.* 75, p. 137, Christ himself is "our rule and instruction." Elsewhere, as in Let. T220 in this volume; Let. T243 (1377), T64 (1378); and various places in *The Dialogue*, he gives his disciples the example of his obedience and self-sacrifice as rule and instruction.

[9] As inseparable as love and truth are in Catherine's thought, both in God and in human virtue, this is one of only five instances of God/Christ being *identified* as "truth and love" together. The others are Let. T11, T123, T259 (all in this volume), and Prayer 17.

[10] Cf. Augustine, *Sermo CCXXXIV* (PL XXXVIII, 1116): "That cross was a school, where the teacher taught the thief. The wood on which he hung became a chair for

So, dearest most gracious[b] father, I want you in sweet wisdom[c] and with the greatest zeal to keep your mind's eye on this book of life, which affords you such gentle and agreeable instruction. Be concerned only about God's honor and the salvation of souls, about serving Christ's dear bride. In this light[11] you will shed your self-centeredness and be clothed in divine love. You will seek God because of his infinite goodness and because he is worthy of our seeking and our love. For God's sake you will love yourself and virtue, and you will hate sin. And with this same love you will love your neighbors.

You know very well that divine Goodness has set you within the mystic body of holy Church and nourished you at the breast of this dear bride[12] only to have you eat the food of God's honor and the salvation of souls at the table of the most holy cross. It is his will that this food be eaten only on the cross,[13] that is, by bearing physical difficulties with constant restless desire.[14] This is what God's Son did. As he endured torments in his body he endured also the pain of desire, and the cross of desire was greater than the physical cross. And this was his desire: hunger for our redemption in fulfillment of his eternal Father's commission—and he suffered until he saw this accomplished.[15] Also, since he is the eternal Father's wisdom, he saw those who would share in his blood as well as those who through their own fault would not. Because his blood was given to all, he grieved for the foolishness of those who would be unwilling to share in it.[16] This was the crucified desire he bore from beginning to end.

---

teaching." Also Cavalca, *Specchio di croce, prologo*, p. 2: "Christ . . . on the cross is like a teacher occupying his chair, for he teaches . . . every perfect doctrine."

[11] "This light," judging from similar passages, must be the light of knowledge and faith that comes from the teaching of Christ.

[12] This (with its occurrence in this letter's partial twin, Let. T11) is the earliest extant reference in Catherine's works to the Church as a nursing mother. It occurs twenty-one more times in later letters and in *The Dialogue*.

[13] The meaning is both "at" the cross as at a table, and "on" the cross, since eating at this table implies that one is crucified with Christ. Again we see Catherine's interpretation of conformity with Christ identified with a sharing in his redemptive role.

[14] It. *molti anxietati desiderii*.

[15] Cf. Prayer 18, pp. 162–163: "I see that this Word, once written in you, [Mary,] was never without the cross of holy desire. Even as he was conceived within you, desire to die for the salvation of humankind was engrafted and bound into him. This is why he had been made flesh. So it was a great cross for him to carry for such a long time that desire, when he would have liked to see it realized at once." Also Let. T16 to a great prelate (in this volume).

[16] Cf. Let. T12/DT66 to Giovanni di Gano da Orvieto, in which she relates this vision of Christ to his cry of "I thirst!" Though here the reference is to not sharing by deliberate choice, she elsewhere includes those who do not share in the blood because of ignorance, that is, the unbelievers (Let. T133/DT32 in vol. I; Let. T209, T256 in this volume; Prayer 1).

And when he had given his life the cross of desire ended, but not desire itself.

This is what you and every other person ought to be doing: offering both physical effort and the effort of desire, grieving at the offense done to God and the harm done to all the souls we see perishing. It seems to me it is time, dearest father, to be giving honor to God and our best efforts to our neighbors.[17] We must not, then, regard ourselves selfishly or merely on the level of feeling, nor with slavish fear. No, we must act with true love and holy fear of God.[18] And if it is necessary to give our life for God's honor we ought to give it—to say nothing of our material possessions.

I hope in God's infinite goodness that, since you are a courageous man, you will do this, and will persevere in what you have begun, that you will continue to be a faithful son of holy Church. By exercising yourself in virtue you will achieve great perfection. I have been very happy about your constancy and perseverance up to now. I beg you never to turn back, even in the face of death. Act like a virtuous man, a fragrant flower (as you should be) in the mystic body of holy Church.

It is because I know that only those who are courageous in virtue are constant[d] that I said I long to see you a courageous and fearless man, so that you might be better able to fulfill God's will and my desire for your salvation. Keep company with the humble spotless lamb, and you will find our king, coming to us in the street, humble and meek.[19] And then let selfish sensuality be ashamed to lift its head in impatience, seeing God so humbled. To make us great he is made little. And gentle First Truth teaches us how to become great. How? With the lowliness of true humility. That is why I said we should learn from him to be meek and humble of heart.[20]

So up, dearest father! Let's rouse ourselves from the sleep of apathy and

---

[17] In Let. T104 to Raimondo da Capua, written in late 1377, she will place this admonition in the context of a discussion on the use of time and attribute it to an experience she has had in prayer: "In our concern for [souls] we steal time from ourselves—time, that is, that we might have had for our comfort, any comfort, new or old—and we give that time to our neighbors. This is why, when that servant of God asked, 'My Lord, what do you want me to do?' he answered, 'Give honor to me, and your best efforts to your neighbors.' " "Best efforts" translates *fadiga*, which always conveys the connotations of its English cognate, *fatigue*, within the effort or labor.

[18] The present letter has up to this point been identical with Let. T11 except for a few details which could well be ascribed to scribal differences and have no bearing on the meaning of the text or its translation. From here on the content is unique to Let. T242.

[19] Cf. Mt. 21, 5, citing Zec. 9, 9: "Tell the daughter of Zion, 'Your king comes to you meek, seated upon an ass, upon the foal of a beast of burden.' " (Vulg.) This Palm Sunday allusion may be an allusion to the bishop's entry into Siena, which surely would have been without the usual pomp and circumstance attending an episcopal procession.

[20] Mt. 11, 29.

run on courageously, following the teaching of Truth. I'll say no more. Keep living in God's holy and tender love.

Jesus, gentle Jesus. Amen.[e]

Textual Notes

a. Translation based on B; R1: *filially / slavishly*.

b. P5: *most gracious and venerable / dearest and most gracious.*

c. P2: *providence / wisdom* (*providentia / prudentia*).

d. B, P2: *considerando ine che se non quegli che sono virile non sono costanti*; T, R1, P4: *me / ine*; T, P2: *sono / se non*. All versions are lexically and structurally problematic, but the sense seems clear from similar passages elsewhere in Catherine's writings.

e. B ends with *Gentle Jesus! Jesus love!*

LETTER T296/G70[1]
To Don Giovanni dalle Celle
20 to 31 October 1377

Don Giovanni, a noble Florentine (1310-1396), was in his earlier monastic life abbot of Santa Trinità in Florence. Convicted there of incontinence and sorcery, he was imprisoned for a year. After completing his time of penance he left the abbey and went to Vallombrosa outside Florence, to the hermitage *dalle celle* ("of the cells"), by which name he was subsequently known. Renowned for his holiness, wisdom, and knowledge of the Scriptures, he converted many young Florentines through his direction and letters. Among these were Barduccio Canigiani, later one of Catherine's disciples and secretaries, and another disciple, Conte di Ser Conti, to whom Let. T83[2] is addressed.

On 10 October 1376, Giovanni wrote to William Flete, who had accused him of speaking out against Catherine: "Not only do I not want to do such a thing, but I am prepared to die for her honor." Calling her his queen, he says, "I would consider it a glory to be called a heretic with her. ... Oh sweetest heresy of the heavenly Catherine! You turn sinners into just people. Friend of publicans and sinners, you make the angels laugh and heaven rejoice. You honor God; you enlighten the Church of Christ; you raise the dead to spiritual life. ... You have the words of eternal life, and we have believed and known that you are anointed by the Holy Spirit and are the daughter of the living God!"[3]

Two comments in the present letter to Giovanni incline me to place it in late October 1377. First, she refers to their disciples, "those who are there and those who are here." This would make it unlikely that she is writing from Florence, since Giovanni's hermitage was very near that city. Secondly, she speaks of those who should "either leave the place or else prefer death to doing what shouldn't be done," very possibly a reference to the public flaunting of the interdict in Florence on 18 October 1377, when the "Madonna of the Impruneta" and the head of Saint Zanobius were carried in procession to the Piazza della Signoria. There Mass was celebrated and one of the Augustinian friars of Santo Spirito preached an impassioned sermon to the crowd, though the terms of the interdict for-

---

[1] MSS: Mo-*a*, corrected by *b*; S2, P4, P5, R2, T; translation based on Mo-*a*. No relevant variants.

[2] Written after Catherine's arrival in Rome in 1378.

[3] Let. IV, in P. Cividali, *Il beato Giovanni dalle Celle*, *Atti della R. Accademia dei Lincei*, CCCIII, ser. V, vol. XII, 1906, pp. 439–440. Note that all of the biblical allusions which Giovanni refers to Catherine here are in the gospel referred to Jesus. Clearly he sees her as a Christ figure.

bade any public liturgy or preaching.[4] Placing the letter in this context would accord very well with the linguistic evidence.[5]

§

In the name of Jesus Christ crucified and of gentle Mary.

Dearest father in Christ gentle Jesus,

I Caterina, servant and slave of the servants of Jesus Christ, am writing to you in his precious blood. I long to see you eating and savoring souls for God's honor at the table of the most holy cross in the company of the humble spotless Lamb. I don't see, dearest father, how this sweet food can be eaten anywhere else. Why not? Because we cannot eat it in truth without suffering a great deal. We have to eat it with the teeth of true patience and the mouth of holy desire, and on the cross of great trials (no matter where they may come from, whether from gossip or from the world's taking scandal). And we have to suffer all these things even to the point of death.

Now is the time, dearest father, to show whether we are lovers of Christ crucified or not, and whether or not we enjoy this food. It is time to give honor to God and our best efforts to our neighbors—I mean the physical effort of great suffering and the spiritual effort of offering tears and sweat and continual humble prayer in God's presence with bitter sorrow and restless desire. I don't see how God's anger against us can be appeased, his mercy be inclined toward us, and so many little sheep who are perishing in the devils' hands be rescued by his mercy, except in the way I've said, that is, with great sorrow and heartfelt compassion and with very intense prayer.

So I'm inviting you, dearest father, in the name of Christ crucified: let's begin all over again to lose ourselves and to seek only God's honor in the salvation of souls, without any slavish fear. Let's never let anything slow

---

[4] Cf. Gardner, *Saint Catherine of Siena*, p. 224. Catherine's distress over this same incident may well be echoed in Prayer 5 (pp. 48–49), prayed on 26 October 1377.

[5] Three of the six letters which share twelve or more of this one's forty-seven analyzed patterns are, in fact, from the last half of October 1377. One is from early November of that year, and the other two are very long letters from 1378 and 1379. Besides, a striking number of significant clusters within individual patterns begin and/or end precisely in October 1377: ALLENT, ANSIET, BOCCDESI, CORRGIUS, DIAMANTE, EBBRAMOR, EBBRPERD, LINGUANA, ONORFADP, PERDMED, PROPVOL, PUPILFED, SOSPCIBO. Fawtier (II, p. 190) places the letter in 1378 or 1377, but leans toward the latter. Dupré Theseider (unpublished notes) places it either while Catherine was in Florence in 1378, or possibly in 1377, but in any case before the schism of 1378. Gigli (*Opere*, II, p. 462) places it in 1378.

us down—not our own pain, not the desire to please others, not the necessity of suffering death. No, let's run like people drunk with love and sorrow over the persecution of the blood of Christ crucified. For we see it persecuted no matter where we turn. If I turn to ourselves, gangrenous members that we are, [I see us] persecuting the blood with our many sins, with the stench of so many deadly sins and with our poison selfishness that is infecting the whole world.[6]

And if I turn to the ministers of the blood of this gentle and humble Lamb, words can't even describe such evils and sins! If I turn to those ministers who are under the yoke of obedience,[7] I see they are so imperfect (because the cursed root of selfish love is not yet dead in them) that not one has come forward to give his life for Christ crucified. On the contrary, they prefer fear of death and of suffering to holy fear of God and reverence for the blood.

And if I turn to the laity who have already renounced worldly desire, they haven't practiced the kind of virtue that would make them either leave the place or else prefer death to doing what shouldn't be done.[8] They've acted this way either because of their imperfection or because they've been advised to. If I were to give the advice, I would advise them, if they wanted to act perfectly, to prefer death. And if they thought they were weak, then they should run away from the place, the occasion of sin, as fast as they could. And it seems to me that you and every servant of God ought to give the same advice to anyone who comes to you. For you know that under no circumstances are we permitted to commit the least sin, not only for fear of punishment and death but even to perform a great act of virtue.

So no matter which way we turn, we find nothing but sins. I have no doubt that if even one person had been so perfect as to have given his or her life for what has happened and is still happening every day, that person's blood would have cried out for mercy and would have bound the hands of divine justice. It would have shattered the Pharaoh hearts that are hard as diamonds—for I don't see any way to shatter them except with blood.[9]

---

[6] She seems here, by her use of the first person plural, to be including both Giovanni and herself in the state of the interdicted city of Florence.

[7] That is, those who are members of religious orders.

[8] The reference seems to be to the public flaunting of the interdict in Florence on 18 October. She implies that the Florentines ought at that time to have either left the city or been ready to die rather than violate the interdict.

[9] Cf. Ex. 4, 21 (Vulg.): "I will harden Pharaoh's heart." Also *Dial.* 4, pp. 31–32: "They have, with the hand of free choice, encrusted their heart in a diamond rock that can never be shattered except by blood." G. Cavallini, in her note to this passage, cites Vincent de Beauvais, *Speculum naturale*, L, VIII, c. 39, where the fresh warm blood of a goat has power

Oimé! Oimé! Oimé! My unfortunate soul! I see Christian religion lying dead, and I neither grieve nor weep over it! I see that darkness has invaded the light. For people have turned from the light of most holy faith received in the blood of Christ and have become blinded, the pupil of their eye shriveled up. Like blind people, we see them fall into the ditch,[10] that is, into the mouth of the infernal wolf, stripped bare of virtue and dead from the cold. Because they have been stripped of charity for God and for their neighbors and cut loose from the bond of charity, they have lost all reverence for God and for the blood.

Oimé! I believe my sins have been the cause of it! So I beg you, dearest father, to pray to God for me. Let him either take away my sins and not let me be the cause of so much evil, or give me death!

I beg you to take these dead children, bathed in the blood of Christ crucified, and eat them as your food at the table of the most holy cross. I tell you, unless we and God's other servants do our utmost with many prayers, and unless the others turn away from so many evils, divine judgment will come and divine justice will take out her rod—although, if we open our eyes, one of the worst [punishments] we could have in this life is already here, that is, to be deprived of the light and not see the evil and harm, physical as well as spiritual. And those who don't see cannot correct themselves, because they neither hate what is evil nor love what is truly good. And because they don't correct themselves, they fall from bad to worse. This is what seems to me to be happening, and we are worse off now than on the first day.[11]

If we are true servants of God, therefore, we must never quit. We must suffer much and with true patience, giving our best efforts to our neighbors and honor to God with many prayers and restless desires. Let sighs be our food, and tears our drink at the table of the cross. I don't see any other way. This is why I said I long to see you eating and savoring souls at the table of the most holy cross.

Please remember your dearest children and mine, those who are there and those who are here.[12] Nourish them and help them grow in great perfection as best you can. Let us do our best to run, dead to every tem-

---

to shatter the diamond, which resists both iron and fire. This letter is, in fact, the first instance of Catherine's use of the diamond image, although she has earlier written in more than half a dozen letters of the cold hardness of the human heart being melted or shattered by the heat of the blood of Christ (Let. T30/DT1, T28/DT17, T134, T181/DT55, T221, T226, T228).

[10] Mt. 15, 14 (Lk. 6, 39).

[11] She probably means the first day of the interdict.

[12] Several of Giovanni's disciples have, on his advice, become disciples of Catherine. But she probably considers all of her disciples as his, and vice versa.

poral or spiritual self-will, that is, seeking as our food not selfish spiritual consolation but only souls. Let us find our joy on the cross with Christ crucified and, if necessary, give our lives for the glory and praise of his name. As for me, I am dying and cannot die, as I hear and see my Creator offended! So I ask you, you and the others, as an alms, to pray to God for me.

I'll say no more. Keep living in God's holy and tender love.

Gentle Jesus! Jesus love!

LETTER T309/G299[1]
To Giovanni da Parma, in Rome
23 October 1377

We know nothing of the man to whom this letter is addressed, other than that he was in Rome at the time it was sent. There is a Giovanni da Parma who was a correspondent of Petrarch, but Gardner states that this man cannot be the one to whom the present letter is addressed.[2] The occasion for Catherine's letter is Giovanni's perturbation after having read a book others have condemned.

The letter is dated 23 October, without a year. It is highly unlikely that the letter would have been written in 1379, when Catherine herself was in Rome. Nor is a date earlier than 1377 likely, since this letter has so little in common with other letters of that period. In October of either 1377 or 1378 Catherine could have heard of Giovanni's problem through Raimondo, who was in Rome at both times—if not from Giovanni himself. Dupré Theseider places the letter in 1378 because a number of other letters from that year are dated in the rubrics. This, however, does not seem sufficient reason, especially since a number of other letters from 1377 and early 1378 are so dated.[3]

Linguistically, this letter shares far more heavily with others in late 1377 than with those of late 1378. This evidence, though not absolutely conclusive, leads me to place this letter in 1377.[4] Another factor which inclines me toward 1377 is that the letter is characterized in a number of places by awkward structures which render the sense somewhat unclear, a stylistic quality not uncommon during Catherine's stay in the Val d'Orcia.

---

[1] MSS: B, P2, A, P5, F2, P3; translation based on B, as edited by Dupré Theseider. No relevant variants.

[2] *Saint Catherine of Siena*, p. 376, n. 2.

[3] Dupré Theseider, unpublished notes. The other letters in question are T260, T270, T385, and T286. Gardner also, without stating his reasons, places the letter in 1378 (*Saint Catherine of Siena*, pp. 286–287). Fawtier (II, p. 284) places it with "all due reservation" in 1377, having misread Gardner as opting for that date.

[4] Four of the eight letters sharing fifteen or more of this one's seventy-three analyzed patterns are from autumn of 1377. The other four (three of which are very long) are widely scattered through 1378 and 1379. A number of significant clusters within individual patterns are concentrated in autumn of 1377 and do not reappear in late 1378 (AMODCRIS, CAPOVOL, FIELACET, GUERRDIO, OBEDLUNG, PACEBOCC, PACIFICA, SAZFAST).

§

In the name of Jesus Christ crucified and of gentle Mary.

Dearest brother in Christ gentle Jesus,

I Caterina, servant and slave of the servants of Jesus Christ, am writing to you in his precious blood. I long to see you grounded on the living rock, Christ gentle Jesus, since there is no other way we can set the foundation for a building that will last. It would quickly collapse when the wind blew.[5] But those whose foundation is on this dear rock, who follow the teaching of Christ crucified, never fail.

What does this gentle loving Word (whom we call the living rock) teach, and where does he teach us? Not in the midst of worldly pleasure and enjoyment, but at the table of the most holy cross.[6] What he teaches us is to love God in truth, to hate vice and the selfish sensuality that is the reason for vice, and to love virtue and the God who is the reason for all virtue. He teaches us to obey the commandments of the law in order to lead us to love according to the counsels.[7] He makes us conceive the desire to learn these at the table of the most holy cross, where we are clothed in charity for God and for our neighbors.

But note that we cannot learn without the light, nor without a book.[8] Our mind's eye must be enlightened by the light of most holy faith, and the book must be written in such a way that from its writing we may learn what is being taught. If I'm seeing rightly, dearest brother, God has given us our mind's eye, and within it the light of faith. Neither the devil nor anyone else can rob us of this light unless we ourselves have already let go of it in selfish love. And God has given us a written book. I mean the Word, God's Son.[9] This book was written on the wood of the cross

---

[5] Cf. 1 Pt. 2, 4; Mt. 7, 24–27.

[6] While Catherine often combines the theme of eating at the table of the cross with the statement that this is Christ's teaching, and often speaks of Christ mounting the podium or chair of the cross to teach, this is the only place in which she speaks of his teaching at the *table* of the cross.

[7] The evangelical counsels were traditionally counted as voluntary poverty, continence, and obedience.

[8] The image of the book is certainly prompted by the occasion for this letter, Giovanni's worry over having read another book, one that others have apparently told him has been condemned.

[9] *il Verbo del Figliuolo di Dio* could be read as translated here (which is the usual sense of the formula), or as "the word of God's Son," which would seem on the surface to fit the image, but which in fact mutilates the image, since the Word, the second person of the Trinity, is ultimately himself the message. (Besides, Catherine usually uses *parola* to refer to the word as a linguistic entity.)

not with ink but with blood. And its illuminated initials[10] are Christ's wonderful sacred wounds.[11] Who is so simple and dense, so dull-witted, as not to know how to read these chapters? So far as I know, only those who love selfishly. And they become this way not because they don't know how [to read] but because they don't *want* to know how.

Here is how the book is written.

In the chapter that is his feet, we see that they are nailed so that we may nail our affection to him by stripping it of all inordinate willfulness. In this way, it will neither want nor seek anything but Christ crucified.[12] We want to go to the eternal Father with this incarnate Word, this written book, as intermediary. We long to endure any undeserved suffering—physical or spiritual pain, all sorts of diabolical temptations and suggestions as God permits them, problems with other people. We want to endure it all for the glory and praise of God's name. If we keep to this way, we will be following and realizing in ourselves our dear Savior's words: "No one can go to the Father except through me." He is the way; he is the truth,[13] and those who walk by him are walking by the light and will not come to darkness.[14] This is how we nail the feet of our affection, by keeping to the way of truth.[15]

When we come to the open side of Christ crucified, we discover the life of grace. For once we have stripped our affection of vice and selfish sensual passion with a holy hatred (hatred we have found in the written book,

---

[10] Catherine's use of *capoverso* bears the sense not only of the illuminated initial that signals the beginning of a chapter or paragraph, but the chapter or paragraph itself. Cf. Let. T316 to Daniela of Orvieto (1378): "For this is the way and the rule eternal Truth has given you. He wrote it upon his own body in letters so large that no one, no matter how dull-witted, has an excuse for not reading it. And he wrote it not with ink, but with his own blood. You can see clearly the illuminated initials (*capoversi*) of this book, and how large they are. All of them show the eternal Father's truth, the indescribable love with which we were created: only—and this is the truth—so that we might share in his own supreme eternal good." In what follows, *capoverso* is translated as "letter," "initial," or "chapter" as the context requires.

[11] Cavalca, *Specchio di croce*, XXXVI, uses the image of Christ as book, with his five wounds as initials illuminated in red, so large that anyone can read them. Catherine, however, develops the imagery in far more detail. The image is used also in Let. T318 (1378) and Prayer 18, pp. 158–159, but the present letter is the only place in which she specifically develops a significance for each of the five wounds in relation to the book image.

[12] Cf. 1 Cor. 2, 2: "I determined that while I was with you, I would speak of nothing but Jesus Christ, and him crucified." Also Gal. 6, 14: "May I never boast of anything but the cross of our Lord Jesus Christ! Through it, the world has been crucified to me, and I to the world."

[13] Jn. 14, 6.

[14] Jn. 8, 12.

[15] The image of the three "chapters" enumerated here, the wounds of Christ's feet, side, and head, are further developed in *Dial.* 26–87, pp. 64–160, as the stairs on the bridge (the crucified Christ).

since [Christ] so hated these things that he wanted to punish them in his own body), we discover hearty love for true solid virtue in his open heart. This opening has revealed to us his blazing, hearty love. He has made his blood a bath for us, the blood that was steeped in the fire of divine charity because it was shed for love.[16] For it was for love of his Father's honor and our salvation that he ran as one in love to the shameful death of the cross in fulfillment of his eternal Father's command.

It really is true, then, that he teaches us at the table of the cross. There we learn from him to be meek and humble of heart,[17] and with this meekness and humility we keep God's dear commandments. And where have we found these commandments? In the book. How? By the light—that is, the light of most holy faith. And so, when we receive the life of grace, we live in hunger for God's honor and the salvation of souls.

Eventually we come to read at the thorn-crowned head of Christ crucified, at his mouth. There we crucify our own thorn-crowned head.[18] Our selfish wilfulness is indeed a thorn bush that stabs and torments us if we use it as a crown by keeping the head of our will perversely independent of God's dear will. But in our thorn-crowned head, Christ crucified, we shed this pathetic thorn bush.[19] Then we discover peace at his mouth.[20]

---

[16] Cf. Let. T80 to Giovanni Tantucci (1378): "The blood is never without fire. In fact, it is steeped in the fire of divine charity, since it was shed for love. So the fire [fused] with the blood consumes and washes away the rust of sin from our conscience—rust that is like a worm eating away within our conscience." Catherine's consideration of the fusing of fire and blood is sometimes couched in the image of bread, as in Let. T87 to Giovanna Pazza (in this volume): "Only the blood can satisfy our hunger, because the blood has been mixed and kneaded [into one dough] with the eternal Godhead." Elsewhere, as in *Dial.* 27, p. 66, the image is mortar: "But after these stones [the virtues] were hewn on the body of my Word, my gentle Son (I have told you that he is the bridge), he built them into walls, tempering the mortar with his own blood. That is, his blood was mixed into the mortar of his divinity with the strong heat of burning love." Sometimes the mortar is the very cement of the roadway, the bridge, as in *Dial.* 135 and elsewhere. And sometimes, as in Let. Gardner I/DT52 to Bartolomeo Smeducci, this mortar joins individual human beings, the stones, into a single wall that is Christ, and so joins them with God.

[17] Mt. 11, 29 (Vulg.).

[18] Note that the stairs on the bridge are only three: the feet, the heart, and the mouth. In this book imagery, Catherine adds the wounds of Christ's head and hands as further "chapters."

[19] This is Catherine's only reference to "our own thorn-crowned head." But cf. *Dial.* 44, p. 90, which in fact closely parallels what follows here: "I showed myself to you under the figure of a tree. . . . At the foot of the tree, if you recall, was a sort of thorn bush. All who were in love with their own sensuality backed off from that thorn bush. . . . But many, when they recognized the world's deceit, returned to the tree and crossed through the thorn bush, that is, the will's decision. Beforehand, this decision is a thorn bush they seem to encounter when they follow the way of truth. Conscience always pulls in one direction, and sensuality in the other. But as soon as they say, 'I want to follow Christ crucified,' the thorn bush is broken and they discover my immeasurable tenderness."

[20] This is the kiss of peace, described a bit more at length in *Dial.* 76, p. 141.

For our sins truly were a most bitter gall and vinegar. They had sapped us of the strength of grace. But if we conform ourselves with God's gentle will, then in Christ's tasting of this bitter gall and vinegar we taste the peace he won in such great bitterness. I mean his reconciling of humankind with God after we had for so long been at war. This is why the glorious Paul says that the blessed Christ is our peace; he was made the mediator between God and humankind. Indeed, the dear apostle urges us to be reconciled and make peace with God because [Christ] came as our mediator.[21]

If we follow this lovely straight way, we will receive the effects of this peace. Here in this life we will eat the crumbs of grace, and in everlasting life, full and perfect foods that satisfy completely and flawlessly. The glorious doctor Augustine, attempting to express this, says that there is satiety without surfeit and hunger without pain, for hunger will be far from[a] painful, and satiety far from boredom.[22]

For once we have arrived at such joy and tasted peace, we will have read and will continue to read the nailed hands of God's Son by letting all our spiritual and mental activities be nailed to God's will, pursuing them all for the glory and praise of his name. In the case of mental activities, we train our mind to order and direct them according to divine charity. Our heart is always nailed to that charity, no matter what other practices we may take up in view of attaining virtue, no matter what different ways God may allow or that we may be capable of. All are done in holy reverence of God.

All are nailed to the cross, since the true servants of God would not wish to act or to go through this life without suffering.[23] In fact, they want to take up their cross and follow Christ in all truth, with constancy and patience and enduring perseverance, even to the point of death. For

---

[21] Cf. 2 Cor. 5, 18–19. But Catherine seems to be echoing even more the language of Eph. 2, 14; she may not have been aware that the latter passage refers not to the reconciliation of humankind with God but of gentile with Jew.

[22] Cf. Cavalca, *Specchio di croce*, p. 184: "Sated, we shall be hungry, and hungering we shall be sated, but our satiety will be far from boredom, and our hunger far from pain." Also, *Descrizione de' dieci comandamenti*, p. 306: "We shall desire though we are sated, and we shall be sated even in our desiring. Yet satiety will not be a source of boredom, nor desire be accompanied by pain, as happens in this world." The idea is in fact found not in Augustine but in pseudo-Augustine, *Meditatio XXVII* (PL XL, 921).

[23] The last four sentences of the translation are a single long sentence in the original, the precise intent of which is not clear to me. I have rendered the passage in the light of similar passages in Catherine's writings. *Se ella è operazione mentale, che egli eserciti la mente sua in dirizzarla e ordinarla nella divina carità; sempre il cuore vi sta confitto con tutti quanti gli altri esercizi che la creatura piglia per giugnere a virtù in molti e in diversi modi, secondo che Dio permette, ed egli è atto a ricevere: tutte sono fatte col santo timor di Dio, confitte in croce, chè già non vorrebbe il vero servo di Dio adoperare e passare questa vita senza pena.*

they are grounded on the living rock and have learned the teaching written in the book, as I've said, and they have the light of most holy faith. So suffering does not make them retreat from their perseverance in virtue. No, they have found delight in suffering as did the humble Lamb. Neither suffering nor death, neither our ingratitude nor the Jews' saying, "Come down from the cross and we will believe you!"[24] made him retreat from obeying his Father and saving us. They learn the teaching of perseverance from him. If they were not grounded on this rock, they would turn back, afraid of their own shadow. They would fail in everything.

And this is why I said that I long to see you grounded on the living rock, Christ gentle Jesus. And this is how I am begging you to act.

I'm sure, too, that if you read this wonderful book, then that book of yours that seems to be troubling you so will be no problem at all.[25] I can't see why you're fretting so about it.[26] If people are telling you that the book conflicts with the truth of the saints who are approved by the Church, either leave it alone or have it corrected yourself.[b] Stick with those you are certain conform with the truth. And if your conscience is troubling you because the devil is trying to confound you by saying, "Look how long you've been living in this error! You think you've been serving God, but you've been serving and reverencing the devil!"—you mustn't believe him. No, use the light to realize that God looks at the good holy will with which we are acting—even though the book you've been reading may not be of God. For it is an evil will—and nothing else—that makes an action sinful. It is to the will that sin or virtue is attributed, depending on whether the will is loving one or the other.[c] So you don't have to be so perturbed about any of these things. You should instead dispose of every suffering like a courageous man, in the way I've described, and chase away this bitterness with the sweetness of the gentle humble Lamb.

I have no more to say to you. Keep living in God's holy and tender love.

Gentle Jesus! Jesus love!

---

[24] Mt. 15, 32.

[25] Burlamacchi (note to the letter in Gigli, *Opere,* II) speculates that the book in question may have been one of Raymond Lully's (1235?–1315) works. Lully, a Spanish Franciscan tertiary, philosopher, and missionary, had advocated the teaching of Greek, Hebrew, Chaldean, and Arabic to student missionaries. Some persons in the late fourteenth century were saying that his works had been condemned by Gregory XI, while others were suspending judgment.

[26] This last sentence is recorded in Dupré Theseider's unpublished transcription of B, but not in Tommasèo.

Textual Notes

a. The manuscript has *dolceçça / di lunga*, clearly an error, since *dolceçça* ("sweetness") would make no sense here. Besides, the passage is one which occurs frequently in Catherine's writings, with *di lunga*.

b. Tommasèo text adds *and don't use it any more.*

c. The manuscript has *secondo che l'uomo à l'uno o l'altro* (literally "depending on whether a person has the one or the other"), which would leave the sense of the statement unclear. Again the intended sense is clear from similar passages in Catherine's writings.

Letter T38/G184[1]
To Agnesa, widow of Orso Malavolti
October 1377

One of Catherine's very earliest extant letters was addressed to Agnesa Malavolti and others of the Sienese *Mantellate*. The present letter is a more personal one, written to console and encourage Monna Agnesa after the death of her daughter—apparently the last of her children, since Catherine speaks of her "last tie" having been broken.[2] This, however, does not help to date the letter, since it is not known when the daughter died.[3] For this, one must turn to the linguistic evidence, which points most strongly to October 1377.[4]

It would not be surprising if Catherine had received word of the death of Monna Agnesa's daughter while she was in the Val d'Orcia, since news seems to have been traveling back and forth between there and Siena quite regularly.

§

In the name of Jesus Christ crucified and of gentle Mary.

Dearest daughter in Christ gentle Jesus,

I Caterina, servant and slave of the servants of Jesus Christ, am writing to you in his precious blood. I long to see you grounded in true patience, since I believe that without patience we cannot be pleasing to God. Those who are impatient are very pleasing to the devil and to their own selfish sensuality. They take pleasure in nothing but anger when they don't get what their sensuality wants. But on the same score, this is very displeasing

---

[1] MSS: Mo-*a*, M, S5, S6, Ro, B, P2, R1, P5, F2, F1, P3; translation based on Mo-*a*. No other manuscript consulted.

[2] There is a third letter to Agnesa, T53, which I believe is slightly later than this one.

[3] While many of the Malavolti are listed in the San Domenico *Necrologia* (Laurent, *Fontes*, XX), neither Orso nor Agnesa is; therefore, one would not expect to find this daughter there.

[4] I am particularly persuaded by the number of significant clusters within individual patterns which begin and/or end in or very near October, with about as many beginning there (CAPOSPIN, FONDPROP, IMPAZZPRI, MIROLLO, MORTIMMO, ODORPAZ, PERFCOM, REGINA, SALUPERF, SDEGN, SPASIMAT, STATCOM, VIRTSENZ) as ending there (CONFITTO, IMPAZPRI, MOTIMMO, PERFCOM, PROPVOL, RADSUPER, SDEGN, SPEZCOLO, VIRTSENZ, VOLSPIR). Fawtier (II, p. 228) and Dupré Theseider (unpublished notes) decline to date the letter.

to God. The devil, on the other hand, is very pleased, because anger and impatience are the pith of pride.[5]

Impatience forfeits the fruits of these people's efforts and deprives them of God. It makes them begin to experience the earnest of hell, and then gives them eternal damnation. For in hell their perverse and evil will burns with anger and hatred and impatience. But though it burns it is never consumed; [the fire] within is constantly refreshed and never diminishes. This is why I say it is not consumed. What has been very much dried up and consumed in their soul is grace. But their being is not consumed, as I've said, and this is why their pain is everlasting. This is what the saints say, that the damned beg for death but cannot have it because the soul never dies. (It does indeed die to grace through mortal sin, but its being never dies.)

There is no sin, no vice that gives one such a foretaste of hell in this life as anger and impatience. [The impatient] live in hatred of God and in contempt of their neighbors. They are unwilling to bear or tolerate their neighbors' shortcomings; they don't even know how to! Anything that is done or said to them sets them flying, their emotions stirred to anger and impatience like a leaf in the wind! They become unbearable to themselves, because their perverse will is always gnawing at them, wanting what it cannot have. They are out of sorts with God and with their own rationality. And all of this comes from the tree of pride baring its pith of anger and impatience and making incarnate devils of human beings. And fighting these devils we can see is much worse than fighting the devils we can't see! So everyone should really avoid this impatience!

But listen! There are two sorts of impatience.[6]

The first is the ordinary impatience of ordinary worldly people. It comes from their inordinate love for themselves and for temporal things, when they love these apart from God, when to possess them they don't care about losing their souls and putting themselves into the devils' hands. There is no remedy for this unless they learn to know themselves and realize that they have offended God. They have to cut down this tree [of pride] with the knife of true humility. This humility nurtures charity in the soul, and charity is a tree of love whose pith is patience and benevolence toward one's neighbors.

Impatience reveals, more than any other vice, that the soul has lost

---

[5] The same imagery of impatience as the marrow or pith of pride is used in Let. T104 and in *Dial.* 31 and 128.

[6] Let. T39 to Don Jacomo of Pontignano (1378) contains an identical passage, but with a different development.

God. It is judged on the spot. It is, after all, the pith of the tree of pride.[7] By the same token, patience is a better and more perfect witness than any other virtue that God is within the soul by grace. Patience, I say, is grounded in the tree of love, since it is for love of one's Creator that one repudiates the world and loves injury, whatever its source.

I said that anger and impatience are of two sorts, ordinary and special. We have spoken of the ordinary sort. Now I'll tell you about the special sort, that of persons who have already repudiated the world and want to be servants of Christ crucified—but in their own way, that is to the extent that they find pleasure and consolation in him. The reason is that spiritually selfish will is not dead in them. They ask and even demand that God give them consolation and trials according to their own wishes, not God's. So whenever they get the opposite of what their spiritually selfish will wants, they become impatient.

Now spiritual self-will is an offshoot of pride. It comes from genuine pride just as an offshoot put out by a tree off to its side. The offshoot may seem to be separate from the tree, and yet it takes its very substance from that tree. This is how it is with the selfish will of those who choose to serve God in their own way. When they don't get their own way, they are in pain, and that pain leads to impatience. They become unbearable to themselves, and find no more pleasure in serving either God or their neighbors. In fact, if people come to them for advice or help, they would give them nothing but reproach. They wouldn't know how to deal with [their neighbors'] need.[8]

All of this is the product of a spiritually selfish and sensual will. It comes of the tree of pride's having been cut down but not pulled out by the roots. The tree is cut down when we have lifted our desire beyond the world and set it on God, but have set it on God only imperfectly. The root is still there, and this is why it has sent out this offshoot over to the side. It shows itself in regard to spiritual things. So if we are deprived of God's consolation and our spirit is sterile and dried up, right away we are interiorly disturbed and dejected. Under pretext of virtue (because we think we have lost God) we become whiners. We begin to lay down the law to God.[9] But if we were truly humble, with true self-knowledge and self-contempt, we would consider ourselves unworthy of those visits God pays to souls. We would consider ourselves deserving of the pain we are

---

[7] This is one of those grammatically loose sentences which seem to characterize a number of letters from this immediate period.

[8] Note that spiritual self-will manifests, as an "offshoot," the pith of the tree of pride (impatience), just as the "offshoot" of discernment manifests the pith of the tree of love (patience). Cf. *Dial.* 10, p. 42, for the development of the imagery.

[9] Literally, "We become legislators for God."

suffering when we perceive that our spirit is being deprived of God (not in terms of grace but in terms of consolation). We are suffering pain because we are having to work with our own tools![10] We pretend that the pain our spiritual will feels from this is our fear of offending God, but it is really selfish sensuality!

Humble people who have used energetic love to thoroughly uproot pride, who have denied their will by always seeking God's honor and the salvation of souls, are not bothered by pain. In fact, they are more in awe when troubled in spirit than when tranquil, because they have a holy respect for God's giving and granting this for their own good, so that they will rise above imperfection and become perfect. This is how [God] makes them achieve perfection, because it brings them to a better knowledge of their own shortcomings and of God's grace. They discover that grace is in them from the good will God has given them (since deadly sin displeases them).

In fact, consideration of their sins and shortcomings, past and present, has made them conceive hatred for themselves and love for God's supreme eternal will. So they bear [their pains][11] reverently, and are content to endure whatever God may send them, interiorly or exteriorly, from whatever source, if only they can realize within themselves and clothe themselves in the loveliness of God's will. They find joy in everything. The more they see themselves deprived of what they love, whether by God (in the form of consolation, as I've described) or by other people, the happier they are.

It often happens that people love in a spiritual way, and then if they don't find in others the comfort and satisfaction they'd like, or if they think [their friends] are loving or paying attention more to someone else than to them, they feel hurt and depressed. And they take to grumbling about their neighbors and making rash judgments. They pass judgment on the spirit and motivation of God's servants—especially those who have caused them pain. They become impatient, and then they think what they shouldn't be thinking and say aloud what they shouldn't be saying. In their hurt they invoke a stupid sort of humility, a pretense of humility which is really an offshoot of pride, saying to themselves, "I don't want to talk to them! I don't want to bother with them any more! I'll keep my distance; I don't want to be a cause of pain either to them or to myself." And there they stand[12] in a perverse sort of indignation. But the fact that they

---

[10] This imagery is unique here.

[11] The text has simply a feminine plural pronoun as object, but the context seems to make clear that its referent is the pain mentioned shortly before.

[12] Tommasèo in his note interprets the sense of *stare in terra* as "to abase oneself in affected humility, in abjection." However, in the only other instance in which Catherine uses the expression (Let. T213 to Daniela da Orvieto, 1378), it clearly has the sense of physical

are feeling judgment in their heart and are grumbling with their tongue ought to alert them that they are in fact indignant. This is not the way we should act. This is not the way to pull out the roots [of pride] or to chop off with a clean cut its offshoot that keeps us from attaining the perfection we've begun [to work at].

No, we should take our place at the table of the most holy cross to eat the food of souls—with a generous heart, with contempt for ourselves, and passionate desire for God's honor and the salvation of souls, and love for virtue in our soul. We should seek to acquire virtue not through selfish consolation from God or from others, but through sweat and suffering, following the example and teaching of Christ crucified. We should reproachfully say to ourselves, "You, my soul, who are a member [of his body], shouldn't be walking a way different from the way [Christ] your head walked. It isn't right that under a thorn-crowned head there should be delicate members!"

If the winds of emotion and passion[13] should blow (whether from our own weakness or from the devil's trickery or from any other source), we should mount the bench of our conscience and call ourselves to account. We shouldn't let these things pass without chastising and punishing them with hatred and self-contempt. This is how the root [of pride] is pulled out. And self-contempt will dispel contempt for our neighbors. I mean, we will be more displeased about our unruly feelings and our evil thoughts than we are about the pain or other hurt or displeasure others have caused us.

This is the wonderful and holy way of people who are all on fire with Christ. This is how they have pulled out the root of perverse pride along with its pith, impatience. The devil really likes this pride, as we've said above, because it is the principle and source of all sin. On the other hand, it displeases God just as much as it pleases the devil. God is displeased by pride, and pleased by humility.

God was so pleased with Mary's humility that his goodness compelled him to give her the Word, his only-begotten Son—and she was the wonderful mother who gave [that Word] to us. You know well that God's Son did not take flesh within Mary until she had clearly expressed both her will and her humility by saying, "*Ecce ancilla Domini.* Let it be done to me according to your word."[14] But as soon as she had said this, she conceived within her the dear spotless Lamb. By this, gentle First Truth was showing us how excellent this little virtue is, and how much those receive who in humility give their will as an offering to their Creator.

---

standing (on two feet). I have therefore kept the literal sense.

[13] Literally, "the winds of the many movements of the heart."

[14] Lk. 1, 38 (Vulg.). Catherine cites the first sentence in Latin.

So in times of difficulty; when we are harassed or hurt, slandered or vilified by our neighbors; when we are troubled in mind or deprived of spiritual or temporal consolation by Creator or creature (by our Creator in kindness, when he draws our spiritual feelings back into himself (though it seems from the severity of our pain and struggles that he is no longer within us); and by other people when it seems from our conversation and recreation with them that we love them more than they love us)—in all these things, I tell you, those who have been made perfect in humility[15] say, "My Lord, here I am, your maidservant! Let it be done in me according to your will, and not according to what my emotions want."[16] In this way they give off the perfume of patience—to the Creator and to other people and to themselves. They enjoy spiritual peace and calm. In the midst of war they have found peace because they have rid themselves of selfish willfulness grounded in pride.

They have conceived divine grace within their soul. Within their breast they carry Christ crucified. They find their joy in the wounds of Christ crucified. They want to know nothing but Christ crucified.[17] Their bed is the cross of Christ crucified. There they immerse their will and become humble and obedient, since there is no obedience without humility, and there is no humility without charity.

This is what they discover in the Word, since it was in humility and in obedience to his Father that he ran to the shameful death of the cross, nailing and bonding himself there with the nail and bond of charity. He suffered with such patience that no cry of complaint was heard from him.[18] For the nails could never have been enough to hold the God-man nailed and fixed to the cross if love had not held him there. This, I tell you, is what these souls experience. This is why they do not want to find joy except with Christ crucified. For if it were possible to acquire virtue and avoid hell and have eternal life with consolation both spiritual and temporal in this world, and without suffering, they would not want it so. They would rather have eternal life by suffering even to the point of death than to have it in this other way, if only they can be like Christ crucified and be clothed in his humiliation and pain. They have discovered the table of the spotless Lamb!

Oh glorious virtue! Who would not be willing to surrender to death a thousand times over and suffer every sort of pain to acquire you? You are a queen, in possession of the whole world! You live in everlasting life. Even

---

[15] The text is ambiguous: "in humility" may modify either "made perfect" or "say."

[16] It. *secondo quello che voglio io sensitivamente.*

[17] Cf. 1 Cor. 2, 2.

[18] Cf. Is. 53, 7.

while those who are clothed in you are still mortal, you allow them, by the power of love, to make their home with those who are immortal.

As for you, dearest daughter, since this virtue is so excellent, so pleasing to God and so useful for us and for the salvation of our neighbors, rouse yourself from your foolish apathetic sleep! Throw off your heart's weakness and fragility so that it won't feel any pain or impatience on account of anything God may permit us, so that we won't fall into either the ordinary sort of impatience I've described or the special sort. Rather let us serve our Savior courageously, with generous heart and true perfect patience. Otherwise we will by the first sort of impatience lose grace, or by the second sort we will get in the way of perfection and you wouldn't reach what God has called you to.[19]

It does seem that God is calling you to great perfection. I see this from the fact that he is taking away from you every tie that could hold you back. For, according to what I hear, it seems he has called to himself your daughter, your final outward tie.[20] Though I have a holy compassion for you, I am content in God's having set you free and relieved her of her burden. Now I want you to cut off your selfish will completely and be attached to nothing but Christ crucified. In this way you will fulfill his will and my desire. And this is why I said that I long to see you grounded in true holy patience. I know no other way you can fulfill [God's will], since without patience we cannot return to our dear goal.[21]

I'll say no more. Keep living in God's holy and tender love.

Gentle Jesus! Jesus love!

---

[19] Catherine switches abruptly from first person plural to second, this time apparently deliberately.

[20] Agnesa's son Antonio and Deo di Veri Malavolti had been beheaded in 1372 for the rape of a young girl, though it was said that the girl had consented (Orlando Malavolti's *Historia de' fatti e guerre de' Sanesi*, Venice, 1599, cited by Burlamacchi in his notes to the letter in Gigli, *Opere*, II).

[21] The use of "return" is intentional. Cf. Prayer 4 (p. 42), in which Catherine addresses St. Paul: "You, wonderful Paul, . . . truly knew where you had come from and where you were going—and not only where you were going but even the road you were traveling, for you had come to know your origin and your goal."

LETTER T79/G149[1]
To the abbess and nuns of San Pietro in Monticelli a Lignaia in Florence
October 1377 or shortly thereafter

The Benedictine monastery of San Pietro in Monticelli was located on a hill just outside the San Frediano gate of Florence.[2] Since it was very near the Olivetan monastery, Catherine may have become acquainted with the nuns there during one of her stays in the city. After Catherine's death in 1380, her disciple and scribe Barduccio Canigiani (whom Catherine seems not to have met before 1378) would write a letter to Suor Caterina Petriboni of that monastery, describing in great detail Catherine's last days and her passing.[3] Burlamacchi writes, "There is preserved in the monastery a crucifix, left there by the saint, which is highly venerated. This crucifix is referred to in an addition to the *Life*."[4]

There are no clues in the content of the letter to place it chronologically. The linguistic evidence, however, strongly supports placing it in the last months of Catherine's stay in the Val d'Orcia, and more precisely, near Let. T23, T217, and T95, with which it has close parallels.[5]

§

In the name of Jesus Christ crucified and of gentle Mary.

Dearest daughters in Christ gentle Jesus,

I Caterina, servant and slave of the servants of Jesus Christ, am writing to you in his precious blood. I long to see you as true servants and brides of

---

[1] MSS: Mo-*c*, B, P2, R1, P5, F2, F1, P3, P4, S4; translation based on Mo-*c*, with reference to R1. Variants from Tommasèo text noted. (The same lacuna—unmarked as such—occurs in Mo, R1, and the Tommasèo text. Cf. n. 6.)

[2] Burlamacchi's note to the letter in Gigli, *Opere*, I, p. 845.

[3] That letter, often referred to as the *Transito*, is included in a collection in the *Biblioteca comunale* of Siena, MS.T.II, 7. It was first printed in Aldo Manuzio's edition of the *Epistolario* in 1500. It can be found in English as an appendix to Algar Thorold's translation of *The Dialogue* (all editions), and in Italian in *Lettere*, ed. Tommasèo/Misciattelli, vol. VI, pp. 148-153.

[4] In Gigli, *Opere*, I, p. 846.

[5] All five letters sharing eighteen or more of this one's seventy-four analyzed patterns are from October 1377 or later. A number of significant clusters within individual patterns which begin and/or end between October and December 1377 support the letter's placement there: AGNELCON, ALTEZZA, AMORSPIR, CONVERSC, CUORANIM, CUORDOPP, CUORLIBE, NEGLINO, NUDITA, OPERCONG, ORDINVIT, SAZAFFAM, SPOSCONS. Neither Fawtier (II, p. 227) nor Dupré Theseider (unpublished notes) dates this letter.

Christ crucified, following so closely in his footsteps that you would sooner die than violate his dear commandments and counsels, which you have promised to follow.

Oh how sweet and pleasant it is for a bride consecrated to Christ to follow the way and teaching of her Bridegroom![a] And what is his way and teaching? Nothing but love! For it is love that makes every other virtue virtuous. His teaching is not pride or disobedience or selfish love; it is not worldly wealth or honor or prestige; nor is it physical pleasure or enjoyment. It is not love's way to love our neighbors for our own sake. . . .[6]

[Christ] loved us and gave his life for us with such blazing love and, in fact, in profound and genuine humility.[7] Now has anyone ever seen greater humility than this? God humbles himself before humankind! Supreme exaltedness stoops as low as our humanity! He is obedient even to dying the shameful death of the cross. He is patient and so meek that not a cry of complaint is heard from him.[8] He who was supreme eternal wealth chose voluntary poverty—so much so that dear Mary had no blanket to wrap him in, and in the end, dying naked on the cross, he had no place to rest his head.[9] This gentle loving Word was saturated with pain and robed in humiliation. He delighted in insult, mockery, and abuse. He satisfies with such warm and affectionate love all who are hungry; yet he himself endures hunger and thirst. He is our dear God who has no need of us; yet he did not relax his efforts to save us. No, he persevered, and neither our foolish ingratitude nor the Jews' shouting that he should come down from the cross could keep him from accomplishing our salvation.

This, then, is his teaching and his way.[10] And we miserable sin-filled wretches do just the opposite. We are not true spouses but adulteresses, since we look for enjoyment, delight, pleasure, and sensual love—a selfish love that is the source of dissension and disobedience. Our cell becomes our enemy, while we take a fancy to associating with people of the world and with those who live in a worldly way. We want to have plenty and to lack for no temporal provision, and if we don't always have plenty, we

---

[6] The original is obviously missing a substantial piece here. What is missing certainly followed Catherine's usual logic of loving not for our own sake but for God, as is the case in similar passages. The argument then proceeds to the contrast with Christ, who loved us so much as to give his life.

[7] It. *e anco è profonda e vera humiltà*. Again, the text may be a bit mutilated. The translation is therefore somewhat conjectural, based on the context.

[8] Cf. Is. 53, 7.

[9] Mt. 8, 20 (Lk. 9, 58). But cf. also *Dial.* 151, p. 320: "He was so poor on the wood of the cross that neither the earth nor the wood could give him a place to lay his head. He had nowhere to rest it except on his own shoulder."

[10] Literally, "the teaching and the way he has made."

think we are destitute. We distance ourselves from our Creator and forsake our mother, prayer.[11] We even weary sometimes of saying the prayers to which we are obligated. For to those who don't love, every least exertion seems too much to bear, and what is possible seems quite infeasible. The reason for all of this is selfish love, which is both born from pride and in turn gives birth to pride, grounded in a great deal of ingratitude and foolish indifference to good holy deeds.[12]

I don't want this to happen to you, dearest daughters! No, follow as true brides in the footsteps of your Bridegroom, for there is no other way you can observe the poverty,[13] obedience, and continence you have promised and vowed. You know very well that in your profession you gave your freedom of choice to your eternal Bridegroom as a dowry, since you made those promises[b] with a free heart. These are three pillars that hold up the city of our soul and keep it from falling into ruins. Without them, it collapses at once.

So a bride should be poor voluntarily, for love of Christ crucified who has taught her the way. Poverty is the glory and wealth of religious, and it is a great contradiction when they are found to have anything to give away. Do you realize what great evil comes of this? For if you disregard poverty, you will disregard everything else as well. You are supposed to be living in unity with your sisters, living a common life so that the least have as much as the great and the great as much as the least. But if you set your heart on possessions and don't live in unity with your sisters, you will eventually fall into incontinence—if not actually, then in spirit. And you will fall into disobedience, breaking your rule and resisting correction by your superior. You will be going back on what you promised. And that leads to associating with others who live undisciplined lives, whether they be religious or seculars, women or men. Why? Because your relationships are no longer grounded in God but are governed only by whatever gifts or enjoyment or pleasure they may yield. And the love and friendship will last only as long as the gifts and the enjoyment.[14]

---

[11] Cf. Let. T26 to her niece, Suor Eugenia (1379): "Truly this prayer is a mother who conceives the virtues in charity for God and brings them to birth in charity for one's neighbors."

[12] This relationship of pride and selfish love giving birth to each other is expressed only here, in Let. T2 to Andrea dei Vitroni (1378). In all other cases it is pride that is born from selfish love.

[13] It is unusual for Catherine to refer to the religious vow simply as "poverty," rather than as "voluntary poverty," but she make the voluntariness explicit in the very next paragraph.

[14] Cf. *Dial.* 125, p. 243, where it is said of those who do not observe poverty and common life: "For such as these it is impossible to keep the third vow, that of continence, for a full belly does not make for a chaste spirit. Indeed, they become inordinately excited and

This is why I say that if you don't have any possessions, if you have nothing to give away, you don't have to worry about any unseemly relationships! And without such relationships there is nothing to distract your mind or to make you fall into impurity, either physically or spiritually. Instead you seek and want to keep company with Christ crucified and with his dearest servants, who love for Christ's sake and out of love for virtue rather than for their own selfish advantage. You conceive a seemingly insatiable desire and hunger for virtue. You see that prayer is a mother and a fountain from which you can drink the life of grace and the treasure of virtue,[15] and so you cut yourself off from human companionship and flee to the refuge of your cell to look for your Bridegroom, and the two of you embrace on the wood of the most holy cross. There you bathe in tears and sweat, and become drunk on the blood of the Lamb who is consumed with love.[16] You pasture on sighs of sweet burning desire.

Such is [the picture of] the sincere and true bride who really[17] follows her Bridegroom. As I've said, no suffering kept the blessed Christ from accomplishing our salvation. So no suffering or difficulty, no hunger or thirst or deprivation, keeps or should keep his bride from working continually for God's honor. Let her respond to her body's selfish hankering to be pampered by saying, "Be comforted, my soul, for your deprivation here below is moving you on toward eternal life." And let nothing keep her from doing good with holy desire—whether it be diabolical temptation or carnal weakness or those perverse counselors of the devil who are worse than Jews in their saying over and over, "Come down from the cross of penance and disciplined living."[18] Nor should her neighbors' ingratitude

---

lustful, and so go from evil to evil. And much evil comes on them because of their possessions, because if they had nothing to spend they would not live so sumptuously and would not have these capricious affairs. For romance does not last long when one has nothing to give, nor do those friendships that are built not on perfect love but on love of presents or on any delight or pleasure one might find in the other." The Dominican tradition from the beginning made the vow of obedience central, reasoning that if one was obedient to the rule one would necessarily be chaste and poor. In fact, Dominicans have always explicitly pronounced only the vow of obedience at their profession. Yet Catherine consistently puts voluntary poverty in this privileged position.

[15] This is the only place in which Catherine refers to prayer as a fountain. Yet the image is closely related to her other fountain imagery, as well as to all of her imagery of water and blood.

[16] It. *consumato ed innamorato agnello.*

[17] The original *reale* ("sincere") and *realmente* ("really") could also be translated as "royal" and "royally," but since there is no other royal imagery in this letter, I have opted for a broader meaning.

[18] The reference, of course, is to Mt. 27, 40, where those who challenge Christ to come down from the cross if he is God's Son are simply referred to as "people going by." But "worse than Jews" (without an article) clearly reflects (as do all of Catherine's references to "the Jews") the common medieval Christian attitude which considered Jews to be enemies

or lack of recognition or appreciation keep her from serving them and seeking their salvation. If it did, it would seem that she was looking for some reward from them rather than from God, and she should prefer death to that!

Patiently put up with one another's faults, dearest daughters, and lovingly share the burden of one another's shortcomings. In this way you will be joined and made one in the bond of charity, a bond so strong that neither the devil nor anyone else will be able to divide you unless you yourselves so choose. Be obedient even to the point of death. Then you will be true spouses, and when the Bridegroom calls you to account in your last moment, at death, you will have your lamp filled, not empty. You will be like the wise virgins and not like the foolish ones.[19]

Your heart should indeed be a lamp filled with oil. It should carry the light of knowledge of yourself and of God's goodness within you, which is the fire and light of charity, set burning and fed by the oil of sincere and deep humility.[20] For if you don't have the light of self-knowledge, you can't humble yourself, since with pride one never humbles oneself. Once the lamp is readied, you must hold it in your hand with your sight set truly on God.[21] I mean the hand of holy fear that gives direction to our desire and inclinations. I'm talking not about slavish fear, but about holy fear that would not for anything offend God's supreme eternal goodness. Every person has this lamp because the human heart *is* a lamp. And if the hand of holy fear holds the lamp upright and ready, all will go well.

But people who hold it in the hand of slavish fear turn it upside down by serving and loving selfishly and for their own advantage rather than for love of God. They put out the light and spill the oil, since their lamp has no light of charity, no oil of true humility. These are the people of whom our Savior said, "I do not know you; I do not know who you are."[22]

So I want you to be strong and wise. Hold on to your heart, and see

---

of God and of Christ. In her single letter to a Jew (Let. T15 to the Jew Consiglio, vol. I), while she addresses him as "my dear and very loved brother," her whole purpose is to persuade him to "leave hardness behind and come out of the darkness of unbelief."

[19] Cf. Mt. 25, 1–13.

[20] Elsewhere it is charity or desire that actually sets afire, but here, uniquely, the oil of humility is the agent that makes it possible, as it were, for the fire to catch. Also, while Catherine, again uniquely here, seems actually to identify the light of knowledge with the light of charity, what follows seems to bear out rather the very close relationship between the two, in which knowledge of God's charity leads to true self-knowledge and true self-knowledge leads to love. Cf. Let. T211/DT70 to Raimondo da Capua (in this volume): "This humility comes from self-knowledge, and this charity from knowledge of God's goodness. And there the soul becomes drunk and consumed with love."

[21] It. *con una santa e vera intentione in Dio.*

[22] Mt. 25, 12.

that it is a lamp held upright. And just as a lamp is narrow at the bottom and broad at the top, so must your heart be with its inclinations.[23] It should be narrow so far as the world and all its pleasure and delight and vanity and contentment are concerned. But at the top it should be broad, with heart, soul, and strength entirely set on and dwelling in Christ crucified.

This is how you will be daughters and brides and servants. You will run along the way and follow the teaching of Christ crucified.[c] Be robed in suffering and humiliation for his sake. Live in unity, and love one another.

And you, my lady abbess, be a mother and a shepherd ready to lay down your life for your daughters if necessary.[24] Dissuade them from breaches of common life and from socializing. These things are death to the soul and destructive of perfection. Be a mirror of virtue in your own relationships, so that you may admonish more by virtue than by words.

All of you,[25] bathe in the blood of Christ crucified. Keep living in God's holy and tender love.

Gentle Jesus! Jesus love!

Textual Notes

a. Tommasèo: *the Holy Spirit / her Bridegroom.*

b. Tommasèo: *that profession* (*professione*) / *those promises* (*promessione*).

c. Tommasèo: [*This is how. . . . Christ crucified.*]

---

[23] It. *il cuore e l'affetto.*

[24] Jn. 10, 11: "I am the good shepherd. The good shepherd lays down his life for the sheep."

[25] "All of you" is not explicitly in the text but is implied in the shift from second person singular (the abbess) to plural.

LETTER T23/G356[1]
To Nanna, daughter of her brother Benincasa, in Florence
October 1377 or shortly thereafter

Nanna (short for Giovanna) was the daughter of Catherine's eldest brother Benincasa. The date of her birth is not documented, but if Benincasa was already old enough in 1346 to be administering the dyeshop,[2] he could easily have had a daughter near Catherine's age. The rubric in R1, R2, and Nd calls her simply "a virgin," so she was probably not a nun.

There is nothing in the content of the letter to date it. The linguistic evidence, however, points most strongly to the Rocca d'Orcia period. And within that period I would place the letter most probably near the much longer Let. T79 to the abbess and nuns at San Pietro in Monticelli (also in Florence), because of its close and unique parallels with that letter.[3] This would put it in October 1377 or shortly thereafter.

§

In the name of Jesus Christ crucified and of gentle Mary.

Dearest daughter in Christ gentle Jesus,

I Caterina, servant and slave of the servants of Jesus Christ, am writing to you in his precious blood. I long to see you a true spouse of Christ crucified, avoiding whatever might get in the way of your possessing this gentle glorious Bridegroom. But you cannot do this unless you are one of those wise virgins consecrated to Christ who had their lamps filled with oil and the light within them.[4] So you see, if you want to be a spouse of Christ, you must have a lamp, oil, and light.

The lamp symbolizes our heart. Our heart ought to be shaped like a lamp. You can see that a lamp is wide on top and narrow lower down. This is how our heart is shaped as well, to symbolize that we ought always to keep it wide on top by means of holy thoughts and images and continual prayer. We should always hold before our memory God's blessings,

---

[1] MSS: B, P2, R1, P5, F2, F1, P3, R2, Nd; translation based on R1. No relevant variants.

[2] This is known from a document of that year (concerning property), published in Laurent, *Fontes*, I, *Documenti*, pp. 13–19.

[3] The six letters which share nine or more of this one's thirty-five analyzed patterns are widely scattered from October 1377 through 1379. Significant clusters within individual patterns which lend support to placement in or near October 1377 are ADULTER, AMAINEST, LAMPANA, PENAMENT, RICCGRAZ, and VERGSAV. Neither Fawtier (II, p. 309) nor Dupré Theseider (unpublished notes) dates this letter.

[4] Cf. Mt. 25, 1–13, the parable of the ten virgins.

most especially the blessing of the blood by which we were redeemed. For, my daughter, the blessed Christ ransomed us not with gold or silver or pearls or any other precious thing, but with his precious blood.[5] So we should never forget such a blessing but hold it always before our mind's eye with sweet holy thankfulness, seeing that God loves us so unspeakably much that he didn't consider it too much to surrender his only-begotten Son to the shameful death of the cross in order to give us the life of grace.

I said that a lamp is narrow lower down, and so should our heart be.[6] The meaning of this is that our heart ought to be narrow where these earthly things are concerned by not desiring or loving them inordinately. We should not hanker after more than God chooses to give us, but should always be thanking him, seeing how tenderly he provides for us so that we never want for anything.

This is how our heart will truly be a lamp. But reflect, my daughter, that this is not sufficient. There must also be oil inside. The oil symbolizes that dear little virtue, profound humility. For the spouse of Christ must be patient, meek, and humble, and she will be as humble as she is patient, and as patient as she is humble.[7] But we cannot attain this virtue of humility except through true self-knowledge. I mean we must know our own poverty and weakness, that of ourselves we are incapable of a single virtuous act or of freeing ourselves from any pain or struggle. For if we are physically ill or are suffering or struggling spiritually, we cannot free ourselves of it or get rid of it. If we could, we certainly would. So it is indeed true that of ourselves we are nothing, nothing but shame, poverty, filth, weakness, and sins. This ought to make us always lowly and humble.

But it would not be good to dwell exclusively in this knowledge of ourselves, because we would become discouraged and weary, and from discouragement we would end up in despair. Now the devil wants nothing more than to lead us to discouragement, so that he can eventually bring us to despair. So we ought to dwell in knowledge of God's goodness within us, realizing that he has created us in his own image and likeness and created us anew to grace in the blood of his only-begotten Son, the gentle Word incarnate, and that God's goodness is continually at work in us.[8]

---

[5] 1 Pt. 1, 18.

[6] This image of the lamp, large at the top but narrow at the bottom, occurs also in Let. T79 and T112 in this volume, and in T360 in 1379, but in none of these letters is it developed with the detail found here.

[7] This is the only instance in which Catherine places patience in proportion with humility. In several other places (Let. T75 and T95 in this volume; T35 [late 1377 or early 1378]; T84 [1379]; *Dial.* 154 and 159) it is obedience and humility which are in direct proportion with each other.

[8] Cf. *Dial.* 66, p. 124: "Now I do not want her to think about her sins individually, lest her mind be contaminated by the memory of specific ugly sins. I mean that I do not want

But note, on the other hand, that it wouldn't be good to dwell exclusively in this knowledge of God, because we would become proud and presumptuous. So the one knowledge should always be combined with the other.[9] We must dwell in the holy knowledge of God's goodness and in the knowledge of ourselves. Then we will be humble, patient, and meek, and this is how we will have oil in our lamp.

Next there must be light, or the rest is not enough. And this light has to be the light of most holy faith. But the saints say that faith without deeds is dead, that it is neither alive nor holy but dead.[10] So we have to practice living virtuously all the time. We have to leave behind our childish ways, our vanities, and live no longer as worldly youngsters.[11] No, we must live as faithful spouses consecrated to Christ crucified, and in this way we will have lamp and oil and light.

But the gospel says there were five of these wise virgins.[12] So I'm telling you that each of us must be five. Otherwise we cannot enter the wedding feast of eternal life. By "five" is meant that we must so subjugate and discipline our five bodily senses that we will never sin with them by using them (or any one of them) for immoderate pleasure or enjoyment. This is how we shall be five, by having subjugated our five bodily senses.

Reflect, though, that this gentle Bridegroom, Christ, is more jealous of his brides than I can tell you! So if he should notice that you love someone else more than you love him, he will be irritated with you. And unless you change your ways, the door will not be opened for you to the place where Christ the spotless Lamb celebrates his marriage to all his faithful spouses. No, you will be thrown out[13] as were those five foolish virgins who prided themselves (and emptily!) only on their physical integrity and

---

her to, nor should she, think about her sins either in general or specifically without calling to mind the blood and the greatness of my mercy. Otherwise she will only be confounded. For if self-knowledge and the thought of sin are not seasoned with remembrance of the blood and hope for mercy, the result is bound to be confusion. And along with this comes the devil, who under the guise of contrition and hatred for sin and sorrow for her guilt leads her to eternal damnation. Because of this—though not this alone—she would end in despair if she did not reach out for the arm of my mercy."

[9] In Let. T49 to Alessa dei Saracini and in *Dial.* 66, 73, and 86, she says that the two sorts of knowledge must season each other, as condiments.

[10] Cf. Jas. 2, 17.

[11] Cf. 1 Cor. 13, 11 (Vulg.): "When I was a child I spoke like a child, I thought like a child, I reasoned like a child. But when I became an adult, I put childish ways behind me."

[12] Nowhere else does she develop this numerical significance of the "five virgins."And other than here, only in Let. T79 to the abbess and nuns of Monticelli and Let. T360 to Peronella di Masello Pepe does she even refer to the parable of the wise and foolish virgins.

[13] This is not the only instance in which Catherine mixes elements of the parable of the ten virgins with that of the wedding banquet in Mt. 22, 1–14, where the man who is not properly dressed for the feast is thrown out.

virginity and lost their spiritual virginity by the adulteration of their five senses. They did not carry along the oil of humility, and so their lamps went out. They were told, "Go and buy yourselves some oil." In this instance the oil symbolizes human flattery and praise, because this sort of oil is what all flatterers and those who give worldly praise are peddling. It is as if they were told, "You didn't want to use your virginity and your good deeds to buy eternal life but wanted instead to buy human praise. You did what you did to get human praise, so now go and buy yourself praise, for you will not come in here!"

So, my daughter, beware of human praise! Don't look for praise for anything you do, because then the door of eternal life will not be opened for you.

It is because I believe this is the best way that I said that I long to see you a faithful spouse of Christ crucified. So I beg you and I command you to do your best to be just this.

I have no more to say to you. Keep living in God's holy and tender love.

Gentle Jesus! Jesus love!

LETTER T217/G156[1]

To the superior and sisters of the Monastery of Santa Maria delle Vergini in Monteluce and To the prioress and sisters of the Monastery of San Giorgio in Perugia October 1377 or shortly thereafter

Burlamacchi observes that the Monastery of Santa Maria delle Vergini in Monteluce in Perugia was Franciscan, and that the superior would therefore have been called *ministra* (and later, *badessa*), not *priora* as the rubric in the manuscripts has it. As for the second monastery to which this letter is addressed, Burlamacchi says that in Catherine's day the only monastery called San Giorgio, a Dominican house, was about a mile outside the city. It was later named San Tommaso Apostolo, for the church which had originally stood there. The circumstances of Catherine's acquaintance with these monasteries are not recorded in any early source.[2]

There is nothing in the content of the letter to date it. The linguistic evidence, however, strongly supports placing it in October 1377 or a bit later.[3]

§

In the name of Jesus Christ crucified and of gentle Mary.

Dearest mother and daughter in Christ gentle Jesus,

I Caterina, servant and slave of the servants of Jesus Christ, am writing to you in his precious blood. I long to see you as brides who are joined and made one in the bond of true and blazing charity.[4] This is the bond that

---

[1] MSS: Mo-*a*, M, S5, S6, Ro, P4, S4, Bo1; translation based on Mo-*a*. No relevant variants.

[2] Burlamacchi, notes to the letter in Gigli, *Opere*, I, pp. 879–880.

[3] Of the six letters which share nineteen or more of this one's eighty analyzed patterns, four fall between October 1377 and early 1378. The most convincing evidence, however, lies in the number of significant clusters within individual patterns which begin and/or end in or very close to October 1377: ADULTER, CAPOSPIN, CAPOVOL, CONGREGA, CONVERSC, DIOINUOM, DONACONV, MADORAZ, MONDCONT, MORTIMMO, OBEDPENT, SEGNAMOR, SOLITUD, SPOSCONS, SUPERBOB. Because the letter has a great deal in common with Let. T95 (to a group of young men attached to Giovanni dalle Celle), in spite of the fact that the addressees are in quite different circumstances, I would place the two near each other chronologically. Both Fawtier (II, p. 227) and Dupré Theseider (unpublished notes) decline to date the letter.

[4] She is speaking, as the rest of the letter will make clear, not directly of union with Christ the Bridegroom, but of that union with each other in charity which will demonstrate that they are in fact united with Christ.

held the God-man nailed fast to the wood of the cross.[5] It is the bond that united God with humankind and humankind with God, the bond that unites us with our Creator and makes us lovers of true solid virtue.

What is this bond? It is a love that cuts and separates even as it bonds. For while it binds and joins us to God, it also cuts us off and separates us from sin and from that selfish sensual love which is the source of separations and of all evil. It takes away the dead water and gives us the living water of grace. It separates us from the darkness and gives us the light that lets us see and experience the truth.

Oh wonderful fire of love! You fill us with every sweetness and loveliness.

No bitterness or pain can invade those whose spirits burn with so sweet and glorious a fire! Charity never judges wrongly. It judges not by human standards but by God's,[6] because it sees and knows that God wants nothing other than that we be made holy.[7] Now God wants only our good, and everything comes from God, including trial and temptation and every other sort of suffering and trouble and torment. And since God permits all of these things for our good, nothing should cause us pain. (The only exception is sin, which is the opposite of being and therefore does not exist in God. Sin, therefore, is not deserving of love. Sin we should indeed hate, and sooner die than offend our Creator.)

Oh gentleness of love! How can your bride's heart keep from loving you when she reflects that you are a Spouse who is life? You, God eternal, have created us in your own image and likeness, for love alone. When we had lost grace because of our wretched sin, you gave us the Word, your only-begotten Son, and your Son gave his life for us. He punished our wickedness in his own body, paying the debt he had never contracted. Oimé! Oimé! how wretched we are! We are the thieves, and he is executed for us![8]

Shame, shame on the foolish, hard, blind bride who does not love in the face of such love on God's part! This lovely gentle bond is so delightful!

How do we know whether we are loving? If we love God, we follow rationally in the footsteps of the Word, God's only-begotten Son. If we do

---

[5] Cf. Cavalca, *Specchio di croce*, p. 41: "No bond of iron could have held Christ nailed or bound—only charity, the bond of perfection."

[6] Cf. Mt. 16, 23; Rom. 12, 2. Catherine seems to be drawing on the sense of both passages here and elsewhere when she speaks of discerning God's will, often in contrast with judging by human standards, for example, in *Dial.* 100, pp. 187–192, where she dedicates an entire chapter to the theme.

[7] 1 Thes. 4, 3.

[8] Cf. Cavalca, *Specchio di croce*, p. 61: "Saint Bernard, feeling sorry for Christ, said: 'Oh most loving young Man! What have you done in suffering such cruel pain and death? I am the reason for your grief! I am the thief, and you have been executed on the cross! I am the debtor, and you have suffered the penalty and paid the debt for my sins!' "

not love God, we follow the devil and our own selfish sensuality, and we conform to the habits of the world, which are contrary to God. So we are experiencing death without even being aware of it. We lie there in the dark because we don't have the light. We live in continual pain, in disharmony with our neighbors, in constant divisiveness, because we are not bonded in charity and are [in fact] in the devils' hands. We have left our eternal Bridegroom and are adulteresses rather than brides of Christ crucified. For a wife is called an adulteress only if she deserts the love of her husband to love and unite herself illicitly with someone else.

It is mercenary and really dangerous not to love when we see that we are loved.[9] Love, then, love each other! This is how it will be known whether or not you are brides and daughters of Christ. There is no other way of knowing except by love grounded in God, by the love we have for our neighbors.[10]

And the means we must use to get to our goal is following in the footsteps of Christ crucified. Our means is not the Father but the Son; for the Father is not subject to suffering, while the Son is.[11] We must, then, follow the way of the most holy cross, enduring shame, insult, and abuse. We must make light of the world and all its prestige and pleasure. We must suffer hunger and thirst in voluntary poverty. We must be uncompromising in our obedience. We must persevere. We must be pure in mind and body. Our converse must be with persons who reverence God in truth. We must keep to the solitude of our cell and avoid the parlor as if it were poison, because socializing does not become the brides of Christ, whether it be with devout people or with the worldly. And we should be talking with God's true servants, not with the hooded friars.[12]

---

[9] This is related to the stages of love which Catherine addresses in *Dial.* 56 and 60: "The first of these stages is imperfect, the second more perfect, and the third most perfect. The first is a mercenary, the second my faithful servant, and the third my child who loves me with no regard for selfish interests." (p. 111) In the fuller development that follows, there is a stage of friendship after that of faithful servanthood: "This is how it is with dear friends. Their loving affection makes them two bodies with one soul, because love transforms one into what one loves." (pp. 115–116)

[10] Cf. Jn. 13, 35 (Vulg.): "This is how all will know you are my disciples, if you love one another."

[11] Jn. 14, 6. Cf. Let. T271 to Alessa dei Saraceni (1378): "But watch out, dearest daughter, lest you deceive yourself. It would be a delusion for you to want to eat [this food, souls] at the eternal Father's table while disdaining to eat it at the table of the Son. And at what table should we eat it? At the table of the most holy cross, since this food cannot be had without suffering, and it is only the Son, not the Father, who is subject to suffering. And because we would never be able to cross this stormy sea without suffering, this gentle loving Word who endured suffering made himself our way and our rule, cementing the road with his own blood."

[12] Burlamacchi sees this (It. *frati incappucciati*) as a reference to the *Fraticelli*, a group that had split off from the Franciscans in 1294 in pursuit of a more radical poverty. They

It is not right that the members [of a body] with a thorn-crowned head should be pampered, as do those fools who distance themselves from Christ their head and are concerned about nothing but physical pleasure and enjoyment. Most especially should we, who have been taken out of the world and put in the garden of holy religion as brides consecrated to Christ, be fragrant flowers. And truly, if you are true to what you have promised and give forth a really great fragrance, you will share in God's goodness, living in grace. And you will enjoy the eternal vision of God. If you were not to [keep your promises], you would stink of great dishonor; in this life you would experience the earnest of hell, and in the end, the vision of the devils.

In order to follow Christ, you left secular life and renounced the world and its riches, promising true poverty. You renounced your own will, promising true obedience. And you left behind the ordinary way of life, choosing not to be worldly brides, in order to preserve true continence and virginity. This last is a perfume that delights God and the angels, who are pleased to dwell within the spirit of those who live in the fragrance of purity. You are gathered together not to live in divisiveness or in hatred or spite or mutual animosity, but to be joined and made one in the bond of charity. There is no other way you can please God, no other way any virtue can be perfect in you.

What shame and spiritual chagrin must those experience who have made promises and then have not kept them but have done just the opposite![13] These people are not following Christ! They are not following the way of the cross but choose to go the way of sin. This is not the way! No, we must follow the humble Christ, the spotless Lamb, the poor Lamb. So great was his poverty that he had no place to rest his head.[14] He was most pure and the poison of sin was not in him. He was obedient to his Father even to dying in shame on the cross for our salvation. The only reason the saints and our glorious father Saint Dominic established their orders on these three pillars—poverty, obedience, and continence—was to make it possible to be conformed more closely to Christ and to follow his teaching and his counsels.[15] From these three issue all the virtues, and from their opposites issue all the vices.

In poverty, forsake worldly pride and associations and those perverse friendships which are bought only with gifts. If you have nothing to give,

---

were eventually excommunicated. Their mention here may be an indication that the letter was written initially to the Franciscan monastery, and then sent in copy to the Dominicans.

[13] Mo makes this a question.

[14] Mt. 8, 20 (Lk. 9, 58).

[15] One may presume that the letter to the Franciscans had Francis here. It is unusual for Catherine to refer to religious poverty simply as "poverty" and not as "voluntary poverty."

you will find friendship only among God's true servants, who love the gift of your soul.

Give up vanity of heart and levity of spirit and come to live in your cell, where you will experience that prayer is your mother who will preserve and strengthen you in virtue.[16] Come to perfect purity. Keep your vow of continence by abstaining not only from one sin but from all sin.[17] Trample your selfish sensuality underfoot by abstaining from selfish sensual pleasures and by fasting and watching and praying in order to subjugate your body. In this way you will become humble and patient and charitable. You will bear with and share the burden of your neighbors' shortcomings. You will be united with God in love and with your neighbors in God. You will be tolerant of any physical pain or inconvenience your neighbors may cause you, if only you can win your own soul.[18]

Once you have so gently rooted out pride (in the way I've described), you will experience how fragrant holy obedience is. We are as obedient as we are humble, and as humble as we are obedient. So it follows that if we are not proud, we are humble, and if we are humble, we are truly obedient. And there you have the third pillar that holds up the city of your soul—for if you are truly obedient you will be faithful to the order and its customs. If you are obedient you will not lift up your head (your selfish will) against your superior. You won't argue with her but will obey at her first word, bowing your head at once to the yoke. You won't say, "Why are you telling me to do this rather than that?" No, you will think only of how you can be prompt in your obedience.

Oh lovely obedience! You are never in pain. You make us live and run as if we were dead—because you kill our selfish will, and the more dead it is, the faster we run. Why? When our spirit is dead to our perverse sensual will's selfish love, we finish our course more light-footedly and are united with our eternal Bridegroom in single-minded love.[19] Our spirit is so

---

[16] Catherine often refers to prayer as a mother nursing the virtues as children at her breast, but only in Let. T150 to Frate Francesco Tebaldi (1378 or 1379) does she integrate with that the images of fire and blood, thus bringing it into the total mystery of the blood of Christ and all of her imagery for that mystery, describing prayer as "a mother clothed in fire, inebriated with blood, and nursing the virtues as children at her breast."

[17] It is clear from many of Catherine's observations that she does not fall into the common trap of regarding sins of unchastity as the worst of sins.

[18] Cf. Mk. 8, 36 (Vulg.): "What profit does a person have who gains the whole world and loses his or her own soul?" This rather disconnected sequence may be related to a passage from Let. T182 to Suor Bartolomea della Seta (in this volume): "Make your shoulders like those of a porter, and don't refuse any load if you really want to keep earning right up to the end!"

[19] It. *per affetto d'amore.*

wonderfully uplifted that even in this mortal life we begin to taste the fragrance and fruits of the immortals.

So be obedient! Be obedient even to the point of death! Love, love each other! Be joined in the bond of charity, for there is no other way we can reach our goal or achieve the purpose for which we were created. And this is why I said that I long to see you as brides who are joined and made one in the bond of true and blazing charity.

I'll say no more. Keep living in God's holy and tender love.

Gentle Jesus! Jesus love!

Letter T95/G308[1]

To certain Florentine youths,
adopted sons of Don Giovanni dalle Celle
October 1377 or shortly thereafter

Catherine was still at Rocca d'Orcia when Giovanni dalle Celle, the hermit of Vallombrosa near Florence, wrote to his friend Giovanni (called Conte):

> You know that three of these boys of mine went to Catherine at the Salimbeni fortress. She received them graciously and spoke with them. But Maestro Giovanni [Tantucci], who is with her, didn't want to speak with them. In fact, he hid, and said, 'Unless they leave, I will!' I was really astounded at his coldness and ignorance, because he could have spoken with them. ... Again, even if he considered them excommunicated, he could have spoken with them and admonished them in regard to their salvation. And if he hadn't talked about anything else, he would not have sinned.[2] And if you say, 'He did this because he hates the Florentines so,' anyone who hates his brother is a murderer, according to the apostle. ... Here you have three earthly angels, innocent, full of enthusiasm. Burning with love, they travel through dark and dangerous territory to find her who lives at the foot of the mountain of myrrh and incense. They put themselves in danger from rivers, in danger from thieves, led by the Holy Spirit to see the wonder of the world, the marvel of angels, and the joy of sinners. My *maestro* would talk with barbarians, Saracens, and Jews, but is unwilling to talk with three earthly angels who weep day and night over the evils being done in the world. ... I feel a great urgency to write him a letter to show him his error openly, but because he is as I am, because he is as Catherine is, I will forego the pen and only marvel at the wonder of it—because there is no law that would have prevented his speaking with them without sin."

He then asks his friend to write to "those sons of Catherine who are afraid to speak with the innocent, though with others they will speak."[3]

Though Fawtier, and Dupré Theseider after him, hesitate to identify

---

[1] MSS: Mo-*a*, corrected in a few places by *b*; B, P2, T, P5, F2, P3; translation based on Mo-*a*.

[2] The Florentines are still under interdict, which means that others are not to communicate with them. The Augustinian hermit Giovanni Tantucci, who is at Rocca d'Orcia with Catherine, has not therefore wanted to have anything to do with the three young Florentines.

[3] Let. VI, *Il beato Giovanni dalle Celle*, ed. P. Cividali, p. 442.

the young men to whom Catherine's letter is addressed with the three referred to by Giovanni dalle Celle, it seems unlikely, given the chronology, that they are not the same.[4] The linguistic evidence strongly supports placing the present letter in October 1377 or shortly thereafter. Catherine's reference to Sant'Antimo with its implied invitation to "come and see" could easily correspond with the period following her visit there. And the fact that Giovanni in his letter does not so much as mention Raimondo da Capua would seem to indicate that the latter has already left the Rocca. I would therefore conjecture that Catherine wrote this letter shortly after her visit to Sant'Antimo, and that the young men in fact responded by coming to see her at the Rocca a bit later. If her letter was written in October and the young men arrived in late October or even in November, there would still be time for Giovanni dalle Celle's letter to be written while Giovanni Tantucci and Catherine are still at the Rocca.[5]

§

In the name of Jesus Christ crucified and of gentle Mary.

Dearest sons in Christ gentle Jesus,

I Caterina, servant and slave of the servants of Jesus Christ, am writing to you in his precious blood. I long to see you so bound in charity's sweet bond that neither the devil nor anyone else will be able to set you free from it. This is the sweet bond that bound God to us and us to God[a] when the divine nature was joined with human nature.[6] This is the indescribable love that gave us being when God drew us out of his very self by creating us in his image and likeness. And because our soul was made simply of love, it is love that gives our soul its three powers and binds them together.[7]

Our will, wanting to love something, moves our understanding to see. And when our understanding senses that the will (if it is rational) wants to love, it centers its attention on the indescribable love of the eternal Father,

---

[4] Fawtier (II, p. 288) and Dupré Theseider after him (unpublished notes) refer to the letter of Giovanni dalle Celle, but refrain from identifying the three young men to whom Catherine's letter is addressed with the three referred to by Giovanni. They simply place Catherine's letter before or during the Val d'Orcia period.

[5] The four letters which share nineteen or more of this one's sixty-one analyzed patterns are rather widely scattered. There is, however, a concentration of significant clusters within individual patterns beginning and/or ending in October 1377: CHIODI, DIOEUOMO, DIOINUOM, LEGGEPER, NATURDIV, UMILBALI, UMILMANS.

[6] Prayer 17, pp. 146–154, develops the imagery of engrafting in great detail.

[7] Cf. *Dial.* 54, pp. 107–108, for another elaboration of this concept of love as the wellspring and integrating force of the soul's powers.

who has given us the Word, his Son. [And it focuses] on that Son's obedience and humility, on how he meekly and with tremendous love endured pain, insult, anguish, scorn, and abuse. And so our will reaches out with indescribable love for what our understanding has seen. With a firm hand it takes the treasure it has drawn with its love and places it in our memory, so that it acknowledges and is grateful for the graces and gifts it sees it has received from its Creator. For it sees that what it has, it has not by its own efforts but because of grace—for we are the ones who are not, and what we produce is sin, the thing that is not.

Oh what a horrible death is sin, which robs us of life! When we see this in the way I've described, we clothe ourselves in love and in utter humility. In God's goodness we discover and experience charity by seeing that we have shared in this charity through all the gifts and graces we have received and are still receiving. And in knowing ourselves and sin (which we discover through that perverse law within us that has rebelled and is still rebelling against our Creator), we conceive a disgust and hatred for our selfishness.[8] Through that hatred[b] we discover a patience that makes us strong enough to endure pain, scorn, abuse, hunger and thirst, cold and heat, and the devil's torments and temptations; and we despise and run away from the world with all its pleasures. From such self-hatred is born a spring of humility, which in turn is governess and wet-nurse to charity.[9] And once charity, indescribable love, has found her governess, humility, and her servant, hatred of self (which for love serves charity with perfect patience), we are willing to suffer. Self-hatred avenges charity and punishes her enemies. And these are her enemies: selfishness (by which we love ourselves for our own sake, and love whatever we love for our own sake rather than for God's), pleasure, complacency, prestige, honor, and wealth.

And what sort of vengeance does self-hatred take? A vengeance so gentle that words cannot describe it! From the selfishness that brings death[c] it leads us to life-giving divine love. From darkness and hate and disgust for virtue it leads us to such love for virtue that we would prefer death to loss of virtue. In fact, we begin to grasp at whatever methods or directions we see will help us acquire virtue and preserve it. We see the danger of physical pleasure and soft living, of keeping company with people who are evil, perverted, and worldly, and so we avoid them with all our heart and energy. We confront our body with opposition. We take vengeance on it by subduing it with penance, with fasting, vigils, prayer, and discipline—espe-

[8] Cf. Rom. 7, 23: "But I see in my body's members another law at war with the law of my mind."

[9] Cf. *Dial.* 9, pp. 40–42; 63, pp. 118–119, for the development of this relationship of humility and charity within two larger images.

cially when we most need it, that is, when our flesh wants to rebel against the spirit.[10] We take a mortal vengeance on our will; we kill it by submitting it to God's commandments and to the counsels which Christ, God's only-begotten[d] Son, left us to complete the commandments. By doing so we clothe ourselves in God's gentle eternal will. Courageously and securely we navigate this stormy sea by following in the footsteps of Christ crucified.[11]

This, then is the sweet bond that binds us to our Creator. *You, Charity, bound God to us and us to God, as I said before, when you, eternal Father, gave us the Word, your Son, joining your divine nature with our human nature.* Oh dearest sons, this was the bond that held the God-Man nailed fast to the cross; for unless love had held him, neither nails nor cross could have.[12] Christ's love for the Father's honor and for our salvation, together with his hatred and disgust for sin, took vengeance on our iniquities and punished them in his own body with suffering and torment.[13]

So if we are bound to Christ crucified we will follow him by taking vengeance on our selfishness for God's honor and our own salvation as well as our neighbors' by routing our enemies—I mean vice and disobedience to our Creator in flouting his commandments. But our friends—true solid virtues exercised in love and in perfect charity—these we will receive and take in. One of the best friends we have is genuine obedience. If we are as humble as we are obedient, we obey God's[e] holy commandments. And if we are really in love with this obedience, which is a denying and killing[f] of our own will, we will stretch ourselves further still. We will obey Christ's counsels by taking on the yoke of holy obedience in a [religious] order. There is no doubt, my sons, that this is the more secure and tested[g] way. Even though we see weak religious who do not keep the rule, the order itself is never weakened, for it is formed and founded by the Holy Spirit.

So if you sense that God is calling you to obedience, answer him. And if you think you cannot be satisfied by those orders that have declined so and for lack of love abound in abuses, here is my answer. There are many monasteries where all the bad roots have left.[14] So if you have an incli-

---

[10] Cf. 1 Cor. 9, 27: "I chastise my body and bring it into subjection." (Vulg.)

[11] Cf. Ps. 77, 19: "Through the sea was your way, and your path through the deep waters, though your footsteps were not seen." See also Prayer 11, pp. 86–97, where Catherine elaborates at length on the image of the two opposing garments, selfish will and God's will.

[12] Cf. Cavalca, *Specchio di croce*, p. 41: "No bond of iron could have held Christ nailed or bound—only charity, the bond of perfection."

[13] Cf. *Dial.* 155, p. 330; Let. T60 (vol. I), T287 (in this volume).

[14] It. *ogni ghattiva barba*, literally "every bad root." In the few other places in which Catherine uses *barba* the reference is to weeds that must be rooted out. It would be possible

nation toward religious life, the best course and most to God's honor would be to go somewhere that has a good leader. Among others, I can attest to Sant'Antimo, where, as Don Giovanni[15] will tell you, there is an abbot who is a mirror of humility and poverty and unity, for he wants to be not the greatest but the least.[16] May God in his infinite goodness make of it whatever would be most for his honor and best for you.

Bind yourselves, my sons, bind yourselves together in charity. Support each other and bear with each other's faults, so that you may be bound together in Christ gentle Jesus, and not divided. Love, love each other; for you know that this is the sign the blessed Christ left his disciples when he said that God's children would be recognized only by their unity of love one with another in perfect charity.[17] I was so encouraged by the good news I heard about your unity. Grow in it. And don't turn back. Let me be able to say to you what Saint Paul said to his disciples, that they were his joy, his delight, and his crown.[18] Please live in such a way that I will be able to say that.

I'll say no more. Bathe in the blood of Christ crucified, and bind yourselves together in the bond of love. Keep living in God's holy and tender love.

Gentle Jesus! Jesus love![h]

Textual Notes

a. P2: [*and us to God*].
b. B, P2: *In ourselves* (*nel'uomo*) / *Through that hatred* (*nel'odio*).
c. P2: [*that brings death*].
d. B, P2: [*only-begotten*].
e. B, P2: [*God's*].
f. B, P2: [*and killing*].
g. P3: *quick* (*pronta*) / *tested* (*provata*).
h. T adds *Mother Mary!*

---

also to interpret *barba* in its other sense, "beard," and simply translate "all the bad monks," but nowhere else does Catherine use *barba* in this sense.

[15] Giovanni dalle Celle.

[16] The Abbot of Sant'Antimo, Giovanni di Gano da Orvieto. Let. T112/DT66 (in this volume) is addressed to him. He has officiated at the foundation of Catherine's convent at Belcaro in spring of 1377, and during her stay in the Val d'Orcia she has defended him against the accusations of the archpriest of Montalcino, saying that Giovanni is "as great and perfect a servant of God as has lived in these parts in a very long time."

[17] Jn. 13, 35.

[18] Phil. 4, 1.

Letter T56/G86[1]
To Frate Simone da Cortona
October or November 1377

The young Dominican Simone di Neri da Cortona was easily depressed, and was very dependent on expressions of Catherine's affection for him, as is clear not only from references to him in Catherine's letters, but even in his own testimony in the *Processo Castellano*.

The present letter, Catherine's only extant letter directly to Simone, must be related to two letters addressed to Neri di Landoccio Pagliaresi "at the Rocca," one signed "F.S." and the other of which the writer says, "I am not signing my name, because I don't know that I *have* a name."[2] Both of these letters, bemoaning the sender's being cut off from the family because of his sorry state, are surely from Frate Simone.[3] Their spirit corresponds perfectly with the present letter, in which Catherine refers to Simone's getting his name back and being welcomed back into the family. In fact, it is probably the desperation evident in Simone's second letter to Neri that prompts Catherine to take things in hand with her melancholy disciple.

One has only to account for the 1378 date in the manuscript of the two letters to Neri.[4] Grottanelli, who edited the letters, concluded that their true date must be 1377. It seems implausible that both Catherine and Neri could have been at the Rocca at any time in 1378—at least not long enough for the exchange of three letters. Besides, there is no linguistic support whatever for placing Catherine's letter to Simone in 1378. There is, on the other hand, strong linguistic support for placing it in October or November 1377. This would also allow time for Gabriele di Davino Piccolomini to have arrived in Siena with greetings from Neri, and for Simone to have responded not only with his first letter (Let. 7) but also, with his second (Let. 8), to "several" messages from Neri.[5]

---

[1] MSS: Mo-*a*, M, S5, S6, Ro, F3, P4, Pa; translation based on Mo-*a* (which includes an ending not found in other manuscripts), with variants based on an unpublished transcription by Dupré Theseider.

[2] Simone's two letters have been edited as Let. 7 and 8 in Grottenelli's edition of "Lettere dei discepoli," found in MS. T.III.3 of the Biblioteca Comunale di Siena and since appended to the Tommasèo/Misciattelli edition of the *Epistolario* in vol. VI.

[3] He even, in Let. 7, calls Catherine "your Mamma," rather than "our Mamma."

[4] Grottanelli's note is found in MS. T.III.3 of the Biblioteca Comunale di Siena.

[5] The letter which shares most heavily (nineteen patterns) with this one is from November or December 1377. There are, moreover, several significant clusters within individual patterns which begin and/or end in October or November of that year: ABBRACC, ALLENT, AMASERVE, AMORSPIR, ARMETERR, ATTPORT, DIOPERM, NUVOLOCC, NUVOLPR, ODIOAMPR, RICHIAM, SANGLUME. Both Fawtier (II, p.

At the end of the letter, Catherine sends greetings from Neri and to Tommaso d'Antonio Caffarini. So the latter must still be in Siena.

§

In the name of Jesus Christ crucified and of gentle Mary.

Dearest "nameless" son in Christ gentle Jesus,[6]

I Caterina, servant and slave of the servants of Jesus Christ, am writing to you in his precious blood. I long to see you bathed and drowned in the blood of the Lamb, so that you will run like a drunk onto the battlefield to fight as a courageous knight against the devil, the world, and your own weakness. With the light of faith and with indescribable love you will always find joy in the struggle.[7]

But you know that we cannot fight or be victorious except with the light of most holy faith. And we cannot have this light unless we raise our mind's eye from the earth, from all earthly attachments, and get rid of the cloud of selfish love, the perverse cloud that utterly deprives us of all light, whether spiritual or temporal.[8] In the temporal sphere, it keeps us from knowing how weak we are, how fickle and unreliable the world is, how empty and fleeting our life is, and how slyly the devil tricks us with these transitory things (often under the pretext of virtue). In the spiritual sphere, this blindness keeps us from discerning and knowing God's goodness. In fact, we often perceive what God gives us for our good as just the opposite! All of this happens to us because we do not reflect on God's intent in his mysteries, nor on the great love with which he gives them to us. No, like blind persons we perceive things other than they really are.

Sometimes God allows the world to persecute us, or other people to hurt us, or our superiors to impose an obligation on us—and we fail to see it as the will of God, who is doing it to make us holy. Instead of seeing God's will permitting this for our good, we look upon it as a matter of human will. So we often end up angry with our neighbors and do all sorts of wrong and foolish things against God and against them. What is the reason

211) and Dupré Theseider (unpublished notes) decline to date the letter. Neither alludes to Simone's letters to Neri.

[6] Only Mo and Ro have *senza nome* ("nameless") in the salutation, but the rubric in both specifies Simone as the addressee.

[7] Simone has written (Let. 8): "I've wandered so far from the true way that I'm almost convinced it would be impossible for me ever to find or enjoy the food I referred to above [love and charity] or to find any place of rest."

[8] Again, Simone (Let. 8): "I've kept the eye of my understanding closed off with darkness; I've expelled the light from my soul."

for this? The scant light we have because our selfish love has covered over the pupil of our [mind's] eye, most holy faith.

If we are in the midst of diabolical temptations and our eye is afflicted with this blindness, we are so deluded that, when the devil puts these illusory[a] thoughts and suggestions into our heart, we think we have been rejected by God. This leads us to discouragement, which in turn makes us give up the practice of prayer because we imagine God does not find us acceptable—and we become [so] despondent we can't stand ourselves.[9] Obedience then becomes burdensome. We forsake our cell and find our pleasure in socializing. All this, and a multitude of other bad things happen to us because we haven't thrown off the cloud of selfish love either spiritually or temporally. We don't, therefore, recognize the truth. Nor do we yet find our joy on the cross with Christ crucified.

If this is so, we will not be courageous knights fighting against our enemies for Christ crucified. No, we will be so cowardly that we'll be afraid of our own shadow! So what do we need? We need Christ's blood! In that blood we will discover a firm confidence that will free us of all slavish fear. And we will discover living faith when we experience that God wants nothing other than our good. This is why he gave us the Word, his only-begotten Son. And the Son gave his life for us to restore us to grace; he made his blood a bath for us to wash away the leprosy of our wickedness. From this we know and are convinced in living faith that God will not allow the devils to harass us more than we can bear.[10] He will not allow the world to torment us beyond our capacity to accept it. And he will not allow our superiors to impose on us greater obligations than we can carry.

With this sweet glorious light [of faith], no struggle will make you discouraged or despondent.[11] Nor will you forsake your cell or go running to seek the company of others. Instead, you will embrace the cross. You won't throw down the weapon of prayer and the rest of [your] spiritual exercises, but will humble yourself before your Creator and offer continual humble prayers. You will not slacken your pace in time of struggle or in time of calm or in any sort of time at all. Conscientiously and without carelessness or discouragement you will serve God and observe your rule in truth. And what will bring this about? The light of most holy faith that you have discovered in the blood.

And what is the source of the light? The blazing fire of charity that

---

[9] Simone has written (Let. 8): "For a long time already I've found myself canceled, erased, deleted from the book in which I used to feel so sweetly fed."

[10] Cf. 1 Cor. 10, 13.

[11] Quite abruptly Catherine switches to "you," as she begins to address Simone's personal issues very directly.

you have discovered in the blood. For it was for love that this gentle loving Word ran to the shameful death of the cross. And the heat of divine love (which you have discovered in the blood) has consumed and destroyed the darkness of selfish love that was shrouding your [mind's] eye and keeping it from seeing. So now you can see. And because you see, you love. And because you love, you reverence God and serve your neighbors.

Then you have been made a courageous knight. You are fighting with the shield of faith and the weapon of charity. Charity is a two-edged sword, its two edges being hatred and love—love for virtue and hatred for vice and for selfish sensual passion. Like one in love you delight in the cross and in acquiring virtue by means of suffering. Motivated by love, you seek God's honor and the salvation of souls. Where is such desire found? In the blood! There is no other way you can have it!

And this is why I said that I long to see you bathed, drowned, in the blood of Christ crucified. And I am telling you that then you *will* have a name, and I will have found my son again! So bathe, drown yourself, in the blood, without discouragement, without despondency!

I have no more to say to you. Keep living in God's holy and tender love. Wicked Neri, my inattentive son, sends you his greetings. And I urge you to ask God to free him from such inattentiveness![12]

Gentle Jesus! Jesus love!

Remember us to Frate Tommaso d'Antonio[13] and to all my other children. . . .[b]

Textual Notes

a. P4 (literally): *by the work of the devil / by the illusion of the devil.*

b. M, S6, P4: [*Wicked Neri. . . . inattentiveness!* and *Remember . . . children. . . .*]

[12] Possibly Neri is serving as scribe and is ridiculing himself, but Catherine herself may be playfully taunting Neri to make Simone feel better about himself.

[13] Tommaso Caffarini.

Letter T53/G182[1]
To Agnesa, widow of Orso Malavolti
October or November 1377

This is the third of Catherine's three extant letters to Agnesa Malavolti, a widow and a member of the Sienese *Mantellate.*[2]

There is nothing particular in the content of the letter to suggest a very precise placement, but the linguistic evidence would strongly suggest placing it during the Val d'Orcia period, with the strongest indications pointing to October or November.[3] I would place it most probably in November, a bit later than Let. T38, the letter in which Catherine consoles Monna Agnesa on the death of her daughter.

§

In the name of Jesus Christ crucified and of gentle Mary.

Dearest daughter in Christ gentle Jesus,

I Caterina, servant and slave of the servants of Jesus Christ, am writing to you in his precious blood. I long to see you bound in the bond of divine charity. This is the bond that held the God-man nailed fast to the wood of the most holy cross—for nails would not have been enough to hold him had love not kept him there.[4] This is the lovely bond that binds our soul with God and makes us one thing with him, for love unites.

Oh dear love, so loving that you purify our soul![5] You dissipate the cloud of selfish sensual passion and enlighten our mind's eye when we gaze

---

[1] MSS: Mo-*a*, M, S5, S6, Ro, P4, S4; translation based on Mo-*a*. No relevant variants.

[2] I have placed Let. T61 among the earliest of Catherine's letters (vol. I) and Let. T38 in October or November 1377 (in this volume).

[3] The five letters sharing ten or more of this one's twenty-nine analyzed patterns are all from this period or later, but broadly scattered. A number of clusters within individual patterns, however, are particularly significant: CASACOGN, COGNAMA, NUVOLOCC, NUVOLPR, and PAZPROV for the beginning point; DIOEUOMO and SEGNAMOR for the ending point; SOSPCIBO for a specific narrowing to October–November 1377. Both Fawtier (II, p. 228) and Dupré Theseider (unpublished notes) decline to date this letter even broadly.

[4] This comparison, stemming from Cavalca and other sources, appears often in Catherine's writings. See, for example, Let. T34 to the prior of Monteoliveto (1378), where she explicitly names love as the Holy Spirit: "... the mercy and generosity of the Holy Spirit; I mean the indescribable love that held [Christ] nailed to the wood of the most holy cross. For neither nails nor ropes could have held him bound were it not for the bond of charity."

[5] She often calls the Word "loving" (or "in love"—*amoroso*), but only in a few places does she even indirectly use the adjective in regard to love itself, for example in Let. T83 to Conte di Conti da Firenze (1378 or 1379), where God's charity is a "loving fire."

into eternal Truth.[6] You fill our memory with the graces and gifts we receive from our Creator, so that we become grateful for and appreciate these blessings. And you sate our soul with sweet loving desire. So says the holy prophet, "Sighs are a food for me, and tears a drink."[7] What was making him sigh and weep? This sweet lovely bond, love![8] So, dearest daughter, since it is so lovely, so delightful, and so necessary for us, we should not go on sleeping but should rouse ourselves with true holy desire and earnestness, and courageously seek it.

And if you should ask me, "Where can I find it?" here is my answer: in the house of self-knowledge.[9] There you will discover the unspeakable love God has for you—God, who created you in his own image and likeness and for love created you anew to grace in the blood of his only-begotten Son. Once you have discovered love and come to know it within yourself, you will not be able to keep from loving. And the sign that you have discovered and conceived love will be that you bind yourself in charity with your neighbors by loving them and by serving them lovingly. For the good and the service that we cannot do for God we must do for our neighbors, enduring with true patience whatever burden they may be to us.[10] This is the sign that we love our Creator in truth and are bound to him in this lovely bond. There is no other way we can share in grace or be able to return to the end for which we were created.[11] And this is why I said that I long to see you bound in the bond of divine charity.

I have no more to say to you. Keep living in God's holy and tender love.

Gentle Jesus! Jesus love!

---

[6] She may well be drawing this imagery (which first appears in her writings at this time) from the clouds which in autumn almost continually shroud the Rocca.

[7] Cf. Ps. 41, 4 (Vulg., following the Septuagint). The psalmist's tears, however, are tears motivated not, as Catherine says, directly by love, but by regret over the loss of God's presence: "My tears have been my bread day and night, as people say to me every day, 'Where is your God?' "

[8] She will often speak, in *The Dialogue*, of love constraining people to sigh and weep for the Church.

[9] The image of "the cell of self-knowledge" occurred for the first time, in an isolated case, in early 1377, and in autumn of 1377 Catherine began to use it frequently. She has only once before, in Let. T144 to Monna Pavola (summer of 1375, vol. I), related self-knowledge to the image of the *house*, but in that instance the house was the soul. Now she begins to build very steadily and consistently both images, that of "the house of self-knowledge" and that of "the cell of self-knowledge."

[10] The sense of the original (*portando . . . ogni fadiga che noi ricevessimo da lui*) can include both the burden others may be to us and the annoyance or trouble they may cause us.

[11] Cf. Prayer 4, pp. 42–43 (on the feast of Saint Paul, 1377): "You, wonderful Paul, . . . truly knew where you had come from and where you were going . . . for you had come to know your origin and your goal. . . . and [our] goal is the same as [our] origin."

Letter T44/G283[1]
To Ser Antonio di Ciolo
October or November 1377

Antonio di Ciolo (Petraciolo), since he is addressed by the title *Ser*, was almost certainly a notary. If he was Sienese, as Meattini speculates,[2] it would not be surprising if Catherine wrote to him while she was outside the city, though, since he seems not to be a close friend or disciple, it would not be surprising either if she corresponded with him by letter even from nearby.

In this letter, Catherine is both admonishing Antonio in regard to physical purity and encouraging him to enter religious life. As for the chronological placement of the letter, the linguistic evidence points very strongly to the later months of the Rocca d'Orcia period, probably October or November.[3]

Note that there are unusually many instances of pronominal inconsistency, and switching of subjects for example, *servi di Dio* to *ella* (*l'anima*) even within a single sentence. This characteristic of a number of the Val d'Orcia letters may indicate Catherine's occasional use of a scribe other than Neri or Stefano, perhaps her sister-in-law Lisa or Fra Santi (see Let. T119, notes 6 and 7).

§

In the name of Jesus Christ crucified and of gentle Mary.

Dearest son in Christ gentle Jesus,

I Caterina, servant and slave of the servants of Jesus Christ, am writing to you in his precious blood. I long to see you united in holy desire with our gentle Savior, since there is no other way we can reject the world or attain perfect purity and maintain physical and spiritual continence. For if we do not draw near to God and become one with him by the way we direct our love, we will necessarily become identified with creatures, with worldly

---

[1] MSS: B, P2, P5, F2, P3; translation based on Gigli (*Opere*, II) in the absence of access to any of the manuscripts.

[2] *Epistolario*, p. 819.

[3] Two of the four letters which share seventeen or more of this one's sixty-eight analyzed patterns are from the Val d'Orcia period, and two are later. The more convincing evidence, however, lies in a number of patterns which cluster significantly around October and November 1377: CONVERSC, CORPVOL, ELEGMORT, GERMTRIB, MONDSAZI, NONPUO, NUVOLOCC, NUVOLPR. Neither Fawtier (II, p. 290) nor Dupré Theseider (unpublished notes) dates this letter.

pleasures and joys and prestige, apart from God. Why? Because we cannot live without love. We have to love either God or the world. We always become one with the object of our love and in this union we are transformed because we always take on something of what is in the object of our love.

If we love the world, we have nothing but pain in the world, for because of sin the world brings forth the thorns and troubles of great bitterness. Our flesh gives us nothing but the poisonous filth of sin and corruption—so much so that those who conform themselves with the will of the flesh[4] and sensual passion are mortally poisoned by it,[5] because they fall into mortal sin and lose the life of grace. There is nothing else such love can give. It makes one continually sad, unbearable to oneself, because God has permitted that wrongly directed love[6] should make one unbearable to oneself.

Love that is directed to God's gentle will and made one with God because of its basic direction,[7] on the other hand, gives us something of what is in God.

God is supreme eternal loveliness. God's servants, therefore, experience tremendous gratification in bitter and difficult things because they are serene and satisfied when they find that God is within them by grace. For they cannot be satisfied by anything but God. Why? Because God is greater than they are, and they are greater than any created thing. So whatever God has created, he has created to serve humankind, and humankind he has created for himself, so that we should love him with all our heart and all our strength,[8] and serve him in truth. This is why these worldly things cannot satisfy us, because they are less than we. So we have rest and peace when we live in God.[9] We share in such a greatness of heart that the sweep of our charity[10] is big enough to embrace everyone. In fact, we do our best to serve and help our neighbors and so to show our love for our Creator.

God is supreme eternal purity. Both our soul and our body, therefore,

---

[4] Jn. 1, 13 (Vulg.): "born not of the will of the flesh, nor of human will, but of God."

[5] Cf. Let. T21, to an unnamed person, the only close parallel (in this volume): "[N]eutralize the poison in your flesh with remembrance of the scourged flesh of Christ crucified, God and human; for through the union of the divine nature with human nature, our flesh attained such dignity that it is exalted above all the choirs of angels." Note that both letters deal with physical purity.

[6] It. *disordinato affetto.*

[7] It. *l'affetto ch'è ordinato nella dolce volontà di Dio, unita in lui per affetto d'amore.*

[8] It. *affetto.*

[9] Cf. Augustine, *Confessiones*, Bk. I, 1: "Our hearts are restless until they rest in you."

[10] It. *affetto di carità.* There is a paradox here of the direction of love to God being as focused as an arrow shot yet broad enough to embrace everyone within that very directedness, because by it one shares in God's own all-embracing love.

share in that purity because of our union with God, and we keep our mind and body perfectly pure, preferring to die rather than dirty and pollute our body or our mind with impurity. Not that we can't have thoughts in our heart or even physical arousal. But such thoughts and arousals don't dirty our soul. Only our will can do that when it freely consents to our weakness or to the thoughts of our heart. Lacking such consent we commit no sin; in fact, we earn merit by putting up a holy resistance and always picking from these thorns the fragrant rose of perfect purity. For this leads us to a deeper knowledge of ourselves, and then we rise up against our selfish weakness with a holy hatred, and in love run to Christ crucified with continual humble prayer, knowing that there is no other way to escape from such evils. We've already said that the closer we come to him, the more we share in his purity. So it really is true that from these struggles we pick the purest of roses. This is indeed the remedy against this wretched sin of our weak fragile flesh, that we come close to God and conform ourselves with him by the way we direct our love.[11]

And let's not wait for time, dearest brother! Time is short and doesn't wait for us, so we shouldn't wait for it, either! What a business[12] that we should choose to go on sleeping in such blindness, and not rouse ourselves from this sleep! But it's true that we cannot wake up or attain this union [with God] without the light. By the light of most holy faith we have to come to know our wretchedness and our guilt. Then, with our sight purified, we have to concentrate on God's unspeakable love for us. God revealed this love to us in the Word, his only-begotten Son, and the Son revealed it in his blood, shed with such blazing love when he ran like one in love to the shameful death of the cross. When we see that we are loved that much, how can we keep from loving? We cannot!

Oh dearest son, don't stay away from this light, but conscientiously rid yourself of the cloud of selfish love for yourself, and contemplate with lively faith the spotless slain Lamb, who is calling you with such great love. If you respond to him, you will attain this perfect union [with God], and once you are one with God, you will experience the fragrance of perfect purity.[13]

A very good remedy for this vice [of impurity] is to think about the dignity our poor flesh attained because of God's union with us when the divine nature was joined with our human nature. Seeing your human nature exalted higher than all the choirs of angels will shame you and serve

---

[11] It. *per affetto d'amore.*

[12] It. *gran fatto è.*

[13] I can find no other instance of Catherine's linking physical purity with union with God.

as a restraint from giving yourself to such wretchedness. When your mind and your desire rise up so sweetly, the stench of vice must of necessity be smothered.

Beyond this, we must chastise our body and discipline it with watching and with continual humble prayer. We must cling to the tree of the most holy cross. We must as far as possible avoid associating with those who live lecherously. Have no doubt that God will be immensely gracious to you if only you make an effort to cut this knot rather than standing there trying to untie it.[14] Hurry up and put all your affairs in order. Run to the yoke of holy obedience with sweet loving desire. There you will kill your will and discipline your body; there you will experience the earnest of eternal life. And don't look upon this as burdensome, because the burden will turn into a tremendous joy for you! I am certain that if you make your home with the good gentle Jesus[15] by the way you direct your love,[16] you will do it, but not otherwise.

And this is why I said that I long to see you united with our Savior by the way you direct your love, so that you will attain true purity and get rid of the passion that is giving you so much pain. I have no doubt that you will get rid of it if you do this.[17] At least let your will be ready to die rather than choose to sin.

Bathe in the blood of Christ crucified and begin a new life, in trust that your sins will be devoured in the blood and the fire of love. As for me, I want to take your sins and dissolve them with prayers and tears in the fire of divine charity. I want to bear the penance for you. All I ask of you and urge upon you is that you focus on freeing yourself quickly from the world. Give it a swift kick! For if you don't, it will soon enough be the one kicking you! Don't resist the Holy Spirit, who is calling you.

I'll say no more. Keep living in God's holy and tender love.

Gentle Jesus! Jesus love!

---

[14] Catherine repeats this admonition in other letters. In Let. T130 (in this volume) and T318 (1378) she emphasizes that it is the shortness of time that makes it necessary to cut the knot of attachment to the world rather than untie it, and in Let. T72 she specifies that it is with the double-edged knife of love for God and hatred for selfish love of self that it must be cut. She develops the theme at length in Let. T205 (1378) and T329 (1379), when she is trying to prod Stefano Maconi to a decision to enter religious life—the same thing she is prodding Antonio to do in this letter.

[15] Cf. Jn. 14, 23 (Vulg.): "Those who love me will keep my word, and my Father will love them, and we will come to them and make our dwelling with them."

[16] It. *per affetto d'amore.*

[17] "This" is probably a reference to his entering religious life, something she is quite clearly encouraging him to do.

LETTER T335/G56[1]
To Don Cristofano,
Carthusian monk at the Monastery of San Martino in Naples
October or November 1377

The Carthusian Don Cristofano is not identified other than by his location in Naples. Catherine could have become aware of his problems either through a letter from him or through one of his Carthusian brothers, perhaps someone at Gorgona who knew of Cristofano's wish to transfer to the latter monastery, an issue Catherine addresses at the end of the letter.[2]

The letter's content provides no clue as to when it might have been written. The linguistic evidence, however, points strongly to Catherine's time in the Val d'Orcia, with the greatest probability that it was written in October or November.[3] There are also many parallels (though not verbally close) to *The Dialogue* (also to Let. T76 in this volume), as well as a number of unusual and even unique expressions and numerous significant manuscript variations.

---

[1] MSS: Mo-*c*, F4, B, P2, H, P1, P3, R2, P4, Pa, V; translation based on Mo-*c*, with variants based on an unpublished transcription by A. Volpato.

[2] Gorgona is an island in the Mediterranean off the coast from Livorno and Pisa. There was a Carthusian monastery there which Catherine visited in 1375 and with whose prior and monks she was in correspondence.

[3] Four of the seven letters which share twenty-one or more of this one's one hundred two analyzed patterns are from the last four months of 1377. (The other three are later.) More convincing, however, is the number of significant clusters within individual patterns which begin and/or end in that period, with four of these occurring only once or never before October: ABBRACC, AGNELCON, AMASERVE, ARMTERR, BUSSPORT, CONCEPPR, DAFIGLIO, FEDELMER, LEGGEPER, LUMEVEST, PENAMENT, SERVMERC, VIRNTIM, VIRTSENZ, VISIODIO. The number of these clusters which end near October inclines me to place the letter not only within these four months but most probably nearer mid-October. Both Fawtier (II, p. 186) and Dupré Theseider (unpublished notes) consider the letter undatable, except that both think it must be later than Catherine's 1375 visit to the island of Gorgona and earlier than the schism (November 1378), since she does not mention the latter (though to me this silence would not seem strange given the very personal nature of the letter).

§

In the name of Jesus Christ crucified and of gentle Mary.[a]

Dearest father in Christ gentle[b] Jesus,

I Caterina, servant and slave[c] of the servants of Jesus Christ, am writing to you in his precious blood. I long to see in you the light and fire of the Holy Spirit—the light that dispels all darkness, the fire that consumes whatever selfish love[d] and unwillingness to suffer[4] there may be in our soul, whether it has to do with the spiritual or the physical.

Why do I so long to see this light and fire in you? Because, according to what you wrote me, you are suffering from trials and sufferings[5] both physical and spiritual, and for these you need this light.

And why, dearest father,[e] do we need this light? Because it is a way of seeing with the eye of understanding. Just as our happiness consists in seeing God, so in seeing and coming to know ourselves and God's goodness within us we receive the light of the Holy Spirit's grace.[6] And this grace and[f] light strengthen our soul and fire us up to endure with great[g] desire and patience any illness or trial or temptation[h] that may come our way, whether from our own flesh or the devil or other people. We don't ever wish to choose the timing in our own way. No, as persons clothed in God's sweet eternal[i] will, we hold in reverence whatever time or circumstance is ours.[7] For as soon as we turn our mind's eye to knowing ourselves and to seeing God's will for us and what God requires,[j] we discover that God wants and looks for nothing other than that we be made holy.[8] If he had wanted anything else, he would never have given us the Word, his Son,[k] nor would his Son have given his life for us with such blazing love.

---

[4] It. *impazienzia.*

[5] It. *passioni*, which in all but a few ambivalent cases in Catherine's writings signifies suffering rather than an emotional state. This interpretation is borne out by what follows in the letter.

[6] This is a rather obscure summary of what Catherine explains more amply in *Dial.* 45, p. 92: "So you see, my servants' chief happiness is in seeing and knowing me. This vision and knowledge fills their will. They have what their will longs for and so they are satisfied. This is why I told you that most especially, the joy of eternal life is in possessing what the will longs for. But know that its satisfaction is in seeing and knowing me. Even in this life they enjoy the pledge of eternal life, since they have a taste of the very thing that satisfies them. How do they have this pledge in this life? Let me tell you. They see my goodness in themselves and they see my truth when their understanding—which is the soul's eye—is enlightened in me."

[7] Cf. Let. T250 to Giovanni di Gano da Orvieto (in this volume): "We discern God's will for us with due reverence. That is, we see that whatever God permits, whether persecution or consolation, whether from human or diabolic sources, it is all done to make us holy."

[8] 1 Thes. 4, 3.

So we see that whatever physical illness or spiritual temptations God permits us in this life are for our good, and we judge it all by God's standards.[9] And because God's will permits these things only for our good, we realize that not a leaf falls from a tree without God's providence.[l] God allows us to be tempted in order to test our virtue and make us grow in grace, not that we may be conquered but that we may[m] conquer by trusting in divine help rather than in our own strength. We say with the dear apostle Paul: "Through Christ crucified, who is within me and strengthens me, I can do anything."[10,n] When we do this, the devil is left defeated. And the weapon with which he is defeated is our stripping ourselves of our own will and clothing ourselves in God's, discerning that whatever God permits is for our sanctification. For a selfish will is the only source of spiritual suffering.

The devil is aware of this. He cannot trick God's servants with what is obviously evil or with an excessively broad conscience, so he tries to trick them with scrupulosity and unwarranted discouragement, under the pretext of virtue.[o] To the person who is sick he says, "You could be doing a lot of good if only you were healthy." And to the mind of the person who is being harassed and tempted (in whatever way) by evil thoughts and imaginings, the very devil who is doing the tempting says, "If you didn't have these thoughts, you would be more[p] pleasing to God. Your spirit would be at peace, and [your praying of the divine] office and everything else you do would please and gratify God." He wants this person to give up doing these things,[r] wants to give the impression that because of these evil thoughts and strong temptations God's goodness is not pleased with anything this person says or does. The devil cannot use what is obviously evil to make God's servants fall, so he tries to use the appearance of virtue to make them fall. And so he gains more ground with them by means of discouragement than in any other way.

Understand, dearest father, that God allows these ordeals only so that we may test in ourselves the virtues of patience and courage and perseverance. These virtues have their wellspring in self-knowledge—for in struggle I come to know that I am not.[r] If I were anything at all, I would free myself from these things. But I cannot free myself from spiritual struggles or from physical illness. Still, we can keep our will from consenting. In this will we discover God's goodness.[11] In unspeakable love God gave us

---

[9] Literally, "within God's will."

[10] Phil. 4, 13.

[11] Catherine explains elsewhere that we discover God's goodness in temptation when God preserves in us a "good and holy will" which refuses to consent to sin. Cf., for example, Let. T189/DT84 to the monks of San Girolamo at Cervaia (in this volume): "When you know you have a good will, and know you would rather die than actually offend your

this free will, and it is this will which sins or acts virtuously. Free woman that she is, neither the devil nor anyone else can force her to sin any more than she chooses to.[12]

Wise people realize this, and they are happy in time of struggle because they see that God allows it to make them grow into greater and more proven virtue. For virtue is tested and seen to be truly virtue only through what is contrary to it.[13] It is like a woman who has conceived a child. Until she gives birth to the child, it is impossible to see for certain what it is; one can only guess. So it is with us. Unless we give birth to it through the proving ground of suffering (whether this comes from the flesh or the devil or other people), we can never see whether or not we truly have it.[14] For people whose virtue is not yet tested are often ready to endure anything for their God. And God, seeing that desire has been conceived in them, at once puts them to the test. He wants to try their love to see whether it is faithful or mercenary. We prove the love within us when we discover that it is in fact faithful,[s] that trial and consolation affect us equally because we realize that everything is permitted by God. We are happy and glad with whatever we have, because our will has become one with God's.[t] But if [our love] is found to be servile, if in time of trial it wants to avoid suffering, then it is mercenary[u] rather than faithful, and we have reason for conversion.

Creator, then you must let go of your discouragement and walk by the light of the grace hidden within your soul, the grace God has given you in safeguarding your good will. . . . And we discover God in ourselves by discovering our good and holy will."

[12] Cf. Let. T36 to several Monteolivetan novices in Bologna: "Get drunk on the blood of this gentle Lamb, who has made the fortress of your soul strong, who has delivered it from slavery to the devil's perverse tyranny and given it back to you a free woman. For there is no one who can take away your mastery unless you so choose, and this is something he has given to everyone." Also Let. Gardner I/DT52 to Bartolomeo Smeducci (vol. I): "Once this weak body of ours and our sensual nature have been conquered, we will be the victors. Our reason, our soul, will be a free woman, in possession of God the supreme eternal Good."

[13] Cf. *Dial.* 8, p. 39: "You test the virtue of patience in yourself when your neighbors insult you. Your humility is tested by the proud, your faith by the unfaithful, your hope by the person who has no hope. Your justice is tried by the unjust, your compassion by the cruel, and your gentleness and kindness by the wrathful."

[14] Cf. *Dial.* 11, p. 45: "When the soul has thus conceived virtue in the stirring of her love, and through her neighbors proved it and for their sakes brought it to birth, not all the world can rob her of this virtue. Indeed, persecution only serves to prove it and make it grow. But for that very reason, were the soul's virtue not evident and luminous to others in time of trial, it could not have been conceived in truth; for I have already told you clearly that virtue cannot be perfect or bear fruit except by means of your neighbors. If a woman has conceived a child but never brings it to birth for people to see, her husband will consider himself childless. Just so, I am the spouse of the soul, and unless she gives birth to the virtue she has conceived [by showing it] in her charity to her neighbors . . . , then I insist that she has never in truth even conceived virtue within her."

It is indeed true, then, that God permits everything to make us grow in grace and to prove our virtue, as I've said. This makes us come to know ourselves better,[v] and in this knowledge we humble ourselves rather than exalting ourselves in pride. And we come to know God's goodness within us when we discover that God keeps our will from consenting to all these temptations and fabrications of the devil.[15]

Now this is God's will; I mean the fact that God lets these things happen for this purpose. But what is the devil's perverse will?[w] It is this. In order to bring us to weariness and discouragement, to spiritual dejection and a troubled conscience, the ancient enemy doesn't tempt us[x] with abject sin by bothering us repeatedly[y] with physical titillations in any belief that we would give in to this. He knows very well that our will is determined to die rather than consent [to this]. No, he does it to lead us into a different sin[z] by making us think there is sin where there is none. He says, "Your prayer[aa] and the other things you do ought to be done with purity of spirit and heart,[bb] and you are doing them in such filth!" He says this so that prayer will become a source of weariness for us, so that in weary dejection we will abandon both prayer and every other holy and good work. He is interested only in how[cc] he can get us to put down the weapon we are defending ourselves with—for then it is easy for him to get[dd] us in both the first way and the second!

And this is our weapon: holy prayer, along with holy thoughts[ee] grounded in God's eternal will. In this will we seek ourselves not for ourselves but for God, and we seek our neighbors for God.[ff] And we seek God for God rather than for our selfish advantage, in so far as God is supreme eternal Goodness, deserving of our love and service. So we love and serve God[gg] no matter what the time or circumstances. Then we are standing on the secure rock, with a bold blazing[hh] desire. We rise above ourselves, calling ourselves to account with a holy self-contempt, considering ourselves deserving of the suffering and struggles but undeserving of the fruit we see follows upon the suffering. In humility, we consider ourselves undeserving of spiritual peace and calm.

Our joy is to be on the cross with Christ crucified. We are willing to be sated with shame, pain, mockery, and vilification, if only we can be like Christ crucified. For we see that we can be united with our Creator only through love, and Love,[ii] Christ Jesus, chose this way as the best and most perfect he could have. He taught us that this is the way of truth and light when he said, "I am way and truth and life. Whoever walks by this way

---

[15] This is what Catherine calls elsewhere the principle of a good and holy will.

will not go astray but will be walking by the light."[16] God's servants want to follow him.[jj] So even if it were possible to avoid hell[kk] and to take possession of paradise and to leave the world without suffering, they wouldn't want to. No, they *want* to leave the world and escape hell[ll] and take possession of eternal life in suffering in order to be like their beloved Christ. If they are ill they are happy, because they see this as revenge against their body and against that perverse law which is continually fighting against the spirit.[17] If they experience struggles and spiritual darkness, or temptation to blasphemy or despair or infidelity, or anything else the devil might offer, true humility makes them rejoice, because they consider themselves undeserving of peace. Weariness does not trouble them. Their only concern is to keep the rock of their will strong so that it isn't swayed to any sort of consent.[18] They sense that the rock of their will is standing strong by God's grace, for not only does it not consent, but nothing gives it pain except its fear of offending God.

I want you to be cautious in this suffering. For it seems to me the devil is harassing you a lot in this.[mm] In fact, all of your sufferings come down to this. Understand that this pain should be disciplined,[19] as I've said, grounded by humility in self-knowledge and in knowledge of God's goodness guarding your will.[20] In this way the pain will be fattening (making your soul fat with virtue) rather than consuming[nn] you in despair.[21] From

---

[16] Cf. Jn. 14, 6; 8, 12; 11, 9, the elements of which passages Catherine combines rather freely here as elsewhere.

[17] Rom. 7, 23.

[18] The sense of Mo, which has, "to any consent of their own," is not clear. R2 has ". . . that their will not be swayed to any evil consent. So they are happy, because they sense. . . ." This version could be seen as somewhat parallel with a passage in Let. T203 to several novices of Monteoliveto in Perugia (in this volume): "Sometimes, when we are at prayer or saying the [divine] office, the devil casts a dark shadow over our spirit in the form of all sorts of ugly thoughts. But we should never let this make us give up our prayer. No, we should persevere in it, and with a holy thought chase away the evil thought, and keep our good holy will from consenting to these evil thoughts." And Let. T332 to Pietro di Giovanni and Stefano Maconi (1379): "Let the dog of conscience bark to wake up our reason, and let not the least thought pass through our heart without reason examining it. And let no evil stirring pass without its being punished with reproach."

[19] It. *ordinata*.

[20] In the sense of "keeping your will from consenting to evil."

[21] Cf. *Dial.* 78, p. 147: "So it is with these very dear children. When they have attained the third and fourth stage [of love] they are sad as they carry their actual and spiritual cross by actually enduring physical pain as I permit it, and the cross of desire, their crucifying sorrow at the offense done to me and the harm done to their neighbors. They are happy, I say, because the delight of charity that makes them happy can never be taken away from them, and in this they receive gladness and blessedness. Therefore their sadness is called not 'distressing sadness' that dries up the soul, but 'fattening sadness' that fattens the soul in loving charity, because the sufferings increase and strengthen virtue, make it grow and prove it."

it you will draw the little virtue of humility through self-knowledge, and the virtue of charity through knowledge of God, and these are two wings which will let your soul fly to eternal life.[22] For it wouldn't be good to take only the fear of sinning unmixed with hope in divine mercy.

The devil would like nothing better than to lead us into discouragement and dejection, which dry up the soul. This discouragement and spiritual dejection put down the weapon the Holy Spirit has given us; I mean the weapon of our will conformed with God's. Then you begin to want your own will under the pretext of serving God better. You want to get rid of your illness and other spiritual sufferings, saying, "I'd be able to serve my Creator better and more freely."[oo] This is self-deceit, and it comes from the unwarranted fear the devil offers in order to clothe you once again in your own selfish will. From this is born an unwillingness to suffer. You become unbearable to yourself, spiritually preoccupied, opinionated. You want to choose circumstances and paths in your own way rather than as God allows them.

I don't want[pp] any more discouragement, then! No more dejection! No more of your own will! [I want] instead a joyousness, a sweet fire of love and light of the Holy Spirit, a heart brave and not fearful. Clothe yourself in God's gentle eternal will, which has permitted you every one of these physical and spiritual sufferings. God has done and continues to do this for your sanctification. He has given you this out of a special love, not out of hatred.

Up, then, with your weapon! Let's rout this devil with God's[qq] eternal will! Let's chase away the one thought with the other—I mean, with thoughts of God[23] let's chase away the devil's thoughts! You may tell me, "I can't think about God or say the [divine] office or do anything else that's good—both because I'm ill and because of all the contrary things that come into my mind!" My answer is, don't let that make you give up. No, in illness practice patience, because that's where patience is proved. When [you are tormented by] the devil's evil thoughts, say the office and practice holy thoughts of God. Don't preoccupy your mind by standing there arguing with the devil, thinking you can resist him in this way. Don't do this, because your mind would only become more preoccupied. Tell yourself that these thoughts are outside of you. You can do this because they are inside you only to the extent that your will consents to

---

[22] The image occurs also in Let. T175, T189/DT84, T221 in this volume and in Let. T243 in 1378.

[23] Or "God's thoughts." What follows, however, seems to make "thoughts of God" the more likely sense.

them. Lacking that consent, they haven't come into the house but are only knocking at the door.

You shouldn't take the devil's own arrow, thinking to strike him down with it. For standing there arguing with him will never strike him down. No, you must take the arrow of God's will, the arrow of self-contempt and self-hatred, and strike him down with this by saying, "If my Creator wishes to keep me in these pains and difficulties all my life long, I am ready to want it[rr] for the glory and praise of his name."[24] And say to the temptations, "You are very welcome!" and receive them as you would a very dear friend. For they are an effective means of rousing us[ss] from the slumber of apathy and leading us on to virtue.

So be glad! Be happy! Persevere right up to the point of death, and [be ready] to die rather than leave the place God has called you to. Embrace the cross with a willingness[tt] to suffer. Hide between God and suffering,[25] looking with your mind's eye open to the Lamb slain and consumed for you. Be satisfied to stay in whatever situation God puts you or may yet put you in the future. You must, because you[uu] know for certain that God calls and chooses us in the way we will be most pleasing to him. And if you do, you will win light upon light.[26]

Because of Christ crucified, suffering will be a delight for you,[27] and you will consider worldly comforts painful. Even in this life you will begin to experience the earnest of eternal life. For one of the chief [sources of] our happiness in everlasting life is to be securely confirmed in[vv] the eternal Father's will and there to taste the divine sweetness. But we will never experience it up there unless we have clothed ourselves in God's will here below, while we are pilgrims on our journey. When we are so clothed we experience God in our sufferings through grace. Our memory is filled with the blood of the spotless Lamb, our understanding opens up and gazes upon the unspeakable love God has revealed to us in the wisdom of

---

[24] This is the only place in which Catherine uses the arrow image in just this way. Usually the positive sense of the image is charity and the negative is the "poisoned arrow" of sin. (Cf. *Dial.* 78, 116–117, 124, 126.)

[25] There is no parallel to this image anywhere else in Catherine's writings. She speaks often of hiding in the wounds or the open side of Christ, where one will find knowledge of oneself and of God and experience God's mercy. And she speaks in Let. T173 to a friar who has left the order and in Prayer 15, p. 132, of hiding under the wings of God's mercy. The sense here seems to bear out what goes before, that if one sees suffering in terms of God's providence, one can suffer in peace.

[26] Again, the expression is unique here. In *Dial.* 85, p. 156, she speaks of "light beyond any natural light," and in Prayer 14, p. 122, she addresses God as "light above every light." But the sense here seems rather to be "one light after another."

[27] The sense of *la pena per Cristo crocifisso* could also be "suffering for Christ crucified."

his Son, and then the love we discover in the Holy Spirit's mercy drives out our selfish love for ourselves and for any created thing apart from God.

Don't be afraid,[ww] dearest father, but carry on joyfully in conforming yourself well to God's will whether you are healthy or ill or in whatever condition you may be. Right now God is asking of you no other exercise except patience and courage, with sweet perseverance. And you will have this perseverance if you determine in your heart to want nothing but suffering and difficulties. The crown will follow, because it is granted to courage and perseverance. Those who are filled with and enlightened by the fire of the Holy Spirit receive this [gift of perseverance]. Without this guiding light[28] we cannot walk, and this guiding light is won and lost in the way I've already described. And this is why I said that I long to see in you the light and the blazing fire of the Holy Spirit.

So I am praying and will continue to pray supreme eternal Truth[xx] to so completely fill you with this light that you will recognize the treasure (all these trials and temptations) he has put into your hands. He has done it only for love, so that you may be one of his chosen ones and so that he may reward you for your labors with the eternal vision of himself.

I'll say no more. If it should please God's goodness for you to serve on Gorgona, I'm certain God will see to what is best for you. Just be content wherever you are, and see that you don't give in to feeling sorry for and indulging your body.[yy] Be satisfied with the same life your other brothers are living. They have been and are made of the same flesh as you, and the same God who is on their side is on yours too.[29]

Keep living in God's holy and tender love.

Gentle Jesus! Jesus love![zz]

Textual Notes

a. R2 omits both the inscription and the invocation, leaving four lines blank.
b. R2, V: [*gentle*].
c. R2: [*and slave*].
d. F4, R2 add *and self-indulgence.*
e. R2: [*And why do we need*].
f. V: [*grace and*].
g. R2: [*great*]; V: [*with great . . . patience*].
h. V: [*illness or*]; [*or temptation*].
i. R2: [*eternal*].
j. R2 adds *and looks for.*

[28] Literally, "guide."

[29] Cf. Rom. 8, 31: "If God is for us, who can be against us?"

k. V: *God's Son / his Son.*

l. The structures are a bit confused here, with erasures and insertions in Mo, but the meaning is clear. F4: *And because ... our good / These things are all for our salvation.*

m. V: [*be conquered ... may*]—but this is clearly a scribal error.

n. R2: *I will endure anything / I can ... anything.*

o. R2 adds *and good.*

p. V: *much more / more.*

q. R2: [*He wants ... things*].

r. R2: *nothing / not.*

s. R2: *God proves ... and if he finds that it is faithful / We prove ... faithful.*

t. R2: *made our will one with God's / our will ... God's.*

u. R2: *a mercenary servant / mercenary.*

v. V: [*grace ... better*].

w. R2: [*Now .... will?*], clearly a scribal error, since there is a line skipped from one occurrence of "devil" to the next.

x. V: *isn't content* (*non contenta*) / *doesn't tempt us* (*non ci tenta*).

y. R2: [*doesn't tempt ... repeatedly*].

z. H: *But then he gives us another battle / No, ... sin.*

aa. V: *creation* (*creatione*) / *prayer* (*oratione*), clearly a scribal error. (The *o* misread as *cr* results in a word which would not make sense in the context.)

bb. R2: [*and heart*].

cc. R2: *whether / how.*

dd. R2: *defeat / have.*

ee. V: *works* (*operationi*) / *thoughts* (*cogitationi*).

ff. V: [*and we seek our neighbors for God*].

gg. R2: *The soul is servile* (*L'anima è servile*) / *We love and serve God* (*L'ama e serve*).

hh. R2: *enlightened / blazing.*

ii. S2: *for love / Love.*

jj. F4: *it* (that is, the way) / *him.*

kk. V adds *in peace.*

ll. R2: *light / law*—but this is inconsistent with Catherine's allusion to Rom. 7, 23.

mm. R2: [*a lot*].

nn. R2 adds *and distressing.*

oo. R2 adds *if it weren't for these harassments.*

pp. V: *Don't choose* (*Non vogliate*) / *I don't want* (*Non voglio*).

qq. *God's* is supplied from F4; R2 expands to *with our will harmonized with God's gentle eternal will.*

rr. R2: *to endure it willingly / to want it.*

ss. From R2; Mo: *me*; P4, V: *you.*

tt. V, H: *true willingness*; R2: *firm willingness / willingness.*

uu. Mo-*b* corrects *you know* to *we know.*

vv. H: *conformed to / confirmed in.*

ww. R2 adds *of anything.*

xx. V: *Truth, or indeed Goodness / Truth.*

yy. V: *self-indulgence or physical feelings / feeling . . . body* (*o passione / e compassione*). R2: [*If it should please . . . . wherever you are*].

zz. F4 places *Keep living . . . love* above, after *I'll say no more.* R2: *Jesus Christ, gentle love!*; H: *Jesus, etc.*

LETTER T50/G185[1]
To Caterina di Ghetto
October or November 1377

Caterina di Ghetto is listed as one of the *Mantellate* of Siena in 1378.[2] Tommaso Caffarini says that she was a niece of Catherine's first confessor (and cousin) Tommaso dalla Fonte, and that the latter gave the saint's mantle to her after Catherine's death.[3] Both Caffarini[4] and Raimondo da Capua[5] tell us that she was one of Catherine's earliest disciples. We know no more about her role in Catherine's life after the early references, nor whether she accompanied Catherine on any of her journeys.

The linguistic evidence would support placing this letter to Caterina during Catherine's stay in the Val d'Orcia, most probably between October and December. The themes it shares with T335 seem to make it well placed near that letter, and therefore probably before December.[6]

§

In the name of Jesus Christ crucified and of gentle Mary.

My dearest sister and daughter in Christ gentle Jesus,

I Caterina, servant and slave of the servants of Jesus Christ, am writing to you in his precious blood. I long to see you a true servant and spouse of Christ crucified. We should be servants, because we were ransomed by his blood. But I don't see how we could be of any use to him by our service, so we must be of use to our neighbors—for our neighbors are the means by which we acquire and prove our virtue.

---

[1] MSS: B, P2, R1, P5, F2, F1, P3; translation based on R1.

[2] Laurent, *Fontes*, I, *Documenti*, p. 47.

[3] "Et idem confessor, cum ex hac vita migravit, dimisit illam [cappam] cuidam nepoti sue, sorori dicti ordinis, que etiam Catharina Ghetti huc usque dicitur. . . ." (*Processo Castellano*, ed. Laurent, pp. 63–64) Drane (*History of St. Catherine of Siena*, vol. I, p. 100, n. 1) cites a notation by Grottanelli on a copy of the *Mantellate* list: "nipote di S. Cat. Proc. MS. fol. 28, recto." I would take *confessor* to be the antecedent of *sue*, but Grottanelli (as well as Gardner, *Saint Catherine of Siena*, p. 53) apparently assumes that the antecedent is the implied subject of *migravit*, that is, Catherine.

[4] *Processo Castellano*, p. 80.

[5] *Life*, II, viii, 244, p. 231.

[6] The only two letters which share ten or more of this one's thirty-four analyzed patterns fall between October and December 1377. A number of significant clusters within individual patterns begin and/or end in this same period: ANELLO, BARBSUP, CIRCONCI, CUORDOPP, FEDELINF, ORAZING, SENZMEZZ, VIRTVITA. Both Fawtier (II, p. 228) and Dupré Theseider (unpublished notes) decline to date the letter.

Know that every virtue receives life from love. And love is learned in love, by raising the eyes of our understanding to consider how much we are loved by God. When we see how we are loved, we cannot keep from loving, and when we love God, we embrace the virtues in an impulse of love, and we hate and despise vice.

So you see how we conceive the virtues in God and bring them to birth in our neighbors.[7] You know very well that when your neighbors are in need, you give birth to the child within you, charity. And when your neighbors injure you, you give birth to patience.[8] You offer your prayers for [all] your neighbors, but especially for those who injure you. And so we should. If they are unfaithful to us, we should be faithful to them, devotedly working for their salvation, loving them gratuitously and not because they have earned it.[9]

I mean you should beware of loving your neighbors for your own advantage. This would not be faithful love, and you would not be responding to the love that bears you up. For God has loved you gratuitously, and you cannot return this kind of love. So God wants you to give it to your neighbors by loving them gratuitously and not because they have earned your love, as I've said.[10] Nor should you ever lessen or cut back on your love for your neighbors because they've injured you or because you see that their love for you has lessened. No, you should love them in charity, tolerantly putting up with their faults.

---

[7] Cf. *Dial.* 11, p. 45: "When the soul has thus conceived virtue in the stirring of her love, and through her neighbors proved it and for their sakes brought it to birth, not all the world can rob her of this virtue. Indeed, persecution only serves to prove it and make it grow. But for that very reason, were the soul's virtue not evident and luminous to others in time of trial, it could not have been conceived in truth; for I have already told you clearly that virtue cannot be perfect or bear fruit except by means of your neighbors. If a woman has conceived a child but never brings it to birth for people to see, her husband will consider himself childless. Just so, I am the spouse of the soul, and unless she gives birth to the virtue she has conceived [by showing it] in her charity to her neighbors . . . , then I insist that she has never in truth even conceived virtue within her."

[8] Cf. *Dial.* 8, p. 39: "You test the virtue of patience in yourself when your neighbors insult you. Your humility is tested by the proud, your faith by the unfaithful, your hope by the person who has no hope. Your justice is tried by the unjust, your compassion by the cruel, and your gentleness and kindness by the wrathful."

[9] Literally, "not because we owe it to them," but the sense here clearly puts on the neighbors the responsibility of having by their unfaithfulness compromised their claim on love.

[10] Cf. *Dial.* 64, p. 121: "I ask you to love me with the same love with which I love you. But for me you cannot do this, for I loved you without being loved. Whatever love you have for me you owe me, so you love me not gratuitously but out of duty, while I love you not out of duty but gratuitously. So you cannot give me the kind of love I ask of you. This is why I have put you among your neighbors: so that you can do for them what you cannot do for me—that is, love them without any concern for thanks and without looking for any profit for yourself. And whatever you do for them I will consider done for me."

As for God's servants, regard them with respect and [find] great consolation [in them].[11] See that you don't act like those stupid and senseless people who want to appoint themselves as both investigators and judges of what God's servants do and how they live. Such people are deserving of severe reproach. Realize that wanting to make God's servants walk the same way we do is nothing less than an attempt to regulate and legislate for the Holy Spirit—which is absolutely impossible. Let those who make such judgments reflect that the root of pride is not yet outside them, nor is there within them true charity for their neighbors (that is, loving them gratuitously and not because they've earned it). So let's love God's servants, not judge them.[12]

We must in fact love everyone. Those who are living outside of grace we must love with bitter sorrow for their sin, because they are offending God and harming their own souls. Do this, and you will be in harmony with that dear lover Paul. He weeps with those who weep and rejoices with those who rejoice.[13] In the same way, because of our desire for God's honor and their salvation, you will be weeping with those who are in a condition to be weeping. And when you experience God in the stirring of love, you will be rejoicing with God's servants, who are rejoicing.[14]

You see, then, how in charity for God we conceive the virtues and how in charity for our neighbors we bring them to birth. If you act in this way, if you love your neighbors sincerely, not with a false heart or feigned love but freely, without any concern for your own spiritual or material profit, you will be a true servant. Through your neighbors, you will be responding to your Creator's love for you. And you will be his faithful spouse, and not unfaithful.

A bride is lacking in fidelity toward her spouse when she gives to someone else the love she owes him. Now you are a bride. You know very well that God's Son espoused us all at the time of his circumcision, when his flesh was cut to give us just the tiniest bit of a ring as a sign that he wanted to espouse the human race. When you contemplate such unspeaka-

---

[11] It. *Con grande consolatione et reverentia raguardare e servi di Dio.*

[12] These remarks may reflect Catherine's concern about the rumors being spread in Siena about her and her mission in the Val d'Orcia.

[13] Rom. 12, 15, where Paul is actually telling the Romans to "rejoice with those who rejoice, weep with those who weep."

[14] Elsewhere she explains, as in Let. T184 to the Company of the Virgin (in this volume): "We rejoice with God's servants who are rejoicing. We weep with the wicked who are living in a time of weeping, in the compassion and sorrow we bear because of their offense against God. And we willingly surrender ourselves to every kind of pain and torment in order to bring the wicked back to the condition of those who are rejoicing, who are living as lovers of lovely, royal virtue."

ble love, you ought to love him without any interference from anything outside of God.[15]

So you have been made a servant to your neighbors, to serve them in everything to the extent that you can. Just as you are a spouse to Christ, so you must be a servant to your neighbors if you would be a faithful spouse. Because we cannot be of any profit or service to God in our love for him, we must, as I've said, serve our neighbors with a genuinely heartfelt love. There is no other way nor any other vehicle[16] through which we can serve God. And this is why I said that I long to see you a true spouse and servant of Christ crucified.

Bathe, now, dearest sister and daughter, in the sweet blood of Christ crucified.[a]

I'll say no more. Keep living in God's holy and tender love.

Gentle Jesus! Jesus love!

Textual Notes

a. Tommasèo does not record this sentence.

---

[15] There is a play on words in the Italian here which is difficult to convey in translation. The word *mezzo* denotes "what is in between," whether positively as a means or negatively as an interference. Cf. Let. T164/DT58 to Melina Barbani (vol. I): "You know, my dear beloved daughter, that to join two things together there must be nothing between them or there cannot be a perfect fusion. Now realize that this is how God wants our soul to be, without any selfish love of ourselves or of others in between, just as God loves us without anything in between. . . . I want you and my other dear daughters to be transformed in and united with God by love, getting rid of any medium, anything that gets in between—except divine charity, which is a sweet and glorious medium that doesn't separate but unites. Really, it seems just like the master mason. He gathers many stones and fits them together, and the result is called both 'stones' and 'a wall.' He does this by using mortar as his medium. Without the medium the stones would fall apart more scattered and broken than ever. So now imagine how our soul has to gather all people and be united with them in love and desire for their salvation, so that they may be sharers in the blood of the Lamb. So here this wall stands—many people, yet they are one. . . . [Y]ou could say, 'First you tell us that God doesn't want anything between us and him, and now you tell us to put something in between!' My answer is that you must use the medium that doesn't put anything between us and God, the fire of divine charity, which becomes one with [God] as wood put into the fire. Would you say the wood remains wood? No, it becomes one with the fire. But if you were to use as medium your selfish love for yourself, you would be using a medium that would separate you from God, even though it is nothing (because sins have their root in nothing but selfish love and pleasure and enjoyment apart from God)."

[16] It. *forma*.

Letter T292/G129[1]
To William Flete, Matteo di Fazzio dei Cenni, Fra Santi, and other disciples
October or November 1377

The occasion for this letter seems to be a matter of disunity among Catherine's disciples in and around Siena, including William Flete at Lecceto, Matteo Cenni in Siena, and the hermit Fra Santi.[2] Since the last was probably with Catherine at Rocca d'Orcia during at least part of Advent of 1377 (she says in Let. T119 to Alessa dei Saracini that he has been ill), the present letter is probably not from that period. Nor can she be writing from Rome, since Fra Santi accompanied her there.

The very early letters to members of this group of disciples make no reference to discord, the first hint of this being in Let. T77 to William, which I have placed in spring of 1376. But that mention of discord is not nearly so strong as the reference in Let. T124, which clearly was written during Catherine's stay in the Val d'Orcia, probably during Advent.[3]

The linguistic evidence lends at least some support for placing the present letter sometime between October and December of 1377. Because of its necessary relationship with Let. T124 and because of the probable exclusion of Advent, I would place this letter probably in October or November.[4]

§

In the name of Jesus Christ crucified and of gentle Mary.

Dearest sons in Christ gentle Jesus,

I Caterina, servant and slave of the servants of Jesus Christ, am writing to you in his precious blood. I long to see you made one in the bond of

---

[1] MSS: R1, P5, F2, P3, P4, F7; translation based on R1.

[2] Fra Santi is the Sienese hermit at whose hermitage Catherine will later do much of her dictating of *The Dialogue* after her return from Florence. Burlamacchi (notes to the letter in Gigli, *Opere*, I) says he was from Terni or Teramo and that he was an associate of Giovanni Colombini and of the Carthusian Pietro Petroni, at whose death he assisted.

[3] Let. T119, T77, and T124 are in this volume.

[4] Most of this letter's twenty-two analyzed patterns occur very frequently and over the entire range of Catherine's writing years. The letters which share nine or more of these patterns are similarly scattered. Only three patterns show any significant chronological clustering (AMAINSIE, SERVEFIG, SERVMERC), and these are most densely concentrated between October and December 1377.

charity, for I am convinced that without this bonding we cannot be pleasing to God.

This is the lovely sign by which Christ's servants and children are recognized.[5] But reflect, my sons, that this bonding must be unadulterated by any stain of selfish love for yourselves. If you love your Creator, love and serve him not for your own profit but because he is supreme eternal Goodness and deserves to be loved. Otherwise you would be mercenaries, like those avaricious people who love money in order to hoard it for themselves.[6] Your love for your neighbors must be unadulterated.

Love, love each other! You are each other's neighbors! But watch out, for if your love were grounded in self-interest or in the selfish pleasure you took in each other it would not last. It would flounder, and you'd find your souls empty. Love that is grounded in God must be such that we love each other as creatures of God and in regard for virtue. Then, even though you[7] may get less pleasure or profit from those you love, your love will not fail if it is grounded in God, because you are loving with regard to virtue and for God's honor, and not for your own [ends]. If your love is in God, I say, even if those you love become less virtuous, you won't love them less.[a] True, you don't love the virtue that isn't there, but you love them no less as God's creatures, fellow members bound to you within the mystic body of holy Church.[8] In fact, a love of great and sincere compassion will grow in you, and you will give them birth with tears and sighs and continual prayer in God's dear presence.[9]

This is the sort of love Christ bequeathed to his disciples, a love that never falters or slows down. No injury makes it impatient, nor does it get indignant or take to grumbling, because it loves not selfishly but for God. It neither judges nor wants to judge by human standards but only in accord with its Creator's will,[10] which wants only that we be made holy.[11]

---

[5] Cf. Jn. 13, 35.

[6] It. *per propria avarizia.*

[7] Within three sentences, Catherine has switched from second person plural to third person singular to first person singular, and then back to third person. For consistency's sake, I have kept the second person plural vantage point throughout.

[8] This is yet another indication that Catherine did not understand the term "mystic body of the Church" as encompassing just the clergy and hierarchy, since at least two of her addressees here are laity.

[9] She implies a continual giving birth, since it is a question here of persons who have already been born to grace, and she does not seem to say that they necessarily have died to grace. Cf. Let. T141/DT38 to Don Giovanni dei Sabbatini (vol. I): "I call you son as well, since I am continually giving you birth by prayer and desire in God's presence just as truly as a mother gives birth to her child." (Gal. 4, 19: "You are my children, and you put me back in labor pains until Christ is formed in you.")

[10] Cf. Mt. 16, 23; Rm. 12, 2. Catherine seems to be drawing on the sense of both passages here and elsewhere when she speaks of discerning God's will, often in contrast with

It is happy with whatever God permits, in whatever way God permits it, because it seeks only its Creator's honor and its neighbors' salvation. One can truly say that those [who have such love] are bound in the bond of charity, the same bond that held the God-man nailed fast to the wood of the sweet holy cross.

But reflect, my sons, that you could never realize such perfect union without focusing your attention on Christ crucified and following in his footsteps. It is in him that you will discover this love, since he has loved you not out of duty but gratuitously. And because his love is gratuitous, neither our ingratitude nor our foolishness nor our vanity and pride caused his love to slow down.[12] No, he persevered even to the shameful death of the cross to rescue us from death and give us life. This is what you must do, my sons. Learn, learn from him! Love, love each other with a pure and holy love in Christ gentle Jesus![b]

I'll say no more, because I hope to see you again as soon as it pleases divine goodness. Keep living in God's holy and tender love.

Gentle Jesus! Jesus love![c]

Textual Notes

a. Tommasèo: *non ricusa meno l'amore*, which seems to imply a full withdrawal of love. R1 has *non viene meno l'amore.*

b. R1: [*with a pure . . . Jesus!*]

c. R1: *Keep living, etc. Jesus, etc.*

---

judging by human standards, for example, in *Dial.* 100, pp. 187–192, where she dedicates an entire chapter to the theme.

[11] 1 Thes. 4, 3.

[12] Here the verb (*allenta*) is particularly appropriate, since Catherine so often speaks of Christ "running like one in love" to the cross.

LETTER T49/G177[1]
To Monna Alessa dei Saracini
Late October or November 1377

Alessa seems to have been with Catherine only at the beginning of the Val d'Orcia mission, if that. We know that early in that period she and a certain Monna Bruna were in nearby Montegiovi "on assignment."[2] They may have returned to Siena immediately after that. In any case, Alessa was in Siena at least by early October.

The present letter gives no clue as to where it is being written from or when. The linguistic evidence, however, points emphatically to the Val d'Orcia period, and most strongly toward October or November. This is reinforced by the occurrence of passages which closely parallel *The Dialogue*.[3] I would therefore guess that it is from late October or November.

§

In the name of Jesus Christ crucified and of gentle Mary.

Dearest daughter in Christ gentle Jesus,

I your poor unworthy mother am longing for you to achieve the perfection for which God has chosen you. It would seem that if we want to achieve that, we have to proceed with, not without, moderation. [Yet, in another sense,] all our actions should be done both with and without moderation.[4] We must love God[a] without moderation, setting neither qualification nor measure nor rule, but loving him boundlessly. Yet, to arrive at the perfection of love, you have to set priorities in your life.

Let your highest priority be to avoid associating with people socially except as charity requires. Love many people, but keep company with few.[b] Even with those you love with a spiritual love, know how to moder-

---

[1] MSS: Mo-*a*, with few corrections by *b*; M, S5, S6, Ro, F3, P4, S4; translation based on Mo-*a*, with variants based on unpublished notes by A. Volpato.

[2] Cf. Let. T118 to Caterina dello Spedaluccio and Giovanna di Capo, written in the early weeks of Catherine's stay in the Val d'Orcia.

[3] This conclusion is based on a number of significant clusters within individual patterns which begin and/or end in those months: ACQUAVIV, AMORIMPE, AMORSPIR, CELLCOGN, CELLMENT, CONSENZ, LEGGEPER, OBEDCARI, ORDINVIT, SEDIACON, SONNCORP. Fawtier (II, p. 228) declines to date the letter. Dupré Theseider (unpublished notes) places it in autumn of 1377.

[4] The text as it stands literally seems to contradict itself, but what follows confirms that Catherine is addressing a paradox. While all of our human loves must be moderated (*con modo*), God must be loved without qualification or measure of moderation of any sort (*senza modo*).

ate your relationship. Unless you do, realize that, though you might not advert to it, you would be putting a limit on the limitless love you owe to God, because you would be putting a finite person between yourself and God. The love you ought to be giving to God you would be giving to this person by loving him or her without moderation, and this would stand in the way of your becoming perfect. So you should love people with moderation, according to your priorities, and spiritually.[5]

Take, for example, a jug that you'd fill in the fountain and drink from in the fountain.[6] For although you might have drawn love from God, who is the fountain of living water, unless you drank from it always in God it would end up empty. And this will be the sign that you are not drinking entirely in God: that the person or thing you love becomes a source of pain to you, either because of a conversation you have, or because you have been deprived of some comfort you are used to receiving, or because of something else that happens. When these things—or *anything* other than offense against God—cause you pain, it is a clear sign that this love is still imperfect, drawn outside the fountain.[7]

So how can you make perfect what is imperfect? Here is how: by correcting and purifying the movements of your heart with true self-knowledge and with displeasure and hatred for your lack of perfection. (I mean your being so rude as to give to a creature the love you ought to be giving completely to God, by loving God in a limited way and the creature without moderation.) For our love for God must be without measure, and our love for creatures must be measured alongside love for God and not according to our own consolation, whether spiritual or temporal. Love everything and everyone in God, then, and use hatred to[c] correct every affection that is out of order.

My daughter, make yourself two dwelling places. The first is a physical dwelling place, your room. Don't leave it to be running here and there, except as required by necessity, a command of the prioress,[8] or charity.

The other dwelling place is spiritual, and you should carry it with you constantly. This is the cell of true self-knowledge, and there you will find knowledge of God's goodness to you. This cell is really two rooms in one,

---

[5] Cf. Let. T164/DT58 to Melina Barbani, in which Catherine expands on this notion of loving with moderation, developing the concept of mediation in contrast with interference.

[6] In the public fountains of Siena, especially Fonte Branda near Catherine's home, the water from the springs within the rock collects in a roofed reservoir enclosed by a low wall. One could in such a case speak of drinking "in the fountain."

[7] This imagery is developed also in *Dial.* 64, p. 121, and 144, pp. 303–304.

[8] Alessa is not a religious, but as a *Mantellata* (Third Order Dominican, as was Catherine) she is subject in many things (by rule, though not by vow) to a prioress chosen by the Dominican chaplain and a few of the more senior members of the group.

and while you are in the one you must at the same time be in the other; otherwise your soul would end up either in confusion or in presumption. For if you stayed in self-knowledge, spiritual confusion would be the result. And if you stayed only in knowledge of God, you would end up in presumption. So the one has to be seasoned by the other, and the two made to be one. When this is accomplished you will arrive at perfection. Here is why. From knowledge of yourself you will gain hatred for your selfish sensuality, and because of that hatred you will be a judge. You will mount the bench of your conscience and demand an account of yourself,[d] letting no sin pass without doing it justice. From this knowledge issues the spring of[e] humility, which never acts on assumptions, never takes scandal in anything, but bears with joyful patience any injury, any loss of consolation, any suffering from any source whatever. Disgraces appear as a sort of glory, and fierce persecution as refreshment. In all of them it rejoices at seeing itself chastised for that perverse law of selfish sensual will which is constantly rebelling against God.[9] And it sees itself conformed with Christ Jesus crucified, who is [the] way and teaching of truth.

In the knowledge of God you will discover the fire of divine charity, where you will find your pleasure on the cross with the spotless Lamb, searching out God's honor and the salvation of souls in continual and humble prayer. Herein lies all our perfection. There are many other things, but this is the principal one.[10] In this we receive so much light that we cannot be wrong in the lesser works that follow.

My daughter, find your pleasure in conforming yourself with the humiliations of Christ. Keep watch over the movements of your tongue, for sometimes it shouldn't echo the feelings of your heart! Digest what's in your heart first, with self-hatred and self-contempt.[11] Make yourself the least of the least, in humility and patience submissive to everyone else for God's sake. Don't be excusing yourself, but say, "*Mea culpa.*"[12] In this way, with the power of humility, you conquer both your own vices and those of the person of whom you've spoken [ill].

Regulate your time, the night for vigil (once you have given your body the sleep you owe it), and the morning for church and sweet prayer. And don't spend time in chatting until the proper hour. In this respect as in everything else, don't let yourself be distracted except for necessity, obedience, or charity, as I've said. After your mealtime spend a bit of time in

---

[9] Cf. Rom. 7, 23.

[10] An echo of 1 Cor. 13, 13, where "the greatest of these is charity."

[11] This imagery is unique here.

[12] "My fault," a phrase from the *Confiteor* at the beginning of Mass: "I confess . . . that I have sinned, through my own fault. . . ."

recollection. Then do some manual work, depending on what you have to do. So far as Vespers is concerned, go and do a bit; whatever the Holy Spirit prompts you to do, let it be at that.[13] Then go back and take care of your old mother. No carelessness! And see that she has what she needs.

Let this be your responsibility from now till my return.[14] See that you act in such a way as to realize my desire.

I'll say no more. Keep living in God's holy and tender love.

Gentle Jesus! Jesus love!

Textual Notes

a. *God* is written within the text of P4, inserted (by *a*, apparently) above the line in Mo, and omitted in F3.

b. P4: *socially. Love many people, but keep company with few, except as charity requires.* / *socially. . . . few.*

c. P4: [*use hatred to*].

d. P4: [*of yourself*].

e. F3: *true* (*vera*) / *the spring of* (*vena*). Either would be consistent with Catherine's usage.

---

[13] It. *Allora del vespero, e tu va e fa cavelle, e quanto lo Spirito Santo ti fa fare, tanto sta.* The meaning is not clear. Perhaps Alessa is to go to the church for Vespers, praying along with the choir of friars just as much as she may be inspired to. Or perhaps *vespero* is simply the evening, and Alessa is just to do whatever the Spirit prompts her to do. (Tommasèo: *Ad ora del vespero. . . .* "At the hour of Vespers. . . .")

[14] Mo: *E sia tuo questo peso di qui alla mia tornata.* Tommasèo: . . . *sia tuo questo peso. Di più, alla mia tornata.*

Letter T62/G248[1]
To Sano di Maco di Mazzacorno and her other children
October to December 1377

This is another of several letters which Catherine addressed to her disciples in Siena through the good offices of the wool worker Sano di Maco di Mazzacorno.[2] The rubrics in the various manuscripts do not, however, indicate where the letter was sent, nor from where. For this, one must rely on the chronological placement of the letter, which can be determined only on the basis of the linguistic evidence.

That linguistic evidence suggests very strongly that the letter was written during Catherine's stay in the Val d'Orcia, indeed during the latter months of that period.[3]

§

In the name of Jesus Christ crucified and of gentle Mary.

Dearest children in Christ gentle Jesus,

I Caterina, servant and slave of the servants of Jesus Christ, am writing to you in his precious blood. I long to see you faithful servants to our dear Savior. To serve him is not to be a servant but to reign.[4]

A servant without fidelity cannot be a servant in truth, for servants who are not faithful are mercenary, serving either for their own advantage or[a] out of slavish fear. And because their service is not perfect, because it is not enlightened by faith, these people are also neither strong nor persevering but go flying off with every wind. The wind of consolation blows them to lightheartedness, but the wind of difficulty blows them to impa-

---

[1] MSS: Mo-*a*, M, S5, S6, Ro, B, P2, P5, F2, F1, P3; translation based on Mo-*a*. I have not consulted any other manuscript, but have noted where Tommasèo differs from Mo-*a*.

[2] The rubric of Mo adds that it was dictated in ecstasy (*in abstractione*).

[3] The letter has very little in common with letters written before autumn of 1377. All nineteen letters sharing thirteen or more of this one's sixty-eight analyzed patterns are from that period and later, with ten of them occurring during that period. Further, a number of significant clusters within individual patterns begin at that point (AMARVERI, AMASERVE, AMORFEDE, IMPAZPRI, LABORE, LEGGCUOR, LEGRAGIO, LUMEPERF, MAREONDE, MARETEMP, PUPILFED, SERVFDEL, SERVMERC, SERVPROS). Several also end in the same period (FUGVELEN, IMPAZPRI, LABORE, LEGGCUOR, LEGRAGIO, MAREONDE, PAREOFFE, PONSED, SAZFAST). Fawtier (II, p. 289) and Dupré Theseider (unpublished notes) decline to date this letter.

[4] Cf. Augustine, *Meditatio XXXII* (PL XL, 925): "To serve God is to reign." Catherine was most probably familiar with the popular saying either from sermons or from contemporary writers such as Cavalca (*Trenta stoltitie*, p. 32) or Bianco da Siena (*Lauda LIX*, 18).

tience. The wind of struggle or of the devil's harassment makes them become halfhearted[5] and sit down in despondency because they think they have lost God when they see that they have lost consolation and spiritual sensitivity. All of this happens because they love the gifts of grace more than the one who gives them, because they are serving more out of regard for themselves than for the supreme eternal Goodness that is God. And so, because their love is imperfect, so is the light of [their] faith.

But those who love perfectly serve with fidelity and with living faith. They believe in truth that whatever God does or permits is done for their sanctification, because God does not want the sinner to die but to be converted and live.[6] They have seen by the light of most holy faith that it is the very same love that makes God give us great consolations or permit the devil to harass our spirit and allow others to persecute us. We see that God is supremely good, and that nothing other than supreme goodness can come from him. We see that nothing has been made without God except sin alone. Faithful souls, therefore, embrace everything with love because everything is good and is given for our salvation—and we neither can nor should be sad about our own good!

Perhaps, dearest children, you will say to me, "In times of struggle it seems to us that we are rebellious, that we are offending God, and we feel worse about this than we do about the pain." Here is my answer. It is as much your selfish spiritual sensuality as anything else that is feeling bad! And this passion, under the pretext of fearing to offend God, has put a bit of dust in your mind's eye (where the pupil of most holy faith is), to keep you from discerning and knowing the truth.[7] For if your mind's eye were unobstructed, you would know that God's giving is well measured. And you ought to see clearly that no struggle, no harassment from the devil or from our weak flesh, is sinful or offensive to our Creator unless our selfish will consents to the evil thoughts in our heart.

But those who are faithful servants, who have the light of most holy faith, profit handsomely from times of struggle. They build a true foundation by leaving selfish mercenary love behind. Their heart and motivation[8] have become pure and generous.[9,b] In times of intense struggle they wage a fierce war with themselves, and this war (along with the holy hatred they have conceived) makes them willing to suffer as faithful servants.

---

[5] It. *intiepidisce.*

[6] 1 Thes. 4, 3; Ez. 33, 11.

[7] This imagery of the pupil of faith in the eye of understanding begins to appear in Catherine's writings only during the Val d'Orcia period.

[8] It. *affetto.*

[9] It. *liberale,* which has connotations both of freedom and of generosity. Its use here is related to later references to being free.

They are always happy to go to battle for Christ crucified. And they grow in love when they recognize that their good and holy will is not their own doing but that of the supreme eternal goodness of God who has given it as a favor and not because it is their due.

Oh glorious faithful servanthood that frees our soul from perverse servitude to the devil, the world, and ourselves!

We are freed from the devil because we have bound our will in the bonds of reason. We don't consent to his harassments or let ourselves become inordinately discouraged. No, we laugh at the devil. We enjoy being on the battlefield. So the devil is flogged with the rod of charity and bound with the shackles of true humility. We are made masters, so that we no longer fear the devil. Instead, the devil is afraid of us because of Christ crucified, through whom we can do anything.[10]

And, I say, we are made free masters of the world because we don't let ourselves be ruled by inordinate attachment to its grandeur and pleasures. We are masters of these things; we make light of and reject them. Why? Because we have seen and known by the light of most holy faith that the world's wealth is utter poverty. Its pleasures and delights are despicable, so incomparably wretched that we avoid them as if they were poisonous snakes.[11]

We serve others only within God's will, for we don't want to comply with their will except to the extent that it is directed to the search for and love of eternal Truth. We love and serve our neighbors because the sweet light [of faith] has shown us that they are the intermediary God has given us; by [loving and serving] them we can prove our love for God.[12] This sort of service makes us truly free, because we are not serving our neighbors sinfully.

I say too that we are faithful and free in not serving our selfish sensuality.[13] When it has rebelled, we have trampled it under the feet of our

---

[10] Phil. 4, 13: "I can do all things in him who strengthens me."

[11] Cf. *Dial.* 47, p. 98: "For just as venom is painful to the body and ultimately causes death unless a person makes the effort to vomit it out and take some medicine, so it is with this scorpion of the world's pleasure. I am not speaking of material things in themselves. I have already told you that these are good and that they are made by me, the greatest Good, and so you can use them as you please with holy love and truthful fear. What I am speaking of is the venom of a perverted human will, which poisons souls and causes them death."

[12] Cf. *Dial.* 7, p. 36: "Since love of neighbor has its source in me, the more the soul loves me, the more she loves her neighbors. Such is the means I have given you to practice and prove your virtue. The service you cannot render me you must do for your neighbors."

[13] Cf. Let. T50 to Caterina di Ghetto: "You see, then, how in charity for God we conceive the virtues and how in charity for our neighbors we bring them to birth. If you act in this way, if you love your neighbors sincerely, not with a false heart or feigned love but freely, without any concern for your own spiritual or material profit, you will be a true servant. Through your neighbors, you will be responding to your Creator's love for you."

love. We have struck it down with the knife of hatred and of love, of hatred for vice and love for virtue.[c]

So this lovely servanthood has indeed made us masters and sovereigns. We have sought ourselves not selfishly but for God, because God is supreme eternal Goodness and deserves our love and service. And we have sought our neighbors for God's sake, with no regard for self-interest.

What words could ever describe the peace of those who are faithful? Not that it is a peace without waves and stormy seas. But their will is at peace because it has been made one with God's gentle will. So the storm is calm to them, since they have no concern for themselves. They serve their Creator in war as well as in peace. And they hold war as dear as peace, and peace as dear as war, because the light of faith has made them see, and this vision has made them know that one and the same love sends them both.

They are never scandalized by their neighbors, because they judge not by human standards but by God's.[14] So they are liberated from grumbling. I don't think this is true of you; I don't think you are this perfect.[15] No, you are grumbling much of the time, passing judgment on one another under the pretext of compassion and goodness. This sort of thing cannot but be offensive to God. It displeases him, and it very emphatically displeases me! This is not how you were taught. No, you were taught to love one another, to bear with and share the burden of each others' shortcomings. No one is without shortcomings; only God has no shortcomings at all.[d] All of this is happening to you because you have not yet become faithful servants. For if you were faithful servants there would be no sarcasm or grumbling or scandal-mongering or disobedience among you—either in anger or in jest.[16]

I was thinking of your imperfection, and of how the reason for your imperfection is that the light of most holy faith is not perfect in you, and this is why I said that I long to see you faithful servants. To serve in this way is to reign in this life through grace, to rule over the world, the flesh, and the devil. Once you are free, you will be bound in the bond of charity; you will be humble and meek; you will have a true and holy patience. And in the end you will reign with the truly and wonderfully joyful in everlasting life,[17] where we will be rewarded for our every labor. There

---

[14] Cf. Mt. 16, 23; Mk. 11, 18 (Vulg.), where Jesus rebukes Peter, "You are a scandal to me, because you are judging not by what is of God but by what is human."

[15] Cf. Jas. 3, 2 (Vulg.): "The person who does not sin in words is perfect."

[16] These remarks may or may not be related to what she has said in Let. T294 to the same group of disciples, though in that letter she seemed to be directly concerned with grumbling about her and her companions in the Val d'Orcia.

[17] It. *i veri e dolci gustatori*. The expression must be seen in relation to "those who eat

satiety is without boredom and hunger without pain, for hunger is freed from pain and satiety from boredom.[18]

Up then, dearest children, and run this race! See that only one wins it. By this I mean, don't let your heart be split off; let it be joined as one and the same thing with your neighbors in affectionate love.[19] And so that you will be better able to run, drink your fill of the blood of Christ crucified;[e] get drunk on it! This blood challenges us to run. It motivates us to fight. We don't refuse the effort by turning back for fear of our enemies, because we are trusting not in ourselves but in the blood of Christ crucified. Don't go on sleeping, then, but rouse yourselves from the slumber of apathy and run to this blood.[f]

I'll say no more.[g] Keep living in God's holy and tender love.

Gentle Jesus! Jesus love!

Textual Notes

a. Tommasèo: *and / either . . . or.*
b. Tommasèo: *their heart has become pure and their love generous / their . . . generous.*
c. Tommasèo: *We have trampled it under the feet of our love; we have struck it down and cut it to pieces with the knife. . . . / When it has rebelled . . . . knife. . . .*
d. Tommasèo: [*at all*].
e. Tommasèo: *Jesus Christ / Christ crucified.*
f. Tommasèo adds *of Christ crucified.*
g. Tommasèo adds *to you.*

---

and enjoy (*gustano*) souls at the table of the cross" (for example, Let. T283 in vol. I and T83 in 1378 or 1379), as well as to those who enjoy God even in this life because of their union with the divine will (for example, Let. T112 in this volume and T5 in 1378) In heaven this enjoyment of God and of one's neighbors is made perfect.

[18] Cf. Cavalca, *Specchio di croce*, p. 184 (citing Pseudo-Augustine, *Meditatio XXVII*, PL XL, 921): "Sated, we shall be hungry, and hungering we shall be sated, but our satiety will be far from boredom, and our hunger far from pain."

[19] It. *per affetto d'amore.* While she usually simply *states* that "only one wins the race," here she advises her disciples to *see to it* that only one wins, that is, the integrity of love for God and neighbor.

LETTER T259/G222[1]
To Tommaso d'Alviano
October to December 1377

Catherine has already written to Tommaso d'Alviano concerning his military service to God and the Church (Let. T191). The present letter contains no mention of military service, but only of a general Christian service, with apparent specific reference to Tommaso's roles of authority, which could well be an allusion to his office as ecclesiastical administrator of Orvieto, a post he assumed in 1377.

The close parallels between what is written here and in *The Dialogue* concerning the fulfillment of God's truth (chapter 21) and the gathering of the powers of the soul (chapters 51–55) would seem to be an argument for placing this letter close to the period when Catherine was composing the latter work, that is, October 1377 through October 1378. But since the *Dialogue* treatment of these topics is more detailed and developed, I would guess that this letter was written before Catherine had finished those parts of her book.

There is no more direct clue in the letter's content to when it was written.[2] The linguistic data, however, argue very persuasively in favor of placement between October and December of 1377.[3]

§

In the name of Jesus Christ crucified and of gentle Mary.

Dearest brother in Christ gentle Jesus,

I Caterina, servant and slave of the servants of Jesus Christ, am writing to you in his precious blood. I long to see you a faithful servant of our Cre-

[1] MSS: Mo-*a*, S3, M, S5, S6, Ro; translation based on Mo-*a*. No relevant variants.

[2] Fawtier (II, p. 260) places it shortly after Let. T191, which he dates 1377 or early 1378. Dupré Theseider (unpublished notes) places it before Let. T191, but without citing reasons.

[3] Eight other letters share twenty-two or more of this one's eighty-eight analyzed patterns; five of these are dated between September and December of 1377, and three are later. Most persuasive is the very dense concentration of clusters within individual patterns in the last months of 1377. Fifteen patterns show no occurrences at all or only an isolated occurrence or two before September 1377 (AMAINVER, AMASERV, BENEFATT, CONGRPOT, GIUDICVO, LUMEPERF, MEZZPER, OPERCONG, PROSPER, RAGUARD, RICRGRAZ, SANGSANT, SERVFEDE, TENRAGIO, VERITCMP). Another thirteen significant clusters end by December 1377 (BENEFATT, CONCEPPR, CONGRPOT, CUORANIM, DAFIGLIO, GIUDICVO, MEZZPER, OPERCONG, RAGUARD, RIBELCHS, RICRGRAZ, SANGSANT, TENRAGIO).

ator, and that servanthood makes us reign eternally.[4] It would not, however, be a source of life if we were not faithful. I mean faithful with the light of faith.

We acquire this light when with the eye of our understanding we gaze into the boundless charity God showed in so lovingly giving us being. And we discover boundless love in the Word his only-begotten Son as well, for in his blood we discover how God created us anew to the grace we had lost because of our sin. So it was for love that God created us in his own image and likeness, and for love that he gave us his Son to reinstate us by creating us anew to grace in his blood. God wanted, through his Son, to reveal to us his truth and his gentle will—that he seeks and wants only that we be made holy.[5] This is God's truth: that in truth he created us to share and be happy in that eternal vision of him from which we receive our blessedness.

Because of the sin Adam had committed, this truth was not being realized in humankind.[6] So God, wanting to realize this truth, urges himself on by his own charity and gives us what he holds most dear, his only-begotten Son. And he lays on him this task of reinstating humankind and bringing us back from death to life.

God, as I've said, wants the human race to be born again in the blood, and no one can have the fruit of the blood without the light of faith. This is why Christ said to Nicodemus, "No one can enter eternal life without being born again."[7] Christ, then, wanted to show that the eternal Father had given him the task of conceiving this child, the human race, through the impulse of love, and of giving it birth on the wood of the most holy cross in true obedience, in hatred and contempt for the sin of [its first] father.[8]

It seems that this gentle Word is like the eagle who looks up into the sphere of the sun and who always sees from high up the food he wants to

---

[4] Cf. Augustine's "To serve God is to reign" (*Meditatio XXXII*, PL XL, 925), cited in many contemporary writers, for example, Cavalca, *Trenta stoltitie*, p. 32.

[5] 1 Thes. 4, 3.

[6] As she often does with this story of God's mercy, Catherine now switches suddenly to telling it in the present tense.

[7] Jn. 3, 5.

[8] "The sin of [its first] father" is the sin of Adam, said in Christian doctrine to have left its mark on every human being. Usually Catherine uses the image of conceiving and giving birth in reference to charity as mother of the virtues. This is the only place in which she refers it to Christ giving birth to the human race. The closest parallel is in Let. T272 to Raimondo da Capua (in this volume, the letter which will form the basic outline for *The Dialogue*), where the imagery is extended to Christians: "Conceive, my children, and give birth to this child, the human race, with hatred and sorrow for sin and with blazing and yearning love."

capture. Spotting it on the earth, he comes and takes it, and later, back up high, he eats it.[9] This is how our eagle, the gentle Jesus, looks into the sun of the Father's eternal will, and there sees his creatures' sin and rebellion. And in those earthly creatures (whom he has spotted in the Father's exaltedness) he sees the food he must capture. And this is his food: obediently to fulfill in us the Father's truth by taking on this pitiable earth that has sinned and rebelled against God in wretched disobedience.[10] In his obedience he chooses to fulfill in us the Father's truth, to restore grace in us, deliver us from servitude to the devil (which gives eternal death), and lead us back to serve our Creator. After he has seen and taken the food the Father has given him to eat, he sees that he cannot eat it down there on the earth if he wants to draw poor humankind back to its original obedience,[11] so he flies up with his prey to the heights of the most holy cross, and there he eats it in indescribable and anguished desire. In his own person he punishes our sins by suffering physically, and with his will he makes satisfaction by his hatred and contempt for sin. With the power of the divine nature that is in him he offers the sacrifice of his blood to his Father, and his sacrifice is accepted.[12]

So you see him up high in pain and disgrace, mocked, abused, tormented, and insulted, sated with shame and so tortured with thirst that he dies of thirst for our salvation. This is how this gentle Lamb, so in love, ate. And this is why he said, "If I am lifted up high I will draw everything to myself."[13] For because of our rebirth in the blood of Christ crucified we are drawn to love him—if only we follow reason instead of abandoning it in love for our selfish sensuality. Once our heart has been drawn to love our benefactor, everything is drawn: heart, soul, and will, along with everything we do spiritually and physically.

This love [in turn] draws our soul's powers (which are spiritual).

Our memory is drawn by the eternal Father's power and cannot help holding close the favors we have received from him, remembering them in affectionate love and being appreciative and grateful.[14]

---

[9] Iacopo da Varazze describes the qualities of the eagle in the *Legenda aurea*, in his commentary on the feast of Saint Luke: "The eagle is sharp-sighted, for it can look into the sun without blinking, and can see little fishes in the sea from a great height."

[10] Jn. 4, 34 (Vulg.): "My food is to do the will of the one who sent me, and to bring his work to completion."

[11] She contrasts "original obedience" with the "original sin" of Adam.

[12] Cf. Aquinas, *Summa Theologica*, III, q. 48, a. 6: "Because Christ's humanity is the instrument of the Godhead . . . , all of his actions and sufferings operate instrumentally in virtue of his divinity for the salvation of humankind."

[13] Jn. 12, 32.

[14] Augustine, whom Catherine follows in her understanding of the three powers of the soul, sees memory as the power to "hold" God's blessings, rather than as the simple power

Our understanding rises into the wisdom of this spotless Lamb to contemplate in him the fire of his charity. There we see that all God's judgments are just.[15] For no matter what God permits, whether prosperity or adversity, God does it not out of hatred but out of love. So we receive and hold everything as love. For if God's Wisdom, God's Son, had wanted anything else, he would never have given his life for us. Enlightened, then, by this true light, no difficulty we might suffer saddens us, and if our feelings should want to grieve, we quiet them in the light of reason. Not only are we not sad, but we hold these things in reverence. We are happy to suffer in punishment for our sins and to be able to conform ourselves with the sufferings of Christ crucified. If we have worldly prosperity, prestige, and power, we hold them not with inordinate love but with love that is well-ordered. We are zealous for true and holy justice free from any slavish fear because we have raised our mind's eye to the Wisdom that is God's Son. There we see a justice so overwhelming that in order not to leave sin unpunished he took out the punishment on his own humanity, which he had taken from us.

Next our will rises up and runs to the love our mind's eye has seen in God, and thus we win and experience the grace and mercy that is the Holy Spirit. Filled with love and desire for God, our will reaches out in charity to love our neighbors with a familial charity rather than selfishly. (For if we were loving selfishly, we would be neither reasonable nor just with ourselves or our neighbors.) But because the Holy Spirit's grace has freed us from self-centeredness by lifting our affection up into himself, we have been made just and faithful servants of our Creator.

So no matter what our state in life, whether in positions of authority or grandeur or worldly prestige and wealth, whether in the state of continence or of marriage, with children or without them, we are pleasing to God in every way because we love with an affection that is bound to God. And this is what gentle First Truth reveals to us: that God is partial not to states of life or to times or places, but to true and holy desires.

I said that we are drawn spiritually as well as physically, and that is the truth.[16] For once we have put the three spiritual powers of our soul in order and lifted them up high on the energy of love and gathered them in God's name (I mean, tuned our memory to hold God's gifts and graces; our understanding to comprehend what Wisdom, God's Son, wants; and

---

of recalling. She is here developing these three powers as the Trinitarian image within the human person.

[15] Cf. Tb. 3, 2: "You are righteous, O Lord, and all your deeds are just."

[16] Tommasèo omits "that God is partial . . . that is the truth."

our will to love in the gentle mercy of the Holy Spirit), then God dwells within our soul by grace.[17]

This is how we must understand our Savior's meaning when he said, "If two or three or more are gathered in my name, I will be in their midst."[18] So we can understand that he was talking about the gathering of the soul's three powers that I just mentioned, as well as the physical gathering of the servants of God. But note that he puts before us two, three, and more. We have already spoken of the three. By the two we can understand love and holy desire for God, since it is love that has to do the gathering. For if we did not love, our memory wouldn't be ready to receive and hold, nor would our understanding be moved to see and comprehend, nor would our will nurture divine love within us. Once love has gathered the treasure together, holy fear guards it and refuses to let the enemy, deadly sin, get into the city of our soul.

Love was the first motivation even of that holy law of God founded on fear that was given to Moses. For it was out of love that God gave it, so that humankind would be restrained from its evil ways. Later came the gentle loving Word with the law of love, not to dissolve the law that had been given, but to fulfill it, since fear was not giving us life.[19] He harmonized the law of love with the law of fear, and he did it so perfectly that what was imperfect was made perfect. So we have to hold to both the one and the other, because they are so perfectly made one that anyone who doesn't want to be separated from God cannot have the one without the other. They are bound together (to the extent that we are still talking about the ten commandments), and together they give the life of grace. It would be impossible to want to separate them and still have God within oneself by grace. This is why he said "if there are two" rather than "if there is one." For one is incapable of being "gathered together," and thus one can never be more than one. So we cannot reach three without two. No, first we have to have two, and then, little by little, with these two (love and fear of God), we find the soul's three powers, which make but one soul. And that one, adorned with the perfection of charity, is so perfect that it holds the two and the three as well as the "more."

And why does he say, "Either two or three *or more* gathered in my name"? These are people's good and holy actions. For when we have made it our principle to gather and regulate all our powers in God's name, everything we do is directed to God (even though it may appear to be

---

[17] There are close parallels between what follows and *Dial.* 51–56.

[18] Mt. 18, 20.

[19] Cf. Mt. 5, 17: "Do not think that I have come to abolish the law and the prophets. I have come not to abolish them, but to fulfill them."

worldly, such as having great authority and prestige, and living with one's wife and children, which seem to be worldly matters—or anything else at all). Then we know well his truth, that God has given us nothing in this life that will be an impediment to our salvation. If we want, in fact, all these things will be instruments for our practice of virtue, to give us a greater knowledge of our own poverty and of divine goodness.

So we don't complain about the Creator or about other people (nor can we), but only about ourselves, who with the rottenness of deadly sin rebel against our Creator. We can't complain about God, since he has made us so strong that neither the devil nor anyone else can take God away from us. In fact, the wrong worldly people do us often results in our having God more perfectly (if we don't because of our selfish feelings get angry), since it tests our patience and we see whether or not we love our Creator in truth. And then our soul's vessel is even more filled with grace. So we can't complain. Even if impulses of impurity are roused within us because of other people or things and we are tempted to indecent urges or actions or demeanor, I'm saying we can't complain even about this, because such impulses can often enough come from our own weakness as well as from seduction by others. And we can contain these impulses if we are willing to resist reasonably and be sensitive to purity's fragrance.

But whenever you feel you are being attacked by this or any other vice, take out your love and holy fear of God. With your mind's eye look into your memory, where you have stored God's favors, and with your will love him and give him glory and praise. With this holy gratitude you will put out the fires of anger and impurity and injustice and every other sin—but especially injustice.[20]

For those who have to hold office and authority get into all sorts of trouble unless they hold their positions virtuously. The moment they don't keep their eyes fixed on God they begin exercising their authority with selfishly directed love. Such love poisons their soul and robs them of light so that they neither recognize nor understand anything but the transitory things of sense. They always assume the worst and never the best about God's intentions as well as their own and other people's. Their selfishness deprives them of the life of grace and gives them death. Their actions are directed only to the death that is sin, so they pass sentence and impose punishment according to human opinion rather than reason, because of their slavish fear that they will lose their position!

Oh how dangerous this perverted love is! It was the devil's law, and the devil gave it in the very beginning to Eve, with Adam following and carry-

---

20 She seems to be alluding particularly here to Tommaso's role as ecclesiastical administrator of Orvieto.

ing it through.[21] It was a law of diabolical love and fear. But gentle First Truth overthrew this perverse law and set us free so that nothing at all can force us to adhere to it. True, we can with our freedom of choice accept it if we want to, but it cannot be imposed on us any more than we willfully choose. With such a Redeemer, who has given us strength and rescued us from slavery to the law of sin, how ashamed we should be not to follow him in perfect love, with all our heart, with all our will, and with the light of living faith which we discover and experience with our eye of understanding and by which, with our will, we give birth to living deeds, not dead.[22] It [must be] a living faith, because faith without deeds is dead.[23] There is no other way we can be servants of Christ crucified. And serving him makes us reign not only in everlasting life but also by making us masters of ourselves. And those who are masters of themselves have become masters of all the world. For they neither fear nor care about anything except the things of God, whom they love and serve. Many people possess cities and fortresses, but unless they are in possession of themselves in love for virtue they will discover that they aren't anything but empty—both of the world and of God, whether in life or in death.

I said that I long to see you a faithful servant of our Creator because I was reflecting that without the light of faith as intermediary you wouldn't be able to attain this perfection. So I beg you, dearest brother, do it! I mean, do serve God courageously! It's true that you cannot be of any service or profit to God, since God has no need of our service. But he has given us a way, in that he considers done for him whatever service we do for our neighbors for the praise and glory of his name.[24] And of all the services we can do that please God, serving his gentle bride pleases him especially, and it seems you have been called to this service.[25] So serve her

---

[21] Cf. Gn. 3, 1–6.

[22] Cf. Let. T185/DT54 to Pope Gregory XI: "For those who love themselves—whether they are rulers or the ruled—harbor within themselves the evil pride that is the head and origin of all evil. For those who are isolated in their self-centeredness, loving themselves selfishly and not for God, can do nothing but evil; all virtue is dead in them. They are like a woman whose children are stillborn—truly so, because they have none of the life, the charity, that is concerned only for the praise and glory of God's name." In *Dial.* 46, p. 94, she adds the dimension of faith in relation to charity, as she does in the present letter: "Just as a woman bears a living child and presents it living to her husband, so [these people] would have presented me, the soul's spouse, with living virtues. But these wretched people do just the opposite. They reach the age of discernment when they ought to . . . give birth to virtues with the life of grace. Instead they give birth to dead virtues. They are dead because all their actions, being done in deadly sin and bereft of the light of faith, are dead."

[23] Jas. 2, 20–26.

[24] Cf. Mt. 25, 40.

[25] This would seem to imply that Tommaso has only recently been appointed administrator in Orvieto—or that Catherine has just learned of that appointment.

generously. For you will please God by whatever spiritual or temporal service you do her, so long as you do it with a good and upright intention. If you do this, God is appreciative and grateful. He will give you the fruits of your efforts in this life by grace, and in everlasting life you will receive the eternal vision of God and will see the eternal Father's truth and love with perfectly clear light undimmed by any darkness. Here below we see him imperfectly, but up there without any imperfection.[26]

I'll say no more. I pray God's goodness to give you perfect light to serve him perfectly. Keep living in God's holy and tender love.

Gentle Jesus! Jesus love!

[26] Cf. 1 Cor. 13, 12: "Now we see indistinctly, as in a mirror; then we shall see face to face."

LETTER Gardner II[1]
To Samuelle da Rimine, Doctor of Laws
October to December 1377

The addressee is identified only in Nd; I have not found a reference to identify him. Rimini is on the coast southeast of Bologna. Given the fact that the University of Bologna was a center of legal studies, it is quite possible that he was still in that area when Catherine met or heard of him—but it seems impossible to ascertain where and in what context this might have happened. The letter seems truncated, never arriving at the usual summary statement. There is, unfortunately, nothing in the content of the present letter to suggest a placement before or after Gardner III, also addressed to Samuelle (named again only in Nd). That letter seems to be from autumn of 1378. The linguistic evidence would support placing the present letter sometime during the period of the composition of *The Dialogue*, most likely while Catherine was still in the Val d'Orcia, and therefore between late October and the end of December 1377.[2]

§

In the name of Jesus Christ crucified and of gentle Mary.

Dearest son in Christ gentle Jesus,

I Caterina, servant and slave of the servants of Jesus Christ, am writing to you in his precious blood, longing to see your memory filled with the blood of Christ gentle Jesus crucified. Let the eye of your understanding be open to contemplate the fire of divine charity that is revealed to you in this blood of Christ gentle Jesus. Then your will and affection will have their fill of love and be satisfied, since our affection[3] loves what our understanding has seen.[4]

Then we will see the three powers of our soul gathered together, and

---

[1] MSS: R2, Nd; translation based on R2. Gardner in his note calls the manuscript "manifestly corrupt," which it certainly seems to be.

[2] Even with only fourteen patterns analyzed, it is clear that this is not an early letter, since there is next to no significant sharing with letters written before 1377. Most significantly, this letter shares with Let. T259 (late 1377) and *The Dialogue*, and with no other work, the development of the soul's three powers gathered in God's name, so that God becomes present "in their midst" by grace (found in the congruence of the patterns CONGRPOT and MEZZPER).

[3] That is, the will's power to love.

[4] At this point Catherine switches to first person plural and maintains this vantage point through the next paragraph.

our Savior's words will be fulfilled: "When two or three are gathered together in [my] name, I am in their midst."[5] This is really so. It seems our Savior meant to say, "Let the soul's three powers be gathered together, so that the memory is filled with [my] blood and with God's blessings, the eye of understanding sees and focuses on God's inexpressible love for humankind, and[a] the will loves."[6] It follows that when these three powers[b] are gathered together, all our actions and works are gathered together in God's name,[7] because everything is done for him. Then our soul rejoices because we see that God is in our midst[8] through grace and through the sweet effects[9] of love.

I want you then to hurry[10] to the fountain of [Christ's] blood and fill the vessel of your memory with that blood.[11] I'll say no more. I urge you, for love of Christ crucified. . . .[12] Keep living in God's holy and tender love.

Gentle Jesus! Gentle Jesus! Amen.

Textual Notes

a. R2: *nella* (*in the*) / *e la* (*and the*), probably a copyist error.

b. R2: *penitenzie* (*penances*) / *potenzie* (*powers*), certainly a copyist error (reading *en* for *o*), since "penances" would make no sense in this context.

---

[5] Mt. 18, 20.

[6] This analogy is developed in a number of places in *The Dialogue*, with the first significant expansion in ch. 51 (p. 105), where it is the hand of free choice which does the gathering. In *Dial.* 54 (pp. 107–109), love of God and of neighbor are brought into the analogy as the "two," and the three stages of love, the three stairs on the bridge of Christ crucified, are integrated with the three powers of the soul. The only other letters in which the analogy occurs are T259 (in this volume) and T263 (1378).

[7] Gardner conjectures a reading which would either add "and" (*ed operare*) as I have done, or *sa adoperare* ("know how to do"). The latter reading, however, would not be consistent with parallel passages in Catherine's writings, whereas supplying the missing conjunction would. (I have translated the verbs as nouns only for lack of satisfactory paired verbs in English.)

[8] That is, within us, since the present analogy concerns the three powers of a single soul.

[9] It. *effetto*, which perhaps should be read as *affetto*, "affection."

[10] It. *siate sollecito ad andare.*

[11] In *Dial.* 79 the images of the mirror, the sea of peace, and the fountain of living water all occupy this position in the analogy. For Catherine, all of these images (as well as others) merge in the blood of Christ and the life of grace (which in turn are ultimately one).

[12] Here, except for the closing, the letter is ended with simply an *etc.*

Letter T76/G76[1]
To Giovanni di Bindo di Doccio, monk of Monteoliveto
October to December 1377

There is a Domina Margharita Bindi listed among the Sienese *Mantellate* in 1352, and listed again in 1378 as Domina Margarita Bindi Doccii.[2] This is surely Giovanni di Bindo's mother. Of Giovanni himself we know that he is listed as a Monteolivetan monk already in 1373, that in 1379 to 1380 he was at the monastery of Santa Anna in Camprena, and that he died in 1417.[3] But there is no record of his whereabouts at any other time.

The content of the letter seems to indicate that Giovanni is experiencing difficulties both with his superiors and in his friendships within the community, but gives no clue as to when it might have been written. The linguistic evidence would support placing it during Catherine's time in the Val d'Orcia, most probably between October and December.[4]

§

In the name of Jesus Christ crucified and of gentle Mary.[a]

Dearest son in Christ gentle Jesus,

I Caterina, servant and slave of the servants of Jesus Christ, am writing to you in his precious blood. I long to see you constant and persevering in virtue, so that you will not turn back to look at what you have already plowed,[5,b] but will persist in following the path of virtue. It is perseverance that is crowned, and without perseverance we cannot be pleasing or

---

[1] MSS: Mo-*a*, M, S5, S6, Ro, F3, B, P2, H, P1, P3, P4, Pa; translation based on Mo-*a*, consulting H for protocol; relevant variants in Tommasèo text noted.

[2] Laurent, *Fontes*, I, *Documenti*, pp. 24, 47.

[3] *Registro Olivetano*, I, 59, cited in P. Lugano, "L'istituzione di Montoliveto nella seconda metà del Trecento," p. 68. Lugano conjectures that Giovanni di Bindo is the young man born out of wedlock whom Catherine urges the prior of Monteoliveto Maggiore near Siena to receive as a novice (Let. T8, in this volume), but such an identification would require that Let. T8 have been written before 1373, which seems hardly likely.

[4] The seven letters which share fifteen or more of this one's fifty-five analyzed patterns are all from mid-October 1377 or later, with three of them falling between mid-October and December 1377. The heaviest concentration of significant clusters within individual patterns falls in the last three months of 1377, with a number of patterns occurring only once or twice or not at all before then: ANCUD, CELLSANG, COGNFOND, CONVERSC, CORROTT, DAPERVIT, GUSTDESI, NUVOLOCC, VERITDIL. Also, a few significant clusters end before 1378: CELLSANG, CONVERSC, GUSTDESI. Fawtier (II, p. 193) and Dupré Theseider (unpublished notes) decline to date this letter.

[5] Cf. Lk. 9, 62 (Vulg.): "Anyone who puts a hand to the plow but keeps looking back is unfit for the reign of God."

acceptable to God. This is the virtue that, together with the outpouring of charity, brings to our soul the fruition of all our efforts.[6]

Oh how happy are those who run out their entire lives in true holy virtue! Even in this life they experience the earnest of eternal life.[7] But it is impossible to attain this perfection without much suffering. For this life does not pass without struggle, and those who would avoid struggle would be avoiding its fruits as well. They would really not for all that have avoided the struggle, because we have to put up with difficulties no matter what our situation. And our bearing with the struggle is either meritorious or not, depending on whether or not our will is directed toward God.

If people are worldly, everything they do is corrupt and wasted, because the foundation of their love and motivation[8] is corrupt. And so they put up with struggles but gain no merit at all. What pain and burdens they endure in the devil's service! For it often costs them a good deal of suffering and even physical death to commit deadly sin. They are the devil's martyrs.[9] They are children of darkness, and they try to teach the children of the light, giving us great cause for shame and embarrassment in God's sight.[10]

Oh dearest son, how foolish and wretched it is for us to think it unbearably hard to suffer for Christ crucified and to possess the life of grace, when worldly people consider it not difficult at all to endure pain in the service of the devil! This all comes about because we are not grounded in the truth and in genuine self-knowledge, because we are not set firmly upon the living rock, Christ gentle Jesus.[11] Those who do not know themselves cannot know God, and those who do not know God cannot

---

[6] Cf. Let. T150 to Francesco Tebaldi (1378 or 1379): "There will be none that can withstand us or prevent perseverance from enduring until the very end, when charity will establish us in possession in everlasting life, where every good exists unmarred by any evil. There we will receive the fruits of all our efforts." It is charity, she says elsewhere (for example, Let. T279 to Ristoro Canigiani, 1378), which makes it possible for us to persevere to the end in virtue.

[7] That is, they receive, as it were, a down-payment on their eternal reward.

[8] It. *affetto*.

[9] The expression occurs also in *Dial.* 48, 51, 94, 146, and in Let. T315 to Pietro da Milano (late 1378 or early 1379). The expression had been used by the Dominican Humbert de Romans (thirteenth century) in his *De Vita Regulari*: "If they have a good intention and are free of deadly sin they are God's martyrs, presenting their bodies to God as living victims. If, however, they labor so hard out of concupiscence, they are like martyrs of the devil, and present their bodies to the devil as fetid victims." (I thank Stephen C. Córdova for making me aware of this last reference.)

[10] Cf. Lk. 16, 8 (Vulg.): "For the children of this world are wiser in their own generation than the children of light."

[11] Cf. 1 Pt. 2, 4.

love him.[12] Since they do not love God, they learn neither perfect charity nor the self-contempt that enables us to endure patiently every pain and struggle and burden, whether it comes from the devil or from other people.[13]

Sometimes people assault and hurt us by their words or actions, and God allows this so as to prove our virtue. And sometimes the devil assaults us with all sorts of evil thoughts in order to make us lose grace and to lead us to death. These temptations take many forms. Sometimes he will tempt us against our superiors by making their commands seem unwise to us so that we conceive a dislike for them and for our rule. He does this to rob us of obedience. When the devil comes in through this door of disobedience, we don't realize that he wants to drag us away from the rule, because the devil insinuates: "These commands are so unwise, and you are young. You shouldn't be putting up with so much pain. Better for you, then, to keep your distance from this. You'll find some way, some sort of permission, to get yourself excused." And so he makes it seem that this can be right.

These are the temptations that come. But neither these nor any other vile and miserable temptations do any harm just because they come, but only if our selfish will assents to them. For God gives them not for our death but for life, not so that we may be defeated but that we may triumph and that our virtue may be proved. As for us, let us courageously open the eyes of our understanding by the light of most holy faith to contemplate the blood of Christ crucified. Then our weakness will be strengthened and we will in this glorious precious blood come to know virtue and perseverance.[14]

In Christ's blood we discover how serious and how loathsome sin is. There both justice and mercy are revealed. We surely know that if sin were not very displeasing to God and extremely destructive of our salvation, he would not have given up the Word, his only-begotten Son. He

---

[12] Thus she states the kernel of her entire teaching on the dynamic of knowledge of self and knowledge of God as central to the spiritual life.

[13] Catherine makes it clear elsewhere (for example, Let. T226 to Raimondo da Capua in this volume) that it is only sin within oneself that one is to hate. The self created by God is good and is worthy of love.

[14] Cf. Let. T195/DT87 to Stefano Maconi (1379): "In Christ's blood we are made strong, even though weakness persists in our sensuality. So we can see how this strength is gained, since all our weakness is in the sensual side of us. Here, I am saying, is how we gain this glorious virtue of strength and steady perseverance. Because our reason is made strong in Christ's blood, we must drown ourselves in this sweet glorious ransom. How? With our mind's eye and by the light of most holy faith we see it within the vessel of our own soul, in the knowledge that our being comes from God, and that God created us anew to grace in the blood of his only-begotten Son. And in that blood we were freed from our weakness."

would not have been willing to make his Son an anvil in order to take out on his body the punishment for our sins and so work out justice for the sin we had committed.[15] Nor would the Son have given his life for us, paying the price of his blood for us with such blazing love, making of that blood a bath to wash away the leprosy of our sins. He did this in gratuitous mercy, and not because he had to. So it is indeed true that in [Christ's] blood, in his running with genuine humility in ready obedience to his shameful death on the cross, we discover the seriousness and loathsomeness of sin as well as justice and the lavishness of God's mercy.

I tell you, this is the way—by the light of faith and in the true self-knowledge that makes us humble ourselves—to attain perseverance and to resist other people's and the devil's temptations. Such knowledge will lead us to utter contempt for our selfish sensuality, and this contempt will bring our sins to justice. Then we will endure with true patience any injury or torment or scorn or meanness, any imprudent orders, the burdensome aspects of the rule, or any other struggles, whatever their source. And this is the way we will taste the fruit of divine mercy that we have discovered in the movement of [our] love[16] and seen with the eye of our understanding.

I don't want you then, dearest son, to become apathetic. I don't want you to be lacking in holy knowledge, or to close your mind's eye so as not to look at this glorious precious blood. For if you weren't raising your eyes in this way, you would become very ignorant. Rather than knowing the truth, you would make mistakes because your eyes would be clouded over. You would look for pleasure and joy where they do not exist by setting your heart on created things more than on the Creator, and on finding pleasure and joy in creatures.

Sometimes people begin by loving others under the pretext of spiritual love. And if they aren't careful, if they don't practice virtue, they don't know the truth and don't keep their eyes on the blood of Christ crucified, and so this love becomes utterly sensual. Once the devil has brought them to where he wants them (that is, after he has made them get into these relationships under pretext of the spiritual and made them put aside the practice of holy prayer and desire for virtue and knowledge of the truth) he puts into their spirit such a boredom and sadness and despair that they want to put off the yoke of obedience and abandon the garden of religious life. Here they had once enjoyed so many sweet glorious[c] fruits before they

---

[15] Cf. Let. T161 to Nella Buonconti (in this volume): "There he bore the weight of our sins; there they were hammered out as [on] an anvil under the hammer. This is how the soul is shaped—in the sufferings of Christ, with the fire of his charity as agent."

[16] It. *nell'affetto d'amore.*

lost their sense of taste, their holy desire. But that was in the lovely time when the burdens and difficulties of the rule seemed delectable to them. So you see what great evil can come from this.

So I want you to try as hard as you can to behave in such a way and with such genuine desire that this may never happen to you, no matter what might happen. May your spirit never be confounded. No, raise your eyes to the blood and drink in a sweet and expansive hope. Apply the remedy of rising above everything that might get in the way of the truth. Then you will receive immense grace from God. You will begin to reap the fruit of your efforts when you welcome the outpouring of charity into your soul.

Flee now, dearest son, into the cell of self-knowledge. Embrace the wood of the most holy cross. Bathe in the blood of the humble spotless Lamb. And avoid any relationships that might be detrimental to your salvation. And don't go wondering, "What will it look like if I set myself free from these people? I'll disappoint them and they'll take it badly." But don't give in. We are put here to please not creatures but the Creator. You know that at the final moment, at death, none will answer for you except [your] virtue and divine mercy.[17]

How much we need virtue! Without virtue we cannot live the life of grace. This is why I said I long to see you constant and persevering in virtue even to the point of death, so that nothing at all will make you turn back. I hope, in God's goodness, that you will do this, as a true son should. In this way you will be doing what you are obligated to do, and you will fulfill my desire.

I'll say no more. Keep living in God's holy and tender love.

Gentle Jesus! Jesus love!

Textual Notes

a. H: *In the name . . . Christ, etc.*

b. Tommasèo: *the plow / what you have already plowed.*

c. Tommasèo: *mellow / glorious.*

---

[17] Cf. Let. T3 to the Curate of Casole and others (vol. I): "Open the eye of your understanding, and don't wait for the supreme Judge's power and might! A human judge is one thing; the divine Judge is quite another. Before the latter there is no appeal; one can have no advocate or attorney. The true Judge has appointed our conscience to be our advocate. So it is we ourselves who condemn ourselves in the end, we ourselves who judge ourselves deserving of death."

LETTER T116/G326[1]
To Madonna Pantasilea, wife of Ranuccio da Farnese
October to December 1377

Pantasilea was the daughter of Agnolino di Giovanni Salimbeni. It is therefore not unlikely that Catherine wrote this letter to her at the suggestion of someone at Rocca d'Orcia. The linguistic evidence does indeed support placing the letter sometime between October and December of 1377.[2]

§

In the name of Jesus Christ crucified and of gentle Mary.

Dearest sister in Christ gentle Jesus,

I Caterina, servant and slave of the servants of Jesus Christ, am writing to you in his precious blood. I long to see you truly enlightened, knowing yourself and God so that you may recognize how terribly weak the world is. For once we have come to the true and holy knowledge of our own poverty, we will know the world's poverty very clearly. And once we know God's goodness to us (which we find within our own being when we recognize that we are rational creatures made in God's image and likeness), we will in truth love[a] God. Whatever we love, as well as every gift and grace, we will credit to our Creator. We will always be in accord with his will, content with whatever God does or permits to happen to us, because we see that God wants nothing other than that we be made holy.[3]

This is what the gentle Word, God's Son, shows us. For in order that we might be made holy in him he ran like one in love to the shameful death of the cross, suffering a bitterly agonizing death to free us from eternal death. Since Christ's death and his blood, then, have shown us how boundlessly God loves us and how he wants nothing but our good, we

---

[1] MSS: Mo-*a*, S3, M, S5, S6, Ro; translation based on Mo-*a*. No relevant variants.

[2] The letters which share ten or more of this one's twenty-nine analyzed patterns are widely scattered chronologically. There are, however, a number of significant clusters within individual patterns which begin and/or end between October and December of 1377: AMAINVER, ATTPORT, CONFORMC, CORRINAM, COSPREST, NEGLINO, PENSAM, VISIODIO. Fawtier (II, p. 298), because of the addressee's relationship to the Salimbeni, places the letter possibly in the second half of 1377. Dupré Theseider (unpublished notes) considers this "not bad," observing also that "Gigli (*Opere*, I, p. 618) is wrong, then, when he says that Ranuccio died in 1362," since the rubric does not designate Pantasilea as a widow. Besides, the letter advises Pantasilea about her relationship with her husband. (Actually, it was Ranuccio's brother Pietro who died in 1362, leading the Florentine army against Pisa.)

[3] Cf. 1 Thes. 4, 3.

ought to bear patiently indeed every trouble and difficulty, no matter how God gives them to us. We ought always to have a holy trust in him, remembering that he will provide for our every need and will never give us more than we can bear. The more he gives us and the more difficult it becomes, the more he strengthens us to keep us from faltering.[4]

We should, then, put up with these things and reverence them for the sake of Christ crucified and because they are instrumental in bringing about our salvation. For difficulty and trial in this life humble us and blunt our pride. They make us get rid of our inordinate love for the world and put our love in order in God. They conform us with Christ crucified as well, and make us feel some of his humiliation and pain.

So we really need these things if we want to experience the eternal vision of God. They make us alert, rouse us from the sleep of ignorance and apathy, so that in time of need we run to Christ, knowing that only he can help us. In this way we become grateful for the blessings we have received and are still receiving. We have a better knowledge of God's goodness and our poverty, because he is the one who is, while we are the ones who are not and owe him our existence. You can see this very clearly, for just when we would like to live we have to face death; we want to be healthy and we are sick; we want to hold on to our children and the world's wealth and pleasures, but we have to let go of them. How true this is! Either they by divine dispensation leave us, or we leave them behind in death when we depart this dark life. So you see, we are nothing of ourselves except full of sin and wretchedness. This is all that belongs to us. Everything else is God's.

So, dearest sister, open your mind's eye and love your Creator and all that he loves—I mean virtue, especially patience, along with true and perfect humility. Think nothing of yourself. Simply give honor and glory to God, possessing the things of the world, even your husband and children, wealth and every other pleasure, as lent to you and not as your own. For, as I've already said, these things will fail you. You cannot hold or possess them as you like, but only as it pleases divine goodness to lend them to you. If you do as I say, you won't make a god of your children or of anything else. No, you will love everything for God's sake and nothing apart from God, and you will despise sin and embrace virtue.

Lift, lift your desire and affection above the world and set it on Christ crucified, who is stable and constant. He will never fail you, nor can he ever be taken from you against your will. I'm not saying that you shouldn't remain married or in the world if that's what you want, or that

---

[4] Cf. 1 Cor. 10, 13: "He will not let you be tested beyond your strength. Along with the test he will give you a way out of it so that you may be able to endure it."

you shouldn't take care of your children and the rest of the family as your state of life requires. I'm only saying that you should live a well-ordered life. In whatever you do, keep God before your eyes. Walk in holy fear, and live your married life as a sacrament. Respect as much as you can the days ordained by holy church.[5]

Nurture your children in virtue and in God's dear commandments, for it isn't enough for a mother and father to feed their children's bodies only. The animals do as much for their young, but *children* have to be nurtured spiritually in grace according to their capacity. Correct and punish them when they have done wrong. Have them go to confession often and hear Mass every morning or at least on the days commanded by the church. In this way you will be a mother to their souls as well as to their bodies. I'm certain that you will do this if you truly know God and yourself, as I've said; without that knowledge it would be impossible.

I am convinced that there is no other way for you to have God's grace, and that is why I said that I long to see you truly enlightened, knowing yourself and God. I beg you, for love of Christ crucified and for your own good, to do as I say. In that way you will fulfill in yourself both God's will and my desire.

I'll say no more. Keep living in God's holy and tender love.

Gentle Jesus! Jesus love!

Textual Notes

a. After *love* there is in Mo an erasure of five letters (*e teme*, "and fear"?).

[5] Catherine's admonitions reflect the Christian sexual ethics of her day. It was not unusual for wives to leave their husbands to enter religious life. Even within marriage, sexual abstinence was considered virtuous, and was popularly considered mandatory on certain feasts (though not actually so restricted by church law).

LETTER T224/G321[1]
To Niera Gambacorta
October to December 1377

The content of this second of the two extant letters to Niera, wife of Gherardo Gambacorta, is very general, though at the end Catherine refers to a communication from Niera asking about marrying off her servant boy. She is also displeased with Gherardo because "he has not done what every faithful Christian ought to do." What that may be is not hinted at, except that he should "not wait till the end of his life, since he doesn't know when or under what circumstances that will be." The reference is almost certainly to confession. (In Let. T155, the only other letter to Niera, which I have quite tentatively placed in early 1377, Catherine wants Niera to tell her husband to get to confession,because he doesn't know when he will die. This would seem to indicate either that the two letters are not very far apart or that Gherardo was a chronic slacker in this regard.) The linguistic evidence would seem to place this letter most probably at some point between October and December 1377 or possibly a bit earlier, in any case all but certainly before 1378 and all but certainly later than Let. T155.[2]

§

In the name of Jesus Christ crucified and of gentle Mary.

Dearest daughter in Christ gentle Jesus,

I Caterina, servant and slave of the servants of Jesus Christ, am writing to you in his precious blood. I long to see you a faithful servant and daughter of the eternal Father.

You know that it is love that makes us faithful. People always[a] have faith in the object of their love. So we see God's true servants, because of their love for their Creator, losing all faith and confidence in themselves. They don't trust in their own virtue or in their own knowledge because they see and know that they are not. They acknowledge that their being is from God, that they have it as a gift and not because they have a right to it. When people love with faith, they have a lively trust not in them-

---

[1] MSS: B, P2, R1, P5, F2, F1, R2, Nd; translation based on R1, with reference to Nd.

[2] The three letters which share eleven or more of this one's thirty-three analyzed patterns are very widely scattered chronologically. The significant clusters within individual patterns which point most strongly to the last three months of 1377 are AMORFEDE, DIOUMIL, NASCPIAG, OGGIDOM, PIAGCRIS, RICCPOV, RICHIAM, SERVEFIG, SUPERBOB. Both Fawtier (II, p. 309) and Dupré Theseider (unpublished notes) decline to date the letter.

selves but in the one who is. Their faith is not dead but alive with sweet holy deeds.[3]

What are the deeds that prove that faith is alive and grounded in true love? Patience in the face of injury or pain, no matter how God sends it; divine charity in the face of selfish sensual love for self; humility in the face of the bloated pride people take in worldly prestige and pleasure, honor, and enjoyment.

This humility has despised the world with all its pretense. But we cannot have it without the knowledge that we are sinful, that we are nothing. We cannot have it until we see how God has stooped down to us. When we contemplate supreme exaltedness descended as far down as our humanity, our human pride is embarrassed to see God so humiliated!

These, then, are the fruits brought forth by living faith that is focused completely on our Creator. Those who have such faith experience and are happy in God in truth. They feel no suffering, regardless of what pain or torment they may endure, because they firmly believe that God neither seeks nor wants nor permits anything except for our sanctification.[4] All of this comes from love, since without love they would have no faith.

On the other hand, you see how those whose affection and concern are focused on the world put all their faith and trust in themselves and in the world. They live in continual pain and bitterness, because they have set their love on what is neither solid nor dependable. So they end up disillusioned. How dependable are father or mother or honors or wealth or power? Not at all dependable! All of them are as fleeting as the wind! Today alive, tomorrow dead. Now healthy, now ill. Now rich, now poor. Now living happily with one's children, and then gone. So if we love and desire these things too much we suffer, because they do not last and we cannot hold on to what we love.[5]

I don't want you then, my dearest daughter, to have faith or trust in yourself or in perishable things. I want all your delight to be in serving Christ gentle Jesus, in whom is all delight and consolation. In that service[6] our soul becomes drunk on the blood of the spotless Lamb. We catch fire and melt in the fire of blazing charity. We receive such strength that neither the devil nor anyone else can deprive us of this good.[7] So hide yourself

[3] Cf. Jas. 2, 17 (Vulg.): "Faith that does not have deeds is intrinsically dead."

[4] 1 Thes. 4, 3.

[5] Cf. Giordano da Rivalto, ed. Narducci, p. 97: "Now a person is rich, now poor; now happy, now sad. . . . So now I may be healthy, and shortly ill. Everything changes for human beings, for now someone's father dies, now someone's mother, now a brother, now a child; now you have a husband, now you're a widow, and all these things disturb us."

[6] Literally, "there" (*ine*).

[7] Cf. Let. T137/DT45 to Matteo Cenni: "Truly the soul's being united with and trans-

within the wounds of Christ crucified. Put your affection, your faith, and your trust in Christ crucified. With this true gentle Lamb you will pass through this darksome life and reach everlasting life, where those dear [souls] pasture who are truly joyful.[8]

Regarding what you asked me about marrying off your boy,[9] my answer is that you should be concerned not about possessions or high social standing but only about the girl's virtue and good situation.[10] If you find this to be the case, do it confidently. And whatever you do, do it in fear of God, keeping your soul's attention focused always on him.

Bless and encourage Monna Giovanna[11] in Christ gentle Jesus. And tell Gherardo I am about to complain to Christ crucified about him because he hasn't done what every faithful Christian ought to do. Tell him not to wait till the last day of his life, since he doesn't know when that will be nor in what circumstances.[12]

Keep living in God's holy and tender love.

Gentle Jesus! Jesus love!

Textual Notes

a. Tommasèo: [*always*].

---

formed into him is like fire consuming the dampness in logs. Once the logs are heated through and through, the fire burns and changes them into itself, giving them its own color and warmth and power. It is just so with us when we look at our Creator and his boundless charity. We begin to experience the heat of self-knowledge—which consumes all the dampness of our selfish love for ourselves. As the heat increases, we throw ourselves with blazing desire into God's measureless goodness, which we discover within our very selves. We are then sharing in his warmth and in his power, in that we begin at once to feed on and savor souls. And we in turn change every other person into ourselves in love and desire, by giving *them* the color and taste for virtue that we have drawn from the wood of the most holy cross—that noble tree on which hangs, as fruit, the spotless Lamb, God and human."

[8] It. *dove si pascono i veri e dolci gustatori*, that is, those who in their earthly life fed on and enjoyed souls at the table of the cross and who as a result in eternity find true joy. The use of the verb *pascono* ("they pasture"), unique here in this context, suggests their relationship with the Lamb.

[9] The original has not *figliuolo* (which refers explicitly to a son) but *garzone* (which refers simply to any boy or to a young male servant). Catherine uses the word in only two other contexts, in both of which the boy is clearly not the son of the subject. So the boy in question here is not Niera's son but a young servant.

[10] It. *buona condizione.*

[11] From R1and R2, which have simply *Mõ g̅ v*. The identity of this woman is unknown. I have found no reference to a Giovanna Gambacorta, nor to any other Giovanna with whom Catherine was associated in Pisa. (The Tommasèo text has *Gherardo* in place of *Monna Giovanna.*)

[12] In Let. T155, she gave Niera essentially the same message for her husband Gherardo.

LETTER T87/G342[1]
To Giovanna dei Pazzi
November or December 1377

Giovanna dei Pazzi seems to have been one of Catherine's early disciples in Siena, since she occasionally served Catherine as scribe during the first years of the latter's public life.[2] Gigli speculates that she may have been a member of the dei Pazzi family who had moved to Siena in the thirteenth century, one house of their descendants being the Cinughi.[3] Apparently on the basis of this speculation, Meattini assumes that she was a *Mantellata*,[4] since there is a *Domina Iohanna ser Petri Cini* among the Sienese *Mantellate* listed in 1378.[5]

This is Catherine's only letter to Giovanna. In fact, she eventually says, "dearest daughters," which would seem to indicate an intent to address others of her disciples in Siena as well as Giovanna. So Catherine herself must be away from Siena. There is no record of Giovanna having accompanied Catherine on any of her journeys after Pisa. While there is no clue in the content of the letter as to when it was written, the linguistic evidence points very strongly to the last two months of Catherine's stay in the Val d'Orcia, that is, November or December 1377. Note especially that patience is called a queen only here, in *The Dialogue*, and in Let. T104 (also from November or December 1377).[6]

---

[1] MSS: Mo-*a*, M, S5, S6, Ro, F3; translation based on Mo-*a*.

[2] Let. T41/DT3 and T152 in vol. I and T208/DT6 in this volume.

[3] *Opere*, II, p. 687.

[4] *Epistolario*, p. 965.

[5] Laurent, *Fontes*, I, *Documenti*, p. 48.

[6] All eight letters which share fourteen or more of this one's sixty-four analyzed patterns are from October 1377 or later, with four of these during the Val d'Orcia period. Further, there are a good number of significant clusters within individual patterns which begin and/or end in the last three months of 1377 (AFFOCDES, ANELLO, CAPOSPIN, CASACOGN, MEDICRIS, MORTDIST, NUDITA, NUVOLOCC, ODORPAZ, PENREFRI, REALPAZ, REGINA, SALUPERF, SOSPCIBO, VASESANG), with four of these beginning in November. Fawtier (II, p. 309) and Dupré Theseider (unpublished notes) decline to date the letter.

§

In the name of Jesus Christ crucified and of gentle Mary.

Dearest daughter in Christ gentle Jesus,

I Caterina, servant and slave of the servants of Jesus Christ, am writing to you in his precious blood. I long to see you enduring in royal fashion[7] whatever our dear Savior grants you.

You will come to know eternal Truth[a] by loving him. And the only sign we can give of our love is to love everyone else in charity and to suffer with true and royal patience even to the point of death. We must not want to have times and places to our own liking but in God's way—and God neither seeks nor wants anything but that we be made holy.[8]

What outrageous foolishness it would be if we sick people were to demand that Christ our doctor give us medicine according to our liking rather than as he wants, since he sees and knows what we need! So I want you to understand, my daughter, that whatever God grants or permits in this life, he does it either because we need it for our salvation or for our progress in perfection. We should therefore bear it humbly and patiently. We should accept it with reverence, opening our mind's eye to consider the great charity and blazing love with which God gives it to us. Once we realize that he gives it not out of hatred but out of love, we will accept it in love.

This virtue of patience is so essential for us that we must procure it if we don't want to lose the fruit of our labors. And we must get up out of our indifference and diligently go to where it is to be found. Where is it to be found? In Christ crucified. For his patience was such that no cry of complaint was heard from him.[9] The Jews cried, "Crucify!" And he cried, "Father, forgive those who are crucifying me, because they do not know what they are doing."[10]

Oh patience! *You gave us life! By bearing our iniquities with patience, you punished* [b] *them in your own body on the wood of the cross!*[11] In his blood he washed our soul's face, and with true patience created us anew to grace. His blood covered our nakedness, since it clothed us again in grace. In the

---

[7] It. *realmente.* The word can also mean "really" or "solidly," but at the very end of the letter it becomes clear that the intended sense here is "royally," as Catherine refers to patience as queen.

[8] 1 Thes. 4, 3.

[9] Cf. Is. 53, 7: "He opened not his mouth." (Vulg.)

[10] Lk. 23, 34.

[11] She switches quickly from apparently addressing patience, then addressing Christ, and then speaking again in the third person.

heat of his blood he broke humankind's iciness and warmed our tepidity. In his blood darkness fell away and he gave us the light. In his blood our selfish love was consumed. I mean that if we consider how we are loved in the blood, we have good reason to rise above our miserable selfish love and love our Redeemer, who with such blazing love gave us life. He ran like one in love to the shameful death of the cross.

His blood has been made a drink for those who want it, and his body food. For there is no way our appetite can be satisfied, no way our hunger and thirst can be relieved, except with his blood. Even if we possessed the whole world, we could not be satisfied, because the things of the world are less than we are, and we cannot be satisfied by anything less than we are. Only the blood can satisfy our hunger, because the blood has been mixed and kneaded [into one dough] with the eternal Godhead, a nature infinitely[c] greater than we. So there we can satisfy our desire—and with the fire of charity, since it is for love that [the blood] was shed![12]

This blood was given us to overflowing. On the eighth day after his birth, when he was circumcised, the tiny cask of his body was tapped. Yet it was so little that it couldn't satisfy us. But at the time of the crucifixion the lance was thrust into his side. Longinus was the instrument of this, when he opened Christ's heart.[13] When this cask was emptied of physical life through the separation of soul from body, his blood was handed over.[14] It was heralded with the trumpet of mercy, with the fire of the Holy Spirit as trumpeter, so that whoever wants some of this blood can come for it.[15] Where? To this very cask, Christ crucified, by following his way and his teaching.[16]

What is his teaching? To love God's honor and the salvation of souls, and to acquire virtue by means of suffering and by doing force and violence to our selfish sensuality. What path must we keep to if we want to

---

[12] Either the last *and* is superfluous, or something is missing—more probably the latter, since *shed* has no antecedent as the text stands.

[13] The soldier who pierced Jesus' side with a lance is not named in the gospels (Mk. 15:39; Jn. 19, 34). Legend, however, identifies him as Longinus, healed and converted after the crucifixion and later martyred. His feast was celebrated on 15 March. Catherine may have known his legend from the *Legenda aurea*.

[14] It. *messo a mano*.

[15] Nowhere else in Catherine's writings is this image of the trumpet used in this way. Elsewhere she speaks of Paul and other preachers as *banditori* ("heralds"), but only here does she use the word "trumpeter" (*trombatore*) and apply it to the Holy Spirit.

[16] Cf. Let. T136/DT37 to Bishop Angelo Ricasoli (vol. I): "Bleeding from every member, he has made himself cask and wine and cellarer for us. Thus we see that his humanity is the cask that encased the divine nature. The cellarer—the fire and the hands that are the Holy Spirit—tapped that cask on the wood of the most holy cross. And this wisdom, the incarnate Word, sweetest of wines, tricked and defeated the devil's malice, for he caught him on the hook of our humanity."

reach this place and this teaching in order to get the blood? And what vessel do we need, and what light?

[We need] the light of most holy faith, and this faith is the pupil of our mind's eye. For without this glorious light we would lose the way. We would be like worldly people who have blinded their mind's eye with the cloud of selfish love and self-indulgence, and so they wander around in the dark, blinded.[17] Not only do these people not walk [the way of] Christ's blood; they despise and reject it. So we have to have the light, as I've said, and keep to the path of true self-knowledge and knowledge of God's goodness within us, hating vice and loving virtue. This is both a path and a house where we learn and come to know the teaching of Christ crucified. In this house of knowledge of ourselves and of God we discover the blood and find that our soul's face has been washed clean.

What vessel must we carry? The vessel of our heart, I tell you, so that we can put our heart's desire[18] into the blood like a sponge and draw out the blood—and with it the passionate charity with which it was shed. And then, after we have got the light, and walked along the path by following the teaching of Christ crucified, and reached the place and filled our vessel, our soul gets drunk. We taste a food that is patience and experience a fragrance that is virtue, such a desire for suffering that it seems as if we cannot have our fill of carrying the cross for Christ crucified. We act like drunkards who, the more they drink, the more they would like to drink. So the more we suffer, the more we would like to suffer. Suffering is our refreshment. The tears we shed in remembrance of the blood are our drink. And sighs are our food.

This, then, is the path and the way to come to grace and to win this queen, patience. It was of her I was speaking when I said that I long to see you enduring in royal fashion whatever divine Goodness grants you—with true holy patience.

So up, dearest daughters![19] Let's sleep no longer in the slumber of indifference! No, with anguished sorrow and weeping over the offenses against God, let's enter the open storehouse of the side of Christ crucified, where we will find the blood. We truly have nowhere to rest our head

---

[17] The word used here is *abacinati*, which has the sense of being blinded by a bright light, a bit paradoxical in conjunction with being blinded (*accecati*) by a cloud. Cf. Let. T343 to Rainaldo da Capua (1379 or early 1380), where Catherine describes various causes of blindness, among them intense heat or brightness that burns the pupil of the eye. She then goes on to compare selfish love to this intense heat.

[18] It. *affetto*.

[19] The shift to the plural seems to imply that the letter is in fact intended to be shared in some way with others of Catherine's disciples in Siena. (An early scribal error could have been perpetuated in all extant manuscripts, but this seems unlikely, since both the noun and the adjective are plural.)

except in the blood and on the thorn-crowned head of Christ crucified. There thrust the arrows of flaming desire, and the arrows of continual humble prayer for God's honor and the salvation of souls.

I have no more to say to you.[20] Keep living in God's holy and tender love.

Gentle Jesus! Jesus love!

Textual Notes

a. Tommasèo: *Life / Truth.*

b. Tommasèo: *putting them on / bearing them in.*

c. Several letters at the end of *infinita* have been erased by *b*; my conjecture is that the original was *infinitamente*. If not, it would read: *an infinite nature, greater than we.*

[20] The forms are once again singular.

LETTER T51/G133[1]
To Frate Felice da Massa, Augustinian Hermit of Lecceto
November or December 1377

Felice da Massa was one of those who accompanied Raimondo da Capua to Avignon, preceding Catherine and her company there, and remaining with her through the journey back to Siena. This is Catherine's only extant letter to Felice. The rubric of Mo says that is was "done in ecstasy" (*fatta in abstractione*).

Catherine says that Felice is to "give no thought" to her. So it may be that he has had reason to worry. Two possible occasions of such concern could have been Catherine's physical and political troubles during her time in the Val d'Orcia, or the danger in which she was during her 1378 mission to Florence. We do not know whether Felice accompanied her anywhere besides to Avignon, nor whether he was among those she summoned to Rome early in 1379. Here she is clearly encouraging him in his life with his brothers, which would place him at Lecceto.

We are, then, thrown back on whatever linguistic data might give a clue as to the letter's placement. One can say with real confidence that it is almost certainly not earlier than autumn of 1377, since it has so little in common with letters before that period. Nor does it share as heavily with letters after 1377 as it does with those written during the last months of Catherine's stay in the Val d'Orcia. I would therefore place it sometime between September and December 1377. In fact, a number of close parallels with *The Dialogue* lead me to believe it was most probably written some time after Catherine had begun that work, that is, in November or December.[2]

---

[1] MSS: Mo-*a*, M, S5, S6, Ro, P4, Pa; translation based on Mo-*a*. No relevant variants.

[2] Of the six letters which share fifteen or more of this one's fifty-one analyzed patterns, two are from September and two from November or December of 1377. (The other two are from 1378 and 1379.) Also, a number of clusters within individual patterns begin and/or end between August and December 1377, with heavier concentrations from September to December: AMARVERI, AMORFEDE, BENEFATT, CASACOGN, COGNDIFT, COGNFOND, LEGGEPER, MAREONDE, MARETEMP, MIROLLO. Both Fawtier (II, p. 214) and Dupré Theseider (unpublished notes) decline to date the letter.

§

In the name of Jesus Christ crucified and of gentle Mary.

Dearest son in Christ gentle Jesus,

I Caterina, servant and slave of the servants of Jesus Christ, am writing to you in his precious blood. I long to see you grounded in true and perfect humility, since those who are humble are also patient in enduring any hardship for love of truth.[3]

Because humility is the governess and wet-nurse of charity, there can be no humility without charity.[4] Those who are on fire within the furnace of charity are not apathetic. No, they are thoroughly conscientious, because charity is never lazy but is always working.[5] But we cannot have either love (which consumes apathy) or humility (which extinguishes pride)[6] unless we have the light, and unless our enlightened vision has something to look at. For even though our eyes may have the ability to see, and even though they may have light, if they aren't open, their ability to see will do us no good. Our soul's eye is understanding, and it has the light of faith to the extent that the veil of selfish love hasn't covered it up.[7] Once selfish love is removed, our eyes are left clear and we can see. So it is essential that our will wake up and decide to love its Benefactor. Then, when our mind's eye senses that it is being stimulated by our will, it opens and focuses on its object, Christ crucified, and in him (especially in his blood) it recognizes the depths of God's boundless charity.[8]

But where should we see and focus in this way? In the house of self-knowledge. There we come to know our own poverty, since we see with

---

[3] Cf. Let. T23 to her niece Nanna (in this volume): "[S]he will be as humble as she is patient, and as patient as she is humble. But we cannot attain this virtue of humility except through true self-knowledge." Later in this letter as well, Catherine will introduce the role of self-knowledge.

[4] Cf. Let. T33 to the abbot general of Monteoliveto (1378): "Charity's wet-nurse is deep humility. And what food does this nurse give her? The food of light and of self-knowledge, and by this light [the soul] has come to know her poverty and the frail sensuality that is the cause of all poverty. In this knowledge she humbles herself and conceives a contempt for herself with which she nurtures in herself the fire of divine charity, coming to know God's unspeakable goodness, the goodness that is the beginning and end of all her knowing."

[5] In Let T127/DT20 (in this volume) she tells Bartolomeo Dominici that "charity is not lazy. No, it does great things!"

[6] The original has "either love or humility (which consumes apathy and extinguishes pride)," but the context both of this letter and of the whole of Catherine's thought makes clear that the one is the effect of love, the other of humility.

[7] In other letters from this period Catherine is beginning to image faith as the pupil of the eye of understanding, and selfish love as the cloud or cataract with which one sometimes covers that pupil and blocks the light.

[8] Here the movement of the will precedes the movement of understanding. Usually it is the other way around.

our mind's eye—and in truth—our non-being and our sinfulness. By "in truth" I mean that we know both ourselves and God's goodness within us. For knowing only ourselves, or wanting to know God without knowing ourselves, would not be a knowledge grounded in truth; nor would we derive from it the fruit we should derive from self-knowledge. In fact, we would be more likely to lose than gain. Why? All we would derive from knowledge of ourselves alone would be weariness and confusion. So our soul would dry up and, if we were to go on like this without anything to counterbalance it, we would end in despair. And if we wanted to know God without knowing ourselves, the fruit we would derive would be the fetid fruit of a terrible presumption that both feeds pride and feeds on it.[9]

So the light must see and know in truth.[10] It must season knowledge of self with knowledge of God, and knowledge of God with knowledge of self. Then we will reap neither presumption nor despair. When the two sorts of knowledge are in mutual relationship, we will reap the fruit of life. For from knowledge of ourselves we will derive the fruit of true humility. This will give birth to hatred and contempt for sin and for that perverse law which is always ready to fight against the spirit.[11] From this hatred we give birth to patience, which is the pith of charity.[12]

And from knowledge of God's great goodness, which we discover within ourselves, we will derive as fruit the depths of blazing charity for God and for our neighbors. For by the light we see and know that the love we bear our Creator is of no service at all to God, and so we turn right around and, for love of God, we do for our neighbors the service we cannot do for God.[13] We love God's creatures because we see that God loves them supremely. It is of the very nature of love to love everyone and everything that our beloved loves.

So by this light, dearest son, we will acquire the virtues of humility and charity. We will with true holy patience bear with and share the burden of our neighbors' shortcomings. With the perfect conscientiousness we learn in the fire of divine charity we will destroy apathy, and with the water of true humility pride will be extinguished. Famished for God's honor, we

---

[9] This relationship between knowing God and knowing self is developed also in *Dial.* 10, pp. 41–42.

[10] In a few other instances also (Let. T201, T313, T318) Catherine speaks of the light itself as seeing, but this must be taken as a sort of shorthand for her image of the soul's power of understanding seeing by means of the light.

[11] Cf. Rom. 7, 23.

[12] Cf. Let. T38 to Agnesa Malavolti (in this volume), where the image of the tree of charity with its pith of patience is developed at length.

[13] The idea that one can serve God only by serving one's neighbors is ultimately at the heart of Catherine's spirituality, but only in this period does she begin to articulate it very frequently.

will begin to eat and enjoy souls at the table of the humble spotless Lamb.[14] There is no other way for us.

I am convinced that we must keep to this way and to the path of true humility, and this is why I said I long to see you grounded in true and perfect humility. So I want you to do this, without pain or spiritual distress. I want us now to begin once again, with living faith, with firm hope, and with ready obedience.[15] I want you to fatten your soul in this way. I don't want you drying up from spiritual weariness and confusion. No, rouse yourself from the slumber of apathy! When you see virtues in your brothers, steal them for yourself and keep them in your bosom.[16] And let the truth be your delight; let it always be in your mouth, and proclaim it when it is needed. Proclaim it lovingly and to everyone, especially to those you love with a special love—but with a certain congeniality, putting the shortcomings of the other person on your own shoulders.[17] If in the past you haven't done it as sensitively as you should, let's do better in the future.

I don't want this to be at all painful for you. And don't give a thought to me. May all the waves of the stormy sea be royally crossed over with true humility and familial charity and holy patience! I'll say no more. Keep living in God's holy and tender love.

Gentle Jesus! Jesus love!

---

[14] This is the table of the cross, where Christ's food becomes our food. Cf. Jn. 4, 34: "My food is to do the will of the one who sent me, and to accomplish his work." Again, the idea is developed, among other places, in Let. T33 to the Abbot General of Monteoliveto: "This gentle Word, to fulfill his Father's will and command for his creatures, ran as one in love to the table of the most holy cross. There he ate souls as his food by suffering pain and shame and disgrace and ultimately a shameful death." Cf. also Let. T242 to Bishop Angelo Ricasoli (in this volume): "[D]ivine goodness has put you in the mystic body of holy Church and nurtured you at the breast of this dear bride only so that you might eat the food of God's honor and the salvation of souls at the table of the most holy cross. He does not want this food to be eaten anywhere else but on the cross, by your bearing physical toil with many restless desires, just as God's Son did, who endured bodily torments and at the same time the pain of desire—and the cross of desire was greater than the physical cross. This was his desire: his hunger for our redemption in fulfillment of the eternal Father's command."

[15] As she so often does, Catherine uses the first person pronoun to include herself in the admonition.

[16] It. *pecto*. Religious (and I imagine medievals in general) would often hide small items tucked in the folds of their habits above the belt. So the sense here seems to be a bit playful, referring to that expediency as well as to the other sense of *nel pecto*, "in the heart."

[17] Cf. *Dial.* 102, p. 194: "So let silence or a holy argument for virtue be in your mouth to discourage vice. And when you think you discern vice in others, put it on your own back as well as theirs, acting always with true humility. Then if the vice is truly there, such people will change their ways all the sooner, seeing themselves so gently understood. That agreeable reproof will constrain them to change their ways, and they will tell you what you wanted to say to them."

LETTER T287a/G75[1]
To Pietro di Giovanni di Viva of the Carthusian Monastery at Maggiano[2]
November or December 1377

Pietro di Giovanni di Viva will later be prior of the monastery at Maggiano, near Siena. The rubricists give him the title *Don*, as if he were already prior when this letter is addressed to him, but this may be simply in view of his *eventual* office. Catherine, in fact, addresses him here not as father but as son, and admonishes him about obedience to his superior, speaking in fact as if he has just recently entered the monastery.[3]

Since we do not know when Pietro joined the community at Maggiano,[4] and since there is no other chronological clue within the letter, we must rely on the linguistic evidence for its placement. That evidence points strongly toward the final months of 1377, while Catherine is still in the Val d'Orcia, with a greater probability of November or December.[5]

---

[1] MSS: H, P4, S6, with the longer version (Let. T287b to the monk Niccolò) in Mo, S2, F3. I have based the translation on H, but with reliance on Mo (the more reliable manuscript) where H seems in error.

[2] S6 specifies simply that Pietro's monastery is at Siena, but H and P4 explicitly say, "To Don Pietro di Giovanni di Viva, Carthusian monk at Maggiano, near Siena."

[3] A longer version of this letter (T287b) is addressed to Niccolò, an Olivetan monk and son of Catherine's disciple Nanni di Ser Vanni Savini. Of the manuscripts I have been able to examine, Mo, S2, and F3 have only Niccolò as addressee (and have the longer version of the letter). H and P4 have Pietro as the only addressee (and have the shorter version). I am presenting the two separately rather than confuse issues with excess notes. The fact that the *però dissi* summary occurs in both versions in the same place (at the end of Pietro's but before the additional material in Niccolò's) makes me suspect that the letter to Pietro is the prototype.

[4] Nor do we know when Niccolò, the recipient of Let. T287b, entered Monteoliveto Maggiore.

[5] A good number of letters share a heavy proportion of this one's eighty-four analyzed patterns, and they range from mid-1376 through 1379. There are, however, many significant clusters within individual patterns which begin and/or end in the Val d'Orcia period, with several of them more centered on November and December: AMAINVER, AMORFEDE, ATTPORT, CONVERSP, CORPVOL, COSTANT, GRAVPECC, INVIRTU, LEGGEPER, MOSCA, NUVOLOCC, NUVOLPR, SALM, SANTPROP, VISIOPAC. Both Fawtier (II, p. 192) and Dupré Theseider (unpublished notes) simply place both versions of Let. T287 before 1379–1380, when Niccolò di Nanni di Ser Vanni was no longer at Monteoliveto Maggiore.

§

In the name of Jesus Christ crucified and of gentle Mary.

Dearest son in Christ gentle Jesus,

I Caterina, servant and slave of the servants of Jesus Christ, am writing to you in his precious blood. I long to see you constant and persevering in the sincere holy resolve you have taken in your heart and spirit, the resolve to serve God in truth in [your] holy order. Without perseverance you would not receive the fruit of your efforts, since it is only perseverance that is crowned. So you see that this glorious virtue of perseverance is really essential for us. Because we need it so badly, then, how can we have it? I'll tell you.

Every virtue has life because it is motivated by charity.[6] Without charity we would not receive the fruit of grace even though we might have an act of virtue.[7] So we must be motivated by love in our acquisition of virtue. But we cannot attain true love unless our heart and will are stripped of selfish love for ourselves.

This [selfish] kind of love, this pampering we give our selfish sensual passion, robs us of the life of grace. It dims our mind's eye. In fact, it is a cloud over the pupil, the light of most holy faith.[8] We lose our sense of taste, our desire. Virtue once seemed good to us. Once it gave us pleasure to see it in virtuous people, and we sought it for ourselves in Christ crucified. But now that this selfish love has taken over, it seems just the opposite. Selfish love makes us weak and fearful; we are afraid of our own shadow. This is why we don't persevere in what we have begun as long as the root of selfish love is still alive in us. For without the light that we've lost (as I've described), we are walking in the dark. We don't know the truth; we don't know our sinfulness; we don't know the graces and gifts we have received from God's infinite goodness. If we had this knowledge we would not be weak but strong and persevering. We wouldn't be brought down by the devil's wickedness and rascally temptations or by the nagging of our selfish frailty or by the world's flattery or by the difficulties of the rule. No, by the light of most holy faith we would pass through them all with a courageous heart.

---

[6] It. *Ogni virtù a vita dall'affetto della carità.*

[7] Cf. Aquinas, *Summa Theologica*, II–II, q. 23, a. 8: "It is charity that directs the acts of all other virtues and that consequently gives the form to all other acts of virtue. It is precisely in this sense that charity is called the form of the virtues."

[8] Medieval physiology saw the pupil not as an opening in the eye, but as the actual light by which the eye sees.

This, dearest son, is the way to arrive at perfect perseverance. You must strip your heart and will of all selfish love for yourself and stop pampering your body. Avoid thinking about your father, your brothers and sisters, and your relatives. Remember them in holy prayer with desire for their salvation, but don't dwell on them with any other sentiment. You know that our Savior says we must forsake father and mother, sisters and brothers, and our very selves (that is, our selfish will) if we want to be worthy of him. Otherwise it is impossible.[9] You have begun to forsake the world and your selfish will and have taken on the yoke of true obedience. Now, if you want really to keep and fulfill this resolve until you die, you have to renounce the world and its pleasures over and over every day.[10]

But take note: we cannot either accept or reject[a] what we do not know. This is why we need the light of most holy faith in which to set Christ crucified before our mind's eye. By focusing on him you will know the seriousness of the deadly sin we commit when we set our will and our love inordinately on ourselves, on other people, or on created things. Mortal sin is so serious that being bound in just one such sin is enough to send a person to hell. It was and is so displeasing to God that to punish Adam's sin he sent the Word, his only-begotten Son, so that he could punish sin in his body. Even though the poison of sin was not in him, God took out the punishment on the Word, his only-begotten Son, in order to atone for human sin, in order not to let it go unpunished.[11] So the blessed Christ was our justice.[12] The justice and the suffering that humankind should have borne, he bore. Like one in love, to fulfill his Father's command, he ran to the shameful death of the most holy cross. So by focusing on this Word, we see how serious the guilt of deadly sin is.

When we see, then, that deadly sin is so serious and so displeasing to God (when the light of faith has let us know this), we hate sin. We come to detest intensely both sin and its cause. Because we see that the perverse law of our body is an instrument that inclines us to sin, that it is a perverse law that fights against the spirit,[13] our reason, along with free choice and our good and holy will,[14] rises up with hatred and contempt

[9] Cf. Lk. 14, 26.

[10] It would seem very strange for Catherine to be advising Pietro in this way if he were indeed prior. She speaks rather as if he has just recently entered the monastery.

[11] Aquinas, *Summa Theologica*, III, q. 48, a. 4, speaks of "the debt of punishment, to the payment of which humankind was held fast by God's justice," and of Christ's Passion as "a sufficient and more than sufficient atonement for the sin and the debt of the human race."

[12] 1 Cor. 1, 30 (Vulg.): "You are in Christ Jesus, whom God has made our justice and sanctification and redemption."

[13] Cf. Rom. 7, 23.

[14] Catherine often emphasizes that the preservation of "a good and holy will" in the

to discipline our body and our flesh.[15] We kill selfish will with the knife of holy obedience, never rebelling against the rule or our superiors.

But always we persevere, and must persevere, with the same desire for obedience with which we entered [religious life] on that first day. With that same holy fear we must exercise our spirit in continual humble prayer right up to the last day of our life, so that our spirit will never become lazy. We should always be occupied with praying the psalms or meditating or raising our mind to God, pondering[b] within ourselves the blazing charity we discover and see in the blood of the Word, God's Son.[16] For he has made a bath of his blood to wash away our sins.

When we see and consider that God loves us so much, we cannot keep ourselves from loving. And when we love, our mind thinks about the object of our love. Now we cannot live without love. And since two opposing loves cannot exist together, we must of necessity be stripped of perverse love and clothed in God's. Because our heart cannot but be sensitive to the one we love, we use holy thoughts to drive out the evil thoughts the devil would like to put into our heart. And the devil, finding that our heart is ablaze in the fire of divine charity, doesn't come around much, any more than a fly comes around a boiling cauldron. But if the devil were to find our heart fearful and lukewarm, he would come in right away with all his ugly thoughts and imaginings.

So we must keep active so that we will be found not lukewarm or empty but filled with God in holy desire, remembering and meditating on the wonderful blessings we have received from him.[17] And if these [evil] thoughts come anyway (since the devil never sleeps but is constantly tormenting us[18]), this shouldn't weary or discourage our spirit. No, we

---

midst of trial and temptation is not only a gift of God but a sure sign that God is dwelling within us.

[15] The It. *macerare* has the connotation of physical discipline (for example, with chain or flagellation) in view of making the body compliant.

[16] Cf. Let. T213 to Suor Daniela of Orvieto (1378): "They find prayer everywhere, because they always carry with them the place where God dwells by grace and where we ought to pray. I mean the house of our soul, where holy desire is always praying. This desire rises up with the light of understanding to look within us, and into the measureless fire of divine charity which we discover in the blood [Christ] shed—the blood that by love's generosity we find within the vessel of our own soul."

[17] Cf. Mt. 12, 43–45; Lk. 11, 24–26 (Vulg.): "When the unclean spirit has gone out of a person, it wanders through waterless places looking for a spot to rest, but it finds none. Then it says, 'I will return to my house from which I came.' When it comes, it finds it empty and swept and put in order. Then it goes and brings along seven other spirits more evil than itself, and they enter and live there; and the last state of that person is worse than the first." Also, Rev. 3, 16 (Vulg.): "Because you are lukewarm, and neither cold nor hot, I will begin to vomit you out of my mouth."

[18] Cf. 1 Pet. 5, 8 (Vulg.): "Stay sober and awake; for your enemy the devil prowls about like a roaring lion looking for someone to devour."

should resist and see that our will does not give in. For if our will doesn't consent to the devil's suggestions or to the weakness of our flesh, we do not sin. In fact, we earn merit because of the suffering we endure. This means that if we don't sit down in apathy, or let our spirit become weary and discouraged, or give up the practice of prayer, [the struggle] will bring us to true and perfect virtue. Why? In times of struggle we come to know ourselves and our weakness better. And we come to know God's goodness within us better when we see that God has graciously preserved our good and holy will—and it is the will alone that sins or merits. So you see how in times of intense struggle we become more perfect and prove ourselves in virtue.

Next, I want you to believe that God does not burden us with more than we can carry.[19] God's giving is indeed well measured, because he is our God who wants nothing else but that we be made holy.[20]

By the light of faith, then, rise above every sort of selfish love. And to attain the most perfect love, as I've told you, set before your mind's eye Christ crucified and the indescribable charity he has demonstrated for you by shedding his blood with such blazing love. Then, by the light, you will come to know in this gentle Word how serious sin is. And you will come to know your own weakness and his charity. In that charity you will love and pursue virtue, ready to suffer any pain in order to acquire it. And in charity you will live in love with your neighbors.

This must be your study: to love God in truth and your neighbors as yourself;[21] to be humble and obedient; to patiently suffer pain, hurt, disdain and abuse, the burdens of the rule and the heavy obligations placed on you by your superior, and the devil's temptations; and to persevere in enduring all these things right up to the moment of your death. In times of struggle and weariness, run with this light of holy faith to embrace the most holy cross, and there put your hope confidently in the blood of Christ crucified. I haven't the least doubt that if you are humble (with the humility that nurtures charity within us) and obedient and truly patient, you will by the power of this blood be victorious over your enemies, the world, the flesh, and the devil. And you will return triumphant to your city, Jerusalem, the vision of peace.[22] But without persevering effort you will never return there—and that persevering effort is lost by selfish love.

---

[19] Cf. 1 Cor. 10, 13 (Vulg.): "God will not allow you to be tempted beyond your capacity, but with the temptation will give you a way out so that you may be able to bear it."

[20] 1 Thes. 4, 3.

[21] Mt. 19, 19.

[22] Since God (the heavenly Jerusalem) is humankind's true home, Catherine speaks consistently of our "returning" there.

This is why I said that I long to see you constant and persevering in the holy resolve you have taken, even to the point of death. This, dearest son, is what I am asking you to do, since God has been so merciful to you.[23] He has rescued you from the world's filth and has put you in the garden of holy religion to fight against vice and against your selfish will, to acquire virtue and to fulfill God's sweet will for you. So fight courageously, and don't turn back. Be prepared to die rather than resist[24] when it comes to holy obedience.

I have no more to say to you. Keep living in God's holy and tender love.

Gentle Jesus! Jesus love!

Textual Notes

a. H (as well as P3) has *amare* where other manuscripts have *lassare*. *Amare* ("love") makes no sense in this context, which goes on to speak of rejecting sin, so I have accepted the reading of Mo.
b. Note that the manuscripts for Let. T287b (Mo, S2) have *ragunando* ("gathering up") / *rugumando* ("pondering").

[23] From this point on, the letter to Pietro is quickly concluded, while that addressed to Niccolò di Nanni di Ser Vanni continues, first with expansions to this letter's closing sentences, and then with a lengthy addition.

[24] It. *ricalcitrare*.

LETTER T287b/G75[1]
To Niccolò di Nanni di Ser Vanni of Monteoliveto Maggiore
November or December 1377

This letter repeats the greater part of Let. T287a exactly, and is then expanded in a longer conclusion. The young man to whom it is addressed is the son of Catherine's disciple and benefactor, Nanni di Ser Vanni Savini of Siena. It is clear from the tone of the letter that he has just recently, at Catherine's urging, entered the Benedictine monastery of Monteoliveto Maggiore. There is no record of his entrance date.[2]

The linguistic evidence supports placing this letter in the last months of 1377, most probably in November or December.[3]

§

In the name of Jesus Christ crucified and of gentle Mary.

Dearest son in Christ gentle Jesus,

I Caterina, servant and slave of the servants of Jesus Christ, am writing to you in his precious blood. I long to see you constant and persevering in the sincere holy resolve you have taken in your heart and spirit, the resolve to serve God in truth in [your] holy order. Without perseverance you would not receive the fruit of your efforts, since it is only perseverance that is crowned. So you see that this glorious virtue of perseverance is really essential for us. Because we need it so badly, then, how can we have it? I'll tell you.

Every virtue has life because it is motivated by charity.[4] Without charity we would not receive the fruit of grace even though we might have an

---

[1] MSS: Mo-*a*, M, S5, S6, Ro, F3, S2, B, P2, P1, P5, P3, Pa; translation based on Mo-*a*, as corrected by *b*. See notes to Let. T287a.

[2] Placido Lugano, "Santa Caterina da Siena e i monaci di Montoliveto," p. 168, n. 7, says: "This Niccolò di Nanni is the Fr. Nichola Vannis de Eugubio, who in 1379–1380 was at S. Niccolò di Fuligno." In "L'istituzione di Montoliveto nella seconda metà del Trecento," p. 77, Lugano corrects this to say that Nichola Vannis de Eugubio is "in all probability" the Niccolò of this letter. Then, in n. 64, p. 77, he questions Tommasèo's calling him "perhaps" Niccolò di Nanni Savini, saying that "in 1379–1380 there was only one 'Nichola Vannis' in the whole order, and that was the one residing in Fuligno." But the rubric of Mo expressly names him as Niccolò di Nanni di Ser Vanni, though of course the copyist (Neri di Landoccio Pagliaresi) could have been mistaken in this. Lugano has nothing more to say about the present letter in either article.

[3] Though this version of Let. T287, being longer, has about a dozen patterns not found in Let. T287a, none of these patterns is particularly revealing chronologically. So the arguments cited for Let. T287a are valid for this longer letter as well.

[4] It.: *Ogni virtù a vita dall'affetto della carità.*

act of virtue.[5] So we must be motivated by love in our acquisition of virtue. But we cannot attain true love unless our heart and will are stripped of selfish love for ourselves.

This [selfish] kind of love, this pampering we give our selfish sensual passion, robs us of the life of grace. It dims our mind's eye. In fact, it is a cloud over the pupil, the light of most holy faith.[6] We lose our sense of taste, our desire. Virtue once seemed good to us. Once it gave us pleasure to see it in virtuous people, and we sought it for ourselves in Christ crucified. But now that this selfish love has taken over, it seems just the opposite. Selfish love makes us weak and fearful; we are afraid of our own shadow. This is why we don't persevere in what we have begun as long as the root of selfish love is still alive in us. For without the light that we've lost (as I've described), we are walking in the dark. We don't know the truth; we don't know our sinfulness; we don't know the graces and gifts we have received from God's infinite goodness. If we had this knowledge we would not be weak but strong and persevering. We wouldn't be brought down by the devil's wickedness and rascally temptations or by the nagging of our selfish frailty or by the world's flattery or by the difficulties of the rule. No, by the light of most holy faith we would pass through them all with a courageous heart.

This, dearest son, is the way to arrive at perfect perseverance. You must strip your heart and will of all selfish love for yourself and stop pampering your body. Avoid thinking about your father, your brothers and sisters, and your relatives. Remember them in holy prayer with desire for their salvation, but don't dwell on them with any other sentiment. You know that our Savior says we must forsake father and mother, sisters and brothers, and our very selves (that is, our selfish will) if we want to be worthy of him. Otherwise it is impossible.[7] You have begun to forsake the world and your selfish will and have taken on the yoke of true obedience. Now, if you want really to keep and fulfill this resolve until you die, you have to renounce the world and its pleasures over and over every day.[8]

But take note: we cannot either accept or reject[a] what we do not know. This is why we need the light of most holy faith in which to set Christ crucified before our mind's eye. By focusing on him you will know the seriousness of the deadly sin we commit when we set our will and our love

---

[5] Cf. Aquinas, *Summa Theologica*, II–II, q. 23, a. 8: "It is charity that directs the acts of all other virtues and that consequently gives the form to all other acts of virtue. It is precisely in this sense that charity is called the form of the virtues."

[6] Medieval physiology saw the pupil not as an opening in the eye, but as the actual light by which the eye sees.

[7] Cf. Lk. 14, 26.

[8] It would seem very strange for Catherine to be advising Pietro in this way if he were indeed prior. She speaks rather as if he has just recently entered the monastery.

inordinately on ourselves, on other people, or on created things. Mortal sin is so serious that being bound in just one such sin is enough to send a person to hell. It was and is so displeasing to God that to punish Adam's sin he sent the Word, his only-begotten Son, so that he could punish sin in his body. Even though the poison of sin was not in him, God took out the punishment on the Word, his only-begotten Son, in order to atone for human sin, in order not to let it go unpunished.[9] So the blessed Christ was our justice.[10] The justice and the suffering that humankind should have borne, he bore. Like one in love, to fulfill his Father's command, he ran to the shameful death of the most holy cross. So by focusing on this Word, we see how serious the guilt of deadly sin is.

When we see, then, that deadly sin is so serious and so displeasing to God (when the light of faith has let us know this), we hate sin. We come to detest intensely both sin and its cause. Because we see that the perverse law of our body is an instrument that inclines us to sin, that it is a perverse law that fights against the spirit,[11] our reason, along with free choice and our good and holy will,[12] rises up with hatred and contempt to discipline our body and our flesh.[13] We kill selfish will with the knife of holy obedience, never rebelling against the rule or our superiors.

But always we persevere, and must persevere, with the same desire for obedience with which we entered [religious life] on that first day. With that same holy fear we must exercise our spirit in continual humble prayer right up to the last day of our life, so that our spirit will never become lazy. We should always be occupied with praying the psalms or meditating or raising our mind to God, pondering[b] within ourselves the blazing charity we discover and see in the blood of the Word, God's Son.[14] For he has made a bath of his blood to wash away our sins.

---

[9] Aquinas, *Summa Theologica*, III, q. 48, a. 4, speaks of "the debt of punishment, to the payment of which humankind was held fast by God's justice," and of Christ's Passion as "a sufficient and more than sufficient atonement for the sin and the debt of the human race."

[10] 1 Cor. 1, 30 (Vulg.): "You are in Christ Jesus, whom God has made our justice and sanctification and redemption."

[11] Cf. Rom. 7, 23.

[12] Catherine often emphasizes that the preservation of "a good and holy will" in the midst of trial and temptation is not only a gift of God but a sure sign that God is dwelling within us.

[13] The It. *macerare* has the connotation of physical discipline (for example, with chain or flagellation) in view of making the body compliant.

[14] Cf. Let. T213 to Suor Daniela of Orvieto (1378): "They find prayer everywhere, because they always carry with them the place where God dwells by grace and where we ought to pray. I mean the house of our soul, where holy desire is always praying. This desire rises up with the light of understanding to look within us, and into the measureless fire of divine charity which we discover in the blood [Christ] shed—the blood that by love's generosity we find within the vessel of our own soul."

When we see and consider that God loves us so much, we cannot keep ourselves from loving. And when we love, our mind thinks about the object of our love. Now we cannot live without love. And since two opposing loves cannot exist together, we must of necessity be stripped of perverse love and clothed in God's. Because our heart cannot but be sensitive to the one we love, we use holy thoughts to drive out the evil thoughts the devil would like to put into our heart. And the devil, finding that our heart is ablaze in the fire of divine charity, doesn't come around much, any more than a fly comes around a boiling cauldron. But if the devil were to find our heart fearful and lukewarm, he would come in right away with all his ugly thoughts and imaginings.

So we must keep active so that we will be found not lukewarm or empty but filled with God in holy desire, remembering and meditating on the wonderful blessings we have received from him.[15] And if these [evil] thoughts come anyway (since the devil never sleeps but is constantly tormenting us[16]), this shouldn't weary or discourage our spirit. No, we should resist and see that our will does not give in. For if our will doesn't consent to the devil's suggestions or to the weakness of our flesh, we do not sin. In fact, we earn merit because of the suffering we endure. This means that if we don't sit down in apathy, or let our spirit become weary and discouraged, or give up the practice of prayer, [the struggle] will bring us to true and perfect virtue. Why? In times of struggle we come to know ourselves and our weakness better. And we come to know God's goodness within us better when we see that God has graciously preserved our good and holy will—and it is the will alone that sins or merits. So you see how in times of intense struggle we become more perfect and prove ourselves in virtue.

Next, I want you to believe that God does not burden us with more than we can carry.[17] God's giving is indeed well measured, because he is our God who wants nothing else but that we be made holy.[18]

---

[15] Cf. Mt. 12, 43–45; Lk. 11, 24–26 (Vulg.): "When the unclean spirit has gone out of a person, it wanders through waterless places looking for a spot to rest, but it finds none. Then it says, 'I will return to my house from which I came.' When it comes, it finds it empty and swept and put in order. Then it goes and brings along seven other spirits more evil than itself, and they enter and live there; and the last state of that person is worse than the first." Also, Rev. 3, 16 (Vulg.): "Because you are lukewarm, and neither cold nor hot, I will begin to vomit you out of my mouth."

[16] Cf. 1 Pet. 5, 8 (Vulg.): "Stay sober and awake; for your enemy the devil prowls about like a roaring lion looking for someone to devour."

[17] Cf. 1 Cor. 10, 13 (Vulg.): "God will not allow you to be tempted beyond your capacity, but with the temptation will give you a way out so that you may be able to bear it."

[18] 1 Thes. 4, 3.

By the light of faith, then, rise above every sort of selfish love. And to attain the most perfect love, as I've told you, set before your mind's eye Christ crucified and the indescribable charity he has demonstrated for you by shedding his blood with such blazing love. Then, by the light, you will come to know in this gentle Word how serious sin is. And you will come to know your own weakness and his charity. In that charity you will love and pursue virtue, ready to suffer any pain in order to acquire it. And in charity you will live in love with your neighbors.

This must be your study: to love God in truth and your neighbors as yourself;[19] to be humble and obedient; to patiently suffer pain, hurt, disdain and abuse, the burdens of the rule and the heavy obligations placed on you by your superior, and the devil's temptations; and to persevere in enduring all these things right up to the moment of your death. In times of struggle and weariness, run with this light of holy faith to embrace the most holy cross, and there put your hope confidently in the blood of Christ crucified. I haven't the least doubt that if you are humble (with the humility that nurtures charity within us) and obedient and truly patient, you will by the power of this blood be victorious over your enemies, the world, the flesh, and the devil. And you will return triumphant to your city, Jerusalem, the vision of peace.[20] But without persevering effort you will never return there—and that persevering effort is lost by selfish love.

This is why I said that I long to see you constant and persevering in the holy resolve you have taken, even to the point of death. This, dearest son, is what I am asking you to do, since God has been so merciful to you[21]—and the glorious Saint Nicholas as well.[22] God has rescued you from the world's filth and from your miserable toil. He has put you in the garden of holy religion to fight against vice and against your selfish will, to acquire virtue and to fulfill God's sweet will for you. So fight on courageously with the shield and the light of faith, navigating with the yoke of holy obedience.[23] Don't turn back. And be prepared to die rather than

---

[19] Mt. 19, 19.

[20] Since God (the heavenly Jerusalem) is humankind's true home, Catherine speaks consistently of our "returning" there.

[21] From here on this letter differs from the one sent to Pietro di Giovanni di Viva.

[22] The reference to Saint Nicholas could be an indication that Catherine is writing near the feast of that saint, 6 December.

[23] Cf. Let. T36 to several Olivetan novices (in this volume), in which Catherine describes religious life as a ship which "is maneuvered under the yoke of sincere and holy obedience. Just think how great a favor God has done you because he knows how weak your arms are! For those who are in the world navigate this sea on their own power, but those in religious life navigate on the power of others." The original (*La quale navicella è menata col giogo della santa e vera obedienzia*) is a bit problematic, since *giogo* can refer to one of the banks of oars in a galley. This interpretation, however, does not seem possible in light of the present passage, since Catherine a bit further on in this letter describes the *giogo* of obe-

resist when it comes to holy obedience.

If sometimes your sensuality finds it hard to carry on, or if because of all these [evil] thoughts coming into your mind your soul sometimes gets weary of not feeling the peace it would like, rouse yourself with true humility. Reflect that you are undeserving of spiritual peace and calm and deserving of these burdens. Think of the sufferings God's Son endured for you, and the sufferings *you* endured in the service of the devil. Then tell yourself, "Treacherous sensuality! You put up with so much pain while you were in the darkness of mortal sin! How much more you should suffer for Christ crucified now that God has enlightened you! So bear up today, my soul, and tomorrow you shall do whatever God will have you do. Tomorrow perhaps your life will end and by the power of [Christ's] blood you will receive the fruit of your labors." In this way, by regarding yourself as deserving of the burdens both in consideration of your sins and for love of Christ crucified, you will bypass the burdens and be carrying Christ's yoke, which is sweet and mild and will spark in your soul the blaze of his unspeakable charity.[24]

Bathe in the blood of Christ crucified, so that you may be constant and persevering, and fill up the joy my soul has experienced in your being saved, in your taking the habit and assuming the holy yoke of obedience. Think how unbearably sad I would be to have rescued a son from the devil's hands by God's goodness, and then see you not persevering and not being a mirror of religion in true humility and obedience! So I am begging you, ordering you (to the extent that I can and know how) not to turn back to look at what you have plowed.[25] And I beg you to learn to restrain your tongue.

When [evil] thoughts or[a] strong temptations regarding some specific thing (no matter how ugly) come into your heart,[26] never keep them in-

---

dience as *dolce e soave*, echoing the gospel reference to the yoke of Christ (Mt. 11, 29–30). It is therefore probable that, in the context of the ship image, she is thinking of the chains which bind the rowers of the Mediterranean galleys, who in her day are usually slaves or prisoners. She does not, however, anywhere speak of religious as slaves or prisoners, but only as servants. Except for naming herself "servant and slave," she reserves the term "slavery" for servitude to sin.

[24] Mt. 11, 30.

[25] Lk. 9, 62. As usual, Catherine renders it freely but aptly, since one can hardly cut a straight furrow with a hand-held plow if one's attention is on what has already been plowed rather than on the terrain ahead.

[26] Tommasèo has *l'odio*, "hatred," while the manuscripts have *ladia*, "ugly." Though the structure is a bit awkward in that the verb and the subsequent pronoun switch from plural to singular, the original is consistent with (for example) Let. T189/DT84 in this volume, written to several other Olivetan monks as well as to the monks of Cervaia: "Our sin, or any diabolical illusion or temptation, however repulsive, filthy, and ugly it may be, need not make us falter."

side, but reveal them to the father of your soul.[27] For the devil very much likes it when we hold on to these things, and doesn't like it at all when we tell them. Why? When we hold on to them we become confused; then we get discouraged and give up our spiritual exercises. This often leads to despair[b]—just what the devil wants. So we mustn't be afraid, but must reveal our every infirmity to the doctor of our soul, with hope in Christ's blood.

I have no more to say to you. Keep living in God's holy and tender love.

Gentle Jesus! Jesus love!

Textual Notes

a. Tommasèo: *and / or.*

b. *This ... despair* supplied by *b* and other manuscripts. Mo-*a* has simply: "And the devil wants nothing if not to make us fall into despair."

---

[27] That is, your confessor or superior.

LETTER T104/G92[1]
To Frate Raimondo da Capua
November or December 1377

Catherine in this letter calls Raimondo "my remiss and ungrateful son," exhorting him to patience in the face of maltreatment. ("[Our suffering] may be unjust in the sense that we have not offended those who are doing us wrong.") Raimondo is apparently in Rome, since she asks him to "beg the glorious Peter and Paul to give me and my poor children grace." Her own mood is somewhat discouraged: "As for me, if it is [God's] will, let him take me from this dark life, for life is unbearable for me, and I long for death."

All of the above would place the letter some time between mid-September 1377, when Raimondo left for Rome, and November 1378, when Catherine joined him there. For more precision one must look to the linguistic evidence. This would seem to place the letter most probably in November or December 1377 (when we know from other letters that Catherine was in fact discouraged and ill).[2]

§

In the name of Jesus Christ crucified and of gentle Mary.

Dearest and very loved father, remiss and ungrateful son in Christ gentle Jesus,

I Caterina, servant and slave of the servants of Jesus Christ, am writing to you in his precious blood. I long to see you truly and perfectly conscientious about acquiring and preserving virtue, for without conscientiousness we never discover virtue, nor preserve it once we have it. Love is what makes our heart conscientious and moves the feet of our affection to walk to where virtue is found.

A lack of conscientiousness, then, indicates a lack of love. So we must love courageously and sincerely, letting neither our selfish feelings nor any other person get in the way. And to achieve such tender love we have to open our mind's eye to see and know how much we are loved by God.

---

[1] MSS: Mo-*a*, corrected by *b*; M, P4, S2, S5, S6, Ro; translation based on Mo-*a*.

[2] Three of the six letters sharing seventeen or more of this one's sixty-eight analyzed patterns are from these months. (The other three are from late 1378 through 1379.) A number of significant clusters within individual patterns begin and/or end within this brief period: AFFOCDES, CALDCAR, CASACOGN, CELLALET, FRUTPAZ, MENSCIBO, REGINA, SEGNAMOR, SENZMEZZ. Fawtier (II, p. 200) places the letter in late 1377 or early 1378. Dupré Theseider (unpublished notes) places it in late 1377.

But to arrive at that knowledge we have to walk with the feet of our affection into the house of true self-knowledge, because it is in knowledge of ourselves that we conceive hatred for our selfish sensuality and love for God because of his boundless charity, which we have discovered within us. And then our heart rises up at once at the urging of blazing desire and goes in search of how we might best spend our time. For we seem never to have enough time, once we see that in time we can choose either to acquire treasure or lose it.

And we see that there is no way we can acquire true virtue except through charity for our neighbors. We have learned that charity from knowing God, because in God's goodness we have seen and have come to know that his boundless love reaches out not just to us but to everyone, our friends and enemies alike. Granted, we love one person more than another, depending on the virtue we find in them. We love virtuous persons for love of virtue and as creatures [of God]. Unjust and wicked sinners we love both because they were created by God and also so that they might abandon sin and come to virtue. In this way we begin to eat and savor souls for God's honor. And we would give ourselves up to death to rescue souls from the hands of the devils. In our concern for them we steal time from ourselves—time, that is, that we might have had for our own comfort, any comfort new or old—and we give that time to our neighbors. This is why, when that servant of God asked, "My Lord, what do you want me to do?" he answered, "Give honor to me, and your best efforts to your neighbors."[3]

And what efforts do I give them? Physical efforts as well as spiritual. By spiritual efforts I mean holy desire. I mean the offering of holy, humble, and continual prayer in joy for the virtuous and in sorrow for those who lie dead in mortal sin. I mean bearing in true patience their scandalmongering, their detraction, their complaints against us. I mean never for any reason letting up in our prayer, our burning desire, our hunger and concern for their salvation. Then we are conformed with Christ crucified, eating this food on Christ's painful and restless cross of desire, the cross that was greater and more painful than his physical cross.[4]

I said also[a] that God wants us to give our physical efforts. And we give

---

[3] "That servant of God" is Catherine herself.

[4] Cf. Prayer 18, pp. 162–163: "I see that this Word, once written in you, [Mary,] was never without the cross of holy desire. Even as he was conceived within you, desire to die for the salvation of humankind was engrafted and bound into him. This is why he had been made flesh. So it was a great cross for him to carry for such a long time that desire, when he would have liked to see it realized at once." This contrast between the physical cross and the cross of desire occurs also in *Dial.* 78, p. 146; Let. T11 to Cardinal Pierre d'Estaing; and Let. T16 to a great prelate (both letters in this volume).

our physical efforts in the service of our neighbors when we give them any service at all that makes us suffer physical pain and inconvenience. Sometimes God lets us suffer assault, hunger and thirst, and all sorts of persecution, as did the holy martyrs when they endured pain and severe torture. But we are so imperfect that we are not yet worthy of so great a good as to be persecuted for Christ!

This, then, is how we must give our best efforts to our neighbors and honor to God, doing everything for the glory and praise of his name. Otherwise our efforts would bear no fruit for life. On the contrary, even in this life we would experience an earnest of eternal death. Conceive love in God by seeking his honor and the salvation of souls, and in the person of your neighbor let the love you conceive be proved by the virtue of patience.

Oh patience, how peaceable you are! Oh patience, what hope you give to those who possess you! Oh patience, you are a queen in control of and not possessed by anger! Oh patience, you serve sentence on selfish emotion when it would raise its head in anger! You carry a sword, double-edged with hate and love, to cut off and root out anger and pride and the impatience that is the pith of pride.[5] *Your clothing is the sun, alight with the true knowledge of God and warm with divine charity. The rays from [this sun] fall on those who do you wrong, heaping on their heads coals of fire ablaze with charity to burn up and consume the hatred in their hearts.*[6] *You then, sweet patience grounded in charity, are the source of fruit for our neighbors and of honor to God. This garment of yours is covered with stars, all the different virtues, for we can have no patience without the stars of all the virtues along with the night of self-knowledge, which is a sort of moonlight.*[7] And after this knowledge of ourselves comes the day, with the great light and warmth of the sun as a garment for patience. Who then would not fall in love with such a lovely thing as patience, with willingness to suffer for the sake of Christ crucified?

So, dearest and very loved father, let us carry on! Don't lose any time. Try to get to know yourself so that this queen may dwell in your soul, for

---

[5] Charity is often imaged in Catherine's writings (for example, *Dial.* 10, pp. 41–42) as a tree rooted in the soil of humility. The tree's pith is patience. In contrast, the tree of selfish love is rooted in the depths (or on the mountain) of pride, and its pith is impatience. In *Dial.* 128 (p. 252), however, impatience is the pith (or marrow) of pride itself.

[6] Prv. 25, 22; Rom. 12, 20 (Vulg.): "But 'if your enemies are hungry, feed them. If they are thirsty, give them a drink. By doing so, you will heap coals of fire upon their heads.' Do not be conquered by evil, but conquer evil by doing good."

[7] If Catherine had known that moonlight was reflected sunlight, she would have found the image even more appropriate, given her linking of self-knowledge with knowledge of God. But cf. Prayer 19, p. 170: "But if I gaze into your exaltedness, any rising up to there that my soul can manage is as the dark night compared with the light of the sun, or as different as is the moonlight from the sun's globe."

we really do need her. In this way you will find yourself on the cross with Christ crucified and be nourished on his food.[8] It is for this that God chose and called you. It will seem to you that you are in the moonlight when you are suffering, but in that suffering you will discover the light of the sun. Then[b] your soul will be revivified in virtue, and you will keep it and seek it with greater and more thorough conscientiousness until you reach your destination. You will conform yourself with Christ crucified, who suffered pain and torment and shame. Why did he suffer? Because he knew God's wisdom, that punishment had to be the consequence of sin against the Father. But humanity was weakened and unable to make satisfaction; so he with blazing love made satisfaction, though the poison of sin was not in him.[9] In this, if you are virtuous, you will follow in his footsteps in suffering.

[Our suffering] may be unjust in the sense that we have not offended those who are doing us wrong, but as far as God is concerned we are always suffering justly, because we are always doing him wrong. So, just as Christ suffered to the point of death and rose[c] glorious, so it shall be with us and with God's other servants who endure suffering until their self-centeredness is dead. For when self-centeredness is dead and vice is struck down, we come out of it resurrected to grace, glorious with patience as queen, and clothed in the garment patience wears.[10] For as I said earlier, patience perseveres to the end, since it reaches all the way to heaven. All the virtues, it is true, except charity (the garment patience wears) remain here below while charity enters heaven like a lady. Nevertheless, she attracts to herself the fruit of all the virtues, but especially the fruit of patience, which is at the very center of charity, its very pith.

This is why, when we see patience, she is not naked but clothed in love, for patience without charity would not even be a virtue. But when our love is true and perfect, we give evidence of it by bearing with pain and disgrace, scorn and abuse, temptations from the devil and impulses of our flesh, the tongues of critics and the flatteries of the two-faced people who have one thing in their heart and another on their lips. All this we endure with genuine and holy patience, and with sincere concern for the service of God and of our neighbors. And we are brought to dwell within the cell of self-knowledge, within which is encompassed the cell of the

---

[8] She will eventually speak more of this food.

[9] Catherine often refers to sin as poison, but never develops the image.

[10] That is, the garment of love or charity, as is stated below. Elsewhere (for example, in Let. T113 to Bandeçça Salimbeni, in this volume) Catherine specifies that this is a wedding garment—either the dress of the bride or the dress expected of guests at the wedding banquet of the gospel parable, Mt. 22, 1–14 (or sometimes apparently both simultaneously).

knowledge of God's goodness to us.[11] There we become fat; there we are happy. Within that cell we eat souls as our food in our suffering, having made the cross our table. In that cell of[d] glory and praise to God's name we find our rest, having there made our bed. So we have discovered table and food and waiter (the Holy Spirit, I mean), and the eternal Father's honor, where we rest.[12] And once we have so pleasantly found the cell within, we seek it outside as well, in so far as we can.[13]

Remember, dearest father and remiss son, Mary's teaching and that of gentle First Truth. Realize your need to dwell in knowledge of yourself, and to offer continual humble prayer. You have to treasure your cell and come to know the truth, and avoid all company except what is necessary for the salvation of souls, to rescue them from the hands of the devil in holy confession. Where that is concerned, find your pleasure with publicans and sinners. As for other people, love many of them but associate with few. Don't forget the divine office in the proper time and place. Don't be slow or careless when you have things to do for God and in service to your neighbors, either. But though you do have business to attend to, find refuge in your cell and don't be gadding about under the pretext of virtue.

I am sure that if you are perfectly conscientious and hungry for virtue, you will do all of this and will not be so forgetful as not to keep in mind what I've told you. Otherwise (if you are not conscientious) you will never do this or even keep what you have. This is why I said that I long to see you truly and perfectly conscientious. I trust that gentle mother Mary to fulfill my desire. Let go of yourself and seek only Christ crucified, no one else, nothing else.

Beg the glorious Peter and Paul to give me and my poor children grace to drown ourselves in the blood of Christ crucified and clothe ourselves in

---

[11] Cf. Let. T201 to the Roman Carthusian Giovanni (1378), where she explains how these two are really one cell. Also Let. T49 to Alessa dei Saracini (in this volume): "This cell is really two rooms in one, and while you are in the one you must at the same time be in the other; otherwise your soul would end up either in confusion or in presumption. For if you stayed in self-knowledge, spiritual confusion would be the result. And if you stayed only in knowledge of God, you would end up in presumption. So the one has to be seasoned by the other, and the two made to be one. When this is accomplished you will arrive at perfection."

[12] The referents of the images are a bit uncertain here because of Catherine's varying use of the images involved. Usually in the combination of table, food, and waiter, the table is the Father, the food is the Son, and the waiter is the Spirit. But in this case she has just referred to the cross as table, to souls as food, and to the Father as bed; so she seems to carry these meanings over into the trilogy, in which the Spirit is then the only new referent.

[13] The "outside" cell here is one's physical cell or room. Cf. Let. T353 to Catella, Checcia, and Caterina Dentice (1379), where she speaks of the necessity of both. She expands on the same notion below for Raimondo.

gentle Truth. As for me, if it is his will, let him take me from this dark life, for life is unbearable for me, and I long for death. Take heart, and let's be glad and joyful, because our happiness will be complete in heaven.

I'll say no more. Keep living in God's holy and tender love.

Gentle Jesus! Jesus love!

Textual Notes

a. *also* supplied by *b*.

b. *Then* supplied by *b*.

c. *b*: *was raised / rose*.

d. *that cell of* supplied by *b* above the line.

Letter T214/G174[1]
To Caterina dello Spedaluccio and Giovanna di Capo
November or December 1377

The tone of Catherine's remarks about the Church in this letter must place it in a time when she is discouraged about people who "are heaping more and more abuse and dishonor upon Christ's dear bride." In fact, her comments are very similar to those made in Let. T104 to Raimondo da Capua, which I would guess to be from November or December 1377.

The letter must, of course, be from a period when neither of the women to whom it is addressed is with Catherine. We know from Let. T132 (vol. I) that Giovanna di Capo was with Catherine during most of her stay in Pisa in 1375. She was also with Catherine in Florence from early 1378 through late July, and in Rome from November 1378 until Catherine's death. And there is no reason to suppose that both Giovanna and Caterina would not have been in Siena with Catherine during the interlude between those two journeys, since they returned there even before Catherine did. Thus the plausible time for this letter seems to be effectively narrowed to the Val d'Orcia period. Let. T118 (in this volume) makes it clear that Giovanna did not in fact accompany Catherine on that mission.

On the basis of its similarity in tone to Let. T104 to Raimondo da Capua, I would place this letter in November or December 1377.[2]

§

In the name of Jesus Christ crucified and of gentle Mary.

Dearest daughters in Christ gentle Jesus,

I Caterina, servant and slave of the servants of Jesus Christ, am writing to you in his precious blood. I long to see you grounded in true patience and deep humility so that you will be able to follow the gentle spotless Lamb, for there is no other way you can follow him.

Now is the time, my daughters, to prove whether we are virtuous[a] or not, to prove whether you [really] are daughters. You must patiently endure others' persecution and slander, defamation and rumor-mongering.

---

[1] MSS: Mo-*a*, M, S5, S6, Ro, F3, P4, S4; translation based on Mo-*a*, with variants from an unpublished transcription by Dupré Theseider.

[2] The linguistic evidence broadly supports this placement. Seven of the eleven letters which share ten or more of this one's thirty-seven analyzed patterns are from October through December 1377. Two significant clusters within individual patterns in particular (GRATVIRT, MONDOPER) reinforce a placement in November or December. Both Fawtier (II, p. 228) and Dupré Theseider (unpublished notes) decline to date the letter.

You must suffer these things with genuine humility, not taking scandal or becoming impatient or raising your head in pride against anyone. You know very well that this is what you have been taught: that you must eat the food of God's honor and the salvation of souls on the cross, and do it with true holy patience.[3]

Oimé! In the name of gentle First Truth, dearest daughters, I am inviting you to rouse yourselves from the slumber of indifference and of selfish love for yourselves, and to offer up continual humble prayers with frequent vigils in true self-knowledge. For the world is perishing because people are heaping more and more abuse and dishonor upon Christ's dear bride. So let us give honor to God and our best efforts to our neighbors![b] Oimé! Neither you nor God's other servants should want to end your[c] lives in any other way but in sighing and weeping! For there is no other way to placate God's anger, which we see so clearly descending upon us.

Oh unhappy me! My daughters, I believe it is my wretched self who am the reason for so many evils, because of my great ingratitude and the other sins I have committed against my Creator! Oimé! Oimé! Who is God, who is being offended by his creatures? He is the one who is supreme eternal Goodness, who in his charity created us in his own image and likeness, and who after we had sinned created us anew in the blood of the loving spotless Lamb, his only-begotten Son. And who are we ignorant mercenaries who are offending our Creator? We are the ones who of ourselves are not, who would not exist if God had not made us, who of ourselves are full of every sort of wretchedness. We seem intent only on how we might be able to offend God, and on how we might be able to offend each other in contempt of our Creator.

With our own miserable eyes we see [Christ's] blood being persecuted in God's Church—the blood that gives us life.[4] Let our hearts break in pained and anguished desire! Let the life drain from our bodies and let us die rather than see God so mocked! This is a living death for me! I beg my Creator for death and cannot have it! It would be better for me to die than to live, rather than see such great destruction as has come and is yet to come upon the Christian people!

Let us take out the weapon of holy prayer. I see no other remedy. The

---

[3] Cf. Jn. 4, 34 (Vulg.): "My food is to do the will of the one who sent me, and to complete his work." The image of feeding on souls for God's honor at the table of the cross occurs frequently in Catherine's writings, for example, in Let. T256 to Frier Niccolò of the Knights of St. John (in this volume): "Learn from this slain, consumed Lamb, who with delight in the food of his Father's honor and our salvation set himself to eating it at the table of the shameful cross, paying no attention to his weariness and grief." It is further embellished in *Dial.* 76, pp. 140–141.

[4] Cf. Acts 9, 4: "Saul! Saul! Why are you persecuting me?"

time has come for God's servants to be persecuted,[5] and they must hide in the cavern of self-knowledge and knowledge of God, crying out for his mercy through the merits of his Son's blood. I don't want to say any more, my daughters, because if I went on as long as I'd like to, I'd never stop till God took me out of this life!

Now a word to you, Andrea.[6]

It is not those who [simply] begin who are crowned with glory, but those who persevere until death. Oh my daughter, you have begun to put your hand to the plow of virtue by leaving behind the vomit of deadly sin.[7] Now you must persevere if you would receive the fruit of the effort it will take to rein in your youth and keep yourself from running off to be a member of the devil. Oimé, my daughter! Don't you give even a thought to the fact that you were a member of the devil, that you were sleeping in the filth of impurity, and that God plucked you out of the great physical and spiritual wretchedness in which you were living?

So you mustn't be ungrateful or unappreciative, or evil will snatch you up and the devil will return with seven companions and be stronger than he was before.[8] The way to show your gratitude and appreciation for the grace you have received is to be strong in the face of the devil's challenges and against the world and your flesh when they plague you, and to persevere in virtue. If you want to escape such temptations, my daughter, cling to the tree of the most holy cross by physical abstinence,[9] by watching and prayer, bathing with holy desire in the blood of Christ crucified. This is how you will win the life of grace and fulfill my desire—which is that you be a true servant of Christ crucified.

I am begging you, then, to leave childhood behind. Choose as your spouse Christ, who has ransomed you with his blood. But if you still want the world, you must wait till you can get it in a way that is for God's honor and your own good.[10] Be obediently submissive even to the point of

---

[5] Cf. Jn. 15, 20 (Vulg.): "If they have persecuted me, they will also persecute you."

[6] Andrea is not identified, but what follows seems to indicate that Catherine would like her to become a *Mantellata* or even a nun. She is evidently young, and has apparently been converted rather recently from a life of sin, perhaps of prostitution.

[7] Cf. Lk. 9, 62, for the plow image, and 2 Pt. 2, 22 (citing Prv. 26, 11) for the image of the dog returning to its vomit.

[8] Mt. 12, 43–45 (Vulg.): "When the unclean spirit has gone out of a person, it wanders through waterless places looking for somewhere to rest, but it finds nothing. Then it says, 'I will return to my house from which I came.' When it comes, it finds it empty, swept, and tidied. Then it goes and brings along seven other spirits more evil than itself, and they enter and live there. And the last state of that person is worse than the first."

[9] She seems to mean sexual abstinence, but in a future sense, since she urges Andrea to take Christ as her spouse. (What follows clearly implies that she is not married).

[10] It. *E se tu vorrai pur el mondo convienti aspectare tanto che si possa avere el modo di dartelo per modo che sia honore di Dio e bene di te.* By "the world," she seems to mean mar-

death, and don't go against the will of Caterina and Giovanna.[11] I know that they will not tell you anything or give you any counsel that is not for God's honor and your salvation, both physically and spiritually. If you don't do this, you will displease me immensely, and do yourself scant service. I hope that by God's goodness you will act in such a way that God will be honored, and you will have the fruit and will afford me great comfort.

And you, Caterina and Giovanna, work for God's honor and [Andrea's] salvation even to the point of death.

Dear daughters, now is the time for hard work—but it ought to be a consolation for us in Christ crucified.

I'll say no more. Keep living in God's holy and tender love.

Gentle Jesus! Jesus love!

Textual Notes

a. F3: *love virtue* (*amiamo virtù*) / *are virtuous* (*abiamo virtù*).

b. P4: *let us order God's honor and efforts. . . . / let us . . . neighbors* (*ordiniamo . . . e lhonore. . . . / Or diamo . . . lonore*).

c. P4: *your and our / your*.

---

riage. This would seem to imply that Andrea has been involved either in prostitution or in some form of sexual activity outside of marriage.

[11] Certainly Caterina dello Spedaluccio and Giovanna di Capo, to whom this letter is addressed.

Letter Fawtier 15[1]
To an unspecified group of her disciples
November or December 1377

The only manuscript in which this letter occurs is Landau 1415, and even there it is broken off abruptly.[2] (The somewhat awkward style of this letter and others for which there are extant originals leads me to suspect that this is Catherine's own unedited style, while the collections illustrate the polishing done by the compilers.) The letter begins *Carissimi figliuoli.* ... ("Dearest children. . . ."), the only indication of an addressee.

If one is to give any weight to the rubric, "written by the hand of Saint Catherine of Siena, that is, copied by her,"[3] the letter should probably be placed after October 1377, when she is said to have learned to write. A placement in late 1377 is only quite broadly supported by the linguistic data.[4] But there is a strong argument for placement in late 1377 in its sharing with only Let. T104 and *The Dialogue* the theme of charity as lady. I would therefore place it near Let. T104 and near the other letters which refer to her learning to write, in November or December 1377. The disciples to whom it is addressed would then almost certainly be those who are in Siena at this time.

§

In the name of Jesus Christ crucified and of gentle Mary.

Dearest children in Christ gentle Jesus,

I Caterina, servant and slave of the servants of Jesus Christ, am writing to you in his precious blood. I long to see you immersed and bathed in the blood of the humble spotless Lamb. This blood makes the soul drunk. It clothes us in the fire of divine charity, because there is no blood without fire, no fire without blood.[5]

---

[1] MS: Landau 1415 (L), fol. 107v; translation based on L as transcribed by Fawtier and published as number 15 in his *Cateriniana*, pp. 29–31. Toward the end, either the manuscript has many copyist errors, or Fawtier's transcription is faulty. Having no access to the manuscript, I have in each case made the best possible conjecture, giving my reasoning in the notes.

[2] This fact leads Fawtier to wonder whether the manuscript may have once contained more of Catherine's letters.

[3] It. *scripta per mano di sancta Catherina da Siena cioè copiata da quella.*

[4] Only one significant cluster within an individual pattern (DIMONDRM) is concentrated narrowly in November and December 1377. Two others (EBBRPERD, MENSCIBO) end there. Fawtier does not place the letter chronologically.

[5] Cf. Let. T189 to the monks of Cervaia and to Giovanni di Bindo and others (in this

Oh how sweet and wonderful it is to be drunk on and clothed in such a gentle loving fire, to lose ourselves completely in it! It consumes the dampness of selfish love and the delight we take in our own comfort [and] in all human pleasure. We now delight not in pleasing others but only in pleasing our Creator. Why? Because of our self-contempt. For the sole source of our desire to please [others] is the pleasure we take in ourselves. And the fire of charity which we find in [Christ's] blood consumes all of this.

Charity is a food that nourishes our soul at her breasts. This divine charity is waiter, table, and food because of the fire of the Holy Spirit. [But the Holy Spirit] is not separate from the power of the Father or the wisdom of the Son; they are one and the same thing. This is why I said that the Holy Spirit is table and food and waiter. So it is true:[a] the Father is table, and the Son is food roasted on the wood of the most holy cross,[6] and the Holy Spirit waits on us. We see that this dear waiter serves us our being and every grace we have received over and above our being. This means that God gives and is given to us continually, and not out of any obligation but out of love, as a free favor.

[Charity][b] is the dear intermediary that both unites and separates.[7] She unites us to God, and she cuts us off from ourselves, from our disordered selfish love. She makes our heart all strong[8] because she frees us from slavish fear and leaves us living in holy fear.[9] She is not without the light but

---

volume): "[T]he fire is steeped in blood, so it truly does burn. This fire is the love that is the Holy Spirit, for love was the hand that pierced God's Son and made him shed his blood. [The fire and the blood] became one, and so perfect was their uniting that we cannot have fire without blood, nor blood without fire." In Let. T270 to Gregory XI (in the volume) the idea is placed in a slightly different context: "You [as pope] are the mother who nurses us at the breasts of divine charity, giving us neither blood without fire nor fire without blood, since the blood was shed with blazing love."

[6] Cf. Let. T52 to Jeronimo da Siena (in this volume): "*Oh tender Lamb, roasted over the fire of divine charity on the spit of the most holy cross! Oh sweetest of foods, filled with joy and happiness and consolation! You lack nothing, because for those who serve you in truth you are made table and food and waiter.* We see well that the Father is a table for us, and a bed where the soul can rest. And we see the Word, his only-begotten Son, who has given himself to us as food with such burning love. And who has brought him to us? The waiter, the Holy Spirit—and because of his boundless love he is not satisfied to have anyone else wait on us but wants to serve as waiter himself."

[7] This theme is developed in great detail, under the imagery of mortar, in Let. T164/DT58 to Melina Barbani (in this volume).

[8] It. *virile*, which is literally (and here also somewhat figuratively) "manly."

[9] Catherine often contrasts "slavish fear" with "holy fear." The contrast is developed at length in Let. T361 to a Neapolitan woman (1378 or 1379): "[H]oly fear of God ... makes us so courageous that we fear neither suffering nor death nor any sort of persecution; nor are we afraid of displeasing other people, because we want only to please our Creator. The only thing we fear is offending God. What sweetness for those who possess this holy fear! Because it flows from charity's sweetness, it is a reverential fear as it should be, the fear of good children who are afraid of displeasing their parents. It isn't the punishment they

carries with her the lamp of most holy faith, along with firm and perfect hope. She is patient. She is strong, never vanquished, always victorious. Her height[10] extends from heaven to earth, and from the society of this life she reaches eventually the heavenly society of those who are truly joyful,[11] for charity enters heaven as a lady who gathers to herself the fruits of all the other virtues.[12] She is so pleasant and so sweet that she dispels all bitterness. She gladdens the heart and makes it perfectly single and free,[13] not deceitful or two-faced.[14]

So we should diligently seek charity. We must not be apathetic, but run to where she is to be found. And where shall we find her? In Christ crucified, by following his teaching, for it is he who showed us charity in action, with his blood.

Up, then, dearest children! There is no more time for sleeping! It is time to wake up, because our enemies do not sleep.[15] The perverse law that is always fighting against the spirit never sleeps.[16] Nor does the devil with his evil temptations. Nor does the world with its lying flattery and all its troubles. So it would be truly insane[17] to go on sleeping. Keep yourselves awake[18] with watching and with continual humble prayer. Then

---

fear, but the offense itself, because of their love and respect. It's the same with those who have generously and completely given themselves to the service of their Creator with all their heart and all their affection. They serve him not out of fear or with a mercenary love, but with unstinting love. And just as their love and service are free, so is their fear free, for in holy fear they are ready to suffer anything without fear of the pain."

[10] Literally, "length."

[11] It. *i veri gustatori*, literally, "the true enjoyers." That is, those who "eat and enjoy (savor) souls at the table of the cross for God's honor" attain full and perfect enjoyment in God's will in heaven.

[12] Cf. *Dial.* 160, p. 346: "It is charity alone who comes as a lady bringing with her the fruit of all the virtues, leaving the other virtues themselves outside as she enters into me, eternal Life. It is in me that these souls enjoy eternal life because I am eternal Life."

[13] Fawtier's transcription has *tanto e schietto e libero* ("such and single and free"), but I have translated it as "perfectly single and free" on the assumption that the original has *tutto* (more literally, "completely"), as have several parallel passages in Catherine's writings.

[14] Fawtier's transcription has *e non factone danno*. I suspect the original has *e non ficto ne doppio*, which would be parallel to other passages such as Let. T82 to three women of Florence (in this volume): "Your love for God will be sincere, not feigned (*finto*), single-hearted, not two-faced (*doppio*)." Or *Dial.* 33, p. 74: "the deceitful (*finto*) heart that is not sincere and generous but double (*doppio*), that says one thing but thinks another."

[15] Cf. Rom. 13, 11: "It is now the hour for you to wake from sleep." And 1 Pt. 5, 8 (Vulg.): "Stay sober and alert, for your enemy, the devil, prowls about like a roaring lion looking for someone to devour."

[16] Rom. 8, 23.

[17] Fawtier's transcription has *nato* ("born"), but it must be *mato* or *matto*.

[18] Fawtier's transcription has *destinato* ("destined"), which I suspect (again from numerous parallel passages) should be *destatevi* or *destianci*.

we will be doing ourselves a service by preserving[19] and increasing grace within our soul. And we will be . . . our neighbors with hunger for God's honor. . . .[20]

Textual Notes

a. Fawtier's transcription has *life*, but both the immediate context and related texts make me strongly suspect that the original (which I have not seen) has not *vita* but *verità*.
b. Even though the pronoun is masculine (*questo*), the context makes clear that its antecedent is charity. And the next pronominal reference is in fact feminine. Because of the personified references which follow, I have used "she" throughout the paragraph.

[19] Fawtier's transcription has *e servando* ("observing"), which I suspect should be *conservando*. Nowhere else in the entire corpus of her writings does Catherine use the verb *servare* in the sense of preserving, nor does she ever speak of serving (*servendo*) grace.

[20] Here the letter (and in fact the manuscript) is cut off. The final clause actually reads: *e al proximo con fame del honore di Dio ci nutrica. . . .* I have not attempted to fit the last two words ("nourishes us") into the translation, since it is unknown to what the clause relates.

LETTER T94/G84[1]
To Frate Matteo di Francesco Tolomei of the Order of Preachers
November or December 1377

Matteo Tolomei was introduced to the Dominican Order after his conversion by Catherine early in the latter's public life, and became a friar shortly thereafter.[2]

We can deduce with fair certainty from Let. T118 and T120[3] that Matteo was with Catherine at Rocca d'Orcia for at least some of the time in summer and autumn of 1377, and from Let. T272[4] that he was in Rome with Raimondo by October of that year, and from Let. T344 that he was there again in July 1379. Catherine's admonition toward the end of the present letter to him ("... when you left me, I told you to try hard to avoid socializing and spend time in your cell, and not to stay away from choir and the refectory, to the extent that it would be possible for you") seems to indicate that Matteo's responsibilities (or propensities) are going to be such that he will not always be able (or think he is able) to observe the external details of common life. The reference might be to a time he would spend with his sick sister (see Let. T120), except that it seems he went with Raimondo to Rome about the middle of September, and therefore probably did *not* go to visit his sister as his mother had demanded (if indeed my placement of Let. T120 is correct). So the present letter would have to have been written some time between late September 1377 and November 1378, that is, between Matteo's departure from the Val d'Orcia to Rome and Catherine's own journey to Rome. (It could hardly have been from an occasion when he was traveling with Bartolomeo Dominici around the Val d'Orcia, since then he would not likely have had access to choir and refectory on any regular basis at all.)

The linguistic evidence inclines me to narrow the probability even further to November or December 1377, while Matteo is with Raimondo in Rome, and Catherine is still in the Val d'Orcia.[5] This is reinforced by

---

[1] MSS: Mo-*a*, M, S5, P4, Pa; translation based on Mo-*a*. Variants from Tommasèo text noted.

[2] Testimony of Tommaso Caffarini, *Processo Castellano*, ed. Laurent, p. 89.

[3] Both in this volume.

[4] Also in this volume.

[5] All four letters which share twenty-two or more of this one's eighty-four analyzed patterns fall between late October and December 1377. Further, there are a number of significant clusters within individual patterns which begin and/or end in this narrow period: ACCETDES, AMAINVER, BENEFATT, CELLASTUD, CONSMENT, CORO, GIACMORT, LUMEVERO, MANGGUST, SENZMEZZ, SERVMERC, VIRTSENZ. Fawtier (II, p. 211) declines to place this letter even broadly. Dupré Theseider (unpublished notes) places it in October 1377.

her references to loving even those who are scandalized by us and who criticize us, which would put it near Let. T104 and T259, with which it in general shares very heavily. There are also a few patterns which this letter shares only with *The Dialogue*.[6] In fact, the letter sometimes develops themes beyond their development in *The Dialogue*.

§

In the name of Jesus Christ crucified and of gentle Mary.

Dearest son in Christ gentle Jesus,

I Caterina, servant and slave of the servants of Jesus Christ, am writing to you in his precious blood. I long to see you seeking God in truth, with no interference from selfish sensuality or from any other creature.[7] With this sort of interference we could not be pleasing to God.

God gave us the Word, his only-begotten Son, without regard for his own profit.[8] But while it is true that our service doesn't profit God at all, the same is not true of ourselves. Even though we may not serve God for our own profit, the profit is nevertheless all ours! The flower, that is the honor, goes to God. But we get the fruit, the profit.[9] He has loved us without being loved [first], and we love because we are loved. He loves us

---

[6] ANDAROTO, FIGLSERV, RINCHIUS.

[7] Catherine makes a distinction, in her use of the word *mezzo* (literally, "something in between," "means"), between persons or things that come between us and God as an obstacle or interference, and persons and things that function as intermediaries in a positive way. A bit further on, she will speak of our neighbors as the *mezzo* God has appointed to mediate our love.

[8] The It. *utilità* has the sense of profit, advantage, service, usefulness.

[9] Cf. Let. T113 to Bandeçça d'Agnolino Salimbeni (in this volume): "[I]f this worker, free choice, plants the tree . . . in the soil of true humility . . . , then it will produce fragrant blossoms of virtue, especially that topmost blossom of glory and praise for God's name. And all the other sweet blossoms and fruits, its virtuous deeds, will receive fragrance from that topmost blossom. This is the blossom, dearest daughter, that makes our virtues flower; it is the blossom God wants for himself. The fruit he wants to be ours. The only thing he wants from this tree is this blossom of glory, that is, that we give glory and praise to his name. The fruit he gives to us. He has no need of our fruit, because he lacks nothing. He is the one who is, but we (who are the ones who are not) do need it. We have no being of ourselves, but only through him, because he has given us being and every gift we have beyond that. So we can be of no service to him. Supreme eternal Goodness saw that human beings cannot live on blossoms but only on fruit. (If we eat blossoms we die, but on fruit we live.) That is why God took the blossom for himself and gives the fruit to us. And if we foolish people want to feed on the blossom—that is, give ourselves the glory and praise that ought to be God's—it robs us of the life of grace and gives us eternal death if we die without changing our ways, [if we don't learn] to keep just the fruit for ourselves and give the blossom, the glory, to God."

gratuitously, and we love him because it is our duty, because we are obligated to love him. So just as we can't be of any profit to God, neither can we love him gratuitously or without obligation. We are obligated to him, not he to us. For he loved us before he was loved, and so created us in his image and likeness.

Look then. We can't be of any profit to God or love him with this first sort of love.[10] But God, I say, wants to be loved by us just as he has loved us, without any self-interest. He requires this of us. How can this be, since God requires it, and yet we can't relate to him in this way? I'll tell you. By using the means he has appointed. We should love God freely and without any regard for our selfish advantage. That is, we should be useful not to him (which we can't do) but to our neighbors. By using this intermediary we can do as God requires for the glory and praise of his name.[11] To show our love for God, we must love and serve every other person. We must extend our charity to the good and to the evil, to every sort of person—to those who wrong us and find us a scandal as well as to those who serve us. For God shows no partiality except to holy desires, and God extends his charity to sinners as well as to the just.[12]

It is true that God loves some people as his sons and daughters, some as friends, some as servants.[13] And some he loves as persons who have deserted him, for whose return he longs.

These last are the wicked sinners who have lost grace. But how does this best of fathers show his love for them?[14] By lending them time. And in this time he sets before them all sorts of opportunities.[15] Sometimes he gives them the opportunity to repent of their sin by removing the place and the possibility for doing as much evil as they'd like to. He also uses many other ways of making them hate vice and love virtue, and this love for virtue takes away the will to sin. Thus, because of the time God has out of love given them, these enemies become his friends. They now have grace and are in a position to receive their Father's inheritance.

God loves as his sons and daughters those who serve him in truth without any slavish fear. These have drowned and killed their selfish will, and

---

[10] The It. *questo primo amore* refers to God's free love, but the expression also carries the sense of "this original love," in implicit contrast to "original sin."

[11] Cf. Cavalca, *Specchio di croce*, p. 27: "We must love God in service. Not that we can be of any use to him, but we must in his love and by his command be of use to our neighbors."

[12] Cf. Rom. 2, 11; Acts 10, 34; Mt. 5, 45.

[13] Here Catherine takes the opposite perspective from *Dial.* 57–73, where it is souls on the road to perfection who *love God* as servants, as friends, or as children and heirs.

[14] What follows echoes in a number of ways the parable of the "prodigal" son (Lk. 15, 11–31).

[15] Again, the It. is *mezzo*.

are obedient to every other person, for God's sake, even to the point of death. They aren't mercenaries who serve for their own gain. No, they are sons and daughters. They disdain consolation, and delight in affliction. Their whole intent is on how they can be like Christ crucified, finding nourishment in his humiliation[a] and suffering.[16] They do not seek or serve God for the sake of any sweetness or comfort they might receive from God or from others, whether spiritual or temporal. For they are not seeking God and their neighbors for selfish ends. No, they seek God for God's sake because he deserves to be loved. They seek themselves for God's sake and for the glory and praise of God's name. And they serve their neighbors for God's sake, doing for them whatever service they can.

Such persons are following their Father's example.[17] They all find delight in charity for their neighbors. They love God's servants for the love they bear their Creator. They love the imperfect in their progress toward perfection by offering their desire and continual prayers for them. And they love the wicked who are lying dead of mortal sin because they are God's rational creatures, redeemed by one and the same blood as they themselves are. So they grieve over their damnation, and to rescue them they would surrender themselves to bodily death. Persecutors, grumblers, judgmental people who find them a scandal—they love them all because they are God's creatures (as I've said), and because they are instruments of virtue and progress toward perfection for them. They especially [help them acquire] that royal virtue, patience, the lovely virtue that is never scandalized or shaken or toppled by any contrary wind or by any diabolical temptation.

These are the people who seek without any interference,[18] who love in truth, as dear legitimate sons and daughters.[19] And God loves them as

---

[16] Clearly, "child of God" for Catherine means not helplessness and dependence but identification with Christ as Son of God, and with his mission of redemption.

[17] Catherine often says that we cannot follow the Father, because the Father cannot suffer, but that we must follow the Son. Yet here and in a few other places she does speak of following the example (literally, the footsteps) of the Father, clearly referring to the first person of the Trinity. (She does also on occasion refer to Christ as Father.)

[18] Again the Italian is *mezzo* (cf. n. 5).

[19] Catherine in a number of places refers to the unbaptized as bastards in need of legitimization through baptism, for example, in Let. T239/DT81 to Pope Gregory XI (in this volume): "I am not . . . advising you, dear father, to abandon your legitimate children, who feed at the breasts of Christ's bride, in favor of these bastard children who have not yet been legitimized through holy baptism." In Let. T311 to the Defenders of Siena (1379) she seems to include among the illegitimate those who have abandoned the pope as their father: "He is a man who sees much farther than you think. He has both legitimate and illegitimate children resting on his heart, and in due time he will prove that he has known. No more of this now, for love of God! Treat him as Christ's vicar on earth. Treat him as your dear father." In the one case, however, in which she confronts *actual* illegitimacy, she is

a true father would. He reveals to them the secret of his charity[20] in order that they may have their eternal inheritance. So they run, drunk on Christ's blood, set ablaze and perfectly enlightened by the fire of divine charity. They don't run along the path of virtue in their own fashion but in the fashion of Christ crucified, following in his footsteps. And even if it were possible to serve God and acquire virtue without hardship, they would not want to.

They don't act like those others who are servants and friends but whose service is sometimes not quite disinterested. These sometimes look to their own advantage, and so they become very friendly because they know their own need, and they know their benefactor and see that he can and is willing to help them. True, before this they were servants who knew their wickedness and the punishment that must follow it. So in fear of punishment they got rid of vice and with love they embraced virtue.[21] That is, they entered their Lord's service [in love] and began to take hope in his kindness, knowing that he does not want sinners to die but to be converted and live.[22] For if they had done it only out of fear, that would not have been enough to regain their Lord's full favor and have life; they would be mercenary servants.

Nor should we live merely for love of the fruit, the consolation we receive from our Lord, once we have become his friends. For such a love would not be strong, but would falter when we are deprived of the sweetness or consolation or spiritual joy. In fact, it would falter under any contrary wind of persecution or diabolical temptation or promptings of the flesh.[23] The loss of spiritual consolation would lead to discouragement, and persecution and injury from others would lead to impatience.

So you see, this sort of love is not strong. Those who love with this

---

compassionate and non-judgmental. That letter, T8 (in this volume), concerns a young man who has been refused admittance to Monteoliveto Maggiore by its prior, presumably because of his illegitimate birth. She writes, "Don't ever be impressed by eminence, by greatness or lowliness, by legitimacy or illegitimacy of birth. God's Son, whose example we must follow, never despised (nor now despises) anyone, whatever his or her position or parentage, whether just or sinner. No, he receives with love anyone who is determined to get up out of the filth of deadly sin, out of the emptiness of the world, and return to grace."

[20] This is the only place in which Catherine explicitly relates "the secret" of Christ's heart to "the secret" of the Father's charity. She does, however, often say that the Father loved us so much as to give us his Son, and the Son so loved us as to give his life for us.

[21] The original switches here to present tense. Catherine seems to forget that she has been talking specifically about what these "sons and daughters" were before they had reached that point, and she does not in fact come back to that perspective.

[22] Ez. 3, 18.

[23] There is a bit of repetition in the original ("would falter" and "diabolical temptations") which I have not duplicated. Note that the "contrary winds" are here as elsewhere the classic three: the devil, the world (persecution), and the flesh.

sort of love, in fact, act like Saint Peter. Before the passion, he loved Christ tenderly, but he wasn't strong, and so he faltered at the time of the crucifixion. But later, after the coming of the Holy Spirit, he distanced himself from this sweet love.[24] He let go of fear and progressed to a love that was strong, tested in the fire of many tribulations. Once he had progressed to this filial love, he bore all these things with true patience. Indeed, he ran after[b] them as joyfully as if he had been going not to torment but to a wedding. And this was because he had become [God's] son. But if Peter had continued living merely in the sweetness and in his fearfulness during and after Christ's passion, he would never have become so perfect as to be [God's] son and a champion of the Church. He would never have come to find joy in feeding on souls.[25]

But note what Peter and the other disciples did that enabled them to let go of their slavish fear and their weak love of consolation, and to receive the Holy Spirit as gentle First Truth had promised. Scripture says that they shut themselves up at home and stayed there in watching and continual prayer.[26] They remained there for ten days, and then the Holy Spirit came.

The lesson we and everyone else ought to learn from this is that we [too] must shut ourselves up at home in watching and prayer. We must stay there for ten days, and then we will receive the fullness of the Holy Spirit.[27] After the Holy Spirit came, he enlightened [the disciples] with the truth and they saw the secret of the Word's boundless charity and the Father's will, which wants nothing but that we be made holy. The blood of this gentle loving Word revealed this to us when he returned to the disciples—that is, when the fullness of the Holy Spirit came. The Spirit comes with the power that is the Father, with the wisdom that is the Son, and with the compassionate mercy that is the Holy Spirit. Thus the truth of what Christ said to the disciples is realized: "I will go away, and I will return to you."[28] He did return, because the Holy Spirit cannot come without the Son and the Father, since he is one with them. He came, then (as I've said), with the power that is appropriated to the Father, with the wis-

---

[24] "Sweet" (*dolce*) here refers to Peter's tender (*dolce*) but fragile love for Christ before the crucifixion, a love that was not strong enough to keep him from denying Jesus during the latter's trial or to make him follow his Master to Calvary.

[25] It. *gustatore e magiatore dell'anime.*

[26] Cf. Acts 1, 13–14.

[27] The "ten days" is deduced from the times named in Acts, that is, that Christ ascended forty days after his resurrection, and that the Spirit came on the Jewish feast of Pentecost. Though Catherine compares the disciples' waiting at home for the Holy Spirit with the house of self-knowledge in Let. T351 to Pope Urban VI (1379) and in *Dial.* 63 (pp. 120–121), this is the only place she gives a symbolic meaning to the ten days.

[28] Jn. 16, 16.

dom that is appropriated to the Son, and with the benevolent love that is appropriated to the Holy Spirit.[29] The apostles gave strong testimony to this.[30] For in love they at once let go of their fear, and they came to know the truth in true wisdom and went out in great power to face the unbelievers. They cast out devils and toppled idols. They did this not with worldly power or physical strength but with the might of the spirit and the power of God that they had received by divine grace.

It is the same with those who have gotten up from the vomit of deadly sin and from the wretchedness of the world and begin to experience the supreme Good and fall in love with his sweetness. Still, as I've said, they would not escape hell by living merely in fear. They would be acting like thieves who refrain from stealing because they are afraid of the gallows, but who would steal if they thought they wouldn't suffer the penalty.[31] The same is true of those who love God for his sweetness. Their love is not strong or perfect but weak and imperfect, and so they are unstable.[32] They are not truly persevering either in keeping to the path to perfection or in the way they walk it.

The way to reach perfection is the way the disciples followed (as I've described).

Just as Peter and the others shut themselves up at home, so those who have come to love their Father and are [God's] sons and daughters have done and ought to do. Those who want to progress to this state [of perfection] must enter and shut themselves up in the house of self-knowledge, which is the cell in which we should live. And within this cell is another cell, the cell of the knowledge of God's goodness within us.[33] From the knowledge of ourselves we draw a genuine humility, along with holy hatred for the offenses we have committed and continue to commit against our Creator. This leads to true and perfect patience. And in the knowledge

---

[29] Augustine (*De Trinitate*) appropriates these specific attributes to Father, Son, and Holy Spirit. Cf. Aquinas, *Summa Theologica*, I, q. 38, a. 7: "For the manifestation of our faith it is fitting that the essential attributes [of God] should be appropriated to the persons. For although the trinity of persons cannot be proved by demonstration . . . , nevertheless it is fitting that it be declared by things which are more known to us. . . . Such a manifestation of the divine persons by the use of the essential attributes is called *appropriation*." Catherine's only other explicit reference to this concept of appropriation is in *Dial.* 110 (p. 206), but there she does not give the full Augustinian trilogy.

[30] Literally, "witnessed to this well."

[31] Capital punishment for theft was not unheard of in Catherine's day.

[32] Clearly the text has become somehow corrupted here, though the manuscripts give no indication of a lacuna. I am conjecturing that either the *ma* ("but") in the manuscripts was originally *non* ("not") or that a "not" is simply missing. At least this makes the development logical without supposing that any more is missing.

[33] The cell image is usually a single cell of the knowledge of self and of God, or occasionally a double cell. The cell within a cell is unique here.

of God which we discover within ourselves we acquire the virtue of blazing charity, from which we draw holy loving desires.

Staying shut up in such a lovely and glorious house as the knowledge of ourselves and of God is the way to learn[34] watching and continual prayer. By watching I mean not just watching with our bodily eyes but watching with the eyes of our soul. I mean that the eyes of our understanding should never be closed but always open and focused on Christ crucified, ineffable love. There we discover love as well as our own sinfulness, since it was for sin that Christ gave his blood. Then we rise up with immense desire[35] to love what God loves and to hate what God hates. Everything we do we direct to God; we do everything for the glory and praise of his name. And this is the continual prayer of which Paul speaks: "Pray without interruption."[36] This is how we progress beyond being merely servants and friends. That is, we progress from slavish fear and self-indulgent love for our own consolation to true servanthood, true friendship, true filiality. For we don't cease being [God's] servants and true friends once we have become his true sons and daughters. No, now we are servants and friends in truth, with no regard for ourselves or for anything but pleasing God.

I said that [the disciples] stayed for ten days, and then the Holy Spirit came. In the same way, those who want to reach this perfection must stay for ten days; that is, they must live within the ten commandments of the law. And they will observe the counsels along with the commandments of the law, because they are bound up together and we cannot observe the one without observing the other. Those who are in the world must observe the counsels spiritually in holy desire, while those who have left the world behind must observe them both spiritually and in actuality.[37] This is how[c] we receive the outpouring of the Holy Spirit, with true wisdom in true and perfect light and knowledge, and with power and strength that is strong against any temptation and powerful especially against ourselves in mastery of our selfish sensuality.

But you won't be able to do any of this if you go gadding about in all sorts of socializing, staying away from your cell and absenting yourself from choir.[38] This is what I was thinking of when I told you, as you took leave of me, that you should be conscientious about avoiding socializing,

---

[34] Literally, "find."

[35] It. *affetto*.

[36] 1 Thes. 5, 17.

[37] The evangelical counsels are traditionally encompassed in voluntary poverty, continence, and obedience. She is contrasting those who live a secular way of life with those who profess these counsels through the vows of religious life.

[38] That is, the chanting of the liturgical hours with the community.

about keeping to your cell, about not staying away from choir or refectory (as far as possible),[39] and about watching in continual prayer. This is how you will fulfill the desire I expressed when I said I long to see you seeking God in truth, without any interference.

I'll say no more. Keep living in God's holy and tender love.

Gentle Jesus! Jesus love!

Textual Notes

a. Tommasèo adds *and labors.*

b. Tommasèo: *with* / *after.*

c. Tommasèo: *Thus, if* (*Così se*) / *This is how* (*Così si*)

[39] The ministry of preaching could often make it impossible for the friar to pray and eat with the community. Dominican legislation in fact subordinated such specifics of common life to the ministry of preaching for which it had been founded.

Letter T113/G330[1]
To the Countess Bandeçça Salimbeni of Siena[2]
November or December 1377

There is nothing in the context of this letter to indicate whether Catherine wrote it before Let. T112 (in this volume, also to Bandeçça) or after. She makes no mention here of Bandeçça's becoming a nun at the new monastery of Belcaro. She speaks only of being "enclosed" by dwelling in the cell of self-knowledge. Perhaps this is a hint that Catherine has gotten to know the countess better during her stay at Rocca d'Orcia, and has come to the conclusion that Bandeçça is not meant for the cloister.

The rubric of Mo names the countess as "of Siena," which may simply indicate her family origins. She apparently, however, did not live always at the family fortress at Rocca d'Orcia, since in Let. T115 to Isa Salimbeni (in this volume) Catherine suggests that it would be good if the countess would go to the Rocca before Catherine's arrival there, so that they could discern the Holy Spirit's will. This letter could, therefore, have been written before Catherine's departure from the Rocca near the end of the year if Bandeçça was not there the whole time. The linguistic evidence would seem to support such a scenario, and would most strongly support placing it in November or December.[3]

§

In the name of Jesus Christ crucified and of gentle Mary.

Dearest daughter in Christ gentle Jesus,

I Caterina, servant and slave of the servants of Jesus Christ, am writing to you in his precious blood.[4] I long to see you grounded in true and perfect

---

[1] MSS: Mo, M, S3, S5; translation based on Mo.

[2] There is a comment after the rubric in Mo: "Done in ecstasy," perhaps in the hand of the original scribe, perhaps added later.

[3] Ten letters share twenty-two or more of this one's one hundred three analyzed patterns, and all ten are dated from October 1377 and later. A number of significant clusters within individual patterns begin and/or end between October 1377 and very early 1378, but I am especially convinced by those which are concentrated in November and December (CERCCOSE, FRUTVITA, GIARDREL, GIARDINI, LEGRAGIO, MONOARBI, MORTDES, NUDITA, PIANTUMI, REGINA, SPUGNA, TUTTPART, UMILMANS, UTILCAR). Fawtier (II, p. 300) places the letter between January and early April 1377. Dupré Theseider (unpublished notes) puts it in March 1377, probably earlier than Let. T112.

[4] This letter is unusually filled with ambiguous grammatical structures and inconsistencies, as well as a great deal of cumbersome repetition—possibly because of the circum-

charity, a wedding[a] garment that covers all our nakedness and hides our shame. I mean it covers sin,[5] which gives birth to shame. Charity wipes sin out, consumes it in its heat,[6] and without this garment we cannot enter the everlasting life to which we are invited.[7]

What is charity? It is an indescribable love which we have drawn from our Creator, so that we love him with all our heart,[b] all our energy, and all our strength.[8] I said we have drawn it from our Creator, and this is the truth. But how? With love, because love is to be had only with love and from love. But you will say to me, dearest daughter, "How do I have to act in order to find and acquire this love?"[9] This is my answer; here is the way.

You need a light to acquire any sort of love, because we cannot know what we cannot see, and we cannot love what we do not know. So you have to have light in order to see and know what you ought to love. And because we needed light, God provided for our need by giving us the light of understanding, the noblest part of our soul, and within it its pupil, most holy faith.[10]

And I tell you, even if we sin against our Creator, we do not therefore go on living without light or love. For since we are made of love, created for love's sake in the image and likeness of God, we cannot live without love, nor would we love without light. So if we want to love, we have to see. But do you know what seeing is, and what loving is, for worldly people? It is a dark and obscure seeing, and in the shadowy night one cannot discern the truth. And it is a deadly love, because it is death-dealing, depriving the soul of the life of grace. But why is this seeing obscure? Because it is focused on the darkness of the passing things of the world which it has set before itself outside of God. I mean, these people do not look at things within God's goodness, but only for sensual pleasure, and it is this sensual sort of pleasure and love that moved the understanding to see and know only the things of sense.[11] Because they sin, this affection that is nourished by the light of understanding (though it was affection that first

---

stances of its dictation in a state of ecstasy. I have therefore taken more than usual liberty with the translation in the interests of clarity.

[5] Cf. 1 Pet. 4, 8: "Charity covers a multitude of sins." (Vulg.)

[6] Catherine often compares charity with a blazing furnace. Cf. Giovanni dalle Celle, *Lettere*, ed. Cividali, p. 444: "Christ took all our sins upon himself and consumed them all in the fire of his charity in the presence of God the Father."

[7] Cf. the parable of the wedding banquet, Mt. 22, 1–14.

[8] Mk. 12, 30.

[9] In Let. T29/DT18 to Regina della Scala (vol. I) she uses the same rhetorical question to introduce a discussion of the acquisition of charity.

[10] Cf. *Dial.* 45, p. 92; 98, pp. 185–187. Also in her prayers and in other letters Catherine develops this very central image of hers.

[11] Cf. Prayer 11, pp. 86–97, for an elaboration of the conflict of light and darkness.

moved understanding) deals them death and deprives them of the life of grace. For nothing can be seen or loved apart from God and not be death-dealing.

Therefore, whatever we love we ought to love in God and for God, that is, acknowledge that everything, including our very self, is from his goodness.

So you see, worldly people do see and love, because it is impossible to live without seeing and loving. But the love of worldly people, which deals death, is different from the love of God's servants, which gives life. For the love that is acquired from supreme and eternal love gives the life of grace. So since we have both our mind's eye and the light, we should open that eye to the light of most holy faith and focus our attention on the indescribable love God has for[c] us. Then our will, seeing that we are loved, cannot but love what understanding has seen and known in truth.

Oh dearest daughter, don't you see that we are a tree of love, because we were made for love?[12] And this tree is so well made that no one can keep it from growing or take its fruit without the tree's consent. And God has given this tree a worker to tend it as it pleases, and this worker is free choice.[13] Without this worker we (whom I've likened to a tree) would not be free, and if we were not free we would have an excuse for sin. But we can have no excuse because there is nothing, neither the world nor the devil nor our weak flesh, that can force us to any sin at all against our will. For this tree has the gift of reason (if free choice wants to make use of it), and it has the eye of understanding to see and know the truth (unless the cloud of selfishness overshadows it).

By this light the worker, free choice, sees where the tree ought to be planted. Now if this worker didn't have this wonderful power of understanding and didn't see, there might be an excuse. Free choice could say, "I was free, but I didn't see where I could plant my tree, whether up high or down low."[14] But free choice can't say that, because it has understanding that does see, and reason—understanding that is a bond of rational love with which to bind and engraft the tree into the tree of life, Christ gentle Jesus. So if the tree is to produce the fruit of life, free choice ought to plant it only after the eye of understanding has seen the place and the sort of soil it should stand in.

Dearest daughter, if this worker, free choice, plants the tree where it

---

[12] Cf. *Dial.* 10, pp. 41–42.

[13] Cf. Let. T138/DT41 to Giovanna d'Angiò (vol. I) for still more development of the image of the worker.

[14] Cf. *Dial.* 93, p. 171: "The soul who lives virtuously sets her tree's root in the valley of true humility. But those who live wickedly have set their root in the mountain of pride, and because it is badly planted it produces fruit not of life but of death."

ought to be planted, that is, in the soil of true humility (for it should not put it on the mountain of pride, but in the valley of humility), then it will produce fragrant blossoms of virtue, especially that topmost blossom of glory and praise for God's name. And all the other sweet blossoms and fruits, its virtuous deeds, will receive fragrance from that topmost blossom. This is the blossom, dearest daughter, that makes our virtues flower; it is the blossom God wants for himself. The fruit he wants to be ours. The only thing he wants from this tree is this blossom[d] of glory, that is, that we give glory and praise to his name. The fruit he gives to us.

God has no need of our fruit, because he lacks nothing. He is the one who is, but we (who are the ones who are not) do need it. We have no being of ourselves, but only through God, because he has given us being and every gift we have beyond that.[15] So we can be of no service to him.[16] Supreme eternal Goodness saw that human beings cannot live on blossoms but only on fruit. (If we eat blossoms we die, but on fruit we live.) That is why God took the blossom for himself and gives the fruit to us. And if we foolish people want to feed on the blossom[e]—that is, give ourselves the glory and praise that ought to be God's—it robs us of the life of grace and gives us eternal death if we die without changing our ways, [if we don't learn] to keep just the fruit for ourselves and give the blossom, the glory, to God.

Once our tree has been planted so nicely, it grows so high that no one—except the eye of understanding that has guided it—can see its top, our soul's will, where it is united with the infinite God in the impulse of love.

Oh dearest daughter, I want to tell you in what field this sort of soil is, so that you'll not make a mistake. The soil is true humility, as I've said, and the place you'll find it is the enclosed garden of self-knowledge.[17] I say it is enclosed because if you dwell in the cell of self-knowledge, you are enclosed. You are not wide open, because you are not dissipated in worldly delights. You are not looking for wealth, either for yourself or for others, but for voluntary poverty. Your efforts are directed at pleasing not creatures but only the Creator. And when the devil presents you with ugly and distracting thoughts, spiritual difficulties, and unwarranted fears, you don't open yourself to investigate them or to find out why they come or

---

[15] This is a concept she stresses often, for example, *Dial.* 46, p. 94.

[16] Cf. *Dial.* 64, pp. 120–121. Also Let. T94 to Francesco Tolomei: "But while it is true that our service doesn't profit God at all, the same is not true of ourselves. Even though we may not serve God for our own profit, the profit is nevertheless all ours! The flower, that is the honor, goes to God; but we get the fruit, the profit."

[17] Cf. Sg. 4, 12: "You are an enclosed garden, my sister, my bride, an enclosed garden, a fountain sealed."

to argue with them. You don't let confusion or spiritual vexation dissipate your heart, nor do you abandon your [spiritual] exercises. No, you lock yourself up, in the company of trust and the light of most holy faith, with hatred and contempt for your selfish feelings, considering yourself unworthy of spiritual peace and quiet. In true humility you consider yourself worthy rather of conflict and unworthy of fruit—I mean, you consider yourself deserving of the pain that is apparently inflicted on you when you are struggling so.[18] You focus your attention constantly on Christ crucified, pleased to be on the cross with him, and so you use one thought to banish the other.[19] This then is the lovely place where you will find the soil of true humility.

The top of the tree (your soul's will, which follows after understanding, as I've said) has come to know Christ crucified and the fiery abyss of his charity. And charity you have come to know in this Word, because this is where God's love for us is revealed. You came to know the Word in getting to know yourself, in recognizing that you are a rational creature made in God's image and likeness, and created anew in the blood of God's only-begotten Son. And now your will dwells in union with the will of Christ crucified, and with love you attract love. I mean that with well-ordered love, which rises above mere sentiment, you attract to yourself the blazing love of Christ crucified.

For our heart, when it is in love with divine love, is like a sponge absorbing water.[20] Now a sponge, even though it is by nature absorbent, doesn't absorb water unless it is put into the water. Just so, even though it is in keeping with our heart's nature to love, unless the hand of free choice along with the light of reason picks it up and puts it into the fire of divine charity, it will never be filled with grace. But if it is made one with that fire, it will be constantly filled. And this is why I told you that with love and from love we attract love.[21]

Once the heart, like a jug, is full, it waters the tree with the water of divine charity for our neighbors. Such charity is a dew and a rain that waters both the tree and the soil of true humility. It enriches the soil and the garden of self-knowledge, now seasoned with knowledge of God's goodness to us.[22]

---

[18] This is an idea frequently expressed by Catherine, for example, in *Dial.* 4, p. 29.

[19] That is, use the thought of Christ crucified and your identification with him to banish the unwanted thoughts.

[20] Cf. Let. T226 to Raimondo da Capua (in this volume), where the image is applied to St. Paul.

[21] Cf. Let. T196/DT64 to Pope Gregory XI (in this volume): "[T]he human heart is drawn by love as by nothing else, since it is made of love."

[22] Cf. *Dial.* 66, p. 125: "The soul, then, should season her self-knowledge with knowl-

You know very well that unless a tree is watered with the dew and rain and warmed by the heat of the sun, it will never produce or ripen its fruit and will always be incomplete. It is the same with us who, as I've said, are trees. For though we are planted, if we are not watered with the dew of self-knowledge, and warmed by the sun of divine charity, we will never produce lifegiving fruit, nor will our fruit ever ripen.

Once a tree is full-grown it stretches out its branches and offers fruit to its neighbors—I mean the fruit of holy, humble, continual prayer and the example of a good holy life. And it stretches out its branches to them, too, whenever it can, by offering them material help with a great and generous heart, sincere and unfeigning.[23] I mean that it doesn't pretend to be what it is not. It serves others in whatever way it can, sincerely and with energetic charity, doing all it can to meet their needs as it sees them. Charity seeks not what is our own,[24] nor does it seek ourselves selfishly, but for God, in order to give God the blossoms of glory and praise to his name. Charity does not seek God selfishly but for God's own sake, since he in his goodness is deserving of our love. And charity does not seek to serve our neighbors selfishly but only for God, to give our neighbors the service we owe God but cannot give him. For I've already told you that we cannot give any service to God, so God has us do it for our neighbors, whom God has given us as a means of proving our virtue and of showing our love for our dear eternal God.

This charity has a taste of eternal life. It has consumed and continues to consume all our sins. It gives us perfect light and true patience, and makes us so strong and constant that we never turn back to look at what has been plowed.[25] We persevere even to the point of death, pleased to be on the battlefield for Christ crucified and keeping his blood before us to energize us as real knights during the battle. This charity is so useful, so necessary, so delightful that without it we live in continual bitterness. Without it we die and our shame is uncovered, and at the judgment on the last day we are disgraced before the whole world, before the angels and all the citizens of everlasting life (where there is life without death, light without darkness, and perfect and universal charity in which everyone experiences and shares everyone else's good in affectionate love).[26]

So we should embrace this gentle queen, this wedding garment, charity.

---

edge of my goodness, and her knowledge of me with self-knowledge." And 73, p. 135: "Self-knowledge must be seasoned with knowledge of me, or it would end in confusion."

[23] Cf. 1 Tim. 1, 5: "love that springs from a pure heart, a good conscience, and a faith unfeigned." (Vulg.)

[24] 1 Cor. 13, 5.

[25] Cf. Lk. 9, 62.

[26] Cf. *Dial.* 41, pp. 82–83.

In sweet restless desire we should be ready to give our lives in exchange for this queen, and once we have her, be willing to bear any suffering from any source whatever, even to the point of death, in order to keep her and make her grow within the garden of our soul. I see no other way or path for us. And this is why I told you that I long to see you grounded in true and perfect charity.

I beg you for love of Christ crucified, try as hard as you can to build this foundation. Then you will have no cause for slavish fear, or for fear of the contrary winds of devilish or creaturely vexations that would like to get in the way of our salvation. But a tree planted in the valley cannot be hurt by the wind;[27] so be meek and humble of heart.[28]

I'll say no more. Keep living in God's holy and tender love.

Gentle Jesus! Jesus love!

Textual Notes

a. *wedding* partially written over erasure in Mo.
b. S3: [*so that . . . heart and*].
c. S3 (in margin): *has shown / has for*.
d. The text has *questi fiori* (plural) here, but only the singular makes sense in the context.
e. Again the text has plural, but see above.

---

[27] Cf. Simone Fidati da Cascia, *Ordine della vita cristiana*, p. 175: "Humility is the deep trench within which one does not feel any evil wind."

[28] Cf. Mt. 11, 29.

LETTER T282/G39[1]
To Nicola da Osimo
November or December 1377

We have met Nicola da Osimo, notary and secretary to Gregory XI, in Let. T181/DT55. The tone of this second of Catherine's two extant letters to him seems to imply that Nicola is involved in some project which is sufficiently intense to require his absence from the regular liturgical prayers of the Church. She also begs him "to ask the holy father to seize every opportunity possible (always respecting his conscience) for the reform of holy Church and for peace from a war so great that so many souls are being hurt." The context for these concerns could quite possibly be the unrest caused by Florence's public flaunting of the interdict from mid-October 1377 on. At least the linguistic evidence would support such a placement more strongly than any other. I would, on this basis, place the letter in November or December 1377.[2]

§

In the name of Jesus Christ crucified and of gentle Mary.

Dearest reverend father in Christ gentle Jesus,

I Caterina, servant and slave of the servants of Jesus Christ, am writing to you in his precious blood. I long to see you a solid pillar, immovable except in God. Never let the ingratitude and ignorance you encounter in those who feed in this garden, nor the disgust that comes from seeing ecclesiastical affairs so chaotic, make you evade or refuse the effort and hard work that are your lot in the mystic body of holy Church, Christ's dear bride.

It often happens that when we wear ourselves out over something and

---

[1] MSS: Mo-*a*, corrected by *b*; M, P4, S2, S4, S5, S6, Ro; translation based on Mo-*a*. No relevant variants except from *b*.

[2] Four of the seven letters which share thirteen or more of this one's forty-six analyzed patterns are from October to December 1377 (with two in early 1378 and one in 1380). By far the heaviest concentration of significant clusters within individual patterns also lies between October and December 1377 (AFFOCDES, AUTORITA, GIARDCHS, LUMEVEST, MENSDESI, ONORFADP, PENAMENT, SALM, TUTTPART). I am drawn more toward November or December because of two strong clusters (AFFOCDES, SALM) which begin in November. Fawtier (II, pp. 176–177), observes that since the letter does not allude to the pope's return to Rome, it could be from a time somewhat remote, for example, 1372–1373, when Catherine was still not thinking of this. But he also concedes that it could be from 1377. Dupré Theseider (unpublished notes) places it sometime between October 1377 and March 1378.

then it is not completed in the way we wish or does not produce the desired effects, we become spiritually disheartened and sad. We say to ourselves, as it were: "It would be better for you to give up this project that you began and worked at for so long but that still is unfinished, and to look for spiritual peace and quiet." But then, hungry for God's honor and the salvation of souls, we must answer boldly and refuse selfish comfort, saying: "I do not want to avoid or run away from hard work, because I do not deserve spiritual peace and quiet. What is more, I want to persevere in the position for which I have been chosen and courageously give honor to God with my work, and give my best efforts to my neighbors." It is true that sometimes the devil, to make us weary of our undertakings when we are experiencing little spiritual peace in them, will put it into our mind to say, "I am doing more harm than good with this. So I would gladly run away from it—not because of the hard work but because I do not want to sin."

Oh dearest father, when he puts these thoughts into your heart and mind, do not give way or believe either yourself or the devil! No, with joy and holy blazing desire embrace the work without any slavish fear. And have no fear of sinning in this. The sign of sin is a disordered and perverse will, since sin occurs when our will is not conformed to God's. Although we may be deprived of the consolation of reciting the office and all the psalms, or of saying them at the proper time and place with the calm mind we would like to have, this does not mean our time is wasted.[3] This is, in fact, also working for God. So you shouldn't worry about it, especially when you are working and wearing yourself out in the service of Christ's bride. For however and in whatever we wear ourselves out for her, it is more worthwhile and pleasing to God than our mind can see or imagine.

I am reminded, dearest father, of a servant of God to whom it was revealed just how pleasing this sort of service is to him.[4] I say this so that you may be encouraged to be willing to suffer weariness for her.[5] Once (and more than once, as I have heard) this servant of God had a tremendous desire to give her blood and her life, to spend and use up everything within her for Christ's bride, holy Church. Then she lifted up her mind's eye and came to know God's goodness to her. She saw that God had for love given her being and all the graces and gifts she had received above and beyond being, and the sight and experience of such love and such depths

---

[3] Cf. *Dial.* 165, p. 359: "Remember, though, that you should never rise from prayers of obligation except for the sake of charity or obedience." The implication seems to be that Nicola is involved in some project that does indeed prevent his participation in the Divine Office.

[4] The reference is to herself, in her usual third-person narrative of such personal experiences.

[5] That is, the Church.

of charity made her realize that there was no other way to respond to God except by love. But since she could not be of service to him, she could not show him her love.

So she began searching, trying to see if she could find any means by which she could show her love for him. Then she saw that God supremely loved his human creatures, and that the love she had discovered in herself she found in everyone else as well, because all of us are loved by God. This, she found, was the means by which she could be useful and which would show whether or not she loved God. Then she arose, ablaze with charity for her neighbors, and she conceived such love for their salvation that she would willingly have given her life for their salvation. The service she could not do for God she wanted to do for her neighbors. She had seen and experienced that she had to respond through her neighbors, and in that way return love for love, just as God had shown us his love and mercy through the Word, his Son. So, when she saw that she would be pleasing to God[a] through desire for the salvation of souls by giving honor to God and her best efforts to her neighbors, she looked to see in which garden and at what table she could enjoy her neighbors.[6]

Then our Savior made this revelation to her: "Dearest daughter, it is in the garden of my bride that you must eat, and at the table of the most holy cross, that is, with your suffering and with anguished desire, with vigils and prayers, and with everything you can do. And [you must do it] conscientiously. And understand that you cannot have desire for the salvation of souls apart from desire for the salvation of holy Church, for the Church is the universal body of all who share the light of holy faith, and they cannot have life unless they are obedient to my bride. So you must desire to see your neighbors, Christians as well as the unbelievers and everyone else, feeding in this garden under the yoke of holy obedience, clothed in the light of living faith. I mean faith with holy and good deeds, because faith without deeds is dead.[7] This is an ordinary desire and hunger for this universal body.

"But now I want you and am telling you to increase your hunger and desire, and prepare yourself specifically[8] to lay down your life if necessary in the mystic body of the Church for my bride's reform. For if she is reformed, the good of the entire world will follow. Why? Because with her darkness, ignorance, selfishness, impurity, and bloated pride she has gener-

---

[6] "Enjoy" refers to Catherine's much-used image of eating and enjoying souls at the table of the cross. I have found no close parallel to what follows in any of Catherine's other letters, nor in her prayers, nor in *The Dialogue*.

[7] Jas. 2, 17.

[8] It is not clear whether "specifically" (or "in particular") modifies the laying down of her life or "in the mystic body."

ated and continues to generate darkness and death in the souls of those in her charge. So I am inviting you and my other servants to exert yourselves to the extent of whatever capacity I give you, in desires and vigils and prayers and every other sort of exercise. I tell you, this work and service done for her is so pleasing to me that not only will I reward my servants who have a holy and upright intention, but will also reward the servants of the world who serve her sometimes selfishly (though sometimes they do serve out of reverence for holy Church). I tell you, no one who serves her reverently will go unrewarded, so much do I value that service. They will never see eternal death, I say. In the same way, I shall not leave unpunished in one way or another those who disrespectfully wrong my bride."

So, when she saw the tremendous greatness and generosity of God's goodness and what has to be done to be most pleasing to him, the fire of desire so increased that if it had been possible to give her life for holy Church a thousand times a day from then until the day of judgment, it would have seemed to her less than a drop of wine in the sea. And that is truly the case.

I want you, then, and I am inviting you, to work for her as you have always done, so that you who are a pillar set in place to support and help this bride may, as I've said, be so [solid] that neither consolation nor trials will ever move you. Nor must any contrary winds that may come to impede those who travel the way of truth, nor anything else, make us turn back. This is why I said I long to see you a solid pillar.

So up, dearest and sweetest father! It is our time, in this bride, to give honor to God and our best efforts to her. I beg you for love of Christ crucified to ask the holy father to seize every opportunity possible (always respecting his conscience) for the reform of holy Church and for peace from a war so great that so many souls are being hurt. Let him seize it with all eagerness and no irresponsibility, for God will reproach him most severely for any irresponsibility or lack of concern, and will hold him accountable for the souls who are lost because of it.

Commend me to him. Also, I humbly ask his blessing. I'll say no more. Keep living in God's holy and tender love.

Gentle Jesus! Jesus love!

Textual Notes

a. *that . . . God* inserted by *b*, in margin.

Letter T128/G285[1]
To Gabriele di Davino Piccolomini
November or December 1377

Gabriele di Davino Piccolomini, a married Sienese noble, had joined Catherine's circle early in her public life. He was with Catherine for at least some of her stay in the Val d'Orcia, but he can hardly have been there for the entire period, since in October or November he carried messages between Neri di Landoccio Pagliaresi at the Rocca and Simone da Cortona in Siena.[2] There is an explicit record of his having twice been present at the Salimbeni fortress when Catherine freed demoniacs. Both events took place before Raimondo's departure for Rome and therefore before mid-September.[3] Gabriele also accompanied Catherine to Rome in 1378.

Within the content of this single extant letter to Gabriele there is only one possible clue as to when it was written, an allusion to a crusade: "I want you to know what arms you must have. See that you get them now among Christians and begin to use them, so that they won't be rusty when you go against the unbelievers." Such allusions are found very frequently in Catherine's correspondence up to the end of 1376, and after that only twice in 1377 and once in 1379. However, she uses the imagery of battle and armor throughout this letter (which is basically concerned with Gabriele's spiritual life) and only as a sort of afterthought at the conclusion relates it to the projected crusade. Since Catherine continued to nurture the dream of a crusade till the end of her life, it would not be surprising to references to it later than the period during which she most actively promoted the crusade.

The linguistic evidence quite clearly excludes the likelihood of this letter's having been written later than very early 1378.[4] There are, further, a few significant clusters within individual patterns which begin and/or end in the last months of 1377[5] and only one earlier. Besides, Gabriele was almost certainly with Catherine during most of her time in Siena. The

---

[1] MSS: Mo-*a*, M, S5, S6, Ro, B, P2, P5, F2, P3; translation based on Mo-*a*. Relevant differences with Tommasèo text noted.

[2] See the introduction to Let. T56.

[3] Testimony of Francesco Malavolti, *Processo Castellano*, ed. Laurent, p. 396. Gabriele had a son who became a Dominican at Catherine's urging and was eventually declared blessed.

[4] None of the ten letters sharing eight or more of this one's thirty analyzed patterns was written later than the end of 1377. Nor are there any significant clusters within individual patterns after that point.

[5] COSTANT, MOSCA, PIGNATTA.

most plausible period, then, in which to place this letter is late 1377 or possibly very early 1378 (after Catherine's arrival in Florence). I would lean more strongly toward late 1377, when Catherine was still in the Val d'Orcia and Gabriele was most probably in Siena.[6]

§

In the name of Jesus Christ crucified and of gentle Mary.

Dearest son in Christ gentle Jesus,

I Caterina, servant and slave of the servants of Jesus Christ, am writing to you in his precious blood. I long to see you so constant and persevering in virtue that you will never turn back. There is no other way you can be pleasing to God or receive the fruit of the blood of the humble spotless Lamb, since it is only perseverance that is crowned.[7] So we must have perseverance.

You may say, dearest son, "How can I be constant and persevering when I am surrounded by so much opposition and by so many enemies? The world and other people hound and hurt me and spread rumors about me. And my own sensuality often fights[a] and rebels against reason." I answer you that there is no other way to conquer these enemies except by being fearless and well armed, by willingly joining battle [with them], ready to die. And you must be in love with the glory that follows after the fight. We have been sent into the field to combat our enemies, the world, the devil, and the flesh, and unless we are armed there is no way we can fight or survive the blows without injury.

So what are the arms we must have?

You must[b] have a sword in your hand to defend yourself.[8] Let it be double-edged, the one edge being love for virtue and the other hatred of vice. With this you will strike down the world by hating its prestige and

---

[6] Neither Fawtier (II, p. 290) nor Dupré Theseider (unpublished notes) ventures to date this letter.

[7] Cf. Rev. 2, 10: "Remain faithful until death and I will give you the crown of life." Also 2 Tim. 2, 5 (Vulg.): "Those who compete in a contest are not crowned unless they compete according to the rules."

[8] The text has at this point simply *Di coltello* ("Of the sword") as a sort of title. The phrase seems misplaced here, unless it is taken as a note to the effect that Catherine (or a scribe) had later decided that this was the logical place for this paragraph about the sword. In the original the paragraph on the sword comes only much later, after "And be fearless" (see n. 12). If the sword paragraph is thus moved (and the "also" inserted by *b* is ignored), the letter flows smoothly from that point into its conclusion. I have therefore acted on this conjecture and so moved it.

pleasures and ostentation and vanity and bloated[c] pride. You will use true patience (the patience you acquire through your love for virtue) to strike back at those who are striking out at you.[9] You will strike down the devil (since it is only charity than can strike him down), and he will avoid your soul as a fly avoids a boiling cauldron.[10] To strike back at your sensuality and weakness you will use the [self-]contempt you have drawn from holy knowledge of yourself. And you will go into battle with the love for your Creator that you have attained through knowledge of God's goodness within you.

You[d] must have true charity as a cuirass that will fend off the blows dealt us in so many ways by the world, as well as the devil's assaults and the attacks of your own weakness (which, as I've said, fights against the spirit). And over the cuirass you must have the scarlet breastplate that is Christ's blood mingled and joined and fused[11] with the fire of divine charity.[12]

This blood has to be exposed.[13] I mean you must show it plainly to everyone. You must not keep it hidden but must proclaim it in good and holy deeds and, when needed, with words.

Don't be like so many fools who are ashamed in the world's presence to mention Christ or to admit that they are Christ's servants. They are unwilling to put on this breastplate. Oh worldly absurdity! They are ashamed to mention Christ and the blood that has ransomed them with such blazing love, but they aren't ashamed of the wickedness by which they have so miserably squandered the fruit of the blood! They have destroyed their soul's beauty and lost their dignity. They have made themselves brute

---

[9] That is, "the world."

[10] Cf. *Dial.* 90, p. 167: "[T]he soul cannot be tricked as long as she remains united with me. So the devil flees like a fly from a boiling cauldron, because he is afraid of the fire. If the soul were lukewarm he would enter fearlessly—though often he perishes there when he finds it hotter than he had imagined!" The only other occurrence of the boiling cauldron image is in Let. T287 (in this volume, November or December 1377).

[11] It. *unito intriso e impastato.*

[12] This armor imagery is also developed in Let. T159 to Raniere di Santa Caterina (in this volume). In that letter the details are slightly different: "I mean the cuirass of true and deep humility and the breastplate of blazing charity. For just as the cuirass is joined to the breastplate and the breastplate to the cuirass, so is humility the nurse of charity and charity the nourisher of humility. This is the armor I am giving you, since it can withstand all the poisoned arrows the devil, the world, and the flesh can shoot, without being penetrated by a single one. For when we are in love with Christ crucified no arrow of deadly sin will penetrate us—I mean through the consent of our will. We are so strong that neither the devil nor anyone else can force us to do more than we want."

[13] The breastplate, worn over the cuirass (the leather shirt that covers the entire upper torso), is the outermost piece of the upper armor and is thus fully exposed. So Christ's blood, fully exposed to the enemy, is the first defense against the latter's blows. But "exposed" here also has the sense of "put out into the open," "revealed."

beasts and servants and slaves of sin, and they aren't even aware of it! Why? Because they have lost the light of reason, and so they go about blind and frenzied. They cling to the things of this world, though they cannot hold on to them as they would like because these things are as fleeting as the wind. Either they forsake us—or we forsake them when the supreme Judge calls us to account by separating our soul from our body. If such people don't change course either during life or at the moment of death, they will lose the goods of earth and those of heaven as well, and will come to eternal damnation. But really, no one should be so foolish as to procrastinate, since we don't know how or when or in what circumstances we will die!

I don't want you, son, to be among those who are living so dangerously. No, arm yourself in the way I've described. Be constant and persevering in battle even to the point of death. And be fearless.[14] You must keep Christ crucified before your mind's eye, glorying in the shameful load he carried.[15] In him you will see the glory prepared for you and for all who serve him. In that glory you will find and receive the fruit of every load you have carried for the glory and praise of his name.[16]

This, dearest son, is how to reach perfect virtue, to conquer weakness, and to persevere even to the point of death. Without perseverance our tree will produce no fruit.[17] And this is why I said that I long to see you so constant and persevering that you will never turn back.

I have no more to say to you. I've mentioned being armed so that you may be well-provided for when the standard of the most holy cross is raised. I want you to know what arms you must have. See that you get them now among Christians and begin to use them, so that they won't be rusty when you go against the unbelievers.

Keep living in God's holy and tender love.

Gentle Jesus! Jesus love!

---

[14] This is the point at which the paragraph about the sword occurs in the original.

[15] It. *gloriandoti negli obrobri e nelle fadighe sue.*

[16] Cf. Rom. 8, 18: "I consider the sufferings of the present to be as nothing compared with the glory to be revealed in us." Also 1 Cor. 2, 9 (Vulg.): "Eye has not seen, ear has not heard, nor has the human heart imagined what God has prepared for those who love him."

[17] Catherine often refers to the soul as a tree "made for love and living only by love." (for example, *Dial.* 10, p. 41). Cf. also Let. T27 to Abbot Martino of Passignano (vol. I): "[W]e do not and cannot share in grace unless we clothe ourselves, through the movement of love, in the crucified love of God's Son, by following in the footsteps of Christ crucified. For we sterile and completely fruitless trees have to be joined with Christ gentle Jesus, the fruitful tree."

Textual Notes

a. Tommasèo: *disgusts me* / *fights.*

b. *b* inserts *also.*

c. Tommasèo: *infinite* (*infinita*) / *bloated* (*infiata*).

d. Mo has first person plural. I have used second person singular for consistency. Tommasèo: *also have* / *have.*

LETTER T22/G67[1]
To Abbot Martino of Passignano
November to December 1377

This is Catherine's second extant letter to Abbot Martino.[2] The content of the letter gives no clue as to when it was written. Two images, however, serve to place it quite firmly in the last month or two of 1377.

The image of the dog of conscience is developed here in great detail (quite close, in fact, to chapter 129 of *The Dialogue*), and more developed than in Let. T114 (which was written between March and September 1377 and is the first text in which the image occurs).[3] This suggests the probability of a relatively late dating, very likely close to the period in which Catherine was composing *The Dialogue*. The imagery recurs in a cluster of letters with heavy sharing in autumn of 1378, when she was finishing *The Dialogue*, but not with the vivid detail of this letter. So late 1377 or early 1378 seems the most plausible placement, either during Catherine's last months in the Val d'Orcia or near the beginning of her time in Florence. Of these two periods, the second is far less plausible, since letters of that period have little in common with this one. Since the dog of conscience theme appears rather late in *The Dialogue*, and does *not* appear in Let. T272 (the letter which provides the initial outline for *The Dialogue*), one might speculate that Catherine developed it first in this letter and then used it again in *The Dialogue*.

There are also certain elements of Catherine's garden imagery which do not appear except in a few isolated cases (with various elements of the imagery distributed differently) before October 1377, and which show the same scattered distribution after 1377.[4]

Besides these images, there is that of the consumed Lamb,[5] which occurs in only one isolated instance after December 1377.[6]

I would therefore place this letter quite confidently in November or December 1377.

---

[1] MSS: Mo-*c*, B, P2, R1, P5, F2, P3, R2, P4, Pa; translation based on Mo-*c*. Significant differences from Tommasèo text noted.

[2] The other, Let. T27, vol. I, was written in early 1376.

[3] The patterns in question are ABBAI, CANECIBO, CANECONS.

[4] The patterns in question are GIARDANI, GERMTRIB, RIVOLTER.

[5] AGNELCON.

[6] Also, the only two letters which share thirteen or more of this one's forty-two analyzed patterns fall between September and November 1377. Fawtier (II, p. 191) and Dupré Theseider (unpublished notes) decline to date this letter.

§

In the name of Jesus Christ crucified and of gentle Mary.

Dearest father in Christ gentle Jesus,

I Caterina, servant and slave of the servants of Jesus Christ, am writing to you in his precious blood. I long to see you a true gardener, a true manager of the orchard of your own soul and the souls of those in your charge.

We are a garden, an orchard really. And First Truth has made our reason, together with our freedom of choice, to be our gardener. It is the task of reason and free choice, with the help of divine grace, to root out the brambles of vice and plant the fragrant herbs of virtue. But it is impossible to plant the virtues without first turning over the soil, and the brambles with it. I am talking about the soil of our selfish sensual will, which finds pleasure only in fleeting earthly delights filled with the troublesome brambles of vice and sin. Turn over this soil, dearest father, in this bit of time we still have, and let sweet and genuine virtues be planted. To do this, use the power of love, an indescribable love drawn from the spotless Lamb and seasoned with hatred and contempt of self. Let it be seasoned, too,[7] with true patience, with faith that is not dead but alive with true deeds,[8] with disdain for the world. Let it be seasoned with true justice toward those in your charge, tempered with mercy. Let it be seasoned with a ready obedience to Christ and to the rule, persevering even to the point of death.

Regarding the rule, I say, observe it in true holy desire and in watching and continual prayer. That is, let your understanding be always awake to know and ponder[a] your own non-being and the goodness of God, the one who *is*,[9] within you. Then continual prayer will follow, little by little, since continual prayer is nothing else than a holy desire and sweet impulse[10] of love, an impulse that corresponds to our understanding. These are some of the most fragrant plants in this garden.

So I want you to be more zealous. This is where you will discover hunger for God's honor and for the salvation of those in your charge. And this is how you will fulfill God's will and the desire I expressed in saying that I long to see you a true gardener for your soul and the souls of those

---

[7] The text actually continues the same sentence, using "with" phrases. At some point, however, the phrases begin to refer more directly to the abbot's activity, though all of the virtues named in some way "season" love (as fragrant herbs added to a dish).

[8] Cf. Jas. 2, 17 (Vulg.): "Faith that does not have deeds is intrinsically dead."

[9] Catherine frequently refers to God as "the one who is," that is, the one whose being is contingent on no one and nothing else. All creatures, in contrast, "are not."

[10] It. *affetto*.

in your charge. For if you are hungry for their[b] salvation for God's honor, you will be eager to rescue them from wretchedness, to punish their faults and to lift up those who are virtuous and want to live according to the rule.

Once the garden has been well tended in this way, I want you to leash the dog of conscience to the gate, so that if enemies should come while the eyes of understanding are asleep, the dog will bark. When the alarm of conscience sounds,[11] [understanding's] eyes will awake to confront the enemies with contempt and hatred, armed and ready with the weapon of love.[12]

You must feed this dog so that she[13] will really be vigilant. Her food is nothing else but hatred and love, brought in the dish of true humility held in the hand of true and perfect[c] patience (since hatred and love join to give birth to humility and sweet gentle patience).[14] The more food, the more vigilance! This dog will become so alert that she will bark if enemies so much as pass by, so that understanding may get up to see who they are and determine whether or not they are from God. In this way the gardener will not be able to be tricked, and the garden will not be looted. Nor will the enemy come to sow the weeds of selfish love that sprout brambles and choke off the seed of virtue.[15] Give this dog [plenty] to drink! Give her [plenty] to drink! Fill up the dish of your memory with the blood of Christ crucified and keep it set before her continually so that she will not waste away and die of thirst.

Up, dearest father! Let's kick out the world with all its pretense and pleasure and wealth! Then, [once we are] poor, let's follow the Lamb who was forsaken and slain on the wood of the most holy cross. Let's not wait any longer, for love of God! Time is snatched from our hands without our

---

[11] Literally, "when the stimulus of conscience barks."

[12] The role of the will is implied here. Cf. Let. T225 to Lazzarino da Pisa (vol. I): "Always hold fast to a holy will that concentrates only on what Christ loved and on what he hated. When our will is thus armed with hatred and love it will be granted such strength that, as Saint Paul says, neither the world nor the devil nor the flesh will be able to lure us from this way."

[13] Catherine actually matches the pronominal references to *il cane* ("the dog") and therefore makes them masculine. But since, in the English, the dog is conscience (*la coscienza*), feminine pronouns seem more consistent.

[14] Usually humility is portrayed as generated from hatred and nurturing charity, as in *Dial.* 63, p. 118: "Every perfection and every virtue proceeds from charity. Charity is nourished by humility. And humility comes from knowledge and holy hatred of oneself, that is, of one's selfish sensuality." But cf. also Let. T273/DT31 to Raimondo da Capua (vol. I): "I am saying that unless you are drowned in the blood you will not attain the little virtue of true humility, which is born from hatred as hatred is from love."

[15] Catherine merges here elements from the parable of the sower (Mt. 13, 1–9; 18–23) and the parable of the wheat and the weeds (Mt. 13, 24–30).

even noticing. So it makes no sense for us to wait for what we don't have while we are losing what we do have.

I'll say no more. Keep living in God's holy and tender love.

Gentle Jesus! Jesus love!

Textual Notes

a. Tommasèo: *come* (*venga*) / *be always awake* (*vegghi*).

b. Tommasèo: [*their*].

c. Tommasèo: [*and perfect*].

LETTER T124/G142[1]

To Matteo di Fazzio dei Cenni of the Casa della Misericordia in Siena
Late November to December 1377

One can conclude from its references to gossip in Catherine's absence from Siena that this letter is being written from the Val d'Orcia. Because she says that her "return has been delayed by continuing physical weariness as well as by God's will, but primarily by the latter," I would place it nearer the end of her stay but before she knows that she must go to Florence, possibly near the letter (T119) to Alessa dei Saracini in which she also tells of her physical ailments, and therefore during Advent, in late November or December.[2]

§

In the name of Jesus Christ crucified and of gentle Mary.

Dearest son in Christ gentle Jesus,

I Caterina, servant and slave of the servants of Jesus Christ, am writing to you in his precious blood. I long to see you bathed and drowned in the blood of Christ crucified, the blood that makes us so drunk that we completely forget ourselves.[3] We want not a single bit of ourselves to remain apart from the blood. I mean we don't want to choose [anything] in our own way or according to our own opinions—circumstances of time or place, consolations or trials, being wronged or derided or slandered or insulted, or anything else from any source whatever, for ourselves or for anyone else. No, we submit ourselves completely to God's will, which we discover in Christ's blood. How so? Because that blood reveals God's gracious will, which neither wants nor seeks anything but that we be made holy, and whatever he gives or permits is given us out of love, so that we may be made holy in him.[4] This is how his truth is fulfilled.

---

[1] MSS: R1, T, P3; translation based on R1, with variants from unpublished notes of A. Volpato.

[2] While the linguistic evidence broadly supports placement of the letter in the Val d'Orcia period, a few significant clusters within individual patterns are more strongly concentrated between October and December: AGNELCON, BEATITUD, COSADEB, EBBRPERD, SCHIFPEN, SENZMEZZ. Fawtier (II, p. 216) declines to date this letter. Dupré Theseider (unpublished notes) places it in October or November 1377.

[3] Cf. Let. T208/DT6 to Bartolomeo Dominici (in this volume): "Do as a heavy drinker does who loses himself and can no longer see himself." Also Let. T29/DT18 (vol. I), T75/DT62 (in this volume), and T25 (1378).

[4] 1 Thes. 4, 3.

His truth is this, that he created us for the glory and praise of his name and so that we might share in his blessedness and in his boundless charity, and this destiny we receive and experience perfectly when we see God. This is what we have come to know. We have seen with our mind's eye the eternal Father's will in the blood of his Son. And this is why, when we are swallowed up in the blood, and enlightened by God's gracious will which we have discovered in the blood, we have no more pain.[5] We do not walk according to our own way, nor do we want to direct ourselves or anyone else according to our own opinions. And so we do not suffer as do those who go their own way, because we have completely let go of our own opinions. In fact, we concentrate on doing just what we discover in the blood. And what do we discover in the blood? The eternal Father's honor and the salvation of souls. For this Word was never concerned about anything else. He did not evade suffering, but took his place at the table of the cross to eat souls as his food.

So let us, his members, let go of ourselves and be nourished on the blood of the Lamb slain and consumed. If we do we shall have life and shall experience the earnest of eternal life. We shall have light, and in that light we shall be freed from darkness, be freed from all scandal-mongering and gossip, for we shall not be passing judgments that are distorted in the direction of either good or evil. No, just as we ourselves have been immersed and lost in the blood, so we shall immerse and lose others [in that blood], convinced that the Holy Spirit is guiding them.

It is quite otherwise with those who have made some attempt but have not completely let go of themselves. Very often they experience intense suffering when they set themselves up as judges over the ways and customs of God's servants and end up spreading scandal and gossip. And often they make others gossip as well when they peddle their opinions and their pains. Those opinions ought to be buried in the blood, or with the person concerned, without getting all sorts of other people involved. If such people were immersed in and enlightened by the blood this is how they would act. But they don't, because they are not yet so perfect as to have their will immersed [in the blood] as is required of God's servants. So they are still spiritually self-opinionated even though they may have completely let go of worldly things. It turns out that they are ignorant, and in their ignorance they fall into all sorts of faults and improprieties.

Let's run then, dearest and cherished son! Let's all plunge into Christ's

---

[5] Cf. Let. T108/DT49 to Giovanna di Capo and Francesca (late 1377): "We rejoice and are glad in everything, and we see that God permits these things for our profit and perfection. I'm not surprised that we are, then, free from suffering, since we have shed the cause of suffering—I mean self-will grounded in self-centeredness—and have put on God's will grounded in charity."

precious and glorious blood, sparing not one bit of ourselves. Let's endure every difficulty, every wrong and rumor and all else, with patience and reverence as we should. Let's offer God's servants our counsel without gossiping or spreading our own opinions about them. In this way we shall be instrumental in ending the gossip rather than causing it. So let us act, and let nothing be done except in the blood. I don't see how it can be any other way. And this is why I said that I long to see you get drunk on the blood of Christ[a] crucified; it seems to me it is necessary, essential.

This is how I want us to act. And I especially beg you, urge you, to pray to First Truth for me (for I need it), that he so immerse and drown me there [in his blood] that I may be perfectly enlightened to see and know my little sheep, both those I have and those who are lost, and may put them on my shoulders and return with them to the sheepfold.[6]

What great ignorance on the part of a sheep not to recognize its shepherd's voice! You people have been hearing the shepherd's voice for so long that you ought to know it well, but it seems you are being contrary, that you are following your own voices—and you bleat without even knowing what you are saying. You are following human counsel and judgment, and it seems you have all lost the light of faith. It is as if the shepherd, who has called you and wants to give his life for your salvation, had called you with a different voice, not with the divine voice and with God's gracious will but with a human voice. Neither anything anyone might say, nor the sheep's own ignorance, can put them so out of tune with God's voice as to keep them from responding to it both in themselves and in regard to others.

Here is how the most gentle Jesus acted. He let neither the Jews' grumbling and taking scandal nor our ingratitude keep him from accomplishing the Father's honor and our salvation. And this is how those ought to act whom God has appointed to follow this Lamb; nothing at all must make them turn back. And if sick sheep who *ought* to be healthy are bleating like sick sheep, that should not make the shepherd leave those who are at the point of death if it seems possible to give these life, or leave those who are completely blind for the sake of those who simply have sore eyes![7] That isn't how you should act. No, learn from the holy disciples, some of whom stayed home and some of whom went out, depending on what they saw to be for God's greater honor. We have to suppose that both those who stayed and those who went provoked endless gossip. But

---

[6] Cf. the parable of the good shepherd: Jn. 10, 14–15; Mt. 18, 12–13; Lk. 15, 4–7.

[7] The implication seems to be that Catherine's disciples in Siena are "bleating" for her to come back to attend to their minor woes, while she is convinced she must stay where she is to attend to those who are in mortal danger spiritually.

those who went didn't therefore stop working for God's honor. Nor did those who stayed forget the light of faith, or lose their willingness to suffer, or cease to recall and remember their shepherd's voice. In fact, they grew stronger joyfully, because the greater the obstacles, the more perfect the work accomplished.

So be true little sheep. Don't be afraid of your own shadow, and don't think that I've left the ninety-nine for just one. I'll tell you this much: for every one of those ninety-nine I have ninety-nine [others] who are seen only by divine goodness.[8] And uncreated Charity knows this, he who for this hidden purpose lets [me] endure the fatigue of travel, the weight of illness, the burden of gossip and scandal-mongering. For all, may God's name be praised and glorified! For whether I leave or stay is dictated not by human will, but by God's. My return has been delayed by continuing physical weariness as well as by God's will, but primarily by the latter. We will return as soon as possible and as soon as the Holy Spirit allows us to. But be content whether we stay here or leave. Put all your imaginings to rest higher up, in the conviction that divine providence is doing and will continue to do everything—except that I am the one who spoils God's work by my numerous sins, and so I am hurting you and the whole world. I beg you as urgently as I can to ask God to give me perfect light so that I may walk, dead [to myself], in the way of truth.

I'll say no more. Take heart in Christ gentle Jesus. And give our greetings to everyone, particularly the Bachelor and Frate Antonio. . . .[9]

Keep living in God's holy and tender love.[b]

Gentle Jesus! Jesus love!

Textual Notes

a. P3: *Jesus Christ / Christ.*

b. P3: [*Keep . . . love*]; R1, T have *Keep living, etc.*

[8] She probably means that, while she has left "ninety-nine" of her disciples behind, it is not to seek just "one" lost one (as does the good shepherd in the parable), but fully as many as she has left behind, and that only God knows how many that is.

[9] William Flete, who was known as "the Bachelor" because he held a bachelor's degree from Cambridge but had declined to complete his master's degree, and Antonio da Nizza, also an Augustinian hermit at Lecceto near Siena. They were good friends of Matteo, who in fact had been converted by William.

LETTER T119/G178[1]
To Monna Alessa dei Saracini
Advent (29 November to 24 December) 1377

Catherine is concerned here with apparent gossip on the part of a certain unidentified woman and perhaps of Alessa herself, gossip which is causing Catherine pain. There is also mention of a woman (perhaps the same, perhaps another) of whose conversion Alessa has informed Catherine.

The rubric of Mo says that the present letter was written "while Catherine was at the Rocca." And within the letter Catherine refers to its being Advent (29 November to 24 December in 1377). This placement is reinforced by the linguistic data.[2]

§

In the name of Jesus Christ crucified and of gentle Mary.

Dearest daughter in Christ gentle Jesus,

I Caterina, servant and slave of the servants of Jesus Christ, am writing to you in his precious blood. I long to see you following the spotless Lamb's teaching, your heart free, stripped of everything created and clothed only in the Creator with the light of most holy faith. For without light you cannot walk along the straight way of the spotless slain Lamb.

This is why my soul longs to see you and the others honest and courageous, not whipped about by any wind that might come along. See that you don't turn back, but always go forward, keeping in mind the teaching you have been given. Return every day to the garden of your soul to root out any brambles that might choke the seed, the teaching you were given, and to till the soil. I mean, every day strip your heart clean.[3] You really have to do it continually. I've seen many people who *seemed* to have been stripped clean, but I've found—more by their actions than by their words—that they are not. It is their actions that show where their heart is,

---

[1] MSS: Mo-*a*, B, P2, R1, T, P5, F1, F2, P3, S4; translation based on Mo-*a*, with variants based on unpublished notes of A. Volpato.

[2] Two of the three letters which share nine or more of this one's thirty-two analyzed patterns fall between October and December of 1377. Several significant clusters within individual patterns support the Advent placement equally broadly (ACCETDES, ANDLUCE, COGNVERI, CUORLIBE, GRATVIRT, LINGUANA, LUMEVEST, SPOSVERI, UNGUENT) and several more narrowly (FRUTPAZ, GIARDANI, PAROLOP, RIVOLTER). Fawtier (II, p. 225) and Dupré Theseider (unpublished notes) simply affirm the Advent placement.

[3] Cf. the parable of the sower, Lk. 8, 5–15.

though their words might show the opposite. So I want you truly to strip your heart clean by following Christ crucified.

And let your mouth be silent. I have noticed! And I hardly believe that the other woman has been silent.[4] I'm very sorry, if things are as they seem to me. My Creator wants me to put up with it, and I'm happy to put up with it, even though I'm not happy about the offense to God.

You wrote me that it seemed God was prompting you in prayer to pray for me. Thanks to divine Goodness for showing such indescribable love for my soul! You said I should let you know whether I'm in pain, whether I was suffering the weaknesses I usually do in this sort of weather.[5] To that I answer that God has provided for me wonderfully both within and without. Physically he has been very provident this Advent, giving me distraction from my pain in writing.[6] True, by God's goodness the pain is worse than usual. But if God has intensified my pain, he has provided for Lisa's healing, and just at the time Fra Santi became ill! The latter was at the point of death, but now he is, almost miraculously, so much better that one might say he is cured.[7]

It seems, though, that my Spouse, eternal Truth, has chosen to give me an exquisite and real test both within and without, both visibly and invisi-

---

[4] It.: *Sonmi aveduta che poco credo che l'altra l'abbi tenuto*. The "other woman" may be Monna Bruna, also Catherine's disciple, who was at Montegiovi with Alessa earlier in autumn. Or it may be the woman referred to later on, possibly a resident of Montegiovi. From what follows, it seems in any case to be a matter of the rumors being spread about Catherine, which she repeatedly tells her disciples to ignore.

[5] The Italian could also be translated "at this time," meaning either "at this time of year" or simply "whether I'm suffering as much as usual at this time."

[6] Some commentators have included this with the evidence that Catherine knew how to write, and link it with the account of her writing of Prayer 6 (*Processo Castellano*, ed. Laurent, pp. 62–63; cf. introduction to that prayer in my edition, pp. 51–53). Others, including Dupré Theseider (unpublished notes), interpret "writing" here and elsewhere as "dictating." (However, in his later article in *Dizionario biografico*, p. 376, he does not exclude the possibility of Catherine's having learned to write.) The interpretation that Catherine did *not* learn how to write, says Dupré Theseider in his unpublished notes, is buttressed by the almost immediate mention of her sister-in-law Lisa's getting well just when Fra Santi (another disciple, whose hermitage outside Siena Catherine will later use while finishing her *Dialogue*) got sick. Lisa seems to have been literate, and therefore could well have served Catherine as scribe at times, though there is no other specific indication of it beyond this paragraph, and whenever Lisa is listed among Catherine's companions there is always at least one other known scribe among them. In any case, while it is clear that Catherine did often use the verb "write" when she was dictating (for example, the opening of every letter), a collection of other passages in her own writings and those of her contemporaries seem to me sufficient indication that she did learn how to write in her later years.

[7] The reference does not necessarily, I think, imply that the two are with Catherine at the Rocca, since she could know of their condition from her contacts in Siena. If, on the other hand, she mentions their illnesses in relation to their being able to serve her as scribes, they would have to be with her.

bly—the invisible [aspects] being innumerably more than the visible. But along with the testing he has provided so sweetly that words could never express it.[8] So I want pain to be my food, and tears my drink, and sweat my anointing. I want pain to fatten me, pain to heal me, pain to give me light, pain to give me wisdom,[a] pain to clothe my nakedness, pain to strip me clean of all selfish love, spiritual or material. The pain of being deprived of all creaturely consolation has called me [to look at] my lack of virtue, to recognize how imperfect I am and how utterly perfect is the light of gentle Truth, provider and acceptor of holy desires, who plays no favorites. He has not withheld his kindness from me because of my ingratitude or because of my dearth of light and knowledge. No, he has regarded only his own supreme goodness.

I beg you for love of Christ crucified, my dearest daughter, not to relax your prayer. In fact, double it, because I have more need of it than you can see. And thank God's goodness for me. Ask him to give me grace to give my life for him, and ask him, if he will, to relieve me of the burden of my body, because my life is of little use to others. No, because of my sins my life is a burden and pain to everyone, near and far. May God in his mercy free me from so many sins! In the little time I have to live, may he make me live in ardent love for virtue. And in suffering may I offer painful, sorrowful[b] desires in his presence for the salvation of the whole world and for the reform of holy Church.[9] Rejoice, rejoice on the cross with me! May the cross be a bed where my soul may rest, a table where I may enjoy as food the fruit of patience[c] in peace and in quiet!

You wrote saying. . . .[10] I was encouraged[d] by that, first, because I would hope that she will change her ways and live with a heart less vain than up to now. Secondly, I was encouraged because of the children who were brought to the light of holy baptism. May God give them his sweetest grace, and may he let them die[e] if they are not going to be good.[11] Bless them and encourage her in Christ gentle Jesus. Tell her to live in sweet holy fear of God, and to give God the credit for the grace she has

---

[8] Cf. 1 Cor. 10, 13. The testing may be the coolness of Gregory XI to which she refers in Let. T267 (written in October or November), where, within a letter to Raimondo da Capua in Rome, she sends her plea that Gregory not reject her. It could also be the absence of Raimondo and/or the continuing criticism of her ministry by friends and enemies alike.

[9] Cf. *Dial.* 1, p. 26, where Catherine describes herself as praying "for the reform of holy Church" and "for the whole world in general, and in particular for the peace of Christians who are rebelling against holy Church with great disrespect and persecution."

[10] Here, as at the ellipsis below, the editor of the earliest manuscript has omitted personal material considered irrelevant to the edificatory purposes of the first dissemination of the letters. Possibly the omitted reference is to "the other woman" mentioned earlier.

[11] There is no hint as to who these children might be. Perhaps they are the children of the woman in question.

received, for it has been not small but great indeed. And if she were ungrateful for it, she would really displease God, and would perhaps not go unpunished.[f]

Commend us [to] . . . .[12,g] I've had no news at all of them, and I don't know why. May God's will be done. Our Savior has put me on the *Isola*, and the winds are lashing on every side.[13] Let's all be happy in Christ crucified, shut up in the house of self-knowledge, while we are far from one another.

I'll say no more. Keep living in God's holy and tender love.

Gentle Jesus! Jesus love![h]

Textual Notes

a. P2: [patience / wisdom].

b. P5, F2: *sweet / sorrowful.*

c. P5, F2, F1: *wisdom / patience.*

d. P5, F1: *very much encouraged / encouraged.*

e. P2 adds *soon*; R1: *give them love / let them die.*

f. P5, F2, F1: *he would perhaps not let her live / she would . . . unpunished.*

g. P5, F1: [*Commend us. . . .*].

h. P5, F1: *Keep living in Christ gentle Jesus. Amen.* P3: *Keep living. . . . Gentle Jesus! Jesus and Mary, love!*

[12] Again personal material is omitted in the manuscript.

[13] The *Isola* is the promontory (*Rocca*) on which the fortress of the Salimbeni at Tentennano in the Val d'Orcia was built. It is indeed an "island" in the sense of its isolation. But it was (and is still) also so called because its summit is frequently above the clouds that shroud the valley below, and lashed by winds from nearby Mont'Amiata. Catherine may be alluding to the physical environment as a metaphor of her own isolation and the gossip and rumors pounding at her from every side, as she has complained above and also in Let. T123 to the Defenders of Siena (in this volume).

Appendix:
Persons Associated with Catherine of Siena

These notes do not by any means include all who were associated with Catherine. For each volume I have listed those who are referred to in her letters or in the introductions to the letters. Persons who are known only by their given names, who are mentioned only once in the corpus of the letters, and of whom nothing else is known, are ordinarily not listed here. Nor are persons listed who are named only in the footnotes. Because of the inconsistency of family designations, all are alphabetized by given name.

AGNESA DI ORSO MALAVOLTI: Letters T38, T53, T61

Wife of Orso Malavolti, a member of one of the leading families of Siena. She was already widowed and a member of the *Mantellate* when Catherine was associated with her. (She still appears on the *Mantellate* list in 1378.[1])

ALESSA DEI SARACINI: Letters T49, T119, T126, T271, T277, T286

A friend and disciple of Catherine already during the latter's years of solitude. It was Alessa who attempted to teach Catherine to read, and early served as one of her scribes. After the death of Catherine's father, Catherine (and probably her mother Lapa) went to live with Alessa, perhaps for several years. Alessa accompanied Catherine on nearly all of her journeys, and as Catherine lay dying, she deputed Alessa to lead her disciples. Alessa, however, died not long after Catherine.

ANGELO RICASOLI: Letters T88, T136, T242, T341

A member of one of the leading families of Florence, he succeeded Pietro Corsini as bishop of that city on 19 June 1370. Catherine very probably made his acquaintance (by reputation if not in person) while she was in Florence during the Dominican General Chapter in the spring of 1374. Gardner describes him as mediocre and time-serving.[2]

---

[1] M. Hyacinthus Laurent, *Fontes*, I (*Documenti*), pp. 24, 47.

[2] *Saint Catherine of Siena*, p. 171.

When the populist Signoria refused in October 1377 to continue to observe the interdict, Ricasoli left his see and took refuge on his family lands near Siena.

ANTONIO DA NIZZA (i.e., Nice): Letters T17, T326
Augustinian hermit of Lecceto and close friend of William Flete. He had earlier studied canon law at Toulouse. He died probably in 1390.

ANTONIO DI CIOLO (PETRACIOLO): Letter T44
Almost certainly a notary, since he is addressed by the title *Ser.*

BARDUCCIO DI PIERO CANIGIANI
Son of Piero Canigiani of Florence and younger brother of the prominent lawyer and politician Ristoro. He joined Catherine's circle of disciples probably during the early weeks of her 1378 stay in Florence. Almost immediately thereafter he began to serve as her principal scribe, and one of the three to whom she dictated her *Dialogue*. To him we owe the earliest extant and most reliable transcription of that work. From Florence he traveled with Catherine back to Siena and eventually to Rome. During the final year and a half of Catherine's life he was her constant companion, secretary, and personal helper. There are no extant letters from Catherine to Barduccio—but there probably was no such correspondence because he was with her from the time he first met her until her death.

After Catherine's death he told the story of her last days in a long letter to Suor Caterina Petriboni. Not much later, he contracted consumption and, at the suggestion of Raimondo da Capua, moved to Siena "lest the air of Rome would harm him." There he died on 2 December 1382.

BARTOLO and ORSA USIMBARDI: Letters T89, T93, T236, T248, T379
Upper-class Florentines, they became disciples of Catherine at least by the time of her 1378 stay in their city. They are constantly associated in Catherine's letters with Francesco di Pipino and his wife.

BARTOLOMEA D'ANDREA MEI: Letter T71
It is known only that she was of the Buoninsegna family.

BARTOLOMEA DELLA SETA: Letters T182, T221
Nun of the Monastery of Santo Stefano near Pisa.

BARTOLOMEA DI DOMENICO: Letter T278
Probably Sienese. The letter is addressed to her during her stay in Rome.

BARTOLOMEA DI SALVATICO: Letter T165
One of a group of pious women befriended by Catherine on her visits to Lucca.

BARTOLOMEO DI GIACOMO: Letter T14
Catherine's older brother. He married Lisa di Golio (or, according to others, di Chimento) Colombini, who quickly became a favorite companion of Catherine. With Benincasa and Stefano, Bartolomeo inherited their father's wool-dying business, and after the failure of that venture moved to Florence. He died sometime after 1397. The letter is addressed to him and his two brothers in Florence.

BARTOLOMEO DOMINICI (1343–1415): Letters T70, T105, T127, T129, T146, T198, T200, T204, T208
A native of Siena and Dominican friar of San Domenico in that city, he was introduced to Catherine in 1368 by his novitiate companion and Catherine's confessor, Tommaso dalla Fonte. According to his own testimony, he was twenty-four at the time and she about twenty-one.[3] They remained close friends for life. He occasionally served her as confessor and accompanied her on her journeys to Pisa, Lucca, and Avignon. He taught and held office in various houses of the Dominican Order and was very active in the reform movement after Catherine's death. In 1412 he contributed his personal testimony to the *Processo Castellano*.

BARTOLOMEO SERAFINI DA RAVENNA: Letter T323
Originally a monk of the Carthusian monastery of Calci near Pisa, he was the founding prior of the Carthusian monastery on the island of Gorgona in 1373, and disciple of Catherine. He was among those summoned by Catherine to Rome in 1378 at the behest of Urban VI to form "a council of the servants of God." One letter of his to Catherine (*Lettere dei discepoli*, III) survives.

BENEDETTA (BANDEÇÇA) DI GIOVANNI DEI SALIMBENI: Letters T112, T113
Daughter of the deceased Giovanni d'Agnolino Salimbeni and sister of the younger Agnolino, living in exile at the family fortress at Rocca d'Orcia. (See Giovanni d'Agnolino Salimbeni.) After Bandeçça had lost her husband and then her fiancé, Catherine tried to persuade her to enter the monastery she was establishing at Belcaro.

---

[3] *Processo Castellano*, c. 1312.

BENINCASA DI GIACOMO: Letters T10, T18, T20
Catherine's eldest brother. When their father Giacomo died in 1368 the family wool-dying business was left to Benincasa, Bartolomeo, and Stefano. That same September the three were elected *Defensores* of the city, a post they held for less than a year. On 14 October 1370 the three brothers applied for Florentine citizenship.[4] Their business must have done badly after their party's fall from power, and in 1373 they sold their properties in Siena,[5] probably to meet their debts. On 7 October 1373 a group of Florentine merchants petitioned the Commune of Siena to force Benincasa, Bartolomeo, and Stefano's heirs to pay an outstanding debt.[6] Benincasa died sometime after 1397.

BENUCCIO DI PIERO DE' BELFORTI: Letter T103
Distantly related to the Salimbeni family of Siena and Rocca d'Orcia, his mother being Angiola Salimbeni, daughter of Benuccio di Sozzo di Francesco Salimbeni.[7] The letter is addressed to him and his cousin Bernardo di Uberto.

BIANCINA DI GIOVANNI DEI SALIMBENI: Letter T111
Widow of Giovanni d'Agnolino dei Salimbeni, lord of Rocca d'Orcia, and mother of the younger Agnolino and his sisters Isa and Bandeçça. Monna Biancina was primarily responsible for Catherine's coming the Val d'Orcia in 1377 to reconcile Agnolino and his cousin Cione di Sandro.

BIRINGHIERI DEGLI ARZOCCHI: Letter T24
Parish priest of Asciano, a few miles east of Siena.

BUONACCORSO DI LAPO: Letter T234
Member of a mercantile family of Florence and leading figure in the Guelf party of that city. He was Florentine ambassador to Siena in March 1375 and member of the *Signoria* of Florence during March and April 1376. It may well have been he who assured Catherine of the city's support in her negotiations with Gregory XI for peace.

---

[4] Laurent, *Fontes*, I (*Documenti*), doc. VII, pp. 26–28.

[5] T. Tarcisio, "La Casa di S. Caterina: La grande difficoltà del documento del 1346," *S. Caterina da Siena* 12 (1947), nn. 1–6.

[6] Laurent, *Fontes*, I (*Documenti*), doc. VIII, pp. 29–30.

[7] *Istoria genealogica delle famiglie Salimbeni di Siena*, ed. Idlefonso di San Luigi in *Delizie degli Eruditi toscani*, appendix to vol. XXIII, Florence, 1786, p. 80 (cited in Fawtier II, p. 241, n. 1).

CAFFARINI: *See* Tommaso d'Antonio da Siena.

CATERINA DELLO SPEDALUCCIO: Letters T118, T214
Member of the Sienese *Mantellate* and disciple of Catherine.

CATERINA DI GHERARDO BUONCONTI: Letter T161
Wife of Gherardo di Niccolò Buonconti. The letter is addressed to her and her mother-in-law.

CATERINA DI GHETTO
One of Catherine's earliest disciples. In the Sienese *Mantellate* list of 1352 she is called *Katerina Enghecti*, and on the 1378 list, *Caterina Ghetti*, but there is also on the same list the form *Inghetti*.[8] She was a niece of Catherine's first confessor (and cousin) Tommaso dalla Fonte, who gave the saint's mantle to her after Catherine's death. We know no more about her role in Catherine's life after the early references, nor whether she accompanied Catherine on any of her journeys. No letter is addressed directly to her.

CECCA: *See* Francesca di Clemente Gori.

CHARLES V, KING OF FRANCE: Letter T235
King of France, at war with Edward III of England during most of his reign (he died at age thirty-nine). His brother Louis was Duke of Anjou.

CIONE DI SANDRO SALIMBENI:
Lord of Castiglioncello di Trinoro, about ten miles to the east of Rocca d'Orcia. Catherine was called to the Orcia Valley to mediate a dispute between him and his cousin Agnolino over a contested property. Letter T110 is addressed to his wife Stricca.

CONTE DI MONNA AGNOLA: Letter T257
A Florentine and apparently a disciple of Giovanni dalle Celle. At the time Catherine writes to him and his companions, he is interested in joining the projected crusade of the Hospitalers. We know nothing more of him.

CORRADO DE' TRINCI DA FULIGNO: Letter T253
Like his brother Trincio, he was despotic in his power in Fuligno. He

[8] Laurent, *Fontes*, I (*Documenti*), pp. 24, 47, 48.

was at Anagni at the time of Trincio's assassination, but returned to Fuligno on 6 December at the invitation of the people to become lord of the city. Having massacred the rebels who had killed his brother, he ruled until 1386, when he died childless. He was succeeded first by Trincio's son Ugolino, and later by Trincio's widow, Jacoma. The letter is addressed to him and his brother Trincio.

COSTANZA DI NICCOLÒ SODERINI: Letter T314
Wife of Niccolò Soderini of Florence.

CRISTOFANO, CARTHUSIAN: Letter T353
Carthusian monk of San Martino in Naples.

FELICE DA MASSA TANCREDI: Letter T51
Augustinian hermit of Lecceto. He and his confrere Giovanni Tantucci accompanied Raimondo da Capua to Avignon in early 1376. He authored a small book on the childhood of Christ (*La fanciulezza di Gesù*).

FILIPPO DI VANNUCCIO: Letter T36
A young Florentine recommended to the Olivetan order by Catherine in 1378. He became a novice at that order's monastery of San Michele in Bosco near Bologna. The letter is addressed to him and other novices there.

FRANCESCA (CECCA) DI CLEMENTE GORI: Letters T117, T126
A noble Sienese widow with three Dominican sons, all of whom died in the plague of 1374, and a daughter, Giustina, who became a nun at Montepulciano. Francesca served Catherine as scribe in the latter's early letter-writing years and accompanied Catherine on nearly all of her journeys. She is greeted in other letters as well.

FRANCESCHINA OF LUCCA: Letters T162, T163
We know nothing of Franceschina except her name and her association with other women of Lucca befriended by Catherine.

FRANCESCO DI MESSER VANNI MALAVOLTI: Letter T45
A young Sienese nobleman who became Catherine's disciple at the instigation of his friend Neri di Landoccio Pagliaresi, probably early in 1374. He was twenty-five at the time.[9] Like his friend Neri, he de-

[9] *Processo Castellano*, ed. Laurent, pp. 376–412.

lighted in poetry but was also, by his own testimony, "bold and hotheaded, lascivious and unrestrained." He first went to see Catherine only to please Neri, but like so many others, was transformed in Catherine's presence. After a number of lapses he at some point married a girl of fifteen, "beautiful in body but even more so in spirit and virtue," and the two by mutual consent lived for a time "in the same house but not the same bed." On occasion he served Catherine as scribe. After Catherine's death and that of his wife and children he in 1388 became a Benedictine of Monteoliveto Maggiore near Siena. He left that monastery in 1410 to become a "black Benedictine" of San Miliano near Sassoferrato. From that monastery he wrote his testimony for the *Processo Castellano*.

FRANCESCO DI PASCUALE: Letter T36
A novice of the Monteolivetan monastery of San Michele in Bosco near Bologna. The letter is addressed to him and other novices there.

FRANCESCO DI PIPINO and AGNESA HIS WIFE: Letters T91, T93, T174, T176, T179, T190, T248, T249, T251, T265, T274, T288, T289, T290, T300, T378
Francesco di Pipino was a Florentine tailor, originally of San Miniato al Tedesco but highly respected in his adopted city and on friendly terms with leaders among the Guelfs such as the Soderini and the Canigiani. He and his wife Agnesa became Catherine's disciples at least as early as her 1378 visit to Florence. During the final days of that visit she would live with them. Her correspondence with them continued until the end of her life.

GABRIELE DI DAVINO DE' PICCOLOMINI: Letter T128
A married Sienese noble, he joined Catherine's circle early in her public life. He was with Catherine for at least some of her stay in the Val d'Orcia, and also accompanied Catherine to Rome in 1378.

GÉRARD DU PUY
Nephew of Gregory XI, abbot of Marmoutiers and cardinal, he was appointed papal vicar in Perugia in 1373. His government of Perugia was marked by oppression and tyranny. It is he who, as representative of the Church, assented to the condemnation of Niccolò di Toldo (cf. Let. T273).

GHERARDO DI NICCOLÒ DEI BUONCONTI
Son of Niccolò and Nella Buonconti of Pisa. Catherine was his guest during most if not all of her 1375 stay in Pisa, in the home near the

Church of Santa Cristina which was known by contemporaries as one of the most elegant in the city. Gherardo and his brothers Francesco and Tommaso accompanied Catherine on her journey to Avignon in 1376.

GHERARDO GAMBACORTA

Brother of Piero Gambacorta of Pisa. His wife's name is Niera. Catherine seems at every reference to him to be concerned about his spiritual laxity.

GHITA DEGLI ALBIZZI: Letter T75

Widow of Tommaso Corsini and second abbess of the monastery of San Gaggio near Florence.

GIOVANNA D'ANGIÒ (Jeanne d'Anjou): Letters T133, T138, T143, T312, T317, T348, T362

Great-granddaughter of Charles Martel, she became queen of Naples in 1333, when she was only seven. She was licentious, violent, and fickle, an opportunist of the first degree. It was she who had sold Avignon (which she owned as Countess of Provence) to the pope for a nominal sum in 1347 after convincing him of her innocence in the murder of her husband, Andrew of Hungary. She ruled over the liveliest and most splendid court in the peninsula, and eventually sided with the Clementine cause in the schism of 1378. Urban VI excommunicated her in 1380 and enthroned Charles of Durazzo in her place.

GIOVANNA D'AZZOLINO

One of a group of pious women befriended by Catherine on her visits to Lucca.

GIOVANNA DEI PAZZI: Letter T87

One of Catherine's earliest disciples in Siena, occasionally serving Catherine as scribe during the first years of the latter's public life (for Letters T41, T152, and T208). Gigli speculates that she may have been a member of the dei Pazzi family who had moved to Siena in the thirteenth century, one house of their descendants being the Cinughi.[10] Apparently on the basis of this speculation, Meattini assumes that she was a *Mantellata*,[11] since there is a *Domina Iohanna ser Petri Cini*

[10] *Opere*, II, p. 687.

[11] *Epistolario*, p. 965.

among the Sienese *Mantellate* listed in 1378.[12] She is also greeted in several other letters.

GIOVANNA DI CAPO: Letters T108, T118, T214
An early disciple and frequent companion of Catherine, sometimes serving as the latter's scribe. She is listed as *domina Iohanna Capi* in the 1378 *Mantellate* list.[13]

GIOVANNA DI CORRADO MACONI: Letters T241, T247
The very possessive mother of Catherine's disciple Stefano Maconi.

GIOVANNA DI MARTINO DA SIENA: Letter T30
On 19 August 1367 she was named abbess for life of the Monastery of Santa Marta in Siena.[14]

GIOVANNI DA PARMA: Letter T309
Nothing is known of this man except than that he was in Rome at the time Let. T309 was sent.

GIOVANNI DALLE CELLE (1310–1396): Letters T296, T322
A noble Florentine, he was in his earlier monastic life abbot of Santa Trinità in Florence. Convicted there of unchastity and sorcery, he was imprisoned for a year. After completing his time of penance he left the abbey and went to Vallombrosa outside Florence, to the hermitage *dalle celle* ("of the cells"), by which name he was subsequently known. Renowned for his holiness, wisdom, and knowledge of the Scriptures, he converted many young Florentines through his direction and letters. Among these were Barduccio Canigiani, later one of Catherine's disciples and secretaries, and another disciple, Conte di Ser Conti. On 10 October 1376, Giovanni wrote to William Flete, who had accused him of speaking out against Catherine: "Not only do I not want to do such a thing, but I am prepared to die for her honor." Calling her his queen, he says, "I would consider it a glory to be called a heretic with her. . . . Oh sweetest heresy of the heavenly Catherine! You turn sinners into just people. Friend of publicans and sinners, you make the angels laugh and heaven rejoice. You honor God; you enlighten the Church of Christ; you raise the dead to spiritual life. . . . You have the words of

---

[12] Laurent, *Fontes*, I (*Documenti*), p. 48.
[13] Laurent, *Fontes*, I (*Documenti*), p. 49.
[14] From *Archivio di Stato di Siena, Diplomatico, Pergamene di S. Marta.*

eternal life, and we have believed and known that you are anointed by the Holy Spirit and are the daughter of the living God!"[15]

GIOVANNI DEI SABBATINI: Letters T141, T187
Native of Bologna, Carthusian monk of Belriguardo about three miles northwest of Siena.

GIOVANNI DI BINDO DI DOCCIO: Letter T189
Monk of Monteoliveto Maggiore near Siena, listed as such already in 1373. In 1379 and 1380 he was at the monastery of Santa Anna in Camprena. There is no record of his whereabouts at any other time. He died in 1417.[16] The letter is addressed to him and others of the same monastery. Domina Margharita Bindi, listed among the Sienese *Mantellate* in 1352 and listed again in 1378 as Domina Margarita Bindi Doccii, was surely his mother.[17]

GIOVANNI DI GANO DA ORVIETO: Letter T12
Abbot of the Williamite abbey of Sant'Antimo (southeast of Siena) from 1376 until 1393. He assisted Catherine in the establishment of her monastery at Belcaro. She in turn encouraged him in the reform of his abbey and defended him against the attacks of the archpriest of Montalcino.

GIOVANNI TANTUCCI: Letters T80, T219
Augustinian hermit of Lecceto, also known as "the master" because of his degree in theology (probably from Bologna), or as Giovanni Terzo, an early follower of Catherine. He and Felice da Massa accompanied Raimondo da Capua to Avignon in 1376. He was one of those to whom Catherine entrusted her writings before her death, and was asked to deliver her funeral eulogy.

GIUSTO DI GIOVANNI DA VOLTERRA: Letter T8
Prior of Monteoliveto Maggiore sometime before 1378, when he became prior of Sant'Andrea in Volterra. He was prior of San Giovanni sul Venda from 1380 to 1381, and again prior of Sant'Andrea from 1381 to 1383, at which monastery he died in 1384.[18]

---

[15] Let. IV, in P. Cividali, *Il beato Giovanni dalle Celle*, *Atti della R. Accademia dei Lincei*, CCCIII, ser. V, vol. XII, 1906, pp. 439–440.

[16] *Registro Olivetano*, I, 59, cited in P. Lugano, "L'istituzione di Montoliveto nella seconda metà del Trecento," p. 68.

[17] Laurent, *Fontes*, I, *Documenti*, pp. 24, 47.

[18] P. Lugano, "L'istituzione di Montoliveto nella seconda metà del Trecento" and "Santa Caterina da Siena e i monaci di Montoliveto."

GREGORY XI, POPE (1329–1378): Letters T185, T196, T206, T209, T218, T229, T231, T233, T238, T239, T252, T255, T270, T285

Born Pierre Robert de Beaufort, he studied law in Perugia, having been named cardinal at the age of nineteen by his uncle, Pope Clement VI. De Beaufort was elected pope on 30 December 1370. The last of the Avignon popes, he spent all but the final fourteen months of his pontificate in that city. Considered the most able pontiff of the fourteenth century and generally well-intentioned, he was nevertheless often vacillating and irresolute in moral matters. His papacy was in constant tension with the republics of the Italian peninsula. That tension culminated in a general rebellion of the Italian republics in 1375 when Gregory's agents repeatedly used oppressive tactics to reassert papal power in the peninsula. Even the pope's return to Rome in January 1377 did not resolve the conflict. Gregory died on 27 March 1378, having on his deathbed advised the cardinals who attended him "never to listen to busy-body women."

GUILLAUME RAINAUD: Letter T55

Prior general of the Carthusians from 1367 until his death in 1402.[19] Upon his election he refused the title of abbot general offered him by the pope, as well as the rank of cardinal and the dispensation of his monks from abstinence from meat in case of illness. At the time of the schism of 1378 he transferred his loyalty from Urban VI to Clement VII.

IACOMO (GIACOMO) DA PADOVA: Letter T32

Member of the Aldrighetti family and monk of the Benedictine monastery of Monteoliveto Maggiore near Siena. We do not know when Catherine met him, and there is no record of their relationship other than her one letter to him and the fact that he appears as the bearer of a letter to Gregory XI early in 1377 (T209). In 1370 he was among the several Olivetans chosen by the new abbot of Montecassino, Andrea da Faenza, to be transferred to that monastery in order to revitalize it in the wake of its devastation by earthquake and years of poor administration. Although Iacomo appears to have been the only monk not to have protested that transfer (ordered under pain of excommunication), the move never took place because the order was rescinded by Gregory XI after the death of Urban V, who had appointed Andrea da Faenza. This is the last documentation of Iacomo's whereabouts until his appointment as visitator to the monasteries of Subiaco in 1378. The rubric of Let. T32 names him as prior of Monteoliveto in Florence.

---

[19] F. A. Lefébure, *S. Bruno e l'ordre des Chartreux*, Paris, 1883, vol. I, pp. 208–209.

IACOMO DI SANO DI MACO: Letter T36

Son of Catherine's disciple Sano di Maco di Mazzacorno and novice of the Monteolivetan monastery of San Michele in Bosco near Bologna. The letter is addressed to him and other novices there.

IACOMO DI VIVA: Letter Fawtier 16

A Sienese, known to us only from Fawtier's Let. 16, which is addressed to him. He was perhaps a relative of the Carthusian Pietro di Giovanni di Viva of the monastery at Maggiano near Siena.

IACOPO DA ITRI: Letter T183

Archbishop of Otranto. Catherine may have met him as he passed through Pisa as apostolic nuncio in 1375. In 1378 the archbishop was among those who denounced Urban VI, and supported his challenger, Clement VII. Clement named him cardinal and patriarch of Constantinople.

IACOPO (IACOMO) ORSINI: Letters T101, T223, T310

One of a line of twenty-two Orsini cardinals between 1144 and 1562, he was titular cardinal of San Giorgio in Velabro and official protector of Siena at the papal court (salaried as such by the commune). He was known to have papal ambitions. In July 1376 the Florentine *Signoria* used both Cardinals Orsini and Corsini in a sense against Catherine by asking them to use their influence with Gregory XI on behalf of the very ambassadors who were refusing to deal with Catherine. Orsini seems to have taken an outward stance of neutrality in anything that might affect his own political interests, including Gregory's return to Rome. All of Catherine's extant letters to him express dissatisfaction with his personal life.

IPOLITO DEGLI UBERTINI: Letter T130

A Florentine who, after he was widowed, Catherine counseled to enter the Carthusian monastery on the island of Gorgona.

ISA (ELISABETTA) DI GIOVANNI DEI SALIMBENI: Letter T115

Daughter of Giovanni d'Agnolino Salimbeni and, like her sister Bandeçça, a widow at the time of Catherine's correspondence with her.

JACOMA DI TRINCIO DE' TRINCI DA FULIGNO: Letter T264

Born Jacoma d'Este, daughter of the Marquis of Ferrara. Her husband, Trincio de' Trinci, lord of Fuligno and *gonfaloniere* (standard-bearer) of the Church, was assassinated on 28 September 1377 by his political enemies within his own city. After the death of Trincio's successors, his brother Corrado and his son Ugolino, Jacoma took the reigns of the city. The letter was addressed to her on the occasion of her husband's death.

JERONIMO DA SIENA: Letter T52
Native of Siena and Augustinian of Lecceto, Tommaso Caffarini calls him not a hermit but a preacher. After Catherine, during her stay at Rocca d'Orcia in 1377, had written her brief prayer to the Holy Spirit, that document was reportedly given (by Catherine or someone else) to Jeronimo "as a special memento."[20]

LAPA DI PUCCIO DI PIAGENTI: Letters T1, T6, T117, T240
Catherine's mother, daughter of a poet and member of the *popolo minuto* of Siena. Raimondo da Capua calls her "a woman of the old type, very different from the present ungodly generation, a capable manager of her household and her family."[21] An imperious woman, she was very possessive of her daughter Catherine. At some point after her husband's death she became a *Mantellata*. She was present at Catherine's death and outlived her by at least five years.

LAZZARINO DA PISA: Letter T225
A learned Franciscan friar and a popular preacher and teacher of philosophy in Siena, he was converted by Catherine early in her public life and became her disciple.

LISA DI GOLIO COLOMBINI
Catherine's sister-in-law and dear friend and disciple, wife of Bartolomeo di Benincasa. She is referred to in a number of letters, but none is addressed to her.

LOUIS, DUKE OF ANJOU
Brother of King Charles V of France.

LUIGI DELLA VIGNA DA CAPUA: Letter T254
Brother of Catherine's confessor Raimondo da Capua and knight in the service of Queen Giovanna of Naples. In the letter, Catherine intercedes for him after his arrest, asking that he be set free without ransom because of his poverty.

---

[20] *Libellus de Supplemento*, I, i, p. 17.
[21] *Life*, I, i, 23, p. 23.

MADDALENA DI ALESSA: Letter T220
Nun of the Monastery of Santa Bonda near Siena.

MARTINO, ABBOT OF PASSIGNANO: Letters T22, T27
A native of Siena, he became abbot of the Vallombrosan monastery of San Michele in Passignano in 1366, having before been abbot at San Cassiano di Montescalari in Val di Greve (also north of Siena). When Florence was placed under interdict in 1377 he fled to Siena, and when the Florentine *Signoria* broke the interdict in October of that year, he removed much of his monastery's property into Sienese territory.

MATTEO DI FRANCESCO TOLOMEI: Letters T94, T169a
Introduced to the Dominican Order after his conversion by Catherine (early in her public life), he became a friar shortly thereafter.[22]

MATTEO DI TOMUCCIO DA ORVIETO: Letter T197
Known only by name through the letter addressed to him.

MELINA DI BARTOLOMEO BARBANI (also spelled Balbani): Letter T164
One of Catherine's women devotees in Lucca. Catherine stayed at her home during at least one of her visits to Lucca.

NANNA (GIOVANNA) DI BENINCASA: Letter T23
Daughter of Catherine's eldest brother Benincasa. The date of her birth is not documented, but Benincasa was already old enough in 1346 to be administering his father's dyeshop, so he could easily have had a daughter near Catherine's age. Nanna was in Florence at the time the letter was addressed to her. She is called "a virgin" in that letter.

NANNI DI SER VANNI SAVINI
A friend of the Salimbeni family and several times imprisoned by the commune of Siena. He was first sent to Catherine by persuasion of William Flete and converted by Catherine in Raimondo's presence—who then remained Nanni's confessor "for several years." He donated the fortress of Belcaro to Catherine for the establishment of her monastery of Santa Maria degli Angeli (1377).

[22] *Processo Castellano*, ed. Laurent, p. 89.

NELLA DI NICCOLÒ DEI BUONCONTI: Letters T151, T161, T167
Wife of Niccolò dei Buonconti of Pisa. She was widowed probably early in 1376.

NERA SER MICHELIS: Letter T125
She is named as prioress of the Sienese *Mantellate* in the rubric of Let. T125. At the time that letter was written, however, the office was held by Monna Caterina di Ranuccio Saracini, who had been a member of the group at least since 1252, so it may, in spite of the rubric, be to her that the letter is addressed. Dupré Theseider (unpublished notes) states that the prioress to whom this letter is addressed "must be Nera ser Michelis from the list of *Mantellate*, among the oldest by entrance even from the end of 1352, because she is in group A." Nera is not, however, designated as prioress in the 1353 list; the title is given rather to the first name (illegible) on that list.[23]

NERI DI LANDOCCIO PAGLIARESI: Letters T42, T46, T99, T106, T178, T186, T192, T212, T228, T269, T281
A young Sienese nobleman and poet, Catherine's disciple and scribe "almost from the beginning."[24] Letter T99 is Catherine's response to Neri's request to be accepted as her disciple. He served in public office often in Siena (see introduction to Letter T99). After Catherine's death he became a hermit, first at Agromaggio near Florence and later nearer to Siena. He was responsible for much of the earliest gathering and dissemination of Catherine's correspondence. He died on 12 March 1406 and was buried in the Olivetan cemetery outside Siena's Porta Tufi.

NICCOLÒ DEI BUONCONTI
The noble mercantile Buonconti family exercised great power in Pisa. They also owned the Monastery of Berardegna near Siena. Niccolò was father of Gherardo Buonconti, Catherine's host in Pisa in 1375.

NICCOLÒ DEI STROZZI: Letter T256
Commander and prior of the Paduan Hospitalers (Knights of St. John). He may have died in Epirus during 1378, for he is not heard of again from that point on.

NICCOLÒ DI NANNI DE SER VANNI: Letter T287
Son of Catherine's disciple and benefactor Nanni di Ser Vanni Savini,

---

[23] Laurent, *Fontes*, I, *Documenti*, pp. 23, 47.
[24] *Libellus de Supplemento*, III, vi, vii, p. 390.

and monk of Monteoliveto Maggiore near Siena. One of two copies of the letter is addressed to him, the tone of which indicates that he became a Benedictine at Catherine's urging.

NICCOLÒ DI RUGGERO (GERI) SODERINI: Letters T131, T171, T247
A wealthy and prominent Florentine Guelph, frequently a moderating voice in the councils of the party. Catherine quite probably met him and his family during her stay in Florence in May 1374 and often turned to him for support in her dealings with the city. He died just two years after Catherine, in 1382.

NICCOLÒ DI TOLDO
A young Perugian, he had become associated with the court of Sienese senator Pietro Marchese del Monte Santa Maria—perhaps even as an agent of the Perugian papal vicar Gérard du Puy. The *Riformatori*, the ruling party of Siena, were at the time particularly leery of any outside interference in their affairs, and so, when the young Perugian "defamed" the senator, he was arrested and sentenced to death for treason, a sentence eventually concurred in by Gérard du Puy. In Letter T273 Catherine writes to Raimondo da Capua of her ministry to the young man in prison and at his execution.

NICOLÒ DI GHIDA: Letter T189
Monk of Monteoliveto Maggiore near Siena. The letter is addressed to him and others of the same monastery.

NICOLÒ DI PIERO: Letter T36
A young Florentine recommended to the Olivetan order by Catherine in 1378. He became a novice at that order's monastery of San Michele in Bosco near Bologna. The letter is addressed to him and other novices there.

NIERA DI GHERARDO GAMBACORTA: Letter T155
Wife of Gherardo, brother of Piero Gambacorta of Pisa.

NINO DI PUCCETTO DA SPAZZAVENTO: Letter T158
Chaplain of the cathedral in Pisa. A generous man, he gave to the Pisan Carthusians his inheritances from his father and his merchant brother-in-law, Pietro Mirante Virginis, money which helped to build the beautiful monastery of Calci just outside the city. In 1381 he gave the monks there everything he owned, and established the Company of the Stigmata in honor of St. Francis and perhaps also in honor of Catherine of Siena, who had died the previous year. Catherine may have met him during her 1375 stay in Pisa.

PANTASILEA DI RANUCCIO DA FARNESE: Letter T116

Wife of Ranuccio da Farnese and daughter of Agnolino di Giovanni Salimbeni of Siena and Rocca d'Orcia.

PAVOLA DA SIENA: Letters T97, T144

Caffarini names several Florentines who knew Catherine, among them the nuns of the monastery of Santa Maria near Fiesole in the hills above Florence.[25] Dupré Theseider concludes that the Monna Pavola to whom Letter T144 is addressed is from this monastery, and that the title *Monna* designates her as prioress. However, there is no reason not to suppose that Letter T97 is written to the same Monna Pavola, and in that letter one of her "daughters," Bartolomea, is also referred to as *Monna*, so the title cannot, at least in this instance, imply the office of monastic prioress. In Letter Gardner VI (T89), a Monna Pavola from Florence, who Catherine says is in Rome at the time she is writing (May 1379), is said to be "of the monastery of Santo Giorgio," not Santa Maria (and her servant is called "Monna Andrea"). There is no reason not to assume that we are dealing with the same person in each case. Who then is she? Because she is referred to as having "daughters," she is certainly a prioress, either of a monastery or of a group of *Mantellate*. In Letter T144 she and her daughters are invited to prepare to go on a crusade, and it is clear from T97 and other letters that Pavola on at least one occasion travels to Rome. This would not necessarily mean that she and her companions are not nuns. Yet it does not seem too likely that Catherine would refer to her as being "of" a monastery if she were not a nun.

PIERRE D'ESTAING: Letters T7, T11

A Benedictine descended from an illustrious French family. Having been archbishop of Bourges since 1368, he was made cardinal by Pope Urban V in June 1370, and shortly thereafter appointed vicar general to the south of Italy, an appointment confirmed by Gregory XI at his accession to the papacy in January 1371. At the end of 1371 Gregory relieved him of that post and appointed him his vicar general and legate to Bologna. In September 1373 he was named cardinal bishop of Ostia, while still retaining the legation to Bologna until early 1374. He was in Avignon at the time of Catherine's stay there in 1376, and was delegated, along with Cardinal Giles Aycelin de Montaigu, to negotiate with the Florentine ambassadors after the latter had disavowed Cathe-

[25] *Processo Castellano* ed. Laurent, p. 82.

rine's authority to mediate their cause. He was the only French cardinal to support Gregory's return to Rome, and on 21 December 1376 he, along with Cardinals Corsini and Tebaldeschi, won the submission of Rome to Gregory. He died on 25 November 1377 at his titular church in Rome, Santa Maria in Trastevere. The *Cronaca di Bologna* describes d'Estaing as "a very great and upright man ... [with] great legatorial powers, and more authority from the pope than had ever been given to any other representative of the Church."[26] Ammirato Scipione calls him "a man of large heart and great wisdom,"[27] though he could be somewhat overbearing.

PIERO GAMBACORTA: Letter T149

Having assumed power in Pisa in 1370, he championed the papal cause against the Visconti and refused to aid Siena in its defense against the pro-papal Salimbeni in October 1374. Also in 1374 he was apparently the first to invite Catherine to come to Pisa, but Catherine declined that invitation (in Let. T149) citing the risk of scandal.

PIETRO DI GIOVANNI DI VIVA: Letter T287a

Monk of the Carthusian monastery at Maggiano near Siena, and eventually its prior.

PIETRO DEL MONTE SANTA MARIA: T135, T148, T170, T180

Senator in Siena from 18 February 1375 until 18 August 1377. It is obvious from Catherine's four extant letters to him that she respected him and found him a trustworthy ally. In fact, he was on one occasion criticized in Florentine circles for what was seen as his excessive loyalty to the papacy even as they praised him for his virtue. He is the senator with whose court Niccolò di Toldo was associated (cf. Letter T273). Catherine's disciple Neri di Landoccio Pagliaresi also worked under him as a member of the *Consiglio generale* of Siena.

PIETRO DI GIOVANNI VENTURA: Letters T47, T332

An early disciple of Catherine. Sometime after having been converted by her, he became a Dominican friar and is sometimes mentioned as serving as Catherine's emissary. He eventually contributed testimony to the *Processo Castellano*.

---

[26] Della Pugliola, *Cronaca di Bologna*, in *Rerum Italicarum Scriptores*, ed. Muratori, XVIII, coll. 491.

[27] *Istorie Fiorentine*, pt. 1, vol. ii, p. 680.

PIETRO DI MISSERE IACOMO ATTAGHUFI DEI TOLOMEI: Letter T254

Friend of the Florentine prefect Francesco di Vico to whom Catherine appealed for clemency when Luigi, the brother of Raimondo da Capua, had been imprisoned and could not afford the fine exacted.

PIETRO DI TOMMASO CORSINI: Letter T177

Member of one of the old aristocratic families of Florence and bishop of Florence (1363–1370), he was named cardinal in 1369 and bishop of Porto in 1374. Diplomatically astute but of slight moral courage, during the War of the Eight he pleaded with the Florentines to make peace with the pope, but not at the expense of their own interests. He eventually sided with the Clementine cause against Urban VI.

RABE DI FRANCESCO DI TATO TOLOMEI: Letter T120

Born Rabe degli Agazzari. Mother of three of Catherine's disciples: the *Mantellate* Francesca and Ghinoccia, and the friar Matteo. ("Rabe" is a nickname for Orrabile, from Onorabile.)

RAIMONDO DELLE VIGNE DA CAPUA (c.1330–1399): Letters T100, T102, T104, T211, T219, T226, T267, T272, T273, T275, T280, T295, T330, T333, T344, T373

Destined for a legal career, he studied law at Bologna, but after some time abandoned those studies and entered the Dominican Order. In 1374 he was appointed by the Master of the Order, Élias de Toulouse, to be Catherine's confessor and sole authority within the order over her spiritual life and her activities. Certainly he was a major factor in the expansion of Catherine's ministry to ever broader arenas of ecclesiastical and civil affairs. Shortly after her death in 1380 he was elected Master of the Order. He composed a life of Catherine (the *Legenda Major*), begun in 1385 and completed in 1395.

RANIERI: Letter T159

Known only by his given name, he was rector of the church of Santa Cristina in Pisa before joining the Dominicans at the Church of Santa Caterina in the same city. He entered the order on 7 March at the age of thirty-six, and died in Pisa on the same feast at the age of fifty-six.

ROMANO: Letter T72

A flax dresser of the Company of the Bigallo in Florence. The letter concerns his intent to become a religious.

SALVI DI PIETRO: Letter T122
Goldsmith and member of the Company of the Virgin at Santa Maria della Scala in Siena.

SAMUELLE DA RIMINI: Letters Gardner II, III
Doctor of Laws, probably in Bologna.

SANO DI MACO DI MAZZACORNO: Letters T62, T69, T142, T147, T232, T294, T303, T318
A wool-worker and (from at least 1365 on) a member of the Company of the Virgin Mary, a lay confraternity at La Scala Hospital in Siena. He is frequently mentioned in Catherinian sources, and Catherine often directed to him letters intended for her entire Sienese circle.

SANTI DA TERAMO
The Sienese hermit (known as Fra Santi) at whose hermitage Catherine did much of her dictating of *The Dialogue* after her return from Florence. He was an associate of Giovanni Colombini and of the Carthusian Pietro Petroni, at whose death he assisted.

SIMONE DI GIOVANNI: Letter T36
A novice of the Monteolivetan monastery of San Michele in Bosco near Bologna. The letter is addressed to him and other novices there.

SIMONE DI NERI DA CORTONA: Letter T56
A very sensitive young Dominican, he was always fearful of falling out of Catherine's good graces and extremely dependent on expressions of her affection. Innocenzo Taurisano states that Simone was a priest as of 16 June 1374.[28] He may have been ordained about that time, very possibly at Pentecost of that year, 21 May, having been professed as early as 1370 or 1371. After Catherine's death he contributed personal testimony to the *Processo Castallano*. Only Letter T56 is addressed to him, but he is greeted in a number of other letters.

SPINELLO DEI TOLOMEI: Letter T123
A leading citizen of Montepulciano, counted as an enemy of the Sienese government even as late as 1384, but also at odds with the Salimbeni who were living in exile from Siena. He is referred to in the letter.

---

[28] *Santa Caterina nei ricordi dei discepoli*, p. 12. (Taurisano does not give his source.)

STEFANO DI CORRADO MACONI (1347–1424): Letters T195, T205, T222, T298, T319, T320, T324, T329, T332, T365, T368, T369
A member of the lesser nobility of Siena, he became Catherine's disciple early in 1376, having been sent to her by his mother for help in resolving a feud between the Tolomei and the Rinaldini. That spring he accompanied her to Florence and Avignon, probably already beginning to serve as one of her scribes. He was with her also in the Orcia Valley and during much of her 1378 stay in Florence, serving as one of the three principal scribes for her *Dialogue*. After her death he followed her urging that he enter the Carthusian Order, evenually becoming prior of Pontignano, north of Siena, and of Pavia. He was responsible for a major collection of Catherine's letters and contributed testimony to the *Processo Castellano*. He died at Pavia.

STRICCA DI CIONE DI SANDRO SALIMBENI: Letter T110
Wife of Cione di Sandro Salimbeni, lord of Castelioncello di Trinoro.

TADDEO DEI MALAVOLTI: Letter T187
Native of Siena and Carthusian monk of Belriguardo near Siena.

TOMMASO D'ALVIANO: Letters T191, T259
Son of Ugolinaccio lord of Alviano, he was born at the castle there in the early mid-fourteenth century. In 1341 he entered the service of Matteo Orsini, and at some point became a mercenary fighter. In 1366 he was elected Captain of the People in Florence, and in 1377 was appointed ecclesiastical administrator of Orvieto and commissary of Pierre d'Estaing, Cardinal of Ostia.[29]

TOMMASO D'ANTONIO DA SIENA (CAFFARINI): Letter T325
Dominican friar of San Domenico in Siena, an early disciple of Catherine and later the chief promoter of her cult. He was responsible for the solicitation of testimony for the *Processo Castellano* compiled in support of her cause for canonization, an amplification on Raimondo da Capua's *Legenda Major* called the *Libellus de Supplemento*, and a major collection of her letters (S2/S3).

[29] Note to the letters of Colluccio Salutati, I, 50; Pompeo Litta, *Famiglie celebre degli Italiani*, viii. Cf. also A. Theiner, *Codex diplomaticus dominii temporalis S. Sedis*, II, 378, where Tommaso is said to have been, in 1359, in possession of landed properties belonging to Giovanni da Vico. All of the above cited by E. Seckendorff, *Politische Tätigkeit*, p. 75, n. 37.

TOMMASO DALLA FONTE: Letters T25, T41, T98, T139, T283
Catherine's cousin and her first confessor, for whom she always had a special affection. He came to live with Catherine's parents in 1349, having been orphaned during the plague of 1348 at age ten. Later he joined the Order of Preachers at the Church of San Domenico just up the hill from the Benincasa home. While serving as Catherine's confessor, he kept notes concerning her spiritual life; these notes were later used by Raimondo da Capua as he composed his *Legenda major*, but the notes themselves have not survived.

TOMMASO DI GUELFACCIO (also spelled Guelfuccio)
He served as Catherine's courier to carry Let. T252/DT88 to Gregory XI at Corneto, and also as courier for the Sienese government to carry the communication to which Catherine responded with Let. T123.

TORA TRENTA: Letter DTI
Mother of Giovanna di Giovanni Trenta of Lucca.

TRINCIO DE' TRINCI DA FULIGNO: Letter T253
Lord of Fuligno and a *gonfaloniere* (standard-bearer) of the Church, a ferocious despot. On 28 September 1377, the enemies of the Trinci rose against them and Trincio was stabbed to death, and his body hurled from the balcony into the piazza below, where it would remain for several days unburied. His wife was Jacoma d'Este. The letter is addressed to him and his brother Corrado.

URBAN VI, POPE (1318–1389): Letters T291, T302, T305, T306, T346, T351, T364, T370, T371
Born Bartolomeo Prignano, he was named archbishop of Acerenza in 1363 and archbishop of Bari in 1377. An efficient and hard-working chancellor to Pope Gregory XI, he was known as a reformer. After a tumultuous and enigmatic conclave following Gregory's death, he was elected pope on 8 April 1378. By summer he was seen as violent and by some even as mentally deranged. On 2 August the French cardinals gathered in Anagni declared his election invalid and named him antipope. On 20 September Robert de Génève was elected to oppose him, taking the name Clement VII. Catherine and her followers supported Urban's legitimacy, but his papacy continued to lose ground. He spent his last years in Lucca (1387), Perugia (1388), and finally back in Rome, where he died (perhaps poisoned) on 15 October 1389.

WILLIAM FLETE (GUGLIELMO D'INGHILTERRA) (c.1325–c.1390): Letters T55, T64, T66, T77, T227, T292, T326

He became an Augustinian about 1339 and was sent to qualify for a master's degree at Cambridge. He had completed all of the requirements for the degree except for the final exercises when, disillusioned with academic life, he migrated to Tuscany and joined the monastery of his order at Lecetto. (He was ever after familiarly called *il baccelliere*, "the bachelor."). Catherine made his acquaintance very early in her public life. She seems to have found him a good partner in conversation, and he in turn exercised a profound influence on her, especially in regard to Augustinian thought. The two were temporarily alienated when in late 1379 William declined Catherine's invitation to come to Rome as part of a "council of the servants of God," a project he roundly criticized as unwise. In general, however, William was one of Catherine's staunchest defenders both during and after her life.

Bibliography

Patristic and Medieval Works Cited as Possible Catherinian Sources

Albertus Magnus (Albert the Great). *Sermones de tempore et de sanctis.* Augsburg: Johann Wiener, [c. 1476].

Augustinus, Aurelius (Augustine of Hippo). *Confessiones.* PL XXXII; also *The Confessions of Augustine*, ed. John Gibb; text in Latin, introduction and notes in English. New York: Garland, 1980.

——. *Contra Faustum.* PL XLII; also in *Sancti Aurelii Augustini hipponensis episcopi Opera omnia.* Paris: apud editorem, 1841–1842.

——. *De doctrina christiana.* PL XXXIV; also in *Sancti Aurelii Augustini hipponensis episcopi Opera omnia.* Paris: apud editorem, 1841–1842.

——. *De Trinitate.* PL XLII; also in *Sancti Aurelii Augustini hipponensis episcopi Opera omnia.* Paris: apud editorem, 1841–1842.

——. *Enarrationes in Psalmos.* PL XXXVII; also in *Sancti Aurelii Augustini hipponensis episcopi Opera omnia.* Paris: apud editorem, 1841–1842.

——. *In Ioannis evangelium tractatus.* PL XXXV; also in *Sancti Aurelii Augustini hipponensis episcopi Opera omnia.* Paris: apud editorem, 1841–1842.

——. *Meditationes.* PL XL; also in *Sancti Aurelii Augustini hipponensis episcopi Opera omnia.* Paris: apud editorem, 1841–1842.

——. *Propositio ex Epistole ad Romanos.* PL XXXV; also in *Sancti Aurelii Augustini hipponensis episcopi Opera omnia.* Paris: apud editorem, 1841–1842.

——. *Sermones.* PL XXXVIII–XXXIX; also in *Sancti Aurelii Augustini hipponensis episcopi Opera omnia.* Paris: apud editorem, 1841–1842.

——. *Soliloquia.* PL XXXII; also in *Sancti Aurelii Augustini hipponensis episcopi Opera omnia.* Paris: apud editorem, 1841–1842.

Augustinus, pseudo (Pseudo-Augustine). *Ad fratres in eremo sermones.* PL XL.

——. *Meditationes.* PL XL.

Belcari, Maffeo (Feo) de. *Vita del Beato Giovanni Colombini, fondatore de' Poveri Gesuati. Con parte della vita di alcuni primi suoi compagni [Parte della vita di alcuni Gesuati].* Milan: G. Silvestri, 1832.

Bernard de Clairvaux. *De caritate*. PL CLXXXIV; also in *Sancti Bernardi Opera*, ed. J. Leclercq, C. H. Talbot, H. Rochais. Rome: Editiones Cestercienses, 1957–1978 (8 vols.).

——. *De diligendo Deo*. PL CLXXXII; also in *Sancti Bernardi Opera*, ed. J. Leclercq, C. H. Talbot, H. Rochais. Rome: Editiones Cestercienses, 1957–1978 (8 vols.).

——. *De gradibus humilitatis et superbiae*. PL CLXXXII; also in *Sancti Bernardi Opera*, ed. J. Leclercq, C. H. Talbot, H. Rochais. Rome: Editiones Cestercienses, 1957–1978 (8 vols.).

——. *Sermones de tempore et de sanctis diversis*. PL CLXXXIII; also in *Sancti Bernardi Opera*, ed. J. Leclercq, C. H. Talbot, H. Rochais. Rome: Editiones Cestercienses, 1957–1978 (8 vols.).

Bernardino da Siena. *Predicazioni*, in *Opera omnia, iussu et aurtoritate Pacifici M. Peratoni*. Florentiae: Ad Claras Aquas, 1950– .

Bernardus, pseudo. *Vitis mystica*. PL CLXXXIV.

Il bestiario toscano secondo la lezione dei codici di Parigi e di Roma. . . . , ed. M. S. Garver, K. McKenzie. Rome: Società filologica romana, 1912.

Bianco da Siena. *Laude mistiche*, ed. Gennaro Maria Monte Lanciano. [n.p.]: G. Carabba, [1925].

——. *Laude spirituali*. Lucca: Tipi di G. Giusti, 1851.

——. "Lauda alla Beata Caterina da Siena," in *Laude spirituali*. Lucca: Tipi di G. Giusti, 1851.

Bonaventura (Bonaventure, attrib.). *Meditazioni vitae Christi*. Paris: Pierre Levet for Denis Roce, 5 May 1497.

Cavalca, Domenico. *Ammonimento a S. Paula*, in *Opere di frate Domenico Cavalca*, ed. Bartolomeo Sorio, A. Racheli. Trieste: Sezione letterario-artistica del Lloyd Austriaco, 1858.

Cavalca, Domenico (attrib.). *Descrizione de' dieci comandamenti*, in *Opere di frate Domenico Cavalca*, ed. Bartolomeo Sorio, A. Racheli. Trieste: Sezione letterario-artistica del Lloyd Austriaco, 1858.

——. *Disciplina degli spirituali*. Milan: Giovanni Silvestri, 1838.

——. *Medicina del cuore, ovvero trattato della pazienza*. Milan: Giovanni Silvestri, 1838.

——. *Pungilingua*. Milan: Giovanni Silvestri, 1837.

——. *Lo specchio dei peccati*. Milan: Giovanni Silvestri, 1838.

——. *Lo specchio di croce*. Brescia: Moro e Falsina, 1822.

——. *Trattato della mondizia del cuore*. Giovanni Silvestri, 1853.

——. *Trattato dello Spirito Santo*. Imola: Tipi d'I. Galeati, 1886.

——. *Trenta stoltizie*, in *Opere di frate Domenico Cavalca*, ed. Bartolomeo Sorio, A. Racheli. Trieste: Sezione letterario-artistica del Lloyd Austriaco, 1858.

Dante Alighieri. *La Divina Commedia*, ed., trans. Louis Biancolli, Italian and English. New York: Washington Square Press, [1966].

Delizie degli Eruditi toscani, pubblicate e di osservazioni storiche e critiche accresciute da fr. Ildefonso di San Luigi. Florence: Gaetano Cambiagi, 1770–1789.

Dionysius Areopagita (Pseudo-Denis). *De divino nomine* (*Patrologia Cursus Completus, Series Graeca*, III). Also *Il testo tachigrafico del De Divinis nominibus*. Città del Vaticano: Biblioteca apostolica vaticana, 1970. English: *The Divine Names*, trans. John D. Jones. Milwaukee: Marquette University Press, 1980.

Filippo degli Agazzari da Siena. *Gli Assempri, leggende del secolo xiv*, ed. C. F. Carpellini, Siena: I. Gati, 1864.

Fortunatus, Venantius. *Opera*. Paris: Apud editorem, 1850 (also PL LXXXVIII).

Giordano da Rivalto. *Prediche sulla Genesi recitate in Firenze M.CCC.IV dal b. Giordano da Rivalto dell'Ordine dei Predicatori, ora per la prima volta pubblicate*, ed. Domenico Moreni. Florence: Magheri, 1830.

——. *Prediche del beato Giordano da Rivalto, dell'Ordine dei Predicatori recitate in Firenze dal MCCCIII al MCCCVI/Ed per la prima volta pubblicate*, [ed. Domenico Moreni], 2 vols.

——. *Prediche inedite dal b. Giordano da Rivalto dell'Ordine de' Predicatori, recitate in Firenze dal 1302 al 1305 e pubblicate per cura di Enrico Narducci*, ed. Enrico Narducci (vol. 16 of *Collezione di opere inedite o rare dei primi tre secoli della lingua*). Bologna: G. Romagnoli, 1867.

——. *Tre prediche inedite del b. Giordano da Rivalto*, ed. Enrico Narducci. Rome: Tip. delle belle arti, 1857.

Giovanni Colombini. *Le lettere*, ed. Adolfo Bartoli. Lucca: Balatresi, 1856.

Giovanni dalle Celle. *Lettere del beato Don Giovanni dalle Celle monaco Vallombrosiano*, ed. Bartolomeo Sorio. Rome: Tipografia dei classici sacri, 1845.

——. *Lettere*, ed. Cividali, Pia, in "Beato Giovanni dalle Celle." Atti della R. Accademia dei Lincei, Memorie, ser. V, vol. XII, 1906, pp. 354–477.

Giovanni Dominici. *Il libro d'amore di carità*. Bologna: Romagnoli dall'Acqua, 1889.

Gregorius I, Magnus (Gregory the Great). *Libri moralium*. PL LXXVI.

Humbert de Romans. *Opera de Vita Regulari*, ed. J. J. Berthier (2 vols.). Rome: A. Befani. 1888–1889; reprint Torino: Marietti, 1956.

Iacopo da Varazze (Jacobus de Varagine). *Legenda aurea sanctorum sive lombardica historia*. Strassburg: Printer of the 1483 Jordanus, 1483.

Ludolphus de Saxonia. *Vita Christi*. Nuremburg: Anton Koberger, 1478.

Migne, J. P., ed. *Patrologiae Cursus Completus, Series Graeca*. Tournhout: Brepols, 1969.

——. *Patrologiae Cursus Completus, Series Latina*. Paris: Garnier Frères, 1958– .

Passavanti, Jacopo. *Lo specchio di vera penitentia: Trattati della superbia,*

della umilità, e della vanagloria. Florence: Tartini e Franchi, 1725.
Petrus Lombardus (Peter Lombard). *Magistri Petri Lombardi sententiae in 4 libris distinctae.* Grottaferrata, Editiones Collegii S. Bonaventurae ad Claras Aquas, 1971.
Sacchetti, Franco. *I sermoni evangelici, le lettere, ed altri scritti inediti o rari di Franco Sacchetti, raccolti e pubblicati, con un discorso intorno la vita e le sue opere, per Ottavio Gigli*, ed. Ottavio Gigli. Florence: F. Le Monnier, 1857.
——. *Sposizioni di Vangeli*, in *Opere*, ed. Aldo Borlenghi. Milano: Rizzoli, 1951.
Simone Fidati da Cascia. *Expositiones super totum corpus evangeliorum*, in *Il Beato Simone Fidati da Cascia*, ed. Niccola Mattioli. Rome: Antologia Agostiniana 2, 1898.
——. *Ordine della vita cristiana*, ed. Arrigo Levasti, in *Mistici del duecento e del trecento*, 2nd ed., pp. 607–680. Roma/Milano: Rizzoli & Co. 1937.
Thomas Aquinas. *Angelici doctoris Thomae Aquinatis Summa Theologica, cum commentariis Thomae de Vio Card. Cajetani*. Rome: n.p., 1773.
Vincent de Beauvais. *Speculum naturale.* Strassburg: Adolf Rusch, 1478.

General Bibliography, Selected

Acta Sanctorum (*AA.SS.*). Antwerp: Ioannes Meursium, 1643– .
Alessandrini, A. "Il ritorno dei Papi da Avignone e S. Caterina da Siena." *Archivio deputazione romana storia patria*, 1933–1934, pp. 1–132.
Annales Ordinis Cartusiensis ab anno 1084 ad annum 1429. ed. Charles Le Couteulx. Monstrolli: Typis Cartusiae S. Mariae de Pratis, 1887–1891.
Anodal, Gabriella. "Immagini del linguaggio cateriniano e le loro fonti: la chiave." *Rassegna di ascetica e mistica* 22 (1971), pp. 243–254.
——. "Immagini del linguaggio cateriniani e le loro fonti: la madre." *Rassegna di ascetica e mistica* 22 (1971), pp. 227–343.
——. "Immagini del linguaggio cateriniano e le loro fonti: la scala." *Rassegna di ascetica e mistica* 23 (1972), pp. 332–343.
——. "Il libro." *L'arbore della carita*, sp. num., 1970 (Rome: Centro nazionale di studi cateriniani), pp. 68–71.
——. *Il linguaggio cateriniano: indice delle immagini.* Siena: Cantagalli, 1983.
Antonelli, M. "La dominazione pontificia nel Patrimonio negli ultimi venti anni del periodo avignonese." *Archivio della R. Società Romana di Storia Patria* XXX (1907), pp. 269–332, 121–168, 315–355.
Anziani, Jeanne. "La città di S. Caterina." *Bulletino senese di storia Patria* 120, n. 19 (1909), pp. 1–41.
Archivio dello Stato di Siena, Diplomatico, Pergamene di S. Marta. Siena.
Baglione, Astorre. "S. Caterina da Siena e l'Ordine della Certosa," *Inquadramenti storici.* Rome: Edizioni cateriniane, 1975, pp. 65–108.

Baluze, Étienne (Stephanus Baluzius). *Vitae Paparum Avenionensium*, ed. G. Mollat (new ed., 4 vols.). Paris: Librairie Letouzey et Ané, 1914–1927.

Bartoli, P. *Istoria di S. Agnesa di Montepulciano con delle memorie della medesima città e suoi uomini illustri*. Siena: Rossi, n.d.

Battisti, Carlo. "Parlata senese e Santa Caterina." *Studi Cateriniani* 11 (1935), pp. 67–82.

Batzill, Hartmann. *Heilige Sehnsucht: die Gebetsweise der Heiligen Katharina von Siena, dargestellt nach ihren Briefen*. Freiburg/Schweiz: Kanisius-Verlag, [1951?].

Becker, M. "Church and State in Florence on the Eve of the Renaissance (1343–1382)." *Speculum* 37 (1962), pp. 509–527.

Beckwith, Sara. *Christ's Body: Identity, Culture and Society in Late Medieval Writings*. London and New York: Routledge, 1993.

Bell, Rudolph M. *Holy Anorexia*. Chicago/London: University of Chicago Press, 1985.

Bianco, Maria Grazia. "Temi patristici in Santa Caterina." *Congresso internazionale di studi cateriniani, Siena-Roma, 24-29 aprile 1980: Atti*. Rome: Curia generalizia O.P., 1981, pp. 60–75.

Bonifacio, Gaetano. "Santa Caterina e l'isola di Gorgona." *Bollettino Storico Livornese* 4 (1940), pp. 136–140.

Brezzi, Paolo. "Azione politica di s. Caterina da Siena nella storia del suo tempo," in *Inquadramenti storici*. Rome: Edizioni cateriniane, 1975, pp. 7–29.

Brizio, Elena. *Siena nel secondo Trecento: Organismi istituzionali e personale politico dalla caduta dei Dodici alla dominazione viscontea (1368–1399)*. Università degli Studi di Firenze, 1991–1992.

Brucker, Gene A. *Florentine Politics and Society, 1343–1378*. Princeton: Princeton University Press, 1962.

Buonsignori, Vincenzo. *Storia della repubblica di Siena esposta in compendio da V. Buonsignori*. Siena: G. Landi, 1856.

Cabrol, Fernand, and Henri Leclercq. *Dictionnaire d'archéologie chrétienne et de liturgie*. Paris: Letouzey et Ane, 1907– .

Caffarini, cf. Tommaso di Antonio da Siena.

Camaiori, C. "Memorie storiche di Belcaro." *Bullettino Senese di Storia Patria* 20 (1913), pp. 365–367.

Canestrelli, Antonio. *L'abbazia di Sant'Antimo*. Siena: Rivista Siena monumentale editrice, 1910–1912.

Canigiani, Barduccio. *Transito di Santa Caterina*. (This letter to Suor Caterina Petriboni is included in a collection in the *Biblioteca comunale* of Siena, MS.T.II, 7. It was first printed in Aldo Manuzio's edition of the *Epistolario* in 1500. It can be found in English as an appendix to Algar Thorold's translation of *The Dialogue* [all editions], and in Italian in *Lettere*, ed. Tommasèo/Misciattelli, vol. VI, pp. 148–153.)

Carapelli, Angiolo Maria. *Cronotassi della vita di S. Caterina*. Biblioteca Comunale of Siena, MS. T.I.8.
Caterina da Siena. *Briefe der heiligen Caterina von Sienna*, trans. Annette Kolb. Berlin: Hyperion, 1919.
——. *Il Dialogo della divina provvidenza ovvero Libro della divina dottrina*, ed. Giuliana Cavallini. Rome: Edizioni cateriniani, 1968; 2nd ed., Siena: Cantagalli, 1995.
——. *The Dialogue of Catherine of Siena*, trans. Suzanne Noffke. New York: Paulist, 1980.
——. *L'Epistolario di Santa Caterina da Siena*, ed. Eugenio Dupré Theseider: Fonti per la storia d'Italia, pubblicate dal R. Istituto storico italiano per il medio evo. Rome: nella sede dell'Istituto, 1940 (only one of 4 projected volumes).
——. *I, Catherine: Selected Writings of Catherine of Siena*, trans. Kenelm Foster, Mary John Ronayne. London: Collins, 1980.
——. *Lettere*, ed. Lodovico Ferretti. Siena: Tipografia S. Caterina, 1927.
——. *Lettere di S. Caterina da Siena, ridotte a miglior lezione, e in ordine nuovo disposte con note di Niccolo Tommasèo*, ed. Piero Misciattelli. Siena: Giuntini & Bentivoglio, 1913–1922 (6 vols.).
——. *The Letters of St. Catherine of Siena*, ed. Suzanne Noffke, vol. I [1st ed.]. Binghamton: Medieval & Renaissance Texts & Studies, 1988.
——. *Opere di Santa Caterina da Siena, nuovamente pubblicate da Girolamo Gigli*. Siena, Lucca: n.p., 1707–1721 (4 vols.).
——. *The Prayers of Catherine of Siena*, trans. Suzanne Noffke. New York: Paulist, 1983.
——. *Santa Caterina da Siena: Epistolario*, ed. Umberto Meattini. Rome: Edizioni Paoline, 1979.
——. *Selected Letters of Catherine Benincasa: Saint Catherine of Siena as Seen in her Letters*, trans. Vida Scudder. London: J. M. Dent & Sons, Ltd., and New York: E. P. Dutton, 1927.
Cavallini, Giuliana. "Consonanze tomistiche nel linguaggio cateriniano: ‹‹Le vere e reali virtù››." *Rassegna di ascetica e mistica* 25 (1974), pp. 73–82.
——. "Dottrina dell'amore in S. Caterina da Siena: concordanze col pensiero di S. Tommaso d'Aquino." *Divus Thomas* LXXV (1972), pp. 369–388.
——. "Fonti neotestamentarie degli scritti cateriniani." *Congresso internazionale di studi cateriniani, Siena- Roma, 24-29 aprile 1980: Atti*. Rome: Curia generalizia O.P., 1981, pp. 44–59.
Centi, Tito S. "Luci e ombre sul tomismo do s. Caterina da Siena." *Congresso internazionale di studi cateriniani, Siena/Roma, 24–29 aprile 1980: Atti*. Rome: Curia generalizia O.P., 1981, pp. 76–92.
Cerasoli, F. "Gregorio XI e Giovanna I Regina di Napoli: documenti in-

editi dell'Archivio Vaticano." *Archivio Storico per le Provincie Napoletane*, 25 (1900), pp. 6–8.

Chiavacci, Gaetano. "La seconda lettera di S. Caterina a Papa Gregorio XI (T106)." *Studi cateriniani* 10 (1934), pp. 1–21.

Conti, F. "Frate Tommaso d'Antonio e il suo Supplementum." *Santa Caterina da Siena* 3 (1951), pp. 16–25, 51–55.

——. "La ‹‹Legenda B. Catharinae senensis›› di fr. Raimondo da Capua." *Santa Caterina da Siena* 4 (1952), pp. 5–28.

Cristofano di Gano Guidini. *Memorie di ser Cristofano*, ed. Innocenzo Taurisano. Fioretti di Santa Caterina da Siena (2nd ed.), pp. 111–134. Rome: Ferrari, 1927.

Cronaca di Perugia. In *Archivio Storico Italiano*, ser. I, vol. 16.

D'Urso, Giacinto. "Cristo scala di perfezione." *Nuovi Studi Cateriniani* 2. Siena: Cantagalli, 1985, pp. 134–144.

——. *Il genio di Santa Caterina: Studi sulla sua dottrina e personalità*. Rome: Edizioni Cateriniane, 1971.

——. "L'itinerario ascetico di S. Caterina da Siena," in Colosio, Innocenzo (ed.), *Saggi sulla Spiritualita Domenicana*, pp. 100-104. Florence: Lib. Ed. Fiorentina, 1961. (Reprinted from *Rivista di ascetica e mistica* 4, 5 (1961).

——, trans., ed. *La lettera a Raimondo da Capua in lode di Caterina da Siena*. Florence: Tipografica Baccini & Chiappi, 1974 (originally in *Rassegna di ascetica e mistica* 24 (1973), pp. 241–254, 349–358.

De Sanctis, Francesco. *Storia della letteratura italiana*. Milan: Antonio Vallardi, [1942].

Della Pugliola. *Cronaca di Bologna*, in *Rerum Italicarum Scriptores*, ed. Muratori, XVIII.

Denis-Boulet, Noële M[aurice]. *La carrière politique de Ste. Catherine de Sienne*. Paris-Bruges: Desclée, de Brouwer & cie, 1939.

——. "Sainte Catherine di Sienne: le problème historique. L'activité politique de sainte Catherine avant son voyage à Avignon." *Nova et Vetera* 11–12 (1936–37), pp. 361–368, 406–448.

Diario d'Anonimo Fiorentino dall'anno 1358 al 1389, ed. Marco Tabarrini. *Cronache dei secoli XIII e XIV*. Florence: Tipi di M. Cellini, 1876.

Documenti, ed. M. Hyacinthus Laurent. *Fontes vitae s. Catharinae Senensis historici*, vol. I. Siena: R. Università di Siena, 1936.

Drane, Augusta Theodosia. *The History of St. Catherine of Siena and Her Companions*. London: Longmans, Green and co., 1915 (2 vols.).

Dupré Theseider, Eugenio. *Aspetti della città medievale italiana: lezioni tenute nell'università di Bologna durante l'anno accademico 1956–1957*. Bologna: Riccardo Patron, 1956.

——. "Caterina da Siena." *Dizionario biografico degli italiani*, vol. XXII, January 1979, pp. 361–379.

——. *I Papi di Avignone e la questione Romana*. Florence: Felice le Monnier, 1939.

——. "Il mondo cittadino nelle pagini di S. Caterina." *Bulletino senese di storia Patria* 70 (1963), pp. 44–61.

——. "Il purgatorio di S. Patrizio." *Studi cateriniani* 8 (1932), pp. 77–87.

——. "La cronologia delle lettere politiche di S. Caterina e la critica moderna." *Studi cateriniani* 1 (1923), pp. 113–136.

——. "La rivolta di Perugia nel 1375." *Bolletino della R. deputazione di storia patria per l'Umbria* 35 (1938), pp. 69–166.

——. *Problemi del Papato avignonese*. Bologna: Patron, 1961.

——. *Problemi del Papato avignonese: lezioni tenute nell'università di Bologna durante l'anno accademico 1960–1961*. Bologna: Riccardo Patron, 1961.

——. "Santa Caterina nella storia del suo tempo." *Svizzera italiana* 7 (1947), pp. 182–192.

——. "Sono autentiche le Lettere di S. Caterina?" *Vita cristiana* 12 (1940), pp. 212–248.

——. "Un codice inedito dell'Epistolario di S. Caterina da Siena." *Bulletino dell'Istituto storico italiano e Archivio Muratoriano*, 1932, n. 48, pp. 18–56.

Durrieu, Paul. *Les archives angevines de Naples*. Paris: E. Thonin, 1886–1887 (2 vols.).

Elliott, Dyan. *Spiritual Marriage: Sexual Abstinence in Medieval Wedlock*. Princeton: Princeton University Press, 1993.

Eubel, Conrad. *Hierarchia catholica medii aevi*. Patavia: S. Antonio, [1913].

Fawtier, Robert. "Cateriniana." *Mélanges d'archéologie et d'histoire* 34 (1914), pp. 3–95.

——. "La Légende mineure de Sainte Catherine de Sienne." *École française di Rome: Melanges d'archéologie et d'histoire* 32 (1912), pp. 397–509.

——. *Sainte Catherine de Sienne: Essaie de critique des sources. I. Sources hagiographiques*. Paris: De Boccard, 1921 (vol. 121 of *Bibliotèque des Écoles françaises d'Athène et de Rome*).

——. *Ste. Catherine de Sienne: Essaie de critique des sources. II. Les oeuvres de Sainte Catherine de Sienne*. Paris: De Boccard, 1930 (vol. 135 of *Bibliotèque des Écoles françaises d'Athène et de Rome*).

——, and Louis Canet. *La double expérience de Catherine Benincasa* (6th ed.). Paris: Librairie Gallimard, 1948.

Flete, William. *Lettera a Raimondo da Capua in lode di Caterina da Siena* (ed., trans., notes, G. D'Urso). Florence: Tip. Baccini & Chiappi, 1974.

Fortuna, Michele M. "La funzione psicologica delle tre potenze nella dottrina del ponte." *Rassengna di ascetica e mistica* 22 (1972), pp. 55–61.

Fresen, Patricia A. *Self-Knowledge in the Writings of Catherine of Siena*. Doctoral Dissertation, Pretoria: University of South Africa, 1995.

Gams, Pius Bonifacius. *Series Episcoporum Ecclesiae Catholicae, quotquot innotuerunt a Beato Petro apostolo.* Ratisbona: G.J. Manz, 1873–1876.

Gardner, Edmund G. *Saint Catherine of Siena: A Study in the Religion, Literature and History of the Fourteenth Century in Italy.* London: Dent; New York: Dutton & Co., 1907.

——. *The Story of Siena and San Gimignano*, London: J. M. Dent, 1902.

Gebhard, Émile. *Moines et Papes: Essaies de psychologie historique.* Paris: Hachette et Cie, 1896.

Gherardi, Alessandro. *La guerra dei fiorentini con Papa Gregorio XI detta la guerra degli Otto Santi.* Florence: Archivio storico italiano, 1868.

Gougaud, Louis. *Devotional and Ascetic Practices in the Middle Ages*, trans. G. C. Bateman. London: Burns Oates & Washbourne, 1927.

Grottanelli, Francesco, ed. *Leggenda minore di S. Caterina da Siena e Lettere dei suoi discepoli.* Bologna: Gaetano Romagnoli, 1868.

Hackett, Benedict. *William Flete, O.S.A., and Catherine of Siena.* Villanova: Augustinian Press, 1992.

——. "Un profilo del pensiero agostiniano di Caterina nel suo periodo formativo," in *Atti del Simposio Internazionale Cateriniano-Bernardiniano, Siena, 17–20 aprile 1980*, ed. D. Maffei and P. Nardi, pp. 137–147.

——. "Simone Fidati da Cascia and the Doctrine of St. Catherine of Siena." *Augustiniana* 16 (1966), pp. 386–414.

Istoria genealogica delle famiglie Salimbeni di Siena, ed. Idlefonso di San Luigi, in *Delizie degli Eruditi toscani*, appendix to vol. XXIII. Florence: Gaetano Cambiagi, 1770–1789.

Jordan, E. "La date de naissance de Sainte Catherine de Sienne." *Analecta Bollandiana* 40 (1922), pp. 365–411.

Jorgensen, Johannes. *Saint Catherine of Siena*, trans. Ingeborg Lund. London, New York (etc.): Longmans, Green and co., 1939.

Kappeli, T. "Fonti cateriniane nel cod. XIV, 24 dell'Archivio generale domenicano." *Rivista di storia della Chiesa in Italia* 6 (1952), pp. 84–96.

Kirsch, Johann Peter. *Die Ruckkehr der Papste Urban V und Gregor XI von Avignon nach Rom. Auszuge aus den Kameralregestern des Vatikanischenarchivs.* Paderborn: F. Schoningh, 1898.

Landucci, Ambrogio. *Sacra leccetana selva, cioè origine e progressi dell'antico, e venerabile eremo e congregatione di Lecceto in Toscana. ...* Rome: F. Landucci, 1657.

Laurent, Marie-Hyacinthe. "De litteris ineditis Fr. Wilhelmi de Flete." *Annali Augustiniani* 18 (1941–42), pp. 303–327.

——. "Les sources hagiographiques de Ste. Catherine de Sienne et le ms. Marciano Ital. CL.V, 26." *Miscellanea di scritti in memoria di L. Ferrari*, Firenze, 1952, pp. 521–531.

Lauri, Achille. "Origine e sviluppo della poesia in S. Caterina da Siena." *Cultura moderna. Natura ed arte* 52 (1943), pp. 103–110.

——. "Prosa e poesia cateriniana." *Memorie domenicane* 61 (1944), pp. 20–28.

Lazzareschi, Eugenio. "S. Caterina da Siena ed i Lucchesi." *Rosario: Memorie domenicane* 29 (1912), pp. 186–200; 242–257; 296–313.

——. *S. Caterina da Siena in Val d'Orcia.* Florence: Tip. Domenicana, 1915.

Leader, Giovanni Temple and Giuseppe Marcotti. *Giovanni Acuto (Sir John Hawkwood): Storia d'un Condottiere.* Florence: Barbèra, 1889.

Lefébure, F. A. *S. Bruno e l'ordre des Chartreux.* Paris: [n.p.], 1883.

Litta, Pompeo. *Famiglie celebri italiane.* Milan: Giusti, 1819– .

Lucchesi, E. "Santa Caterina da Siena e le sue relazioni con i Monaci di Vallombrosa." *Memorie Domenicane* 65 (1948), pp. 197–227.

Lugano, Placido. "Santa Caterina da Siena e i monaci di Montoliveto." *Rivista storica benedettina* 7 (1912), pp. 161–173.

——. "L'istituzione di Montoliveto nella seconda metà del Trecento," in *Saggi e ricerche nel VII centenario della nascita del B. Bernardo Tolomei (1272–1972).* Siena: Monteoliveto Maggiore, 1972, pp. 49–84.

Luongo, Francis T. (Thomas). "Catherine of Siena: Rewriting Female Holy Authority," in *Women, the Book, and the Godly*, vol. 1, ed. L. Smith. Cambridge: D. S. Brewer, 1995, pp. 89–103.

——. *The Politics of Marginality: Catherine of Siena in the War of Eight Saints, 1374–1378.* Doctoral Dissertation, University of Notre Dame, 1997.

Luttrell, Anthony. "Gregory XI and the Turks." *Orientalia Christiana periodica* 46 (1980), pp. 391–417.

Malavolti, Orlando. *Historia de' fattie e guerre de' Sanesi, cose esterne, come ciuili* ... Ventia: Per Salvestro Marchetti, 1599.

Manaresi, A. "Il mondo cittadino nelle lettere di S. Caterina da Siena." *Memorie domenicane* 75 (1958), pp. 259–278, and 76 (1959), pp. 53–66, 224–258.

Manghi, Aristo. *La Certosa di Pisa—Storia (1366–1866) e descrizione.* Pisa: F. Mariotti, 1911.

Manni, Domenico Maria. *Cronichetta d'Incerto* (in *Cronichette antiche di vari scrittori del buon secolo della lingua toscana.* Florence: Appresso Domenico Maria Manni, 1733).

Mirot, Leon. *La politique française en Italie de 1380 a 1422* ... Paris: A. Picard, 1934– .

——. *La politique pontificale et le retour du S. Siège a Rome en 1376.* Paris: E. Bouillon, 1899.

Misciattelli, Piero. "Caterina Benincasa: l'attività politica." *Mistici senesi*, Siena, 1913, pp. 132–161.

——. "La Regola del Terzo Ordine di S. Domenico e il ruolo delle Mantellate nel Trecento." *Studi Cateriniani* 3 (1926), pp. 45–60.

Missionario vincenziano, ed. *Il Messagio di Santa Caterina da Siena, dottore della chiesa: Tutto il pensiero della vergine senese sposto con le sue parole ridotte a forma moderna.* Rome: Edizioni vincenziane, 1970.

Mollat, G. *Lettres secrètes et curiales du pape Grégoire (1370–1378) intéressant les pays autres que la France.* Paris: E. de Boccard, 1962–1965.

——. "Relations politiques de Grégoire XI avec les Siennois et les Florentins." *Mélanges archéologiques et d'histoire* 68 (1956), pp. 335–376.

Monti, Gennaro Maria. *L'Italia e le crociate in Terra Santa.* Naples: Edizioni della Mostra d'oltremare, [1940].

——. *Le confraternite medievali dell'alta e media Italia*, 2 vols. Venice: "La nuova Italia," 1927.

Necrologia di San Domenico in Camporeggio. Fontes vitae s. Catharinae Senensis historici, ed. Marie-Hyacinthe Laurent, vol. XX. Siena: R. Università di Siena, 1937.

Neri di Donato. *Annales Senensis, auctore Nerio Donati filio, a anno 1352 usque ad annum 1381*, in *Cronaca Senese*, ed. Muratori. Italia: H. Bentivoglienti, 1729.

——. *Annales Senensis*, in *Cronache Senesi*, ed. A. Lisini and F. Iacometti, in *Rerum Italicarum Scriptores*, n.s., XV, part vi, Bologna: Nicola Zanichelli, 1932–1937.

Noffke, Suzanne. *Catherine of Siena: Vision Through a Distant Eye.* Collegeville: Liturgical Press/Michael Glazier, 1996

——. *The Texts and Concordances of the Works of Caterina da Siena.* Madison, Wis.: The Hispanic Seminary of Medieval Studies, 1987 (microfiche).

O'Driscoll, Mary. *Catherine of Siena: Passion for the Truth and Compassion for Humanity.* New Rochelle: New City Press, 1993.

Orlandi, Stefano, ed. *Il "Necrologia" di S. Maria Novella.* Florence: [n.p.], 1955 (2 vols.).

Palmarocchi, Roberto. *Cronisti del Trecento.* Milan/Rome: Rizzoli & Co., [c.1935].

Pecci, Giovanni Antonio. *Memorie storico-critiche della città di Siena.* Siena: Cantagalli, 1988.

——. *Notizie storiche della città di Montalcino.* Sinalunga: Viti-Riccucci, 1989.

Il Processo Castellano. Fontes vitae s. Catharinae Senensis historici, ed. Marie-Hyacinthe Laurent, vol. IX. Milan: Bocca, 1942.

Prunai, Giulio. "L'assoluzione dell'arciprete di Montalcino in un documento del diplomatico fiorentino del 1379." *S. Caterina da Siena*, n.s. 17 (1966, n. 1), pp. 11–15.

Rapisardi-Mirabelli, Andrea. "Caterina da Siena e la concezione della guerra." *Letture cateriniane.* Siena, 1928, pp. 173–214.

Raymundus de Vineis (Raimondo da Capua). *Beati Raymundi Capuani . . . opuscula et litterae*, ed. Hyacinthe-Marie Cormier. Rome: Typographia Polyglotta, S. C. de Propaganda Fide, 1899.

——. *Legenda major*, trans. Giuseppe Tinagli. Siena: Cantagalli, 1934.
——. *The Life of Catherine of Siena*, trans. Conleth Kearns. Wilmington, Del.: Michael Glazier, Inc., 1980.
——. *The Life of Saint Catherine of Siena*, trans. George Lamb. New York: P. J. Kenedy & Sons, 1960.
Raynaldus, Odoricus (Caesar Card. Baronius). *Annales Eccesiastici*. Barri-Ducis: Lud. Guerin, Eques Ord. S. Sylvestri, 1864–1883.
Renouard, Yves. *The Avignon Papacy*, trans. Denis Bethell. Hamden: Archon Books, 1970.
Rothbarth, Margarete. *Urban VI. und Neapel (Inaugural-Dissertation zur Erlangung der Doktorwürde der hohen philosophischen Fakultät der Albert-Ludwigs-Universität zu Freiburg im Breisgau)*. Berlin/Leipzig: Dr. Walther Rothschild, 1913.
Rousset, Paul. "L'idée de Croisade chez Sainte Catherine de Sienne et chez les théoriciens du XIVe siècle." *Congresso internazionale di studi cateriniani, Siena/Roma, 24–29 aprile 1980: Atti*. Rome: Curia generalizia O.P., 1981, pp. 362–372.
Rovasenda, Enrico di. "Sette lettere a una regina," in *Inquadramenti storici*. Rome: Edizioni cateriniane, 1975, pp. 49–64.
Scipione, Ammirato. *Istorie Fiorentine*, ed. Luciano Scarabelli. Torino: Cegini Pompa, 1853.
Seckendorff, Eleonore Maria Franziska. *Die Kirchenpolitishe Tätigkeit der Heiligen Katharina von Siena unter Papst Gregor XI (1371–1378). Ein Versuch zur Datierung ihrer Briefe*. Berlin/Leipzig: W. Rothschild, 1917.
Segre, A. "I dispacci di Cristofora da Piacenza, procuratore mantovano alla corte pontificale." *Archivio storico italiano*, ser. 5, xliii, (1909).
Setton, Kenneth M. *The Papacy and the Levant: 1204–1571*. Philadelphia: American Philosophical Society, 1976.
Spiazzi, R. "L'etica politica di Santa Caterina da Siena." *Stato sociale (Roma)* 15 (1971), pp. 135–154.
Stella, Alessandro. *La révolte de Ciompi: Les hommes, les lieux, le travail*. Paris: Les Éditions de l'École des Hautes Études en Sciences Sociales, 1993.
Tabularium S. Mariae Novae (cited in *Spicilegium Montolivetense*, II). Florence, 1903.
Tartaro, Achille. *La letteratura civile e religiosa del Trecento*. Bari: Laterza, 1972.
Taurisano, Innocenzo M. *Fioretti di Santa Caterina da Siena* (3rd ed.). Rome: Ferrari, 1950.
——. *Little Flowers of St. Catherine of Siena*, trans. Charlotte Dease. St. Paul: E. M. Lohmann Co., 1926.
——. "Santa Caterina e Gregorio XI." *Memorie domenicane*, 1929, pp. 89–111.

——. *Santa Caterina nei ricordi dei discepoli* (2nd ed.). Rome: Ferrari, 1957.

Theiner, A., ed. *Codex diplomaticus dominii temporalis S. Sedis*. Rome: Imprimerie du Vatican, 1861–1862.

Tommasèo, Niccolo. "Moti fiorentini del 1378 de' quali ebbe Caterina da Siena a patire." *Archivio storico italiano* 12 (1860), pp. 21–45.

Tommasi, Giugurta. *Historie di Siena*. Bologna: A. Forni, [1973].

Tommaso di Antonio da Siena (Caffarini). *Leggenda minore di S. Caterina da Siena e lettere dei suoi discepoli*, ed. Francesco Grottanelli. Bologna: G. Romagnoli, 1868.

——. *Libellus de Supplemento: Legende prolixe Virginis Beate Catherine de Senis*, ed. Giuliana Cavallini, Imelda Foralosso. Rome: Edizioni cateriniane, 1974.

——. *Supplemento alla vulgata leggenda di S. Caterina da Siena*, trans. Ansano Tantucci. Rome: Tipografia in Piazza di Monte Citorio, 1866.

——. *Tractatus de ordine ff. de penitentia S. Dominici* , ed. Marie-Hyacinthe Laurent. *Fontes vitae S. Catharinae Senensis historici*, vol. XXI. Siena: R. Università di Siena, 1938.

——. *Vita di Santa Caterina da Siena* (translation of *Supplemento*, trans. Marie-Hyacinthe Laurent). Siena: Cantagalli, 1938.

Trexler, Richard C. *Economic, Political, and Religious Effects of the Papal Interdict on Florence, 1376–1378: A Study of the Secular Penal Power of the Papacy in the Late Middle Ages*. Frankfurt am Main: Johann Wolfgang Goethe-Universität, 1964.

Il tumulto dei Ciompi: Un momento di storia fiorentina ed europea. (Comune di Firenze: Istituto Nazionale di Studi sul Rinascimento.) Florence: Leo S. Olschki Editore, 1981.

Ugurgieri Azzolini, Isidoro. *Le pompe sanesi, o' vero relazione delle hvomini, e donne illvstri di Siena, e svo stato*. Pistoia: Pier'Antonio Fortunati, 1649.

Undset, Sigrid. *Catherine of Siena*, trans. Kate Austin-Lund. New York: Sheed and Ward, 1954.

Verdiani Bandi, A. *I Castelli della Val d'Orcia*. Siena: Cantagalli, 1926.

Volpato, Antonio. "Analisi diplomatistica delle Lettere di S. Caterina" (unpublished paper, 1985).

——. "L'onore di Dio e la salute delle anime in S. Caterina," in *Atti del simposio internazionale Cateriniano-Bernardiniano*. Siena: Accademia Senese degli Intronati, 1982, pp. 301–308.

Zucchelli, Niccola, and Eugenio Lazzareschi. *S. Caterina da Siena ed i Pisani*. Florence: Tip. domenicana, 1916 (date on cover, 1917).

INDEX